Property of
FAMILY OF FAITH
LIBRARY

HABITS OF MIND

HABITS
of MIND

An Introduction to the Philosophy of Education

BY
ANTONIO T. de NICOLÁS
WITH EDITED TEXTS

PARAGON HOUSE

New York

First edition, 1989

Published in the United States by

Paragon House
90 Fifth Avenue
New York, NY 10011

Copyright © 1989 by Antonio T. de Nicolás

Due to constraints of space, all acknowledgments of permission to reprint will appear on page xi.

All rights reserved. No part of this book may be reproduced, in any form, without written permission from the publishers, unless by a reviewer who wishes to quote brief passages.

Library of Congress Cataloging-in-Publication Data
Habits of mind: an introduction to the philosophy of education /
   written and edited by Antonio T. de Nicolás — 1st ed.
      p. cm.
  Bibliography: p.
  Includes index.
  ISBN 0-913729-38-8   ISBN 0-913729-74-4 (pbk.)
  1. Education, Higher—1965– 2. Education—Philosophy. I. de
Nicolás, Antonio T., 1932–
LB2322.H32 1989
378′.001—dc19   88-28349
                                         CIP

Manufactured in the United States of America

To My Students

EPIGRAPHS

Now, here, my dear Glaucon, is the whole risk for a human being. . . . And on this account each one of us must, to the neglect of other studies, above all see to it that he is a seeker and a student of *that study* by which he might be able to learn and *find out* who will give him the capacity and the knowledge to distinguish the good and the bad life, and so everywhere and always *choose* the better *from among those* that are possible. . . .
                                    Plato/Socrates, The *Republic* 618b

[Plato's] city is built to music,
therefore never built.
And, therefore, built for ever.
                                    Tennyson in "Camelot"

In the Temple were forged the hammers which destroyed the Temple.
                                    Anatole France

Like you, I disapprove of the restoration of the Jesuits, which seems to portend a backward step from light into darkness.
                                    Thomas Jefferson to John Adams, 1816.

Let us have a Jesuit for breakfast.
                                    Voltaire, *Candide*

One no longer studies, one no longer observes, one dreams; and we are gravely presented with the dreams of some bad nights as philosophy. I will be told that I, too, dream, I agree; but I give my dreams as dreams, which others are not careful to do, leaving it to the reader to find out whether they contain something useful for people who are awake.
                                    Rousseau, *Emile*

CONTENTS

ACKNOWLEDGMENTS

I wish to remember and thank my first professor of philosophy, Richard DeSmet, who taught me as an undergraduate the philosophical difference between *saying* and *doing*.

The notes on medieval logic appearing in this volume were gathered from my undergraduate classes on logic with Professor DeSmet and from the compendium on medieval philosophy, *Philosophiae Scholasticae Summa*, by Leovigildo Salcedo and Clemente Fernandez (1964, Biblioteca de Autores Cristianos, Madrid). I first used these resources while teaching at the University of San Francisco.

The following publishers have granted me permission to reprint the selections appearing in this volume:

Jude P. Daugherty for "Marx, Dewey, and Maritain: The Role of Religion in Society," from *The World and I*, N.D. Grove Press for The Marquis de Sade, "Dialogue Between a Priest and a Dying Man," from *One Hundred Twenty Days in Sodom and Other Writings*, 1966.

Kappa Delta Pi, An International Honor Society in Education, for John Dewey, *Experience and Education*, 1963.

W.W. Norton and Company for José Ortega y Gasset, *The Revolt of the Masses*, 1966.

Princeton University Press for José Ortega y Gasset, *Mission of the University*, trans. Howard Lee Nostrand. Copyright 1944, © 1972 renewed by Princeton University Press.

University Press of America, Inc. for John Locke, *Some Ideas Concerning Education*, from Lynchburg College Symposium Readings, Classical Selections on Great Issues. Series 1, volume 2: *Education: Ends and Means*.
The World and I for John Bremer, "Translating Plato: Some Reflections on Rhetoric," N.D.

The World and I for Colin N. Turbayne, "The Sciences Now Have Masks on Them," N.D.

Foreword

Habits of Mind is not simply a text on the philosophy of education; it is a primer on reading the *Zeitgeist*. Antonio de Nicolás awakens memories of Robert Bellah's *Habit of the Heart,* a treatise that supports the restoration of community as a refuge from unfettered individualism. But this book treats the habits of intellectual discourse as an organic thread from the ancient past to the present. Professor de Nicolás shatters the contemporary mythology that students have been Nietzscheanized—to use Allan Bloom's expression. In fact, students have been misled by a variety of philosophical assumptions that are either wrongheaded or deceptive.

If one considers scientific reasoning as *a* habit of mind rather than *the* habit of mind, the justification of this book is apparent. Rationalists assume the solution to problems based on scientific analysis. If ideas don't fit the model then the ideas must be reformulated; the model, of course, is not revised. This is not to suggest that scientific achievements can be denied or denigrated. However, science is a perspective on the world that excludes the *transcendent,* what the scientists would describe as the *inexplicable.* From a student's point of view, this habit is reflexive; it is in the educational air one breathes. Religious thought is as alien to the typical student as arcane languages.

Perhaps as important as the prevailing habit of thought is the relativism it promotes. After all, if the proof is in the pudding, any proof that gets you to the pudding is acceptable. There aren't noble ideas or ideals. There is that which is measurable, treatable, and easily understood. The lamentable part of this analysis is that the student barely recognizes the limited reaches of his power. His attachment to a habit has prompted a mind atrophied by restricted experience.

Since relativism is in the ascendancy, students don't have to read

primary sources. They are assigned Foucault's interpretation of the classics or Stanley Fish's analysis of the humanistic tradition. The disciplines
have been eviscerated of rigor, and rely instead on the trendy. Struc-
turalism, semiotics, Lacanism, and deconstruction are modes of thought
pegged into intellectual fashion. They are devoid of real meaning, yet
have the glow of superficial sophistication. Students repeat the psycho-
babble of instructors as if "subliminate" and "projection" have a meaning
outside of a Freudian context. Derivative ideas drive the learning process
in a mad quest for instant erudition. What one gets is the pseudo-
sophistication of instructors leading the narrowly parochial and miseedu-
cated students. It is not that either party in this "dance around the quad"
is malevolent; the issue is the surrender to the fashionable and relative.

In part this is understandable since scholars themselves have generally lost a sense of what Walter Lippman called "the deposited wisdom of
western civilization." The great ideas, those books elevated to classic
status, are often cut down to size as educational standards are lowered.
If educators assume that students can't read Aeschylus, then educators
assign pabulum for them to read.

The capitulation to the lowest common denominator along with the
ambient relativism has conceived "the university without learning." And
it is astonishing that students of education are often among the least
educated.

It is therefore with special delight that I welcome this volume on the
philosophy of education as a primer on what should be known and on
the evolution of philosophic thought. If anything is required in the
present academy, it is a course of study that explains our epistemological
heritage. It is something of a cliche to contend that ideas have consequences. They do when applied or misapplied. The consequence of
the present educational philosophy is applied educated incapacity. The
idea of education is vapid and its application jejune. It is therefore
hardly coincidental that colleges and universities are desperately trying
to regain their legitimacy.

But it is one thing to suggest what is wrong and quite another matter
to set things right. Here is where Antonio de Nicolás skillfully insinuates
himself into the current debate on higher education. His answer to the
critics is not simply the rhetorical request for rigor. He argues for
candor. The candor of ideas, the explanation of our habit of mind
through an exegesis of educational thought from the Jesuits to Ortega y
Gasset. He raises the issue of why ideas matter and answers with a plea
for the tolerance of tradition. His is not simply the historicism of a
scholar fed up with what is, but rather a scholar in search of answers that
will lead the unwary out of the thickets of intellectual confusion. Those
who derive "meaning" from the instrumentation of their own imagination without resort to the refinements of the past are the crusaders for

nihilism. As de Nicolás has noted, the language of the classroom has been appropriated by those bent on radicalizing the process of education. The substitution of theory for essence has emboldened claims in the classroom and left a student population unable to resist propagandistic exercises. Ortega y Gasset said "the universe is not discovered by philosophy." Alas, it is not. Yet the aspiration to explain its many dimensions, to at least ask the requisite questions, was once, and might well be again, the basis for formal education. It seems to me that this book is such a beginning.

HERBERT LONDON

INTRODUCTION

In an age of ideology, obvious truths need stating—and stating them is the project of *Habits of Mind*. My argument is based on the simple theory that if American education is to serve its students, then the whole range of mental possibilities of the students must be developed by our universities—and only secondarily may universities proceed to specialization.

If we acknowledge that the universities represent communities of free people, then we will see it as an imperative that universities develop habits of mind enabling individuals to think and act freely. Students cannot be considered free in thought or action if their universities have failed them in their development of inner faculties enabling such freedom—without indoctrination or manipulation by either teachers or the outside world. To be a free individual means being able to perform acts free from external manipulation.

Habits of mind are identified as the whole range of mental operations people perform, and have performed in history, giving them an individual and social identity, to include cultural diversity and individual uniqueness. Plato identified these plural acts in his "divided line" and, with few additions, the identification still holds. These habits of mind are: the abstraction of images from objects already in the world, the forming of opinions, cognitive operations with their diverse levels of abstraction as exemplified in the operations of science and art and the whole range of imaginative operations for original creation without borrowing from the outside, by recollecting from the past those memories of images, and acts that represent the best of what is human and cultural.

Plato proposed these plural habits of mind and their development as the curriculum and project of education. This project never took root in our educational system, but was discarded by those who came after him, who offered instead something more narrow in the name of certain ideological promissory notes to be cashed at a distant future date. We have thus developed certain habits of mind while burying others, using education to indoctrinate rather than to recall from the past those habits of mind that made us different and diverse, and which guaranteed our continuity as a species and as a multiplicity of cultures.

The project of this book is to rescue from oblivion our original past by recalling those habits of mind that made us and the cultures we represent who and what we are.

The rest of the project and of the argument is sheer repetition and habit formation. The classroom becomes the place of exercise where a whole range of habits of mind is developed, while the students are enabled to reproduce the habits of mind presented in class. Thus each student feels linked to society at large as the source of those original acts. But these habits of mind demand that they be *exercised* in a style suitable to the particular habit to be developed: It is not enough to speak of imagination and to create only concepts.

The development of this set of mental habits has the ultimate aim of enabling the students to decide for themselves which, from among those possible, is the best choice, and to be able to make such decisions consistently. A habit of indecision or the inability to make independent decisions exhibits a failure of education.

There is, however, a preliminary hurdle to overcome in this project: Our American system of education did not start the system of education of the West. We have not stopped to consider if our American system of education serves, or is representative of, the people of America. But American education started by legitimizing the habits of mind of the Founding Fathers, and no one would think today that the habits of mind of that era are the ones best suited today for an open and representative education. Those products of the Reformation were themselves busy burying habits of mind repugnant to them but essential to our present democracy. This initial problem is also part of the solution for, given the present agreement among critics that the state of education is in mortal crisis, if our resources as a culture had already been exhausted, then any proposals for improvements would prove useless and ineffective.

We take it, therefore, that the failure of our educational system stems from the fact that only certain habits of mind are in use in the classroom, and that these habits of mind neither represent those making up this nation, nor the possibilities inherent in the species.

The remedy to our educational impasse is not to be found in developing a strict curriculum with the classics, nor in training for the ability to sustain a theoretical argument to the end, nor in some other new or old theory of education. The actual remedy lies in our ability to identify those habits of mind that are actually present in our culture, and to make those habits apparent in the classroom so that the students may recognize themselves while reaching out in the exercise that is education. This exercise, hopefully, will contribute to their ability to make free decisions.

To make the use of this book as practical as possible, it has been divided into three parts. The first focuses on the actual history of our habits of mind as we inherited them originally from the medievals, and the subsequent habits of mind we developed up to the present. The second part offers selections from the original writings of those authors who most contributed to the formation of the habits of mind we exhibit today. The third part is a return to our cultural origins in Greece and a reexamination of this period. Our emphasis is on Plato, for we take it that his project of education and philosophy has not yet entered our culture, despite claims to the contrary. Plato's importance in this project is vital, for he is a footnote to those other cultures now present in this nation which have been systematically excluded from representation in our educational system.

The rest of the book is literally in the hands of the students. For the power of this book rests on the fact that we are neurophysiologically linked to one another and to the whole species. The exercises presented in this book are geared to awaken memory in the way memory links us to our own bodies. In this manner the efficacy of this book does not depend on establishing a national policy of education, but rather on the exercise of those habits of mind we have been able to perform in history, and on which each culture depends for innovation and continuity. The exercises proposed here may serve to provide an instant reversal of those trends and attitudes in education that have now reached crisis proportions: apathy, cultural illiteracy, passivity, and the dominance of theory. Besides, these exercises need not wait for their implementation into national policies or for universal consent: they may be set into motion at once in the classroom by an individual instructor and by individual students, since education is ultimately an individual exercise practiced in communities of individuals. This book is written to serve such audiences.

ANTONIO T. de NICOLÁS

HABITS OF MIND

PART ONE

Our Habits

1

Higher Education Today

How Bad Is Our System of Education?

Out of a class of 300 students I found ten who plagiarized papers. These papers were a partial requirement for the final grade, and I felt justified in lowering the final grade of these students, thinking the students would be able to read into this lower grade a warning, and that the matter would thus be put to rest. I was wrong. Two of the penalized students came to see me. They candidly admitted they had plagiarized their papers, but they took great pains to inform me how they had done it: they had plagiarized by copying other students' papers in their own hand, while the other eight students who had plagiarized had done so by photocopying original papers. And this was their argument: Was I not being unjust punishing the two of them as severely as the others? Could I not see they had made an effort while plagiarizing, absent in the case of other plagiarizers? Shouldn't I revise their grade upwards?

My counter-examples fell on deaf ears. Should a murderer be rewarded because he breaks the fall of his already dead victim? Should a thief be given kudos because he used gloves while stealing, thus saving the furniture from his own dirt? The two students listened politely but were adamant with their request. "You should evaluate our argument," they said. For, I was told, they respected my opinions and I should respect theirs.

Was this an exceptional case of moral turpitude? Unfortunately not. These two people shared with others a righteous

3

ground to claim injustice. They had learned, while at the university, that anything taught in the humanities were mere opinions. Facts and knowledge were reserved for the sciences. And the students are not alone in becoming confused while at the university.

A friend of mine, a famous scholar, writer, and professor, became suddenly concerned with a feeling of imminent death. He was not interested in prolonging life, he wrote, but in dying heroically. Would I have any suggestions? Since my friend was familiar with the East I wrote back telling him of my own desire to travel to the Himalayan mountains and discover Shangri-la. I would start my journey walking from Katmandu, I expanded, and would follow the trail to the depths and heights of the mountains until I came face to face with my Maker.

I did not hear from my friend and scholar for more than a year. Then he wrote:

> Your suggestion to meet my Maker in the clear and free air of the Himalayas moved me and filled me with joy and determination. The roof of the world was going to be my exit from the world. What a way to cheat technological society and leave with freedom and dignity! So, I applied for a grant from the Chinese Government to do research in Tibet. I have just been informed that a grant has been awarded to me. . . . So, my friend, I guess this is it, my last journey!

He had been in the academic world for so long he could no longer die independently. He had to do it following proper channels.

How can a scholar, my friend, a man, have lost sight of the simple fact that a heroic act and a bureaucratic act exclude one another? He would die as he lived, a bureaucrat, not a hero. When, in his long academic life, did the bureaucratic take over as a habit of life able to keep the names of other acts but reducing all of life to a bureaucratic habit? Only that is human can be reached through bureaucratic channels. What training is imparted to students that forces them from their early years to develop a habit of legalism in the absence of knowledge and moral judgment? The point to be made in both previous examples is not what is missing in those people—morality, knowledge, heroism—but rather what habits of mind have they been asked to develop in the absence of morality, knowledge, and heroism?

And this is the problem of habits of mind. No one preaches them. No one has to. The structure of the system, the classroom, the course; the demand on the student as to what to focus on—what he or she is expected to select, repeat, take down in notes, defend, make public, store in memory—all these suffice for the student to perform habitually, to develop along legalistic and conformist lines as a habit of his or her education. We do not claim that bureaucratic and legalistic habits are all that the universities reinforce. But it is sufficient for us to state that a large number of students and many members of the faculty need learn only these habits to carry on apparently successful careers.

The truth of the matter is that no one has thus far made the connection between education and our habits of mind. We have always presumed that our habits are common, and have proceeded to examine education externally, as if we were empty containers waiting for the right liquid to fill us up. Another habit we share is that we expect education to come to us mostly from the outside—from objects, external worlds, readings, information, right images, right opinions, the knowledge of the experts. But if this is the case, where is our freedom? Where is the ability to act freely that an education is supposed to lead us to? If everything we learn is from others, from where are we to get the ability to act in a creative, free way that we are entitled to in a free society? Where did we go wrong?

Democracy, Freedom, and Education

The claim that ours is an open society is misleading and self-contradictory. It is misleading because we fail to do anything about being an open society, taking for granted the status quo. On the other hand a society that has no limiting boundaries is not a society, but rather chaos. In our open-mindedness we have tried to solve the problem by being open to people's ideas, but in the process we have allowed only one main habit of mind to develop: the habit of theory forming. We are open-minded because we are capable of turning other people's particularities into abstract, theoretical forms. Thus, in our democracy, differences disappear and homogeneities of abstract forms take their place. Individualities are recognized only as biases, deviations from the theoretical norm, and if these individuals have a common voice we recognize them politically in programs of equal opportunity and the like. While theoretically liberal, we are concerned with human particulars only insofar as they have not yet melted in our theoretical equality, the paradise we envision for our open society.

Formulation of theories is our most cherished habit of mind, and we use it to measure the success or failure of our educational system.

One need only visit any classroom to see firsthand what this habit of theory making is doing and how it is being used against the students.

American education as it is presently practiced shares with its founders—Protestant divines—belief in the "scientific image." The Protestant divines teaching theology, and the contemporary humanists and social scientists looking for scientific-appearing theories to apply to their disciplines, share the same belief, that what they are doing in the classroom is justified by their claim that it is scientific. Thus the scientific image fulfills the function of a myth, as the belief that the scientific method is sufficient to organize the whole of life. These same educators, however, have never stopped to consider the fact that "science," as practiced in the hard sciences, is neither a myth nor an image. Science, as Kant noted, can only be expressed in concepts, never in images, and "this is a problem that has no solution." If this restriction is removed and science acts in education as a myth, the results upon the students are not only confusing but truly catastrophic. Social scientists and humanists fabricate daily abstractions and impose them on the human and social fabric with such quickness that the students are left reeling, wondering about their human whereabouts. Social scientists and humanists exchange places with philosophers multiplying the interpretations of the philosophers of the past to fit the theories of the present. Needless to say none of these faculty members has ever received a license in philosophy to allow them to teach it. In the name of science these humanists and social scientists feel entitled to impose their theories on the whole activity of humans by simply raising them to the level of abstraction that their theories demand. It does not matter whether these theories coincide with the people, the period, or the epistemologies under examination. The theoretical habits thus imposed on the students follow the many contradictory dogmas imposed on them: only "the empirico-quantitative method is legitimate and reliable in the access to reality and truth"; "humans are to be studied as if they were machines"; "humans belong to the animal kingdom"; "there must not be any transcendent realm of being"; "scientific investigation into reality will disclose no supernatural agency in phenomena"; "God and religion will ultimately yield to scientific or natural explanation"; "any religion that claims revelation or inspiration conflicts with science and must be kept mute"; "experience is only a category"; "experience is the result of language, not vice versa"; "all human acts are posterior to ethics." Thus, "all human values are relative, and so are anyone's opinions, for all opinion is biased and, therefore, "all texts are deconstructable." Literature, therefore, "must conform to theory, not the other way around"; "theory determines facts, facts determine theory," and "facts are names." "Adjectives should be kept out of language"; "there is no such thing as poetry"; "there is no such thing as history, and even if there were, it would make no difference, for only theory lives, and in the end only theory is perfect, regardless of its truth or verifiability." "Human life in any concrete, individual form, present or past, is trivial and inconsequential, for tomorrow's theory will prove today's life trivial and inconsequential"; "An honest man is one who is not caught"—and so it goes.

Does it make educational sense to teach Marcuse's *One Dimensional Man* as the only text for critical theory in a class of Sixteenth Century Spanish Literature in a Spanish Department? Is it academically honest to force graduate students to write their doctoral dissertations only by the method of critical theory and quoting only the approved authors of critical theory, particularly if their theses are on Plato's contemporaries? Is it not a travesty to open a Humanities Institute run by critical theorists who deny poetry, have never read the classics, affirm the primacy of theory over experience, and have never written a significant contribution to the humanities? (In the interests of accuracy, this should have been called a Marxist Seminary.)

The present structure of the university is such that these acts against freedom and democracy are permitted in the name of freedom and democracy. Contradictory and insufficient theories are allowed in the mistaken belief that they conform to

our democratic reality. How can an educational system subscribe to error and still claim to be educational? Is there no
accountability in education? In fact, after tenure there is hardly
any. Error has tenure in the universities. Those in administration consider only what *is* and in no way raise the question of
what *ought to be*. Individual faculty members find asylum within
the autonomy of their departments or disciplines. Disagreeing
professors do not challenge one another to public debate. No
one wants to become aware that there is a war going on, much
less the rules of that war. Neither the Sciences nor the Humanities are responsible for that war; they are themselves at war
against those who use them for less than what they have been
traditionally. Ideology is now used in their name, hiding behind administrative bureaucracy, proper channels, and the
freedoms of our Constitution.

The Critics of Education

Three major reports have appeared in the last three years
criticizing higher education in the United States, particularly
undergraduate education. These three negative reports pale in
comparison with the sustained, mordant, presumably deep
criticism of undergraduate education by Professor Allan
Bloom in his book *The Closing of the American Mind: How Higher
Education has Failed Democracy and Impoverished the Souls of To-
day's Students* (New York: Simon and Schuster, 1987). It could
be expected that such criticisms by the experts would put the
matter of education to rest, since all we would need to do would
be to implement the critics' programs of education. Unfortunately, the critics have no program to implement.

What these critics of higher education have achieved is to
make the obvious trivial: the American college is in crisis,
again. In *A Nation at Risk*, David Gardner's National Commission on Education bluntly remarks: "If an unfriendly foreign
power had attempted to impose on America the mediocre
educational performance that exists today, we might well have
viewed it as an act of war." The commission goes on to recommend the following curriculum as the foundation of a high
school education: 1) four years of English; 2) three years of
mathematics; 3) three years of science; 4) three years of social

studies; 5) one-half year of computer science; and for those going on to college, two years of a foreign language.

William Bennett's Report *To Reclaim a Legacy* (1984) cites four specific areas in which education is deficient in America: 1) the jumble of courses offered; 2) the downgrading of the humanities in the college curriculum; 3) the disappearance of requirements; and 4) the indifference of administrators and faculty toward the basic question of what constitutes an education. Like Gardner's commission, Bennett's report recommends a curriculum centered on the Western classics, and warns administrators not to support the encroachment of professional and vocational requirements so that the curriculum does not become all things to all people.

The most recent criticism of college education comes from Ernest L. Boyer (ex-chancellor of the State University of New York), in *College, the Undergraduate Experience in America* (New York: Harper & Row, 1987). Boyer's temperate and liberal account establishes that colleges have lost "their sense of mission," for they suffer a "paralysis" in the definition of the "essential purposes and goals," and are responsible for a loss of faith in general education that is reflected in the failure to provide an integrated core curriculum. In short, colleges suffer a deep malaise, their goals are obscure or nonexistent, their mission is suffering a breakdown, students are driven by careerism, faculty is driven by professional advancement rather than teaching, and their intellectual core is threatened with meltdown.

These reports sound tough and alarming, as, I suppose, they are meant to sound. But they are more effective in the political rear than in the actual battlefield, being politically tough, but contradictory in practice. They are at once a blend of general pessimistic analysis and a general unsinkable optimism about the value and the possibilities of education. They diminish the actual performance of college education while conjuring up the dream that a college education is the key to a good life. Yet, these reports fail to address, in any concrete way, what this education is supposed to accomplish, and for whom. If anything, these reports leave us more in the dark as to what education really is, and are not sufficiently urgent. How can we establish a policy of education if we do not have a clear idea of what education is supposed to accomplish? Who are we educating? Is our multiplicity of cultures represented in our universities? Do we understand what democracy and freedom mean in education? Does the university—or the critics of education, for that matter—have a background, a global image of what this nation is about so that education is geared to fill that image? Are we presupposing all those things and dictating policies for the blind to lead the blind?

Professor Bloom's recent criticism of American higher education addresses some of these questions, being also the more passionate in giving its account of education's failure. Unfortunately, Professor Bloom's heart and mind travel separate paths. The mind misses more often than the heart, and the result is a book full of contradictory claims, insufficient criticisms, and the most absurd presuppositions about the act of teaching, learning, democracy, freedom, and philosophy. But somehow Professor Bloom's gloomy path, despite its flaws, is full of the things a lot of people care about and that all of us must face when dealing with education. The American mind, so runs his thesis, was "closed" in the sixties when it capitulated to the activists. (Many would find such a claim to be the most surprising of the book. Does he claim that the American mind was open before the sixties?) The American university abandoned the classics for the trendy, teaching "relevant" courses in which all ideas have equal value. The university thus surrendered to "cultural relativism," a flawed American adaptation of Nietzsche's nihilism. Higher education thus failed learning and the students, those "nice and empty" creatures who, in the professor's opinion, are sex-ridden moneygrubbers marching to the beat not of reason but of rock music, "commercially prepackaged masturbational fantasy," the professor calls it.

He proposes as the way to attainment of educational health a return to the classical disciplines of the liberal arts with all those European wise men at the heart of the curriculum. But here again the professor flounders. Where is our intellectual freedom as Americans if we are to depend eternally on those Europeans? What, specifically, do those dead Europeans have to contribute to the present problematic life of Americans? Professor Bloom is not clear on this. But if we take his own example of rational discourse, we realize that Professor Bloom aims at educating people so that they may carry and sustain an argument from beginning to end, with a flourish, this being the number one criterion for identifying an educated person. Unfortunately, it is one thing to seem to carry and sustain an argument, and another to actually do so. Notwithstanding the fact that if a nation had to wait for its educated people to carry and sustain their arguments so that the nation would come to rational decisions, the nation would become paralyzed with indecision. If, as Professor Bloom states, the classics will educate us, and if this education consists of carrying and sustaining an argument, then Professor Bloom does not know the classics, or what he proposes as the remedy is insufficient to constitute an education. Professor Bloom translated Plato's *Republic* and nowhere does it offer such a program of education. In fact, if Professor Bloom recalls, Thrasymachus, that master of argumentation, is excluded from the community of Socrates and of young men that goes on to discover the foundations of education in the *Republic*.

Professor Bloom is against the teaching of "values" instead of morality, and in this he has everyone's sympathy. But then he strays when he grounds morality on "nature," and on the teachings of Rousseau. Nature is the most relative of all grounds, as the Marquis de Sade had a field day showing, and Rousseau is the one who introduced into Western culture the individual point of view, grounded on values and not morality. And if Professor Bloom is so keen on the Greeks, why did he not mention the training of the students to perform "virtue by habit" rather than morality through imitation of theoretical principles? If values substitute for morality, morality also substituted for virtue in our own culture. This, in fact, was the way the Greeks died culturally at the hands of the Romans. This is the deep flaw in the critics' presuppositions: all of them presumed that we have temporarily forgotten something we have had all along when in fact this is false. We, as a culture, have never had in our educational practice the Greek model. Instead we have had the Roman model to serve as the foundation of our education, with its penchant for theory and lists of names, while pretending to embrace the Greek model. This fact, at a time of crisis in education, is not a bad piece of news, for it means that our path to recovery is not in recovering what we thought we had, and thus exhausting our resources, but rather a shift to what we never had because we never used it, and thus reaching our resources at a time when we need extra capital. Our possibilities as a culture, or many cultures, consist in activating through education that same set of acts that constitutes the cultures individually and different from one another within the soul of the student, so that he or she may recognize them when seen for what they are. Professor Bloom's Hegelian rhapsody is a clear example of how the critics demand that education be the practice they themselves exhibit, even if it is historically blind—a sheer exercise in theoretical fantasy as close to cultural isolation as rock music, only more abstract, since it is an ahistorical practice and incomplete, and therefore wrong. (This abstract, ahistorical bias of Professor Bloom's book is what made the book so pleasurable to people of every political shading.)

What is obviously needed is a complete philosopical reflection that carries the criticism of education to the roots of the soul. We must analyze those acts we perform to become educated and not stop short by imposing certain habits of mind we have inherited, and thus act against the education of the young. We need to define our society, our culture, our nation, as what it is rather than as what it is not. We are not Romans, Germans, or English primarily, but we are those and also Greeks, Orientals, and all of them at once. As a culture we are neither scientific nor humanistic, but we have adopted a hybrid called technology. Technology, for Americans, is the instrumentalization of both science and humanities, and as such is our universal culture and our philosophy, against which we view both past and future. The fact that it is insufficient should increase our urgency to fill the gaps, direct our training to figure the alternatives, or focus on training that would reestablish the actual practice of doing science and doing humanities. It is because we have accepted the culture of technology, that what the critics see as an aberration of reason is from the viewpoint of technological culture, seen as the outcome of a fully legitimate culture. From an ontological point of view this is not only legitimate but true. Absolute claims are possible only in logical or human isolation. The appearance of the "other" takes care of the absolute claim. It would take a Hegel or a Marx to change the absolute from claim to thought itself, an act exercised in exclusivity because of its inner necessity. And this seems to be the choice of Professor Bloom—a choice that would destroy our previous commitment to democracy and freedom.

The culture of technology, shared by the faculty and imparted to the students, undercuts the mental operations of a free education for other shortcuts of the mind that avoid the accumulation of experience in exercising mental operations. Technological society believes in the instrumentation of reason—that is, it makes of reason an instrument to achieve quantitative efficiency, in the name of which more rather than less is produced; universities become centers for the production, transmission, and storage of information; and all mental operations are reduced to an "intellectual economy" where complicated logical operations are carried out without mentally performing them. In the *Eclipse of Reason* (1974, p. 23) Horkheimer wrote:

> this mechanization is indeed essential to the expansion of industry, but if it becomes the characteristic feature of the mind, it takes on a kind of materiality and blindness, becomes a fetish, a magic entity that is accepted rather than intellectually experienced.

What begins as the instrumentation of reason, the narrowing and routinizing of thinking, ends up as a habit by which all thinking is measured: the ultimate habit of alienation where all subjects are excluded from the actual decision-making process determined by the systems of technology in use. An education controlled by such habits of mind ends as the mechanization of an education that allows no room either for freedom or dignity.

The Roots of Our Crisis in Education

The critics are wrong in proposing cosmetic face-lifts where deeper surgery is needed. Given the habits of mind of the faculty and the institutions providing education, more of the same can be expected for generations to come. What does a theoretical, instrumentalist, bureaucratic habit of mind do with the classics? Memorize them? Catalogue them? Do the critics see the classics as also problematic? Who is going to recreate for the students (or teach the students to recreate) the background, the ultimate image, against which each classic was created? Who is going to teach the students to recreate both the background and the written classic? Who teaches the students that it is not possible to create anything if a background is not first created and imagined? Who teaches the building of backgrounds, those large controlling images bursting out in prose or poetry, as the complete testimony of a period, a culture, a scientific leap? There is, no doubt, a large amount of confusion in the critics themselves. An in-depth philosophical spring cleaning is needed before curricula reforms are proposed. Let the skeletons walk out of the closet.

Professor Bloom blames the Germans—Nietzsche, Freud, Heidegger—for the present state of education, or parts of it. But he is wrong. The German Protestants came to America under the tutelage of a familiar way of thinking, since Americans "thought" in that manner before the Germans arrived on the scene. Protestant Americans already shared a habit of self-absorption inherited from their traditional Whig politics and the Protestantism of the Reformation. The American version, however, is more radical than its progenitors and ultimately more subversive. We need only mention Ralph Waldo Emerson, admired by Nietzsche; Walt Whitman; and the Protestant divines from whom we inherited the habits of thought we now find insufficient in education. "Undoubtedly we have no questions to ask which are unanswerable," wrote Emerson in his *Essays*. Does this sound as brash as anything we hear today from our students? "These problems," he writes elsewhere, referring to original sin, the origin of evil, and the like—"never presented a practical difficulty to any man." And this for a simple reason: "Whenever a mind is simple and receives a divine wisdom, old things pass away—means, teachers, texts, temples fall; it lives now, and absorbs past and future into the present hour." For ultimately God and "I" are one: "Let us stun and astonish the intruding rabble of men and books and institutions by a simple declaration of the divine fact. Bid the invaders take the shoes from off their feet, for God is here within." But is this the God of religion? Certainly not: "As men's prayers are a disease of the will, so are their creeds a disease of the intellect." How does Emerson view himself in relations with others and society? His attitude does not seem salutary or even civil: "Men cease to interest us when we find their limitations. . . . Infinitely attractive was he to you yesterday, a great hope, a sea to swim in; you have found his shores, found it a pond, and you care not if you never see it again." "Leave me alone and I should relish every hour and what it brought to me, the potluck of the day, as heartily as the oldest gossip in the bar-room. I am thankful for small mercies."

Denis Donoghue (*Reading America: Essays on American Literature:* (New York: Knopf, 1987)) joins Santayana in making the same points about Walt Whitman. The poet reduces experience to a succession of moods: and in this Whitman is a barbarian, one "who regards his passions as their own excuse for being"; for the passions are not to be understood or controlled, they are merely to be entertained. And this is Whitman's primitivism: he has gone back "to the innocent style of Adam, when the animals filed before him one by one and he called each of them by its name." Whitman tried "the imaginary experiment of beginning the world over again": no past is acknowledged as in any degree a restraint. Whitman ignores "the fatal antiquity of human nature." To him, the past was an alien place and, comparing his own world, he declared the latter a fresh creation. The first result was that he confirmed himself in his chief interest, his own sensations: nothing else was really alive.

It is obvious that our habits of self-absorption are home-grown, inherited or educated into us by our being born or having attended college in this country: one inherits these habits the way one inherits a surname. The whole range of our literature of alienation is only a confirmation of this absorption with ourselves. At times we label this habit the pursuit of happiness, at others the experience of discrimination, but in the end we are all familiar with the experience of alienation.

But alienation is only one side of the coin: the other side is the habit of mind of theoretical abstraction. An educated American joins the mainstream of American life when he or she is able to be absorbed as a theoretical entity, and absorbs the rest of the world as theoretical entities. Modesty and good manners demand that whatever is personal be kept silent and not allowed to interfere with this objective mirage. An educated American lets objective theory live through him or her— perfect theory, disembodied theory, with no room for subjective deviations. An educated American believes the world, objects, and people may be handled in a purely scientific manner, with subjectivity kept out of the picture and lived privately, in alienation or exultation depending on our potluck.

The Protestant habits of thought we inherit through our institutions operate on two important assumptions. First, thanks to them, we could establish a system of such open-mindedness that in America there would be room for everyone. Except that, and this was the second assumption, everyone coming to America to reside would have to stop being who they were, culturally and individually, and become the abstract entity that the Protestant habit of mind would allow. This habit of thought solved the problem of cultural plurality by divesting each one of us of the particularities of our own cultures and individualities in exchange for a place as a theoretical cypher in the American melting pot. And if this process proved slow or imperfect, we soon were taught habits of civility so that we would not address each other as to what we individually were but in abstract terms that would offend no one.

As Americans, we have labored under the need to identify as a culture. Traditionally the Protestant founders believed that they were doing science when they were doing theology: for them theology was science, an easy transition for the Protestant mind to make. After all, the scientists of the past shared absolute images as their background for an activity they were performing as scientists which was outside the domain of the humanities. America seemed to sell out to the scientific enterprise, except for a few incongruities and confusions still affecting the project of education.

Ours is not a scientific culture, but rather a culture which uses scientific principles to solve the problems of everyday living—at home, abroad, understanding the past, projecting the future. We adopted a technological culture, but this culture, as it became entrenched in our educational program, brought with it original flaws of conception that make any reform in education problematic if not impossible. The critics of education have not even addressed the problem, much less tried to solve the encroachment of technology on education. The confusion of the critics on this point is shared by most faculty; and we are less than honest in placing blame on the students when they show their own confusion.

To assume that we are dealing in the universities with two cultures, that of science and that of the humanities, is not only wrong but reinforces the false division. The humanities are identifiable as the repository of our backgrounds, our original images of tradition, and the tradition of those images. Though the tradition of the humanities may be expressed in prose, poetry, music, or painting, the primary identifiable criterion for the humanities is that they store our images, and the main exercises of the humanities are to keep those images alive and teach the creation and recreation of images so that we may remain alive as a culture and as a species. The operations of science, on the other hand, are concepts, and systems of concepts expressible only as concepts. Now technology as used in education inverts the roles, giving images to science and expressing the humanities only in concepts. It is a dedicated effort to subvert the classical role of education as we understand it or presume it, giving images where they are not needed, and removing them where they are an absolute necessity. This reinterpretation of the world for the expansion of the new culture of technology has become an ideology, rather than a rational, scientific, or humanistic enterprise. It is no surprise that the critics are clamoring for a return to the humanities, a return that is impossible unless the habits of mind imprinted by technology on the young are changed by other habits that make room for both science and the humanities. American education has surrendered to the dictates of a hybrid ideology which, in the name of science, has found a place in our universities because we already had habits of mind hospitable to its presence. But this type of education can only be imparted if students surrender their freedom and dignity.

It would be wrong to read what I have said above as an attack on technology. Technology, like science or the humanities, is one of the things we do, and may be judged by the kinds of acts it elicits from us. We cannot allow any of them to take over the whole range of mental operations, and still presume that we impart an education. Technologizing education is a form of inquisition, and contrary to our freedoms and our democratic ideals, since ours is a democratic society and our education should elicit from the students free acts, and not just provide indoctrination in the name of the general good, or the reigning fashion, or ideology. For education means the exercise of *educere,* bringing out those acts that the students have because they are the repository of the species, or of culture, and in no way canceling their dignity to perform as free agents in the name of more immediate rewards.

It is imperative that we face the problem of education as the problem of our habits of mind, rather than as the gathering of information or the imitation of teachers. A habit of mind is not simply a technique, but rather the repetition of mental operations, learned as techniques, which become embodied in a subject to the point of transparency. Software becomes hardware through repetition. Logic becomes epistemology and very soon metaphysics. The skills of reading become transparent— we are not aware of them—when we learn to read. Through these inner technologies humans extend themselves as far and as wide as the technology is able to reach. Language, through its internal and external tokens, is a technology. It not only creates the visible and the intelligible aspects of human life but also sensitizes individuals to those aspects of the visible and the intelligible that they reach in this manner. The only condition for this human fluidity through practiced technologies is that they be kept alive, remembered through education and through the exercise that education is.

Knowing the history of higher education is important if we are to implement certain habits of mind over others. Our present habits of mind have come about because we have actualized them through repetition in some historical sequence. But the habits of mind we presently use are not all the habits we have or have had as a culture or a species—hence the possibility of educating.

Where do we stand in the history of the habits of mind either present in our contemporary culture, or in the history of which we are a continuation? Are we the heirs of the mental habits of the Greeks, the Romans, the Protestant divines? Of all of them, or some? Have we exhausted the possibilities of our culture?

2

Our Philosophical Roots

Not too long ago being a faculty member at a university was a simple enough matter. Interpretation was handed down from an accepted common experience or an undisputed authority, and the role of the faculty member was that of mediation between that tradition and the student. Thus the tradition was kept alive from generation to generation, along with the abuses of the tradition. American education was founded by those who were abused by their dominant tradition and had lost the freedom to act. The liberty those early Protestants wanted to restore was the freedom to practice religion without restriction from church or state. Since the contents of education, in the old countries, were reduced to philosophy and theology, the persecuted Protestants found no other alternative than to emigrate to America.

The American colleges of the colonial period followed the British models of Oxford and Cambridge. The early colonial colleges were established under religious auspices and, like those of England, they served the upper social classes. The curriculum included grammar, rhetoric, logic, music, astronomy, geometry, mathematics, philosophy, and theology. Harvard University was established by the Massachusets General Court in 1636. Yale, founded in 1701 as an alternative to Harvard, came to be regarded by some as too liberal in theological matters. Virginia's William and Mary was granted a Royal Charter in 1693, Princeton was chartered in 1746 as a

Presbyterian College, and King's College, known later as Columbia University, was chartered in 1754 to serve the New York Anglicans.

Like the European colleges they imitated, the American colleges were elitist and religiously oriented. Primary or vernacular schools were opened for the lower socioeconomic classes, where students were taught reading, writing, arithmetic, and religion. But the preparatory schools and the colonial colleges were reserved for the sons of the upper classes. Women and the poor were excluded. Through social reforms and several local and world wars, education changed its colonial face more or less in step with changes in Europe. But we in America did not seriously consider the state of our educational system until the political cold war had set in and we felt inferior in education to the Europeans. But by the time we tried to do something about it we found certain forces already in place in our colleges and universities, and discovered to our amazement that a trend was in progress in education that had not been there before.

For one thing, the curriculum was no longer religious; in fact, religion had been excluded from the curriculum. For another, education was in the hands of experts from the social sciences or the positivist schools of scientism, and philosophy was no longer the decisive force on matters of curriculum or education. Thirdly, any critic could attack education as long as the attack was radical, advocating that nothing of the past should be allowed to stand.

How did we pass from a faculty of Protestant divines to a faculty of "modernists"—Cartesian, Hegelian, Positivist, Marxist? How did modernism find tenure at the universities? And principally, what was there in the habits of mind of the Protestant divines that made it possible for them to become the umbrella under which the so-called enemies of our nation live, thrive, and educate our young people? How can we fight Marxist governments, but allow Marxists to educate our young?

An Open Mind

None of us coming from repressive traditions will be able to praise sufficiently the open mind we found in America. A breath of fresh air crossed our souls as soon as we set foot on this land. Gone were the shadows and the people inhabiting them, and the fear that sooner or later they would catch up to us. But those of us engaged in education soon found out that an open mind may become the only habit of mind of a people and that this habit could be turned into a calamity because it could be manipulated by those who use it as an instrument of repression. There are those who have translated an open mind into a theoretical mind never able to find itself among the particulars, never able to judge particulars, never able to do more than the habit allows: they gather theory after theory with the same uncommitted lack of emotion as one gathers lumber in the hope of building a house.

I remember first the relief, then the shock I experienced when people talked so openly in America of the political right and left. They could have talked with equal dispassion of cabbages and kings. I had just arrived from Spain, where any talk of right and left was sufficient to land people in jail, or at least to start a physical fight. What had happened to us in America to be able to talk about anything, the most profane and sacred, the most cherished and hated, the most intimate and trivial, all with the same lack of passion? We had developed an open mind, for better or worse.

Our English Protestant founders left to us the habits of mind they themselves inherited from the Protestant Reformation. The human soul divides into private and public. The private part includes emotions, revelations, all the subjective traits that form individual conscience. Though this individual conscience is autonomous and above public dogmatism, it is ultimately a private affair between the individual and his or her God. The public part of the soul must be objective, free from all subjective biases, and rational on the model of the sciences. It is this objective claim that made of theology a science. How these early Protestants understood religion determined also how they understood education, and the habits they promoted in its pursuit. John Cotton (1585–1642), Benjamin Colman (1673–1747), William Ellery Channing (1780–1842), and Ralph Waldo Emerson (1803–1882) may serve as their early models. All these preachers emerged from the Puritan tradition with a deep concern for shaping the *rational* and *emotional* aspects of religion and religious experience. And there is no doubt that while engaged in their life's mission they contributed also to a revival in education, spreading literacy and their versions of the spiritual and social life. More significantly they show us how their preaching, their way of teaching, was also their own spiritual practice and how it formed the educational and spiritual practice of their time. It is significant that even today most people in America understand religion and education the way they did, and what was foreign to them is foreign to most today.

The early Protestant preacher and educator took education as the gift of prophecy. Education was the art of bringing out this gift. They shared a belief in progress—a progress guaranteed by the accumulation of knowledge through objective science. Prophecy to them was the inspired act of speaking forth the Spirit, but since the Spirit comes forth through hearing, the preacher must direct his words to his audience in such a way as to persuade them, or at least one member of such an audience. Protestant thought thus established a "true" connection between Spirit and external form, inspiration of a sermon and its delivery. In this manner it broke away from other biblical and nonbiblical traditions (Catholic, mystical, Hindu, Buddhist, etc.). All the preacher needs to do is touch the individual with the Spirit, for if the Spirit touches the individual, then the Spirit is its own *interpreter*. This frees the individual from any mediation of other humans or even institutions. Interpretation, as much as experience, is private, and its privacy is not the result of reason but of experience itself. This conclusion might have opened a Pandora's box of anarchism, but Calvin came to the rescue. He proposed that the Bible contained knowledge that was "objective and informational," as well as knowledge reserved for the elect. Thus acts of interpretation of the Bible are legitimate and can be delivered to the masses through education, for they have not only an individual but also a social dimension. And in this project, even those who do not share the status of elect may participate.

Thus the model of the spiritual practice of the Protestant preacher is the task of bridging the gap between piety—that mysterious and overwhelming sense of ecstatic union with a transcendent whole—and everyday concerns about moral judgments and decisions in the world.

Our inherited Protestant habits of mind thus establish a

separation between the rational and the private. For starters, there is no room in this tradition for the development of emotional and affective technologies. They are systematically marginalized as private, when many cultures now present in our nation were shaped by the development of those technologies. This, in practice, is tantamount to saying that Protestantism in its early foundational role closed the door to the education of any other faculties, any other habits of mind, than those approved by Protestantism as rational. The rational, on the other hand, was presumed to be primarily "disembodied objectivity," an assumption that has proved so costly in education, since theories have a quick way of becoming human flesh: our students are the embodied result of such theories, rather than their agents or choosers. Nor does it help very much to try to keep the conversation open by declaring, like some Protestant teachers such as Tillich, that all claims from whatever source are symbolic or metaphorical. This is the kind of claim one would not dare to inflict even on one's enemies. The thirteenth to nineteenth century Inquisition could have been avoided by such a claim. But I wonder if any of those killed by the Inquisition would have preferred to be branded heretics, or be dismissed because they had created a world of fancy and believed in it to the point of being declared demented? Are all the cultures we call oral-audial demented because they shaped their rationality on the emotional structures of imagining? Or are we short in rationality because we have not been able to discover the rationality of the emotional?

The argument hardly needs to be made that American democracy cannot be built on a plurality of *symbols* declared to be so by those who hold the interpretation of the public domain. Only true realities will create a democracy, political and individual. And this is the challenge of education.

The Modern and the Postmodern American University

Americans held with blind faith to their belief in the progress of science. It is, therefore, not surprising to find that the authors in our curricula are predominantly of the seventeenth to nineteenth centuries—men who justified with their philosophies the enterprise of science: Descartes, Leibnitz, Kant,

Hegel, Hume, Locke, and few more. The medievals were ignored, and the classics, Plato included, were used only as an extension of the moderns. But the progress of these thinkers was not on a par with the urgency of the problems to be solved. Furthermore, they were too heavy for the new clientele of the universities.

The early university served exclusively the priestly class, with education conducted in Latin, the language of the clergy. In the eighteenth century the university served as a gentlemen's club—a school of languages, diplomacy, wit, and manners. In the nineteenth century the university opened its doors to the mercantile class, and was now dedicated to modern studies and applied science. But the American university opened to the proletarian class and had to invent new methods of instruction, new colleges, diverse curricula, and shortcuts to knowledge so that education would be universally efficient. Americans, almost single-handedly, invented the social sciences, and certainly were the most devoted, outside of the Russians, to legitimize and implement them in the university. Our hero in this endeavor was John Dewey. He succeeded because so many Americans agreed with him that the place of the sciences was the core of the curriculum, and anyone trained in the sciences was an educated man or woman. But the social sciences are not science in the strict sense but borrow principles from science and apply them to nonscientific domains, like populations, human behavior, human knowing, human predictability, and human aspirations and dreams. The verifiability of the claims of the social sciences is not as important as the fact that they have established themselves as substitutes for the humanities, philosophy included, claiming conclusively to justify the work of the sciences and their own work. In the process of such boisterous and false claims they have also reduced thinking to achieving results, quantification, statistical probability, approximation, doubt, relativism, confusion, and the exteriority of all mental life.

The social sciences have emptied the classroom of any spiritual images, substituting in their place masses of numbers and facts, mountains of information that make image making difficult, if not impossible. Facts, figures, and platitudes are no substitute for philosophy. Experts now take the place of the earlier priests, and they advise the educated and the superstitious about all facets of their lives, from belief in God to sexual behavior. The expert appears routinely around every corner where opinions or knowledge are needed, in foreign policy, in the press, in how to take care of a toothache. Indecision and confusion seem to appear all around us, and we have taught it.

Nor are only the students and the superstitious affected by the new trend. Whole departments of philosophy await the results of experiments by the social scientists to pronounce on matters of philosophy. Positivism and language analysis do not take a new step without the aid of the social sciences. And even then they express themselves in the subjunctive mood and no longer in straight, declarative sentences: "If it were the case that such an x existed . . ."

The old metaphysics, the assertion of how things are, is dead for most philosophers and the few adhering to such an antiquated philosophical style are affected by the new fashions from the social sciences. Where once the categories of thought were abstracted from the internal structure of thought itself, now any external structures, provided they are general enough, will serve as the architectonics of all thought. In such systems of metaphysics everything, even the foundation, becomes a category, and thus nobody flinches when "experience" is proposed as such an abstract category. But how would anyone flinch when almost everyone accepts the definition of epistemology as a theory of knowledge, regardless of the fact that cultures including our own are testimony to the contrary: epistemologies are historically many and none is a theory, but rather a concrete set of rules and presuppositions that make knowledge possible.

If any feature characterizes our contemporary age more than any other as to what is being taught at the universities, it is total freedom. No one is able to restrict, oppose, or turn the tide of freedom as it is presently exercised in the universities. In the name of this freedom, individual or departmental, a host of narratives is inflicted on the students under the protection of education. Sociologists and critical theorists are the more visible proponents of the new freedoms. Under their auspices our civilization has entered the *postmodern* condition in highly developed societies. Since science, on whose model they claim to act, has always been in conflict with narratives, science is obliged to legitimize the rules of its own game. This discourse of legitimization produced by science with respect to its own status is *philosophy*. Its first assertion is that the narratives of the past, judged by the yardstick of science, are mere fables. And if the narratives are false so are the meta-narratives of legitimization on which they rested. "The most notable falsity," so a postmodern professor argues (Lyotard, *The Postmodern Condition: A Report on Knowledge*, Minneapolis-University of Minnesota, 1979), "is the university institution which in the past relied on it. Thus the society of the future falls less within the province of a Newtonian anthropology . . . than a pragmatics of language games. . . . They only give rise to institutions in patches—local determinism. The old principle that the acquisition of knowledge is indissociable from the training of minds, or even of individuals, is becoming obsolete and will become even more so."

The postmoderns believe that all knowledge is informational, and as such is indispensable for the production of power, and the competition for power. Only the knowledge that can be exteriorized will survive; knowledge is only interesting if it contributes to the mercantilization of knowledge. How does one legitimize such a claim? According to Lyotard one needs only to establish a working hypothesis, and this working hypothesis does not need to make a claim of being original or true: "What is required of a working hypothesis is a fine capacity for discrimination." In other words, that it be a theory, and that it be stated, supposedly with discrimination. In actual practice discrimination is not necessary in most cases, for the people teaching theory do so to students who mostly lack training in discriminating. The humanities have been lately invaded by such theoretical exercises. A newly established Humanities Institute defines itself with the following three missions: 1) To stimulate research in theory, criticism, and interpretation across the humanities; 2) To become an international center for a unique theoretical perspective, combining traditional critical methods with newer ones, such as semiotics, post-structuralism, feminism, psychoanalysis, speech-act theory, and hermeneutics; and 3) To develop new interdisciplinary courses for graduate students and faculty. Needless to say this institute is funded by the university where it resides.

The Question of the Curriculum

It is an obvious truth that contemporary technology has expanded the field of knowledge well beyond the grasp of undergraduates and even of the faculty. It is also unquestionable that industry and research have contributed to the social welfare. The problem lies in the fact that a selection must be made of what is and what is not relevant to education, what can and cannot be taught, what can and cannot be learned. Contemporary critics of American education have all insisted that undergraduate education should once more be based on the classics, that a curriculum should be structured around the classics. This is a laudable goal, except that in practice it does not solve the problem of undergraduate education. This unhappy result is not the fault of the classics, but of the habits of mind of those who conceived such a program and teach it. Nor is it the fault of the students—bright young men and women, able to digest in one semester what took generations to create and formulate, and yet condemned to carry within themselves an existential doubt as the result of their training.

I shall mention only two different models of how the classics are used in education: together they give us the range of possibilities from the sublime to the stupid. The first model, the best one available, is the program of undergraduate education offered by St. John's College, Annapolis, Maryland, and Santa Fe, New Mexico. The other is offered at my own university under the device of "core curriculum."

St. John's program is exemplary. It mixes the sciences and humanities of each classical period, using the language of the period, engaging students and faculty in rebuilding the culture from the cellar up. Pythagorean and atomist science are not only discussed but are exercised previous to being discussed. Science and humanities face one another historically as students and faculty engage in bringing to life the past, dead once, now alive through their inquiry. A sense of community and mutual dependence between faculty, students, and the classical tradition is established in such a way that it becomes visible to the outsider. The commitment to the intellectual life is so evident no one even questions what to others might appear an overdose of intellectualism. The classics are alive and well at St. John's.

A closer look, however, reveals several factors that demand a revision of such a program. The homogeneity of tradition presumed for the nineteenth century is no longer tenable in America. None of the other classics representing many of the cultures now present in this continent are represented in such a program. Does it mean that becoming an educated American requires first that one become an educated European? What tradition is our American tradition? Is education a mirror, a model, or both?

St. John's program is, no doubt, overly *heady*. The eye of the student seems to be always reading from a book inside of his or her brain, in search of the perfect theoretical formulation, the theory that explains by itself. The classics are read with a theoretical bias, born much later than they were, and now dictating the moves the students may follow with their support. There is a lot of argumentation, a lot of self-doubt, a lot of retracing of steps, a lot of intellectual insecurity—just the opposite of what the student should carry within to make decisions in the culture he or she inhabits.

There are several reasons for such intellectual gropings, the most evident being that the classical authors became public, by writing or stating the results of their private and public experiences in a book, while for the student the book is the experience. The classical work became a classic by putting down something new, being a reformulation of a background the author shared with his contemporaries. This background that the classical authors shared with their contemporaries is not made relevant to the present. An intellectual life without absolute images, absolute background shared with others is a unique experience of our times but not of the classical authors. And if this is the case then we fail to teach the students the main ingredient of a democratic life: how to perform free acts that are not dictated by the imitation of others who demand that our acts resemble theirs: teacher-student, past-present, theory-theory. The classic became a classic by projecting thought against imagination, foreground against background, not by simply thinking. But despite these criticisms, a program like St. John's could develop the model for the future of American education, for all it needs is to enlarge upon an ongoing experiment with the right people already involved in the dialogue that education requires.

Next to this program at St. John's the patchwork of courses offered as "core curriculum" at the university where I teach, and the way the classics are taught shows the other side of the coin of freedom—sheer irresponsibility.

Literary theory is big, or very vocal, at this university. The program offered in combination with English leading to a Master's and a Ph.D. in Comparative Literature is an attempt to build an independent department dedicated to literary theory exclusively. Students are required to be versed in contemporary literary theory, with no other readings required—in fact, they should be avoided. The required reading list is confined to Plato's *Ion* and *Republic*, Aristotle's *Poetics*, and Horace's *Art of Poetry*. Significantly, of Plato's *Republic*, the students are required to read only chapters II, III, and X. It is easily apparent that the purpose of those selected readings is to prove Plato a forerunner of Marx. No wonder one of their instructors was teaching undergraduates that the sun was inside the cave in Plato's *Republic*. This department devised a "core course" for the Humanities Department entitled: "Sin and Sexuality in Literature." Needless to say the course drew a large number of students. The reading list included Plato's *Symposium* and Euripides's *Hippolytus*. The rest of the reading list is more titillating: *The Story of O, The Color Purple, Madame Bovary, Portnoy's Complaint*, plus, for good measure, excerpts from *Penthouse Forum*.

The exam for such a course consisted of multiple choice questions such as:

The event which brought together the speakers in Plato's "The Symposium" was
a. a wine-tasting party given by Phaedrus the Sophist
b. a celebration for Agathon after his victory in the competition for best tragedy (This is their desired answer.)
c. a celebration for Aristophanes after his victory in the competition for best comedy.

Or see this other confusing question:

In Socrates' (Diotima's) speech in Plato's "Symposium" and in Christian doctrine we are told
a. sexual love is always benevolent and healthy.
b. the values (where did they find this formulation?) of the spirit are

greater than those of the physical senses. (This is their desired answer.)

c. it is better to pluck out an eye than to commit adultery in one's heart

d. none of the above.

Regardless of the intentions of the authors of such a course, it is evident that the results on the undergraduates are educational: sin and sexuality are literary theories, disembodied beliefs appearing in literature, which again is also an instrument of literary theory with the power to level all the classics to the heights of *Penthouse Forum*. Once this is established, students are not required to exercise anything more than to signal which of the multiple choice questions seem the most accurate. Where is the literary exercise? Furthermore, courses taught in this manner also raise the question of credentials. Is everyone teaching at the university entitled to teach anything they want, theology, philosophy, without any credentials to do so? Can a few dictate to the rest of the university community what the humanities are? How can a discipline like comparative literature which is *not* normative, dictate to philosophy, which *is* normative?

The problem of the curriculum, ultimately, rests on clearly separating the domains of the sciences and the humanities. Students learn from the hard sciences—mathematics, physics, biology—what concepts to use and how to use them. The humanities primarily teach images and their creation. Between the domains of science and the humanities we have the professions whose function it is to apply scientific principles to technology and other fields. Although they create knowledge, the sciences and the professions do not justify the human use of such knowledge. We have no way of knowing, within those sciences, if we ought to use such discoveries for human life. We never question the use of technology because reason has surrendered to power—this because we have given up on educating our young and ourselves, choosing instead the inertia of power and comfort. If this is the case, we should give up the universities and build professional schools, become trained in technological skills, surrendering the humanities and our decision-making privileges to machines. Let's give up freedom altogether and settle for liberties. The fact that we do not do so, but rather fight our own educational system while we teach is perhaps a sign that freedom is not completely lost.

The memory of our Western tradition should liberate us from complete failure with regard to the American problem in education. Much of what we complain about is inherited, and we should uncover our inheritance in order to continue with our program of education for Americans.

3

An Alternative Philosophy of Education

Our educational policy is primarily a theoretical exercise. The classics, the moderns, the contemporaries are dispensed in the classroom within an egalitarian wrapper of theory that levels all historical and cultural differences. To teach is to theorize, either in the heroic manner of the classics or in the indecisive manner of the contemporaries. The critics of American education seem unaware of this obvious fact, against which any reforms of the present system will end up as a mere exercise to provide "food for thought." Thus, not only the teachers in the classroom, but the critics as well, presuppose a history of education that is not true, not only of other cultures present in our nation but also of the so-called Western culture. Secondly, teachers and critics fail to see that the way in which they teach is limited to one particular and historical habit of thought that reduces education to the virtuosity of its performance, thus reducing education to less than it is capable of producing. Both teachers and critics obliterate the lines separating what is internal and what is external in education. If all we teach is theory and information about a world already in progress, where is the free act? What acts may a student perform that are not dictated from the outside? Where is the change, the novelty, the transformation, the freedom?

Students are creatures of habit, with education primarily an exercise to bring out (*educere*, educate) these habits. From an educational point of view, the history of education is the history

32

of the formation and implementation of these habits of mind. But habits of mind are not only the forming of ideas; they include a whole range of operations that act through the human body to the point of total transparency to the subjects using them. The philosophy of education is, or ought to be, primarily concerned with the formation of these habits in the students before it proceeds to any other projects. A habit of mind is the technological lifeline of the human body. Through these technologies the human body stretches to reach the past and the future while sensitizing itself individually. What we call the objective world is shaped by these subjective structures of human knowing, and knowledge is impossible without them. They are also the sensual life of the body, and since the body abhors a vacuum they must be kept in exercise at all times. Habits can only be changed by other habits, and the history of education is the best reminder of such a struggle for certain habits to dominate over others. The more radical and transparent the habit, the more radical and difficult the change, and the deeper the concentration and dedication needed for the implementation and development of the new habit. Habits of thought are the most difficult to change. Other thoughts, true or false, sublime or stupid, only reinforce the already existing habit of thought. Nor will psychologizing or sermonizing about thought help. Education alone will do if it understands its mission as the concerted effort and ability to bring out all those habits of mind that make up the whole human ground of the culture and of the individual mind and soul.

Habits of Mind as Used, and Their History

A habit of mind is not simply a physical technique, like the use of tools. A habit of mind should provide more than the ability to use a hammer. A habit of mind becomes embodied in the subject and, once acquired, affects all the operations of the subject while affecting also the configuration of the environment. A habit of mind is an embodied technique that through repetition becomes transparent to the subject. Reading, for example, is a learned technique that becomes transparent to the subjects once they start reading. They can only read if they forget the technique while reading. Software becomes hardware through repetition and, like the invention of the printing press, habits of mind form cultural loops that transform the culture and the individuals using them. As a culture we have several such habits of mind: deductive logic, inductive logic, transcendental method, dialectical thought, the borrowing of images, the constructing of images, the forming of opinions, the skills of fantasy. Through language—its materiality, its measures, its rhythms, its repeatability, its ordering of mental life—humans extend themselves as far, wide, and deeply as language allows them through the habits they have developed. In practice, habits of mind act as detachable organs in humans and the abuse of one against the others creates individual and social paralysis.

Language, as much through its internal as its external tokens, is a technology. It not only creates the visible and the intelligible aspects of human life but also sensitizes individuals to those aspects of the visible and intelligible that it can reach. In this creation of the visible and intelligible, language and technology become coextensive. The visible and intelligible adapt to the language used, so that language determines the shape of the visible and intelligible. The mere act of teaching, the act of speaking to students, determines the shape of their education, regardless of what the teacher says. A language attached to the purely deductive habit of thought assumes a human power attributable only to a divine intellect. Those defending the inductive habit of thought assume a human impotence attributable only to our complete dependence on the givenness of objective events, and those using the transcendental or critical habit of thought assume that their categorizing mind and its data are the only measures of the real.

But neither the conceptual system, nor the habit of mind accompanying the use of such a system, assert anything about reality. A conceptual system and the accompanying habit of thought are only the preconditions for meaning or asserting anything about reality. Conceptual systems take on existential import when the system as a whole is used to refer to what is not in the mind or the senses, though having a system to refer to presupposes having a meaningful notion of knowledge or reality. Neither the contents of a conceptual system nor their counterparts—the organic states of the sensory system—are in their own right significant or intentional. They only signify or represent a state of affairs (itself experienced) because *we* take them to do so. The natural intentionality and disposition of the mind can be committed to a knowledge and a reality which are constructed so by us in response to an already-committed way of viewing the world. Thus, reinforcing the students to perform only certain mental acts to favor certain ontologies is not only fallacious but noneducational. In education, more than anywhere else, there is perplexity about how to decide what ontology to adopt, and the answer is: education rather than indoctrination.

Judgments, opinions, or values cannot be taught to the students if those judgments, opinions, or values are not shown as being part of the system of concepts to which the student or teacher belong. For they are not factors in our conscious experience but rather a presupposition of our conscious experience.

It is this lack of correspondence between our teaching and the background through which our teaching is done that is mainly responsible for the present crisis in education. The answer is that we must focus on the background from which our teaching is done so that education, rather than indoctrination, is made possible.

Our Inherited Habits of Mind

The history of higher education is important, not because it is history, but because higher education has been shaped by the adoption and repetition of certain habits of mind in historical sequence. (See chapters 6, 7, and 8.) While these habits of mind are mostly transparent to their users, examination from a historical perspective may make them visible, with surprising results.

The most significant result is that from the point of view of our habits of mind, we have been teaching the wrong history of education. What we call our history of Western culture is mostly the reduction of that culture to what we could accommodate to *one* habit of mind, *our* theoretical propensity.

Secondly, this habit of mind present and transmitted to us by the early Protestant founders of the American university was already present in Europe as the legacy of the Romans.

Thirdly, the claim that our culture dates all the way back to the Greeks, Plato in particular, is false when we examine the habits of mind of the Greeks.

Opposing these three conclusions, which appear negative for American higher education, one positive fact does exist: If the actual state of education in America is bad, it is not because we have exhausted our possibilities as a culture, but rather because we have not even used the possibilities we have had at our disposal.

The limited number of habits of mind we have put to use since the birth of the university in the Western world date only from habits of thought inherited from the Romans, through the medievals, and through the application of scientific ways of thinking to educate. These exclude the habits of mind that the Greeks proposed as the project of education. Plato's project of education has never, with the Romans or with us, been adopted in our educational system, though Plato's words have been used as a theoretical justification for completely different habits of mind already in use.

The university appears in Western culture with the translations of Aristotle's logic into Latin by the medievals, and these skills of logic became the different disciplines of epistemology, ontology, metaphysics, cosmology, etc., that Avicenna invented and contributed to the spread of the universities. A rational system of concepts was developed to justify the claims of theological belief, and the content of the curriculum of the universities was philosophy and theology only.

The habits of mind of the medievals reinforced a theological narrative that in turn reinforced the habits of mind for which it was born. Where the medievals thought they were establishing the will of God in society, they were in fact rediscovering the Roman values of family, nation, fatherland, law—classifications inherent in the habit of thought inherited from them, along with bureaucracy and the fear of the original, the different, the feminine, the source. Conservatism became an inquisition for control of other habits of mind that would give rise to other worlds, and the liberals of those days were right when they affirmed that at the center of the claims of conservatism was nothing but the fear of losing the power to control and exploit society. But the liberals failed to bring to the culture other habits—liberating ones—to counteract the reigning conservative habits. Only the mystics of those days, at the risk of their lives, kept alive a tradition of liberating habits of mind, but the mystics were prevented from speaking their own language in public.

Descartes introduced in the culture the narrative of modernity with a new habit of mind, derived partly from the previous tradition, partly from the hidden rivers of mystical practice. The world was to be apprehended from mathematical models, while the subjects doing the thinking would see themselves as disembodied observers. Thinking itself was not to *be* thought, as by the previous tradition, but it would mean only *having* thoughts. The new habits of mind Descartes shaped with rules was soon implemented through education and the narratives of Locke, Rousseau, and others.

What we know under the name of science is the accumulation of several traditions with different habits of thought. The view that nature was to be best understood as a machine or a set of machines, what we call the mechanical tradition, was the one that came to dominate nineteenth century scientific thinking and influenced so deeply American attitudes in the universities. In this image, a machine is something made up of interlocking (atomic or molecular) parts that perform cyclic motions, but are devoid of intrinsic purpose, in an otherwise empty space-time container. Nature, in this mechanistic version, has no spiritual, rational, or preternatural powers, except, perhaps, the human spirit.

This mechanical explanation was a substitute view of the one held by the medievals. The Middle Ages conceived the cosmos holistically as a living thing, full of finite powers and limited rational purposes, a legacy of Rome, and this model perdured in biology and medicine up to the nineteenth century, influencing science, as in physical cosmology.

Another habit of mind present in the scientific revolution and in so many quarters of contemporary American life is the habit of mind present in the followers of the Hermetic tradition. This tradition stemmed from the Neoplatonic revival of literature of the fifteenth century Renaissance. It based itself on numerology and older Christian and Gnostic sources from Egypt and the Middle East in particular. Alchemy, astrology, and the science of mnemonics (or memory) were the constituent features of this tradition. The habits of mind of the practitioners of these traditions touched religion at one extreme and magic at the other. These practitioners conceived themselves as agents of divine or preternatural powers in nature, either controlling such powers to serve private or communal purposes (magic) or working in conjunction with such powers for the greater glory of God (religion). Copernicus, Kepler, Gilbert, and Newton, as well as Francis Bacon and the Puritan divines were deeply involved in and influenced by this tradition. They saw themselves as engaged in solving the cosmic riddle and also as guarding the secret formulae. American Protestantism favored the new sciences, particularly those with a strong Hermetic component such as chemistry or alchemy, while it distrusted mechanical explanations as dangerously antireligious.

With the rise of modern science new habits of mind developed. The method of the sciences and the image of scientific narratives became unquestioned and reinforced the new habits of mind, becoming an accomplice to those that would best accommodate the new image. These habits of mind became a duplication in the classroom of what the sciences were supposed to be doing in the laboratory. They developed clear and distinct ideas imitating mathematical models that are hypothetical, abstract, ahistorical, and humanly disembodied. Descartes, Newton, Galileo, Locke, and Rousseau are the best examples. The mind was trained to repeat certain logical operations until a habit was developed of reading the world according to those skills. Even if the reading was supposed to be disembodied and therefore objective, the result was that the viewpoints and skills became embodied in those using them. For the older habits of mind, external cosmologies (now considered outdated) were substituted in all classrooms.

It is with Hegel and Marx that thinking as a purely abstract operation, justified as the evolution of the spirit or as being demanded by material dialectics, becomes crystallized as the present habit of thought of most of contemporary teaching. This is the top of the mountain, the habit of mind speaking through the mouth of the critics of education, as a Hegelian or a Marxist rhapsody. This exclusively used habit of mind buries the history of our species, our own history, and those inner acts we need to develop in a democracy both for freedom and for recognition of those present in the democracy.

Today's educational critics demand that education be the

practice they themselves exhibit—historically blind, theoretical, abstract, ahistorical, incomplete. (This may well be the reason why the book by Allan Bloom was so well received by both sides of the political spectrum.) But all of these critics fail to see that this practice would destroy our democratic commitment. Our society, as well as the individual souls it serves, is a composite of internal acts, a democracy of acts. Some of those acts are alive, others are buried. Education is the practice of bringing all those acts into equal presence by making them active through the exercise that is education. But American education is involved not only with the past but also with its own present, and while we need to revive habits of the past, it is also obvious that we need to discover what needs to be done today in the American educational and social context, and this cannot be an imitation of something from the past. It might have to be invented. Where are the technologies of invention in the classroom?

In the *Republic*, Plato devised for education a project based on inner acts and acts of invention. He proposed as a project of education a classification of those inner acts and the way to keep them active, and rejected viewpoints and philosophies as substitutes for the exercise of those acts. He also proposed a project of education where inventiveness would be given top priority as the legitimate exercise of all those entering the gymnasium and not left to the genius. But what happened to this project?

Plato and Our Greek Heritage

The *Republic* is still the primer of education (see chapter 11). It begins with these enigmatic words: "Yesterday I went down to Peiraeus. . . ." and with them Plato launches the listener into one of the most astonishing quests of the human spirit: wisdom. Plato/Socrates envisions education as a training in particular habits of mind that would guarantee a habitual practice of virtue. Virtue for the Greeks was the habit of being able to choose the best from among the possible, and this by habit. Hence Plato's project is the training of the young to make visible to themselves (in the soul) and others (in the polity) the performance of "virtue by habit."

As the narrative of the *Republic* unfolds we find that Socrates agrees to the initial "robbery" of his own person by the young men and that he uses this opportunity to form a "community" in search of those technologies (training) that would make justice visible to all. While a lot of talk goes on for five long chapters in a search for what appears to be a definition of justice, we are made aware of a number of spaces—the house of Polemarchus, the Cave, the region of Er, the desolate region of the dead. Within each of these spaces, different intellectual acts, using different communications media, intelligible and visible, are performed. All acts performed during the whole narrative of the *Republic* concide with those acts which Plato/ Socrates divides with his famous "divided line." And each space demands a different language, a different inner technology for its use and participation in the community. Each use demands a different embodiment from the practitioner. The totality of these embodiments is the criteria for an educated young person to be able to recognize in society what he or she inwardly recognizes: the need for justice inside to bring justice outside. Thus the *Republic* includes the quality of a number of acts to be performed, and also the partial narratives of each space of discourse. No universal narrative from one space takes over the narratives from any other—there is no universal philosophy.

In appearance the prose of the *Republic* leads the listener along a smooth path. There are changes of direction and delays in the journey, but all in all there appears to be a progressive development, an intimation that the listener is nearing home. But suddenly Socrates takes over and introduces sudden shocks and abrupt discontinuities, setting the familiar expectations on their head. At the end of Book Six of the *Republic* he introduces the divided line, followed by the Cave, and the narrative of Er.

The divided line ought to be a simple exercise in reading (509b–511e). How difficult could it be to divide a line into two unequal segments? One, according to Socrates, must be larger than the other; one must be labeled *intelligible*, the other *visible*. Which one is which? (Depending on which habit of mind educators use, they will name the two parts differently, but this is not in the *Republic*.) Are images abstracted from empirical objects, opinions, objects of art and science, visible or intelligible? Is the larger portion (which Plato in the *Sophist* 236b and

The Visible	IDEAS Imagining: The Making of Images	WISDOM Certain knowledge
	Objects of Science and Art. Theoretical Thought	Shadow of Knowledge
	Opinions, Beliefs	
The Intelligible	Images from Objects	

II. THE DIVIDED LINE AS EMBODIED TECHNOLOGIES

Nowhere in the *Republic* does Plato say which part of the divided line is the intelligible and which is the visible. The fact, however, that Plato describes in detail the acts by which objects and mental operations are performed makes it impossible on hermeneutical grounds to identify the larger part of the line as corresponding to objects and acts of just thinking. The technologies of thinking are identifiable with the other parts of the divided line. The upper part and longest part is the world of Er and the technologies connected with "practicing death," "remembering," and "imagining" as described in this study.

This interpretation sets the history of philosophy on its head. No lesser an authority than Kant in his *Critique of Pure Reason* A 313/B 384 writes:

Plato made use of the expression 'idea' in such a way as quite evidently to have meant by it something which not only can never be borrowed from the senses but far surpasses even the concepts of the understanding. . . . For Plato, ideas are archetypes of the things themselves, and not, in the manner of categories, merely keys to possible experiences. In this view they have issued from the highest reason, and from that source have come to be shared in by human reason.

Kant, however, modifies Plato's "ideas" and reduces mental life to sets of concepts of pure reason. And he adds:

The absolute whole of all appearance . . . is only an idea. Since we can never represent it in images, it remains a problem to which there is no solution (*Critique*, A 327-328/B 384)

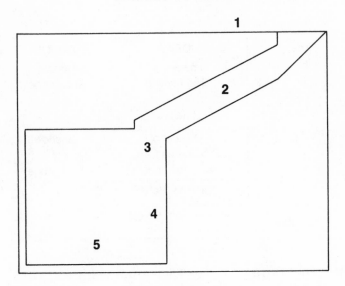

1. THE REPUBLIC:

ACT 1:

The physical place of Peiraeus in relation to Athens: 1. Athens; 2. the way of the descent; 3, 4, 5 Peiraeus.

ACT II and III:

The Divided line and the Cave. 1. The Sun; 2. ". . . the rough, steep way up." 3. . . . "the fire burning far above and behind them"; 4. "human beings carrying all sorts of artifacts"; 5. "the prisoner, facing the wall of shadows." The intelligible casts shadows only, and it is seen such.

ACT IV:

The narrative of Er. All life, human life, takes place in the cave. There are no humans who make human life in the Sun region. Therefore the descent into the Cave which now becomes the ground of death. Out of the death of the past new life emerges through the technologies of imaging. One must, however, be adept at "practicing death." Memories and imagining are capable of resurrecting the past to make it present life. Through this practice the technologies of the visible are kept alive.

264c divides into *icons,* or good images, and *simulacra,* semblances without likeness, or bad images) visible or intelligible? Educators feel that they must make a decision as to which part is which. If they decide a priori which is which, the result will be disastrous to their teaching, closer to indoctrination than actual teaching. If they do not decide on which part is which, then they will have to settle for a program of exercises in the hope that the students will be able to discern by themselves the visible and the intelligible. Plato's answer to this problem is to give no answer at all, for in no place in the *Republic* does he settle the question of which part is which. All Plato does is to describe the acts that through performance prepare the student always to choose the best from among the possible. Besides, a commitment to either side of the divided line or to any one of the narratives from either side would ruin the educational project.

Plato's whole educational enterprise is concerned with developing *quality* in the performance of our inner acts. It is in relation to this quality of performance that he is able to sort out different worlds and the claims of the members of his community. These inner acts performed through education and training rely on their similarity to an original, invisible form. Yes, Plato demands that we accept models. It is in view of these models of acts internally performed (if they are good acts) that will make the invisible visible. The only criterion for judging their validity is how good are the effects produced, for the better the effect the closer the acts performed internally were to the invisible model. The life of the Cave is the image of a life where the intelligibles predominate as *simulacra* (bad images) because they negate the need and existence of original, invisible models. Er appears in the *Republic* as the journey of memory to keep alive those dead by recreating the acts that made them immortal. Er is the reminder that education is an exercise in bringing to life what has already happened, the activating of memory and imagining in such a way that we, the living, keep the whole story of the culture or the species alive. Memory, in this exercise, turns to images which turn the past into new life.

Plato's journey of education acknowledges the body as the primary vehicle (inter-text) of those acts humans performed in the past which serve us as models to perform on our own, to preserve ourselves in innovation and continuity. As humans we

are neurophysiologically connected to one another and to a
common enterprise: the fitting of our souls to the good, while
discarding all those external goods that are not permanent.
This "fitting of the soul" is the primary task of education, is
coextensive with habits of mind found in our human past, and
therefore is historical. For this reason remembering texts and
inter-texts in the present is also the building of our history.
(This remembering of acts to be performed has little to do with
the remembering of information by heart—but without the
heart that created it in the first place.)

By the end of Book Six of the *Republic* the house of Polemarchus is transformed into the Cave. The sun is now up and
the Cave is down. In between there is the mid-region of the fire
where the intelligible forms and the teachers are seen as being
the cause of the shadows on the walls, and how these shadows
are the guiding light of the prisoners. Prisoners and teachers
live under the power of these shadows, are sensitized by them,
and feel their own human emptiness. The region of the sun is
obviously "the solitary region" and different technologies are
needed from those of the shadows to allow the prisoners to
reach there. Human life is always in the Cave and education
should bring the technologies of seeing the sun into the classroom. For the Cave gives birth to simulacra, ideology, the
repetition of one single human habit of mind and its narratives
of liberation. The enemy is within the classroom. The negativity of the Cave is exactly the power it has to negate, the power
to negate models, and the substitution for non-centered viewpoints of the speaker.

Plato introduces imagining as the foundation of education—
not the imagining that we attribute to our selfish acts of fantasy
where the act starts and ends for the benefit of the performer,
nor those acts of imagining that we perform by abstracting
images from objects already present in the world. Plato would
have education build in the student the technologies of invention by making visible what is absent, the sun as it sets over
Athens in the *Republic,* or Love as found in the earlier *Symposium* by tracing its genealogy. Love is the offspring of *Poros*
(abundance) and *Penia* (scarcity) (*Symp.* 203c–204a). Consequently love lives in midair, in a region as vast as it is endless, in
a homeless land (*Symp.* 203c–d). Love is never entirely full,
never entirely empty (*Symp.* 203e). It rests somewhere between

complete wisdom and complete ignorance as the eternal mediator between heaven and hell (*Symp.* 202e) and must remain in midair: a move too close to either side would be the demise of love. Since love has no home it is only in *loving* (repeating the act) that love makes a home. Of itself it has no nature but finds itself only in the acts of love performed. It gives birth to goodness (*Symp.* 206b) and through these acts prolongs itself into immortality (*Symp.* 207a). It is in the creation of goodness and beauty that we become rid of the indeterminateness of the mid-region, the homeless ground, and become one with the immortal (Symp. 207a).

How does a mortal perform this fantastic transformation? In *Symposium* 210a–212a, Plato discards as proper to this goal but not to be absent from education the technologies of logic, rhetoric, acts of logic, and acts of thinking. He proposes instead technologies closer to initiation exercises into mystery religions than to Aristotle, Hegel, or Marx. In *Symposium* 109a–210a he indentifies these technologies with acts of imagining of the kind we might call creative imagining. For this imagining is not an abstraction from objects empirically given to the senses, but rather an imagining that begins to act only when the senses, all information coming from the outside, and all images are canceled. As in the *Republic,* one enters this world by drinking of the "milk of forgetfulness." Here Plato is specific: "[This imagining] will not take the form of a face, or of a hand, or of anything that is of the flesh. It will neither be words, nor knowledge, nor something that exists in something else, such as a creature, or the earth, or the heavens, or anything that is. . . . (*Symposium* 210a–211a)." In the *Phaedo* he gives us the positive clues:

> the real earth . . . is multicolored and marked out by different colors, of which the colors we know here are only limited imitations . . . there, the whole earth is made up of such colors and many others far brighter and purer still.

For in this world of imagining, colors are sharper, mountains and stones smoother and even transparent, better than the precious stones our senses know empirically (*Phaedo* 110c–e).

But it is in the *Republic* that Plato summarizes for us the technologies of imagining (*Republic,* 508e–511e; 532a–534e):

1) the soul must be turned into an opposite direction;

2) a different faculty must be used than the ones we use to create opinion, images, thinking, theorizing;

3) different objects and different reading signs must be created;

4) a different kind of knowledge is created in the whole composite of body and soul, thus

5) enabling us to choose from among the possible the best.

Plato repeats these criteria for imagining in the *Phaedo* 67c–d and in 79e–81a, as the exercise for creating "experience after death," or of achieving experience "through practicing death," by accustoming the soul to "withdraw from all contact with the body and concentrate itself on itself . . . alone by itself."

In short, Plato understands education as a unique concern and a unique motivation for the *quality* of all the acts it performs to educate. Quality of performance concerns itself with directing the will to select and sort out those acts that are historically capable of being remembered and thus repeated. Distinctions and divisions leading to those acts are to be found in the quality itself of the acts performed, not in the external property of objects and their external relations. For it is in these internal acts, without intimation from the outside, that human freedom resides. Divisions, in Plato's scheme of education, are made for the sake of establishing an inner genealogy that separates the pure from the impure, the authentic from the inauthentic, but in no way is it concerned with any classification through genus and species. Plato establishes things and images, originals and copies, models and simulacra. And this can equally hold when sorting out gold, as in the *Republic,* or when sorting out claims, as in the *Statesman,* the *Phaedrus,* or the *Symposium,* "I am the shepherd of men," "I am the possessed," "I am the lover."

The Education of Habits of Mind

Private industry and graduate schools are entitled to concentrate on any habit of mind. The members of those groups are supposed to have been educated. In order to be able to perform in private industry or graduate school students should receive an education based on the ability to make use of the habits of mind inherited from the traditions that educate them. Measured by Plato's standards, which we claim to be our own but which remain mostly ignored, the life of the undergraduate student is not just in a cave, but in a cave within a cave within a cave within a cave. Protestant habits of mind are inserted within Roman habits of mind, rendered visible by the medieval schoolmen. Theorizing for its own sake at the hands of literary critics is served up by Marx and Hegel, through Kant and the medieval Suarezian version of Aristotle's first act of the mind being the apprehension of essences. Imagining as prescribed by Plato as the foundation of education, even when tempered by the public discourse and the acceptance of the public domain, has been removed from education. The classroom has a closer resemblance to what Plato called the simulacrum than the training for the good life. In the classroom, models are not accepted, not even copies of copies, but instead degraded icons and simulacra appear daily to establish images without resemblances. We are teaching so that the students internalize a dissimilitude. The simulacrum includes within its power the capacity to cover up and exclude all originality, all history, by forming those constructions that include within them the angle of the observer, the teacher, the professor. This blind center, this non-centered perspective is the true flight from the original image, progressing toward the unbound, a gradual subversion of history, an avoidance of the limit, of the same and the like. It is also the negation of both copies and originals, models and reproductions. It is the birth of simulation, pretense, and the inauthentic, providing no criteria for repudiating the false claimant. This is as close as we can come to social madness.

It is in this context that the soul of the student suffers an eternal night of the shadows of the cave. The soul finds itself split in an agonizing dualism: on the one hand the student has been taught to develop a habit of reading the world through theories that give rise to possible experiences and legitimize them and, on the other hand, the soul has to contend with a theory of verification that establishes that it is a reflection of real experience (empiricism). Under this metaphysical constraint, human life defines itself as a continuous series of experiments, as temporary commitments, the absence of maps, a decentered chaos at the root of identity—for the only center left is difference, and this difference lets out an internal shout of the soul affirming its own power, in an imitation of madness, as its own eternal movement of eternal difference. The soul of the student has witnessed in itself the rise of the spectral simulacra in its own non-centered affirmation. The false has risen to power through the tenure track offered at the universities. The same and the like, the model and the copy have fallen under the power of the false (the simulacrum). Hierarchies have been made to disappear and thus there is no possible participation of the soul in anything, in determining and distributing value. The world of the university, and thus of the student, has become an eternal difference of nomadic and consecrated anarchies. Foundations have floundered in the soul and in society, and the only hope left is the hope of total collapse, the joyous event the modern soul looks forward to, with no power to stop the race toward the end. Nor are there any narratives left to sustain the individual student in this flight from the past. Skepticism is total except in the belief in constant change for, thanks to this perpetual change, the modern individual is capable of sustaining the incommensurable.

It is better that we have as clear as possible a picture of the student facing us, for unless we understand that student from the inside of his or her own modern habits of mind, we will never understand what needs to be done or why what he or she does is closer to virtue, as the Greeks understood it, than to such ethics as the Romans left us or to Christianity reiterated. The modern student is opening a path in spite of living in the darkest cave the soul has ever inhabited in our history, and most of the defects we detect in the students—the self-absorption, the relativism, the appropriation of meanings without actually carrying out the work of making meanings—are no more and no less than the defects of the culture educating him or her. With the failure of the churches to educate their own, and the families relegating education to the schools, the only temple left for young men and women today is the university. We may well admire their faith, when all their beliefs have been destroyed; and these are the people we need to educate, for they carry the future of our tradition.

What lessons would the *Republic* have to offer to the present-day university? Or perhaps we should ask, how distant were the Greeks from our present-day university?

Like the modern university, the *Republic* unfolds in Peiraeus, "the land beyond," the land beyond the limits, a place not in Athens and "yet within the defensive walls of Athens" (Bremer, 1984, p.3). "Peiraeus," like the modern university, is both in and not in Athens; it is the place that gives common interests to the assembled speakers, the young men from Athens ready to take on the responsibility of running the republic. And this is as close as we come to any resemblance between the model Greek university and ours. The Greeks never had a university to develop and cultivate the mind. They had *gymnasia*, universities for the body, where men and women would gather together naked for the sake of exercise. Strength, agility, and character were to be developed through the physical exercises of racing, jumping, boxing, throwing the discus and the javelin, swimming, wrestling ("Men and women should wrestle naked in the gymnasium," asserted Socrates).

Greek language, law, medicine, and science were native— they did not borrow them from anyone. "Are you a Greek or a barbarian?" simply meant, are you original or a borrower? For this reason they never relied on authority, but instead practiced philosophy as an exercise in intrinsic achievement. A single Greek philosopher could, for this very reason, synthesize in himself a whole university, as the *Republic*. All the acts that created the sciences and philosophies, as well as the people who were the creators, were at the tip of the philosopher's tongue. Since the philosopher was the synthesizer of the culture, it was from him alone that the students could learn whatever was necessary for them to know in the field of public affairs.

The Romans, on the other hand, started by borrowing from the Greeks their own speech. Horace put it thus in his *Ars Poetica* 53:

> which fell from Grecian well-spring,
> but slightly changed.

They also borrowed their laws, though the Romans tried to cover up this robbery by grafting them into their own political system with great ingenuity. The Romans did not think of establishing universities either but for very different reasons

than those of the Greeks. The Romans had given up on the
ideal of wisdom, or understood wisdom to be the art and
practice of law. By the time the "academies" were established in
Rome, Constantinople, and Beirut, the republic had become a
principate and the purpose of the "academies" was to propa-
gate the science of law as legal doctrine.

And yet, there are intimations in Plato's *Republic* as to what
to expect from a university (But first, a word about the spon-
sor. Now that ideology has tried to apply ethics and separate
ethical from unethical money, whatever that means, we should
be reminded that our primer in education, the *Republic,* was
sponsored by Cephalus, a weapons manufacturer employing
thirteen slaves, in whose house the dialogues take place.)

Plato/Socrates agrees that education is in "community." Five
books of the *Republic* are spent gathering the "community."
And when Thrasymachus, the master of the logical overkill,
could disrupt this community, preventing it from reaching the
experience of its own acts, Plato/Socrates simply leaves him out
of the "community." Today we might promote him to teaching
or administration at the graduate school. The students forming
the "community" must be given the dignity and freedom of
their own acts. They must perform all the acts described in the
divided line by themselves, without imitating others or being
forced by others to agreement. Finally they, the students, know
only when they *see* by themselves—not when they *think* by
themselves.

The teacher, in the role of Socrates, must avoid teaching any
philosophy to them even when he or she has one. He or she
must lead the students through acts that would cover the whole
range of habits of the culture. Teaching a philosophy would
cancel the plurality of the exercises for the proficiency of one
skill.

But above all, the university is a place where the soul experiences both death and resurrection: the death of selfish habits
and the resurrection of "the community of the dead." And Er is
the model Socrates offers to his community of students.

Er is the student of every tribe. He is not a Greek, an
Athenian, a Thracian, or a Persian. He is a *Pamphylian,* an
immigrant, a man who makes his home everywhere. He is
every student. He is also Socrates and Plato. He is punished
alone, born alone, and alone he gives his testimony. He is a

pure child of education, and also a warrior for whom every place is all the life there is. He lives in the presence of death, in the presence of the past, and is also a messenger of the future with no freedom to refuse. He is the student/teacher.

Er, the student, Plato, Socrates, is the opposite of Homer, that bad poet who not only imitated others but also buried the dead. The student needs to resurrect the past the way Plato rewrites the *Iliad*. Plato does not name Achilles or how he buried Hector and thus he holds back the hand that killed memory, the purpose being to be able now to tell "the whole story."

The place of Er is Hades, a place of total bereavement. None of the familiar sensations are present. The worlds are forgotten, canceled; images upon images keep rising from the past to become alive in "community." Er, the student, is systematically dismembered by lending those images of the past—sight, sound, touch, smell, taste, and movement, so that they again become alive in the present. Only what is thus imagined is real. This dismemberment, this participation of the student through his or her own internal acts is the necessary condition for the message not to be forgotten, so that the messenger delivers it accurately. Remembering is injecting the past with the live sensations of the student in the present. Thus a neural link is established between the past and the present, and among the members of the community.

But education, in this performance described by Plato in the *Republic,* is a humble exercise for both students and teachers. It is work done in the dark until the students produce their first public acts. Their training is visible in the way they affect the public domain, how they perform, how they make decisions.

The good life of the individual or of the republic is not possible if the student has not had a taste of it, has not seen it in his or her own soul while in training.

4

An Alternative University

The American university and the habits of mind it promotes in the education of the young are modeled mostly on the European Protestant university. Its most distinctive feature is theoretical abstraction, the definitive activity of the high priests in education. Under the protection of this habit of mind, all sorts of theories (and their advocates) have found refuge in the university, notably dialectical materialism in its many varieties, and ideologies of all sorts. Surprisingly enough, no one has seen fit to question this original determinism of our universities, as if the model followed were the only possible one and its goals were clearly delineated and unchangeable. But this would be a wrong assumption: the university has a surprisingly short history, and its goals have been neither clearly delineated nor unchangeable.

Protestant Reformation and Counter-Reformation.

The Protestant university was born as a protest against the medieval schoolmen, while the Catholic university of the Counter-Reformation was an alternative to both. But all these people saw education and the university disrupted by war, and Protestant reformers and Catholic counter-reformers agreed to leave education in the hands of the Church. Significantly, however, Europeans had several models of universities and often were able to taste more than one.

52

How bad was the education of those days? Luther summarized the disarray of the times more dramatically than the present critics of education in American have done:

> [the students] learn only enough bad Latin to become priests and read Mass . . . and yet remain all their lives poor ignoramuses fit neither to cackle nor to lay eggs.
>
> —*Works* IV, 128

Luther called the universities "dens of murderers, temples of Moloch, synagogues of corruption, only worthy to being reduced to dust" (*Janssen* III, 355). Luther's companion Melanchton complained that the "universities were turning students into pagans." Thus Luther and Melanchthon took it upon themselves to reform German education. In an *Epistle to the Burgomasters* (1524), Luther requests from the civil authorities permission to establish schools. In 1530 Luther proposed that elementary education be made compulsory and provided at public expense (Paulsen, *German Education*, 56–57). To the universities reformed under Protestant rule, Luther proposed a curriculum based on the Bible, with Latin, Greek, Hebrew, German, law, medicine, history, and "poets and orators, heathen and Christian" (*Luther* IV, 128). One by one, the German universities came under Protestant control: Wittenberg (1522), Marburg (1527), Tubingen (1535), Leipzig (1539), Koningsburg (1544), Jena (1558). But soon the politics of control started: professors who were opposed to the "right, true, evangelical doctrine" were dismissed. Calvinists were excluded from teaching or attending Lutheran colleges, and Protestants were barred from universities where Catholics controlled the teaching. After 1555, German students were forbidden to attend schools of a different faith than that of the territorial prince (*Janssen* XIII, 260, 264).

The English Schools, Luis Vives

English schools suffered even more than those of the rest of Europe with the wars of Reformation. Monastic, guild, cathedral, and chantry schools practically disappeared. The supply of university students provided by those schools also ceased. In 1548 Oxford graduated only 173 bachelors of art and Cambridge 191; in 1547 and 1550 Oxford had none to graduate. Henry VIII established Trinity College (Cambridge) in 1546, and private philanthropy founded Corpus Christi College, Christ Church College, St. John's College, Trinity College at Oxford, and Magdalene College at Cambridge (1546). But faculty and curriculum came under government control. Scholasticism came to an end in English schools and canon law was set aside. The curriculum was largely secularized by law (1553) and all candidates for degrees had to subscribe to the Anglican Articles of Religion.

The most progressive treatise on education at this time was written in 1519 under the auspices of Henry VIII, *On the Education of Children* by Luis Vives, a Catholic Spaniard teaching at Louvain. "Education," he wrote, "should be directed to the necessities of life, to some bodily and mental improvement and to the cultivation and increase in reverence" (Haydn, *Counter Renaissance*, 242). Vives proposed that formal studies should cover the whole of life, and that the subjects to be taught should show the interrelation of those studies to life. Nature, he proposed, should also be studied, for the experience of things is more instructive than books and theories; students should also study the human body in its anatomy and activity, and not just in a book; students should also consult farmers, hunters, shepherds, and gardeners, for this will be more useful "than the scholastic babblement which has corrupted every branch of knowledge in the name of logic" (Haydn, *Counter Renaissance*, 199). Francis Bacon is not far behind.

These examples from the sixteenth century are important because they show concern with reform and the use of the universities to implement those reforms. In every case a curriculum was established and in every case a crisis in education meant a rally around a reform in the curriculum. Yet, we need to be mindful of the past and to see the aberrations. What in Europe begins as a cry for individual freedom, the unified experience of the curriculum, and the political forces implementing it, ends as the tyranny of homogeneous beliefs. And thus, tyranny is equally visible in the pulpit as in the universities. It is as undemocratic to demand through education assent to the religious narratives of the sixteenth century as it is today about the narratives of scientism. It is obvious that the curriculum by itself is not sufficient to guarantee an education, even when education is always done through a curriculum, as demonstrated in the *trivium* and the *quadrivium* of the ancients. The crucial question is not about the curriculum, but what to do with the curriculum in order to guarantee the students an education and to reduce to a minimum the possibility of indoctrination. What we need to know first is if there is any other model of the university we have not examined in our past which might give us some guidance in our present search.

The Universities of the Counter-Reformation

The European Counter-Reformation has not yet entered the American Constitution the way the Reformation has. For this reason, its models of education are not likely to be found in the public institutions or the consciousness of America. It is, therefore, always a danger that while we are very conscious of the harm the Inquisition did to individuals, we forget that we could be under collective inquisitions imposed on us by our institutions of learning.

The European Jesuits, founded by Ignatius de Loyola (1540) mounted the Counter-Reformation against Luther and Protestantism. Their goal of reforming the reformers was a far cry from the inquisitorial methods of other religious groups: their main weapon was education.

No other group since the sixteenth century has had more influence on education or used education with greater ability. As Roland Barthes has noted: "They (the Jesuits) taught Europe how to read and write with style." (*Sade, Fourrier, Loyola* p. 39). The Jesuits grounded their system of education on *studia inferiora,* corresponding to the German *Gymnasien* and the French *Lycées,* and *studia superiora,* or colleges. In many cases they took over existing universities, like Coimbra (this being the first, 1542) and Louvain, and shocked the competition by offering free instruction. On February 22, 1551, a wooden sign appeared outside a doorway at the Capitoline Hill in Rome which read: "School of Grammar, Humane Letters, and Sacred Studies. GRATIS." This sign marked the birth of the Jesuit Collegio Romano, later to become the Papal Gregorian University. By 1580, the Jesuit monopoly on higher education was secure from Portugal to Poland. The major universities of

South Germany as well as Prague, Vienna, and Ingolstadt were collectively under Jesuit control, and the universities of Wurzburg and Graz were built expressly for them.

Externally the curriculum did not offer very much diversity from those at Protestant universities. The Jesuits did not, like other religious orders, decide to stand or fall with the old scholasticism, but grounded their education on what was known as the *Ratio atque Institutio Studiorum Societatis Jesu*, approved and collected by the then-General of the Jesuit Order Fr. Aquaviva in 1599. The *Ratio* takes education to consist neither in repeating scholasticism, the Bible, or humanism. Education is not a repetition of the past, nor is content or information to be considered the measure of education. The *Ratio* views education as consisting of a series of exercises performed by the students with the aid of able teachers. These exercises should include all the human faculties, and the best curriculum is the one that provides the widest range. Narratives are used only as exercises of discovery, not of belief. The following example should clarify this project which for so many years was the educational lifeline of Europe. By the time Ignatius de Loyola died (1556), the Jesuits were operating 100 colleges. By 1615 they had 372 colleges, and by 1700 the number had grown to 769, as well as 24 universities, spread all over the world. They also left an impressive list of names attesting to their system of education: Galileo, Descartes, the famous heretics of the French Renaissance, as well as Voltaire, Anatole France, Pascal, Renan, Molière, Pierre Corneille—even the Marquis de Sade had a Jesuit tutor.

It might be easier to narrate the workings of this model of education through two of its best products, Descartes and Galileo.

While the European Jesuits stood officially for the public narrative of the Church, the actual practice of education deviated from orthodoxy under the guise of speculation. Under this guise, even scholastic philosophy was made interesting. It became so for Descartes and Galileo, though in different ways.

Every student of the Jesuits knows that the beginning of logic, which all must study, is to establish which is the first act of the mind. Is it an act (judgment) or is it the apprehension of essences (needed to make judgments)? Descartes had to go through this exercise which divides the Jesuits themselves into conservative and progressive theological positions, a division marked by the followers of Thomas Aquinas as contrasted to those following Suarez. The "essencialism" of the first act of the mind reached Descartes as an exercise in *Logica Minor* through the writings of Francisco Suarez. While in the classroom students could play the game of "what if . . ." as an exercise in education, this game became in the hands of Descartes a method serving as the foundation of modern science together with the Suarezian "essencialism." Descartes did not have to undergo an epistemological change adopting the new method; he just used the epistemological exercises of the classroom as they were applied to one particular field where they became a fixed narrative.

The case of Galileo is more complex. William A. Wallace in *Galileo and his Sources: The Heritage of the Collegio Romano in Galileo's Science* (Princeton University Press, 1984) makes a very convincing case for the thesis we are advancing here.

Galileo received his education at the hands of the Jesuits at the Collegio Romano (founded 1551) and, as Wallace shows in his book, there they practiced exercises in speculative epistemology and mathematical modeling, establishing a link of continuity between medieval and modern science. Galileo compiled his early *Latin Notebooks*, the *Logical Questions*, while at his first academic appointment at the University of Pisa (1589–91). These writings deal with epistemological topics such as the presuppositions of scientific inquiry, and the nature of scientific proof. In the *Physical Questions* he deals with the nature of heavenly bodies and of terrestrial elements and change. Wallace's analysis of these books shows that the Aristotelian content and scholastic structure of the *Notebooks* were mostly copied, adapted, or otherwise compiled from unpublished lectures and notes or public works of Jesuit professors at the Collegio Romano, which can be specifically identified.

The *Logical Questions*, Wallace shows, provide a clear case of the "what if . . ." type of reasoning, i.e., hypothetical or suppositional thinking; the fact that this suppositional thinking was also filled with mathematics is also in accord with his Jesuit mentors, the progressive Clavius, Blancanus, and Guevara, though other Jesuits at Pisa and Padua objected to this mathematization of hypothetical thinking. It is, however, obvious that the discoveries that Descartes and Galileo came upon would not have been possible without the exercises of the classroom. The student does not have to agree or disagree with the teacher or professor; his is an exercise and the public domain may judge it when the student becomes public—even if the success is so great as to bring the Inquisition on his head.

There is much more irreverence toward one's teachers among the disciples of the Jesuits than those of other systems. But this irreverence is part of a deeper acknowledgment of love not easy to find in other systems. Jesuit education is famous for the numbers of rebels it has created among its disciples. Anatole France summarized this insight with his famous acknowledgment-rejection: "In the Temple we forged the hammers which destroyed the Temple." Again, it is not their education that they rejected (they were all proud of it, as is so clear in the case of Voltaire) but the ideologies they received with the information and the official curriculum of the Church.

Voltaire summarized for us the main purpose of education in view of prevailing ideologies filtering through it: "Let us cultivate the garden."

The Shape of an Alternative University

It should be clear by now that the crisis of the university and the crisis in undergraduate education are not due primarily to certain isolated abuses by some. The fact of the matter is that abuses have become the norm, and some would even go as far as to claim that the mission of the university is the propagation of the abuses we condemn.

And here we must be fair. The modern American university seems to be clear about the following:

1. Research and graduate teaching;
2. The training of the professions.

But it seems to be confused about:

3. The education of undergraduates;
4. The role of philosophy in the education project as a whole.

In order to best serve the needs of education at the under-graduate level, the following changes must occur. Namely, the curriculum of the sciences and the humanities should be geared to exercise the mind of the students and to eventually develop the habits of mind needed to:

1. become adept at handling the conceptual operations of science, mathematics, physics, biology;
2. become adept at creating and judging the "images" of the humanities, literature, art;
3. become versed in reading different interpretations of the same events, literary theory, criticism;
4. become familiar with other cultures, their images and narratives.

The university should make sure that the goals of the un-dergraduate education are not mixed or dispensed as if they were delivered to professionals or graduate students. The university should make sure that the classroom is an exercise in pluralism of inner acts. Also, the departments should accept the responsibility of reducing ideology to a minimum. This responsibility can only be accomplished effectively if classroom hours are not marked to satisfy the needs of the sciences. The humanities have other needs and other ways of occupying the minds of the students that are not to be measured by hours sitting at a desk in a classroom. The humanities should liberate themselves from the tyranny of the sciences in determining the length of class hours that students and teachers should spend together.

The university should seriously consider the present state of affairs regarding philosophy. All the disciplines of the university owe their foundations to philosophy, having been born of its questions or of its answers. And that means that philosophy alone is normative, being the only discipline completing the full circle of reflection and justification of its own act, unlike the other disciplines, including the sciences. This means that while the university may do all it can to promote its participation in the culture, the university or the sciences cannot say if the society they claim to serve *ought* to use their discoveries. The discussion of the public domain and of the actual policies of the

university cannot be decided without the intervention of philosophy. This simple truth separates the university from being
an institution at the service of truth or of power, and the same
applies to teaching policies at the undergraduate level. The
physical structure of the disciplines at this level need be less
rigidly separated and more interconnected to avoid the abuses
of ideology, or the promotion of power for its own sake. Undergraduate studies should function more independently from
the rest of the university than up to now, when they seem to be
a requirement for preparation of future graduate students
toward fulfilling their required steps for graduation.

But the purpose of this book is not to offer global policies,
or to remedy the crisis of education by demanding that everyone should take this or any other lead, nor even to offer the
negativity of criticism as the only thing we can all do while we
carry on in the classroom—as if by opening our mouths in
public we had already corrected the situation while doing
nothing new in the classroom. The criticism offered so far is
aimed only as the context for the rest of the book. It is within
this context of present-day education that the project of this
book—the exercises proposed in the following chapters—is
offered as a counter-reform in the education of undergraduates. I believe that individuals carry the modulation of cultures,
and not vice versa, and fifteen years of teaching at this university have made me believe even more in the power of inner
human spirit over the indoctrinating power from outside technologies.

5

The Experiment

If inquisitions, biases, and ideologies have always been with us in higher education, and if contemporary inquisitions, biases, and ideologies are engaged mostly in giving us a totally negative picture of people, students, the culture, and the institutions of our education, could not the opposite also be institutionalized in the universities and colleges? Do we need a complete program of positive education approved by the institutions, or could a single instructor create a positive, exuberant, creative course that would be educationally and philosophically sound, and thus subvert the murky current?

Tucked away between "Sexual Deviance" and "The Philosophy of Love and Sex" I found a very unpopular course listed in the undergraduate catalogue as "The Philosophy of Education." In an age when departments need warm body counts for their politics of budgetary appropriation this course had died for lack of demand.

When we started teaching this course fifteen years ago the demand went quickly up from a small fifteen to more than 700 pre-registered students per semester. It has been my experience that the course is not as easily manageable when the number of students exceeds 200 per semester. Thus there are many students left out on a waiting list, and this explains their eagerness to pre-register.

The students are divided into groups, as many groups as authors are presented—and the authors presented include only the giants of education from Plato to Dewey. In fact, they include the authors in this volume. No judgment is made a priori for or against such a selection. Making judgments is left to the students after their presentations.

The groups are formed by the students themselves without any external influence from the professor or the teaching assistants. The role of the teaching assistants is to supervise attendance of the students at discussions and class participation. In no way should the teaching assistants lead or guide the groups. The reasons why students come easily into groups vary: they either know, like, or are intrigued by the author (Marquis de Sade is very popular), or because they live in the same dormitory, or because they have no other option left. It is not very important why the students get together in groups; most likely they do it for the wrong reasons—and it makes no difference.

Each group is responsible for presenting, as a group, a dramatized version of the author or the text chosen to the rest of the students on an assigned date. The group is graded as a whole. The interpretation, dramatization, props, costumes, the actual play is entirely up to the students without any "leading help" from the faculty. For a period of a few weeks they read the author, invent their own image of how the presentation ought to go, and bring it to the whole group to start rehearsals. By that time each member of the group has a different image of the presentation and a different interpretation of what is relevant. And then the fights begin. It is to be made clear to the students that after they are assigned to a group they cannot move to another. So they are forced to fight it out and, ready or not, they make the presentation on the assigned date. I have not known of any group which thought it was ready on the actual day of the presentation, or failed to deliver. In a very short time—two weeks at most for the early presentations—the students have discovered the difficulty of forming communities out of their own individual paths, and how quickly they as a community stand against the other groups. They argue among themselves, read and reread passages, fight and share a common image, and start sitting around the classroom and the university in their own communal groups. All this time, even outside class-time, they are engaged in shaping their presentation. Suddenly the students find themselves making decisions, instructing others, distributing roles, looking out for the good of the group, sacrificing their own rights for those of the group, and even deciding when someone should be expelled from the group for lack of work, attendance, or both. Learning in this manner far surpasses listening (in boredom) to the wisdom of one professor, regardless of how good he or she might be.

The course or experiment has additional requirements. An individual written test is given toward the end of the semester to make sure the students have done other readings prescribed in lectures and assigned in books to promote their cognitive skills. The teaching assistants take care of the other require-ment—attendance at classes, and in group forming and pre-sentation.

It is advisable to use undergraduate students who have taken the course previously. The students are more open in their presence and do not try to cheat as frequently.

Requirements for Teachers and Students

This course is designed for the students to exercise their faculties: making images (presentation), answering questions in a written test (cognitive skills and information), reflection of their experience (philosophy). Other side benefits accrue from participation in communities. It should be stressed that while the presentation is communal, the written test is individual. Teachers should not worry too much in making the require-ments clear every semester. They will be surprised at the easy way students take to the rules. The dissemination of language on campus makes this task easier every semester. Students seem to know everything the first day of classes; all they want to do is get on with the presentations.

Professors might find a course like this a very heavy burden to carry. It makes no difference how enthusiastic the students may become: it is a large load to carry, but the benefits are also great.

Professors should use a lot of restraint. Make a vow to give the students the dignity of conducting the whole affair by themselves. This means, particularly, not leading them in the question of what image they should present in class. If the students are told which image to present, their creativity is taken over by the teacher, and the result will not be the same. The exercise consists in the students making an image out of something they do not know, know vaguely, or need to know. It is only after they have performed this exercise that one can see how easy it is for them later on to add the information needed, correct the image, or even go beyond the accepted images.

For this reason the professor should place this course on a space beyond Nietzsche's negativity and the negativity of structuralists, deconstructionists, modernists, Marxists, critical theorists, or whoever thinks he or she has the truth. This needs to be a postmodern course with the guarantee that the original acts needed to create, sense, speak, and reflect may be performed without inquisitions from the outside. Let whoever gives the course keep out of the picture as much as possible except to direct traffic.

It is advisable, in order to make a course like this work, to load the grading, at least initially, in favor of the student. This does not mean to become arbitrary. There is a lot of creativity, imagination, decision making, and qualitative education for which we have no grading available. Students consume weekends and night hours preparing the presentations. The professor could use the presentation or the written test as the high grade and use the lower one to descend rather than to climb from the lower to the higher.

Since the presentations last for about thirty to forty minutes, the professor should make sure there is time left over for other students to get together at that time to prepare theirs. This is the only way commuters may participate in this course.

This course allows for a great variety of modification in authors to be presented. Texts from other cultures are always included, like the Gita, or women from the past as a model of education for women, and texts from American minorities, like Afro-American poetry. It is up to the instructor to read his or her audience and quickly come to decisions as to what would be most pertinent to the particular audience in the classroom.

Any course, particularly if it becomes popular, may be easily taken by the students for the wrong reasons. Large numbers may cover inactive students hoping to pass through the activity of others. All the students see is the joy, the good word, and the spontaneous claim that it is easy. People seldom realize how much more work is done when things are easy than when they

are hard. Professors should not mind misunderstandings before the students join the course; once inside they are his or her
responsibility. But I have also learned to live with something
only America may be proud of: waste. Where there is waste
there is wealth.

Abuses are not the norm and their occasional presence
should not make the professors try to control it at the cost of
stopping creativity. In all of these years I have only failed one
group for its presentation. They mistakenly took the Marquis
de Sade as an occasion to show a dirty movie; they justified
their work by mounting on the movie with great ingenuity the
bodies of the participants in the presentation. They failed not
because the movie was filthy, but because they failed to see that
the Marquis de Sade had the opposite message in his writings.
Language for the Marquis de Sade sustains whole cities, and
the people of those cities, with its own dry power of sheer
emptiness. His language is empty of images and action and yet
sustains those who believe that to name things is enough, or
tantamount to doing things or knowing, as people in education
believe, that to know is being able to name and repeat those
names.

But most of the presentations are memorable and people
speak of them and themselves even years later.

I remember them from time to time and cannot help smil-
ing, for I have seen that the Greeks were right when they took
it that having ideas was actually "seeing." I have seen my students *see,* and later on reflect on this seeing and become good
philosophers, writers, lawyers, or simply people who could
taste quality in silence and make others do so.

It is to me incomprehensible that students are blamed for so
much of the crisis in education. The students at this university
are not what one would call pusillanimous. They stand no
nonsense and are very bright. They are at their best when their
creativity is challenged.

I remember the presentation of the Gita somewhere in the
Middle East around an arranged wedding of the son of a king
while the Six-Day War was going on.

Or the presentation of Voltaire's *Candide* when the students
chose instead of the proposition of Voltaire: "This is the best of
all possible worlds," the proposition from the social sciences
that "Man is a machine." They had a scene, still unsurpassed by

its sheer creativity, where two professors from the behavioral sciences were conducting a seminar on "Beyond Freedom and Dignity," while bowling at a bowling alley. The pins were students dressed in white robes and brown necklaces to look like pins, and the bowling balls were other students the professors would pull by the hair and casually roll against the standing pins. Score was kept by a referee as the professors made their theoretical points while playing the game. The miracle was how the students could deliver their lines with a straight face when the audience was roaring at every word and gesture.

And then there are some unforgettable lines and insights. The students' version of Nietzche's criticism of Christian prayer was to have a little old lady praying for Christ to listen to her prayer for the whole presentation until at the end a booming voice is heard over the loudspeaker saying: "Woman, I am his Father, haven't you heard he is hung up?"

And there was the group of seven students which had to use a large table in the middle of the room which could not be removed and decided to pretend they were on a boat from a capsized ship, and delivered *The Revolt of the Masses* as they were sinking. We are so used to the mixing of cultures and races at this university that we did not pay attention to the fact that of the seven students only two were Anglo-Saxon Americans, while the other five were Koreans. While delivering the Bill of Rights one of the Anglo-Saxons forgot his lines. The other one immediately improvised: "Just as well, for where we are going they speak no English and have no Bill of Rights."

After all the years of teaching this course I can safely say that the favorite author is *Plato,* with the *Republic* and the *Symposium* being the most popular presentations. It would make a book by itself to set down the varieties of caves I have been introduced to—all very real. The *Symposium,* on the other hand, is excellent for bringing out the performing talents of many students, particularly the understated homosexual, but I must confess with great sadness that Love has not found the right performance yet at this University.

The Plan of This Book

The chapters that follow are arranged in the actual order in which we discovered our habits of thought; that is, in the historical sequence we have used them. Thus we start with the medievals and their use of Aristotle's Logic. We then move to modernity, with the narratives of Descartes, Locke, Rousseau, Voltaire, Marquis de Sade, Nietzsche, and Dewey. And we end up with the actual beginnings of our culture: Plato, the poets.

It is, therefore, obvious that my proposal is for a return to our origins if we are to educate, and not contribute further to indoctrination of our undergraduate students.

This short history of our habits of mind is sufficient to make us aware that what we call Western tradition is only the result of a few of those habits of mind: the realist logic the medievals borrowed from Aristotle and transformed, the abstract mathematical operations of Cartesian methodology, the abstract-dialectical reason of Hegel and Marx. Nowhere in this history of the West is Plato's project of education present, nor has it been implemented or even tried, except indirectly by the Jesuit system of education that the Jesuits developed in Europe, which produced such good students as Galileo, Descartes, Voltaire, Pascal, and many more. It is this system, and the belief that any one professor is more powerful than any system, that I propose as an alternative to the present impasse. This system is based on the exercise of all the faculties of the students. It is so clear in its goals and practice that any ideological moves within it easily give rise to the critical, mordant attacks of a Voltaire in *Candide,* or in some similar fashion, for ideology is instantly detectable.

The last justification for this system is that at last we will be practicing what we have been preaching all along, namely, that our education is based on our Greek origins in Plato and Aristotle. But remember Socrates' teaching method. He never taught facts, or gave information; he was satisfied with moving the soul constantly, and in so doing established communities that shared the same goal of justice—just nations, just souls, just life for free citizens.

It is for this reason that I have placed Plato at the end of this volume, though I have introduced him with the force of a *foreigner* earlier on. If the Plato I present here were familiar to all, then it would be true that we have exhausted our resources. But to the degree that what I say about him sounds strange, to that degree there is hope.

But our most urgent task in this time of crisis is to stop the mind from repeating the theoretical habit of accepting the platitudes that emanate from the belief that language educates by duplicating natural principles (there is hardly any principle as arbitrary as nature); or the belief that language educates by the sheer power of its use, either as a way of appropriating meanings created by others (critical theory) or simply by repeating it: "By the power invested upon me by the State I grant you a degree. . . ."

To refocus on the primacy of exercising the soul as the way to educate our undergraduates will suspend the wrong belief that if we keep the students listening to the narratives of the past, or to the latest theory emanating from "the thought of the month club" that we educate them, while in practice we subjugate them to habits of thought that keep them prisoners of apathy and boredom. There must be something more we can offer to our young people.

PART TWO

Our Models

6

The Medieval Version of Aristotle

Historians have marked the years between the fall of Rome and the Renaissance (A.D. 500–1400) as the Middle Ages, the medieval period, or the Dark Ages. Though this period is chronologically the successor of the classical periods of Greece and Rome, it is in no way their continuation. A dramatic gap occurs between the medievals and the classical cultures of Rome and especially Greece. The Middle Ages appear in history more like an isolated island in an unknown ocean rather than as a continent linking past and present. The Middle Ages start from scratch.

It could have been a very creative period filled with models of creativity for the generations that followed, but instead proved to be a period in which small pieces of literature appeared from time to time, applied by the medievals to the task they thought was theirs: spreading the Christian faith they had inherited from the earlier Christians. Their passion seemed to be reduced to finding a viable reasoning method, to marry it to the faith they believed in, and in this manner to make that faith universally acceptable.

The reasoning method the medievals stumbled upon was not their own; they claimed it to be that of the Greeks, of Aristotle in particular, but this was not exactly true.

During the tenth and eleventh centuries, Arabic learning was spreading and influencing western scholars to the point of dictating the norms of learning and education in mathematics,

natural science, medicine, and philosophy—from Baghdad,
Cairo, to Córdoba, Granada, Toledo, Seville, and the rest of
Europe. Avicenna (980–1037) and Averroes (1126–1198) were
the major thinkers to influence Western thought and education. Avicenna translated the works of Aristotle into Arabic,
starting with his logic, and it is this discovery by Western
scholars that most influenced the development of the universities. Before this point all educational possibilities were enclosed in convents and monasteries, the parish, the chantry,
and the monastery school. The nobility was trained in the
palaces, and women imitated their elders or absorbed whatever
education or knowledge of the times they could in those enor-
mously long sermons, from six to ten hours, that priests would
deliver on Sundays with the showmanship of a country fair.

The Arabs translated to Arabic; the scholastics translated
into Latin, and through Latin, Greek names and philosophies
spread. But were they Greek? Did the medievals perform the
kinds of acts the Greek philosophers like Plato proposed for
the philosopher, or did they perform some other acts?

The medievals lay down for us habits we still exhibit in our
deals with others, but they borrowed them from the Romans,
and from the Romans we repeat many of those habits of
thought and custom, including what we call our values. Our
understanding of family, fatherland, country of origin, the
training of administrators, bureaucracy, our pragmatic propensity to prefer those theories that translate into results, the
institutionalization of informal educational practices into formal school curricula, our common practice of cultural and
educational borrowing and readaptation, even the bringing of
the hand upon the left side of the chest to salute the flag—all
are customs handed down to us from the Romans. And this is
not a pejorative comment, if we contain the claim of the possibilities of our culture to these Roman origins, but it would be
a deadly blow to our human possibilities if in the face of all the
difficulties we encounter in education or in the political life of
conservatives and liberals, we do not agree that our resources
are not exhausted, that we have only touched the surface of our
culture, that we have several other cultural possibilities that are
our own, so that we have no need to borrow from others and be
inauthentic.

Gilbert Highet, in *The Classical Tradition*, remarks that while

". . . in Latin there is an unbroken line of intellectual succession from ancient Rome to the present day . . . the knowledge of Greek in Western Europe died out almost completely in the Dark Ages. . ." (p. 13). Classical Greek culture has been virtually lost under the literary varnish of borrowing and reinterpretation, often performed by various political factions, vying for historical authenticity and using Greek names to legitimize their point of view. And this practice was also a Roman habit we have inherited, and it continued to be present with such examples as the Marxist appropriation of Prometheus as their "archetypal" mascot.

The Medievals used their Scholastic Logic to establish and justify a theoretical orthodoxy. This penchant for theoretical orthodoxy was an inherited habit of mind that the Medievals inherited from the Romans, and their cousins the Greek Sophists. In this manner our educational origins are later than they should have been. And the price has been heavy. Theory and orthodoxy will mark the boundaries of Western education determining who and what is in or out, who and what is acceptable or should be eliminated or marginalized, who or what is with us or against us. But what is left behind, what is buried, unnamed, rejected, is what the Greeks took as the most intimate component of human life and creativity: Chaos, the origin of the cosmos and of all those acts that create, renew, and transform. In Plato's words, we lost "the models." Western culture begins in what Plato took to be "the shadow of knowledge," the technologies of the cave, of the lower section of the divided line, of the manipulation of names without the power of creation hiding behind the names: Chaos.

The selections of this chapter are primarily concerned with showing habits of mind, acts performed, and only secondarily with information. I know that this act of focusing on acts primarily and leaving information by the wayside is new to most faculty and students. Our own habit of mind is to gather information and miss the acts performed in this task, and those not performed. But an inversion of priorities here would undermine the project of this book and the revival of *education* it intends.

The important exercise for the students is to compare Greek and Romans texts and to see their *differences,* not so much in the stories they narrate but in the kinds of acts involved by those giving us the narration. Homer and Virgil, for example, could be compared, an eighth-century Greek and a first-century Roman; or the text we offer here between Plato's *Myth of Er* and Cicero's *Scipio's Dream*, a fourth-century Greek and a first-century Roman. The student and faculty will soon realize that there are deep and unbridgeable differences between the two sets of texts. Virgil borrows from Homer the way Cicero borrows from Plato: a story line to advance political ideals. The Roman texts have certain additions, emphases, omissions, praises, and silences that should make the reading interesting and educative. Virgil's *Aeneid*, written to glorify the victory of Augustus at the Battle of Actium, described the search of Aeneas for the founding of a fatherland, a clever way to trace the origins of the Roman people back to the Trojans. The Greek narrative, on the other hand, merely recounts, act by act, the homeward voyage of a warrior, and there are no other side missions expected from Odysseus; it is a description of acts performed without any accompanying ideology.

Plato's *Myth of Er* in the hands of Cicero is transformed into a pseudo-politico-philosophical proclamation about the rewards in the afterlife guaranteed to the political conservative, ". . . for all who have given security, support and increase to the fatherland, there has been ordained in heaven a special place. . ." One needs to compare Cicero's *Somnium Scipionis* (Scipio's Dream) to Plato's *Myth of Er,* or even other parts of the *Republic* to see what we have really inherited from the historical past, and what we have lost. The Roman text emphasizes *pietas*, devoted loyalty, to the gods, the fatherland, the country, the Republic, the nation, and the family. (Only that there are many orthodoxies around defining them). The Greek text praises and describes "virtue," the ability and cunning to see what needs to be done in every situation, and to choose from among the possible the best action. The Roman Aeneas, the humble, at times cowardly, at times confused warrior-hero, on the other hand, is praised for his determination, his commitment to reach the fatherland, even at the expense of his own happiness.

It is very important for the students and faculty to realize that it is this last model that served the Founding Fathers as their model of selfless public virtue. The Greek model of virtue is not our model, but the Roman *pietas* for devotion to our theoretical orthodoxies. Our Founding Fathers found in Rome a republic that emerged from monarchy, free people who were farmers, and the institutions they recognized, the family, religion, morality, and law. In fact our founders were so infatuated with the Romans that they used to write on constitutional issues under Roman pseudonyms, Publius, Camillus, Brutus, and Cassius. George Washington so loved the character of Cato the Younger in Joseph Addison's 1713 play *Cato* that he made the Roman Republican his role model. He went to see the play *Cato* numerous times and had it performed for his troops at Valley Forge, despite a congressional resolution that plays were inimical to republican virtue (Forrest McDonald, *Novus Ordo Seculorum: The Intellectual Origins of the Constitution*, Lawrence, Kan.: University Press of Kansas, 1985, 71).

The habits of mind we inherited from the Medievals and Romans were made institutionally possible thanks to the discovery of Aristotle's logic. It is this logic that most contributed to shaping our Western habits of mind.

The scholastics debated for centuries whether this logic is a science or an art. Regardless of the answer, the truth of the matter is that this logic is present in all of us the way good social manners are present or absent, and we are judged accordingly. This logic is more prevalent a habit of mind than even subsequent logics, and for this reason it should be made available to students. I have translated it and edited it from Latin sources and notes the way I was taught it by the traditions of Louvain and Spain. I mention these two traditions, for they are significant in the way they formed the bases for the development of modern habits of thought. The Louvain tradition is the Scholastic tradition that following St. Thomas Aquinas took the first act of the mind to be judgment, thus affirming the roots of a philosophy that stressed *existence* to be prior to *essence*. Modern existentialism and phenomenology are the outcome of this move. On the other hand the Spanish tradition following Francisco Suarez, who was followed closely in this by Descartes, took the first act of the mind to be the apprehension of *essences*, and from this tradition we have the development of science, philosophy of science, and those phenomenologist and analytic philosophers who took *essence* as the ground of philosophical activity. In concrete we may align to this trend not only the philosophers of science but also the modern metaphysicians of the Hegel-Marxist style. In short, the first habit of mind brought by the medievals into our culture is also the foundation of the two habits of mind that followed.

Aristotle is the founder of so-called formal logic. He wrote six books pertaining to the logic here discussed: *The Categories; On Interpretation,* dealing with propositions; *First Analytics,* dealing with the syllogism; *Posterior Analytics,* dealing with argumentation; *The Topics,* dealing with arguments on the probable, what he calls dialectics; and the *Summary of the Sophists,* dealing with fallacies. The commentators gathered all these books under the title of the *Organum,* or instrument, since logic was considered the instrument of all the other sciences. It was also considered by the commentators as the highest monument of human culture.

These works by Aristotle became known to the scholastics in the twelfth century through the Arabic translations of Avicenna, the commentary of Averroes, and subsequently in its Latin translation. Porphyry and Boethius in the *Isagogue* made references to the problem of universals and the logic, but it was only with St. Albert the Great (1200–1280) and St. Thomas Aquinas (1225–1274) that the whole logic was used on its own and as the basis for all the other branches of philosophy and theology.

The rationalists, in particular Descartes (1596–1650), considered this logic harmful rather than helpful, and a new logic was advanced. Descartes is followed by Malebranche (1638–1715), A. Guelincx (1624–1669), and Ch. Wolf (1679–1754).

It is with Kant (1724–1804) that this logic becomes merely formalistic, dealing with forms that are a priori and merely subjective, and this is the type of logic that Hegel (1770–1831) uses to inject necessity into the reading of the metaphysics of the world, so that logic becomes metaphysics.

Contemporary logic aims at the right use of the mind for the discovery of new truths, just as classical logic did, but the method is different. It follows the axiomatic model of mathematics and the geometry of Euclid, from simple principles, through simple laws or operations, to true or false conclusions. It has been reduced to the verification and clarification of scientific claims. In the process, modern habits of thought have been reinforced, and in the name of clarification philosophy has suffered a mortal paralysis, leaving it unable to move in any direction. Where the sciences used to come to philosophy for verification, through the use of modern logic philosophy depends on the sciences for its own activity.

Leading exponents of this logic are: R. Lullius; G. Leibniz (1646– 1716); W. Hamilton (1788–1856), the founder of mathematical propositions; F. Brentano (1838–1917); G. Boole (1815–1868); A. Morgan (1806–1868); G. Frege (1848–1925); B. Russell and A. N. Whitehead, who wrote *Principia Mathematica;* and E. Husserl (1859–1938).

Scholastic Logic
(The ART and SCIENCE of ascertaining the TRUTH)

Antonio T. de Nicolás

INTRODUCTION

The END and NATURE of LOGIC (The *why* and *what* of Logic)

Man has many needs corresponding to the various levels of his nature: material, biological, animal, and rational. But what distinguishes him from all other animals is his intellect, through which he is capable of rational knowledge and, therefore, of personal love.

Animals know realities insofar as they "affect" them—their senses.

MAN goes beyond the world of the senses—phantasm or image—and knows realities as they are in themselves—though not their mode of being—and is therefore capable not only of using them to satisfy his animal needs but also to love them in a disinterested way, to appreciate their own goodness, and even to surrender himself to those among them whose goodness is such that they become lovable for their own sake: persons, God, etc.

However this kind of love is conditioned by the *nature* of intellectual knowledge, which resides in complete reflection.

While an animal is affected by reality and can only know the particular material object that affects him, MAN can virtually know all realities because MAN *knows that he knows:* he is capable of complete reflection.

Therefore Man's nature is such that his chief desire is the desire of knowledge and of the best kind of knowledge:

a) intellectual—characterized by complete reflection
b) true—adequating realities as they are in themselves (outside of mind)
c) certain—aware of this adequate grasping (due to evidence)
d) universal—leaving nothing outside its grasp.

The fulfillment of this desire would bring about the end of *ignorance*. Consequently the chief natural desire of Man and his duty is to *love truth* and to pursue it by all the means he can avail himself of.

LOVE expressed in *diligence* (opposed to laziness) and *sincerity* (opposed to prejudices and personal inclinations)

TRUTH. Our intellectual powers do not equal our desire for truth. But they can eventually be supplemented by God's personal Revelation.

Meanwhile we climb from one level of certainty (greater or lesser evidence) to another in our pilgrimage to the Absolute truth. At each level truth is obtained according to a degree of certainty and so we speak of moral, physical, mathematical, logical, and ontological truth.

> Logical truth: the known conformity that exists between our judgments about things and the things themselves.
>
> Ontological truth: the things themselves insofar as they conform with the intellect.
>
> End: whatever is intended for itself (either a thing or an action).
> End "which" or objective: the thing intended for itself.
> End "in which" or subjective: last action where the end "which" is achieved.
>
> Universal Ontological Truth: the end "which" of Man.
>
> Universal Logical Truth: the end "in which" of Man.

Both ends, "which" and "in which" are so universal that no other end is hiding behind them. In other words, there are no other Ends more ultimate to man than the ontological and logical truth.

In order to achieve any END, proper *means* should be used.

Means: whatever is intended, not for itself, but because it leads to an END.

Means can be classified as:

$$\begin{cases} \text{APT} \begin{cases} \text{necessary} \begin{cases} \text{hypothetical (if end is contingent).} \\ \text{compulsory (if End is necessary).} \end{cases} \\ \text{arbitrary} \end{cases} \\ \text{INEPT} \end{cases}$$

APT MEANS to achieve logical truth are the "acts of the intellect rightly used or used according to the rules of Logic."

In order to be more accurate as to the use of LOGIC (formal) we must remember that the intellectual act of complete reflection implies five different aspects:

1. *Subject:* the person who thinks.

2. *The act of thinking* (noesis): operation of the intellect of Subject.

3. *The thought* (noema or noemata): the result or product of act of thinking.

4. *The object* (either real or ideal) about which the subject thinks.

5. *The sign* (oral or written) which expresses the thought.

LOGIC (formal) deals not with n° 1, 2, or 4, *but* primarily with n° 3 and secondarily with n° 5, insofar as it expresses n° 3.

Even more n° 3 is not considered by LOGIC as the result of the intellect (this is the study of psychology) but only insofar as n° 3 is produced *correctly* or in a valid manner.

This LOGIC (in general) does the:

a) studying the *nature* of the different thoughts (noemata) and this is studied in MAJOR LOGIC, and

b) determining the conditions of validity or rules of the noemata (thought) and this is done in MINOR LOGIC or FORMAL LOGIC.

In other words: *Major Logic* deals with the content or subject matter of thought; *Formal Logic* with the rules of thought so that it becomes at all times a valid exercise.

Since Logic (formal) is an art and a science and its study aims at creating habits of sound reasoning in us,

Art is the habit of rightly using (ordering) means to achieve ends.

Habit: a stable (permanent) disposition to act.

Science: speculative science (the what and why it is right reasoning).

Causes of Formal Logic

1. *material:* near: noemata (thoughts) or the results of act of thinking.
remote: the objects upon which the intellect thinks.

2. *formal:* necessary order so that the acts of the intellect are valid.

3. *efficient:* the intellect reflecting upon the noemata (thoughts).

4. *final:* near: right use of acts of the intellect.
remote: ascertaining the truth.

A Brief Outline on the History of Logic

A. In Greece (V B.C.–III A.D.)

Prepared: by the Sophists and Plato (Eristica)
Invented: by Aristotle (384–322 B.C.)

Aristotle wrote six books: TO ORGANON
1. The Categories
2. On Interpretation
3. Prior Analytics
4. Posterior Analytics
5. The Topics
6. On Sophistic Refutation

B. In Medieval EUROPE (IX–XVI A.D.)

St. Thomas Aquinas comments on the ORGANON and Aristotelian Logic is taught again. XIII–XV Ockam.

C. In Modern Europe (XVII–XX A.D.)

Fr. Bacon: (inductive methodology)
Leibniz (De Arte Combinatoria)
Modern Logic: (Symbolic): A. de Morgan, G. Boole, E. Schröder, G. Frege, A. N. Whitehead, B. Russell, I. M. Bochenski, etc.

THE ACTS OF THE MIND

Slogan: Know what it is you are doing.

The whole activity of our intellect is an unceasing pursuit of truth, punctuated by successful but partial grasps of it. If our intellect were intuitive, we would in each case see the truth immediately without having to hunt for it through complicated processes. But in this life, truth is found in a *discursive* way and only intuitively (improper intuition) in some cases. To discover truth discursively we proceed *through acts* of various kinds which it is important to understand well in order to perform them correctly.

Some of these acts, such as direct judgment of perception, questioning, apprehending current concepts, paying attention, and remembering, are so spontaneous that it is useless to determine rules about them, though they can be improved by training. Others, such as reflective judgment, inference, definition, and division of concepts, are more elaborately performed and require a practical knowledge of their own rules. These acts of the mind will be the object of our present study.

Since the whole aim of any activity of our intellect is to ascertain the truth and the truth is conformity with reality, we can only start our study with that act of the mind which puts ourselves in direct contact with reality. This act of the mind is *judgment*. This is the most important act of the mind because with this act we establish the truth by ourselves, asserting that *this* (world of the mind) is *so* (world of reality) and not otherwise. Unfortunately it can be performed incorrectly, i.e. be false. Judgments are, therefore, true or false. *Any act of the intellect in which there is logical truth or logical falsehood is a judgment.* But it may contain something else besides, such as an emotion (pain, admiration, etc.) or be implied in something else, for instance, in an injunction, a prayer, or an act of love. It can refer to any reality, either physical or ideal, material or spiritual, creaturely or divine.

When we make our first judgment it is of this type: "This (somehow felt by my senses) exists now as pleasant (or painful) to me." This is still very vague; yet it is

a) an assertion of existence
b) of a subject related to me through sensation, and
c) determined by a positive predicate.

Subject and predicate are the *terms* of the judgment. They are *concepts* which my intellect had to abstract from the sensible *"phantasm"* or image before it could assert. This *formation of concepts is called: psychological simple apprehension.* It is a part of the complex process of judging. In the case of direct judgments it is *spontaneous* and *unconscious,* implicit but not expressed.

But after making several judgments we spontaneously reflect upon and compare them. In this way we isolate such concepts from the complexity of the full judgment and we grasp them clearly (express them) in themselves. *This clear grasping of a concept* (already formed or conceived) is called: *logical simple apprehension.* This is a second act, really different from the judgment itself. Later on we systematically try to form more difficult, i.e. scientific concepts; then their formation (conception) and clarification (expression) coincide. Similarly when we learn them from others. Once clearly grasped, concepts can of course be used to form new judgments which we have not to form anew.

Simple apprehensions are not judgments, but, when we wish to express them, we do it in the form of a judgment, called *analytic judgment:* i.e. "man" means "rational animal."

Analytic judgments, such as the above example, a definition, are not real judgments, because they do not affirm that any *reality* is what their predicate means, but simply that the meaning of the subject is given in the predicate. They can be *correct* or *incorrect,* but they cannot be true or false.

The third act of the mind is *inference* or *reasoning.* It consists in discovering that a certain judgment (called conclusion) is true because 1 or 2 more judgments are true and imply it, or because 1 other judgment plus a definition are valid (true or correct) and imply it; or also in discovering that a certain definition is correct because 2 other definitions are correct and imply it. For instance:

All hounds are dogs   No devil is beast, therefore no beast is devil
Rover is a hound   All germs are organisms, therefore some or-
Rover is a dog   ganisms are germs.

All men are loved by God
All Russians are men
Krushchev is a Russian
Therefore *Kruschev* is loved by God

Angel means pure finite spirit   Man means rational animal
St. Michael is an angel   Animal means sentient organism
St. Michael is a pure finite spirit Man means rational sentient or-
                                 ganism

It is obvious then that inference is a special way of arriving at the truth. Its goal is a true judgment (or a correct simple apprehension) which was included (implicitly, not explicitly) in previous valid knowledge and is yet new to us. Because of its complexity this act of the mind is often performed incorrectly and that is why the chief aim of Minor Logic is to provide the rules of correct inference.

Important Note:

When we speak of the acts of the mind we are trying to study the acts of the mind that are particularly human as opposed to the animal and his particular way of knowing at the level of sensation. To understand something means to know it beyond the level of sensation.

The data received by animal and men through their external senses is coordinated by a common, central, or synthetic sense into a unified whole. This unified whole is called "phantasm" or image. This phantasm is the sensory representation of the individual object at hand. Please do not confuse it with the "concept" which is universal and which may be applied to many. Phantasm is concrete and particular.

Concept is born by abstraction from the phantasm by the intellect.

SUMMARY: Chief acts of the mind:1) Judgment
                                  2) Logical simple apprehension
                                  3) Reasoning

1) Judgment: Act of the intellect in which there is either logical truth or logical falsehood (also act of the intellect in which I affirm or deny something about something else).

2) Logical Simple Apprehension: Act of the intellect in which I form a concept (act of the intellect in which I say something about something else without affirming or denying it).

Complete definition: "man is a rational animal."
Incomplete definition: "man is an animal" or "Man is rational."

Expression of properties: "organism is mortal."
Simple Apprehension is erroneously called analytical judgment.

3) Reasoning: Act of the intellect in which by the strength of a valid knowledge I find a new valid knowledge.

The known valid knowledge is called Antecedent. It can be one or many judgments, one or many simple apprehensions.
The new knowledge found on the strength of the antecedent is called the consequence or conclusion.

FOUNTAINS (sources) of knowledge and valid judgments

All logicians are most interested in the sources of knowledge and the validity of the acts of the mind.
Validity or authoritativeness (authority) is the capacity which a kind of action has of doing correctly what it pretends to do. Its contrary is invalidity or lack of validity (authority). Each act has a validity of its own.

a) Validity of the judgment: truth; its contrary falsehood.
b) Validity of Simple Apprehension: correctness; its contrary fallacy (incorrectness).
c) Validity of reasoning: the same as Simple Apprehension

IMMEDIATE sources

1) Judgment of perception (of sensible reality). It is sensitive-rational, i.e. a) an intellectual determination; b) of sensation or sensitive intuition. (I perceive the desk.)

2) Semi-intuition (intellectual) of oneself. (It is *I* who perceives the desk.)

3) Understanding of first principles: or that truth is possible. Principles of objectivity or identity, and principles of non-contradiction. (What is cannot at the same time and under the same circumstances not be.)

4) Semi-intuition of activity of intellect: I understand that I think when I think about something.

5) Mystic intuition.

6) Beatific intellectual Vision.

SEMI-IMMEDIATE sources

1) Eutochia or Modern meaning of intuition: (insight, inventiveness) what we call quick grasp of the relevant fact, or concept, etc. It is an act of complex reasoning but very fast.

2) Knowledge which is connatural or derived from personal inclination. (Quick grasp born from moral habit, or from affection.) Fitness to one's own dispositions of things, persons, actions. Quick decisions about right and wrong, etc.

3) Identification: applying concepts to things not well known: "This must be a rhinoceros, since I have been told that a rhinoceros is a one-horned animal somewhat smaller than an elephant, and this is like that."

4) Natural mysticism (acquired): can be philosophical or religious: Yoga, etc.

MEDIATE sources

1) *Reasoning:* can be positive or negative.

  A. Positive

    1. Rational induction: from a limited number of instances to a universal statement (if no contrary instances).

      a) incomplete: from individual subjects to their nature. This and that and that piece of copper conduct electricity, therefore copper conducts electricity.

      b) complete: from species to genus. Copper, iron, etc. conduct electricity; therefore metals conduct electricity.

    2. Deduction: from universal to particular statements: cfr. reasoning expl.

    3. Dialectic assumption: deduction of truth not perceived but required by the inconsistency of the data. My neighbor is fat, though he never eats during the day, so he must eat at night. Finite beings exist, since of themselves they are nothing, therefore there must be an uncaused Cause, whose essence is "to be."

  B. Negative: Refutation

    1. Errors about facts.

    2. Errors about terms (contradiction in the terms of a judgment).

    3. Contradiction between the act of saying and what is said. Elenchic retorsion.

2) *Authority:* which I accept because of the authority of the person.

THE "COPULA" AND THE TERMS IN PROPOSITIONS
Slogan: Know what it is you are saying.

Part A—Signs and Language

Knowledge makes things present to us, not materially but intentionally. This means that when things become objects of our knowing, they are not changed in themselves but remain what they are and where they are; yet, we can say that they are somehow in us, insofar as we have (they have) produced in our minds something else which stands for them and manifests them. These are the *noemata* produced by the three acts of the mind, and they are signs of the realities known to us. Thus, *concepts, judgments,* and *reasonings* are signs: *mental signs* of reality.

Man, being by nature a social animal (and political) wishes to communicate his knowledge and other states of mind to other men, and for that he again requires another kind of signs, material and thus accessible to the senses, producible at will, and versatile enough to manifest clearly even intricate noemata or mental signs. *Any system of such signs of noemata is called language.* It is usually oral or audible, can be also written and visual, or written and tangible (in Braille) or made of touchings and tangible, or gesticulatory and visual.

There are also natural signs, such as footprints, smoke, etc. and man-made signs, such as statues or traffic signs, which are neither mental nor verbal, but are objects capable of signifying something else, either because they are effects, or a normal accompaniment of it, or a representation of its form, or simply due to an accepted convention. These are *extra logical signs.*

> SUMMARY: Sign: anything which points to something beyond itself.
> The signified: what is signified by the sign.
> Signification (meaning): the relation of sign to the signified.

DIVISION OF SIGNS

a) *Formal* signs: point to something without them (signs) being known. Inner signs produced in knower, man or animal: images, noemata, concepts, judgments, reasoning, copula, quantifiers, demonstratives, etc. Infused ideas. Innate ideas (in angels).

b) *Objective* signs: point to something else because they are known. All non-mental signs: language, statues, smoke, traffic signals.

c) *Natural* signs: which are signs by themselves. Crying of pain; smoke of fire.

d) *Conventional* signs: out of convention. The olive branch, language of noemata, white flag, etc.

e) *Representative* signs: take the place of the signified. Statues of saints, photographs, mental images in animals and men, innate ideas, etc.

f) *Merely significative* signs: point to something else without taking its place. Olive branch, speech, alphabet.

IMPORTANT DISTINCTIONS

1. Noemata are formal, natural, and merely significative signs.

2. Language is objective, many times a conventional and merely significative sign.

Definitions of language: Word: significative sound pronounced by the mouth.
elemental word: vowels and consonants.
oral term: word signifying a concept: man, cow, I.

Phrase: a complex of significative words

a) incomplete: (mere phrase): fastest man alive, 2 big melons.

b) complete: *proposition:* a phrase having complete sense.

    i. enunciative: sign of judgment: (declarative or attributive prop.).

    ii. non-enunciative: question, exclamation, wish, command.

    iii. apparently enunciative: sign Simple Apprehension. (Man is rational animal.)

c) discourse, speech: complex of propositions. Argument: Sign reasoning.

Part B—Judgment and Attributive Proposition

A child makes judgments long before he can express them in propositions, and even grown ups make many more judgments than they can express in language. Reality, indeed, assails us every moment and we are forced to judge about it. Wherever our intellect thus reacts to the impressions of reality upon our senses, it is bound to be either true or false, and this reaction is therefore a judgment, whether we express it or not.

Expression is secondary, and it may be imperfect and even misleading, because the resources afforded by the various languages are not equal. All will not manifest equally well the various elements in which a judgment consists. We must therefore ascertain them not so much on the basis of the particular language we happen to use, but through an analysis of what an act has to be if it is to assert truth.

Logical truth can only exist in the intellect; it exists whenever an intellect asserts its conformity with a reality, and is right in asserting it; if not we have logical falsehood; if it does not assert we have no judgment at all.

The reality asserted is normally something else than the intellect itself; but to be asserted it must be present to the intellect, which focuses on it at least through the intermediary of an indicative mental sign or pointer-concept: "this thing," "that reality," etc. This pointer is called logical subject (S), whereas the pointed reality is the real subject. Each subject is something that exists in its own way. Concerning it we can ask at least two questions: 1) Is it? (Does it exist?) and 2) What is it? If the answers are positive it has *existence* and *essence*.

To have existence means to exercise the act of existing. This also cannot be present to the intellect unless it is signified in it by a special mental sign, namely the act of asserting or affirming, which we call "verbal copula" or *"existential copula"* (or simply copula): *is* (am, are) Its contrary is the negative verbal copula: *is not* (am not, are not).

As to the "essence" of the real subject it must also be signified in the intellect by a special mental sign, called attributive or Predicate (P). Properly speaking it does not signify the sole essence, but the subject as having its own essence. And it can express either the basic essence or nature (man, oxygen, tree), some of its accidents (strong, liquid, high), or more or less completely the whole essence (big, blue, sweet-smelling lotus flower, old, blossoming apple tree, my father, etc.).

In practice the logical subject is often made of a pointer-concept plus a previous predicate; for instance, "this man," "that boy," "that girl who is playing ping-pong with my friend," etc.

When we put together a logical subject and a predicate, we make a "concreting synthesis." This is simply a synthesis of mental or formal signs; these are not yet referred to their significate, the real subject. Therefore the concreting synthesis is not yet a judgment. The mental signs, though, are the same ones used for the judgment, unfortunately: S and P, and is and is-not. The copula does not posit existence, only unites S and P. We can signify this synthesis in this manner: S-P and its contrary S + P.

In a question, there is a concreting synthesis plus a doubt whether there is a real subject corresponding to it or not. This synthesis is proposed but not yet asserted or denied: Is this your pen? S-P?

When we refer a concreting synthesis or even a single logical subject to a real subject as to their significate, we also make a synthesis since we put together or unite the sign or signs and their significate. This synthesis is called "objectifying synthesis." It is symbolized as S *is* P or (inverted capital E) SP (or S is or $\exists$S). This symbol stands for the copula and signifies that there exists a real subject which verifies S or S-P. *Any objectifying synthesis is a judgment and vice versa.*

The elements of the judgment are always reduced to the scheme S is P. It may be hidden in another verb or language, or implied in the context or tone of voice.

The horse runs = The horse is running.
I shall leave by the next train = I am going to leave by . . .
Ouch! = something is hurting me plus a corresponding emotion.
Ah! = something is beautiful plus admirative emotion.
There are mangoes for dessert = Some mangoes are today's dessert.

The functions of the copula are double:
a) unites S and P; b) asserts existence of a real subject corresponding to those signs (SP) or the sole S.

SUMMARY: Judgment formed by two terms (S and P) and the copula (is). Or at least of S and is.

Real subject: About which we judge.
Logical subject: concept indicating real subject (pointer-concept).
Subject-term: word or phrase signifying logical subject.
Remember: Thing = the signified.
concept = intellectual sign of thing.
word or oral term = sign of concept.
Predicate: what the intellect identifies with subject.
Copula: sign of synthesis (concretive or objective).
two functions: 1) unites; 2) affirms.
Concretive synthesis: union of logical subject and predicate.
Objective synthesis: union of real Subject and logical subject, or union of real subject and concretive synthesis.

Part C—Simple Apprehension, Concepts and Terms

Concepts can be considered separate from the judgment. This is simple apprehension. All concepts that can be either a subject or a predicate are called *categorematic*. But there are others which do not express realities and therefore not usable as S or P. (Unless it is spoken about themselves) and are employed in an ancillary manner. These are called *syncategorematic*. They accompany categorematic concepts. They are:

1. quantifiers: all, some, none, a few, the, a or an, one, two, etc.

2. prepositions: in, to, into, toward, with, without, up, etc.

3. conjunctions: and, but, if, when, soon, as soon as, whereas, as, etc.

4. adverbs: well, quickly, softly, quietly, legibly, fast, etc.

With these considerations in mind we may now proceed to the different divisions of categorematic terms.

Part D—Categorematic Terms and Their Division

Concepts can be grasped correctly or incorrectly. Therefore S.A. can be doubted or denied quite as well as judgments. The *is* can be doubted and turned into an *is?* or denied, *is not.*

If our concepts are invalid or incorrectly grasped, our judgments will also become invalid. It is therefore very important to be able to recognize the various sorts of concepts, their mutual relationships, the diverse ways of using them, etc. In other words, we must be able to *distinguish.* This is our present slogan: MAKE THE PROPER DISTINCTIONS.

All categorematic concepts can be divided and subdivided from various standpoints. We concentrate here in those divisions which are required for the study of *inference.*

However, before we do that we must consider two *properties* which every term has, namely, *comprehension* (connotation) and *extension* (denotation).

Comprehension designates the total meaning of a concept. This total meaning is a complex unit of meaning. Hence, when we wish to render it explicit we must use many terms. These constituent terms are called *notes* of that concept. Comprehension can be expressed at various levels: a) by expressing those *notes only* which constitute the basic comprehension (definition by genus and specific difference, or quasi definition if the concept defined is a primary notion); b) by expressing the properties which follow necessarily from that basic meaning and form the *complementary comprehension.* For instance:

basic comprehension of "man": rational animal
complete comprehension of "man": capable of laughter, of judg-
                                  ment, of moral change, etc.
The more special a comprehension is, the richer it is.
The more general a comprehension is, the poorer it is.

As to *extension,* it designates the whole collection of real subjects of which a concept can be predicated. The poorer the comprehension, the larger the extension; and the richer the comprehension, the poorer the extension. However, this rule needs certain clarifications. The concept may apparently be poorest, but actually be the richest, as in the case of "transcendental concepts," like being, reality, affirmable, etc. Then the rule is that both comprehension and extension are maximum.

			Extension			
Substance	Substance	Angel	Mineral	Plant	Brute	Man
Body	Corporeal Subst.		Mineral	Plant	Brute	Man
Organism	Animate corporeal Subst.			Plant	Brute	Man
Animal	Sentient animate corporeal Subst.				Brute	Man
Man	Rational sentient animate corporeal Subst.					
	Comprehension					

Summary:

Two main properties of concepts: Comprehension
Extension.

Comprehension: the complex of essential notes of concept.
Extension: sum total of real subjects of which a concept can be predicated.

Rule about extension and comprehension (applicable with universals): The greater the comprehension, the poorer the extension and vice versa.

Slogan: Make the Proper Distinctions!

It is most important that the student goes again and again over these distinctions so that slowly he comes to realize their implications.
To begin with we may divide all concepts into:

Real: (also called of the first intention) which stand for things as they are in themselves, independent of their way of knowing them. Like: *I* am *able to laugh,* since *I* am a *man,* and *every man* is *able to laugh,* since *he* is *animal* and *rational.*

Logic: (or of the second intention) which stands for things as they are in the mind and according to the different ways of knowing them. In the above sentence: "I" is *logical subject;* "able to laugh" predicate and *logical property* and *quality* and *a concrete term;* "a man" is *predicate, concrete term, logical species, middle term* in that syllogism; "every man" is *distributive universal, concrete, major term;* "animal" is *predicate, concrete, near genus, logical substance;* "rational" is *co-predicate, concrete, specific difference.*

It should be obvious that, since logic considers not things in themselves, but their "noemata," most of the technical terms of this art are terms of the second intention.
Again, if we neglect this division, we shall easily mistake the signs for

their significates, images for realities, thoughts for things, logical for real relations or distinctions, etc. For example:

Man is definable.
I am a man.
Therefore, I am definable.

It will help—not to commit the above error—to consider terms from the point of view of *their origin,* or the amount of concrete information they yield, in connection with the degree of *abstraction* which characterizes the S.A. by which they are grasped. With this in mind we may divide concepts into:

1. *Concepts of the first degree of abstraction:* which stand for things as they are known both by the intellect and the exterior senses: the biological description of man and each of its terms, "mammal," "vertebrate," "biped," "upright," etc.; "red," "sour," "blue," "sweet," "noisy," "soft," etc., all such concrete terms as well as their corresponding abstract terms.

2. *Concepts of the second degree of abstraction:* which stand for things as they are in space and time. For example: (as they are known by the intellect and the interior sense, not exterior senses) "square," "round," "small," "old," "young" . . . and examples given for quantity, time, how much, and when. Here we have concrete and corresponding abstract terms.

3. *Concepts of the third degree of abstraction:* which stand for things as they are thought only by the intellect; as beings, true, good, beautiful, act, form, effect, potency, act, accident, creature, person. They are concrete and their corresponding abstract terms.

These terms in turn fall under the category of *real distributive terms.*

It is clear that concepts 1 and 2 are sensitive and rational, whereas concept 3 is purely rational or intentional. The first two numbers are proper to ordinary knowledge and all positive sciences (based on observation); the third is exclusive of Metaphysics.

We may further point out that *abstract terms* correspond to Metaphysical Categories while *concrete terms* correspond to Logical Categories. (1. goodness; 2. good).

Abstract = Form   Concrete = Subject plus Form

All concepts and their expression "terms" are divided into two groups:

1. Positive (or finitans): they say what the thing is—man, mortal.

2. Negative (or *infinitans*): they say what the thing is not = non-man, immortal.

According to the act of simple apprehension, concepts are:

1. incomplex
{
  incomplex in itself and incomplex in the grasping = man.
  incomplex in itself and complex in the grasping = rational animal.
}

2. complex
{
  complex in itself but incomplex in the grasping = philosopher.
  complex in itself and complex in the grasping.
}

According to properties, concepts are:

1. comprehension
{
  concrete
  {
    absolute = man.
    connotative = tall.
  }
  abstract
  {
    absolute = tallness, whiteness, rationality.
  }
}

2. extension
{
  divisive = man.
  collective = army.
}

Since concepts are signs of objects, they manifest their essences. But they can do this more or less efficiently; their power of signifying has degrees. Accordingly, they are divided as follows:

1. Adequate: when their comprehension gives us a complete intelligibility of the signified. In other words it posits the complete essence of the thing. All the definitions by proximate genus and specific difference: Man is a rational animal. But very few realities can be thus defined, except in mathematics, and even there they are only significative signs, not representative, just like angelic ideas are.

2. Inadequate: When their comprehension does not give us a complete intelligibility of the signified.

    a) *obscure:* not enough to distinguish a species from another species: all the transcendental terms of the genuses, differences, and logical accidents separately considered.

    b) *clear:* sufficient to distinguish species from species.

        i: *confuse:* not giving main notes of species: (A horse is) a neighing animal; (a cat is) a mewing beast; (milk is) an opaque white liquid with which mammals feed their young, etc.

ii. *distinct:* giving main notes (especially properties) of species: good biological
descriptions of animals, plants; chemical names, or, even better, formulae.

NOTE THAT: concepts are *formal* signs of their objects.

terms: are only instrumental signs of objects (a word or
combination of words which conventionally signifies an object of thought).

From the point of view of their extension TERMS may be divided as
follows:

1. *Singular:*

   a) individual: referring to one individual only (John, my father).

   b) collective: referring to one collection (Catholic Ch. Jesuits).

2. *Particular:*

   a) individual: of one or several non-mentioned individuals; a few
   men, some sheep, hardly anyone.

   b) collective: of one and several collections not mentioned; a good
   many nations; some families, plenty of ears of corn.

3. *Distributive:*

   may be said of each one and also of all.

   a) Transcendental: whose extension excludes nothing. May be said of
   God and all the classes of Being: being, reality, ontological truth,
   etc.

   b) Transcendental "secundum quid" (in some way): its extension
   includes more than one class but not all.

      i. Quasi-transcendental: may be said of God and the majority of
      classes of Being but not of all: spirit, understanding, free, with
      a will, knowing, etc.

      ii. Universal: can be said of only one class. And it is subdivided
      according to the 5 PREDICABLE (most important for defini-
      tion and division).

         1. *Genus:*

            answers the question what is the essence of this finite being?
            it can be:

            a) *remote:*

               i. supreme: containing all the other genuses: finite
               being.

ii. intermediate: in between g.sup. and g. proximate: organism, body.

iii. proximate: just above the species: "animal" referred to man; "automobile" ref. to motor-car.

2. *Difference:*

completes definition or quasi definition.

i. generic: a superior genus becomes inferior: sub. spiritual becomes material substance, living body becomes sentient organism.

ii. specific: a proximate genus becomes species: (animal) rational; (irrational anim.) baying, barking, roaring, etc.

3. *Species:*

expresses the whole nature of the thing (finite): man or rational animal; ass or braying animal; "bomber" a bombing plane.

4. *Properties:*

a necessary predicate following definition. It may derive from:

genus: mortal.
difference: efficient cause; able of knowledge (rational).
species: able to laugh, think, speak, etc.

in the logical order or follow and not be derived physically, from:
genus: subject to law of gravitation (all bodies).
difference: exoskeletonic (all six legged).
species: carbon is of atomic n° 6, atomic weight 12.

NOTE: The first 4 predicables are *necessary* predicates, i.e., each finite reality has a set of them attached to itself. But the 5th predicable is *contingent,* i.e. happens to be had or not. This is why it is called:

5. *Accident:*

not necessary predicate.
(A horse happens to be) black or bay, fast or slow.
(A man can be) tall, slender, brown-eyed, dark, or brown.
(A beetle is) black or brown; small or large; crawling or resting.

4. *Collective:*

may be said of all considered as a whole, but not individually:
(All American citizens form) America (but not LBJ).
(All men form) humanity but not (BB).
(All players on a soccer team) are the team (not one of them).

Note that collective terms are also either:

singular: humanity, C. Church, S.J. or
particular: a team, some nations, or
universal: society, team, order

Among the GENUS there are 10 which have a particular importance, because they are the names for 10 general categories according to which we can divide all the kinds of finite reality.

But before we define them it will be convenient to bring here to mind a clarification of Substance from the point of view of Metaphysics and Logic so that there is no confusion in the mind of the student.

"Being" is the basic transcendental term.

It is first divided into "infinite Being," which is a singular term, designating the unique Reality: God, and "finite being," which is the first or supreme genus, predicable of many.

"Finite being" designates any "composite of *esse* (is) and essence." On account of its *esse* (is), it exists; *esse* is not a concept but a verb, which designates the inner cause of existence, or the *act of being* (actus essendi). On account of its essence, a finite being is "only that": man, dog, fly, etc.

Every finite essence is composed of a basic part, called "predicamental substance," and a set of complementary parts, called "physical accidents."

The full finite being is called "first or primary substance" (substantia prima). It is made of esse plus essence (predc. substance plus physical accid.) and nothing else.

Since the concept "substance" is only the sign of either primary or predicamental substance, it is secondary with regard to them and is therefore called "secondary substance" (substantia secunda).

Therefore when we talk of the 10 Logical Categories or Predicaments we refer to the concepts which designate directly (term) what the "first substance is," i.e., a real subject, having an essence made of 2 kinds of parts, *and only indirectly* those parts themselves. Thus man, good, big, shouting, etc.

Hence the distinction of 2 kinds of Categories, Metaphysical and Logical, and the division of terms into abstract and concrete.

Metaphysical = abstract   Logical = concrete

NOTE: except in the case of talking about God, who has nothing and

IS everything "eminenter" we may indiscriminantely use both concrete and abstract terms: God is good and goodness; love and to love, etc.

Another NOTE of importance: Please do not be confused with the names: *Predicables* (5) and *Predicaments* (10).

Logical Predicament: concrete concept, positive, irreducible, saying what is the first substance.

1. *Substance:* (complete 2nd substance) concept saying what the first substance is: man, dog, horse, melon, etc.

Concrete Predicamental Accident: concept saying about the first substance as having some physical accident.

a) Absolute: in themselves

2. *Quantity:* quantity, characteristic of bodily substance: gigantic, six feet, small, etc.

3. *Quality:* characteristics: delicious, smooth, healthy, virtuous, skillful, good, intelligent, etc.

b) Relative: as regards others

4. *Action:* speaking, writing, walking.

6. *Relation:* father, son, boss, student, lover of God.

7. *When:* situated in time.

8. *Where:* situated in space, home, Rome.

9. *Posture:* seated, on my back.

10. *"Habitus":* means apparel, costume, physical equipment, saddled, married, ornated, arms, parachute = (as having external things).

The Porphyrian Tree (233–304) classified the various kinds of 1st. Subst. thus:

> Substance: Body, Organism, Animal, Man.
> Corporeal: animate, sentient, rational or
> Incorporeal: inanimate, nonsentient, irrational.

1. *Not notably related*

2. *Significantly related:* This we subdivide into:

a) *Positive:*

i. *convertible:* having the same extension (though not same comprehension).
any concept and its properties: "man," "able to laugh."
any concept and its definition: "man," "rational animal."

any singular term and its correct description: "George Bush, President of USA."

    ii. *not convertible*

  b) *Negative:* one must be denied of the other.

      i. *disparate:* opposed by no certain rule (improperly opposed) angel-dog; salt-man.

      ii. *opposed:* according to a certain rule.

        1. *Contradictory:* one denies the other: man—non-man.

        2. *Contrary:* positive terms which within the same genus distant the most: virtue-vie; love-hatred.

        3. *Possessive-Privative:* one asserts perfection, other absence of perfection: seeing-blind; wise-stupid, healthy-ill.

        4. *Correlated:* joined by a relation: professor-pupil, father-son.

As regards the division 1. Not-notably related terms may mean terms whose association cannot yield a unit of meaning, i.e. a real concept, but can only be verbal, i.e. non-sensical:

"There existed absolutely nothing, and I, the son of a barren woman, was reading in a closed book, in the light of an extinguished lamp, munching away square circles with divine appetite. . . ."

However, not every association of irrelevant terms is illogical, as long as it is not taken literally. We speak of 7 stars as the "Great Bear" and of a constellation as the "Dog" and of Christ as "The Lamb." In other words that means that we use *terms analogically,* i.e., beyond their normal extension and according to some notes only of their full comprehension, hence in some secondary sense. There are also terms whose unity of meaning is so imperfect that we cannot use them twice exactly. These are, not only by use, but by *nature analogical.* And this brings us to the last distinction and division of distributive terms.

1. *Univocal:* it is said of many according to the same meaning. All the universal concepts: man, boy, house (but can be used analog.).

2. *Analogous:* it is said of many according to a meaning which is partly the same and partly different.

    i. *intrinsic:* "if that what is meant" is the same "the way of meaning" different. ("that what is meant = definit. all the transcendental (being, affirmable, good) and quasi-transcendental concepts: (intelligent, living, free).

    ii. *extrinsic:* if also that what is meant is partly different so many terms with meaning hovering over two or more related meanings: Religion, air.

3. *Equivocal:* a mere oral term, which is said of many according to a completely different meaning. Same word: different meaning: egg-to-egg; son-sun; lean-to lean; knight-night, etc.

Synopsis of Concepts and Terms

A. Categorematic
  Aa *Positive*
  Aaa *According to S. A.*
      1. incomplex
      2. complex

      According to Properties
      1. comprehension (concrete—abstract)
      2. extension (divisive—collective)
  Aab *According to degree of signification*
      1. Adequate
      2. Inadequate
        a) obscure
        b) clear
          i. confuse
          ii. distinct
  Aac *Point of View of Extension*
      1. singular—individual and collective
      2. particular—individual and collective
      3. distributive—transcendental; somehow transcendental; universal
      4. collective

      Five Predicables:
      1. Genus—proximate and remote
          i. supreme
          ii. intermediate
      2. Difference—generic and specific
      3. Species
      4. Properties
        a) logical: generic, differential, specific
        b) physical: generic, differential, specific
      5. Accident
  Aa *Negative*
      Ten Logical Categories

1. Substance	*Relative*	7. situated in time: When
Absolute	4. Action	8. situated in space: Where
2. Quantity	5. Passion	9. Posture
3. Quality	6. Relation	10. Habitus

Aad *According to origin or abstraction*
    1. 1st, 2nd, and 3rd degree of abstraction
Aae *According to use*
    1. univocal
    2. analogous: intrinsic and extrinsic
    3. equivocal
Aaf *Compared to one another*
    1. unconnected
    2. connected: positively/negatively: disparate or opposed
       a) contradictory
       b) contrary
       c) possessive-privative
       d) correlated
B. Syncategorematic
    1. Quantifiers
    2. Prepositions
    3. Conjunctions
    4. Adverbs

Part E—The Functional Signification of Terms in Propositions

We have, so far, studied terms in isolation from any context. Thus, for instance, we have seen that a universal is distributive, i.e., can be said of each and all in a class. But about how many it *is* actually said, is a question whose answer is not uniform. Similarly, a term can stand for a thing, or for the concept of that thing or for the oral sign of that concept. In order, therefore, to avoid ambiguity, we must determine what it stands for in each proposition. This is normally easily done through a consideration of the whole context, proximate or remote.

The *functional signification* of a term is its *actual meaning in a proposition*. It always presupposes its absolute meaning, which it cannot contradict. To obtain it we must ascertain:

a. the nature and number of the actual significates of the term (*supposition*/functional extension).
b. whether that significate(s) is considered materially or are formally (*material or formal appellation*).
c. whether it is considered according to the time implied by the verb of the proposition, or other times (*status*, or *ampliation*, or *distraction*).

1. APPELLATION: material or formal

Whenever we attribute a P to an S, we give an appellation to that S. We say that P is the appellant, and S the appellate. The appellant can suit

S either considered materially, i.e., as a certain existent which happens to deserve that P, or considered formally, i.e., according to the concept by which we have signified that S.

Appellant: Predicate

Appellate: Subject

Material appellation: appellation of the subject according to the form under which it is meant. Like: that horse (as horse) is a neighing animal. Man (as man) is endowed with sensitive and rational knowledge. The devil, as devil, is bad; but as a being, he is good.

2. STATUS, AMPLIATION, DISTRACTION

Status: if it is only taken at the time of the proposition. Emperor Napoleon I was defeated at Waterloo (he was then Emperor).

Ampliation: if it is taken as of all the time (of its existence): Your teacher is a rational animal (always).

Distraction: if it is taken as meaning a different time of the time of the proposition: Your teacher was born in 1932 (he was not then a teacher); Emperor Napoleon I won the Battle of Austerlitz (he was not Emporer then); The blind will see (they will no longer be blind then).

3. SUPPOSITION: The Functional Extension of Terms.

Supposition: actual extension of term in proposition (Functional extension or actual denotation). It can be divided:

1. Material: if it is only taken as a word.
   i. natural: "man" is a three-letter, English, monosyllabic word.
   ii. artificial: "does" is a word, present indicative, third person, verb "to do."
2. formal: if it is taken for the nature it signifies:
   i. Logic: if it is taken as a concept (as the nature which is in the mind). "man" is a logical species, subject-term or predictates, etc.
   ii. Real: if it is understood according to the real predicates:
      a. absolute: if it is taken according to the definition (or quasi-definition) therefore as it is *equally* in the thing and in the mind, excluding the differences.

      man is an animal (genus).

      man is a rational substance (difference).

      man is a rational animal (full definition).

      man is capable of conceptual abstraction (property).
      b. personal: taken for the nature as it is found in the thing; it is subdivided according to the *extension:*
         1. Common: taken for all affected by it.
            a) collective: taken at the same time. The Apostles were 12.

    b) distributive: for all and each.
        i. complete: for all and each of one class: All men are
           mortal. All trees are creatures.
        ii. incomplete: taken for all but not for each individual
           of one class. All animals were in Noah's ark.
  2. Discrete: only for part of the extension.
    a) singular: one individual or group: Aristotle was a phi-
       losopher. These four men are blind.
    b) particular: for one or several not determined: lost: a
       horse; he owes him some money; etc. Wanted: a monkey.

ON REASONING

Slogan: Know why you affirm a certain conclusion.

A. *Reasoning of various kinds.*

Since the intellect has no other aim than truth, it always endeavors to perform TRUE judgments. Any other kind of act the intellect may perform is subordinated to this end. Thus, questioning, S.A., and even more obviously inference of reasoning. Indeed, the very fruit or result of reasoning is generally a new judgment, and, if it happens to be a new S.A., this is, like every S.A., in view of making further judgments.

According to the scheme of Fountains of Knowledge and valid judgments, every judgment-conclusion is a *mediate judgment,* since it is discovered as implied in some previously accepted judgment or judgments (or even S.A. plus judgment), called antecedent.

Such a conclusion plus its antecedent (plus possibly all the antecedents of that antecedent, cfr. "supposition") form an ordered or *per se* series of judgments. It is impossible that a number of judgments in such a series be infinite. Indeed if we could not regress in each such series to a first judgment, the truth of which be immediately certain, it would be impossible for us to be certain of the truth of any judgment in the series, since the foundation of that truth would forever escape us. The possible immediate judgments, which can initiate such series in the natural order, have been recorded in the schema of page 6 of the Notes, as 1), 2), 3), 4), under the heading of Immediate sources. We thus obtain the following principle regarding *infinite regress:* Princ.: Infinite regress is not possible in a *per se* series,
  a) of judgments,
  b) of reasonings,
  c) of S.A.,
  d) of relations (i.e., causes and effects).
(This is of course possible in a *per accidens* series).

In consequence of the above principle there exist *first judgments,* and among them *first principles, first notions* (which cannot be defined, but only quasi-defined), *first causes,* etc.

Elements of a series of related through *implication,* either backward or forward. Implication can be either *contingent* (purely *de facto*) or *necessary (de jure).*

When the implication is necessary, we can *pass from the implicant to the necessary implicate. Every such passing is a case of reasoning.*

We have therefore *2 general kinds of reasoning:*

a) from some *exercise* to what is necessarily "exercised" in it;

b) from the *content* of an act to what is necessarily *implied* by it. (*implied* is used here in a restricted sense).

a) *Reasoning "from the exercise":*

We must distinguish 2 kinds of exercise: a) that which is proper to man as such, i.e., as rational animal, and b) any other kind of exercise found in man or in other things. a) is quite distinct, because it is fully covered by the immediate reflective awareness, which characterizes human action as such. Cf. St. Thomas: "When I perceive the stone, I perceive also that I am the one who perceives the stone and the nature of this act." In the same way when we want something, or feel, or desire in a sensitive way. Since such exercises are known from inside, we have greater evidence of their nature and necessary implications.

A. 1. REASONING *"from the human exercise as such."*

The usual textbooks of Logic fail to consider this type of reasoning, and this is regrettable and misleading since concepts of the 3rd. degree or abstraction and Metaphysics are based upon it.

We can make such reasoning for ourselves or for refuting certain kinds of objections made by others. We may call the first "intellective induction" and the second "elenchic retorsion" The latter consists in requesting the opponent to perform an "intellective induction" leading him up to it by our questions. In both cases, it consists in manifesting anything that is exercised in an undeniable human act (exercise of intellect, will, or senses) i.e., *that is at work in it in such a way that without it that act could not have been performed.*

Here are some examples:

a) I perform human acts, therefore they are possible: (from being to being possible).

b) Therefore, their necessary condition of possibility exists.

c) For instance: I judge, hence, I am.

d) I make a sensitive-rational judgment, hence, I am a rational animal.

e) Therefore, I am endowed with intellect and senses.

f) And my intellect can do what it pretends to do, namely, a true judgment: (Principle of truth or objectivity).

g) If you deny this, you do it through a judgment opposed to mine, and which you hold as valid; therefore, you accept willynilly that judgment can be valid, and agree with me.

h) And you accept willynilly that a contradicting judgment can do what it pretends to do, namely, reject as false the judgment it contradicts.

i) Therefore, not every judgment is true, but there are pairs of judgments such as if one is true the the other one is false, and vice versa *(Principle of contradiction).*

A. 2. RATIONAL INDUCTION: *Reasoning "from physical exercises to universal law."*

Principle of Induction: There are physical laws, which are made explicit and which may be deduced from physical facts. This is proved by retorsion.

Indeed, my opponent cannot inform me of this negation without relying on certain constancies of the facts of matter, for instance, that air will usually carry his voice, or paper will not dissolve but will carry his writing or his gesture of denial can be transmitted by light to my eyes; in short, he relies on the constancy of behavior of matter and material means, i.e., on the truth of my own statement. And, in general, from the moment he begins to act intellectually through material means, such as his own body and his physical surroundings, every man acts on the secure confidence that the material world will not betray him. This reliability of behavior of material entities is a necessary condition of possibility of his own sensitive-rational acts, and is therefore as undeniable as those acts.

However, the detailed discovery of the many physical laws is not easy, nor does it reach the same (metaphysical) certainty as the discovery obtained through reasonings of the A. 1.-type. This is due to the fact that mere physical happenings do not fall within the scope of that immediate perfect reflection through which we apprehend the nature of human acts as such. We do not attain those mere physical events from inside, so as to grasp their very nature and, hence, laws of behavior, but only from outside, thus reaching their inner laws only to the extent to which they happen to be manifested.

The rules of Induction belong more properly to Major Logic, and from the point of view of *their use* are more practical in everyday knowledge and positive sciences. However, it will be useful to present them here summarily:

When several, or even one, physical happenings show some constant characteristic(s), it is allowed to generalize the latter, provided no contrary instance is observed. We thus formulate a universal law. If, later on, a contrary instance is observed, we must either give up completely that formulation, or, more often, restrict its scope so as to exclude that instance, while yet retaining the law as valid. Thus we may find that water boils at 100 degrees centigrade and freezes at 0 degrees centigrade, but we must afterward add the restriction: under the atmospheric pressure at sea level. We may find that all metals are good electricity conductors, but not at temperatures approaching absolute zero. When our formulation of physical laws obtained through induction becomes rigorous and, normally, formulable in mathematical terms, we are in the domain of the physico-chemical sciences. Such rigorous formulation can only be approached by what is nowadays called the human sciences, such as sociology, economics, experimental psychology, etc., because they deal with facts which human freedom often enough disturbs.

In that case, the scientists fall back upon mere statistical formulations of the laws at work. The same is the case in subatomic physics, insofar as chance here has a scope limited by the principle of indeterminacy, formulated by Heisenberg.

We may add here what we have already stated regarding judgment as the first act of the mind in the order of knowledge: what is antecedent in the real order of events is consequent in the order of knowledge; conversely, what is antecedent in the order of our knowledge is consequent in the order of events. Thus, the starting point of our knowledge in an inductive problem is some real consequent (effect, data, phenomenon); the aim of induction is to trace this real consequent to its real antecedent (cause or combination of causes).

We may conclude this short study by saying that there is no such thing as a single method of induction to which all others are reducible.

FALLACIES—DEFINITION AND DIVISION

The student will better understand the need to attain a "habit" of right reasoning by first considering certain common "deceptive arguments" found in everyday use. It will, further, help the student to form habits of right reasoning to be able to make first proper definitions about the terms he uses in any discussion and to ask from his opponent the same accuracy. Definitions about terms and proper division, or partial considerations of a whole for its better understanding, will help the student to avoid many of the pitfalls into which the human mind so often blunders. This is the scope of this chapter.

I. *FALLACIES*

A fallacy is a faulty act of the mind, especially a *deceptive argument.* The term "fallacy" may apply to any intellectual act which happens to be invalid, but only broadly to mere errors of fact or principle. It applies strictly to faulty definitions and invalid inferences, whatever may be the rule they fail to observe. (A sophism is a faulty reasoning *deliberately* calculated to deceive.)

The following classification of fallacies, does not, in any way, try to be complete, but will register only the main types of fallacies.

Main types of fallacies:
1.   fallacies of mere language (linguistic or ambiguity)
2.   not of mere language (non-linguistic, of relevance)

1. *FALLACIES OF MERE LANGUAGE:* (linguistic or ambiguous)

   1. *Equivocation:* (the ambiguous middle term in syllogisms) Use of terms that are equivocal (hide—pen) or extrinsically analogous (democracy, progress, religion, science). To avoid it pay attention to the *comprehension* and *supposition* of each term. Better still ask opponent to define his terms.

       Ex: Every philosopher is a scientist.
          Every man is a philosopher.
          Every man is a scientist.

   2. *Amphibology:* (not amphiboly as most textbooks put it; from the Greek: amphibolos = doubtful, and logia, legein = to speak): Use of sentences with an ambiguous sense, i.e., Delphic utterances: "If Croesus went to war with Cyrus, he would destroy a mighty kingdom" (whose?) or H. Macmillan to dismissed Minister S. Lloyd: "You can rest assured that we intend to continue on the path that you have prepared" (in the same or different direction?) ". . . loosely wrapped in a newspaper, she carried three dresses." Read in the newspapers for this type of fallacy.

   3. *Composition:* a conclusion reached from the use of a divisive term in one proposition and collectively in another, i.e., J. Stuart Mill concludes that "since each person's happiness is a good to that person *(divisive)* therefore the general happiness is a good to the aggregate of all persons *(collectively)*."

   4. *Division:* The previous one vice versa from collective to divisive. "It is the last straw that broke the camel's back" (by itself alone, or with all the others?).

   5. *Accent:* Emphasis on words. The sentence changes according to the accent.
       You (not others) may think as you please.

You *may* think as you please. (I allow you)
You may *think* (not act) as you please.
It also applies to phrases out of context, misquoting, as when the student tells the professor, "You said . . ." Did he, really?

6. *Parallel Word Construction:* (figure of speech) a conclusion reached from the similarity of words to similarity of meaning. "immortal"—not mortal; therefore "immemorable"—not memorable. A clearer example in Mill:

"The only proof capable of being given that an object is *visible* is that people actually see it. The only proof that a sound is *audible* is because people hear it; in like manner, I apprehend, the sole evidence it is possible to produce that anything is *desirable* is that people do actually desire it." (It is wrong to reason that because visible means "what can be seen" and audible "what can be heard" therefore "desirable" means "what can be desired." In actual fact "desirable" means "worthy, capable of being desired".

2. *FALLACIES NOT OF MERE LANGUAGE:* (non-linguistic, of relevance)

1. *Accident:* when the "particular" case is not taken into consideration in applying the general rule. Youth is inexperienced.

2. *Converse Accident:* The reverse of no. 1. Considering only exceptional cases and generalizing for all, i.e. opiates are good for some ill people and administered by doctors, therefore opiates are good for all. He is an excellent thief, therefore he is an excellent man. Man is rational, hence its definition is "rational being." This fallacy is called also by modern logicians: hasty generalization.

3. *Ignoring the Issue:* (Ignoratio elenchi): the issue is ignored and a different conclusion, from the one supposed to be established, is reached. The following are the main sub-forms:

a. *argumentum ad hominem:* ignores the issue and attacks the person instead. E.G. "This man tries to prove that we, the managers of the Trade Union, are not honest. But he is a dirty foreigner. What, then, is the value of his accusation?"

b. *argumentum ad populum:* (to the gallery) ignores issue plus appeal to popular prejudices and likes. (the trick to "sell") Phrases like: "the will of the people," "patriotic duty," "thrilling experience."

    c. *argumentum ad misericordiam:* (pity) appeal to pity. A substitution of emotional appeal for rational argument. Special in law court.

    d. *argumentum ad verecundiam:* (shame) based on authority (wrongly mostly) Every *somebody* drinks Johnny Walker (whiskey). "I tell you and that should be enough for you."

    e. *argumentum ad baculum:* abuse of threats, violence, votes made to win a demand.

4. *Petitio Principii:* (Begging the question) assuming as proved the very point to be proved, e.g. "Whiskey causes drunkenness, because it is intoxicating" (because it causes drunkenness) "The soul is immortal, because it cannot die."—b. is immortal. Also used with "question-begging epithets": "the people's candidate, the favorite of millions; the dark ages; the car was what the world was waiting for; the best detergent."

5. *False Cause:* confusing what is not a cause for a cause. Three different forms:

    a) *post hoc, ergo propter hoc:* I was cured after I rubbed my nose with rabbit's brains . . . therefore . . .

    b) *mistaking a mere condition for a cause:* I cannot think without my brain, therefore my brain is the efficient cause of my thinking.

    c) *mistaking a non-premise for a premise:* You said that this is a just punishment, since it is proportioned to the crime; and, besides, it will be an effective deterrent from that type of crime. But, if a punishment is just because it is an effective deterrent from that type of crime, then it would be just to inflict the death penalty for mere pocket-picking.

6. *Complex Question:* Have you stopped beating your wife? If you haven't, then you are a brute, and if you have, then you did beat her and are equally a brute. Beware of "loaded" questions!

7. *Argumentum ad Ignorantiam:* (from ignorance) infers that A should be accepted, because non-A cannot be established. You are guilty, because you cannot prove that you are not guilty. And "there must be ghosts because no one has ever been able to prove that there aren't any."

8. *False Assumption:* (mostly understood, or not explicit) there is no soul because I haven't seen any.

9. *Argument to Silence:* concludes to the absence of a fact because there is no record of it, though it should normally have been recorded (at times can be legitimate). E.G., the

Kumran community did not know Jesus, since there is no reference to him in any of their writings.

Cfr. exercises pages: 69–88 in *Introduction to Logic* of I. M. Copi; and 248–287 in *Logic for Undergraduates,* Kreyche.

II. DEFINITION

Broadly speaking, to define is to clarify the primary "comprehension" of a concept or term; but, in a more strict sense, only secondary concepts can be defined, i.e., clarified by means of less secondary concepts and, ultimately, primary concepts. That is to say, there is no infinite regress in the process of defining.

The primary concepts are self-clarified. But we can make them more explicitly clear by quasi-defining them. And this is done by reference to the basic experiences in which they are "at work", i.e., *implicitly* present, and thus immediately available to our clarifying reflection.

Secondary concepts are those which are strictly definable. The definition of such a concept is an equivalent consisting of less secondary and, therefore, better-known concepts. These are either strictly definable or only quasi-definable.

In a defining statement, such as "man is (or "man" means, or man:) a *rational animal*," only the P. (the underlined part) is, correctly speaking, the definition, i.e., the result of the act of defining S. The term "definition" signifies both that act and its result. It is used more weakly to signify the "nominal definition" i.e. the better-known term or phrase by which you explain a word without declaring its proper comprehension or the nature which it signifies (e.g., "hombre" means "man").

We are not equally successful in defining all terms. There is, therefore, an order of best, fairly good, and poor definitions. And in some cases, we can only give a negative definition.

Things can be defined only insofar as their specific concept can be defined. As individuals, they are undefinable. (We define symbols, not individuals). Hence, the "supposition" of a definition is *absolute,* i.e. it abstracts from the existential manner of being of the thing as well as from the logical manner of being of its concept; it simply expresses what they have in common, i.e., the "quiddity" or nature which the thing has and which its concept signifies. (conf. pages 21, 22 of the Notes).

Etymologically, "definire" means "to mark boundaries of." Thus, in our case, it means "to distinguish a finite thing from all things specifically different from it" (or Infinite Being from all others).

But this is only the first function of a definition. The second is "to declare positively the 'quiddity' or nature signified by the term to be defined." Definitions do not always perfectly fulfill this second function and sometimes not at all.

A definition, either broad or strict, is a complete Simple Apprehension. As such, it is not an existential judgment. But, when we express it together with its S in the form of S is P, it looks like a judgment; hence, we may call it a simili-judgment. It is equivalent to a hypothetical statement; both express simply a nexus of consequence between an S-term and a P-term, but in the case of the definition, this nexus is normally a nexus of identity.

No intellectual life is humanly possible without some definitions of some kind. And no science is possible without at least fairly good definitions. Thus, definitions constitute one of the most essential parts of the intellectual heritage of mankind.

Definition: (broad sense) clarification of the primary "comprehension" of a concept or term.

As an act of the mind: act of the intellect in which I clarify the primary comprehension of a concept or term.

As an oral sign: a phrase signifying the "quiddity" of the concept.

Quasi-definition: clarification of primary comprehension of primary concept, therefore it is intuitive, immediate, implicit in some fundamental experience of man, e.g.:

in the experience of judgment and will: "being" and its transcendental properties, such as "ontological truth," "ontological goodness," "ontological beauty," "act," "active," "lasting," . . . etc.; quasi-transcendentals: "Intelligent," "knowing," "willing," "free"; metaphysical terms: "Passive potency," "relation," "substance," etc; supreme genera: "finite being," "substantial being," "time," "space," "man," "rational animal," "I," "that," etc.

in sensitive experience as such: "sensation," "color" (and the various colors), "sound" (and the various sounds), "taste," etc.

in the experience of organic-animal action: "local movement," "breathing," and other movements. Since these terms are many and hierarchically related, the quasi-definition of one may consist of some of the others.

The so-called "improper definition": does not constitute a true defintion but is similar or extrinsically analogous to the true definition, insofar as it clarifies a certain term. It is called *Nominal Definition,* and can be of different types:

a. *Etymological:* clarifies the linguistic origin of the term.

b. *Def. by synonyms:* clarifies an obscure term by using other, better-known terms of the same or of different language: "Beatitude" means bliss; bliss means happiness.

c. *Def. by description:* Elephant means a very large animal, with ears as large as umbrellas, a rather short tail, and a trunk almost as large as its legs.

d. *Def. by example:* show a piece of chalk and say "this is chalk."

REAL DEFINITIONS: clarification of the primary comprehension of a secondary concept. Therefore mediate, non-intuitive. (This clarification may or may not imply a simultaneous formation of the clarified concept.)

Double role of the real definition:
  a. Distinguishes the defined from all other species.
  b. Declares its "quiddity" or specific nature.
  It fulfills the second role more or less well and therefore we have the following hierarchy of real definitions.

1. *Def. by proximate genus and specific difference:* essential metaphysical def. It is the most perfect and the model that we should imitate as closely as possible in other types of definitions. Indeed, it is the briefest, fullest, and most precise answer to the question, "What is this kind of thing?" Unfortunately only a few concepts can be defined in that way. Should be: by proximate and propium (its own) genus, and by its own specific, positive, and essential difference.

2. *Def. by substitutes of proximate genus and specific difference:*
  a. *by proximate genus and specific logical property.*
  b. *by proximate genus also remote g. and physical property.*   56
  Iron: metal whose atomic number is 26, atomic weight 55.85 (Fe 26).
  c. *by all integral parts of substance: essential physical def.*
  man: composed of "materia prima" and intellectual soul. Water: H_2O.
  or by integral parts of the defined being:
  Finite being: composed of "esse" and complete essence.
  or by integral parts inadequately distinct:
  man: composed of body and intellectual soul.
  or by integral parts considered quantitatively:
  insect: invertebrate animal with body divided into 3 segments (head, thorax, abdomen), 6 legs upon thorax, and (usually) 2 or 4 wings.
  d. *by genus and some now and here characteristic accident:*
  whale: the largest extant sea animal.
  e. *by genus and a complex of accidents characteristic enough:*
  man: tool-using animal that cooks much of its food. Carbon monoxide: colorless, practically odorless gas, density 0.967, boiling point $-192°$, freezing point $-207°$.
  f. *by genus and final cause:*
  Minor Logic (Formal): the art of ascertaining the truth. Barometer: instrument for measuring atmospheric pressure.
  g. *by genus and efficient cause:*
  Malaria: febrile disease caused by animal parasites introduced into man's blood by the bite of the female anopheles mosquito.

h. *by genus and genetic process* (Def. genetic or operatory):
   Circle: figure formed by revolving a line in a plane around one of
   its ends. Bread: article of food made from flour or meal by
   moistening, kneading, and baking.
i. *by genus and characteristic relation:*
   Satellite: celestial (natural or man-made) body that turns around a
   larger celestial body.
   by transcendental term and characteristic relation:
   God: creative cause.
j. *by terms intrinsically analogous and taken "eminenter"* (without limitations): God: is Being itself, Understanding and Will or God is
   Love. or Satyam, Jnanam-Anantam Brahma = is Reality, Knowledge, Infinite (Taitiriya Upanishad, 2, 1).
k. *by transcendental term and characteristic negations:*
   God is *In*finite Being, *Im*material, non-caused: *Im*mortal.
l. *by distributive terms and characteristic illusory attribute:*
   a magician is a man who can draw eggs from the air and rabbits
   from an empty hat.

That which is to be defined is called the "definiendum." That which
defines it is called the "definiens."

The student should, by now, be capable of drawing his own conclusions on the different types of definitions he encounters daily and
come to realize that definitions not only try to give us an inside into the
nature of reality outside of us but also that they form one of the best
guides for measuring the progress man is making in the understanding
of that reality. However, the student should be cautious and realize that
sometimes definitions do not demonstrate the progress of humanity but
rather the contrary. To define man as a "neurotic animal" like psycho-
analysts do is not a sign that man has gone deeper into the knowledge of
human nature, but rather that human nature has degenerated and some
scientists along with it. (Fallacy of composition)

RULES TO GUIDE DEFINITIONS:

1. The definition should be clearer than the defined.
2. The definition must be coextensive with the thing defined, or should
   accommodate only the thing defined.
3. Definitions should be made of terms previously known, not simply
   figurative. Hence the above variety of possible definitions.
4. Definitions should not be redundant, or with non-necessary terms,
   nor circular, and should be brief so that they does not become
   obscure.
5. A definition should, whenever possible, be expressed in positive

terms. (Exercises pp. 121–122, 127–129 of Copi's *Introduction to Logic*. Also from Kreyche's *Logic for Undergraduates*, pp. 7, 76–80.

III. **DIVISION:**

To divide means to state all the parts of a whole. There are 3 kinds of wholes: logical, integral, and potestative. Hence, there are 3 kinds of parts: logical (or subjective), integral, and potestative.

Logical division consists in dividing a distributive term into its sub-concepts i.e. *in stating its full extension.* It is reciprocal to definition, and equivalent to a strict disjunctive proposition: A is divided into a, b, c, = is either a or b or c. Any class whose membership is divided into subclasses is the *genus,* the various subclasses are the *species.*

Each division is made from a certain standpoint, which is called the *basis* of that division. Since we can divide the same whole according to certain different standpoints, there are co-divisions of the same whole.

Division, in general: to state all the parts, adequately distinct, of a whole.

Whole: one having parts; or one in the unity of composition; or composite.

Parts adequately distinct: which can be added in the composite, like a plus B, plus c = A (had plus trunk plus limbs—man) If the parts cannot be added in this manner, they are inadequately distinct—(hand plus its fingers = ?).

Division as an act of the mind: act of the intellect in which I state all the parts, adequately distinct, from a whole.

As an oral sign: phrase stating these parts. The logical division can be expressed either as the P of a strict disjunctive propr. or in the form of a diagram or in any other equivalent manner.

DIVISION OF THE WHOLE: Basis: Is any part equal to its whole (at least to some extent) or is it not?

1. *Logical whole, or universal or distributive:* what is predicated of each part according to all its comprehension and meaning (quality).
   Any distributive term.
   Logical parts or subjective: Its distributive sub-concepts.
   Real singular subjects are not logical parts of a whole, but these subjects plus logical parts are its inferiors.
   Government: executive, legislative, judicial.
   Government: democratic, monarchical, dictatorial, socialist.
2. *Integral whole:* what is not predicated of its parts (neither acc. to comprehension, nor meaning (quality) Can be:
   a. *quantitative:* any material being, insofar as it can be divided into parts equally material, which, in turn could (de jure, at least) be subdivided into quantitative parts in infinitum.

b. *essential:* any finite essence: This essence can be divided in 2 ways:
   1. *metaphysical:* essential metaphysical definition (which is not a thing, but a complex concept), i.e., by proximate genus and spec. difference. These two are integrating parts of this definition, since itself is int. esset. metaph. whole.
   2. *physical:* essential physical definition: what is called real division as opposed to logical.
   Integral parts, or integrating parts: part which is not its whole. It can be quantitative or essential (metaphy. or physically)
3. *Potestative whole:* is stated of all parts according its whole comprehension not its whole meaning or (qualities). Some thing or concept which can be considered according to one meaning separate from all others. Human soul is vegetative, sensible, rational. Each partial soul is the only human soul.

Logical Division: division of a logical whole; distributive terms.

Rules of division: one only basis of division; 2. Make in upon opposite parts (which exclude each other) (no overlapping); 3. Make it adequate (convertible with the whole or complete); 4. Start in proximate parts.

ON REASONING (From Valid Premises)
DEDUCTION

Critical Note:
   In the tradition of the Formal Logic we have been studying so far, Simple Apprehension and Reasoning—Inductive or Deductive—have as their formal object or scope their validity or correctness. The validity or correctness of these acts of the mind is assured by certain sets of rules— definitions, laws of thought, syllogisms, avoiding fallacies, etc. We have seen so far the rules concerning Simple Apprehension, Induction, how to avoid fallacies, etc. All that, in traditional Logic, is left to study would be the syllogism. Assuring the correct use of all these rules, avoiding the pitfalls of the fallacies, and putting into daily use the correct syllogism the student was practically guaranteed to be able to form by himself right or true judgments. In other words he was assured of the correct use of the mechanism that governs the complicated world of the mind, so that the student could by himself find Logical and Ontological Truth. However, though what we have just said may sound to be very much, in practice it is nothing. Formal Logic is *everything* only in potency, for in *act* or formally it does not deal with the truth, as such: the truth, the content to be fed into the sets of rules given in Formal Logic, was supposed to be scattered in the different disciplines of knowledge, science or philoso-

phy. The logician would, eventually, become a scientist or a philosopher.

The mathematician changed, radically, this state of affairs with the invention of Symbolic Logic and its applications to empirical sciences. Logic has found its own truth and its own independence in the relational world of the mathematician.

It is important for the student to realize the different aims of both logics—for there are two—so that he does not use the methods of one for the other and vice versa. Traditional Logic is concerned with relations of things—S-P—rather than with relations denuded of their terms, which is the scope of modern mathematics and Symbolic Logic. One has only to look into the modern theories of algebra, calculus, the theories of equations and functions, of sets and series. The same tendency appears in modern physics where, according to Cassirer, the great conceptual revolution consists in displacing substance—things—by function, and the causal interaction of substances by functional relationships and systems of order. Such substitutions obviously parallel the shift in Logic—from the consideration of terms related as subjects and predicates, to the consideration of relations without regard to differences in the terms related.

Let the student, therefore, become aware of the different scopes and different methods both Logics use in the concrete study of Deduction. Both attitudes are explained by Kant in the following manner:

"The exactness of mathematics depends on definitions, axioms, and demonstrations. . . . None of these can be achieved or imitated by the philosopher in the sense in which they are understood by the mathematician" because according to Kant, the validity of the mathematician's definitions and demonstrations ultimately depends on the fact that he is able to *construct* the concepts he uses. The point is not that mathematics obtains its objects from reason rather than experience, but rather that it obtains them from reason by construction; as, for example, Euclid begins by constructing a triangle which corresponds with his definition of that figure.

Hence, Kant maintains, "we must not try in philosophy to imitate mathematics by beginning with definitions. . . . In philosophy, in fact, the definition in its complete clearness ought to conclude rather than begin our work"; where in mathematics we cannot begin until we have constructed the objects corresponding to our definitions.

With this "critical note" in mind, we may now proceed to the study of Deduction. However, since deduction is mostly concerned with manifesting the implications of the content or synthesis of terms of *propositions,* and the latter differ mostly in regard to their content, we cannot, yet, study deduction without first inquiring about the nature and divisions of propositions. In other words, *what is a proposition?*

I. *The Analysis of Propositions*

A. *A proposition* may be defined as anything which can be said to be true or false. Therefore, from the point of view of Deduction, both premises and conclusions are propositions. However, in order to better understand the above definition of propositions let us see first what a proposition is not.

    1. A proposition is not the same thing as the sentence which states it. The three sentences, "I think, therefore I am," "Je pense, donc je suis," and "Cogito, ergo sum" all state the same proposition. A sentence is a group of words, and words, like other symbols, are in themselves physical objects, distinct from that to which they refer or which they symbolize. The proposition is distinct from the visual marks or sound waves of the expression. Sentences have physical existence and they may or may not conform with the standards of usage or taste. (It is only in this last sense that they are spoken of at times as true or false.) Truth or falsity can be predicated only of the propositions they signify.

    2. Nevertheless, though distinct from the symbols that express them, propositions cannot be expressed without those symbols. The structure of the symbols must correspond to the structure of the propositions, so that not every combination of symbols can convey a proposition. "Susan, cat, ribbon, sandals," and "Water, garage, eye, octopus," are not symbols expressing propositions, but simply nonsense. Only certain arrangements of symbols can express propositions. That is why the grammar of language will clarify many distinctions which are logical in nature.

    3. In sentences like the following two of Hamlet: "Oh, from this time forth, my thoughts be bloody, or be nothing worth!" or "Why wouldst thou be a breeder of sinners?" he is not asserting propositions *except implicitly*. For wishes, questions, or commands, cannot, as such, be true or false. Note however that for these sentences to have the implications of propositions, they would have to be turned inside out—like a sock—and the assumptions upon which they are based made evident. These assumptions involve propositions. The assumptions of the second sentence of Hamlet's would be, among others, that the person addressed exists, is capable of breeding children, and that such children are certain to be sinners. Similarly, the first one assumes that the speaker is capable of having ideas, that these ideas can be murderous, that they may have some kind of value, etc. Moreover, commands or wishes may be turned into propositions when the original sentence is turned into its logical form. "I wish you would come = I shall be pleased if you come" or "You will be sorry if

you do not come." To the extent that the declarations state something that may be true or false they are propositions.

4. There is no need to insist here on the usual confusion between propositions and the mental act required to think them. In the same manner we distinguish proposition from sentence or the symbol which expresses it, we must distinguish it from the act of the mind or the judgment which thinks it.

5. Propositions must not be identified with any concrete object, thing, or event. For propositions are at most only the abstract and selected relations between things. When we affirm or deny the proposition: The moon is nearer to the earth than the sun, neither the moon alone, nor the earth, nor the sun, nor the spatial distance between them is a proposition. The proposition *is the relation asserted to hold between them.* The relations which are the objects of our thoughts are elements or aspects of actual, concrete situations. These aspects, while perhaps not spatially or temporally *separable* from other characters in the situation, are *distinguishable* in meaning. That is why sense experience never yields knowledge without a reflective analysis of what it is we are experiencing. For knowledge is *of* propositions. And propositions can be known only by discriminating within some situation = relations between abstract features found therein.

6. Also note that while a proposition is defined as that which is true or false, it does not mean that we must *know* which of these alternatives is the case. *Cancer is preventable* is a proposition, though we do not know whether it is true.

Sentences like "Three feet make a yard" are not propositions but rather conventional resolutions, in this case about a unit of measure. They take the form of propositions and are treated like them, though they must be distinguished from them.

7. To avoid other difficulties in the interpretation of propositions the student should be most familiar with comprehension (connotation) and extension (denotation); and pages 21–22 about supposition, appellation, status, ampliation, and distraction of terms.

B. *The Division of Propositions*

Modern Logic is faithful in recording the traditional division of Categorical Propositions according to Quantity, Quality, and Distribution of Subject and Predicate. Modern Logic is also faithful in recording the Square of Opposition of Propositions and the immediate inference from Categorical Propositions or the Form (i.e., reducing all propositions to a Logical form by Obversion, Conversion, Contraposition, inversion, and opposition). There is, therefore, no need of explaining those facts any further in these notes.

However there are two points of interest and difference between tradition and modern logic. Tradition is based mostly on the view that all propositions are of the subject-predicate form. The subject being regarded as a substance in which various qualities adhere, and the quality of any inquiry would be to discover the inhering predicates in some concrete subject. Aristotle maintained that the ultimate subject of predication is some concrete, individual substance, and that there is an irreducible plurality of such, but that these substances are systematically related. The student should observe how, in the proses of Symbolic Logic, he will be dealing with the consideration of relations only, without regard to differences in the terms related.

The second important and divergent point is what the modern logicians call the "existential import of categoricals." Particular propositions alone will carry existential import, while universal propositions will be considered simple hypotheses, just as in science universal propositions are taken as hypotheses, i.e., Newton's first law, "if a body were free from impressed forces, it would persevere in its state of rest or in uniform motion in a straight line forever!"

Also, it should be noted that existential import does not refer only to physical existence. For example in "Did Jupiter have a daughter?" we do not speak of physical existence, but of the existence of individuals within a universe of discourse controlled by certain assumptions, such as Homer's statement.

When, therefore, it is said in formal logic that universal propositions do not imply, while particulars do imply, the existence of instances, the student may find it helpful to interpret this (in part at least) on the basis of the different function each type of proposition plays in scientific inquiry. In other words, the student of Modern Logic is asked to validly infer the truth of a proposition concerning some matter of observation from premises obtained through observation and not from universal propositions alone.

This shift from the universal to the particular is one more instance of the positivist and empirical trend of our modern world of science.

We consider that, after these critical remarks and words of caution, the student will be able to amble, on his or her own feet, into the labyrinthine ways of "his own chosen text book on Logic." However we would like to remind him or her of the dangers of taking any absolute position in these matters. Let no one disdain the old and become too infatuated with the new. He or she might find himself or herself advised to follow the same course that the Venecian Lady advised Jean-Jacques Rousseau to follow: "Zanetto," she said, "lascia le donne, et studia la matematica." Which means, "Leave women (philosophy) alone and study mathematics."

Scipio's Dream, from On the Republic,

Cicero

Cicero wrote Scipio's Dream *between 54 and 52 B.C. as part of the sixth book* On the Republic. *The Roman Republic was divided between the conservative Cato and the liberal Julius Caesar. Cicero thought it to be the ripe time to rally the upper classes round his political and philosophical ideal. He borrowed from the* Republic *of Plato and the* Politics *of Aristotle "theories" that promised to do justice to Cicero's political claims: the life of the statesman, the definition of the commonwealth, its generation, its ideal, which Cicero equates with the actual Roman aristocratic republic of 129 B.C.*

Scipio's Dream should be read in comparison and side by side with Plato's Myth of Er. *The* Myth of Er *is Plato's model of rebuilding the present through the technologies of bringing the dead back to life and keeping memory alive. For Cicero* Scipio's Dream *is the propaganda agenda for Roman conservatives against Roman liberals. Only the conservatives inherit the heavens for only they have given support, security, and increase to the fatherland. The conservative mind is the microcosmos of God's mind, and theirs is the heavens; others, the liberals, the members of other political parties must be first purged of much dross before they can share that heaven with the conservatives.*

The students should compare the fact that while for Plato's Er, creation is the result of dividing and subdividing memories until they surrender the dead to us, for the Roman Cicero the heavens coincide with a theoretical orthodoxy reinforced in opposition to other theoretical orthodoxies, and the subsequent result is that self identity is always through the others who reject or accept us, rather than the exacted and virtue of our own acts, as in the Myth of Er.

The translation of Scipio's Dream *is by F. E. Rockwood (Boston, 1903), with Arabic numbers referring to the smaller paragraphs of the Teuner text.*
The translation of Myth of Er *is by Benjamin Jowett.*

The younger Scipio, on duty in Africa, dreams of his grandfather.

"After I had reported in Africa to the consul, Manius Manilius, as military tribune (you recall) of the Fourth Legion, what I wanted most was to meet King Masinissa, who was for good reasons a very close family friend. When I paid him a visit, the old man embraced me, the tears streaming down his face, then looked up to heaven and said: 'Thanks to the sun in the highest, and to the moon and stars, that before I die I see in my kingdom and under my roof a Publis Cornelis Scipio, the very mention of whose name refreshes me, so clearly stamped on my mind is the memory of that splendid and invincible man, his grandfather.' Then I asked him questions about his kingdom, he asked me about our republic, and that day passed for both of us in a long conversation.

"After a regal banquet, we prolonged our talk far into the night. My grandfather was the sole subject of the old king's conversation; he remembered the things he had said as well as the things he had done. Then, when we parted for the night, I fell into a deeper sleep than usual, because I was tired from my journey and had stayed up late. (I believe the subject of our conversation was responsible for what followed; for it quite often happens that what we think and talk about has an effect on our sleep, as in Ennius' account of his vision of Homer, whom of course he used often to think and talk about during his waking hours.) At any rate my grandfather appeared to me, in a likeness which I recognized more from his portrait bust than from personal recollection. To tell the truth, I shuddered when I saw who it was, but he said, 'Be brave; fear not, Scipio, and hand on my words to posterity.'

Scipio's grandfather foretells the young man's future honors and possible murder.

"From a high place brightly illuminated by full starlight he pointed down toward Carthage, and said, 'Do you see that city, which once I humbled before the Roman people, now taking up again the old war, and incapable of keeping the peace? Now you have come, a mere private, to besiege it. Within these three years you will become consul and overturn it, and thereby earn in your own right the nickname "Africanus," which up to now you have worn as a mere inheritance. When you have destroyed Carthage, you will hold a triumph, you will become censor, you will go on missions to Egypt, Syria, Asia Minor and Greece; in your absence from Rome you will again be elected consul; you will win a major war, you will level Numantia to the ground. But when you ride again in your triumphal chariot onto the Capitoline Hill, you will find the republic in turmoil over the policies of my grandson Tiberius Gracchus.

"'This is the time, Africanus, when you must reveal to your fatherland the keenness of your mind, your talents, and your judgment. But at this time too I see destiny opening before you a parting of the ways. For when the years of your life have completed seven times eight solstices, and when these two numbers, each of which is considered perfect for a different reason, in nature's round have reached the sum that is foreordained for you, the whole state will turn to you alone and to your proud name; it is to you that the Senate, all the aristocrats, the allies, Latin and Italian, will look for guidance; on you alone the state will depend for security; in short, you will be needed as dictator to restore public order, if only you escape the treacherous hands of your own kin.' At this point Laelius broke out into an exclamation, and the rest uttered heavy groans, but Scipio smiled gently and said, 'Sh! You'll wake me from my dream! Hear the rest of my story; it will take only a little while.'

Incentives to patriotism: eternal life for good conservatives.

"'But to spur you on to greater eagerness to preserve the republic, Africanus, be assured of this: for all who have given security, support, and increase to the fatherland, there has been ordained in heaven a special place where they may enjoy in blessedness eternal life; for to that director god who rules the universe there is nothing, at least on earth, closer to his heart than that united assembly of mankind, joined together under law, which we call the State, whose rulers and preservers, sent from heaven, to heaven return.'

Incentives to conservatives: the true life is the life after death.

"At this point, stricken as I was by fear not so much of death as of plots within my own family, I plucked up courage to ask him, 'Are you, and my father Paulus, and the others whom we think of as dead, really still alive?' 'The truth is,' he replied, 'that it is those who have escaped from the bonds of the body as from a prison who are really living; your so-called life is the real death. Look! Your father Paulus approaches.' As I caught sight of him, I dissolved in tears, but with an embrace and a kiss he bade me stop my weeping.

This blessedness may not be attained by suicide.

"As soon as I could check the flood of tears and speak, I said, 'Most reverend and best of fathers, since this life of yours is really life, as I have just heard my grandfather say, why do I stay on earth instead of hurrying to come to you?' 'That is not the solution,' he replied. 'For unless that God, whose temple is all that your eye can see, releases you from his galling prison house of the body, you cannot gain entrance here. For man was given life on condition that he would inhabit that globe, the earth, which you see in the midst of this firmament, and the source of man's soul is those eternal fires which you mortals call planets and stars, which, as spheres each endowed with the living breath of divine minds, complete the circuit of their orbits with a speed that wakes our wonder. Therefore both you, my son, and all loyal Romans must keep your souls in the custody of your bodies, and not leave mortal life unbidden by him by whom your souls were given you. Otherwise you will appear to have deserted the post among men assigned you by God.

But by a life of devotion to the conservative cause.

" 'But, like your grandfather here, like me who begot you, Scipio, practise justice and loyalty, virtues which, important as they are in the case of parents and kinsfolk, are most important of all as they affect the fatherland. Such a life is the road to heaven and to this assemblage of those who have finished with mortal life, and, released from the body, dwell in that place which you see.'

Which will lead to an eternity among the wonders of the universe.

"Pointing to a ring of light blazing with uncommon splendor among the other flames, he continued. 'And this, as the Greeks have taught you, you call the Galaxy or Milky Way.' As I looked at it, it seemed to make the rest of the heavens wondrous bright. Moreover there were stars there such as we never see from this earth, and all of a size beyond our wildest conjecture; the smallest of these was the moon, farthest from the sphere of heaven, closest to the earth, shining with a borrowed light. Furthermore, the stellar spheres were far larger than the earth. The result was that the earth itself seemed to me so small that I was vexed at the small size of our empire, which gives us access to the merest pinpoint, as it were, of earth.

The nine spheres, the planets, and the stars.

"As I kept looking down, my grandfather said, 'How long, pray, will your mind remain earth-bound? Do you not see that you have come into the temple of the sky? The universe, you must know, is built of nine circles or rather hollow spheres, one within the other, of which one is the sphere of heaven, the outermost, embracing all the rest, identical with God himself, the all-highest, limiting and containing the others; studded in this heavenly sphere are the eternal rolling orbits of the fixed stars; and beneath it are the seven spheres which revolve the opposite way from the heavenly sphere; one of these spheres is occupied by that planet which on earth men call Saturn. Next comes the glow of that good-omened and health-bringing planet called Jupiter; next below is Mars, red and hateful to the earth; next, about half-way between heaven and earth, comes the sun, the leader, chief, and regulator of all other sources of light, the mind and guiding principle of the universe, so large that it surveys and fills all things with its light. One of the two orbits that follows close upon the sun is Venus, the other Mercury, and in the inmost sphere the moon turns, lit by the sun's rays. Beneath the sphere of the moon there is nothing that is not mortal and frail, except the souls granted as a gift of the gods to the race of men, but above the moon all things are eternal. For the core of all the hollow spheres, the ninth, the earth, does not move, but is the lowest, so that all heavy objects gravitate toward it of their own weight.'

The music of the spheres.

"After I had collected myself following the amazement with which I viewed the spheres, I asked, 'What is this music, so mighty and so sweet, that fills my ears?' 'It is the driving motion of the spheres themselves that produces it,' he replied; 'though the intervals that separate them are unequal, yet the spheres are arranged in an exact proportion; the harmony of bass and treble makes a series of matched chords. For so mighty a motion cannot proceed in silence, and naturally at one extreme of the universe the sound is high, at the other low. That is, that outermost orbit, the heavenly one that carries the stars, because it moves the fastest, moves with a high-pitched, lively sound, while this lowest, or lunar, sphere moves with a deep bass note. I leave the ninth, the earth, out of account, for it remains forever fixed, and motionless is one place, occupying the midpoint of the universe. But the other eight orbits, two of which (Mercury and Venus) move at the same speed, strike seven notes with fixed intervals. This number is the key of almost everything; imitating this music with stringed instruments and the voice, expert musicians have opened for themselves a pathway back to heaven, just as others have whose massive intellects have followed divine pursuits in the midst of this human life.

" 'When the ears of mere mortals are filled with this music, they grow deaf; indeed, hearing is the dullest of your senses. Just as the people who dwell in the high mountains at the cataracts of the Nile have lost their sense of hearing entirely, because the roar is so deafening, even so this music, resulting from the turning of the whole universe at high velocity, is so great a thing that men's ears cannot hear it, just as you cannot look straight at the sun without its rays blinding your eyes.'

By comparison with this eternal life, the reputation of the conservative on earth is unimportant, because limited in space and time.

"Marvel as I did at this, I could not keep my eyes from perpetually looking at the earth.

"Just then my grandfather said, 'I perceive that you still cannot take your mind off the habitat and abode of men; but if it seems to you to be as small as it really is, keep this heavenly sphere ever in view, and despise that mortal one. For what reputation can you gain from the converse of mere men, or what glory that is worth the striving? You see from here that the earth is inhabited only here and there in confined spaces, and that desert wastes lie between these inhabited blots or patches. You see too that dwellers on earth are not only so cut off from one another that there can be no intercommunication; but that some live in the same longitude as you but in the opposite latitude, others in the same latitude but in the opposite longitude, while still others live at the antipodes. Surely you cannot expect your reputation to spread among any of these.

" 'From here also you can see that this same earth is girdled round, as it were, by several zones, two of which, as far apart as possible, and supported by the opposite poles of the heavens, you see to be frozen solid, while the middle and widest zone is parched by the heat of the sun. Only the remaining two are habitable. The South Temperate Zone, where, from your point of view, men walk upside down, has nothing to do with Romans; this other, buffeted by the north wind, where you live—see how small a part of it belongs to you. For the whole territory you inhabit, narrowly limited from north to south, wider from east to west, is nothing but a sort of tiny island, surrounded by that sea which though on earth you call it the Atlantic, the Great Sea, the Ocean, or some grandiose name, is really, as you see, quite infinitesimal.

" 'Out of the area of this known and inhabited world, small as it is, how likely is it that your name, or that of any one of us, can climb the Caucasus which you see here, or swim the Ganges there? Who at the other ends of the earth, east or west, north or south, will hear your name? When you have lopped off these areas, surely you see what narrow limits your fame would have to spread itself in. As for those who actually do talk about us, how long will they do so?

In the passage of millennia of the Great Year, temporal reputation will be forgotten.

" 'And this is not all. Even if *our* posterity should want to hand on to theirs the eulogy of any one of us which they received as a heritage from their fathers, the floods and conflagrations which must occur at fixed intervals would make it impossible for us to achieve a temporal, much less an eternal glory. In any case what does it matter that posterity will talk about you, when you consider that your ancestors never did? And yet those same ancestors are at least as numerous as posterity, and they were certainly better men.

" 'These considerations become especially striking when you reflect that not one of those who can hear our name mentioned have memories a year long. For men unscientifically calculate a year on the basis of the revolution of the sun alone, a single star; but when all the stars return to their starting point, and after eons the whole heaven again looks the same as it did at the beginning, then that can really be called the revolving cycle of a true year, and in it I scarcely dare to mention how many generations of men are included. Perhaps I can express it this way. When the sun suffers eclipse in the same quarter of heaven and on the same day of the year as once it seemed to men to do, at the time the soul of Romulus made its way hither, and when all the constellations have been called back to the positions they held then, you may consider the year to have come full circle; but you must know that of that year scarce a twentieth part has so far passed.

Entrance to heaven is based not on vulgar reputation but on virtue and nobility.

" 'If then you have no hope of return hither to heaven, where great and eminent men find their just reward, consider on the other hand how little that petty human reputation is worth, which can scarcely last the smallest fraction of a single year. If therefore it is your wish to look on high and contemplate this dwelling, this eternal home, you will not debase yourself to seek the good will of vulgar men, nor centre your hopes upon any rewards that mere men can give. Let virtue, shining by her own light, attract you to the true reward. As for what others may say about you, leave that to them, in the assurance that there will be gossip in any case. Remember that all such gossip is confined to these zones which you see; no man's reputation, for good or ill, ever lasted forever. Men die, and their fame is buried; posterity forgets, and reputation is snuffed out.'

"When he had finished, I said, 'Grandfather, if it is really true that for those who have deserved well of the fatherland a straight path, as it were, leads to the gate of heaven, in that case, even though from boyhood I have followed in your footsteps and my father's, and have given you nothing to be ashamed of, now that you have revealed to me so great a reward I shall strive all the more vigilantly.'

It is the mind and not the body that attains eternal life.

" 'Strive you must,' he answered, 'and keep in mind that it is not you that is mortal, but this outward body; for what your mere outline reveals is not the real you; essentially it is each person's mind that *is* that person, and not the bodily shape which the finger can point to. Know then that you are a god, if indeed energy, thought, memory, and foresight are godlike. For the mind is ruler, director, and mover of the body, which it commands exactly as the great director God rules this unvierse; and as the eternal God himself moves the universe which is in part mortal, so the eternal mind moves the body which is subject to decay.

It is the godlike motion of mind or soul that makes the world go round.

" 'For what is always in motion is eternal; but whatever is the source of motion to another object and itself derives its motion from some source must find the limit of its existence in the limit of its motion. Only the self-mover, since it never deprives itself of motion, never stops, but is rather the source and origin of motion for other moving objects. Bu such a first principle has no starting point; for all things originate from a first principle, while the first principle itself can originate from no other thing; for what came into being from some other source would not be a first principle; but if it never begins, it never ceases either. For once a first principle has ceased to exist, it will not come into being again from some other source, nor create another first principle out of itself; at least it will not, if it is true that all things must start from a first principle. That is why the first principle of motion rises out of what is self-moved; but this self-mover cannot be born or die, or else the whole heavens would fall of necessity and all nature come to a stop and find no other source of motion which would impel it to start its motion again from the beginning.

" 'Since then it is obvious that whatever is self-moved is eternal, who can deny that self-motion is the natural attribute of souls? For whatever is moved by an external force is without soul or inanimate; but what has a soul or is animate has within itself the source of its own motion; for this self-motion is the unique quality and force of the soul; and if it is the only thing in the universe which is self-moved it is clearly not subject to birth and is therefore eternal.

The conservative's use of his divine mind is politics is his best hope of heaven; Epicureans cannot be admitted without a long term in purgatory.

" 'Use it therefore to the best ends. For example, it is the best man's sense of responsibility for the security of the fatherland which rouses the soul and uses it so as to make it wing its way more swifly to this its proper dwelling-place. This it will do the more rapidly, if, while it is still enclosed in the body, it will look abroad, and, in the contemplation of the things beyond the body, will withdraw itself as far as possible from it. For when men surrender themselves and, as it were, cater to the bodily pleasures, which desire impels them to minister to, they violate the laws of gods and men, and their souls, when they escape the body, flit about the earth itself and return not to heaven until after many centuries of torture.'

"My grandfather's image faded away: I was loosed from the bondage of my dream."

The Myth of Er, from the **Republic,**

Plato

[Socrates is speaking to Glaucon.]

These, then, are the prizes and rewards and gifts which are bestowed upon the just by gods and men in this present life, in addition to the other good things which justice of herself provides.

Yes, he said; and they are fair and lasting.

And yet, I said, all these are as nothing, either in number or greatness in comparison with those other recompenses which await both just and unjust after death. And you ought to hear them, and then both just and unjust will have received from us a full payment of the debt which the argument owes to them.

Speak, he said; there are few things which I would more gladly hear.

Well, I said, I will tell you a tale; not one of the tales which Odysseus tells to the hero Alcinous, yet this too is a tale of a hero, Er the son of Armenius, a Pamphylian by birth. He was slain in battle, and ten days afterwards, when the bodies of the dead were taken up already in a state of corruption, his body was found unaffected by decay, and carried away home to be buried. And on the twelfth day, as he was lying on the funeral pile, he returned to life and told them what he had seen in the other world. He said that when his soul left the body he went on a journey with a great company, and that they came to a mysterious place at which there were two openings in the earth; they were near together, and over against them were two other openings in the heaven above. In the intermediate space there were judges seated, who commanded the just, after they had given judgment on them and had bound their sentences in front of them, to ascend by the heavenly way on the right hand; and in like manner the unjust were bidden by them to descend by the lower way on the left hand; these also bore the symbols of their deeds, but fastened on their backs. He drew near, and they told him that he was to be the messenger who would carry the report of the other world to men, and they bade him hear and see all that was to be heard and seen in that place. Then he beheld and saw on one side the souls departing at either opening of heaven and earth when sentence had been given on them; and at the two other openings other souls, some ascending out of the earth dusty and worn with travel, some descending out of heaven clean and bright. And arriving ever and anon they seemed to have come from a long journey, and they went forth with gladness into the meadow, where they encamped as at a festival; and those who knew one another embraced and conversed, the souls which came from earth curiously enquiring about the things above, and the souls which came from heaven about the things beneath. And they told one another of what had happened by the way, those from below weeping and sorrowing at the remembrance of the things which they had endured and seen in their journey beneath the earth (now the journey lasted a thousand years), while those from above were describing heavenly delights and visions of inconceivable beauty. The story, Glaucon, would take too long to tell; but the sum was this:—He said that for every wrong which they had done to any one they suffered tenfold; or once in a hundred years— such being reckoned to be the length of man's life, and the penalty being thus paid ten times in a thousand years. If, for example, there were any who had been the cause of many deaths, or had betrayed or enslaved cities or armies, or been guilty of any other evil behaviour, for each and all of their offences they received punishment ten times over, and the rewards of beneficence and justice and holiness were in the same proportion. I need hardly repeat what he said concerning young children dying almost as soon as they were born. Of piety and impiety to gods and parents, and of murderers, there were retributions other and greater far which he described. He mentioned that he was present when one of the spirits asked another, 'Where is Ardiaeus the Great?' (Now this Ardiaeus lived a thousand years before the time of Er: he had been the tyrant of some city of Pamphylia, and had murdered his aged father and his elder brother, and was said to have committed many other abominable crimes.) The answer of the other spirit was: 'He comes not hither and will never come. And this,' said he, 'was one of the dreadful sights which we ourselves witnessed. We were at the mouth of the cavern, and, having completed all our experiences, were about to reascend, when of a sudden Ardiaeus appeared and several others, most of whom were tyrants; and there were also besides the tyrants private individuals who had been great criminals: they were just, as they fancied, about to return into the upper world, but the mouth, instead of admitting them, gave a roar, whenever any of these incurable sinners or some one who had not been sufficiently punished tried to ascend; and then wild men of fiery aspect, who were standing by and heard the sound, seized and carried them off; and Ardiaeus and others they bound head and foot and hand, and threw them down and flayed them with scourges, and dragged them along the road at the side, carding them on thorns like wool, and declaring to the passers-by what were their crimes, and that they were being taken away to be cast into hell.' And of all the many terrors which they had endured, he said that there was none like the terror which each of them felt at that moment, lest they should hear the voice; and when there was silence, one by one they ascended with exceeding joy. These, said Er, were the penalties and retributions, and there were blessings as great.

Now when the spirits which were in the meadow had tarried seven days, on the eighth they were obliged to proceed on their journey, and, on the fourth day after, he said that they came to a place where they could see from above a line of light, straight as a column, extending right through the whole heaven and through the earth, in colour resembling the rainbow, only brighter and purer; another day's journey brought them to the place, and there, in the midst of the light, they saw the ends of the chains of heaven let down from above: for this light is the belt of heaven, and holds together the circle of the universe, like the under-girders of a trireme. From these ends is extended the spindle of Necessity, on which all the revolutions turn. The shaft and hook of this spindle are made of steel, and the whorl is made partly of steel and also partly of other materials. Now the whorl is in form like the whorl used on earth; and the description of it implied that there is one large hollow whorl which is quite scooped out, and into this is fitted another lesser one, and another, and another, and another, and four others, making eight in all, like vessels which fit into one another; the whorls show their edges on the upper side, and on their lower side all together form one continuous whorl. This is pierced by the spindle, which is driven home through the centre of the eighth. The first and outermost whorl has the rim broadest, and the seven inner whorls are narrower, in the following proportions—the sixth is next to the first in size, the fourth next to the sixth; then comes the eighth; the seventh is fifth, the fifth is sixth, the third is seventh, last and eighth comes the second. The largest [or fixed stars] is spangled, and the seventh [or sun] is brightest; the eighth [or moon] coloured by the reflected light of the seventh; the second and fifth [Saturn and Mercury] are in colour like one another, and yellower than the preceding; the third [Venus] has the whitest light; the fourth [Mars] is reddish; the sixth [Jupiter] is in whiteness second. Now the whole spindle has the same motion; but, as the whole revolves in one direction, the seven inner circles move slowly in the other, and of these the swiftest is the eighth; next in swiftness are the seventh, sixth, and fifth, which move together; third in swiftness appeared to move according to the law of this reversed motion the fourth; the third appeared fourth and the second fifth. The spindle turns on the knees of Necessity; and on the upper surface of each circle is a siren, who goes round with them, hymning a single tone or note. The eight together form one harmony; and round about, at equal intervals, there is another band, three in number, each sitting upon her throne: these are the Fates, daughters of Necessity, who are clothed in white robes and have chaplets upon their heads, Lachesis and Clotho and Atropos, who accompany with their voices the harmony of the sirens—Lachesis singing of the past, Clotho of the present, Atropos of the future; Clotho from time to time assisting with a touch of her right hand the revolution of the outer circle of the whorl or spindle, and Atropos with her left hand touching and guiding the inner ones, and Lachesis laying hold of either in turn, first with one hand and then with the other.

When Er and the spirits arrived, their duty was to go at once to Lachesis; but first of all there came a prophet who arranged them in order; then he took from the knees of Lachesis lots and samples of lives, and having mounted a high pulpit, spoke as follows: 'Hear the word of Lachesis, the daughter of Necessity. Mortal souls, behold a new cycle of life and mortality. Your genius will not be allotted to you, but you will choose your genius; and let him who draws the first lot have the first choice, and the life which he chooses shall be his destiny. Virtue is free, and as a man honours or dishonours her he will have more or less of her; the responsibility is with the chooser—God is justified.' When the Interpreter had thus spoken he scattered lots indifferently among them all, and each of them took up the lot which fell near him, all but Er himself (he was not allowed), and each as he took his lot perceived the number which he had obtained. Then the Interpreter placed on the ground before them the samples of lives; and there were many more lives than the souls present, and they were of all sorts. There were lives of every animal and of man in every condition. And there were tyrannies among them, some lasting out the tyrant's life, others which broke off in the middle and came to an end in poverty and exile and beggary; and there were lives of famous men, some who were famous for their form and beauty as well as for their strength and success in games, or, again, for their birth and the qualities of their ancestors; and some who were the reverse of famous for the opposite qualities. And of women likewise; there was not, however, any definite character in them, because the soul, when choosing a new life, must of necessity become different. But there was every other quality, and they all mingled with one another, and also with elements of wealth and poverty, and disease and health; and there were mean states also. And here, my dear Glaucon, is the supreme peril of our human state; and therefore the utmost care should be taken. Let each one of us leave every other kind of knowledge and seek and follow one thing only, if peradventure he may be able to learn and may find some one who will make him able to learn and discern between good and evil, and so to choose always and everywhere the better life as he has opportunity. He should consider the bearing of all these things which have been mentioned severally and collectively upon virtue; he should know what the effect of beauty is when combined with poverty or wealth in a particular soul, and what are the good and evil consequences of noble and humble birth, of private and public station, of strength and weakness, of cleverness and dullness, and of all the natural and acquired gifts of the soul, and the operation of them when conjoined; he will then look at the nature of the soul, and from the consideration of all these qualities he will be able to determine which is the better and which is the worse; and so he will choose, giving the name of evil to the life which will make his soul more unjust, and good to the life which will make his soul more just; all else he will disregard. For we have seen and know that this is the best choice both in life and after death. A man must take with him into the world below an adamantine faith in truth and right, that there too he may be undazzled by the desire of wealth or the other allurements of evil, lest, coming upon tyrannies and similar villainies, he do irremediable wrongs to others and suffer yet worse himself; but let him know how to choose the mean and avoid the extremes on either side, as far as possible, not only in this life but in all that which is to come. For this is the way of happiness.

And according to the report of the messenger from the other world this was what the prophet said at the time: 'Even for the last comer, if he chooses wisely and will live diligently, there is appointed a happy and not undesirable existence. Let not him who chooses first be careless, and let not the last despair.' And when he had spoken, he who had the first choice came forward and in a moment chose the greatest tyranny; his mind having been darkened by folly and sensuality, he had not thought out the whole matter before he chose, and did not at first sight perceive that he was fated, among other evils, to devour his own children. But when he had time to reflect, and saw what was in the lot, he bagan to beat his breast and lament over his choice, forgetting the proclamation of the prophet; for, instead of throwing the blame of his misfortune on himself, he accused chance and the gods, and everything rather than himself. Now he was one of those who came from heaven, and in a former life had dwelt in a well-ordered State, but his virtue was a matter of habit only, and he had no philosophy. And it was true of others who were similarly overtaken, that the greater number of them came from heaven and therefore they had never been schooled by trial, whereas the pilgrims who came from earth having themselves suffered and seen others suffer were not in a hurry to choose. And owing to this inexperience of theirs, and also because the lot was a chance, many of the souls exchanged a good destiny for an evil or an evil for a good. For if a man had always on his arrival in this world dedicated himself from the first to sound philosophy, and had been moderately fortunate in the number of the lot, he might, as the messenger reported, be happy here, and also his journey to another life and return to this, instead of being rough and underground, would be smooth and heavenly. Most curious, he said, was the spectacle—sad and laughable and strange: for the choice of the souls was in most cases based on their experience of a previous life. There he saw the soul which had once been Orpheus choosing the life of a swan out of enmity to the race of women, hating to be born of a woman because they had been his murderers; he beheld also the soul of

Thamyras choosing the life of a nightingale; birds, on the other hand, like the swan and other musicians, wanting to be men. The soul which obtained the twentieth lot chose the life of a lion, and this was the soul of Ajax the son of Telamon, who would not be a man, remembering the injustice which was done him in the judgment about the arms. The next was Agamemnon, who took the life of an eagle, because, like Ajax, he hated human nature by reason of his sufferings. About the middle came the lot of Atalanta; she, seeing the great fame of an athlete, was unable to resist the temptation: and after her there followed the soul of Epeus the son of Panopeus passing into the nature of a woman cunning in the arts; and far away among the last who chose, the soul of the jester Thersites was putting on the form of a monkey. There came also the soul of Odysseus having yet to make a choice, and his lot happened to be the last of them all. Now the recollection of former toils had disenchanted him of ambition, and he went about for a considerable time in search of the life of a private man who had no cares; he had some difficulty in finding this, which was lying about and had been neglected by everybody else; and when he saw it, he said that he would have done the same had his lot been first instead of last, and that he was delighted to have it. And not only did men pass into animals, but I must also mention that there were animals tame and wild who changed into one another and into corresponding human natures—the good into the gentle and the evil into the savage, in all sorts of combinations.

All the souls had now chosen their lives, and they went in the order of their choice to Lachesis, who sent with them the genius whom they had severally chosen, to be the guardian of their lives and the fulfiller of the choice: this genius led the souls first to Clotho, and drew them within the revolution of the spindle impelled by her hand, thus ratifying the destiny of each; and then, when they were fastened to this, carried them to Atropos, who spun the threads and made them irreversible, whence without turning round they passed beneath the throne of Necessity; and when they had all passed, they marched on in a scorching heat to the plain of Forgetfulness, which was a barren waste destitute of trees and verdure; and then towards evening they encamped by the river of Unmindfulness, whose water no vessel can hold; of this they were all obliged to drink a certain quantity, and those who were not saved by wisdom drank more than was necessary; and each one as he drank forgot all things. Now after they had gone to rest, about the middle of the night there was a thunderstorm and earthquake, and then in an instant they were driven upwards in all manner of ways to their birth, like stars shooting. He himself was hindered from drinking the water. But in what manner or by what means he returned to the body he could not say; only, in the morning, awaking suddenly, he found himself lying on the pyre.

And thus, Glaucon, the tale has been saved and has not perished, and will save us if we are obedient to the word spoken; and we shall pass safely over the river of Forgetfulness and our soul will not be defiled. Wherefore my counsel is that we hold fast ever to the heavenly way and follow after justice and virtue always, considering that the soul is immortal and able to endure every sort of good and every sort of evil. Thus shall we live dear to one another and to the gods, both while remaining here and when, like conquerors in the games who go round to gather gifts, we receive our reward. And it shall be well with us both in this life and in the pilgrimage of a thousand years which we have been describing.

TR. BENJAMIN JOWETT

FOCUSING QUESTIONS

1. What "reason" became the foundation of the Middle Ages' education?

2. What was the influence of the Arabic thinkers on Western education?

3. What was the Roman influence on the education of the Middle Ages?

4. Was Greek education in any way present in the education of the Middle Ages?

5. Compare Odysseus and Aeneas in relation to the acts they performed.

6. What differences are most significant in the narratives of Odysseus and Aeneas?

7. From where did Cicero borrow *Scipio's Dream?*

8. What is the difference between dreaming and remembering?

9. How did Aristotle's logic become the foundation of the Western university in the Middle Ages?

10. What are categories, propositions, definitions, and syllogisms?

11. What are fallacies, probable arguments, and dialectics?

12. Note some differences between classical and modern logic, particularly about method and about universals.

13. What kind of habit of mind did Hegel develop for his metaphysics?

SUPPLEMENTARY READINGS

Barnes, Ronna R. *For Court, Manor, and Church: Education in Medieval Europe.* Minneapolis: Burges, 1971.

Cassidy, Frank P. *Molders of the Medieval Mind: The Influence of the Fathers of the Church on the Medieval Schoolmen,* Port Washington, N.Y.: Kennikat Press, 1966.

Donohue, John W. *St. Thomas Aquinas and Education.* New York: Random House, 1968.

Piltz, Anders. *The World of Medieval Learning.* New Jersey: Barnes & Noble, 1981.

Rassam, Amal, and Bates, Daniel G. *Peoples and Cultures of the Middle East.* New Jersey: Prentice Hall, 1983.

Rashdall, Hastings. *The Universities of Europe in the Middle Ages,* 3. vols. Oxford University Press, 1936.

Thorndyke, Lynn. *University Records and Life in the Middle Ages.* New York: Norton, 1975.

Wolff, Philippe. *The Awakening of Europe.* London: Penguin, 1968.

7

Modernity with Galileo, Descartes, Newton

Galileo Galilei, in June of 1633 at the age of seventy, was asked to kneel before the Inquisitorial Tribunal in Rome and recant the Copernican theory that the earth moved around the sun and not vice versa. Was he asked to recant a fact, a hypothesis, or was he debunking an old science and burying the cosmology of the people?

With Galileo we witness the birth of a new habit of thought in our culture. Facts, things, problems, revolutions, and beliefs are less effective than the birth of a new habit of thought. It is the new habit of mind, the new way of focusing and dealing with facts, hypotheses, evidence, proofs, and methods which brings in new worlds and makes the old ways obsolete. What is it that Galileo really did? Rather than trying to catalogue the facts around him like a passive spectator, as the previous habit of mind required, he "imagined" bodies moving in space without any impediment: "I conceive by the work of my mind a moving object sent on a horizontal plane with all impediments removed," is his introductory statement in the fourth book of his treatise on *Mechanics and Local Movement.* What if objects moved in space without friction? Obviously none of this is observable, since the reality to be created is first imaginary, but this imagination developed what we know today as Classical Physics. Regardless of the fact that Galileo might not have been aware of the consequences of such a new habit; regardless of the fact that the destruction of the old cosmology would have

135

damaging effects on the souls of those who became the bene-
ficiaries of the new science; regardless of the fact that even
Galileo might not be fully aware of what he himself was doing,
the fact remains that the new habit of mind revolutionized our
civilization. No general, dictator, or revolutionary can achieve
greater success than can the change of one habit of mind for
another. Habits of mind are difficult to fight. The users are
normally unaware that they are dealing with a habit of mind;
they think rather that they are dealing with facts. Besides,
regardless of the benefits Scholasticism might have had on the
culture, it is obvious that one only habit of mind bores the soul
silly and burdens it with tremendous amounts of debris.

Equal consideration may be given to the success of Marxism
and Hegelianism. In both cases the most successful practitioners of both trends are not dealing with facts, but rather
imposing a new habit of thought, the necessity of abstract
dialectics to reading and reorganizing the facts around them
and also the societies. It is impossible to be a Marxist or a
Hegelian out of sheer belief. One must be educated first into
the habit of mind that creates Marxism and Hegelianism in the
first place. Ideology has as great a need for a habit of mind as
does "virtue," in the Platonic sense.

The selections that follow are geared to make the student
aware of this new habit of mind operating in Newton and
Descartes. It is then expected that the student will be able to
read these authors directly.

Modern Logic

The RULES *of Descartes, the implied logic of Newton, and the subsequent moves
in modern logic may be summarized in a few logical terms, definitions, axioms,
and formulae as it is here presented.*

*The selection by Colin M. Turbayne exemplifies the confusion in modern
science between acts performed and theoretical orthodoxy by scientists and those
who want to universalize its methods beyond the controlled limits of the laboratory.
Turbayne's is an exemplary reflection of what needs to be focused on by readers
before they read the original texts.*

*Mr. Turbayne is Professor of Philosophy at the University of Rochester.

Some Logical Terms, Definitions, Axioms and Formulae

I. By classical logic is meant Boolean algebra of sentences.

A. A Boolean algebra is a set B of at least two distinct elements with two binary operations $\cup$ (cup) $\cap$ (cap) and one unary operation ' (prime), such that B is closed with respect to each of these three operations, and for all a, b, and c belonging to B, the following axioms are satisfied:

A1 $a \cup b = b \cup a$
A2 $a \cap b = b \cap a$
A3 $a \cup (b \cup c) = (a \cup b) \cup c$
A4 $a \cap (b \cap c) = (a \cap b) \cap c$
A5 There is an element $\emptyset$ belonging to B such that $a \cup \emptyset = a$
A6 There is an element I belonging to B such that $a \cap I = a$
A7 $a \cup a' = I$
A8 $a \cap a' = \emptyset$
A9 $a \cup (b \cap c) = (a \cup b) \cap (a \cup c)$
A10 $a \cap (b \cup c) = (a \cap b) \cup (a \cap c)$

A9 and A10 are the distributive laws.
Def.: $a \subseteq b$ if and only if $a \cup b = b$

B. A Boolean algebra of sentences is obtained by adding the following interpretation to the formal syntax A:

a, b, c stand for sentences
$\emptyset$ stands for the absurd sentence (always false)
I stands for the trivial sentence (always true)
$a \cup b$ stands for a and/or b (the logical sum)
$a \cap b$ stands for a and b (the logical product)
a' stands for not-a
$a \subseteq b$ stands for a implies b

The Sciences Now Have Masks On Them

Colin M. Turbayne

In this piece I try to do two things. *First,* in order to give content to the distinction between using metaphor and being used by it, I offer some illustrations of actual victims of metaphor from the history of science. My main examples are Descartes and Newton, two scientists who first invented or developed procedures for describing the process of nature and then confused ingredients of their procedures with the process they described. *Second,* in order to find a method that may help me to avoid the errors of these giants, I present their methods in some detail.

More than others in modern times, Descartes and Newton have influenced the attitudes of subsequent scientists, philosophers, and ordinary people, so that our vision of the world remains largely a complication of the Newtonian and the Cartesian. Moreover, they were both philosophers of science as well as scientists, having left us not only their own descriptions of nature but also higher level accounts of what they thought they were doing in making these descriptions. Finally, in spite of their mistaken beliefs about what they thought they were doing, their methods worked.

In different degrees Descartes and Newton were aware and unaware of what they were doing. To some degree they did not confuse the ingredients of their procedures with the process they described. But they also thought that many ingredients of procedure were duplicated in the process. They thus added qualities to the world, thinking that these ingredients were not just inventions or decisions in the realm of procedure but actual discoveries of fact. In this respect they were like cooks who first use a recipe with great skill and then add the pages of their recipe to the stew.

To change the picture, they were in part victims of Bacon's Idols of the Theatre, "because in my judgment all the received systems are but so many stage-plays representing worlds of their own creation . . . neither only of entire systems but also of many principles and axioms in science which by tradition, credulity, and negligence have come to be received."[1] I shall show how these scientists confused their "stage-plays" with the events they depicted in the way Bacon describes. Then, following the lead given by Descartes, I shall try to do away with the "stage-plays":

1. *Novum Organum* (London, 1626), 1.44.

"The sciences now have masks on them; if the masks were taken off they would appear supremely beautiful."[2] Finally, I shall show how the "stage-plays" may be reperformed, or the "masks" put back, but with this crucial difference, with awareness that they are only "stageplays" or only "masks."

The best way to understand the methods of these scientists is to see them as inherited from a most ancient tradition known for about two thousand years as the double procedure of analysis and synthesis. And the best way to understand this procedure is to start with the account given by its great progenitor, Plato. Indeed we shall see that the modifications made upon the original by those who came later are slight.

ANALYSIS AND SYNTHESIS

The scientific procedures now in vogue were invented by the Greeks. Since their time scientists have been trying to rediscover them, to improve upon them, and to apply them. In order, first, to discover truth or to solve concrete problems in practical matters and, second, to present their discoveries or solutions, the Greeks devised two distinct procedures. To discover truth they invented inductive argument considered as the means whereby general conclusions or principles could be derived from the facts. To present their discoveries they invented the axiomatic method in which from axioms and definitions they derived theorems by deduction.

These two procedures were subsequently called by a variety of Greek and Latin names, the most common being the Greek "analysis" and "synthesis" and the Latin "resolution" and "composition." Although the names "analysis" and "synthesis" were commonly used in these senses until the nineteenth century, there is now some risk of confusion in using them in their old senses. This is because Kant unhappily decided to use the names "analytic" and "synthetic" both in the old way and in a way diametrically opposed to the old. As a result, it is now fashionable to call deduction what they do not really know, their reasoning may be self-consistent, but how can it produce science [*episteme*]?"

The correct solution avoids this mistake. This is because the scientist starts from the bottom of the other side of the arch. In the upward journey he "treats his assumptions, not as first principles, but as *hypotheses* in the literal sense—things 'laid down' like a flight of steps up which he may mount all the way to something that is not hypothetical [in the metaphorical sense]." Not until this is done can the scientist proceed to set up or, rather, lay down, his system. Not until he has grasped certain truths (for Plato, it should be noted, there is one that is ultimate) can he

2. *Private Thoughts* (Composed 1619).

use them as first principles to start his demonstration. The scientist "turns back," and through a series of consistent steps, "descends at last to a conclusion" by deduction. Not until all this is done do the special skills of arithmetic, geometry, astronomy, harmonics, etc., become sciences. They take their proper places within the structure of the arch. Their "first principles," so-called, are used as steps to knowledge of the things at the top of the arch, the real *archai* or beginnings of demonstration. Thus is achieved a *hierarchy,* in at least two senses, of the sciences, for their "first principles," previously used as steps in the ascent, may become theorems in the descent. What once were hypothetical now, "when connected with a first principle, become intelligible."

The upward journey has two main stages. The first or preliminary stage consists in engaging in all the special skills and in becoming clever at them. Here Plato mixed in another metaphor. Engaging in these skills is only a "prelude to the main melody" called the dialectic. Invented by Socrates, it amounts to the proposal of hypotheses which are then tested, "done away with," and "converted" into truths by induction. Corresponding to this last step in the inductive procedure is the *mental state* present when we "grasp" truth. It is called intuition. Among the hypotheses proposed for testing are the "first principles" of the special skills previously used without question. It is the dialectic, therefore, that enables us to convert the practical arts or skills into sciences. Accordingly, the "dialectic will stand as the coping-stone of the whole structure."

Reducing Plato's account to terms of analysis and synthesis: In the incorrect solution the synthesis proceeds without previous analysis. This entails deduction without demonstration. In the correct solution, analysis must precede synthesis; that is, there should be no synthesis without previous analysis; and in Plato's own doctrine, all the stress is upon analysis. This enables two sorts of things to become intelligible: the first principles themselves, and the theorems deductively derived from them.

The methods of subsequent scientists are illuminated by treating them as variants upon Plato's original. From his point of view their users make two classes: those who really are scientists and those who are technicians. Before treating Descartes and Newton, it will helpful to consider briefly two earlier followers of Plato, namely, Aristotle and Euclid, the one a "scientist," the other a "technician."

Aristotle was a "scientist" because he adopted Plato's distinction between analysis and synthesis. But he used a different illustration—that of "analytic" and induction "synthetic." Whatever names are chosen, the two procedures have been used with different degrees of rigor by scientists since Plato's time. Thus Descartes's *Meditations,* Newton's *Opticks,* Berkeley's *Essay on Vision,* and Kant's *Prolegomena* were presented in the inductive or analytical manner, while Plato's *Republic,* Euclid's *Elements* and *Catoptrics,* Spinoza's *Ethics,* Descartes's *Principles* (in part), Newton's

Principia, Berkeley's *Vindication,* and Kant's three *Critiques* were presented in the deductive or synthetical style. Of these, Euclid's application of the deductive method to geometry and optics, and Newton's to mechanics are still regarded as models of the axiomatic method generally. The others, lacking in rigor by recent standards, offer a challenge to the student interested in setting up their contents more systematically.

Right at the start, however, Plato posed a problem whose two main solutions guided and divided all subsequent scientists. This is the problem of the nature and derivation of the axioms or basic premises. Are they true descriptions of the world, or are they merely hypotheses or calculating devices? If the axioms are true, then the theorems are true. But what guarantees the truth of the axioms? The axioms are not demonstrable in the way that what follows from them is demonstrable. Is it therefore a case *first,* of establishing the truth of the axioms in some other way, and then, *afterwards,* of setting up the true system as economically as possible? Or is it a case of *freely inventing* those axioms that will most economically account for the facts?

In presenting the two solutions, Plato gave his version of the nature of scientific method.[3] He enriched his account with a host of metaphors drawn from space-relations, travel, cave-dwelling, hand-grasping, music, and architecture. He conceived the whole structure of the correct solution as a stepped arch one side of which the scientist must mount before he descends the other side.

In the incorrect solution the technician—according to Plato he is not really a scientist—merely descends part of one side of the arch, leaving the whole structure hanging in the air. That is to say, he begins and completes a deductive argument without having first established the truth of his premises. This is the way of geometers who invent hypotheses about figures and angles and other such data, and with these proceed forthwith to set up a deductive system. "Having adopted their hypotheses, they decline to give any account of them, either to themselves or to others, on the assumption that they are self-evident. Then, starting from these assumptions, they descend deductively by a series of consistent steps, until they arrive at all the conclusions they set out to investigate." This procedure is certainly useful in technical matters: it works. Because it works in all phases of earth-measuring, this procedure is perfectly accommodated to the purpose of the geometers. But their purpose is wrong. "Geometers constantly talk as if their object were *to do,* whereas the true purpose of the whole subject is *to know.*" If this is so, then the procedure fails. How can we know that the conclusions are true unless we know that the premises are true? They are not known to be true because "the geometers leave the hypotheses they use unexamined."

3. *Republic,* 509–11, 533–34.

In which case, "if their premises are things they do not really know, and their conclusions and the intermediate steps are deduced from things like a race-course: "There is a difference between arguments *from* and those *to* the first principles. For Plato, too, was right in raising this question and asking, as he used to do, 'Are we on the way from or to the first principles?' There is a difference as there is in a race-course between the course from the judges to the turning point and the way back."[4] Moreover, he laid all the stress upon analysis—the arguments *to* the first principles—and he accepted the doctrine that there should be no synthesis without previous analysis. That is, he held that the premises of science must be principles: they must be known to be true before demonstration. This is true even of hypotheses, for it was left to a later age to make hypotheses hypothetical. He followed his teacher, though with added detail in his account of the derivation of premises by the method of induction—now known as scientific discovery—and he too isolated that mental state corresponding to the last stage of the inductive procedure by which we apprehend truth, intuition. Nevertheless, he clarified Plato's distinction between knowledge of a principle and knowledge of what is "connected with a principle." Only the latter properly belongs to science. That is to say, all science is synthesis or demonstration. It is knowledge not of the premises but of what comes after the premises. But it rests upon the previously acquired "more accurate" unscientific knowledge just mentioned. All this was more tersely put by Aristotle himself in four assertions:[5] "We come to grasp the first principles only through [the *method* of] induction"; "it is [the *mental state* of] intuition that apprehends the first principles"; "Scientific knowing and intuition are always true"; and "All scientific knowledge is discursive."

Euclid, on the other hand, was a "technician" because his *Elements* satisfy the proscribed doctrine of synthesis without previous analysis. His common notions and postulates are all hypotheses because he "declined to give any account of them either to himself or to others on the ground that they were self-evident" and proceeded forthwith to set up his deductive system, thus leaving the structure of his argument hanging in the air. But these remarks fit Euclid's works as they now stand. Perhaps he left another book, now lost, in which he showed how he had derived his postulates from higher principles like those attempts made later by Ptolemy, Proclus, Nasiraddin at-Tusi, and Legendre to prove Euclid's own fifth postulate. Or, more likely, he left a book, also lost, written in the same analytical style as Newton's *Opticks,* in which he showed how he had derived his postulates by induction. Or, most likely, he thought that all his premises were true for good reasons but, preferring to write only

4. *Nicomachean Ethics,* 1095a.
5. *Posterior Analytics,* 81b, 100b.

in the synthetical style, never showed how he had derived them. Considerations like these prompted a later geometer to conclude:

> It was this synthesis alone that the ancient geometers used in their writings, not because they were wholly ignorant of the analytic method but, in my opinion, because they set so high a value on it that they wished to keep it to themselves as an important secret.[6]

The geometer was Descartes. The "important secret" he tried to reveal.

DESCARTES

Both Descartes and Newton were Platonists in their adoption of the doctrine that analysis precedes synthesis. Descartes wrote:

> It is certain that, in order to discover truth, we should always begin with particular notions in order to reach general notions afterwards, though reciprocally, after having discovered the general notions, we may deduce from them others which are particular.[7]

Newton was just as explicit:

> As in mathematics, so in natural philosophy, the investigation of difficult things by the method of analysis ought ever to precede the method of composition.[8]

In the matter of the ingredients of the two procedures, however, they differed from Plato and between themselves. But even here there is enough resemblance to enable us to see the two later accounts as different interpretations of the one original.

Descartes was primarily a physicist. Although his *Discourse on Method, Geometry,* and *Meditations on First Philosophy* have had tremendous influence in their respective fields, his main interest lay neither in method, nor in abstract geometry, nor in metaphysics but in the application of these subjects to physics. He "designed to devote all his life" to the discovery of "a practical philosophy" which, replacing the speculative philosophy of the Schools, would make ourselves masters and owners of nature.[9] Accordingly, the pattern of his life was made up of the early discovery of the method, a general science, restricted to no special subject, and called *"Mathesis Universalis";* then its application to geometry,

6. *Second Replies.*
7. *Letter to Clerselier.*
8. *Opticks* (1704), Query 31.
9. *Discourse,* Part Six.

optics, and astronomy; and finally the discovery of the foundations of his physics. Throughout all this, however, he was doing nothing but geometry. His method, devised to solve "problems about order and measurement," was geometrical. The special subjects to which he applied it were geometrical. And when he gave up abstract geometry he said: "I am doing this purposely in order to have more time to study another kind of geometry," for "my physics are nothing else but geometry."[10]

If metaphysics was secondary, what was its specific role in his entire scheme? It was to provide the foundations of physics. Descartes's quest was for certainty. He could get certainty in physics only by getting true premises. And these could be true only if they were grounded in metaphysics. The search for the foundations ended in 1641, only nine years before his death.

Having finished his *Meditations,* he privately admitted: "I shall tell you between ourselves that these six meditations contain the entire foundation of my physics."[11] Why were these so relevant? The search had been long. Evidently his first venture into physics, *The World,* begun in 1629 and never published, had been composed without satisfactory foundations. As late as 1638 he had said that it is impossible to provide a demonstration of matters that depend on physics "without having proved the principles of physics previously by metaphysics," and he implied that neither he nor anyone before him had done so.[12] In 1640, however, the "breakthrough" was imminent, for he said, "having reduced physics to the laws of mathematics, the demonstration is now possible."[13] But still this was not enough because the premises might not be true. Their referents, material objects, might not exist. "I already know," he wrote at the start of the sixth meditation, "the *possibility* of their existence in so far as they are the subject-matter of pure mathematics since I clearly and distinctly perceive them." But for the same reason that an atheist can infer he is awake but can never be certain,[14] so he cannot be certain of the existence of material objects and thus of the premises of physics. This certainty must come from God the nondeceiver, and His certainty must come from metaphysical proof. This the *Meditations* provided. Accordingly, the things clearly and distinctly perceived exist. Therefore the objects of solid geometry exist, that is things extended in length, breadth, and depth. And these are nothing but the referents of the premises of physics. Thus Descartes reached the end of his search, the beginning of demonstration. This was the ultimate justification of his method.

10. Letter to Mersenne (1638).
11. Letter to Mersenne (1641).
12. Letter to Mersenne (1638).
13. Letter to Mersenne (1640).
14. *Third Replies.* The objector was Hobbes.

In one passage in Part Six of his *Discourse* Descartes revealed the working sequence of his method. This I divide into two parts:

> My general order of procedure has been this. First I have tried to discover in general the principles or first causes of all that exists or could exist in the world. To this end I consider only God, who created them, and I derive them merely from certain root-truths that occur naturally to our minds.
>
> Then I consider the first and most ordinary effects deductible from these causes, and it seems to me that in this way I discovered the heavens, the stars, and earth, and even on the earth, water, air, fire, the minerals, and some other such things. . . . And then I tried to descend to more special cases. But in view of their wide variety I thought it impossible to distinguish those actually found on earth from those that could be found there. . . . It thus appeared impossible to proceed further deductively, and if we were to understand and make use of these things, we should have to discover causes by their effects, and make use of many experiments. . . . My greatest difficulty usually is to find out which is the true explanation, and to do this I know no other way than to seek several experiments such that their outcomes would be different according to the choice of hypothesis.

This is Descartes's vision of the two Greek procedures of analysis and synthesis illustrated by Plato as the ascent and the descent of a stepped arch, and even similarly illustrated by Descrates as "ascending in steps" and "descending," respectively. Now the first strange fact about his account of method is his complete neglect in all the rules specified in the *Regulae* and the *Discourse* of the method of synthesis (characterized in the second part of the passage). What explains it? His interest—like Plato's and unlike Euclid's—lay less in system building than in scientific discovery. And this was because, while the former was so well known and easy and ought to be transferred to rhetoric, the latter was unknown and difficult, Euclid and others having "grudged the secret to posterity." The one "does not teach the fashion in which the matter in question was discovered"; the other does.[15]

Yet the details of his analysis are much the same as Plato's. In the quoted passage (first part) he said that from certain "root-truths" we derive "the principles." But this describes only the second of the two movements, both of which he gave in Rule V of the *Regulae:* "We reduce complex and obscure propositions step by step to simpler ones, *and then,* by retracing our steps, try to rise to intuition of all the simplest ones to knowledge of all the rest"; and which he repeated in the four specified rules of the *Discourse:* We "divide into parts," accepting as true only what is "clearly and distinctly" presented to the mind, *and then* "ascend little by

15. *Regulae,* IV and X; *Second Replies.*

little, in steps as it were, to the knowledge of the most complex." Thus within the analysis itself there are two movements: the "descent," involving the famous method of doubt which, after a series of deductive steps, culminates in intuitions of certainties, such as our own existence and the nature of a triangle; and the "ascent" from these, by a series of intuitions, to such truths as the laws of motion which may become principles. The two dominant "intellectual activities" here, both of which originate from "the light of reason," are intuition or indubitable conceiving, and deduction, which is the same thing applied to more than one step of an argument. The whole analysis then, begins with "complex and obscure" propositions and ends with only "complex" ones, the obscurity having been dispelled. This is much the same as Plato's dialectic which begins with hypotheses and ends with their conversion into known truths by intuition, their hypothetical content having been eliminated. But by trying to transfer the certainty of geometrical demonstration to the procedure of scientific discovery, that is, the certainty of synthesis to analysis, Descartes thought he had found the secret of the ancient geometers.

His account of the synthesis, however, contains a startling disclosure. Having laid down his rules of method, Descartes proceeded to deviate from them. We expect a demonstration of the truth *after* principles have already been found, such as had been prescribed by Plato. But we get a different way of accounting for the facts: "the way of hypothesis" proscribed by Plato. Unable to proceed further deductively, he resorted to the invention of and choice among different hypotheses, the choice being determined by crucial experiments. Thus he gave up the certainty of the *a priori* method in favor of the conjectural *a posteriori*. This meant that in his practice the synthesis preceded analysis, for it preceded that form of it known as inductive testing. The second half of the quoted passage describes this deviation. His actual work in physics and optics reflects it.

In the third part of the *Principles* he said: "I will put forward everything that I am going to write just as a hypothesis. Even if this be thought to be false, I shall think my achievement worth while if all inferences from it agree with experience"; and "I shall also here assume some propositions which are agreed to be false"; to which he added that "the falsity of these propositions does not prevent what may be deduced from them from being true." The hypothesis in question, contrary to the church doctrine of full creation, was that the matter of the universe originally consisted of small particles of the same shape each moving round its own center; or, in other words, as he said in the fourth part: "I have described the Earth and the whole visible universe *as if it were* a machine, having regard only to the shape and movement of its parts."

Nevertheless, it seems that all Descartes's make-believe was only make-believe. Although his big hypothesis may have been freely invented, there is little doubt that he thought it was true. For he preceded his introduction of hypothesis in the *Principles* with the remark: "It can hardly be otherwise than that the principles from which all phenomena are clearly deduced are true." In the sixth part of the *Discourse*, with regard to the hypotheses he had used in optics and astronomy, he said that "the truth of the hypotheses is proved by the actuality of the effects," and "I think I can deduce them from the first truths." Moreover, it should be noted that the content of his big hypothesis is the physical world shorn merely of the secondary qualities of color, smell, taste, and so on. It is extended matter, the defining feature of the physical world, the long sought after and scrupulously argued for conclusion of all the *Meditations*. And this is nothing but the object of solid geometry which, with the addition of another primitive, motion, makes it the object of physics. It would be queer to suppose that Descrates thought his hypothesis false. Finally it should be noted that this "hypothesis" of extension plus motion was used in conjunction with some things not hypothetical, namely, the three "laws of nature" previously deduced. Given extension and motion these laws of motion enabled Descartes to construct the world.

Why then did Descartes use the word "hypothesis"? Its use, fairly obviously, was dictated by prudence. Now in 1633 he had suppressed his *The World* after hearing of Galileo's censure by the church. This book showed how a world would inevitably form from the laws of motion operating upon an original chaos. But it must not be thought that he suppressed it because the chaos was not expressed hypothetically. It was. The "hypothetical" chaos fully satisfied the injunction of Cardinal Bellarmine, the inquisitor of Bruno: "Galileo will act prudently if he will speak hypothetically [*ex suppositione*]." He suppressed it partly because in it he had maintained the motion round the sun not only of the "hypothetical" earth but, like Galileo, of the real earth; and partly because "there might be," he said, "other opinions of mine in which I was misled." It seems likely that, long before all this, he had decided to adopt "the way of hypothesis" in expounding his physics. He had decided to "*speak* hypothetically" though not to think in that way.

NEWTON

We are greatly helped in our understanding of Newton's method by seeing it not only as a variation within the classical tradition but as a reaction against the method of Descartes. In the preface of the *Principia*, Newton showed the direction he was taking: "The whole burden of philosophy seems to consist in this—from the phenomena of motions to investigate the forces of nature, and then from these forces to demon-

strate the other phenomena." Thus, like Descartes, he accepted the
Platonic distinction between analysis and synthesis as well as the Platonic
sequence in which the analysis comes first. Nevertheless, he corrected
Descartes in two main ways. First, like Plato, he rejected "the way of
hypothesis." Second, although like Plato and Descartes, he stressed the
way of analysis, he restored one of its defining features: the conclusions
of analysis are discovered not by intuition independently of experience
but by experiment and observation. He thus rejected Descartes's "The
Light of Reason" in favor of his own "The Light of Nature."

But Newton's extraordinary rejection of hypotheses from physics and
his denial that he used them create an initial problem in understanding
him. In the second edition (1713) of the *Principia* he claimed: **"Hypotheses non fingo"**—literally, "I do not invent (or frame or feign) hypotheses"—and in the *Opticks* he wrote: "Hypotheses are not to be regarded
in experimental philosophy." These are strange claims, for Newton did
frame hypotheses time out of mind. The *Opticks* indeed is riddled with
hypotheses about the nature of light, the existence of aether, the nature
of the first cause, and so on. From this apparent discrepancy it would be
easy to conclude that Newton said one thing and did another. But it is
unlikely that this is the correct answer. How are we to reconcile what he
said he did with what he did? We are hindered rather than helped by his
careless negative definition of "hypothesis": "What is not deducible from
phenomena," which includes almost everything. We need, then, to turn
to the context in which he rejected hypotheses, specifically to the rule of
method that he set down at the end of his *Opticks* long after he had
applied them.

> The method of analysis ought ever to precede the method of composi-
> tion. This analysis consists in making experiments and observations, and
> in drawing general conclusions from them by induction, and of admit-
> ting no objections against the conclusions but such as are taken from
> experiments or other certain truths. For hypotheses are not to be re-
> garded in experimental philosophy. . . . By this way of analysis we may
> proceed . . . from effects to their causes. . . . And the synthesis consists in
> assuming the causes discovered and established as principles, and by
> them explaining the phenomena proceeding from them and proving the
> explanations.

It is clear from this remarkable passage, essential to the understanding of Newton, what he was advocating. He was advocating no synthesis
without previous analysis from experience, that is, no use of the axiomatic method without having first derived the axioms from experience
by induction. It is equally clear what he was rejecting. He was rejecting
"the way of hypothesis," which is nothing but the method of Descartes:
synthesis without previous analysis was what Descartes *said* he practiced,

while analysis without experience was what he preached. The former is actually "the way of hypothesis" or the way of *inventing* the premises to start a demonstration, but the latter also involves the same way, at least from Newton's point of view, because the premises are not derived from experience.

Accordingly, when Newton said, "Hypotheses are not to be regarded," he meant simply that induction from experience ought to precede deduction. When he uttered his *"Hypotheses non fingo"* he was saying in a very abbreviated, and hence cryptic, way: In induction, I do not invent hypotheses, and in deduction I do not demonstrate from them. More fully, he meant that the inductive side of scientific method has a beginning, a middle, and an end, and all must be complete before any deductive system is set up. The beginning consists in "hinting several things" or making "conjectures" about the causes of phenomena. Such hinting is consistent with "I do not invent hypotheses" because they are "plausible consequences" drawn from the facts. That is, they are not derived, like Descartes's conclusions, merely by the Light of Reason or intuition. Although hypothetical in character, Newton did not call them "hypotheses." The middle consists of examining these "hints" and improving them by observations and the tests of experiment. The end is defined by his remark: "And if no exception occur from phenomena, the conclusion may be pronounced generally" and considered "proved" as a "general law of nature." *"Afterwards,"* the deduction proceeds by assuming the conclusions established as principles, and from them demonstrating the phenomena. This procedure is consistent with "I do not demonstrate from hypotheses" because the first principles, although they are *assumed* true, are grounded in experience. The peculiar character of this method, the stress upon experience and the rejection of hypotheses of the Cartesian kind, may be briefly described as follows in Berkeley's words: "It is one thing to arrive at general laws of nature from a contemplation of the phenomena, and another to frame an hypothesis, and from thence deduce the phenomena (*S*, 229)." Had Newton said this, his code words *"Hypotheses non fingo"* would need little deciphering. The characteristic example of the sort of hypothesis proscribed in this view is the epicycle.

Let us see whether the explanation of Newton's meaning just given saves the appearances, where the appearances are Newton's actual applications of method. The *Opticks* is the best illustration of Newton's method, for it not only contains every feature but the stress is where he wanted it, on induction. Structurally this is a very strange work. It begins with "definitions" and "axioms." The axioms, Newton said, "I content myself to assume under the notion of principles in order to what I have farther to write." Then follow "propositions," "theorems," and their "proofs." All this suggests that the *Opticks* is a work of synthesis, a deductive system after the manner of Euclid's *Optics*. But it is not. None of the theorems follows from the axioms. Each proof, except for three at the end of Book I, is a "proof by experiments" although the axioms are assumed in these proofs. Accordingly, the *Opticks* is almost entirely an illustration of the inductive procedure. Books I and II show how Newton derived laws of nature by experiment and observation. Here the book is like a cookbook written by an expert chef long after all the recipes have been tried. In a typical "proof" there is an autobiographical account of experiments actually performed, thus giving a recipe that anyone can use if he has the ingredients. From the experiments, the laws of nature are "manifest." In many cases Newton contented himself merely with recording "observations." In Book III, on the other hand, Newton had "only begun the analysis." It contains what we should call "hypotheses" framed as twenty-nine "queries" and two "questions." While, in the first two books, certain "manifest qualities" of light, such as that white light is a compound of all the primary colors had been "proved," here queries are proposed for further research by others.

The queries are a revelation of an extraordinary mind, disciplined yet free, marvelously keen on detail, yet bold in imagination. These negative queries are really positive conclusions of arguments that are all empirical, all going from effect to cause, and all inductive. The conclusions, however, are nothing but hypotheses which, more optical and less speculative in the first edition, become increasingly less optical and more hypothetical in later editions. This third book of the *Opticks* is not only a commentary on optics; it is a commentary on physics, a work in empirical metaphysics, and a work in empirical theology—all of which, Newton held, are legitimately included in physics. Its premises, mainly implicit in this part, are drawn from optical and other physical phenomena, and the ultimate conclusion is God. In 1704, Newton argued for such things as the mutual interaction of bodies and light, and for the existence of vibrations in the retina, the effect of light, and the cause of sight. In 1706, he argued for the existence of aether, a new medium "swifter than light," and "exceedingly more rare and subtile than the air," and once again for the existence of vibrations in the retina, this time chiefly the effect of aether. In 1717, he speculated that light is made of small unbreakable bodies, and he made conjectures about the existence and nature of God: "Was the eye contrived without skill in optics. . . ," and "Does it not appear from phenomena that there is a being incorporeal, living, intelligent, omnipresent . . ." who alone is directly acquainted with physical objects, while mortals perceive only their images? All these conjectures were "plausible consequences" of the empirical procedure, but since they were not yet "proved," they were not ready for use as premises in demonstration.

Because induction must precede deduction, the *Opticks* was a preparation for a demonstration that Newton never offered. That he intended to set up a deductive system of optics is suggested by the fact that the whole of the *Opticks* is styled "Part I." From this account we see that the *Opticks* is perfectly consistent with *"Hypotheses non fingo":* all the "hypotheses," Newton would have argued, are conclusions from induction, and none are yet to be used as premises in a deduction.

In the *Principia,* however, Newton's good resolutions broke down, for there is one disconfirming instance of the explanation I have offered. In the first edition at the beginning of Book III Newton had presented nine "hypotheses." In the second edition (1713), in line with his rejection of hypotheses, he transformed all of them into "rules," not used in demonstration, with one exception which he retained as "Hypothesis I: That the centre of the system of the world is immovable." From this he proceeded to demonstrate. This, surely, is a case of *hypotheses fingere.* But, after stating it, Newton said immediately: "This is acknowledged by all." This remark echoes what he had said about the axioms of his *Opticks* in 1704: "What *has been generally agreed on* I content myself to assume under the notion of principles." He was doing the same thing here. But whereas the optical axioms might be shown to appear from phenomena, it would be difficult to do the same with this hypothesis. Nevertheless, Newton evidently had to use it, and, accordingly, broke his resolution *"Hypotheses non fingo."*

The rest of the *Principia* does jibe with what he said about method. Force, gravity, and attraction are used here as principles in demonstration. It is clear from question 31 of the *Opticks* that Newton thought that none of them are "occult qualities" or hypotheses. They are all consequences from analysis, "active principles," "manifest qualities," "general laws of nature," or "causes" of motion. While the causes of motion had been discovered, *their* cause had not. Nevertheless, consistent with his rejection of hypotheses, Newton was able to speculate about their cause, that is, to make the hypothesis in the General Scholium to Book III of the *Principia* that it was "a certain most subtle spirit," namely, "aether." In the same place he also speculated about the nature of God, "to discourse of whom" is a proper part of physics. Again it should be noted, however, that he used neither aether nor God as a principle of demonstration.

The main features of Newton's method, it seems, are: the rejection of hypotheses, the stress upon induction, the working sequence (induction precedes deduction), and the inclusion of metaphysical arguments in physics. For final confirmation that Newton so regarded his own method I refer to query 28 of the *Opticks* where he appealed to the authority of the best tradition of the Greeks against the fashion of "late philosophers" who "feigning hypotheses for explaining all things mechanically and referring other causes to metaphysics," banish nonmechanical causes from physics. Then he summed up his own view: "The main business of natural philosophy is to argue from phenomena without feigning hypotheses, and to deduce causes from effects till we come to the very first cause which certainly is not mechanical."

THE SCIENCES NOW HAVE MASKS ON THEM

Having extracted the features of their methods that I need, I now begin to show how Descartes and Newton were victimized by their metaphors, victimized because they presented the facts of one sort as if they belonged to another, but without awareness. They were engaged in sort-crossing. But because they did not know that they were, they confused their own peculiar sorting of the facts with the facts. It was as though, having found that wolf-properties were eminently suitable for illustrating man, they came to believe that he was indeed a wolf. Of their many sort-crossings I shall isolate three.

The first is that of the deductive relation with the relation between events. The former relation belongs to procedure. It is, therefore, the sort of thing that is invented; it was, in fact, invented by the Greeks as the best way of teaching. The latter relation belongs to the process going on in nature. It is, therefore, the sort of thing that is discovered. Now Descartes and Newton adopted the deductive procedure was a most powerful instrument. It was a defining feature of their *"more geometrico"* and "mathematical way," respectively. Descartes's "long chains of reasoning" were deductively linked. Newton's demonstrations were reduced to "the form of propositions in the mathematical way." These ways involved, as we have seen, the deduction of conclusions (theorems) from premises (principles). According to Descartes, "we deduce an account of the effects from the causes." According to Newton "the synthesis consists in assuming the cause discovered and established as principles, and by them explaining the phenomena." It is clear that both men thought that principle and theorem were necessarily connected—necessarily, because this had been a matter of decision by their teachers, the Greeks. All this, it was decided, occurs in the procedure.

What did they think they found, however, going on in the process? The answer is astonishing. The physicist's procedure is duplicated in the physical process. The principle of procedure that starts a demonstration is repeated in the "active principle" that starts a causal process. Moreover, the relation between a principle of procedure and its deduced consequences is exactly the same as that between an "active principle," such as gravity, and its effects. This relation is that of necessary connection. Both men thought that physical causes produce the existence of their effects, and that the effects necessarily follow from the causes, for

Newton described the effects as "proceeding from them," and Descartes supposed that all the phenomena now in the world would be produced by necessary consequence from the laws of motion acting upon either the chaos of the poets or the originally ordered extended particles.

Just to set down this still familiar view is enough to show its strangeness and enough to suggest the aetiology of the confusion involved. The law of nature that explains it is the Principle of Association according to which things noticed constantly to go together first suggest each other, then get the same names, and finally come to be thought the same thing or of the same sort. Since the time of Euclid, physical process and the deductive procedure used to explain it have been constantly associated in the minds of scientists. Thus a procedure-process shift has occurred, at first one suggesting the other, then both sharing the same names: "principle," "necessary connection," "necessary consequence," "proceeding from," and "system"; but then, inexorably, becoming things of the same sort. In this fashion a defining feature of deductive argument was exported to the external world—a prominent page of the recipe was mixed in with the stew. Nature, it was concluded, obeys the logic of the deductive method.

The second sort-crossing I exhibit is the inadvertent identification of explanation with physical explanation and this with causal explanation, that is, the reduction of one to the other. The main elements of this confusion appear from the account just given. Here are additional details. According to Newton the main task of physics was to find the forces of nature, "and then from these forces to demonstrate the other phenomena," the other phenomena being bodily motions. Descartes's view, although earlier in time, was an advance on this, for he saw the task as that of finding the laws of these motions and using the laws to demonstrate the motions. But both men thought the explanation had to be causal, the one holding that physical forces, the other that physical laws, cause events. Moreoever, Newton's three "laws of motion" and Descartes's three "natural laws" reveal that the ultimate constituents of their world were of two sorts: the effects, such as "bodies moving" and "bodies at rest"; and the causes, such as "power of going," "external causes," and "resistance," in the case of Descartes, and "impressed forces," in the case of Newton, specifically described elsewhere as "gravity" and "attraction." These entities were described either as "clear and distinct ideas" or as "manifest qualities" to distinguish them from "obscure notions" or "occult qualities." It should be noted once more that the word "principle" was used to refer ambiguously: to the premise or statement of the law in the procedure, and, under the name "active principle," to the supposed cause in the process.

The Treatise of Man

. . . The nerves of the machine that I am describing to you may very well be compared to the pipes of the machinery of these fountains, its muscles and its tendons to various other engines and devices which serve to move them, its animal spirits to the water which sets them in motion, of which the heart is the spring, and the cavities of the brain the outlets. Morover, respiration and other such functions as are natural and usual to it, and which depend on the course of the spirits, are like the movements of a clock or a mill, which the regular flow of the water can keep up. External objects which, by their presence alone, set upon the organs of its senses, and which by means determined to move in many different ways, according as the particles of its brain are arranged, are like visitors, who, entering some of the grottoes of these fountains, bring about of them- selves, without intending it, the movements which occur in their pres- ence; for they cannot enter without stepping on certain tiles of the pavement so arranged that, for example, if they approach a Diana taking a bath, they make her hide in the reeds; and, if they pass on in pursuit of her, they cause a Neptune to appear before them who menaces them with his trident; or if they turn in some other direction they will make a marine monster come out, who will squirt water into their faces, or something similar will happen, according to the fancy of the engineers who construct them. And finally, when the *reasonable soul* shall be in this machine, it will have its principal seat in the brain, and it will be there like the fountain-maker, who must be at the openings where all the pipes of these machines discharge themselves, if he wishes to start, to stop, to change in any way their movements.

I desire you to consider next that all the functions which I have attributed to this machine, such as the digestion of food, the beating of the heart and arteries, the nourishment and growth of the members, respiration, waking, and sleeping; the impressions of light, sounds, odors, tastes, heat and other such qualities on the organs of the external senses; the impression of their ideas on the common sense and the imagination; the retention of imprinting of these ideas upon the mem- ory; the interior motions of the appetites and passions; and, finally, the external movements of all the members, which follow so suitably as well as the actions of objects which present themselves to sense, as the passions and impressions which are found in the memory, that they imitate in the most perfect manner possible those of a real man; I desire, I say, that you consider that all these functions follow naturally in this machine simply from the arrangement of its parts, no more or less than do the move- ments of a clock, or other *automata,* from that of its weights and its wheels; so that it is not at all necessary for their explanation to conceive it in any other soul, vegetative or sensitive, nor any other principle of motion and life, than its blood and its spirits, set in a motion by the heat of the fire which burns continually in its heart, and which is of a nature no different from all fires in inanimate bodies.

—Descartes

Now although no one since the time of Descartes and Newton has been able to find these forces or active principles in the physical world, many have thought they were investigating them. What is the aetiology of this prejudice? It is easy to accept that corollary of Newton's first law of motion, itself a corollary of Descartes's first law, that every body alters its state only if compelled by impressed forces. But this law has its psychological foundation in another very simple law known by us much more intimately: We are aware that we can make and do things, push and pull them, act with and react to them; we are aware of ourselves as agents, causes, forces, or minds; and this awareness comes to us in infancy and remains as secure as ever. Here, it seems, lies the origin of all our notions of cause. It is often associated with movement, the movement of our limbs and muscles, though it need not be, for we can decide to think of giraffes or kangaroos without the flicker of an eyelid. At an early age we make three inferences: (1) there are other agents or forces besides ourselves; (2) every body alters its state only if forced; (3) bodies are or contain forces. Many of us retain such beliefs throughout our lives. We ought, however, to be suspicious of, at least, the third, because it seems impossible to find the force or power referred to. The only actual experience I have of power, force, or activity is in myself. Outside myself I notice events following each other in time, and I find it very hard to resist the tendency to ascribe power or activity to many of the earlier events. When primitive societies ascribe power to clouds, mountains, and rocks, we are amused. When Descartes and Newton and their followers ascribe force to bodies, it seems to make sense. But surely both are cases of what might be called hylopsychism, because in both something that we find only in oursleves, something that belongs to persons or living things, is ascribed to matter.

It would be a mistake, however, to conclude from this that efficient causes are to be excluded from science. For this would be to equate science with physical science, which only someone steeped in the parochialism of a particular age would want to do. From the analysis of what it is to be a cause, I conclude that there are efficient causes. This allows us to have a science of persons, for we have knowledge of them, and, if so, we can systematize it. Such efficient causes, then, are to be admitted as objects into the principles of science but are to be excluded from the princples of physics.

The third case of sort-crossing I want to exhibit is the unwarranted identification of deduction with computation or calculation or any other form of metrical reckoning or counting. This confusion accompanies a narrow view of the nature of science and scientific demonstration. For some have so narrowly conceived the Cartesian "geometrical method" or the Newtonian "mathematical way," that they (including the authors) have not realized that this method or way—paradoxical as it may seem—need be neither geometrical nor mathematical. Its defining property is demonstration, not the nature of the terms used in it. Whether these terms are used to denote measurable qualities, lines, or angles, or the god's portion of the anatomy of wallaroos is accidental to demonstration itself, and thus accidental to science. What is the aetiology of this prejudice? Measurable qualities, treated mathematically, are used with great advantage in the sciences, but, once more, we must beware of the wide subliminal applications of that law of nature by which frequent associations—especially successful ones—are confused with identity. Because mathematical computation is constantly used in science, we must not regard it as a defining property. Because lines and angles are used to enormous advantage in optical demonstration, and have been so used constantly since Euclid's time, we must not therefore succumb to the tendency to think that explanation by means of lines and angles exhausts optical explanation. We might just as well say that mechanical explanation exhausts science or that we cannot set up a deductive system without using differential equations.

These confusions, because they involve sort-crossing without awareness, seem to be nothing but disguises or masks placed by men on the faces of nature and procedure. It seems, then, that all we have to do is to lift them or take them off in order to see what really occurs and what the scientist actually does. Accordingly, necessary connection illegitimately held to obtain between the events occurring in the process or nature, is restored to its proper place as an ingredient only of procedure. Moreover, when it is said that motion and change in the world are caused by attraction or other active principles, it seems likely that all that is meant is that bodies move in a certain order. Accordingly, the "active principles," star performers in process, are restored to their proper role as principles only in procedure. The principles of physics or any science are premises from which other statements are deduced that describe the way events unfold. The phrase "deduce effects from causes" is simply translated in terms of premises and conclusions, and causal explanations are replaced by explanations in terms of laws or rules; rules because, having lifted the disguise from the face of nature, all we find are bodies moving in a certain order, that is, regularly, that is, according to rule. Thus the causal statement "x attracts y" is replaced by "x and y move according to rule"; and similarly for a thousand similar statements. Finally, the deductive procedure is defined as a special relation between symbols whose interpretation, either numerical or not, is merely accidental.

What I have been doing resembles what Socrates did in the *Phaedo* in his rejoinder to the argument of Cebes. When young he was enthralled by that wisdom called Physical Science, and was "completely blinded" by these studies. He fell for the "mechanism" of the times and identified explanation with mechanical explanation, cause with physical cause. With great difficulty he extricated himself from the use of this appealing procedure and invented a new one. He replaced explanation in terms of causes and effects by explanation in terms of reasons and their deduced consequences. For example, he replaced the mechanical explanation of his "sitting here now," in which nothing was considered but the parts of his body and their motions, by explanation in terms of reasons. He rejected physical causes as causes at all. "To call these things causes is too absurd." His own advance, however, he spoiled by assigning causal power to his reasons.

REPLACING THE MASK

But there was something inadequate and naive about the attempt made in the last section. It was overambitious. Who am I to say what is the correct sorting as though the sorts, having been made in Heaven, were then laid out for us to observe? Moreover, the methods I have been describing worked in spite of their authors' beliefs about them. I would be more sophisticated, therefore, to leave the sort-crossing as it was, except for this important difference: We have now become aware of it. It is, then, as though we now agree with Descartes and Newton that the wolf-properties are peculiarly suited to illustrate man. But, unlike them, we merely refrain from being taken in by this device.

This brings me back to the subject with which I began this chapter, that of hypotheses. Plato, we saw, extended the metaphor in the word "hypothesis" in order to assign to hypotheses their proper role. They were to be treated not as *archai* to start the demonstration (things at the top of the arch) but as *hypo-theses* to start the analysis (steps at the bottom of the arch) from which, after their hypothetical content had been destroyed, the *archai* might be derived. I concluded that Descartes and Newton adopted much of this view, for they too held that we ought to start the analysis with hypotheses, the "obscure propositions" of Descartes and the "hints" or "conjectures" of Newton, and finish it with those established truths called laws of nature, which can function as first principles to start the demonstration. Both were really advocates of the Platonic view that hypotheses were not to be used in demonstration. Newton asserted *"Hypotheses non fingo"* and meant it. Descartes asserted the equivalent of *Hypotheses fingo"* but did not mean it. He acted prudently by deciding to *"speak* hypothetically" while continuing, in line with his formal rules of method, to *believe* otherwise. This might well have been the "mask" he was referring to when he wrote the first of his *Private Thoughts:* "Now that I am to mount the stage of the world, where I have so far been a spectator, I come forward in a mask."

Nevertheless, in all their explanations of nature, both men were constantly making use of hypotheses. The "manifest qualities" that Newton found in bodies and that Descartes "clearly and distinctly" perceived in them were not discoveries of fact but were, from one point of view, occult qualities, and from another, free inventions of their highly imaginative minds. While they believed that they were giving true descriptions of the process of nature they were actually projecting the devices of one into the facts of the other.

Thus from one point of view (that of section 5), they were metaphysicians *malgre eux,* and their metaphysics was mechanism. But from another point of view (that of this section) they were inventing hypotheses, and their big hypothesis was that the whole physical world is one giant machine. Although Descartes himself even spoke from these two points of view, saying in the *Discourse* that "the laws of mechanics are *identical* with those of nature," and in the *Principles* that he had described the whole world "*as if* it were a machine," there is little doubt about which utterance he believed. The one implies belief, the other only make-believe. From the point of view attained in this section, both utterances reveal sort-crossing: the former, sort-trespassing; the latter, sort-crossing with awareness. From the same point of view, the former is a case of being victimized by a metaphor, while the latter is a case of using a metaphor. From the same point of view, the former characterizes the "reductionism" of physics to Euclidean geometry, while the latter characterizes either the extended application of geometry to the physical world or the physical interpretation of Euclid's geometry. Descartes and Newton gave slightly different meanings to "the geometrical way" and "the mathematical way," respectively. They invented slightly different hypotheses.

Moreover, within the classical tradition, both men thought that they derived their first principles by analysis, using the light of reason in one case and the light of nature in the other. Because they thought there was nothing hypothetical about them, they gave their results the dignified title of "laws of nature." Much of their written work they presented in the analytical style showing, they thought, the sequence of their investigation that ended in their discovery of these laws. They did not realize, it seems, that they were presenting, not their patterns of discovery, but detailed autobiographical accounts of their experiences undergone in testing their freely invented hypotheses. Einstein's discerning remark about Newton's *Opticks,* "It alone can afford us the enjoyment of a look at the personal activity of this unique man," applies just as appropriately to much of Descartes's written work. If this was so, if they first invented hypotheses and then subjected them to analysis in the form of inductive testing of their deduced consequences, then, while only one of them was following Cardinal Bellarmine's injunction to speak hypothetically, both were acting in that way. If this was so, then they were following the doctrine of the geometers, rejected by Plato, of setting up deductive systems based upon hypotheses or conjectures: They were "technicians."

But if we consider Plato's masterpiece, the *Republic,* we must conclude that Plato himself, in actual practice, was following the same doctrine—the doctrine he rejected. For in it we see, not the derivation by analysis of first principles, but the arbitrary invention of one big hypothesis that is then used with extraordinary success to account for the facts about man.

Now all hypotheses, by definition, involve make-believe. Many of them, like those under consideration, involve sort-crossing, and are therefore metaphors. The conclusion of this section is the decision to try to adopt the actual technique of Plato and, in addition, to follow the advice of Cardinal Bellarmine. Then, whether we suppose that man is a state, or that the world is a machine, or that man is a wolf, the risk of confusing the facts of one sort with those of the other will be lessened.

FOCUSING QUESTIONS

1. Why did Galileo have to recant to the Inquisition?
2. What did Galileo recant?
3. What is the difference between facts, hypotheses, and habits of mind?
4. What is the habit of mind Galileo introduced in our culture?
5. Is the human body a machine?
6. How would you solve the problem of using one habit of mind in the laboratory and another outside?
7. Would it be legitimate to use only one habit of mind in every context?
8. What is scientism as opposed to science?
9. Can you detect scientism in education?
10. In view of the new habit of mind of science, would you say that facts are evident, hidden, discovered, or made?
11. Does classical physics have a cosmology?
12. Why are cosmologies important?
13. Can anyone be a scientist or claim to be such without the habit of mind to go along?
14. Can anyone be a scientist in every context?
15. Is there a relationship between the habit of mind of the scientist and the instruments he uses doing science, and the habit of mind of a Marxist and the backup of the state?

16. Can a Marxist convince by the power of his reasoning if the audience of one or many does not share his habit of mind?

17. How can facts be recognized without sharing the same habit of mind that created the fact?

18. What is argumentation in a pluralistic society?

SUPPLEMENTARY READINGS

Descartes, R. *The Philosophical Works* (1955) Dover, New York *Discourse on Method, Optics, Geometry and Meterology*, Trans. Oldscamp, P. Bobbs-Merrill, Indianapolis (1965).

de Santillana, Georgio.　*The Crime of Galileo* (Ideal selection for a presentation)

8

The Narratives: Locke, Rousseau, Marquis de Sade

John Locke (1632–1704) was born in Wrington, England, was educated at Oxford University, and later studied medicine. He has been called the intellectual ruler of the eighteenth century for his educational, political, philosophical, and psychological theories. As a member of the Whig political party, Locke opposed the efforts of King James II to establish an absolute monarchy in England. When King James II was exiled, after the Glorious Revolution of 1688, Locke became famous as the philosophical champion of religious tolerance and political liberalism.

With the change in habit of thought between the earlier educational theories of the medievals and those of the post-Cartesian world there is a definite change in "narrative." A "narrative" is not a theory, but rather a set of theories presenting in the form of a comprehensive story an explanation of how things hang together in a general or particular manner. Narratives, besides, serve as a reinforcement of the particular habit of mind adopted. Regardless of what those narratives say, their practical activity is to repeat through education the particular habit of mind the educators have an affinity to, believe in, are adept at, or are unaware of, but necessarily transmit to the students.

The old medieval schoolman believed in a natural law, created by God and which could be known through those acts of the mind well performed in the third degree of abstraction where Truth, One, Beautiful were found, somewhere in the mental operations of their deductive method.

God could not be known directly, but He could be known indirectly through the laws He had created and which together formed what we call Nature. The method, that is the deductive method of logic, was not only appropriate for this task of knowing God indirectly but was also appropriate to dictate human behavior in every context, on this earth, in limbo, in purgatory, in heaven, and in hell. And it was not only adequate for the believers but also for the nonbelievers. Every creature was known as such creature, including God, in the measure that he or she was a character in this story.

In his *Essay Concerning Human Understanding* (not reprinted here), Locke's major philosophical work (1690), we can see at once how the new habit dictates the new theories and the whole narrative in such a manner that it will affect education radically. Ideas are not innate, nor acquired through reading the classics, nor developed through elaborate logical skills. The mind, at birth, was blank, *tamquam tabula rasa,* as blank as a slate. All information, knowledge, and ideas, come from the senses: "Our observation employed either about external sensible objects, or about the internal operations of our minds perceived and reflected on by ourselves is that which supplies our understanding with all the materials of thinkings" (*Essay Concerning Human Understanding* Book II, Chapter I, sec. 2). Once experience enters the mind, knowledge comes whenever agreement or disagreement of ideas is perceived by the mind. Thus *empiricism* entered the classroom with all its consequences. The scientific method becomes thus the narrative of the classroom.

In *Some Thoughts Concerning Education* (1697) Locke recommends a utilitarian approach to education. It should cultivate the ability to manage social, economic, and political affairs in a practical manner. Education should produce the ethical manager, someone who could manage economic affairs prudently, and who would participate in government effectively.

Since the "narrative" of Locke presupposed that all knowledge comes through the senses, the result of the sensuous investigation of nature, he equated nature with the social, and education had to be regulated to be successful from early childhood with rigorous discipline. Thus nature was innocent, while the student was guilty until educated.

Jean Jacques Rousseau (1712–1778) a Swiss-born French philosopher, became famous for his social, political, and educational ideas alive to this day in so many contemporary quarters. His two main works *On The Origin of the Inequality* and *The Social Contract* had enormous political influence. His novel *Emile* (1762) summarizes his theories of education.

Like his predecessor Locke he establishes the hypothetical method of thought to propound his theories. Like Locke and the medievals he also establishes Nature as the ground or model of his theories.

Rousseau turns around Locke's disciplinary education by proclaiming in a visionary's fashion that if learning is only in the senses and the student is blank at birth, then learning is the process by which the student becomes corrupt. Society is guilty, man is innocent. Rousseau's model of nature is neither the medieval's nor that of Locke. Nature is the paradise of the individual. Nature equated with society is a hell to be avoided. In *Origins of Inequality* Rousseau states as much: if you can avoid entering society, do not enter; if you must enter society, then avoid civilized societies with states and sovereigns (choose primitive societies of Africa or the New World); or at the very least, if you cannot avoid entering society with a state, avoid tyranny and enter a small community governed according to the "general will." There is no reason to enter society since reasoning powers are the consequence and not the cause of social life. Reason, for Rousseau, is a mark of degeneration, for he who calculates is ready to cheat and exploit.

Rousseau's understanding of Locke's society as a system that imprisons us within a set of institutions leads him to proclaim that the child needs to be set free from the most coercive of these institutions—the school.

Emile is a journey of education through infancy, childhood, boyhood, adolescence, and youth to help isolate *Emile* from the corruption of society and the cultivation of his own interests and personal experiences.

Emile's sensations and feeling are not those of the school, but those of nature, a sentimentalized, good, romantic nature.

What in fact Rousseau proclaims is that besides the social there is an individual dimension that should be cultivated and that needs a different education from that of the social being.

Donatien-Alphonse-Francois de Sade, better known as the

Marquis de Sade (1740–1814) has been called by Apollinaire "The freest spirit that has ever lived," and Baudelaire wrote that "it is necessary to keep coming back to Sade, again and again." In fact, it is claimed that the Marquis de Sade is constantly with us through the intermediary of other authors, as *Beyond Good and Evil* instead of *Philosophy in the Bedroom.*

Why is he so important and why is he so condemned? Why is he in any way important to education?

The Marquis de Sade should be compulsory reading for all those people who claim to be the owners of a liberal education and who claim to be free citizens. There is no better test to find out how deep our habits of mind are impressed in us through the education we have received. This is equivalent to saying that if we want to find out how our education failed us or how we failed it, we should read the works of Marquis de Sade. And what are we testing? Beliefs or habits of mind? The Marquis de Sade will force us to seek our habits of mind.

The medieval Church grounded education on the laws of nature and through nature it endeavored to reach the heavens and hells of humanity together with the conduct leading to either. The moderns used the same external source of nature to ground their educational practice, either as an independent source of knowledge (Descartes) or an an autonomous one (Rousseau). By the time of the Marquis de Sade, nature was conceived as the only source of knowledge by the encyclopedists, Voltaire, Diderot, and others.

The Marquis de Sade would use the same notion of nature as ground and carry it, in scientific fashion, beyond the limits of verification to the realities of falsification. If nature is carried on to experiential limits nature will collapse as a principle of origin. The laws of nature in human behavior are only the fears and limits imposed on it by humans and the controllers of human freedom. The practice of libertinage ensures not only that objects are destroyed as objects, but that the senses are perverted in their own search for pleasure. What needed to be done to achieve pleasure needs to be changed, for pleasure will be achieved only through pain. In short, nature is not the external, firm ground it has been claimed to be. As a principle of origin it is contradictory and therefore false.

A man who claims that any external source of knowledge is a power of coercion but not of freedom is dangerous to any form of government, and so the Marquis de Sade spent thirty years of his life in various bastilles, fortresses, or keeps of the monarchy, of the Republic, of the Terror, of the Consulate, and of the Empire. The freest spirit became the most imprisoned body. And in jail was his writing executed.

What is left when we remove external agents from the claims of educators? What is left when we remove nature as the referent of education? What is left when we remove the book from the classroom?

Education, in the view of the Marquis de Sade, behaves like a book. While the book contains all the information, none of it happens *in* the book. It all leads outside of the book, outside of the classroom. This leads to dependence and lack of freedom. Above all, it leads to reading the world on the model of the book. A habit of mind is established by which language refers always to things outside, things that are real, things that are good or bad, things already classified to force students into submission. But suppose the *outside* is false, a convenient myth used by the powers that be for the sake of control, what is the student left with? Language and the problem of language. The student might not know anything except the place in the book where the answers can be found, but this already implies a habit of mind of surrender to a model of language that uses him or her, but in no way encourages an individual search for freedom.

Language and its manipulation is the only *constant* in education. Through language, books and their habits of thought become the imprinted text of flesh we call the student. These habits not only read the external way but also determine the acts to be performed internally. They not only inform but also control the students.

One needs to read the Marquis de Sade and to compare the classroom to his "solitary" cities of debauchery. Both are built outside the pale of social life. Both are built for training, both are built only through language. Both cities are "imaginary." They have special times, habits, customs, and populations and both are totally supported by words. In both cities—the Chateau of Silling for example and the classroom—people not only tell, but they tell that they are telling. In both, the central hero or heroine is the storyteller, the narrative's preeminent place in the classroom as the whole schedule of days and nights converge toward this moment. The storyteller is the only actor and what can be done must first be said by him. Education, in this view, is not only the use of language with all its habits, but also the discovery of the interiority of language, where action and language share the same limits. The Marquis de Sade, like education, is boring and repetitive if we fix our attention on the crimes reported or the information to be gathered, but not if we focus on how language is being formed. The universe of discourse is the only universe present in both education and the Marquis de Sade cities. Nothing of what happens in the novels of the Marquis de Sade is "possible." His is an impossible universe if we consider language to refer to some actual human or external world. These external impossibles are in fact the possible language constructs and become the control of the storyteller. All the creatures of the classroom, as much as those of the Marquis de Sade novels, are creatures of discourse, not creatures of reality. To represent them either favorably or unfavorably is to miss the whole point. The characters of the Marquis de Sade's works enthrall or become repulsive in discourse, but all are paper characters, the same as those creatures presented in the classroom. Education exists only by words, and classrooms, as much as the Chateau of Silling, are not sanctuaries of enlightenment or debauchery, but places where only the story, the narrative, lives.

Some Thoughts Concerning Education
John Locke

A sound mind in a sound body, is a short, but full description of a happy state in this world. He that has these two, has little more to wish for; and he that wants either of them, will be but little the better for any thing else. Men's happiness or misery is most part of their own making. He whose mind directs not wisely, will never take the right way; and he whose body is crazy and feeble, will never be able to advance in it. I confess, there are some men's constitutions of body and mind so vigorous, and well fram'd by nature, that they need not much assistance from others; but by the strength of their natural genius, they are from their cradles carried towards what is excellent; and by the privilege of their happy constitutions, are able to do wonders. But examples of this kind are but few; and I think I may say, that of all the men we meet with, nine parts of ten are what they are, good or evil, useful or not, by their education. 'Tis that which makes the great difference in mankind. The little, or almost insensible impressions on our tender infancies, have very important and lasting consequences: and there 'tis, as in the fountains of some rivers, where a gentle application of the hand turns the flexible waters in channels, that make them take quite contrary courses; and by this direction given them at first in the source, they receive different tendencies, and arrive at last at very remote and distant places.

I imagine the minds of children as easily turn'd this or that way, as water it self: and though this be the principal part, and our main care should be about the inside, yet the clay-cottage is not to be neglected. I shall therefore begin with the case, and consider first the *health* of the body, as that which perhaps you may rather expect from that study I have been thought more peculiarly to have apply'd my self to; and that also which will be soonest dispatch'd, as lying, if I guess not amiss, in a very little compass.

How necessary *health* is to our business and happiness; and how requisite a strong constitution, able to endure hardships and fatigue, is to one that will make any figure in the world, is too obvious to need any proof.

The consideration I shall here have of *health,* shall be, not what a physician ought to do with a sick and crazy child; but what the parents, without the help of physick, should do for the *preservation and improvement of an healthy,* or at least *not sickly constitution* in their children. And this perhaps might be all dispatch'd in this one short rule, *viz.* That gentlemen should use their children, as the honest farmers and substantial yeomen do theirs. But because the mothers possibly may think this a little too hard, and the fathers too short, I shall explain my self more particularly; only laying down this as a general and certain observation for the women to consider, *viz.* That most children's constitutions are either spoil'd, or at least harm'd, by *cockering* and *tenderness*.

The first thing to be taken care of, is, that children be not too *warmly clad or cover'd,* winter or summer. The face when we are born, is no less tender than any other part of the body. 'Tis use alone hardens it, and makes it more able to endure the cold. And therefore the *Scythian* philosopher gave a very significant answer to the *Athenian,* who wonder'd how he could go naked in frost and snow. *How,* said the *Scythian, can you endure your face expos'd to the sharp winter air? My face is us'd to it,* said the *Athenian. Think me all face,* reply'd the *Scythian.* Our bodies will endure any thing, that from the beginning they are accustom'd to.

Due care being had to keep the body in strength and vigour, so that it may be able to obey and execute the orders of the *mind;* the next and principal business is, to set the *mind* right, that on all occasions it may be dispos'd to consent to nothing but what may be suitable to the dignity and excellency of a rational creature.

If what I have said in the beginning of this discourse be true, as I do not doubt but it is, *viz.* That the difference to be found in the manners and abilities of men is owing more to their *education* than to any thing else, we have reason to conclude, that great care is to be had of the forming children's *minds,* and giving them that seasoning early, which shall influence their lives always after: For when they do well or ill, the praise and blame will be laid there; and when any thing is done awkwardly, the common saying will pass upon them, that it's suitable to their *breeding.*

As the strength of the body lies chiefly in being able to endure hardships, so also does that of the mind. And the great principle and foundation of all virtue and worth is plac'd in this: that man is able to *deny himself* his own desires, cross his own inclinations, and purely follow what reason directs as best, tho' the appetite lean the other way.

The great mistake I have observ'd in people's breeding their children, has been, that this has not been taken care enough of in its *due season:* that the mind has not been made obedient to discipline, and pliant to reason, when at first it was most tender, most easy to be bow'd. Parents being wisely ordain'd by nature to love their children, are very apt, if reason watch not that natural affection very warily, are apt, I say, to let it run into fondness. They love their little ones and it is their duty; but they often, with them, cherish their faults too. They must not be cross'd, forsooth; they must be permitted to have their wills in all things; and they being in their infancies not capable of great vices, their parents think they may safe enough indulge their irregularities, and make themselves sport with that pretty perverseness which they think well enough becomes that innocent age. But to a fond parent, that would not have his child corrected for a perverse trick, but excus'd it, saying it was a small matter, *Solon* very well reply'd, *aye, but custom is a great one.*

The usual lazy and short way by chastisement and the rod, which is the only instrument of government that tutors generally know, or ever think of, is the most unfit of any to be us'd in education, because it tends to both those mischiefs; which, as we have shewn, are the *Scylla* and *Charybdis*, which on the one hand or the other ruin all that miscarry.

1. This kind of punishment contributes not at all to the mastery of our natural propensity to indulge corporal and present pleasure, and to avoid pain at any rate, but rather encourages it, and thereby strengthens that in us, which is the root from whence spring all vicious actions, and the irregularities of life. For what other motive, but of sensual pleasure and pain, does a child act by, who drudges at his book against his inclination, or abstains from eating unwholesome fruit, that he takes pleasure in, only out of fear of *whipping?* He in this only prefers the greater *corporal pleasure,* or avoids the greater *corporal pain.* And what is it, to govern his actions, and direct his conduct by such motives as these? What is it, I say, but to cherish that principle in him, which it is our business to root out and destroy? And therefore I cannot think any correction useful to a child, where the shame of suffering for having done amiss, does not work more upon him than the pain.

2. This sort of correction naturally breeds an aversion to that which 'tis the tutor's business to create a liking to. How obvious is it to observe, that children come to hate things which were at first acceptable to them, when they find themselves *whipp'd,* and *chid,* and teas'd about them? And it is not to be wonder'd at in them, when grown men would not be able to be reconcil'd to any thing by such ways. Who is there that would not be disgusted with any innocent recreation, in itself indifferent to him, if he should with *blows* or ill language be *haled* to it, when he had no mind? Or be constantly so treated, for some circumstances in his application to it? This is natural to be so. Offensive circumstances ordinarily infect innocent things which they are join'd with; and the very sight of a cup wherein any one uses to take nauseous physick, turns his stomach, so that nothing will relish well out of it, tho' the cup be never so clean and well-shap'd, and of the richest materials.

3. Such a sort of *slavish discipline* makes a *slavish temper.* The child submits, and dissembles obedience, whilst the fear of the rod hangs over him; but when that is remov'd, and by being out of sight, he can promise himself impunity, he gives the greater scope to his natural inclination;

which by this way is not at all alter'd, but, on the contrary, heighten'd and increas'd in him; and after such restraint, breaks out usually with the more violence; or,

4. If *severity* carry'd to the highest pitch does prevail, and works a cure upon the present unruly distemper, it often brings in the room of it a worse and more dangerous disease, by breaking the mind; and then, in the place of a disorderly young fellow, you have a *low spirited moap'd* creature, who, however with his unnatural sobriety he may please silly people, who commend tame unactive children, because they make no noise, nor give them any trouble; yet at last, will probably prove as uncomfortable a thing to his friends, as he will be all his life an useless thing to himself and others.

Beating them, and all other sorts of slavish and corporal punishments, are not the discipline fit to be used in the education of those we would have wise, good, and ingenuous men; and therefore very rarely to be apply'd, and that only in great occasions, and cases of extremity. On the other side, to flatter children by *rewards* of things that are pleasant to them, is as carefully to be avoided. He that will give to his son *apples* or *sugar-plumbs,* or what else of this kind he is most delighted with, to make him learn his book, does but authorize his love of pleasure, and cocker up that dangerous propensity, which he ought by all means to subdue and stifle in him. You can never hope to teach him to master it, whilst you compound for the check you gave his inclination in one place, by the satisfaction you propose to it in another. To make a good, a wise, and a virtuous man, 'tis fit he should learn to cross his appetite, and deny his inclination to *riches, finery,* or *pleasing his palate,* &c. whenever his reason advises the contrary, and his duty requires it. But when you draw him to do any thing that is fit by the offer of *money,* or reward the pains of learning his book by the pleasure of a luscious morsel; when you promise him a *lace-cravat* or a *fine new suit,* upon performance of some of his little tasks; what do you by proposing these as *rewards,* but allow them to be the good things he should aim at, and thereby encourage his longing for 'em, and accustom him to place his happiness in them? Thus people, to prevail with children to be industrious about their grammar, dancing, or some other such matter, of no great moment to the happiness or usefulness of their lives, by misapply'd *rewards* and *punishments,* sacrifice their virtue, invert the order of their education, and teach them luxury, pride, or covetousness, &c. For in this way, flattering those wrong inclinations which they should restrain and suppress, they lay the foundations of those future vices, which cannot be avoided but by curbing our desires and accustoming them early to submit to reason.

I say not this, that I would have children kept from the conveniences or pleasures of life, that are not injurious to their health or virtue. On the contrary, I would have their lives made as pleasant and as agreeable to them as may be, in a plentiful enjoyment of whatsoever might innocently delight them; provided it be with this caution, that they have those enjoyments, only as the consequences of the state of esteem and acceptation they are in with their parents and governors; but they should never be offer'd or bestow'd on them, as the *rewards of this or that particular performance,* that they shew an aversion to, or to which they would not have apply'd themselves without that temptation.

But if you take away the rod on the one hand, and these little encouragements which they are taken with, on the other, how the (will you say) shall children be govern'd? Remove hope and fear, and there is an end of all discipline. I grant that good and evil, *reward* and *punishment,* are the only motives to a rational creature: these are the spur and reins whereby all mankind are set on work, and guided, and therefore they are to be made use of to children too. For I advise their parents and governors always to carry this in their minds, that children are to be treated as rational creatures.

Rewards, I grant, and *punishments* must be proposed to children, if we intend to work upon them. The mistake I imagine is, that those that are generally made use of, are *ill-chosen.* The pains and pleasures of the body are, I think, of ill consequence, when made the rewards and punishments whereby men would prevail on their children; for, as I said before, they serve but to increase and strengthen those inclinations, which 'tis our business to subdue and master. What principle of virtue do you lay in a child, if you will redeem his desires of one pleasure, by the proposal of another? This is but to enlarge his appetite, and instruct it to wander. If a child cries for an unwholesome and dangerous fruit, you purchase his quiet by giving him a less hurtful sweet-meat. This perhaps may preserve his health, but spoils his mind, and sets that farther out of order. For here you only change the object, but flatter still his *appetite,* and allow that must be satisfy'd, wherein, as I have shew'd, lies the root of the mischief: and till you bring him to be able to bear a denial of that satisfaction, the child may at present be quiet and orderly, but the disease is not cured. By this way of proceeding, you foment and cherish in him that which is the spring from whence all the evil flows, which will be sure on the next occasion to break out again with more violence, give him stronger longings, and you more trouble.

The *rewards* and *punishments* then, whereby we should keep children in order, are quite of another kind, and of that force, that when we can get them once to work, the business, I think, is done and the difficulty is over. *Esteem* and *disgrace* are, of all others, the most powerful incentives to the mind, when once it is brought to relish them. If you can once get into children a love of credit, and an apprehension of shame and disgrace, you have put into 'em the true principle, which will constantly work and incline them to the right. But it will be ask'd, How shall this be done?

I confess it does not at first appearance want some difficulty; but yet I think it worth our while to seek the ways (and practise them when found) to attain this, which I look on as the great secret of education.

First, children (earlier perhaps than we think) are very sensible of *praise* and commendation. They find a pleasure in being esteem'd and valu'd, especially by their parents and those whom they depend on. If therefore the father *caress and commend them when do well, shew a cold and neglectful countenance to them upon doing ill,* and this accompany'd by a like carriage of the mother and all others that are about them, it will, in a little time, make them sensible of the difference; and this, if constantly observ'd, I doubt not but will of itself work more than threats or blows, which lose their force when once common, and are of no use when shame does not attend them; and therefore are to be forborne, and never to be us'd, but in the case hereafter-mention'd, when it is brought to extremity.

But *secondly,* to make the sense of *esteem* or *disgrace* sink the deeper, and be of the more weight, *other agreeable or disagreeable things should constantly accompany these different states;* not as particular rewards and punishments of this or that particular action, but as necessarily belonging to, and constantly attending one, who by his carriage has brought himself into a state of disgrace or commendation. By which way of treating them, children may as much as possible be brought to conceive, that those that are commended, and in esteem for doing well, will necessarily be belov'd and cherish'd by every body, and have all other good things as a consequence of it; and on the other side, when any one by miscarriage falls into disesteem, and cares not to preserve his credit, he will unavoidably fall under neglect and contempt; and in that state, the want of whatever might satisfy or delight him will follow. In this way the objects of their desires are made assisting to virtue, when a settled experience from the beginning teaches children that the things they delight in, belong to, and are to be enjoy'd by those only who are in a state of reputation. If by these means you can come once to shame them out of their faults, (for besides that, I would willingly have no punishment) and make them in love with the pleasure of being well thought on, you may turn them as you please, and they will be in love with all the ways of virtue.

The great difficulty here is, I imagine, from the folly and perverseness of servants, who are hardly to be hinder'd from crossing herein the design of the father and mother. Children discountenanc'd by their parents for any fault, find usually a refuge and relief in the caresses of those foolish flatterers, who thereby undo whatever the parents endeavour to establish. When the father or mother looks sowre on the child, everybody else should put on the same coldness to him, and nobody give him countenance, 'till forgiveness ask'd, and a reformation of his fault has set him right again, and restor'd him to his former credit.

You will wonder, perhaps, that I put *learning* last, especially if I tell you I think it the least part. This may seem strange in the mouth of a bookish man; and this making usually the chief, if not only bustle and stir about children, this being almost that alone which is thought on, when people talk of education, makes it the greater paradox. When I consider, what ado is made about a little *Latin* and *Greek*, how many years are spent in it, and what a noise and business it makes to no purpose, I can hardly forbear thinking that the parents of children still live in fear of the school-master's rod, which they look on as the only instrument of education; as a language or two to be its whole business. How else is it possible that a child should be chain'd to the oar seven, eight, or ten of the best years of his life, to get a language or two, which, I think, might be had at a great deal cheaper rate of pains and time, and be learn'd almost in playing?

Forgive me therefore if I say, I cannot with patience think, that a young gentleman should be put into the herd, and be driven with a whip and scourge, as if he were to run the gantlet through the several classes, *ad capiendum ingenii cultum.* What then? say you, would you not have him write and read? Shall he be more ignorant than the clerk of our parish, who takes *Hopkins* and *Sternhold* for the best poets in the world, whom yet he makes worse than they are by his ill reading? Not so, not so fast, I beseech you. Reading and writing and *learning* I allow to be necessary, but yet not the chief business. I imagine you would think him a very foolish fellow, that should not value a virtuous or a wise man infinitely before a great scholar. Not but that I think *learning* a great help to both in well-dispos'd minds; but yet it must be confess'd also, that in others not so dispos'd, it helps them only to be the more foolish, or worse men. I say this, that when you consider the breeding of your son, and are looking out for a school-master or a tutor, you would not have (as is usual) Latin and *logick* only in your thoughts. *Learning* must be had, but in the second place, as subservient only to greater qualities. Seek out somebody that may know how discreetly to frame his manners: place him in hands where you may, as much as possible, secure his innocence, cherish and nurse up the good, and gently correct and weed out any bad inclinations, and settle in him good habits. This is the main point, and this being provided for, *learning* may be had into the bargain, and that, as I think, at a very easy rate, by methods that may be thought on.

When he can talk, 'tis time he should begin to *learn to read*. But as to this, give me leave here to inculcate again, what is very apt to be forgotten, *viz.* That great care is to be taken, that it be never made as a business to him, nor he look on it as a task. We naturally, as I said, even from our cradles, love liberty, and have therefore an aversion to many things for no other reason but because they are enjoin'd us. I have always had a fancy that *learning* might be made a play and recreation to children: and that they might be brought to desire to be taught, if it were proposed to them as a thing of honour, credit, delight, and recreation, or as a reward for doing something else; and if they were never chid or corrected for the neglect of it. That which confirms me in this opinion is, that amongst the *Portuguese,* 'tis so much a fashion and emulation amongst their children, to *learn to read* and write, that they cannot hinder them from it: they will learn it one from another, and are as intent on it, as if it were forbidden them. I remember that being at a friend's house, whose younger son, a child in coats, was not easily *brought* to his book (being taught *to read* at home by his mother) I advised to try another way, than requiring it of him as his duty; we therefore, in a discourse on purpose amongst our selves, in his hearing, but without taking any notice of him, declared, that it was the privilege and advantage of heirs and elder brothers, to be scholars; that this made them fine gentlemen, and beloved by every body: and that for younger brothers, 'twas a favour to admit them to breeding; to be taught to *read* and write, was more than came to their share; they might be ignorant bumpkins and clowns, if they pleased. This so wrought upon the child, that afterwards he desired to be taught; would come himself to his mother to *learn,* and would not let his maid be quiet till she heard him his lesson. I doubt not but some way like this might be taken with other children; and when their tempers are found, some thoughts be instill'd into them, that might set them upon desiring of *learning,* themselves, and make them seek it as another sort of play or recreation. But then, as I said before, it must never be imposed as a task, nor made a trouble to them. There may be dice and play-things; with the letters on them to teach children the *alphabet* by playing; and twenty other ways may be found, suitable to their particular tempers, to make this kind of *learning a sport* to them.

Thus children may be cozen'd into a knowledge of the letters; be *taught to read,* without perceiving it to be any thing but a sport, and play themselves into that which others are whipp'd for. Children should not have any thing like work, or serious, laid on them; neither their minds, nor bodies will bear it. It injures their healths; and their being forced and tied down to their books in an age at enmity with all such restraint, has, I doubt not, been the reason, why a great many have hated books and learning all their lives after. 'Tis like a surfeit, that leaves an aversion behind not to be removed.

I have therefore thought, that if *play-things* were fitted to this purpose, as they are usually to none, contrivances might be made to *teach children to read*, whilst they thought they were only playing. For example, what if an *ivory-ball* were made like that of the royal-oak lottery, with thirty two sides, or one rather of twenty four or twenty five sides; and upon several of those sides pasted on an A, upon several others B, on others C, and on others D? I would have you begin with but these four letters, or perhaps only two at first; and when he is perfect in them, then add another; and so on till each side having one letter, there be on it the whole alphabet. This I would have others play with before him, it being as good a sort of play to lay a stake who shall first throw an A or B, as who upon dice shall throw six or seven. This being a play amongst you, tempt him not to it, lest you make it business; for I would not have him understand 'tis any thing but a play of older people, and I doubt not but he will take to it of himself. And that he may have the more reason to think it is a play, that he is sometimes in favour admitted to, when the play is done the ball should be laid up safe out of his reach, that so it may not, by his having it in his keeping at any time, grow stale to him.

To keep up his eagerness to it, let him think it is a game belonging to those above him: and when, by this means, he knows the letters, by changing them into syllables, he may *learn to read*, without knowing how he did so, and never have any chiding or trouble about it, nor fall out with books because of the hard usage and vexation they have caus'd him. Children, if you observe them, take abundance of pains to learn several games, which, if they should be enjoined them, they would abhor as a task and a business. I know a person of great quality (more yet to be honoured for his learning and virtue than for his rank and high place) who by pasting on the six vowels (for in our language Y is one) on the six sides of a die, and the remaining eighteen consonants on the sides of three other dice, has made this a play for his children, that he shall win who, at one cast, throws most words on these four dice; whereby his eldest son, yet in coats, has *play'd* himself *into spelling*, with great eagerness, and without once having been chid for it or forced to it.

I have seen little girls exercise whole hours together and take abundance of pains to be expert at *dibstones* as they call it. Whilst I have been looking on, I have thought it wanted only some good contrivance to make them employ all that industry about something that might be more useful to them; and methinks 'tis only the fault and negligence of elder people that it is not so. Children are much less apt to be idle than men; and men are to be blamed if some part of that busy humour be not turned to useful things; which might be made usually as delightful to them as those they are employed in, if men would be but half so forward to lead the way, as these little apes would be to follow. I imagine some wise *Portuguese* heretofore began this fashion amongst the children of his country, where I have been told, as I said, it is impossible to hinder the children from *learning to read and write:* and in some parts of *France* they teach one another to sing and dance from the cradle.

The *letters* pasted upon the sides of the dice, or polygon, were best to be of the size of those of the folio Bible, to begin with, and none of them capital letters; when once he can read what is printed in such letters, he will not long be ignorant of the great ones: and in the beginning he should not be perplexed with variety. With this die also, you might have a play just like the royal oak, which would be another variety, and play for cherries or apples, &c.

Besides these, twenty other plays might be invented depending on *letters,* which those who like this way, may easily contrive and get made to this use if they will. But the four dice above mention'd I think so easy and useful, that it will be hard to find any better, and there will be scarce need of any other.

Thus much for *learning to read,* which let him never be driven to, nor chid for; cheat him into it if you can, but make it not a business for him. 'Tis better it be a year later *before he can read,* than that he should this way get an aversion to learning. If you have any contest with him, let it be in matters of moment, of truth, and good nature; but lay no task on him about A B C. Use your skill to make his will supple and pliant to reason: teach him to love credit and commendation; to abhor being thought ill or meanly of, especially by you and his mother, and then the rest will come all easily. But I think if you will do that, you must not shackle and tie him up with rules about indifferent matters, nor rebuke him for every little fault, or perhaps some that to others would seem great ones; but of this I have said enough already.

When by these gentle ways he begins to *read,* some easy pleasant book, suited to his capacity, should be put into his hands, wherein the entertainment that he finds might draw him on, and reward his pains in reading, and yet not such as should fill his head with perfectly useless trumpery, or lay the principles of vice and folly. To this purpose, I think *Æsop's Fables* the best, which being stories apt to delight and entertain a child, may yet afford useful reflections to a grown man; and if his memory retain them all his life after, he will not repent to find them there, amongst his manly thoughts and serious business. If his *Æsop* has *pictures* in it, it will entertain him much the better, and encourage him to read, when it carries the increase of knowledge with it: for such visible objects children hear talked of in vain and without any satisfaction whilst they have no ideas of them; those ideas being not to be had from sounds, but from the things themselves or their pictures. And therefore I think as soon as he begins to spell, as many pictures of animals should be got him as can be found, with the printed names to them, which at the same time will invite him to read, and afford him matter of enquiry and knowledge. *Reynard the Fox* is another book I think may be made use of to the same purpose. And if those about him will talk to him often about the stories he has read, and hear him tell them, it will, besides other advantages, add encouragement and delight to his *reading*, when he finds there is some use and pleasure in it. These baits seem wholly neglected in the ordinary method; and 'tis usually long before learners find any use or pleasure in reading, which may tempt them to it, and so take books only for fashionable amusements, or impertinent troubles, good for nothing.

The Lord's Prayer, the Creeds, and Ten Commandments, 'tis necessary he should learn perfectly by heart; but, I think, not by reading them himself in his primer, but by somebody's repeating them to him, even before he can read. But learning by heart, and *learning to read*, should not I think be mix'd, and so one made to clog the other. But his *learning to read* should be made as little trouble or business to him as might be.

What other books there are in *English* of the kind of those abovementioned, fit to engage the liking of children, and tempt them to *read*, I do not know: but am apt to think, that children being generally delivered over to the method of schools, where the fear of the rod is to inforce, and not any pleasure of the employment to invite them to learn, this sort of useful books, amongst the number of silly ones that are of all sorts, have yet had the fate to be neglected; and nothing that I know has been considered of this kind out of the ordinary road of the horn-book, primer, psalter, Testament, and Bible.

As for the *Bible*, which children are usually employ'd in to exercise and improve their talent *in reading*, I think the promiscuous reading of it through by chapters as they lie in order, is so far from being of any advantage to children, either for the perfecting their *reading*, or principling their religion, that perhaps a worse could not be found. For what pleasure or encouragement can it be to a child to exercise himself in reading those parts of a book where he understands nothing? And how little are the law of *Moses*, the song of *Solomon*, the prophecies in the Old, and the Epistles and *Apocalypse* in the New Testament, suited to a child's capacity? And though the history of the Evangelists and the *Acts* have something easier, yet, taken altogether, it is very disproportional to the understanding of childhood. I grant that the principles of religion are to be drawn from thence, and in the words of the scripture; yet none should be propos'd to a child, but such as are suited to a child's capacity and notions. But 'tis far from this to read through *the whole Bible,* and that for reading's sake. And what an odd jumble of thoughts must a child have in his head, if he have any at all, such as he should have concerning religion, who in his tender age reads all the parts of the *Bible* indifferently as the word of God without any other distinction! I am apt to think, that this in some men has been the very reason why they never had clear and distinct thoughts of it all their lifetime.

And now I am by chance fallen on this subject, give me leave to say, that there are some parts of the *Scripture* which may be proper to be put into the hands of a child to engage him to read; such as are the story of *Joseph* and his brethren, of *David* and *Goliath*, of *David* and *Jonathan*, &c. and others that he should be made to read for his instruction, as that, *What you would have others do unto you, do the same unto them;* and such other easy and plain moral rules, which being fitly chosen, might often be made use of, both for reading and instruction together; and so often read till they are throughly fixed in the memory; and then afterwards, as he grows ripe for them, may in their turns on fit occasions be inculcated as the standing and sacred rules of his life and actions. But the reading of the whole Scripture indifferently, is what I think very inconvenient for children, till after having been made acquainted with the plainest fundamental parts of it, they have got some kind of general view of what they ought principally to believe and practise; which yet, I think, they ought to receive in the very words of the scripture, and not in such as men prepossess'd by systems and analogies are apt in this case to make use of and force upon them. Dr. *Worthington*, to avoid this, has made a catechism, which has all its answers in the precise words of the Scripture; a thing of good example, and such a sound form of words as no Christian can except against as not fit for his child to learn. Of this, as soon as he can say the Lord's Prayer, Creed, the Ten Commandments, by heart, it may be fit for him to learn a question every day, or every week, as his understanding is able to receive and his memory to retain them. And when he has this catechism perfectly by heart, so as readily and roundly to answer to any question in the whole book, it may be convenient to lodge in his mind the remaining moral rules scatter'd up and down in the Bible, as the best *exercise of his memory,* and that which may be always a rule to him, ready at hand, in the whole conduct of his life.

When he can read *English* well, it will be seasonable to enter him in *writing:* and here the first thing should be taught him is to *hold his pen right;* and this he should be perfect in before he should be suffered to put it to paper: For not only children but any body else that would do any thing well, should never be put upon too much of it at once, or be set to perfect themselves in two parts of an action at the same time, if they can possibly be separated. I think the *Italian* way of holding the pen between the thumb and the forefinger alone, may be best; but in this you may consult some good writing-master, or any other person who writes well and quick. When he has learn'd to hold his pen right, in the next place he should learn how to *lay his paper, and place his arm and body to it.*

These practices being got over, the way to teach him to write without much trouble, is to get a plate graved with the characters of such a hand as you like best: but you must remember to have them a pretty deal bigger than he should ordinarily write; for every one naturally comes by degrees to write a less hand than he at first was taught, but never a bigger. Such a plate being graved, let several sheets of good writing-paper be printed off with red ink, which he has nothing to do but go over with a good pen fill'd with black ink, which will quickly bring his hand to the formation of those characters, being at first shewed where to begin, and how to form every letter. And when he can do that well, he must then exercise on fair paper; and so may easily be brought to *write* the hand you desire.

When he can write well and quick, I think it may be convenient not only to continue the exercise of his hand in writing, but also to improve the use of it farther in *drawing;* a thing very useful to a gentleman in several occasions; but especially if he travel, as that which helps a man often to express, in a few lines well put together, what a whole sheet of paper in writing would not be able to represent and make intelligible. How many buildings may a man see, how many machines and habits meet with, the ideas whereof would be easily retain'd and communicated by a little skill in *drawing;* which being committed to words, are in danger to be lost, or at best but ill retained in the most exact descriptions? I do not mean that I would have your son a *perfect painter;* to be that to any tolerable degree, will require more time than a young gentleman can spare from his other improvements of greater moment. But so much insight into *perspective* and skill in *drawing,* as will enable him to represent tolerably on paper any thing he sees, except faces, may, I think, be got in a little time, especially if he have a genius to it; but where that is wanting, unless it be in the things absolutely necessary, it is better to let him pass them by quietly, than to vex him about them to no purpose: and therefore in this, as in all other things not absolutely necessary, the rule holds, *nil invita Minerva.*

Short-hand, an art, as I have been told, known only in *England,* may perhaps be thought worth the learning, both from dispatch in what men write for their own memory, and concealment of what they would not have lie open to every eye. For he that has once learn'd any sort of character, may easily vary it to his own private use or fancy, and with more contraction suit it to the business he would employ it in. Mr. *Rich's,* the best contriv'd of any I have seen, may, as I think, by one who knows and considers grammar well, be made much easier and shorter. But for the learning this compendious way of writing, there will be no need hastily to look out a master; it will be early enough when any convenient opportunity offers itself at any time, after his hand is well settled in fair and quick writing. For boys have but little use of *short-hand,* and should by no means practise it till they write perfectly well, and have throughly fixed the habit of doing so.

As soon as he can speak *English,* 'tis time for him to learn some other language. This no body doubts of, when *French* is propos'd. And the reason is, because people are accustomed to the right way of teaching that language, which is by talking it into children in constant conversation, and not by grammatical rules. The *Latin* tongue would easily be taught the same way, if his tutor, being constantly with him, would talk nothing else to him, and make him answer still in the same language. But because *French* is a living language, and to be used more in speaking, that should be first learned, that the yet pliant organs of speech might be accustomed to a due formation of those sounds, and he get the habit of pronouncing *French* well, which is the harder to be done the longer it is delay'd.

When he can speak and read *French* well, which in this method is usually in a year or two, he should proceed to *Latin,* which 'tis a wonder parents, when they have had the experiment in *French,* should not think ought to be learned the same way, by talking and reading. Only care is to be taken whilst he is learning these foreign languages, by speaking and reading nothing else with his tutor, that he do not forget to read *English,* which may be preserved by his mother or some body else hearing him read some chosen parts of the scripture or other *English* book every day.

Latin I look upon as absolutely necessary to a gentleman; and indeed custom, which prevails over every thing, has made it so much a part of education, that even those children are whipp'd to it, and made spend many hours of their precious time uneasily in *Latin,* who after they are once gone from school, are never to have more to do with it as long as they live. Can there be any thing more ridiculous, than that a father should waste his own money and his son's time in setting him to learn the *Roman language,* when at the same time he designs him for a trade, wherein he having no use of *Latin,* fails not to forget that little which he brought from school, and which 'tis ten to one he abhors for the ill usage it procured him? Could it be believed, unless we had every where amongst us examples of it, that a child should be forced to learn the rudiments of a language which he is never to use in the course of life that he is designed to, and neglect all the while the writing a good hand and casting accounts, which are of great advantage in all conditions of life, and to most trades indispensably necessary? But though these qualifications, requisite to trade and commerce and the business of the world, are seldom or never to be had at grammar-schools, yet thither not only gentlemen send their younger sons, intended for trades, but even tradesmen and farmers fail not to send their children, though they have neither intention nor ability to make them scholars. If you ask them why they do this, they think it as strange a question as if you should ask them, why they go to church. Custom serves for reason, and has, to those who take it for reason, so consecrated this method, that it is almost religiously observed by them, and they stick to it, as if their children had scarce an orthodox education unless they learned *Lilly's* grammar.

But how necessary soever *Latin* be to some, and is thought to be to others to whom it is of no manner of use and service; yet the ordinary way of learning it in a grammar-school is that which having had thoughts about I cannot be forward to encourage. The reasons against it are so evident and cogent, that they have prevailed with some intelligent persons to quit the ordinary road, not without success, though the method made use of was not exactly what I imagine the easiest, and in short is this. To trouble the child with no *grammar* at all, but to have *Latin,* as *English* has been, without the perplexity of rules, talked into him; for if you will consider it, *Latin* is no more unknown to a child, when he comes into the world, than *English:* and yet he learns *English* without master, rule, or grammar; and so might he *Latin* too, as *Tully* did, if he had some body always to talk to him in this language. And when we so often see a *French* woman teach an *English* girl to speak and read *French* perfectly in a year or two, without any rule of grammar, or any thing else but prattling to her, I cannot but wonder how gentlemen have overseen this way for their sons, and thought them more dull or incapable than their daughters.

If therefore a man could be got, who himself speaking good *Latin,* would always be about your son, talk constantly to him, and suffer him to speak or read nothing else, this would be the true and genuine way, and that which I would propose, not only as the easiest and best, wherein a child might, without pains or chiding, get a language, which others are wont to be whipt for at school six or seven years together: but also as that, wherein at the same time he might have his mind and manners formed, and he be instructed to boot in several sciences, such as are a good part of *geography, astronomy, chronology, anatomy,* besides some parts of *history,* and all other parts of knowledge of things that fall under the senses and require little more than memory. For there, if we would take the true way, our knowledge should begin, and in those things be laid the foundation; and not in the abstract notions of *logick* and *metaphysicks,* which are fitter to amuse than inform the understanding in its first setting out towards knowledge. When young men have had their heads employ'd a while in those abstract speculations without finding the success and improvement, or that use of them, which they expected, they are apt to have mean thoughts either of learning or themselves; they are tempted to quit their studies, and throw away their books as containing nothing but hard words and empty sounds; or else, to conclude, that if there be any real knowledge in them, they themselves have not understandings capable of it. That this is so, perhaps I could assure you upon my own experience. Amongst other things to be learned by a young gentleman in this method, whilst others of his age are wholly taken up with *Latin* and languages, I may also set down *geometry* for one; having known a young gentleman, bred something after this way, able to demonstrate several propositions in *Euclid* before he was thirteen.

But if such a man cannot be got, who speaks good *Latin,* and being able to instruct your son in all these parts of knowledge, will undertake it by this method; the next best is to have him taught as near this way as may be, which is by taking some easy and pleasant book, such as *Æsop's Fables,* and writing the *English* translation (made as literal as it can be) in one line, and the *Latin* words which answer each of them, just over it in another. These let him read every day over and over again, till he perfectly understands the *Latin;* and then go on to another fable, till he be also perfect in that, not omitting what he is already perfect in, but sometimes reviewing that, to keep it in his memory. And when he comes to write, let these be set him for copies, which with the exercise of his hand will also advance him to *Latin.* This being a more imperfect way than by talking *Latin* unto him; the formation of the verbs first, and afterwards the declensions of the nouns and pronouns perfectly learned by heart, may facilitate his acquaintance with the genius and manner of the *Latin tongue,* which varies the signification of verbs and nouns, not as the modern languages do by particles prefix'd, but by changing the last syllables. More than this of grammar, I think he need not have, till he can read himself *Sanctii Minerva,* with *Scioppius* and *Perizonius's* notes.

In teaching of children, this too, I think, is to be observed, that in most cases where they stick, they are not to be farther puzzled by putting them upon finding it out themselves; as by asking such questions as these, *(viz.)* which is the nominative case, in the sentence they are to construe; or demanding what *aufero* signifies, to lead them to the knowledge what *abstlere* signifies, &c., when they cannot readily tell. This wastes time only in disturbing them; for whilst they are learning, and apply themselves with attention, they are to be kept in good humour, and every thing made easy to them, and as pleasant as possible. Therefore, wherever they are at a stand, and are willing to go forwards, help them presently over the difficulty, without any rebuke or chiding, remembering, that where harsher ways are taken, they are the effect only of pride and peevishness in the teacher, who expects children should instantly be masters of as much as he knows; whereas he should rather consider, that his business is to settle in them habits, not angrily to inculcate rules, which serve for little in the conduct of our lives; at least are of no use to children, who forget them as soon as given. In sciences where their reason is to be exercised, I will not deny but this method may sometimes be varied, and difficulties proposed on purpose to excite industry, and accustom the mind to employ its own strength and sagacity in reasoning. But yet, I guess, this is not to be done to children, whilst very young, nor at their entrance upon any sort of knowledge: then every thing of itself is difficult, and the great use and skill of a teacher is to make all as easy as he can: but particularly in learning of languages there is least occasion for posing of children. For languages being to be learned by rote, custom and memory, are then spoken in greatest perfection, when all rules of grammar are utterly forgotten. I grant the grammar of a language is sometimes very carefully to be studied, but it is not to be studied but by a grown man, when he applies himself to the understanding of any language critically, which is seldom the business of any but professed scholars. This I think will be agreed to, that if a gentleman be to study any language, it ought to be that of his own country, that he may understand the language which he has constant use of, with the utmost accuracy.

There is yet a further reason, why masters and teachers should raise no difficulties to their scholars; but on the contrary should smooth their way, and readily help them forwards, where they find them stop. Children's minds are narrow and weak, and usually susceptible but of one thought at once. Whatever is in a child's head, fills it for the time, especially if set on with any passion. It should therefore be the skill and art of the teacher to clear their heads of all other thoughts whilst they are learning of any thing, the better to make room for what he would instill into them, that it may be received with attention and application, without which it leaves no impression. The natural temper of children disposes their minds to wander. Novelty alone takes them; whatever that presents, they are presently eager to have a taste of, and are as soon satiated with it. They quickly grow weary of the same thing, and so have almost their whole delight in change and variety. It is a contradiction to the natural state of childhood for them to fix their fleeting thoughts. Whether this be owing to the temper of their brains, or the quickness or instability of their animal spirits, over which the mind has not yet got a full command; this is visible, that it is a pain to children to keep their thoughts steady to any thing. A lasting continued attention is one of the hardest tasks can be imposed on them; and therefore, he that requires their application, should endeavour to make what he proposes as grateful and agreeable as possible; at least he ought to take care not to join any displeasing or frightful idea with it. If they come not to their books with some kind of liking and relish, 'tis no wonder their thoughts should be perpetually shifting from what disgusts them; and seek better entertainment in more pleasing objects, after which they will unavoidably be gadding.

'Tis, I know, the usual method of tutors, to endeavour to procure attention in their scholars, and to fix their minds to the business in hand, by rebukes and corrections, if they find them ever so little wandering. But such treatment is sure to produce the quite contrary effect. Passionate words or blows from the tutor fill the child's mind with terror and affrightment, which immediately takes it wholly up, and leaves no room for other impressions. I believe there is nobody that reads this, but may recollect what disorder hasty or imperious words from his parents or teachers have caused in his thoughts; how for the time it has turned his brains, so that he scarce knew what was said by or to him. He presently lost the sight of what he was upon, his mind was filled with disorder and confusion, and in that state was no longer capable of attention to any thing else.

'Tis true, parents and governors ought to settle and establish their authority by an awe over the minds of those under their tuition; and to rule them by that: but when they have got an ascendant over them, they should use it with great moderation, and not make themselves such scare-crows that their scholars should always tremble in their sight. Such an austerity may make their government easy to themselves, but of very little use to their pupils. 'Tis impossible children should learn any thing whilst their thoughts are possessed and disturbed with any passion, especially fear, which makes the strongest impression on their yet tender and weak spirits. Keep the mind in an easy calm temper, when you would have it receive your instructions or any increase of knowledge. 'Tis as impossible to draw fair and regular characters on a trembling mind as on a shaking paper.

The great skill of a teacher is to get and keep the attention of his scholar; whilst he has that, he is sure to advance as fast as the learner's abilities will carry him; and without that, all his bustle and pother will be to little or no purpose. To attain this, he should make the child comprehend (as much as may be) the usefulness of what he teaches him, and let him see, by what he has learnt, that he can do something which he could not do before; something, which gives him some power and real advantage above others who are ignorant of it. To this he should add sweetness in all his instructions, and by a certain tenderness in his whole carriage, make the child sensible that he loves him and designs nothing but his good, the only way to beget love in the child, which will make him hearken to his lessons, and relish what he teaches him.

Nothing but obstinacy should meet with any imperiousness or rough usage. All other faults should be corrected with a gentle hand; and kind engaging words will work better and more effectually upon a willing mind, and even prevent a good deal of that perverseness which rough and imperious usage often produces in well disposed and generous minds. 'Tis true, obstinacy and wilful neglects must be mastered, even though it cost blows to do it: but I am apt to think perverseness in the pupils is often the effect of frowardness in the *tutor;* and that most children would seldom have deserved blows, if needless and misapplied roughness had not taught them ill-nature, and given them an aversion for their teacher and all that comes from him.

Inadvertency, forgetfulness, unsteadiness, and wandering of thought, are the natural faults of childhood; and therefore, where they are not observed to be wilful, are to be mention'd softly, and gain'd upon by time. If every slip of this kind produces anger and rating, the occasions of rebuke and corrections will return so often, that the tutor will be a constant terror and uneasiness to his pupils. Which one thing is enough to hinder their profiting by his lessons, and to defeat all his methods of instruction.

Let the awe he has got upon their minds be so tempered with the constant marks of tenderness and good will, that affection may spur them to their duty, and make them find a pleasure in complying with his dictates. This will bring them with satisfaction to their tutor; make them hearken to him, as to one who is their friend, that cherishes them, and takes pains for their good: this will keep their thoughts easy and free whilst they are with him, the only temper wherein the mind is capable of receiving new informations, and of admitting into itself those impressions, which, if not taken and retain'd, all that they and their teachers do together is lost labour; there is much uneasiness and little learning.

But under whose care soever a child is put to be taught during the tender and flexible years of his life, this is certain, it should be one who thinks *Latin* and *language* the least part of education; one who knowing how much virtue and a well-temper'd soul is to be preferred to any sort of *learning* or *language,* makes it his chief business to form the mind of his scholars, and give that a right disposition; which if once got, though all the rest should be neglected, would in due time produce all the rest; and which, if it be not got and settled so as to keep out ill and vicious habits, *languages* and *sciences* and all the other accomplishments of education, will be to no purpose but to make the worse or more dangerous man. And indeed whatever stir there is made about getting of *Latin* as the great and difficult business, his mother may teach it him herself, if she will but spend two or three hours in a day with him, and make him read the Evangelists in *Latin* to her: for she need but buy a *Latin* Testament, and having got some body to mark the last syllable but one where it is long in words above two syllables, (which is enough to regulate her pronunciation, and accenting the words) read daily in the *Gospels,* and then let her avoid understanding them in *Latin* if she can. And when she understands the Evangelists in *Latin,* let her, in the same manner, read *Æsop's* Fables, and so proceed on to *Eutropius, Justin,* and other such books. I do not mention this, as an imagination of what I fancy may do, but as of a thing I have known done, and the *Latin* tongue with ease got this way.

But, to return to what I was saying: he that takes on him the charge of bringing up young men, especially young gentlemen, should have something more in him than *Latin*, more than even a knowledge in the liberal sciences: he should be a person of eminent virtue and prudence, and with good sense, have good humour, and the skill to carry himself with gravity, ease and kindness, in a constant conversation with his pupils. But of this I have spoken at large in another place.

At the same time that he is learning *French* and *Latin*, a child, as has been said, may also be enter'd in *Arithmetick, Geography, Chronology, History* and *Geometry* too. For if these be taught him in *French* or *Latin*, when he begins once to understand either of these tongues, he will get a knowledge in these sciences, and the language to boot.

Geography I think should be begun with: for the learning of the figure of the *globe*, the situation and boundaries of the four parts of the world, and that of particular kingdoms and countries, being only an exercise of the eyes and memory, a child with pleasure will learn and retain them. And this is so certain, that I now live in the house with a child whom his mother has so well instructed this way in *geography*, that he knew the limits of the four parts of the world, could readily point, being ask'd, to any country upon the globe, or any county in the map of *England;* knew all the great rivers, promontories, straits and bays in the world, and could find the longitude and latitude of any place, before he was six years old. These things, that he will thus learn by sight, and have by rote in his memory, are not all, I confess, that he is to learn upon the *globes*. But yet it is a good step and preparation to it, and will make the remainder much easier, when his judgment is grown ripe enough for it: besides that, it gets so much time now; and by the pleasure of knowing things, leads him on insensibly to the gaining of languages.

When he has the natural parts of the globe well fix'd in his memory, it may then be time to begin *arithmetick*. By the natural parts of the globe, I mean the several positions of the parts of the earth and sea, under different names and distinctions of countries, not coming yet to those artificial and imaginary lines which have been invented, and are only suppos'd for the better improvement of that science.

Arithmetick is the easiest, and consequently the first sort of abstract reasoning, which the mind commonly bears or accustoms itself to: and is of so general use in all parts of life and business, that scarce any thing is to be done without it. This is certain, a man cannot have too much of it, nor too perfectly: he should therefore begin to be exercis'd in *counting*, as soon, and as far, as he is capable of it; and do something in it every day, till he is master of the art of *numbers*. When he understands *addition* and *subtraction,* he then may be advanced farther in *geography,* after he is acquainted with the *poles zones, parallel circles,* and *meridians,* be taught *longitude and latitude,* and by them be made to understand the use of maps, and by the numbers placed on their sides, to know the respective situation of countries, and how to find them out on the terrestrial globe. Which when he can readily do, he may then be entered in the celestial; and there going over all the circles again, with a more particular observation of the Ecliptick, or Zodiack, to fix them all very clearly and distinctly in his mind, he may be taught the figure and position of the several constellations, which may be shewed him first upon the globe, and then in the heavens.

When that is done, and he knows pretty well the constellations of this our hemisphere, it may be time to give him some notions of this our planetary world; and to that purpose, it may not be amiss to make him a draught of the *Copernican* system, and therein explain to him the situation of the planets, their respective distances from the sun, the centre of their revolutions. This will prepare him to understand the motion and theory of the planets, the most easy and natural way. For since astronomers no longer doubt of the motion of the planets about the sun, it is fit he should proceed upon that hypothesis, which is not only the simplest and least perplexed for a learner, but also the likeliest to be true in itself. But in this, as in all other parts of instruction, great care must be taken with children, to begin with that which is plain and simple, and to teach them as little as can be at once, and settle that well in their heads before you proceed to the next, or any thing new in that science. Give them first one simple idea, and see that they take it right, and perfectly comprehend it before you go any farther, and then add some other simple idea which lies next in your way to what you aim at; and so proceeding by gentle and insensible steps, children without confusion and amazement will have their understandings opened and their thoughts extended farther than could have been expected. And when any one has learn'd any thing himelf, there is no such way to fix it in his memory, and to encourage him to go on, as to set him to teach it others.

When he has once got such an acquaintance with the globes, as is above mentioned, he may be fit to be tried in a little *geometry;* wherein I think the first six books of *Euclid* enough for him to be taught. For I am in some doubt, whether more to a man of business be necessary or useful. At least, if he have a genius and inclination to it, being enter'd so far by his tutor, he will be able to go on of himself without a teacher.

The *globes* therefore must be studied, and that diligently; and I think may be begun betimes, if the tutor will be but careful to distinguish what the child is capable of knowing, and what not; for which this may be a rule that perhaps will go a pretty way, *viz.* that children may be taught anything that falls under their senses, especially their sight, as far as their memories only are exercised: and thus a child very young may learn, which is the *Æquator,* which the *Meridian,* &c. which *Europe,* and which *England,* upon the globes, as soon almost as he knows the rooms of the house he lives in, if care be taken not to teach him too much at once, nor to set him upon a new part, till that which he is upon be perfectly learned and fixed in his memory.

With geography, *chronology* ought to go hand in hand. I mean the general part of it, so that he may have in his mind a view of the whole current of time, and the several considerable *epochs* that are made use of in history. Without these two, history, which is the great mistress of prudence and civil knowledge, and ought to be the proper study of a gentleman, or man of business in the world; without geography and *chronology,* I say, history will be very ill retain'd, and very little useful; but be only a jumble of matters of fact, confusedly heaped together without order or instruction. 'Tis by these two that the actions of mankind are ranked into their proper places of time and countries, under which circumstances they are not only much easier kept in the memory, but in that natural order, are only capable to afford those observations which make a man the better and the abler for reading them.

When I speak of *chronology* as a science he should be perfect in, I do not mean the little controversies that are in it. These are endless, and most of them of so little importance to a gentleman, as not to deserve to be enquir'd into, were they capable of an easy decision. And therefore all that learned noise and dust of the chronologist is wholly to be avoided. The most useful book I have seen in that part of learning, is a small treatise of *Strauchius,* which is printed in twelves, under the title of *Breviarium Chronologicum,* out of which may be selected all that is necessary to be taught a young gentleman concerning *chronology;* for all that is in that treatise a learner need not be cumbred with. He has in him the most remarkable or useful *epochs* reduced all to that of the *Julian Period,* which is the easiest and plainest and surest method that can be made use of in *chronology.* To this treatise of *Strauchius, Helvicus's* tables may be added, as a book to be turned to on all occasions.

As nothing teaches, so nothing delights more than history. The first of these recommends it to the study of grown men, the latter makes me think it the fittest for a young lad, who as soon as he is instructed in chronology, and acquainted with the several *epochs* in use in this part of the world, and can reduce them to the *Julian Period,* should then have some *Latin history* put into his hand. The choice should be directed by the easiness of the stile; for wherever he begins, chronology will keep it from confusion; and the pleasantness of the subject inviting him to read, the language will insensibly be got without that terrible vexation and uneasiness which children suffer where they are put into books beyond their capacity; such as are the *Roman* orators and poets, only to learn the *Roman* language. When he has by reading master'd the easier, such perhaps as *Justin, Eutropius, Quintius Curtius, &c.* the next degree to these will give him no great trouble: and thus by a gradual progress from the plainest and easiest *historians,* he may at last come to read the most difficult and sublime of the *Latin* authors, such as are *Tully, Virgil,* and *Horace.*

The knowledge of *virtue,* all along from the beginning, in all the instances he is capable of, being taught him more by practice than rules; and the love of reputation, instead of satisfying his appetite, being made habitual in him, I know not whether he should read any other discourses of morality but what he finds in the Bible; or have any system of *ethicks* put into his hand till he can read *Tully's Offices* not as a school-boy to learn *Latin,* but as one that would be informed in the principles and precepts of virtue for the conduct of his life.

When he has pretty well digested *Tully's Offices,* and added to it, *Puffendorf de Officio Hominis & Civis,* it may be seasonable to set him upon *Grotius de Jure Belli & Pacis,* or, which perhaps is the better of the two, *Puffendorf de Jure naturali & Gentium;* wherein he will be instructed in the natural rights of men, and the original and foundations of society, and the duties resulting from thence. This *general part of civil-law* and history, are studies which a gentleman should not barely touch at, but constantly dwell upon, and never have done with. A virtuous and well-behaved young man, that is well-versed in the *general part of the civil-law* (which concerns not the chicane of private cases, but the affairs and intercourse of civilized nations in general, grounded upon principles of reason) understands *Latin* well, and can write a good hand, one may turn loose into the world with great assurance that he will find employment and esteem every where.

It would be strange to suppose an *English* gentleman should be ignorant of the *law* of his country. This, whatever station he is in, is so requisite, that from a Justice of the Peace to a Minister of State I know no place he can well fill without it. I do not mean the chicane or wrangling and captious part of the law: a gentleman, whose business is to seek the true measures of right and wrong, and not the arts how to avoid doing the one, and secure himself in doing the other, ought to be as far from such a study of the *law,* as he is concerned diligently to apply himself to that wherein he may be serviceable to his country. And to that purpose, I think the right way for a gentleman to study *our law,* which he does not design for his calling, is to take a view of our *English* constitution and government in the antient books of the *common-law,* and some more modern writers, who out of them have given an account of this government. And having got a true idea of that, then to read our history, and with it join in every king's reign the *laws* then made. This will give an insight into the reason of our *statutes,* and shew the true ground upon which they came to be made, and what weight they ought to have.

Rhetorick and *logick* being the arts that in the ordinary method usually follow immediately after grammar, it may perhaps be wondered that I have said so little of them. The reason is, because of the little advantage young people receive by them: for I have seldom or never observed any one to get the skill of reasoning well, or speaking handsomely, by studying those rules which pretend to reach it: and therefore I would have a young gentleman take a view of them in the shortest systems could be found, without dwelling long on the contemplation and study of those formalities. Right reasoning is founded on something else than the *predicaments* and *predicables,* and does not consist in talking in *mode* and *figure* it self. But 'tis beside my present business to enlarge upon this speculation. To come therefore to what we have in hand; if you would have your son *reason well,* let him read *Chittingworth;* and if you would have him speak well, let him be conversant in *Tully,* to give him the true *idea* of *eloquence;* and let him read those things that are well writ in *English,* to perfect his style in the purity of our language.

If the use and end of right reasoning be to have right notions and a right judgment of things, to distinguish betwixt truth and falsehood, right and wrong, and to act accordingly; be sure not to let your son be bred up in the art and formality of disputing, either practising it himself, or admiring it in others; unless instead of an able man, you desire to have him an insignificant wrangler, opiniator in discourse, and priding himself in contradicting others; or, which is worse, questioning every thing, and thinking there is no such thing as truth to be sought, but only victory, in disputing. There cannot be any thing so disingenuous, so misbecoming a gentleman or any one who pretends to be a rational creature, as not to yield to plain reason and the conviction of clear arguments. Is there any thing more consistent with civil conversation, and the end of all debate, than not to take an answer, though never so full and satisfactory, but still to go on with the dispute as long as equivocal sounds can furnish (a *medius terminus*) a term to wrangle with on the one side, or a distinction on the other; whether pertinent or impertinent, sense or nonsense, agreeing with or contrary to what he had said before, it matters not. For this, in short, is the way and perfection of logical disputes, that the opponent never takes any answer, nor the respondent ever yields to any argument. This neither of them must do, whatever becomes of truth or knowledge, unless he will pass for a poor baffled wretch, and lie under the disgrace of not being able to maintain whatever he has once affirm'd, which is the great aim and glory in disputing. Truth is to be found and supported by a mature and due consideration of things themselves, and not by artificial terms and ways of arguing:

these lead not men so much into the discovery of truth, as into a captious and fallacious use of doubtful words, which is the most useless and most offensive way of talking, and such as least suits a gentleman or a lover of truth of any thing in the world.

There can scarce be a greater defect in a gentleman than not to express himself well either in writing or speaking. But yet I think I may ask my reader, whether he doth not know a great many, who live upon their estates, and so with the name should have the qualities of gentlemen, who cannot so much as tell a story as they should, much less speak clearly and persuasively in any business. This I think not to be so much their fault, as the fault of their education; for I must, without partiality, do my countrymen this right, that where they apply themselves, I see none of their neighbours outgo them. They have been taught *rhetorick,* but yet never taught how to express themselves handsomely with their tongues or pens in the language they are always to use; as if the names of the figures that embellish'd the discourses of those who understood the art of speaking, were the very art and skill of speaking well. This, as all other things of practice, is to be learn'd not by a few or a great many rules given, but by exercise and application according to good rules, or rather patterns, till habits are got, and a facility of doing it well.

Agreeable hereunto, perhaps it might not be amiss to make children, as soon as they are capable of it, often to tell a story of any thing they know; and to correct at first the most remarkable fault they are guilty of in their way of putting it together. When that fault is cured, then to shew them the next, and so on, till one after another, all, at least the gross ones, are mended. When they can tell tales pretty well, then it may be the time to make them write them. The Fables of *Æsop,* the only book almost that I know fit for children, may afford them matter for this exercise of writing *English,* as well as for reading and translating, to enter them in the *Latin* tongue. When they have got past the faults of grammar, and can join in a continued coherent discourse the several parts of a story, without bald and unhandsome forms of transition (as is usual) often repeated, he that desires to perfect them yet farther in this, which is the first step to speaking well and needs no invention, may have recourse to *Tully,* and by putting in practice those rules which that master of eloquence gives in his first book *de inventione,* § 20, make them know wherein the skill and graces of an handsome narrative, according to the several subjects and designs of it, lie. Of each of which rules fit examples may be found out, and therein they may be shewn how others have practised them. The antient classick authors afford plenty of such examples, which they should be made not only to translate, but have set before them as patterns for their daily imitation.

When they understand how to write *English* with due connexion, propriety and order, and are pretty well masters of a tolerable narrative style, they may be advanced to writing of letters; wherein they should not be put upon any strains of wit or compliment, but taught to express their own plain easy sense, without any incoherence, confusion or roughness. And when they are perfect in this, they may, to raise their thoughts, have set before them the examples of *Voitures,* for the entertainment of their friends at a distance, with letters of compliment, mirth, raillery or diversion; and *Tully's Epistles,* as the best pattern whether for business or conversation. The writing of letters has so much to do in all the occurrences of human life, that no gentleman can avoid shewing himself in this kind of writing. Occasions will daily force him to make this use of his pen, which, besides the consequences that, in his affairs, his well or ill managing of it often draws after it, always lays him open to a severer examination of his breeding, sense, and abilities, than oral discourses; whose transient faults dying for the most part with the sound that gives them life, and so not subject to a strict review, more easily escape observation and censure.

Had the methods of education been directed to their right end, one would have thought this so necessary a part could not have been neglected whilst themes and verses in *Latin,* of no use at all, were so constantly every where pressed, to the racking of children's inventions beyond their strength and hindering their chearful progress in learning the tongues by unnatural difficulties. But custom has so ordain'd it, and who dares disobey? And would it not be very unreasonable to require of a learned country school-master (who has all the tropes and figures in *Farnaby's Rhetorick* at his fingers' ends) to teach his scholar to express himself handsomely in *English,* when it appears to be so little his business or thought, that the boy's mother (despised, 'tis like, as illiterate for not having read a system of *logick* and *rhetorick*) outdoes him in it?

To write and speak correctly gives a grace and gains a favourable attention to what one has to say: and since 'tis *English* that an *English* gentleman will have constant use of, that is the language he should chiefly cultivate, and wherein most care should be taken to polish and perfect his style. To speak or write better *Latin* than *English,* may make a man be talk'd of, but he would find it more to his purpose to express himself well in his own tongue, that he uses every moment, than to have the vain commendation of others for a very insignificant quality. This I find universally neglected, and no care taken any where to improve young men in their own language, that they may thoroughly understand and be masters of it. If any one among us have a facility or purity more than ordinary in his mother tongue, it is owing to chance, or his genius, or any thing rather than to his education or any care of his teacher. To mind what *English* his pupil speaks or writes, is below the dignity of one bred up amongst *Greek* and *Latin,* though he have but little of them himself. These are the learned languages fit only for learned men to meddle with and teach; *English* is the language of the illiterate vulgar: tho' yet we see the polity of some of our neighbours hath not thought it beneath the publick care to promote and reward the improvement of their own language. Polishing and enriching their tongue is no small business amongst them; it hath colleges and stipends appointed it, and there is raised amongst them a great ambition and emulation of writing correctly: and we see what they are come to by it, and how far they have spread one of the worst languages possibly in this part of the world, if we look upon it as it was in some few reigns backwards, whatever it be now. The great men among the *Romans* were daily exercising themselves in their own language; and we find yet upon record the names of orators, who taught some of their emperors *Latin,* though it was their mother tongue.

'Tis plain the *Greeks* were yet more nice in theirs. All other speech was barbarous to them but their own, and no foreign language appears to have been studied or valued amongst that learned and acute people; tho' it be past doubt that they borrowed their learning and philosophy from abroad.

I am not here speaking against *Greek* and *Latin;* I think they ought to be studied, and the *Latin* at least understood well by every gentleman. But whatever foreign languages a young man meddles with (and the more he knows the better) that which he should critically study, and labour to get a facility, clearness and elegancy to express himself in, should be his own; and to this purpose he should daily be exercised in it.

Natural philosophy, as a speculative science, I imagine we have none, and perhaps I may think I have reason to say we never shall be able to make a science of it. The works of nature are contrived by a wisdom, and operate by ways too far surpassing our faculties to discover or capacities to conceive, for us ever to be able to reduce them into a science. *Natural philosophy* being the knowledge of the principles, properties and operations of things as they are in themselves, I imagine there are two parts of it, one comprehending *spirits,* with their nature and qualities, and the other *bodies.* The first of these is usually referred to *metaphysicks:* but under what title soever the consideration of *spirits* comes, I think it ought to go before the study of matter and body, not as a science that can be methodized into a system, and treated of upon principles of knowledge; but as an enlargement of our minds towards a truer and fuller comprehension of the intellectual world to which we are led both by reason and revelation. And since the clearest and largest discoveries we have of other *spirits,* besides God and our own souls, is imparted to us from heaven by revelation, I think the information that at least young people should have of them, should be taken from that revelation. To this purpose, I conclude, it would be well, if there were made a good history of the Bible, for young people to read; wherein if every thing that is fit to be put into it, were laid down in its due order of time, and several things omitted which are suited only to riper age, that confusion which is usually produced by promiscuous reading of the Scripture, as it lies now bound up in our Bibles, would be avoided. And also this other good obtained, that by reading of it constantly, there would be instilled into the minds of children a notion and belief of *spirits*, they having so much to do in all the transactions of that history, which will be a good preparation to the study of *bodies*. For without the notion and allowance of *spirit*, our philosophy will be lame and defective in one main part of it, when it leaves out the contemplation of the most excellent and powerful part of the creation.

Of this *History of the Bible*, I think too it would be well if there were a short and plain epitome made, containing the chief and most material heads, for children to be conversant in as soon as they can read. This, though it will lead them early into some notion of *spirits*, yet it is not contrary to what I said above, that I would not have children troubled, whilst young, with notions of *spirits*; whereby my meaning was, that I think it inconvenient that their yet tender minds should receive early impressions of *goblins*, *spectres*, and *apparitions*, wherewith their maids and those about them are apt to fright them into a compliance with their orders, which often proves a great inconvenience to them all their lives after, by subjecting their minds to frights, fearful apprehensions, weakness and superstition; which when coming abroad into the world and conversation they grow weary and ashamed of, it not seldom happens, that to make, as they think, a thorough cure, and ease themselves of a load which has sat so heavy on them, they throw away the thoughts of all *spirits* together, and so run into the other, but worse, extream.

These are my present thoughts concerning *learning* and *accomplishments*. The great business of all is virtue and *wisdom*:

Nullum numen abest si sit Prudentia.

Teach him to get a mastery over his inclinations, and *submit his appetite to reason*. This being obtained, and by constant practice settled into habit, the hardest part of the task is over. To bring a young man to this, I know nothing which so much contributes as the love of praise and commendation, which should therefore be instilled into him by all arts imaginable. Make his mind as sensible of credit and shame as may be; and when you have done that, you have put a principle into him, which will influence his actions when you are not by, to which the fear of a little smart of a rod is not comparable, and which will be the proper stock whereon afterwards to graff the true principles of morality and religion.

I have one thing more to add, which as soon as I mention I shall run the danger of being suspected to have forgot what I am about, and what

I have above written concerning education all tending towards a gentleman's calling, with which a trade seems wholly inconsistent. And yet I cannot forbear to say, I would have him *learn a trade, a manual trade;* nay two or three, but one more particularly.

The busy inclination of children being always to be directed to something that may be useful to them, the advantages proposed from what they are set about may be considered of two kinds: 1. Where the skill itself that is got by exercise is worth the having. Thus skill not only in languages and learned sciences, but in painting, turning, gardening, tempering and working in iron, and all other useful arts is worth the having. 2. Where the exercise itself, without any consideration, is necessary or useful for health. Knowledge in some things is so necessary to be got by children whilst they are young, that some part of their time is to be allotted to their improvement in them, though those employments contribute nothing at all to their health. Such are reading and writing and all other sedentary studies for the cultivating of the mind, which unavoidably take up a great part of a gentleman's time, quite from their cradles. *Other manual arts,* which are both got and exercised by labour, do many of them by that exercise not only increase our dexterity and skill, but contribute to our health too, especially such as employ us in the open air. In these, then, health and improvement may be join'd together; and of these should some fit ones be chosen, to be made the recreations of one whose chief business is with books and study. In this choice the age and inclination of the person is to be considered, and constraint always to be avoided in bringing him to it. For command and force may often create, but can never cure, an aversion: and whatever any one is brought to by compulsion, he will leave as soon as he can, and be little profited and less recreated by, whilst he is at it.

Emile
(1762)

Jean Jacques Rousseau (1712–1778)

Note: *While Locke assumes that between Nature and the student there is no other mediation than discipline, Rousseau attacks this position by establishing* society *as mediating between Nature and the student. The student is not guilty, as Locke presumed, but innocent, for only society is guilty.*

Furthermore, Rousseau assumes that individuals can be found or imagined in isolation from society. His "noble savage" is such an isolated and innocent individual, and this belief is still present in much of our American habitual way of seeing ourselves.

Translation by Barbara Foxley

BOOK II

With our foolish and pedantic methods we are always preventing children from learning what they could learn much better by themselves, while we neglect what we alone can teach them. Can anything be sillier than the pains taken to teach them to walk, as if there were anyone who was unable to walk when he grows up through his nurse's neglect? How many we see walking badly all their life because they were ill taught?

As their strength increases, children have also less need for tears. They can do more for themselves, they need the help of others less frequently. With strength comes the sense to use it. It is with this second phase that the real personal life has its beginning; it is then that the child becomes conscious of himself. During every moment of his life memory calls up the feeling of self; he becomes really one person, always the same, and therefore capable of joy or sorrow. Hence we must begin to consider him as a moral being.

Men, be kind to your fellow-men; this is your first duty, kind to every age and station, kind to all that is not foreign to humanity. What wisdom can you find that is greater than kindness? Love childhood, indulge its sports, its pleasures, its delightful instincts. Who has not sometimes regretted that age when laughter was ever on the lips, and when the heart was ever at peace? Why rob these innocents of the joys which pass so quickly, of that precious gift which they cannot abuse? Why fill with bitterness the fleeting days of early childhood, days which will no more return for them than for you? Fathers, can you tell when death will call your children to him? Do not lay up sorrow for yourselves by robbing them of the short span which nature has allotted to them. As soon as they are aware of the joy of life, let them rejoice in it, so that whenever God calls them they may not die without having tasted the joy of life.

How people will cry out against you! I hear from afar the shouts of that false wisdom which is ever dragging us onwards, counting the present as nothing, and pursuing without a pause a future which flies as we pursue, that false wisdom which removes us from our place and never brings us to any other.

Now is the time, you say, to correct his evil tendencies; we must increase suffering in childhood, when it is less keenly felt, to lessen it in manhood. But how do you know that you can carry out all these fine schemes; how do you know that all this fine teaching with which you overwhelm the feeble mind of the child will not do him more harm than good in the future? How do you know that you can spare him anything by the vexations you heap upon him now? Why inflict on him more ills than befit his present condition unless you are quite sure that these present ills will save him future ill? And what proof can you give me that those evil tendencies you profess to cure are not the result of your foolish precautions rather than of nature? What a poor sort of foresight, to make a child wretched in the present with the more or less doubtful hope of making him happy at some future day. If such blundering thinkers fail to distinguish between liberty and licence, between a merry child and a spoilt darling, let them learn to discriminate.

Let us not forget what befits our present state in the pursuit of vain fancies. Mankind has its place in the sequence of things; childhood has its place in the sequence of human life; the man must be treated as a man and the child as a child. Give each his place, and keep him there. Control human passions according to man's nature; that is all we can do for his welfare. The rest depends on external forces, which are beyond our control.

Absolute good and evil are unknown to us. In this life they are blended together; we never enjoy any perfectly pure feeling, nor do we remain for more than a moment in the same state. The feelings of our minds, like the changes in our bodies, are in a continual flux. Good and ill are common to all, but in varying proportions. The happiest is he who suffers least; the most miserable is he who enjoys least. Ever more sorrow than joy—this is the lot of all of us. Man's happiness in this world is but a negative state; it must be reckoned by the fewness of his ills.

Every feeling of hardship is inseparable from the desire to escape from it; every idea of pleasure from the desire to enjoy it. All desire implies a want, and all wants are painful; hence our wretchedness consists in the disproportion between our desires and our powers. A conscious being whose powers were equal to his desires would be perfectly happy.

What then is human wisdom? Where is the path of true happiness? The mere limitation of our desires is not enough, for if they were less than our powers, part of our faculties would be idle, and we should not enjoy our whole being; neither is the mere extension of our powers enough, for if our desires were also increased we should only be more miserable. True happiness consists in decreasing the difference between our desires and our powers, in establishing perfect equilibrium between the power and the will. Then only, when all its forces are employed, will the soul be at rest and man will find himself in his true position.

There is only one man who gets his own way—he who can get it single-handed; therefore freedom, not power, is the greatest good. That man is truly free who desires what he is able to perform, and does what he desires. This is my fundamental maxim. Apply it to childhood, and all the rules of education spring from it.

There are two kinds of dependence: dependence on things, which is the work of nature; and dependence on men, which is the work of society. Dependence on things, being non-moral, does no injury to liberty and begets no vices; dependence on men, being out of order, gives rise to every kind of vice, and through this master and slave become mutually depraved. If there is any cure for this social evil, it is to be found in the substitution of law for the individual; in arming the general will with a real strength beyond the power of any individual will. If the laws of nations, like the laws of nature, could never be broken by any human power, dependence on men would become dependence on things; all the advantages of a state of nature would be combined with all the advantages of social life in the commonwealth. The liberty which preserves a man from vice would be united with the morality which raises him to virtue.

Keep the child dependent on things only. By this course of education you will have followed the order of nature. Let his unreasonable wishes meet with physical obstacles only, or the punishment which results from his own actions, lessons which will be recalled when the same circumstances occur again. It is enough to prevent him from wrong doing without forbidding him to do wrong. Experience or lack of power should take the place of law. Give him, not what he wants, but what he needs. Let there be no question of obedience for him or tyranny for you. Supply the strength he lacks just so far as is required for freedom, not for power, so that he may receive your services with a sort of shame, and look forward to the time when he may dispense with them and may achieve the honour of self-help.

Nature provides for the child's growth in her own fashion, and this should never be thwarted. Do not make him sit still when he wants to run about, nor run when he wants to be quiet. If we did not spoil our children's wills by our blunders their desires would be free from caprice. Let them run, jump, and shout to their heart's content. All their own activities are instincts of the body for its growth in strength; but you should regard with suspicion those wishes which they cannot carry out for themselves, those which others must carry out for them. Then you must distinguish carefully between natural and artificial needs, between the needs of budding caprice and the needs which spring from the overflowing life just described.

There is such a thing as excessive severity as well as excessive indulgence, and both alike should be avoided. If you let children suffer you risk their health and life; you make them miserable now; if you take too much pains to spare them every kind of uneasiness you are laying up much misery for them in the future; you are making them delicate and over-sensitive; you are taking them out of their place among men, a place to which they must sooner or later return, in spite of all your pains. You will say I am falling into the same mistake as those bad fathers whom I blamed for sacrificing the present happiness of their children to a future which may never be theirs.

Not so; for the liberty I give my pupil makes up for the slight hardships to which he is exposed. I see little fellows playing in the snow, stiff and blue with cold, scarcely able to stir a finger. They could go and warm themselves if they chose, but they do not choose; if you forced them to come in they would feel the harshness of constraint a hundred-fold more than the sharpness of the cold. Then what becomes of your grievance? Shall I make your child miserable by exposing him to hardships which he is perfectly ready to endure? I secure his present good by leaving him his freedom, and his future good by arming him against the evils he will have to bear. If he had his choice, would he hesitate for a moment between you and me?

Do you think any man can find true happiness elsewhere than in his natural state; and when you try to spare him all suffering, are you not taking him out of his natural state? Indeed I maintain that to enjoy great happiness he must experience slight ills; such is his nature. Too much bodily prosperity corrupts the morals. A man who knew nothing of suffering would be incapable of tenderness towards his fellow-creatures and ignorant of the joys of pity; he would be hardhearted, unsocial, a very monster among men.

Do you know the surest way to make your child miserable? Let him have everything he wants; for as his wants increase in proportion to the ease with which they are satisfied, you will be compelled, sooner or later, to refuse his demands, and this unlooked-for refusal will hurt him more than the lack of what he wants. He will want your stick first, then your watch, the bird that flies, or the star that shines above him. He will want all he sets eyes on, and unless you were God himself, how could you satisfy him?

Man naturally considers all that he can get as his own. In this sense Hobbes's theory is true to a certain extent: multiply both our wishes and the means of satisfying them, and each will be master of all. Thus the child, who has only to ask and have, thinks himself the master of the universe; he considers all men as his slaves; and when you are at last compelled to refuse, he takes your refusal as an act of rebellion, for he thinks he has only to command. All the reasons you give him, while he is still too young to reason, are so many pretences in his eyes; they seem to him only unkindness; the sense of injustice embitters his disposition; he hates every one. Though he has never felt grateful for kindness, he resents all opposition.

How should I suppose that such a child can ever be happy? He is the slave of anger, a prey to the fiercest passions. Happy! He is a tyrant, at once the basest of slaves and the most wretched of creatures. I have known children brought up like this who expected you to knock the house down, to give them the weather cock on the steeple, to stop a regiment on the march so that they might listen to the band; when they could not get their way they screamed and cried and would pay no attention to any one. In vain everybody strove to please them; as their desires were stimulated by the ease with which they got their own way, they set their hearts on impossibilities, and found themselves face to face with opposition and difficulty, pain and grief. Scolding, sulking, or in a rage, they wept and cried all day. Were they really so greatly favoured? Weakness, combined with love of power, produces nothing but folly and suffering. One spoilt child beats the table; another whips the sea. They may beat and whip long enough before they find contentment.

Let us come back to the primitive law. Nature has made children helpless and in need of affection; did she make them to be obeyed and feared? Has she given them an imposing manner, a stern eye, a loud and threatening voice with which to make themselves feared? I understand how the roaring of the lion strikes terror into the other beasts, so that they tremble when they behold his terrible mane, but of all unseemly, hateful, and ridiculous sights, was there ever anything like a body of statesmen in their robes of office with their chief at their head bowing down before a swaddled babe, addressing him in pompous phrases, while he cries and slavers in reply?

On the other hand, do you not see how children are fettered by the weakness of infancy? Do you not see how cruel it is to increase this servitude by obedience to our caprices, by depriving them of such liberty as they have, a liberty which they can scarcely abuse, a liberty the loss of which will do so little good to them or us. If there is nothing more ridiculous than a haughty child, there is nothing tht claims our pity like a timid child. With the age of reason the child becomes the slave of the community; then why forestall this by slavery in the home? Let this brief hour of life be free from a yoke which nature has not laid upon it; leave the child the use of his natural liberty, which for a time at least, secures him from the vices of the slave. Bring me those harsh masters, and those fathers who are the slaves of their children, bring them both with their frivolous objections, and before they boast of their own methods let them for once learn the method of nature.

I return to practical matters. I have already said your child must not get what he asks, but what he needs; he must never act from obedience, but from necessity.

The very words *obey* and *command* will be excluded from his vocabulary, still more those of *duty* and *obligation;* but the words strength, necessity, weakness, and constraint must have a large place in it. Before the age of reason it is impossible to form any idea of moral beings or social relations; so avoid, as far as may be, the use of words which express these ideas, lest the child at an early age should attach wrong ideas to them, ideas which you cannot or will not destroy when he is older. The first mistaken idea he gets into his head is the germ of error and vice; it is the first step that needs watching. Act in such a way that while he only notices external objects his ideas are confined to sensations; let him only see the physical world around him. If not, you may be sure that either he will pay no heed to you at all, or he will form fantastic ideas of the moral world of which you prate, ideas which you will never efface as long as he lives.

"Reason with children" was Locke's chief maxim; it is in the height of fashion at present, and I hardly think it is justified by its results; those children who have been constantly reasoned with strike me as exceedingly silly. Of all man's faculties, reason, which is, so to speak, compounded of all the rest, is the last and choicest growth, and it is this you would use for the child's early training. To make a man reasonable is the coping stone of a good education, and yet you profess to train a child through his reason! You begin at the wrong end, you make the end the means. If children understood reason they would not need education, but by talking to them from their earliest age in a language they do not understand you accustom them to be satisfied with words, to question all that is said to them, to think themselves as wise as their teachers; you train them to be argumentative and rebellious; and whatever you think you gain from motives of reason, you really gain from greediness, fear, or vanity with which you are obliged to reinforce your reasoning.

Most of the moral lessons which are and can be given to children may be reduced to this formula:

Master: You must not do that.
Child: Why not?
Master: Because it is wrong.
Child: Wrong! What is wrong?
Master: What is forbidden you.
Child: Why is it wrong to do what is forbidden?
Master: You will be punished for disobedience.
Child: I will do it when no one is looking.
Master: We shall watch you.
Child: I will hide.
Master: We shall ask you what you were doing.
Child: I shall tell a lie.
Master: You must not tell lies.
Child: Why must not I tell lies?
Master: Because it is wrong, etc.

That is the inevitable circle. Go beyond it, and the child will not understand you. What sort of use is there in such teaching? I should greatly like to know what you would substitute for this dialogue. It would have puzzled Locke himself. It is no part of a child's business to know right and wrong, to perceive the reason for a man's duties.

Nature would have them children before they are men. If we try to invert this order we shall produce a forced fruit immature and flavorless, fruit which will be rotten before it is ripe; we shall have young doctors and old children. Childhood has its own ways of seeing, thinking, and feeling; nothing is more foolish than to try and substitute our ways; and I should no more expect judgment in a ten-year-old child than I should expect him to be five feet high. Indeed, what use would reason be to him at that age? It is the curb of strength, and the child does not need the curb.

Treat your scholar according to his age. Put him in his place from the first, and keep him in it, so that he no longer tries to leave it. Then before he knows what goodness is, he will be practicing its chief lesson. Give him no orders at all, absolutely none. Do not even let him think that you claim any authority over him. Let him only know that he is weak and you are strong, that his condition and yours puts him at your mercy; let this be perceived, learned and felt. Let him early find upon his proud neck, the heavy yoke which nature has imposed upon us, the heavy yoke of necessity, under which every finite being must bow. Let him find this necessity in things, not in the caprices of man; let the curb be force, not authority. If there is something he should not do, do not forbid him, but prevent him without explanation or reasoning; what you give him, give it at his first word without prayers or entreaties, above all without conditions. Give willingly, refuse unwillingly, but let your refusal be irrevocable; let no entreaties move you; let your "No," once uttered, be a wall of brass, against which the child may exhaust his strength some five or six times, but in the end he will try no more to overthrow it.

It is very strange that ever since people began to think about education they should have hit upon no other way of guiding children than emulation, jealousy, envy, vanity, greediness, base cowardice, all the most dangerous passions, passions ever ready to ferment, ever prepared to corrupt the soul even before the body is full-grown. With every piece of precocious instruction which you try to force into their minds you plant a vice in the depths of their hearts; foolish teachers think they are doing wonders when they are making their scholars wicked in order to teach them what goodness is, and then they tell us seriously, "Such is man." Yes, such is man, as you have made him. Every means has been tried except one, the very one which might succeed—well-regulated liberty.

Give your scholar no verbal lessons; he should be taught by experience alone; never punish him, for he does not know what it is to do wrong; never make him say, "Forgive me," for he does not know how to do you wrong. Wholly unmoral in his actions, he can do nothing morally wrong, and he deserves neither punishment nor reproof.

Let us lay it down as an incontrovertible rule that the first impulses of nature are always right; there is no original sin in the human heart, the how and why of the entrance of every vice can be traced. The only natural passion is self-love or selfishness taken in a wider sense. This selfishness is good in itself and in relation to ourselves; and as the child has no necessary relations to other people he is naturally indifferent to them; his self-love only becomes good or bad by the use made of it and the relations established by its means. Until the time is ripe for the appearance of reason, that guide of selfishness, the main thing is that the child shall do nothing because you are watching him or listening to him; in a word, nothing because of other people, but only what nature asks of him; then he will never do wrong.

I do not mean to say that he will never do any mischief, never hurt himself, never break a costly ornament if you leave it within his reach. He might do much damage without doing wrong, since wrong-doing depends on the harmful intention which will never be his. If once he meant to do harm, his whole education would be ruined; he would be almost hopelessly bad.

But if, in spite of your precautions, the child contrives to do some damage, if he breaks some useful article, do not punish him for your carelessness, do not even scold him; let him hear no word of reproval, do not even let him see that he has vexed you; behave just as if the thing had come to pieces of itself; you may consider you have done great things if you have managed to hold your tongue.

May I venture at this point to state the greatest, the most important, the most useful rule of education? It is: Do not save time, but lose it. I hope that every day readers will excuse my paradoxes; you cannot avoid paradox if you think for yourself, and whatever you may say I would rather fall into paradox than into prejudice. The most dangerous period in human life lies between birth and the age of twelve. It is the time when errors and vices spring up, while as yet there is no means to destroy them; when the means of destruction are ready, the roots have gone too deep to be pulled up. If the infant sprang at one bound from its mother's breast to the age of reason, the present type of education would be quite suitable, but its natural growth calls for quite a different training. The mind should be left undisturbed till its faculties have developed; for while it is blind it cannot see the torch you offer it, nor can it follow through the vast expanse of ideas a path so faintly traced by reason that the best eyes can scarcely follow it.

Therefore the education of the earliest years should be merely negative. It consists, not in teaching virtue or truth, but in preserving the heart from vice and from the spirit of error. If only you could let well alone, and get others to follow your example; if you could bring your scholar to the age of twelve strong and healthy, but unable to tell his right hand from his left, the eyes of his understanding would be open to reason as soon as you began to teach him. Free from prejudices and free from habits, there would be nothing in him to counteract the effects of your labours. In your hands he would soon become the wisest of men; by doing nothing to begin with, you would end with a prodigy of education.

Reverse the usual practice and you will almost always do right. Fathers and teachers who want to make the child, not a child but a man of learning, think it never too soon to scold, correct, reprove, threaten, bribe, teach, and reason. Do better than they; be reasonable, and do not reason with your pupil, more especially do not try to make him approve what he dislikes; for if reason is always connected with disagreeable matters, you make it distasteful to him, you discredit it at an early age in a mind not yet ready to understand it. Exercise his body, his limbs, his senses, his strength, but keep his mind idle as long as you can. Distrust all opinions which appear before the judgment to discriminate between them. Restrain and ward off strange impressions; and to prevent the birth of evil do not hasten to do well for goodness is only possible when enlightened by reason. Regard all delays as so much time gained; you have achieved much, you approach the boundary without loss. Leave childhood to ripen in your children. In a word, beware of giving anything they need today if it can be deferred without danger to tomorrow.

There is another point to be considered which confirms the suitability of this method: it is the child's individual bent, which must be thoroughly known before we can choose the fittest moral training. Every mind has its own form, in accordance with which it must be controlled; and the success of the pains taken depends largely on the fact that he is controlled in this way and no other. Oh, wise men, take time to observe nature; watch your scholar well before you say a word to him; first leave the germ of his character free to show itself, do not constrain him in anything, the better to see him as he really is. Do you think this time of liberty is wasted? On the contrary, your scholar will be the better employed, for this is the way you yourself will learn not to lose a single moment when time is of more value. If, however, you begin to act before you know what to do, you act at random; you may make mistakes, and must retrace your steps; your haste to reach your goal will only take you further from it. Do not imitate the miser who loses much lest he should lose a little. Sacrifice a little time in early childhood, and it will be repaid you with usury when your scholar is older.

Remember you must be a man yourself before you try to train a man; you yourself must set the pattern he shall copy. While the child is still unconscious there is time to prepare his surroundings, so that nothing shall strike his eye but what is fit for his sight. Gain the respect of every one, begin to win their hearts, so that they may try to please you. You will not be master of the child if you cannot control everyone about him; and this authority will never suffice unless it rests upon respect for your goodness. There is no question of squandering one's means and giving money right and left; I never knew money to win love. You must neither be harsh nor niggardly, nor must you merely pity misery when you can relieve it; but in vain will you open your purse if you do not open your heart along with it, the hearts of others will always be closed to you. You must give your own time, attention, affection, your very self; for whatever you do, people always perceive that your money is not you.

In the village a tutor will have much more control over the things he wishes to show the child; his reputation, his words, his example, will have a weight they would never have in the town; he is of use to everyone, so everyone is eager to oblige him, to win his esteem, to appear before the disciple what the master would have him be; if vice is not corrected, public scandal is at least avoided, which is all that our present purpose requires.

Zealous teachers, be simple, sensible, and reticent; be in no hurry to act unless to prevent the actions of others. Again and again I say, reject, if it may be, a good lesson for fear of giving a bad one. Beware of playing the tempter in this world, which nature intended as an earthly paradise for men, and do not attempt to give the innocent child the knowledge of good and evil; since you cannot prevent the child learning by what he sees outside himself, restrict your own efforts to impressing those examples on his mind in the form best suited for him.

The explosive passions produce a great effect upon the child when he sees them; their outward expression is very marked; he is struck by this and his attention is arrested. Anger especially is so noisy in its rage that it is impossible not to perceive it if you are within reach. You need not ask yourself whether this is an opportunity for a pedagogue to frame a fine disquisition. What! No fine disquisition, nothing, not a word! Let the child come to you; impressed by what he has seen, he will not fail to ask you questions. The answer is easy; it is drawn from the very things which have appealed to his senses. He sees a flushed face, flashing eyes, threatening gestures, he hears cries; everything shows that the body is ill at ease. Tell him plainly, without affectation or mystery, "This poor man is ill, he is in a fever." You may take the opportunity of giving him in a few words some idea of disease and its effects; for that too belongs to nature, and is one of the bonds of necessity which he must recognize. By means of this idea, which is not false in itself, may he not early acquire a certain aversion to giving way to excessive passions, which he regards as diseases; and do you not think that such a notion, given at the right moment, will produce a more wholesome effect than the most tedious sermon? But consider the aftereffects of this idea; you have authority, if ever you find it necessary to treat the rebellious child as a sick child; to keep him in his room, in bed if need be, to diet him, to make him afraid of his growing vices, to make him hate and dread them without ever regarding as a punishment the strict measures you will perhaps have to use for his recovery. If it happens that you yourself in a moment's heat depart from the calm and self-control which you should aim at, do not try to conceal your fault, but tell him frankly, with a gentle reproach, "My dear, you have hurt me."

I do not propose to enter into every detail, but only to explain general rules and to give illustrations in cases of difficulty. I think it is impossible to train a child up to the age of twelve in the midst of society, without giving him some idea of the relations between one man and another, and of the morality of human actions. It is enough to delay the development of these ideas as long as possible, and when they can no longer be avoided to limit them to present needs, so that he may neither think himself master of everything nor do harm to others without knowing or caring. There are calm and gentle characters which can be led a long way in their first innocence without any danger; but there are also stormy dispositions whose passions develop early; you must hasten to make men of them lest you should have to keep them in chains.

Our first duties are to ourselves; our first feelings are centered on self; all our instincts are at first directed to our own preservation and our own welfare. Thus the first notion of justice springs not from what we owe to others, but from what is due to us. Here is another error in popular methods of education. If you talk to children of their duties, and not of their rights, you are beginning at the wrong end, and telling them what they cannot understand, what cannot be of any interest to them.

Your ill-tempered child destroys everything he touches. Do not vex yourself; put anything he can spoil out of his reach. He breaks the things he is using; do not be in a hurry to give him more; let him feel the want of them. He breaks the windows of his room; let the wind blow upon him night and day, and do not be afraid of his catching cold; it is better to catch cold than to be reckless.

I have already said enough to show that children should never receive punishment merely as such; it should always come as the natural consequence of their fault. Thus you will not exclaim against their falsehood, you will not exactly punish them for lying, but you will arrange that all the ill effects of lying, such as not being believed when we speak the truth, or being accused of what we have not done in spite of our protests, shall fall on their heads when they have told a lie. But let us explain what lying means to the child.

There are two kinds of lies: one concerns an accomplished fact, the other concerns a future duty. The first occurs when we falsely deny or assert that we did or did not do something, or to put it in general terms, when we knowingly say what is contrary to facts. The other occurs when we promise what we do not mean to perform, or in general terms, when we profess an intention which we do not really mean to carry out. These two kinds of lie are sometimes found in combination, but their differences are my present business.

He who feels the need of help from others, he who is constantly experiencing their kindness, has nothing to gain by deceiving them; it is plainly to his advantage that they should see things as they are, lest they should mistake his interests. It is therefore plain that lying with regard to actual facts is not natural to children, but lying is made necessary by the law of obedience; since obedience is disagreeable, children disobey as far as they can in secret, and the present good of avoiding punishment or reproof outweighs the remoter good of speaking the truth. Under a free and natural education why should your child lie? What has he to conceal from you? You do not thwart him, you do not punish him, you demand nothing from him. Why should he not tell everything to you as simply as to his playmate? He cannot see anything more risky in the one course than in the other.

The lie concerning duty is even less natural, since promises to do or refrain from doing are conventional agreements which are outside the state of nature and detract from our liberty. Moreover, all promises made by children are in themselves void; when they pledge themselves they do not know what they are doing, for their narrow vision cannot look beyond the present. A child can hardly lie when he makes a promise; for he is only thinking how he can get out of the present difficulty, any means which has not an immediate result is the same to him; when he promises for the future he promises nothing, and his imagination is as yet incapable of projecting him into the future while he lives in the present. If he could escape a whipping or get a packet of sweets by promising to throw himself out of the window tomorrow, he would promise on the spot. This is why the law disregards all promises made by minors, and when fathers and teachers are stricter and demand that promises shall be kept, it is only when the promise refers to something the child ought to do even if he had made no promise.

The child cannot lie when he makes a promise, for he does not know what he is doing when he makes his promise. The case is different when he breaks his promise, which is a sort of retrospective falsehood; for he clearly remembers making the promise, but he fails to see the importance of keeping it. Unable to look into the future, he cannot foresee the results of things, and when he breaks his promises he does nothing contrary to his stage of reasoning.

Children's lies are therefore entirely the work of their teachers, and to teach them to speak the truth is nothing less than to teach them the art of lying. In your zeal to rule, control, and teach them, you never find sufficient means at your disposal. You wish to gain fresh influence over their minds by baseless maxims, by unreasonable precepts; and you would rather they knew their lessons and told lies, than leave them ignorant and truthful.

We, who only give our scholars lessons in practice, who prefer to have them good rather than clever, never demand the truth lest they should conceal it, and never claim any promise lest they should be tempted to break it. If some mischief has been done in my absence and I do not know who did it, I shall take care not to accuse Emile, nor to say, "Did you do it?" For in so doing what should I do but teach him to deny it? If his difficult temperament compels me to make some agreement with him, I will take good care that the suggestion always comes from him, never from me; that when he undertakes anything he has always a present and effective interest in fulfilling his promise, and if he ever fails this lie will bring down on him all the unpleasant consequences which he sees arising from the natural order of things, and not from his tutor's vengeance.

The detailed treatment I have just given to lying may be applied in many respects to all the other duties imposed upon children, whereby these duties are made not only hateful but impracticable. For the sake of a show of preaching virtue you make them love every vice; you instill these vices by forbidding them. Would you have them pious, you take them to church till they are sick of it; you teach them to gabble prayers until they long for the happy time when they will not have to pray to God. To teach them charity you make them give alms as if you scorned to give yourself. It is not the child, but the master, who should give; however much he loves his pupil he should vie with him for this honour; he should make him think that he is too young to deserve it. Alms giving is the deed of a man who can measure the worth of his gift and the needs of his fellow men. The child, who knows nothing of these, can have no merit in giving; he gives without charity, without kindness; he is almost ashamed to give, for, to judge by your practice and his own, he thinks it is only children who give, and that there is no need for charity when we are grown up.

Silly children grow into ordinary men. I know no generalization more certain than this. It is the most difficult thing in the world to distinguish between genuine stupidity, and that apparent and deceitful stupidity which is the sign of a strong character. At first sight it seems strange that the two extremes should have the same outward signs; and yet it may well be so, for at an age when man has yet no true ideas, the whole difference between the genius and the rest consists in this: the latter only take in false ideas, while the former, finding nothing but false ideas, receives no ideas at all. In this he resembles the fool; the one is fit for nothing, the other finds nothing fit for him. The only way of distinguishing between them depends upon chance, which may offer the genius some idea which he can understand, while the fool is always the same.

Hold childhood in reverence, and do not be in any hurry to judge it for good or ill. Leave exceptional cases to show themselves, let their qualities be tested and confirmed, before special methods are adopted. Give nature time to work before you take over her business, lest you interfere with her dealings. You assert that you know the value of time and are afraid to waste it. You fail to perceive that it is a greater waste of time to use it ill than to do nothing, and that a child ill taught is further from virtue than a child who has learnt nothing at all. You are afraid to see him spending his early years doing nothing. What! Is it nothing to be happy, nothing to run and jump all day? He will never be so busy again all his life long. Plato, in his *Republic*, which is considered so stern, teaches the children only through festivals, games, songs, and amusements. It seems as if he had accomplished his purpose when he had taught them to be happy; and Seneca, speaking of the Roman lads in olden days, says, "They were always on their feet, they were never taught anything which kept them sitting." Were they any the worse for it in manhood? Do not be afraid, therefore, of this so-called idleness. What would you think of a man who refused to sleep lest he should waste part of his life? You would say, "He is mad; he is not enjoying his life, he is robbing himself of part of it; to avoid sleep he is hastening his death." Remember that these two cases are alike and that childhood is the sleep of reason.

The apparent ease with which children learn is their ruin. You fail to see that this very facility proves that they are not learning. Their shining, polished brain reflects, as in a mirror, the things you show them, but nothing sinks in. The child remembers the words and the ideas are reflected back; his hearers understand them, but to him they are meaningless.

Although memory and reason are wholly different faculties, the one does not really develop apart from the other. Before the age of reason the child receives images, not ideas; and there is this difference between them: images are merely the pictures of external objects, while ideas are notions about those objects determined by their relations. An image when it is recalled may exist by itself in the mind, but every idea implies other ideas. When we image we merely perceive, when we reason we compare. Our sensations are merely passive, our notions or ideas spring from an active principle which judges. The proof of this will be given later.

I maintain, therefore, that as children are incapable of judging, they have no true memory. They retain sounds, form, sensation, but rarely ideas, and still more rarely relations. You tell me they acquire some rudiments of geometry, and you think you prove your case: not so, it is mine you prove; you show that far from being able to reason themselves, children are unable to retain the reasoning of others; for if you follow the method of these little geometricians you will see they only retain the exact impression of the figure and the terms of the demonstration. They cannot meet the slightest new objection; if the figure is reversed they can do nothing. All their knowledge is on the sensation level, nothing has penetrated to their understanding. Their memory is little better than their other powers, for they always have to learn over again, when they are grown up, what they learnt as children.

I am far from thinking, however, that children have no sort of reason. On the contrary, I think they reason very well with regard to things that affect their actual and sensible well-being. But people are mistaken as to the extent of their information, and they attribute to them knowledge they do not possess, and make them reason about things they cannot understand. Another mistake is to try to turn their attention to matters which do not concern them in the least, such as their future interest, their happiness when they are grown up, the opinion people will have of them when they are men—terms which are absolutely meaningless when addressed to creatures who are entirely without foresight. But all the forced studies of these poor little wretches are directed towards matters utterly remote from their minds. You may judge how much attention they can give to them.

The pedagogues, who make a great display of the teaching they give their pupils, are paid to say just the opposite; yet their actions show that they think just as I do. For what do they teach? Words! words! words! Among the various sciences they boast of teaching their scholars, they take good care never to choose those which might be really useful to them, for then they would be compelled to deal with things and would fail utterly; the sciences they choose are those we seem to know when we know their technical terms—heraldry, geography, chronology, languages, etc., studies so remote from man, and even more remote from the child, that it is a wonder if he can ever make any use of any part of them.

You will be surprised to find that I reckon the study of languages among the useless lumber of education; but you must remember that I am speaking of the studies of the earliest years, and whatever you may say, I do not believe any child under twelve or fifteen ever really acquired two languages.

If the study of languages were merely the study of words, that is, of the symbols by which language expresses itself, then this might be a suitable study for children; but languages, as they change the symbols, also modify the ideas which the symbols express. Minds are formed by language, thoughts take their colour from its ideas. Reason alone is common to all. Every language has its own form, a difference which may be partly cause and partly effect of differences in national character; this conjecture appears to be confirmed by the fact that in every nation under the sun speech follows the changes of manners, and is preserved or altered along with them.

By use the child acquires one of these different forms, and it is the only language he retains till the age of reason. To acquire two languages he must be able to compare their ideas, and how can he compare ideas he can barely understand? Everything may have a thousand meanings to him, but each idea can only have one form, so he can only learn one language. You assure me he learns several languages; I deny it. I have seen those little prodigies who are supposed to speak half a dozen languages. I have heard them speak first in German, then in Latin, French, or Italian; true, they used half a dozen different vocabularies, but they always spoke German. In a word, you may give children as many synonyms as you like; it is not their language but their words that you change; they will never have but one language.

In any study whatsoever the symbols are of no value without the idea of the things symbolised. Yet the education of the child is confined to those symbols, while no one ever succeeds in making him understand the thing signified. You think you are teaching him what the world is like; he is only learning the map; he is taught the names of towns, countries, rivers, which have no existence for him except on the paper before him. I remember seeing a geography somewhere which began with: "What is the world?"—"A sphere of cardboard." That is the child's geography. I maintain that after two years' work with the globe and cosmography, there is not a single ten-year-old child who could find his way from Paris to Saint Denis by the help of the rules he has learned. I maintain that not one of these children could find his way by the map about the paths on his father's estate without getting lost. These are the young doctors who can tell us the position of Peking, Ispahan, Mexico, and every country in the world.

You tell me the child must be employed on studies which only need eyes. That may be; but if there are any such studies, they are unknown to me.

It is a still more ridiculous error to set them to study history, which is considered within their grasp because it is merely a collection of facts. But what is meant by this word "fact"? Do you think the relations which determine the facts of history are so easy to grasp that the corresponding ideas are easily developed in the child's mind? Do you think that a real knowledge of events can exist apart from the knowledge of their causes and effects, and that history has so little relation to words that the one can be learnt without the other? If you perceive nothing in a man's actions beyond merely physical and external movements, what do you learn from history? Absolutely nothing; while this study, robbed of all that makes it interesting, gives you neither pleasure nor information. If you want to judge actions by their moral bearings, try to make these moral bearings intelligible to your scholars. You will soon find out if they are old enough to learn history.

Such words as king, emperor, war, conquest, law, and revolution are easily put into their mouths; but when it is a question of attaching clear ideas to these words the explanations are very different from our talk with Robert the gardener.

Without the study of books, such a memory as the child may possess is not left idle; everything he sees and hears makes an impression on him, he keeps a record of men's sayings and doings, and his whole environment is the book from which he unconsciously enriches his memory, till his judgment is able to profit by it.

All children learn La Fontaine's fables, but not one of them understands them. It is just as well that they do not understand, for the morality of the fables is so mixed and so unsuitable for their age that it would be more likely to incline them to vice than to virtue. "More paradoxes!" you exclaim. Paradoxes they may be; but let us see if there is not some truth in them.

I maintain that the child does not understand the fables he is taught, for however you try to explain them, the teaching you wish to extract from them demands ideas which he cannot grasp, while the poetical form which makes it easier to remember makes it harder to understand, so that clearness is sacrificed to facility.

Let us make a bargain, M. de la Fontaine. For my part, I undertake to make your books my favorite study; I undertake to love you, and to learn from your fables, for I hope I shall not mistake their meaning. As to my pupil, permit me to prevent him studying any one of them till you have convinced me that it is good for him to learn things three-fourths of which are unintelligible to him, and until you can convince me that in those fables he can understand he will never reverse the order and imitate the villain instead of taking warning from his dupe.

When I thus get rid of children's lessons, I get rid of the chief cause of their sorrows, namely their books. Reading is the curse of childhood, yet it is almost the only occupation you can find for children. Emile, at twelve years old, will hardly know what a book is. "But," you say, "he must, at least, know how to read." When reading is of use to him, I admit he must learn to read, but till then he will only find it a nuisance.

People make a great fuss about discovering the best way to teach children to read. They invent "bureaux" and cards, they turn the nursery into a printer's shop. Locke would have them taught to read by means of dice. What a fine idea! And the pity of it! There is a better way than any of those, and one which is generally overlooked—it consists in the desire to learn. Arouse this desire in your scholar and have done with your "bureaux" and your dice—any method will serve.

Present interest, that is the motive power, the only motive power that takes us far and safely. Sometimes Emile receives notes of invitation from his father or mother, his relations or friends; he is invited to a dinner, a walk, a boating expedition, to see some public entertainment. These notes are short, clear, plain, and well written. Some one must read them to him, and he cannot always find anybody when wanted; no more consideration is shown to him than he himself showed to you yesterday. Time passes, the chance is lost. The note is read to him at last, but it is too late. Oh! if only he had known how to read! He receives other notes, so short, so interesting, he would like to try to read them. Sometimes he gets help, sometimes none. He does his best, and at last he makes out half the note; it is something about going tomorrow to drink cream—Where! With whom! He cannot tell—how hard he tries to make out the rest! I do not think Emile will need a "bureau." Shall I proceed to the teaching of writing? No, I am ashamed to toy with these trifles in a treatise on education.

I will just add a few words which contain a principle of great importance. It is this—What we are in no hurry to get is usually obtained with speed and certainty. I am pretty sure Emile will learn to read and write before he is ten, just because I care very little whether he can do so before he is fifteen; but I would rather he never learnt to read at all, than that this art should be acquired at the price of all that makes reading useful. What is the use of reading to him if he always hates it?

BOOK III

Our island is this earth; and the most striking object we behold is the sun. As soon as we pass beyond our immediate surroundings, one or both of these must meet our eye. Thus the philosophy of most savage races is mainly directed to imaginary divisions of the earth or to the divinity of the sun.

What a sudden change you will say. Just now we were concerned with what touches ourselves, with our immediate environment, and all at once we are exploring the round world and leaping to the bounds of the universe. This change is the result of our growing strength and of the natural bent of the mind. While we were weak and feeble, self-preservation concentrated our attention on ourselves; now that we are strong and powerful, the desire for a wider sphere carries us beyond ourselves as far as our eyes can reach. But as the intellectual world is still unknown to us, our thoughts are bounded by the visible horizon, and our understanding only develops within the limits of our vision.

Let us transform our sensations into ideas, but do not let us jump all at once from the objects of sense to objects of thought. The latter are attained by means of the former. Let the senses be the only guide for the first workings of reason. No book but the world, no teaching but that of fact. The child who reads ceases to think, he only reads. He is acquiring words not knowledge.

Teach your scholar to observe the phenomena of nature; you will soon rouse his curiosity, but if you would have it grow, do not be in too great a hurry to satisfy this curiosity. Put the problems before him and let him solve them himself. Let him know nothing because you have told him, but because he has learnt it for himself. Let him not be taught science, let him discover it. If ever you substitute authority for reason he will cease to reason; he will be a mere plaything of other people's thought.

You wish to teach this child geography and you provide him with globes, spheres, and maps. What elaborate preparations! What is the use of all these symbols; why not begin by showing him the real thing so that he may at least know what you are talking about?

One fine evening we are walking in a suitable place where the wide horizon gives us a full view of the setting sun, and we note the objects which mark the place where it sets. Next morning we return to the same place for a breath of fresh air before sunrise. We see the rays of light which announce the sun's approach; the glow increases, the east seems afire, and long before the sun appears the light leads us to expect its return. Every moment you expect to see it. There it is at last! A shining point appears like a flash of lightning and soon fills the whole space; the veil of darkness rolls away, man perceives his dwelling place in fresh beauty. During the night the grass has assumed a fresher green; in the light of early dawn, and gilded by the first rays of the sun, it seems covered with a shining network of dew reflecting the light and colour. The birds raise their chorus of praise to greet the Father of life; not one of them is mute; their gentle warbling is softer than by day, it expresses the langour of a peaceful waking. All these produce an impression of freshness which seems to reach the very soul. It is a brief hour of enchantment which no man can resist; a sight so grand, so fair, so delicious, that none can behold it unmoved.

Fired with this enthusiasm, the master wishes to impart it to the child. He expects to rouse his emotion by drawing attention to his own. Mere folly! The splendor of nature lives in man's heart; to be seen, it must be felt. The child sees the objects themselves, but does not perceive their relations, and cannot hear their harmony. It needs knowledge he has not yet acquired, feelings he has not yet experienced, to receive the complex impression which results from all these separate sensations. If he has not wandered over arid plains, if his feet have not been scorched by the burning sands of the desert, if he has not breathed the hot and oppressive air reflected from the glowing rocks, how shall he delight in the fresh air of a fine morning? The scent of flowers, the beauty of foliage, the moistness of the dew, the soft turf beneath his feet, how shall all these delight his senses? How shall the song of the birds arouse voluptuous emotion if love and pleasure are still unknown to him? How shall he behold with rapture the birth of this fair day, if his imagination cannot paint the joys it may bring in its track? How can he feel the beauty of nature, while the hand that formed it is unknown?

Never tell the child what he cannot understand: no descriptions, no eloquence, no figures of speech, no poetry. The time has not come for feeling or taste. Continue to be clear and cold; the time will come only too soon when you must adopt another tone.

Brought up in the spirit of our maxims, accustomed to make his own tools and not to appeal to others until he has tried and failed, he will examine everything he sees carefully and in silence. He thinks rather than questions. Be content, therefore, to show him things at a fit season; then, when you see that his curiosity is thoroughly aroused, put some brief question which will set him trying to discover the answer.

Should the method of studying science be analytic or synthetic? People dispute over this question, but it is not always necessary to choose between them. Sometimes the same experiments allow one to use both analysis and synthesis, and thus to guide the child by the method of instruction when he fancies he is only analysing. Then, by using both at once, each method confirms the results of the other. Starting from opposite ends, without thinking of following the same road, he will unexpectedly reach their meeting place and this will be a delightful surprise. For example, I would begin geography at both ends and add to the study of the earth's revolution the measurement of its divisions, beginning at home. While the child is studying the sphere and is thus transported to the heavens, bring him back to the divisions of the globe and show him his own home.

His geography will begin with the town he lives in and his father's country house, then the places between them, the rivers near them, and then the sun's aspect and how to find one's way by its aid. This is the meeting place. Let him make his own map, a very simple map, at first containing only two places; others may be added from time to time, as he is able to estimate their distance and position. You see at once what a good start we have given him by making his eye his compass.

No doubt he will require some guidance in spite of this, but very little, and that little without his knowing it. If he goes wrong let him alone, do not correct his mistakes; hold your tongue till he finds them out for himself and corrects them, or at most arrange something, so opportunity offers, which may show him his mistakes. If he never makes mistakes he will never learn anything thoroughly. Moreover, what he needs is not an exact knowledge of local topography, but how to find out for himself. No matter whether he carries maps in his head provided he understands what they mean, and has a clear idea of the art of making them. See what a difference there is already between the knowledge of your scholars and the ignorance of mine. They learn maps, he makes them. Here are fresh ornaments for his room.

Remember that this is the essential point in my method—Do not teach the child many things, but never let him form inaccurate or confused ideas. I care not if he knows nothing provided he is not mistaken, and I only acquaint him with truths to guard him against the errors he might put in their place. Reason and judgment come slowly, prejudices flock to us in crowds, and from these he must be protected. But if you make science itself your object, you embark on an unfathomable and shoreless ocean, an ocean strewn with reefs from which you will never return. When I see a man in love with knowledge, yielding to its charms and flitting from one branch to another unable to stay his steps, he seems to me to like a child gathering shells on the seashore, now picking them up, then throwing them aside for others which he sees beyond them, then taking them again, till overwhelmed by their number and unable to choose between them, he flings them all away and returns empty handed.

Time was long during early childhood; we only tried to pass our time for fear of using it ill; now it is the other way; we have not time enough for all that would be of use. The passions, remember, are drawing near, and when they knock at the door your scholar will have no ear for anything else. The peaceful age of intelligence is so short, it flies so swiftly, there is so much to be done, that it is madness to try to make your child learned. It is not your business to teach him the various sciences, but to give him a taste for them and methods of learning them when this taste is more mature. That is assuredly a fundamental principle of all good education.

This is also the time to train him gradually to prolonged attention to a given object; but this attention should never be the result of constraint, but of interest or desire; you must be very careful that it is not too much for his strength, and that it is not carried to the point of tedium. Watch him, therefore, and whatever happens, stop before he is tired, for it matters little what he learns; it does matter that he should do nothing against his will.

If he asks questions let your answers be enough to whet his curiosity but not enough to satisfy it; above all, when you find him talking at random and overwhelming you with silly questions instead of asking for information, at once refuse to answer; for it is clear that he no longer cares about the matter in hand, but wants to make you a slave to his questions. Consider his motives rather than his words. This warning, which was scarcely needed before, becomes of supreme importance when the child begins to reason.

There is a series of abstract truths by means of which all the sciences are related to common principles and are developed each in its turn. This relationship is the method of the philosophers. We are not concerned with it at present. There is quite another method by which every concrete example suggests another and always points to the next in the series. This succession, which stimulates the curiosity and so arouses the attention required by every object in turn, is the order followed by most men, and it is the right order for all children. To take our bearings so as to make our maps we must find meridians. Two points of intersection between the equal shadows morning and evening supply an excellent meridian for a thirteen-year-old astronomer. But these meridians disappear, it takes time to trace them, and you are obliged to work in one place. So much trouble and attention will at last become irksome. We foresaw this and are ready for it.

There are various regions of the earth, and these regions differ in temperature. The variation is more evident as we approach the poles; all bodies expand with heat and contract with cold; this is best measured in liquids and best of all in spirits; hence the thermometer. The wind strikes the face, then the air is a body, a fluid; we feel it though we cannot see it. I invert a glass in water; the water will not fill it unless you leave a passage for the escape of the air; so air is capable of resistance. Plunge the glass further in the water; the water will encroach on the air space without filling it entirely; so air yields somewhat to pressure. A ball filled with compressed air bounces better than one filled with anything else; so air is elastic. Raise your arm horizontally from the water when you are lying in your bath; you will feel a terrible weight on it; so air is a heavy body. By establishing an equilibrium between air and other fluids its weight can be measured, hence the barometer, the siphon, the air gun, and the air pump. All the laws of statics and hydrostatics are discovered by such rough experiments. For none of these would I take the child into a physical cabinet; I dislike that array of instruments and apparatus. The scientific atmosphere destroys science. Either the child is frightened by these instruments or his attention, which should be fixed on their effects, is distracted by their appearance.

We shall make all our apparatus ourselves, and I would not make it beforehand, but having caught a glimpse of the experiment by chance we mean to invent step by step an instrument for its verification. I would rather our apparatus was somewhat clumsy and imperfect, but our ideas clear as to what the apparatus ought to be, and the results to be obtained by means of it. For my first lesson in statics, instead of fetching a balance, I lay a stick across the back of a chair, I measure the two parts when it is balanced; add equal and unequal weights to either end; by pulling or pushing it as required, I find at last that equilibrium is the result of a reciprocal proportion between the amount of the weights and the length of the levers. Thus my little physicist is ready to rectify a balance before ever he sees one.

Undoubtedly the notions of things thus acquired for oneself are clearer and much more convincing than those acquired from the teaching of others; and not only is our reason not accustomed to a slavish submission to authority, but we develop greater ingenuity in discovering relations, connecting ideas and inventing apparatus, than when we merely accept what is given us and allow our minds to be enfeebled by indifference, like the body of a man whose servants always wait on him, dress him and put on his shoes, whose horse carries him, till he loses the use of his limbs. Boileau used to boast that he had taught Racine the art of rhyming with difficulty. Among the many short cuts to science, we badly need some one to teach us the art of learning with difficulty.

The most obvious advantage of these slow and laborious inquiries is this: the scholar, while engaged in speculative studies, is actively using his body, gaining suppleness of limb, and training his hands to labour so that he will be able to make them useful when he is a man. Too much apparatus, designed to guide us in our experiments and to supplement the exactness of our senses, makes us neglect to use those senses. The theodolite makes it unnecessary to estimate the size of angles; the eye which used to judge distances with much precision, trusts to the chain for its measurements; the steel yard dispenses with the need of judging weight by the hand as I used to do. The more ingenious our apparatus, the coarser and more unskillful are our senses. We surround ourselves with tools and fail to use those with which nature has provided every one of us.

But when we devote to the making of these instruments the skill which did instead of them, when for their construction we use the intelligence which enabled us to dispense with them, this is gain not loss, we add art to nature, we gain ingenuity without loss of skill. If instead of making a child stick to his books I employ him in a workshop, his hands work for the development of his mind. While he fancies himself a workman he is becoming a philosopher. Moreover, this exercise has other advantages of which I shall speak latter; and you will see how, through philosophy in sport, one may rise to the real duties of man.

Let the child do nothing because he is told; nothing is good for him but what he recognises as good. When you are always urging him beyond his present understanding, you think you are exercising a foresight which you really lack. To provide him with useless tools which he may never require, you deprive him of man's most useful tool—common-sense. You would have him docile as a child; he will be a credulous dupe when he grows up. You are always saying, "What I ask is for your good, though you cannot understand it. What does it matter to me whether you do it or not; my efforts are entirely on your account." All these fine speeches with which you hope to make him good, are preparing the way, so that the visionary, the tempter, the charlatan, the rascal, and every kind of fool may catch him in his snare or draw him into his folly.

A man must know many things which seem useless to a child, but need the child learn, or can he indeed learn, all that the man must know? Try to teach the child what is of use to a child and you will find that it takes all his time. Why urge him to the studies of an age he may never reach, to the neglect of those studies which meet his present needs? "But," you ask, "will it not be too late to learn what he ought to know when the time comes to use it?" I cannot tell; but this I do know, it is impossible to teach it sooner, for our real teachers are experience and emotion, and man will never learn what befits a man except under its own conditions. A child knows he must become a man; all the ideas he may have as to man's estate are so many opportunities for his instruction, but he should remain in complete ignorance of those ideas which are beyond his grasp. My whole book is one continued argument in support of this fundamental principle of education.

As soon as we have contrived to give our pupil an idea of the word "Useful," we have got an additional means of controlling him, for this word makes a great impression on him, provided that its meaning for him is a meaning relative to his own age, and provided he clearly sees its relation to his own well-being. This word makes no impression on your scholars because you have taken no pains to give it a meaning they can understand, and because other people always undertake to supply their needs so that they never require to think for themselves, and do not know what utility is.

"What is the use of that?" In the future this is the sacred formula, the formula by which he and I test every action of our lives. This is the question with which I invariably answer all his questions; it serves to check the stream of foolish and tiresome questions with which children weary those about them. These incessant questions produce no result, and their object is rather to get a hold over you than to gain any real advantage. A pupil, who has been really taught only to want to know what is useful, questions like Socrates; he never asks a question without a reason for it, for he knows he will be required to give his reason before he gets an answer.

See what a powerful instrument I have put into your hands for use with your pupil. As he does not know the reason for anything you can reduce him to silence almost at will; and what advantages do your knowledge and experience give you to show him the usefulness of what you suggest. For, make no mistake about it, when you put this question to him, you are teaching him to put it to you, and you must expect that whatever you suggest to him in the future he will follow your own example and ask, "What is the use of this?"

Perhaps this is the greatest of the tutor's difficulties. If you merely try to put the child off when he asks a question, and if you give him a single reason he is not able to understand, if he finds that you reason according to your own ideas, not his, he will think that what you tell him is good for you but not for him; you will lose his confidence and all your labour is thrown away. But what master will stop short and confess his faults to his pupil? We all make it a rule never to own to the faults we really have. Now I would make it a rule to admit even the faults I have not, if I could not make my reasons clear to him; as my conduct will always be intelligible to him, he will never doubt me and I shall gain more credit by confessing my imaginary faults than those who conceal their real defects.

I hate books; they only teach us to talk about things we know nothing about. Hermes, they say, engraved the elements of science on pillars lest a deluge should destroy them. Had he imprinted them on men's hearts they would have been preserved by tradition. Well-trained minds are the pillars on which human knowledge is most deeply engraved.

Is there no way of correlating so many lessons scattered through so many books, no way of focusing them on some common object, easy to see, interesting to follow, and stimulating even to a child? Could we but discover a state in which all man's needs appear in such a way as to appeal to the child's mind, a state in which the ways of providing for these needs are as easily developed, the simple and stirring portrayal of this state should form the earliest training of the child's imagination.

Eager philosopher, I see your own imagination at work. Spare yourself the trouble; this state is already known, it is described, with due respect to you, far better than you could describe it, at least with greater truth and simplicity. Since we must have books, there is one book which, to my thinking, supplies the best treatise on an education according to nature. This is the first book Emile will read; for a long time it will form his whole library, and it will always retain an honoured place. It will be the text to which all our talks about natural science are but the commentary. It will serve to test our progress towards a right judgment, and it will always be read with delight, so long as our taste is unspoilt. What is this wonderful book? Is it Aristotle? Pliny? Buffon? No; it is *Robinson Crusoe*.

Robinson Crusoe on his island, deprived of the help of his fellowmen, without the means of carrying on the various arts, yet finding food, preserving his life, and procuring a certain amount of comfort; this is the thing to interest people of all ages, and it can be made attractive to children in all sorts of ways. We shall thus make a reality of that desert island which formerly served as an illustration. The condition, I confess, is not that of a social being, nor is it in all probability Emile's own condition, but he should use it as a standard of comparison for all other conditions. The surest way to raise him above prejudice and to base his judgments on the true relations of things, is to put him in the place of a solitary man, and to judge all things as they would be judged by such a man in relation to their own utility.

At the beginning of this second period we took advantage of the fact that our strength was more than enough for our needs, to enable us to get outside ourselves. We have ranged the heavens and measured the earth; we have sought out the laws of nature; we have explored the whole of our island. Now let us return to ourselves, let us unconsciously approach our own dwelling. We are happy indeed if we do not find it already occupied by the dreaded foe who is preparing to seize it.

What remains to be done when we have observed all that lies around us? We must turn to our own use all that we can get, we must increase our comfort by means of our curiosity. Hitherto we have provided ourselves with tools of all kinds, not knowing which we require. Perhaps those we do not want will be useful to others, and perhaps we may need theirs. Thus we discover the use of exchange; but for this we must know each other's needs, what tools other people use, what they can offer in exchange. Given ten men, each of them has ten different requirements. To get what he needs for himself each must work at ten different trades; but considering our different talents, one will do better at this trade, another at that. Each of them, fitted for one thing, will work at all, and will be badly served. Let us form these ten men into a society, and let each devote himself to the trade for which he is best adapted, and let him work at it for himself and for the rest. Each will reap the advantage of the others' talents, just as if they were his own; by practice each will perfect his own talent, and thus all the ten, well provided for, will still have something to spare for others. This is the plain foundation for all our institutions. It is not my aim to examine its results here; I have done so in another book *(Discours sur l'inegalite)*.

According to this principle, any one who wanted to consider himself as an isolated individual, self-sufficing and independent of others, could only be utterly wretched. He could not even continue to exist, for finding the whole earth appropriated by others while he had only himself, how could he get the means of subsistence? When we leave the state of nature we compel others to do the same; no one can remain in a state of nature in spite of his fellow-creatures; and to try to remain in it when it is no longer practicable, would really be to leave it, for self-preservation is nature's first law.

Thus the idea of social relations is gradually developed in the child's mind, before he can really be an active member of human society. Emile sees that to get tools for his own use, other people must have theirs, and that he can exchange what he needs and they possess. I easily bring him to feel the need of such exchange and to take advantage of it.

Remember I demand no talent, only a trade, a genuine trade, a mere mechanical art, in which the hands work harder than the head, a trade which does not lead to fortune but makes you independent of her. In households far removed from all danger of want I have known fathers to carry prudence to such a point as to provide their children not only with ordinary teaching but with knowledge by means of which they could get a living if anything happened. These far-sighted parents thought they were doing a great thing. It is nothing, for the resources they fancy they have secured depend on that very fortune of which they would make their children independent; so that unless they found themselves in circumstances fitted for the display of their talents, they would die of hunger as if they had none.

As soon as it is a question of influence and intrigue you may as well use these means to keep yourself in plenty, as to acquire, in the depths of poverty, the means of returning to your former position. If you cultivate the arts which depend on the artist's reputation, if you fit yourself for posts which are only obtained by favour, how will that help you when, rightly disgusted with the world, you scorn the steps by which you must climb. You have studied politics and state-craft, so far so good; but how will you use this knowledge, if you cannot gain the ear of the ministers, the favourites, or the officials? If you have not the secret of winning their favour, if they fail to find you a rogue to their taste? You are an architect or a painter; well and good; but your talents must be displayed. Do you suppose you can exhibit in the salon without further ado? That is not the way to set about it. Lay aside the rule and the pencil, take a cab and drive from door to door; there is the road to fame. Now you must know that the doors of the great are guarded by porters and flunkeys, who only understand one language, and their ears are in their palms. If you wish to teach what you have learned, geography, mathematics, languages, music, drawing, even to find pupils, you must have friends who will sing your praises. Learning, remember, gains more credit than skill, and with no trade but your own none will believe in your skill. See how little you can depend on these fine "Resources," and how many other resources are required before you can use what you have got. And what will become of you in your degradation? Misfortune will make you worse rather than better. More than ever the sport of public opinion, how will you rise above the prejudices on which your fate depends? How will you despise the vices and the baseness from which you get your living? You were dependent on wealth, now you are dependent on the wealthy; you are still a slave and a poor man in the bargain. Poverty without freedom, can a man sink lower than this!

When we review with the child the productions of art and nature, when we stimulate his curiosity and follow its leads, we have great opportunities of studying his tastes and inclinations, and perceiving the first spark of genius, if he has any decided talent in any direction. You must, however, be on your guard against the common error which mistakes the effects of environment for the ardour of genius, or imagines there is a decided bent towards any one of the arts, when there is nothing more than that spirit of emulation, common to men and monkeys, which impels them instinctively to do what they see others doing, without knowing why. The world is full of artisans, and still fuller of artists, who have no native gift for their calling, into which they were driven in early childhood, either through the conventional ideas of other people, or because those about them were deceived by an appearance of zeal, which would have led them to take to any other art they saw practised. One hears a drum and fancies he is a general; another sees a building and wants to be an architect. Every one is drawn towards the trade he sees before him if he thinks it is held in honour.

I know I have said too much for my agreeable contemporaries, but I sometimes let myself be carried away by my argument. If any one is ashamed to be seen wearing a leathern apron or handling a plane, I think him a mere slave of public opinion, ready to blush for what is right when people poke fun at it. But let us yield to parents' prejudices so long as they do not hurt the children. To honour trades we are not obliged to practice every one of them, so long as we do not think them beneath us. When the choice is ours and we are under no compulsion, why not choose the pleasanter, more attractive and more suitable trade. Metal work is useful, more useful, perhaps, than the rest, but unless for some special reason Emile shall not be a blacksmith, a locksmith nor an ironworker. I do not want to see him a Cyclops at the forge. Neither would I have him a mason, still less a shoemaker. All trades must be carried on, but when the choice is ours, cleanliness should be taken into account; this is not a matter of class prejudice, our senses are our guides.

In conclusion, I do not like those stupid trades in which the workmen mechanically perform the same action without pause and almost without mental effort. Weaving, stocking-knitting, stone-cutting; why employ intelligent men on such work? It is merely one machine employed on another.

All things considered, the trade I should choose for my pupil, among the trades he likes, is that of a carpenter. It is clean and useful; it may be carried on at home; it gives enough exercise; it calls for skill and industry, and while fashioning articles for everyday use, there is scope for elegance and taste. If your pupil's talents happened to take a scientific turn, I should not blame you if you gave him a trade in accordance with his tastes; for instance, he might learn to make mathematical instruments, glasses, telescopes, etc.

When Emile learns his trade I shall learn it too. I am convinced he will never learn anything thoroughly unless we learn it together. So we shall both serve our apprenticeship, and we do not mean to be treated as gentlemen, but as real apprentices who are not there for fun; why should not we actually be apprenticed? Peter the Great was a ship's carpenter and drummer to his own troops; was not that prince at least your equal in birth and merit? You understand this is addressed not to Emile but to you—to you, whoever you may be.

BOOK IV

We have reached the moral order at last; we have just taken the second step towards manhood. If this were the place for it, I would try to show how the first impulses of the heart give rise to the first stirrings of conscience, and how from the feelings of love and hatred spring the first notions of good and evil. I would show that justice and kindness are no mere abstract terms, no mere moral conceptions framed by the understanding, but true affections of the heart enlightened by reason, the natural outcome of our primitive affections; that by reason alone, unaided by conscience, we cannot establish any natural law, and that all natural right is a vain dream if it does not rest upon some instinctive need of the human heart. But I do not think it is my business at present to prepare treatises on metaphysics and morals, nor courses of study of any kind whatsoever; it is enough if I indicate the order and development of our feelings and our knowledge in relation to our growth. Others will perhaps work out what I have here merely indicated.

Hitherto my Emile has thought only of himself, so his first glance at his equals leads him to compare himself with them; and the first feeling excited by this comparison is the desire to be first. It is here that self-love is transformed into selfishness, and this is the starting point of all the passions which spring from selfishness. But to determine whether the passions by which his life will governed shall be humane and gentle or harsh and cruel, whether they shall be the passions of benevolence and pity or those of envy and covetousness, we must know what he believes his place among men to be, and what sort of obstacles he expects to have to overcome in order to attain to the position he seeks.

To guide him in this inquiry, after we have shown him men by means of the accidents common to the species, we must now show him them by means of their differences. This is the time for estimating inequality natural and civil, and for the scheme of the whole social order.

Society must be studied in the individual and the individual in society; those who desire to treat politics and morals apart from one another will never understand either. By confining ourselves at first to the primitive relations, we see how men should be influenced by them and what passions should spring from them; we see that it is in proportion to the development of these passions that a man's relations with others expand or contract. It is not so much strength of arm as moderation of spirit which makes men free and independent. The man whose wants are few is dependent on but few people, but those who constantly confound our vain desires with our bodily needs, those who have made these needs the basis of human society, are continually mistaking effects for causes, and they have only confused themselves by their own reasoning.

It must be admitted that this method has its drawbacks, and it is not easy to carry it out; for if he becomes too soon engrossed in watching other people, if you train him to mark too closely the actions of others, you will make him spiteful and satirical, quick and decided in his judgments of others; he will find a hateful pleasure in seeking bad motives, and will fail to see the good even in that which is really good. He will, at least, get used to the sight of vice, he will behold the wicked without horror, just as we get used to seeing the wretched without pity. Soon the perversity of mankind will be not so much a warning as an excuse; he will say, "Man is made so," and he will have no wish to be different from the rest.

But if you wish to teach him theoretically to make him acquainted, not only with the heart of man, but also with the application of the external causes which turn our inclinations into vices; when you thus transport him all at once from the objects of sense to the objects of reason, you employ a system of metaphysics which he is not in a position to understand; you fall back into the error, so carefully avoided hitherto, of giving him lessons which are like lessons, of substituting in his mind the experience and the authority of the master for his own experience and the development of his own reason.

To remove these two obstacles at once, and to bring the human heart within his reach without risk of spoiling his own, I would show him men from afar, in other times or in other places, so that he may behold the scene but cannot take part in it. This is the time for history; with its help he will read the hearts of men without any lessons in philosophy; with its help he will view them as a mere spectator, dispassionate and without prejudice; he will view them as their judge, not as their accomplice or their accuser.

To know men you must behold their actions. In society we hear them talk; they show their words and hide their deeds; but in history the veil is drawn aside, and they are judged by their deeds. Their sayings even help us to understand them; for comparing what they say and what they do, we see not only what they are but what they would appear; the more they disguise themselves the more thoroughly they stand revealed.

Unluckily this study has its dangers, its drawbacks of several kinds. It is difficult to adopt a point of view which will enable one to judge one's fellow-creatures fairly. It is one of the chief defects of history to paint men's evil deeds rather than their good ones; it is revolutions and catastrophes that make history interesting; so long as a nation grows and prospers quietly in the tranquillity of a peaceful government, history says nothing; she only begins to speak of nations when, no longer able to be self-sufficing, they interfere with their neighbours' business, or allow their neighbours to interfere with their own; history only makes them famous when they are on the downward path; all our histories begin where they ought to end. We have very accurate accounts of declining nations; what we lack is the history of those nations which are multiplying; they are so happy and so good that history has nothing to tell us of them; and we see indeed in our own times that the most successful governments are least talked of. We only hear what is bad; the good is scarcely mentioned. Only the wicked become famous, the good are forgotten or laughed to scorn, and thus history, like philosophy, is for ever slandering mankind.

Moreover, it is inevitable that the facts described in history should not give an exact picture of what really happened; they are transformed in the brain of the historian, they are moulded by his interests and coloured by his prejudices. Who can place the reader precisely in a position to see the event as it really happened? Ignorance or partiality disguises everything. What a different impression may be given merely by expanding or contracting the circumstances of the case without altering a single historical incident. The same object may be seen from several points of view, and it will hardly seem the same thing, yet there has been no change except in the eye that beholds it. Do you indeed do honour to truth when what you tell me is a genuine fact, but you make it appear something quite different? A tree more or less, a rock to the right or to the left, a cloud of dust raised by the wind, how often have these decided the result of a battle without any one knowing it? Does that prevent history from telling you the cause of defeat or victory with as much assurance as if she had been on the spot? But what are the facts to me, while I am ignorant of their causes, and what lessons can I draw from an event, whose true cause is unknown to me? The historian indeed gives me a reason, but he invents it; and criticism itself, of which we hear so much, is only the art of guessing, the art of choosing from among several lies, the lie that is most like truth.

Have you ever read Cleopatra or Cassandra or any books of the kind? The author selects some well-known event, he then adapts it to his purpose, adorns it with details of his own invention, with people who never existed, with imaginary portraits; thus he piles fiction on fiction to lend a charm to his story. I see little difference between such romances and your histories, unless it is that the novelist draws more on his own imagination, while the historian slavishly copies what another has imagined; I will also admit, if you please, that the novelist has some moral purpose good or bad, about which the historian scarcely concerns himself.

You will tell me that accuracy in history is of less interest than a true picture of men and manners; provided the human heart is truly portrayed, it matters little that events should be accurately recorded; for after all you say, what does it matter to us what happened two thousand years ago? You are right if the portraits are indeed truly given according to nature; but if the model is to be found for the most part in the historian's imagination, are you not falling into the very error you intended to avoid, and surrendering to the authority of the historian what you would not yield to the authority of the teacher? If my pupil is merely to see fancy pictures, I would rather draw them myself; they will, at least, be better suited to him.

The worst historians for a youth are those who give their opinions. Facts! Facts! And let him decide for himself; this is how he will learn to know mankind. If he is always directed by the opinion of the author, he is only seeing through the eyes of another person, and when those eyes are no longer at his disposal he can see nothing.

I leave modern history on one side, not only because it has no character and all our people are alike, but because our historians, wholly taken up with effect, think of nothing but highly coloured portraits, which often represent nothing. The old historians generally give fewer portraits and bring more intelligence and common-sense to their judgments; but even among them there is plenty of scope for choice, and you must not begin with the wisest but with the simplest. I would not put Polybius or Sallust into the hands of a youth; Tacitus is the author of the old, young men cannot understand him; you must learn to see in human actions the simplest features of the heart of man before you try to sound its depths. You must be able to read facts clearly before you begin to study maxims. Philosophy in the form of maxims is only fit for the experienced. Youth should never deal with the general, all its teaching should deal with individual instances.

To my mind Thucydides is the true model of historians. He relates facts without giving his opinion; but he omits no circumstance adapted to make us judge for ourselves. He puts everything that he relates before his reader; far from interposing between the facts and the readers, he conceals himself; we seem not to read but to see. Unfortunately he speaks of nothing but war, and in his stories we only see the least instructive part of the world, that is to say the battles. The virtues and defects of the Retreat of the Ten Thousand and the Commentaries of Caesar are almost the same. The kindly Herodotus, without portraits, without maxims, yet flowing, simple, full of details calculated to delight and interest in the highest degree, would be perhaps the best historian if these very details did not often degenerate into childish folly, better adapted to spoil the taste of youth than to form it; we need discretion before we can read him. I say nothing of Livy, his turn will come; but he is a statesman, a rhetorician, he is everything which is unsuitable for a youth.

History in general is lacking because it only takes note of striking and clearly marked facts which may be fixed by names, places, and dates; but the slow evolution of these facts, which cannot be definitely noted in this way, still remains unknown. We often find in some battle, lost or won, the ostensible cause of a revolution which was inevitable before this battle took place. War only makes manifest events already determined by moral causes which few historians can perceive.

The philosophic spirit has turned the thoughts of many of the historians of our times in this direction; but I doubt whether truth has profited by their labours. The rage for systems has got possession of all alike, no one seeks to see things as they are, but only as they agree with his system.

Add to all these considerations the fact that history shows us actions rather than men, because she only seizes men at certain chosen times in full dress; she only portrays the statesman when he is prepared to be seen; she does not follow him to his home, to his study, among his family and his friends; she only shows him in state; it is his clothes rather than himself that she describes.

I would prefer to begin the study of the human heart with reading the lives of individuals; for then the man hides himself in vain, the historian follows him everywhere; he never gives him a moment's grace nor any corner where he can escape the piercing eye of the spectator; and when he thinks he is concealing himself, then it is that the writer shows him up most plainly.

What then is required for the proper study of men? A great wish to know men, great impartiality of judgment, a heart sufficiently sensitive to understand every human passion, and calm enough to be free from passion. If there is any time in our life when this study is likely to be appreciated, it is this that I have chosen for Emile; before this time men would have been strangers to him; later on he would have been like them. Convention, the effects of which he already perceives, has not yet made him its slave, the passions, whose consequences he realizes, have not yet stirred his heart. He is a man; he takes an interest in his brethren; he is a just man and he judges his peers. Now it is certain that if he judges them rightly he will not want to change places with any one of them, for the goal of all their anxious efforts is the result of prejudices which he does not share, and that goal seems to him a mere dream. For his own part, he has all he wants within his reach. How should he be dependent on any one when he is self-sufficing and free from prejudice? Strong arms, good health, moderation, few needs, together with the means to satisfy those needs, are his. He has been brought up in complete liberty and servitude is the greatest ill he understands. He pities these miserable kings, the slaves of all who obey them; he pities these false prophets fettered by their empty fame; he pities these rich fools, martyrs to their own pomp; he pities these ostentatious voluptuaries, who spend their life in deadly dullness that they may seem to enjoy its pleasures. He would pity the very foe who harmed him, for he would discern his wretchedness beneath his cloak of spite. He would say to himself, "This man has yielded to his desire to hurt me, and this need of his places him at my mercy."

One step more and our goal is attained. Selfishness is a dangerous tool though a useful one; it often wounds the hand that uses it, and it rarely does good unmixed with evil. When Emile considers his place among men, when he finds himself so fortunately situated, he will be tempted to give credit to his own reason for the work of yours, and to attribute to his own deserts what is really the result of his good fortune. He will say to himself, "I am wise and other men are fools." He will pity and despise them and will congratulate himself all the more heartily; and as he knows he is happier than they, he will think his deserts are greater. This is the fault we have most to fear, for it is the most difficult to eradicate. If he remained in this state of mind, he would have profited little by all our care; and if I had to choose, I hardly know whether I would not rather choose the illusions of prejudice than those of pride.

Great men are under no illusion with respect to their superiority; they see it and know it, but they are none the less modest. The more they have, the better thay know what they lack. They are less vain of their superiority over us than ashamed by the consciousness of their weakness, and among the good things they really possess, they are too wise to pride themselves on a gift which is none of their getting. The good man may be proud of his virtue for it is his own, but what cause for pride has the man of intellect? What has Racine done that he is not Pradon, and Boileau that he is not Cotin?

The circumstances with which we are concerned are quite different. Let us keep to the common level. I assumed that my pupil had neither surpassing genius nor a defective understanding. I chose him of an ordinary mind to show what education could do for a man. Exceptions defy all rules. If, therefore, as a result of my care, Emile prefers his way of living, seeing, and feeling to that of others, he is right; but if he thinks because of this that he is nobler and better born than they, he is wrong; he is deceiving himself; he must be undeceived, or rather let us prevent the mistake, lest it be too late to correct it.

Provided a man is not mad, he can be cured of any folly but vanity; there is no cure for this but experience, if indeed there is any cure for it at all; when it first appears we can at least prevent its further growth. But do not on this account waste your breath on empty arguments to prove to the youth that he is like other men and subject to the same weaknesses. Make him feel it or he will never know it. This is another instance of an exception to my own rules; I must voluntarily expose my pupil to every accident which may convince him that he is no wiser than we. The adventure with the conjurer will be repeated again and again in different ways; I shall let flatterers take advantage of him; if rash comrades draw him into some perilous adventure, I will let him run the risk; if he falls into the hands of sharpers at the card table, I will abandon him to them as their dupe. I will let them flatter him, pluck him, and rob him; and when having sucked him dry they turn and mock him, I will even thank them to his face for the lessons they have been good enough to give him. The only snares from which I will guard him with my utmost care are the wiles of wanton women. The only precaution I shall take will be to share all the dangers I let him run, and all the insults I let him receive. I will bear everything in silence, without a murmur or reproach, without a word to him, and be sure that if this wise conduct is faithfully adhered to, what he sees me endure on his account will make more impression on his heart than what he himself suffers.

The time of faults is the time for fables. When we blame the guilty under the cover of a story we instruct without offending him; and he then understands that the story is not untrue by means of the truth he finds in its application to himself. The child who has never been deceived by flattery understands nothing of the fable I recently examined; but the rash youth who has just become the dupe of a flatterer perceives only too readily that the crow was a fool. Thus he acquires a maxim from the fact, and the experience he would soon have forgotten is engraved on his mind by means of the fable. There is no knowledge of morals which cannot be acquired through our own experience or that of others. When there is danger, instead of letting him try the experiment himself, we have recourse to history. When the risk is comparatively slight, it is just as well that the youth should be exposed to it; then by means of the apologue the special cases with which the young man is now acquainted are transformed into maxims.

It is not, however, my intention that these maxims should be explained, nor even formulated. Nothing is so foolish and unwise as the moral at the end of most of the fables; as if the moral was not, or ought not to be so clear in the fable itself that the reader cannot fail to perceive it. Why then add the moral at the end, and so deprive him of the pleasure of discovering it for himself. The art of teaching consists in making the pupil wish to learn. But if the pupil is to wish to learn, his mind must not remain in such a passive state with regard to what you tell him that there is really nothing for him to do but listen to you. The master's vanity must always give way to the scholar's; he must be able to say, I understand, I see it, I am getting at it, I am learning something. One of the things which makes the Pantaloon in the Italian comedies so wearisome is the pains taken by him to explain to the audience the platitudes they understand only too well already.

When I see the studies of young men at the period of their greatest activity confined to purely speculative matters, while later on they are suddenly plunged, without any sort of experience, into the world of men and affairs, it strikes me as contrary alike to reason and to nature, and I cease to be surprised that so few men know what to do. How strange a choice to teach us so many useless things, while the art of doing is never touched upon! They profess to fit us for society, and we are taught as if each of us were to live a life of contemplation in a solitary cell, or to discuss theories with persons whom they did not concern. You think you are teaching your scholars how to live, and you teach them certain bodily contortions and certain forms of words without meaning. I, too, have taught Emile how to live; for I have taught him to enjoy his own society and, more than that, to earn his own bread. But this is not enough. To live in the world he must know how to get on with other people, he must know what forces move them, he must calculate the action and reaction of self-interest in civil society, he must estimate the results so accurately that he will rarely fail in his undertakings, or he will at least have tried in the best possible way. The law does not allow young people to manage their own affairs nor to dispose of their own property; but what would be the use of these precautions if they never gained any experience until they were of age. They would have gained nothing by the delay, and would have no more experience at five-and-twenty than at fifteen. No doubt we must take precautions, so that a youth, blinded by ignorance or misled by passion, may not hurt himself; but at any age there are opportunities when deeds of kindness and of care for the weak may be performed under the direction of a wise man, on behalf of the unfortunate who need help.

Mothers and nurses grow fond of children because of the care they lavish on them; the practice of social virtues touches the very heart with the love of humanity; by doing good we become good; and I know no surer way to this end. Keep your pupil busy with the good deeds that are within his power, let the cause of the poor be his own, let him help them not merely with his money, but with his service; let him work for them, protect them, let his person and his time be at their disposal; let him be their agent; he will never all his life long have a more honourable office. How many of the oppressed, who have never got a hearing, will obtain justice when he demands it for them with that courage and firmness which the practice of virtue inspires; when he makes his way into the presence of the king himself, to plead the cause of the wretched, the cause of those who find all doors closed to them by their poverty, those who are so afraid of being punished for their misfortunes that they do not dare to complain?

But shall we make of Emile a knight-errant, a redresser of wrongs, a paladin? Shall he thrust himself into public life, play the sage and the defender of the laws before the great, before the magistrates, before the king? Shall he lay petitions before the judges and plead in the law courts? That I cannot say. The nature of things is not changed by terms of mockery and scorn. He will do all that he knows to be useful and good. He will do nothing more, and he knows that nothing is useful and good for him which is unbefitting his age. He knows that his first duty is to himself; that young men should distrust themselves; that they should act circumspectly; that they should show respect to those older than themselves, reticence and discretion in talking without cause, modesty in things indifferent, but courage in well-doing, and boldness to speak the truth. Such were those illustrious Romans who, having been admitted into public life, spent their days in bringing criminals to justice and in protecting the innocent, without any motives beyond those of learning, and of the furtherance of justice and of the protection of right conduct.

So Emile loves peace. He is delighted at the sight of happiness, and if he can help to bring it about, this is an additional reason for sharing it. I do not assume that when he sees the unhappy he will merely feel for them that barren and cruel pity which is content to pity the ills it can heal. His kindness is active and teaches him much he would have learnt far more slowly, or he would never have learnt at all, if his heart had been harder. If he finds his comrades at strife, he tries to reconcile them; if he sees the afflicted, he inquires as to the cause of their sufferings; if he meets two men who hate each other, he wants to know the reason of their enmity; if he finds one who is down-trodden, groaning under the oppression of the rich and powerful, he tries to discover by what means he can conteract this oppression, and in the interest he takes with regard to all these unhappy persons, the means of removing their sufferings are never out of his sight. What use shall we make of this disposition so that it may re-act in a way suited to his age? Let us direct his efforts and his knowledge, and use his zeal to increase them.

I am never weary of repeating: let all the lessons of young people take the form of doing rather than talking; let them learn nothing from books which they can learn from experience. How absurd to attempt to give them practice in speaking when they have nothing to say, to expect to make them feel, at their school desks, the vigour of the language of passion and all the force of the arts of persuasion when they have nothing and nobody to persuade! All the rules of rhetoric are mere waste of words to those who do not know how to use them for their own purposes.

I am aware that many of my readers will be surprised to find me tracing the course of my scholar through his early years without speaking to him of religion. At fifteen he will not even know that he has a soul, at eighteen even he may not be ready to learn about it. For if he learns about it too soon, there is the risk of his never really knowing anything about it.

If I had to depict the most heart-breaking stupidity, I would paint a pedant teaching children the catechism; if I wanted to drive a child crazy I would set him to explain what he learned in his catechism. You will reply that as most of the Christian doctrines are mysteries, you must wait, not merely till the child is a man, but till the man is dead, before the human mind will understand those doctrines. To that I reply, that there are mysteries which the heart of man can neither conceive nor believe, and I see no use in teaching them to children, unless you want to make liars of them. Moreover, I assert that to admit that there are mysteries, you must at least realize that they are incomprehensible, and children are not even capable of this conception! At an age when everything is mysterious, there are no mysteries properly so-called.

"We must believe in God if we would be saved." This doctrine wrongly understood is the root of blood-thirsty intolerance and the cause of all the futile teaching which strikes a deadly blow at human reason by training it to cheat itself with mere words. No doubt there is not a moment to be lost if we would deserve eternal salvation; but if the repetition of certain words suffices to obtain it, I do not see why we should not people heaven with starlings and magpies as well as with children.

The obligation of faith assumes the possibility of belief. The philosopher who does not believe is wrong, for he misuses the reason he has cultivated, and he is able to understand the truths he rejects. But the child who professes the Christian faith—what does he believe? Just what he understands; and he understands so little of what he is made to repeat that if you tell him to say just the opposite he will be quite ready to do it. The faith of children and the faith of many men is a matter of geography. Will they be rewarded for having been born in Rome rather than in Mecca? One is told that Mahomet is the prophet of God and he says, "Mahomet is the prophet God." The other is told that Mahomet is a rogue and he says, "Mohamet is a rogue." Either of them would have said just the opposite had he stood in the other's shoes. When they are so much alike to begin with, can the one be consigned to Paradise and the other to Hell? When a child says he believes in God, it is not God he believes in, but Peter or James who told him that there is something called God, and he believes it after the fashion of Euripides—"O Jupiter, of whom I know nothing by thy name."

We hold that no child who dies before the age of reason will be deprived of everlasting happiness; the Catholics believe the same of all children who have been baptised even though they have never heard of God. There are, therefore, circumstances in which one can be saved without belief in God, and these circumstances occur in the case of children or madmen when the human mind is incapable of the operations necessary to perceive the Godhead. The only difference I see between you and me is that you profess that children of seven years old are able to do this and I do not think them ready for it at fifteen. Whether I am right or wrong depends, not on any article of the creed, but on a simple observation in natural history.

From the same principle it is plain that any man having reached old age without faith in God will not, therefore, be deprived of God's presence in another life if his blindness was not willful; and I maintain that it is not always willful. You admit that it is so in the case of lunatics deprived by disease of their spiritual faculties, but not of their manhood, and therefore still entitled to the goodness of their Creator. Why then should we not admit it in the case of those brought up from infancy in seclusion, those who have led the life of a savage and are without the knowledge of the true God. Reason tells that man should only be punished for his willful faults, and that invincible ignorance can never be imputed to him as a crime. Hence it follows that in the sight of the

Eternal Justice every man who would believe if he had the necessary knowledge is counted a believer, and that there will be no unbelievers to be punished except those who have closed their hearts against the truth.

Let us beware of proclaiming the truth to those who cannot as yet comprehend it, for to do so is to try to inculcate error. It would be better to have no idea at all of the Divinity than to have mean, grotesque, harmful, and unworthy ideas; to fail to perceive the Divine is a lesser evil than to insult it. The worthy Plutarch says, "I would rather men said, 'There is no such person as Plutarch,' than that they should say, 'Plutarch is unjust, envious, jealous, and such a tyrant that he demands more than can be performed.'"

The chief harm which results from the monstrous ideas of God which are instilled into the minds of children is that they last all their life long, and as men they understand no more of God than they did as children. In Switzerland, I once saw a good and pious mother who was so convinced of the truth of this maxim that she refused to teach her son religion when he was a little child for fear lest he should be satisfied with this crude teaching and neglect a better teaching when he reached the age of reason. This child never heard the name of God pronounced except with reverence and devotion, and as soon as he attempted to say the word he was told to hold his tongue, as if the subject were too sublime and great for him. This reticence aroused his curiosity and his self-love; he looked forward to the time when he would know this mystery so carefully hidden from him. The less they spoke of God to him, the less he was himself permitted to speak of God, the more he thought about Him; this child beheld God everywhere. What I should most dread as the result of this unwise affectation of mystery is this: by overstimulating the youth's imagination you may turn his head, and make him at the best a fanatic rather than a believer.

But we need fear nothing of the sort for Emile, who always declines to pay attention to what is beyond his reach, and listens with profound indifference to things he does not understand. There are so many things of which he is accustomed to say, "That is no concern of mine," that one more or less makes little difference to him; and when he does begin to perplex himself with these great matters, it is because the natural growth of his knowledge is turning his thoughts that way.

We have seen the road by which the cultivated human mind approaches these mysteries, and I am ready to admit that it would not attain to them naturally, even in the bosom of society, till a much later age. But as there are in this same society inevitable causes which hasten the development of the passions, if we did not also hasten the development of the knowledge which controls those passions we should indeed depart from the path of nature and disturb her equilibrium. When we can no longer restrain a precocious development in one direction we must promote a corresponding development in another direction, so that the order of nature may not be inverted, and so that things should progress together, not separately, so that the man, complete at every moment of his life, may never find himself at one stage in one of his faculties and at another stage in another faculty.

What a difficulty do I see before me! A difficulty all the greater because it depends less on actual facts than on the cowardice of those who dare not look the difficulty in the face. Let us at least venture to state our problem. A child should always be brought up in his father's religion; he is always given plain proofs that this religion, whatever it may be, is the only true religion, that all others are ridiculous and absurd. The force of the argument depends entirely on the country in which it is put forward. Let a Turk, who thinks Christianity so absurd at Constantinople, come to Paris and see what they think of Mahomet. It is in matters of religion more than in anything else that prejudice is triumphant. But when we who profess to shake off its yoke entirely, we who refuse to yield any homage to authority, decline to teach Emile anything which he could not learn for himself in any country, what religion shall we give him, to what sect shall this child of nature belong? The answer strikes me as quite easy. We will not attach him to any sect, but we will give him the means to choose for himself according to the right use of his own reason.

Remember that to guide a grown man you must reverse all that you did to guide a child. Do not hesitate to speak to him of those dangerous mysteries which you have so carefully concealed from him hitherto. Since he must become aware of them, let him not learn them from another, nor from himself, but from you alone; since he must henceforth fight against them, let him know his enemy, that he may not be taken unawares.

As there is a fitting age for the study of the sciences, so there is a fitting age for the study of the ways of the world. Those who learn these too soon follow them throughout life, without choice or consideration, and although they follow them fairly well they never really know what they are about. But he who studies the ways of the world and sees the reason for them, follows them with more insight, and therefore more exactly and gracefully. Give me a child of twelve who knows nothing at all; at fifteen I will restore him to you knowing as much as those who have been under instruction from infancy; with this difference, that your scholars only know things by heart, while mine knows how to use his knowledge. In the same way plunge a young man of twenty into society; under good guidance, in a year's time, he will be more charming and more truly polite than one brought up in society from childhood.

For the former is able to perceive the reasons for all the proceedings relating to age, position, and sex, on which the customs of society depend, and can reduce them to general principles, and apply them to unforeseen emergencies; while the latter, who is guided solely by habit, is at a loss when habit fails him.

If in order to cultivate my pupil's taste, I were compelled to choose between a country where this form of culture has not yet arisen and those in which it has already degenerated, I would progress backwards. I would begin his survey with the latter and end with the former. My reason for this choice is, that taste becomes corrupted through excessive delicacy, which makes it sensitive to things which most men do not perceive; this delicacy leads to a spirit of discussion, for the more subtle is our discrimination of things the more things there are for us. This subtlety increases the delicacy and decreases the uniformity of our touch. So there are as many tastes as there are people. In disputes as to our preferences, philosophy and knowledge are enlarged, and thus we learn to think. It is only men accustomed to plenty of society who are capable of very delicate observations, for these observations do not occur to us till the last, and people who are unused to all sorts of society exhaust their attention in the consideration of the more conspicuous features. There is perhaps no civilised place upon earth where the common taste is so bad as in Paris. Yet it is in this capital that good taste is cultivated, and it seems that few books make any impression in Europe whose authors have not studied in Paris. Those who think it is enough to read our books are mistaken; there is more to be learnt from the conversation of authors than from their books; and it is not from the authors that we learn most. It is the spirit of social life which develops a thinking mind, and carries the eye as far as it can reach. If you have a spark of genius, go and spend a year in Paris; you will soon be all that you are capable of becoming, or you will never be good for anything at all.

I will go still further in order to keep his taste pure and wholesome. In the tumult of dissipation I shall find opportunities for useful conversation with him; and while these conversations are always about things in which he takes a delight, I shall take care to make them as amusing as they are instructive. Now is the time to read pleasant books; now is the time to teach him to analyse speech and to appreciate all the beauties of eloquence and diction. It is a small matter to learn languages, they are less useful than people think; but the study of languages leads us on to that of grammar in general. We must learn Latin if we would have a thorough knowledge of French; these two languages must be studied and compared if we would understand the rules of the art of speaking.

There is, moreover, a certain simplicity of taste which goes straight to the heart; and this is only to be found in the classics. In oratory, poetry, and every kind of literature, Emile will find the classical authors as he found them in history, full of matter and sober in their judgment. The authors of our own time, on the contrary, say little and talk much. To take their judgment as our law is not the way to form our own judgment.

If I am not mistaken, the attention of my pupil, who sets so small a value upon words, will be directed in the first place to these differences, and they will affect his choice in his reading. He will be carried away by the manly eloquence of Demosthenes, and will say, "This is an orator;" but when he reads Cicero, he will say, "This is a lawyer."

Speaking generally Emile will have more taste for the books of the ancients than for our own, just because they were the first, and therefore the ancients are nearer to nature and their genius is more distinct. Whatever La Motte and the Abbe Terrasson may say, there is no real advance in human reason, for what we gain in one direction we lose in another; for all minds start from the same point, and as the time spent in learning what others have thought is so much time lost in learning to think for ourselves, we have more acquired knowledge and less vigour of mind. Our minds like our arms are accustomed to use tools for everything, and to do nothing for themselves. Fontenelle used to say that all these disputes as to the ancients and the moderns came to this—Were the trees in former times taller than they are now. If agriculture had changed, it would be worth our while to ask this question.

After I have led Emile to the sources of pure literature, I will also show him the channels into the resenvoirs of modern compilers; journals, translations, dictionairies, he shall cast a glance at them all, and then leave them forever. To amuse him he shall hear the chatter of the academies; I will draw his attention to the fact that every member of them is worth more by himself than he is as a member of the society; he will then draw his own conclusions as to the utility of these fine institutions.

I take him to the theatre to study taste, not morals; for in the theatre above all taste is revealed to those who can think. Lay aside precepts and morality, I should say; this is not the place to study them. The stage is not made for truth; its object is to flatter and amuse; there is no place where one can learn so completely the art of pleasing and of interesting the human heart. The study of plays leads to the study of poetry; both have the same end in view. If he has the least glimmering of taste for poetry, how eagerly will he study the languages of the poets, Greek, Latin, and

Italian! These studies will afford him unlimited amusement and will be none the less valuable; they will be a delight to him at an age and in circumstances when the heart finds so great a charm in every kind of beauty which affects it. Picture to yourself on the one hand Emile, on the other some young rascal from college, reading the fourth book of the *Aeneid,* or Tibullus, or the *Banquet* of Plato: what a difference between them! What stirs the heart of Emile to its depths, makes not the least impression on the other! Oh, good youth, stay, make a pause in your reading, you are too deeply moved; I would have you find pleasure in the language of love, but I would not have you carried away by it; be a wise man, but be a good man too. If you are only one of these, you are nothing. After this let him win fame or not in dead languages, in literature, in poetry, I care little. He will be none the worse if he knows nothing of them, and his education is not concerned with these mere words.

My main object in teaching him to feel and love beauty of every kind is to fix his affections and his taste on these, to prevent the corruption of his natural appetites, lest he should have to seek some day in the midst of his wealth for the means of happiness which should be found close at hand. I have said elsewhere that taste is only the art of being a connoisseur in matters of little importance, and this is quite true; but since the charm of life depends on a tissue of these matters of little importance, such efforts are no small thing; through their means we learn how to fill our life with the good things within our reach, with as much truth as they may hold for us. I do not refer to the morally good which depends on a good disposition of the heart, but only to that which depends on the body, on real delight, apart from the prejudices of public opinion.

Dialogue between a Priest and a Dying Man

The Marquis de Sade

Note: *For the Marquis de Sade neither Nature nor society are foundations upon which education or morality or law may be built. For the Marquis de Sade* language *is the only foundation of all education and of all claims, for it makes people believe in the realities they build through names, and names are the boundaries of their cities and of their education, or lack of it.*

PRIEST—Come to this the fatal hour when at last from the eyes of deluded man the scales must fall away, and be shown the cruel picture of his errors and his vices—say, my son, do you not repent the host of sins unto which you were led by weakness and human frailty?

DYING MAN—Yes, my friend, I do repent.

PRIEST—Rejoice then in these pangs of remorse, during the brief space remaining to you profit therefrom to obtain Heaven's general absolution for your sins, and be mindful of it, only through the mediation of the Most Holy Sacrament of penance will you be granted it by the Eternal.

DYING MAN—I do not understand you, any more than you have understood me.

PRIEST—Eh?

DYING MAN—I told you that I repented.

PRIEST—I heard you say it.

DYING MAN—Yes, but without understanding it.

PRIEST—My interpretation—

DYING MAN—Hold. I shall give you mine. By Nature created, created with very keen tastes, with very strong passions; placed on this earth for the sole purpose of yielding to them and satisfying them, and these effects of my creation being naught but necessities directly relating to Nature's fundamental designs or, if you prefer, naught but essential derivatives proceeding from her intentions in my regard, all in accordance with her laws, I repent not having acknowledged her omnipotence as fully as I might have done, I am only sorry for the modest use I made of the faculties (criminal in your view, perfectly ordinary in mine) she gave me to serve her; I did sometimes resist her, I repent it. Misled by your absurd doctrines, with them for arms I mindlessly challenged the desires instilled in me by a much diviner inspiration, and thereof do I repent: I only plucked an occasional flower when I might have gathered an ample harvest of fruit—such are the just grounds for the regrets I have, do me the honor of considering me incapable of harboring any others.

PRIEST—Lo! where your fallacies take you, to what pass are you brought by your sophistries! To created being you ascribe all the Creator's power, and those unlucky penchants which have led you astray, ah! do you not see they are merely the products of corrupted nature, to which you attribute omnipotence?

DYING MAN—Friend—it looks to me as though your dialectic were as false as your thinking. Pray straighten your arguing or else leave me to die in peace. What do you mean by Creator, and what do you mean by corrupted nature?

PRIEST—The Creator is the master of the universe, 'tis He who has wrought everything, everything created, and who maintains it all through the mere fact of His omnipotence.

DYING MAN—An impressive figure indeed. Tell me now why this so very formidable fellow did nevertheless, as you would have it, create a corrupted nature?

PRIEST—What glory would men ever have, had not God left them free will; and in the enjoyment thereof, what merit could come to them, were there not on earth the possibility of doing good and that of avoiding evil?

DYING MAN—And so your god bungled his work deliberately, in order to tempt or test his creature—did he then not know, did he then not doubt what the result would be?

PRIEST—He knew it undoubtedly but, once again, he wished to leave to man the merit of choice.

DYING MAN—And to what purpose, since from the outset he knew the course affairs would take and since, all-mighty as you tell me he is, he had but to make his creature choose as suited him?

PRIEST—Who is there can penetrate God's vast and infinite designs regarding man, and who can grasp all that makes up the universal scheme?

DYING MAN—Anyone who simplifies matters, my friend, anyone, above all, who refrains from multiplying causes in order to confuse effects all the more. What need have you of a second difficulty when you are unable to resolve the first, and once it is possible that Nature may all alone have done what you attribute to your god, why must you go looking for someone to be her overlord? The cause and explanation of what you do not understand may perhaps be the simplest thing in the world. Perfect your physics and you will understand Nature better, refine your reason, banish your prejudices and you'll have no further need of your god.

PRIEST—Wretched man! I took you for no worse than a Socinian— arms I had to combat you. But 'tis clear you are an atheist, and seeing that your heart is shut to the authentic and innumerable proofs we receive every day of our lives of the Creator's existence—I have no more to say to you. There is no restoring the blind to the light.

DYING MAN—Softly, my friend, own that between the two, he who blindfolds himself must surely see less of the light than he who snatches the blindfold away from his eyes. You compose, you construct, you dream, you magnify and complicate; I sift, I simplify. You accumulate errors, pile one atop the other; I combat them all. Which one of us is blind?

PRIEST—Then you do not believe in God at all?

DYING MAN—No. And for one very sound reason: it is perfectly impossible to believe in what one does not understand. Between understanding and faith immediate connections must subsist; understanding is the very lifeblood of faith; where understanding has ceased, faith is dead; and when they who are in such a case proclaim they have faith, they deceive. You yourself, preacher, I defy you to believe in the god you predicate to me—you must fail because you cannot demonstrate him to me, because it is not in you to define him to me, because consequently you do not understand him—because as of the moment you do not understand him, you can no longer furnish me any reasonable argument concerning him, and because, in sum, anything beyond the limits and grasp of the human mind is either illusion or futility; and because your god having to be one or the other of the two, in the first instance I should be mad to believe in him, in the second a fool. My friend, prove to me that matter is inert and I will grant you a creator, prove to me that Nature does not suffice to herself and I'll let you imagine her ruled by a higher force; until then, expect nothing from me, I bow to evidence only, and evidence I perceive only through my senses: my belief goes no farther than they, beyond that point my faith collapses. I believe in the sun because I see it, I conceive it as the focal center of all the inflammable matter in Nature, its periodic movement pleases but does not amaze me. 'Tis a mechanical operation, perhaps as simple as the workings of electricity, but which we are unable to understand. Need I bother more about it? when you have roofed everything over with your god, will I be any the better off? and shall I still not have to make an effort at least as great to understand the artisan as to define his handiwork?: By edifying your chimera it is thus no service you have rendered me, you have made me uneasy in my mind but you have not enlightened it, and instead of gratitude I owe you resentment. Your god is a machine you fabricated in your passions' behalf, you manipulated it to their liking; but the day it interfered with mine, I kicked it out of my way, deem it fitting that I did so; and now, at this moment when I sink and my soul stands in need of calm and philosophy, belabor it not with your riddles and your cant, which alarm but will not convince it, which will irritate without improv-

ing it; good friends and on the best terms have we ever been, this soul
and I, so Nature wished it to be; as it is, so she expressly modeled it, for
my soul is the result of the dispositions she formed in me pursuant to her
own ends and needs; and as she has an equal need of vices and of virtues,
whenever she was pleased to move me to evil, she did so, whenever she
wanted a good deed from me, she roused in me the desire to perform
one, and even so I did as I was bid. Look nowhere but to her workings
for the unique cause of our fickle human behavior, and in her laws hope
to find no other springs than her will and her requirements.

PRIEST—And so whatever is in this world, is necessary.

DYING MAN—Exactly.

PRIEST—But if everything is necessary—then the whole is regulated.

DYING MAN—I am not the one to deny it.

PRIEST—And what can regulate the whole save it be an all-powerful
and all-knowing hand?

DYING MAN—Say, is it not necessary that gunpowder ignite when you
set a spark to it?

PRIEST—Yes.

DYING MAN—And do you find any presence of wisdom in that?

PRIEST—None.

DYING MAN—It is then possible that things necessarily come about
without being determined by a superior intelligence, and possible hence
that everything derive logically from a primary cause, without there
being either reason or wisdom in that primary cause.

PRIEST—What are you aiming at?

DYING MAN—At proving to you that the world and all therein may be
what it is and as you see it to be, without any wise and reasoning cause
directing it, and that natural effects must have natural causes: natural
causes sufficing, there is no need to invent any such unnatural ones as
your god who himself, as I have told you already, would require to be
explained and who would at the same time be the explanation of
nothing; and that once 'tis plain your god is superfluous, he is perfectly
useless; that what is useless would greatly appear to be imaginary only,
null and therefore nonexistent; thus, to conclude that your god is fiction
I need no other argument than that which furnishes me the certitude of
his inutility.

PRIEST—At that rate there is no great need for me to talk to you about
religion.

DYING MAN—True, but why not anyhow? Nothing so much amuses
me as this sign of the extent to which human beings have been carried
away by fanaticism and stupidity; although the prodigious spectacle of
folly we are facing here may be horrible, it is always interesting. Answer
me honestly, and endeavor to set personal considerations aside: were I
weak enough to fall victim to your silly theories concerning the fabulous

existence of the being who renders religion necessary, under what form would you advise me to worship him? Would you have me adopt the daydreams of Confucius rather than the absurdities of Brahma, should I kneel before the great snake to which the Blacks pray, invoke the Peruvians' sun or Moses' Lord of Hosts, to which Mohammedan sect should I rally, or which Christian heresy would be preferable in your view? Be careful how you reply.

PRIEST—Can it be doubtful?

DYING MAN—Then 'tis egoistical.

PRIEST—No, my son, 'tis as much out of love for thee as for myself I urge thee to embrace my creed.

DYING MAN—And I wonder how the one or the other of us can have much love for himself, to deign to listen to such degrading nonsense.

PRIEST—But who can be mistaken about the miracles wrought by our Divine Redeemer?

DYING MAN—He who sees in him anything else than the most vulgar of all tricksters and the most arrant of all impostors.

PRIEST—*O God, you hear him and your wrath thunders not forth!*

DYING MAN—No my friend, all is peace and quiet around us, because your god, be it from impotence or from reason or from whatever you please, is a being whose existence I shall momentarily concede out of condescension for you or, if you prefer, in order to accommodate myself to your sorry little perspective; because this god, I say, were he to exist, as you are mad enough to believe, could not have selected as means to persuade us, anything more ridiculous than those your Jesus incarnates.

PRIEST—What! the prophecies, the miracles, the martyrs—are they not so many proofs?

DYING MAN—How, so long as I abide by the rules of logic, how would you have me accept as proof anything which itself is lacking proof? Before a prophecy could constitute proof I should first have to be completely certain it was ever pronounced; the prophecies history tells us of belong to history and for me they can only have the force of other historical facts, whereof three out of four are exceedingly dubious; if to this I add the strong probability that they have been transmitted to us by not very objective historians, who recorded what they preferred to have us read, I shall be quite within my rights if I am skeptical. And furthermore, who is there to assure me that this prophecy was not made after the fact, that it was not a stratagem of everyday political scheming, like that which predicts a happy reign under a just king, or frost in wintertime? As for your miracles, I am not any readier to be taken in by such rubbish. All rascals have performed them, all fools have believed in them; before I'd be persuaded of the truth of a miracle I would have to be very sure the event so called by you was absolutely contrary to the laws of Nature, for only what is outside of Nature can pass for miraculous;

and who is so deeply learned in Nature that he can affirm the precise
point where her domain ends, and the precise point where it is infringed
upon? Only two things are needed to accredit an alleged miracle, a
mountebank and a few simpletons; tush, there's the whole origin of your
prodigies; all new adherents to a religious sect have wrought some; and
more extraordinary still, all have found imbeciles around to believe
them. Your Jesus' feats do not surpass those of Apollonius of Tyana, yet
nobody thinks to take the latter for a god; and when we come to your
martyrs, assuredly, these are the feeblest of all your arguments. To
produce martyrs you need but have enthusiasm on the one hand, resistance on the other; and so long as an opposed cause offers me as many of
them as does yours, I shall never be sufficiently authorized to believe one
better than another, but rather very much inclined to consider all of
them pitiable. Ah my friend! were it true that the god you preach did
exist, would he need miracle, martyr, or prophecy to secure recognition?
and, if, as you declare, the human heart were of his making, would he
not have chosen it for the repository of his law? Then would this law,
impartial for all mankind because emanating from a just god, then
would it be found graved deep and writ clear in all men alike, and from
one end of the world to the other, all men, having this delicate and
sensitive organ in common, would also resemble each other through the
homage they would render the god whence they had got it; all would
adore and serve him in one identical manner, and they would be as
incapable of disregarding this god as of resisting the inward impulse to
worship him. Instead of that, what do I behold throughout this world?
As many gods as there are countries; as many different cults as there are
different minds or different imaginations; and this swarm of opinions
among which it is physically impossible for me to choose, say now, is this
a just god's doing? Fie upon you, preacher, you outrage your god when
you present him to me thus; rather let me deny him completely, for if he
exists then I outrage him far less by my incredulity than do you through
your blasphemies. Return to your senses, preacher, your Jesus is no
better than Mohammed. Mohammed no better than Moses, and the
three of them combined no better than Confucius, who did after all have
some wise things to say while the others did naught but rave; in general,
though, such people are all mere frauds: philosophers laughed at them,
the mob believed them, and justice ought to have hanged them.

PRIEST—Alas, justice dealt only too harshly with one of the four.

DYING MAN—If he alone got what he deserved it was he deserved it
most richly; seditious, turbulent, calumniating, dishonest, libertine, a
clumsy buffoon, and very mischievous; he had the art of overawing
common folk and stirring up the rabble; and hence came in line for
punishment in a kingdom where the state of affairs was what it was in
Jerusalem then. They were very wise indeed to get rid of him, and this

perhaps is the one case in which my extremely lenient and also extremely tolerant maxims are able to allow the severity of Themis; I excuse any misbehavior save that which may endanger the government one lives under, kings and their majesties are the only things I respect; and whoever does not love his country and his king were better dead than alive.

PRIEST—But you do surely believe something awaits us after this life, you must at some time or another have sought to pierce the dark shadows enshrouding our mortal fate, and what other theory could have satisfied your anxious spirit, than that of the numberless woes that betide him who has lived wickedly, and an eternity of rewards for him whose life has been good?

DYING MAN—What other, my friend? that of nothingness, it has never held terrors for me, in it I see naught but what is consoling and unpretentious; all the other theories are of pride's composition, this one alone is of reason's. Moreover, 'tis neither dreadful nor absolute, this nothingness. Before my eyes have I not the example of Nature's perpetual generations and regenerations? Nothing perishes in the world, my friend, nothing is lost; man today, worm tomorrow, the day after tomorrow a fly; is it not to keep steadily on existing? And what entitles me to be rewarded for virtues which are in me through no fault of my own, or again punished for crimes wherefor the ultimate responsibility is not mine? how are you to put your alleged god's goodness into tune with this system, and can he have wished to create me in order to reap pleasure from punishing me, and that solely on account of a choice he does not leave me free to determine?

PRIEST—You are free.

DYING MAN—Yes, in terms of your prejudices; but reason puts them to rout, and the theory of human freedom was never devised except to fabricate that of grace, which was to acquire such importance for your reveries. What man on earth, seeing the scaffold a step beyond the crime, would commit it were he free not to commit it? We are the pawns of an irresistible force, and never for an instant is it within our power to do anything but make the best of our lot and forge ahead along the path that has been traced for us. There is not a single virtue which is not necessary to Nature and conversely not a single crime which she does not need and it is in the perfect balance she maintains between the one and the other that her immense science consists; but can we be guilty for adding our weight to this side or that when it is she who tosses us onto the scales? no more so than the hornet who thrusts his dart into your skin.

PRIEST—Then we should not shrink from the worst of all crimes.

DYING MAN—I say nothing of the kind. Let the evil deed be proscribed by law, let justice smite the criminal, that will be deterrent enough; but if by misfortune we do commit it even so, let's not cry over spilled milk; remorse is inefficacious, since it does not stay us from crime, futile since it does not repair it, therefore it is absurd to beat one's breast, more absurd still to dread being punished in another world if we have been lucky to escape it in this. God forbid that this be construed as encouragement to crime, no, we should avoid it as much as we can, but one must learn to shun it through reason and not through false fears which lead to naught and whose effects are so quickly overcome in any moderately steadfast soul. Reason, sir—yes, our reason alone should warn us that harm done our fellows can never bring happiness to us; and our heart, that contributing to their felicity is the greatest joy Nature has accorded us on earth; the entirety of human morals is contained in this one phrase: *Render others as happy as one desires oneself to be,* and never inflict more pain upon them than one would like to receive at their hands. There you are, my friend, those are the only principles we should observe, and you need neither god nor religion to appreciate and subscribe to them, you need only have a good heart. But I feel my strength ebbing away; preacher, put away your prejudices, unbend, be a man, be human, without fear and without hope forget your gods and your religions too: they are none of them good for anything but to set man at odds with man, and the mere name of these horrors has caused greater loss of life on earth than all other wars and all other plagues combined. Renounce the idea of another world; there is none, but do not renounce the pleasure of being happy and of making for happiness in this. Nature offers you no other way of doubling your existence, of extending it.—My friend, lewd pleasures were ever dearer to me than anything else, I have idolized them all my life and my wish has been to end it in their bosom; my end draws near, six women lovelier than the light of day are waiting in the chamber adjoining, I have reserved them for this moment, partake of the feast with me, following my example embrace them instead of the vain sophistries of superstition, under their caresses strive for a little while to forget your hypocritical beliefs.

NOTE: The dying man rang, the women entered; and after he had been a little while in their arms the preacher became one whom Nature has corrupted, all because he had not succeeded in explaining what a corrupt nature is.

FOCUSING QUESTIONS

1. How did John Locke modify the traditional concept of natural Law?
2. How did John Locke modify the definitions of knowledge, education, ideas, and politics?

3. John Locke held that humans are born like blank slates, empty of ideas. What developed in education on this principle?

4. Why is John Locke called the inventor of disciplinary education?

5. How did Rousseau turn the tables on Locke regarding education and society?

6. Why did Rousseau consider society evil?

7. Would Emile's education ever contribute anything to society?

8. Compare the ideas of nature in the medievals, Locke, Rousseau, and the Marquis de Sade.

9. Why is Nature not a valid ground to educate?

10. What is the relation between language and Nature?

11. Why do the classroom and the cities of the Marquis de Sade equate to one another?

12. What is the absolute ground of education according to the Marquis de Sade?

13. Do you think the Marquis de Sade is a pervert, a philosopher, or the most influential educator?

14. Do you think the writings of the Marquis de Sade are true, false, good, evil, beyond all four, educational?

SUPPLEMENTARY READINGS

Barthes, Roland. *Sade, Fourier, Loyola.* Translated by Richard Miller. New York: Farrar, Straus and Giroux, 1976.

de Sade, Marquis. *The Marquis de Sade,* Translated by Rechard Seaver and Austryn Wainhouse. New York: Grove Press, 1965.

Gay, Peter. *John Locke on Education.* New York: Teachers College, Columbia University, 1964.

Locke, John. *An Essay Concerning Human Understanding.* Edited by Alexander Fraser. New York: Dover, 1959.

————. *Two Treatises of Government.* Edited by Peter Laslett. New York: New American Library, 1965.

Rousseau, Jean Jacques. *The Social Contract.* Edited by R. D. Masters. Baltimore: Penguin, 1969.

————. *Emile or On Education.* Translated by Allan Bloom. New York: Basic Books, 1979.

9

The Critics: Vico, Voltaire

In 1725 Giambattista Vico published his new book: *Principles of a New Science concerning the Nature of the Nations by which are Found the Principles of Another System of the Natural Law of the Gentes.* This title, of course, was shortened in subsequent editions and we know it today as *The New Science.*

In this book Vico is concerned with origins and his criticism of others is based on a new method which should provide the investigator with a sense of

> how the founders of gentile humanity by means of their natural theology (or metaphysics) imagined the gods; how by means of their logic they invented languages; by morals, created heroes; by economics, founded families, and by politics, cities; by their physics, established the beginnings of things as all divine; by the particular physics of man, in a certain sense created themselves.
>
> *The New Science,* par. 367

This means that there is no one nature to be grasped by one method and imposed on all contexts of human conduct, but rather that there are several natures, as many as disciplines or subject matters and each should be studied within its own context.

Vico understood very quickly that humans become intoxicated by the progress of their own rationality and thus tend to measure and evaluate all periods of culture and all human disciplines as if they had been created by that contemporary rationality, though all fail by its measure and come up short.

Vico, on the other hand, took it that men developed by the exercise of their faculties, and the first exercise being imagination. Early human beings were people with great imagination who felt the world through poetry and music. He quotes Aristotle to clarify his own direction:

> On this there is a fine passage in Aristotle in which he remarks that men of limited ideas erect every particular into a maxim. The reason must be that the human mind, which is indefinite, being constricted by the vigor of the senses, cannot otherwise express its almost divine nature than by thus enlarging particulars in imagination. It is perhaps on this account that in both the Greek and the Latin poets the images of gods and heroes always appear larger than those of men.
>
> *New Science,* par. 816

Vico is the only voice in the history of modern education which raises in praise of other forms of knowing besides the "rational" as we understand it today.

> Man in his ignorance makes himself the rule of the universe, for in the examples cited he has made of himself an entire world. So that, as rational metaphysics teaches that man becomes all things by understanding them, this imaginative metaphysics shows that man becomes all things by *not* understanding them; and perhaps the latter proposition is truer than the former, for when man understands he extends his mind and takes in the things, but when he does not understand he makes the things out of himself and becomes them by transforming himself into them.
>
> *New Science,* par. 405

This strong and vivid imagination was needed for those early people to make the world, and because they made it so and used it so they left for us an inheritance of faculties:

> In that human indigence, the peoples, who were almost all body and almost no reflection, must have been all vivid sensation in perceiving particulars, strong imagination in apprehending and enlarging them, sharp wit in referring them to their imaginative genera, and robust memory in retaining them. It is true that these faculties appertain to the mind, but they have their roots in the body and draw their strength from it. Hence memory is the same as imagination which for that reason is called *memoria* in Latin.
>
> *New Science,* par. 819

According to Vico, therefore, we are internally divided, for on the one hand we are capable of creating while on the other we develop faculties to understand worlds already created, on the one hand we create, on the other we understand, on the one hand we are capable of abstracting the mind from the senses and on the other we are capable of submerging the poetic faculty deep into particulars. Cognition and imagination are not subservient to one another; they are autonomous and need different cultivation in education, according to Vico. What stands in the way of this way of education is what Vico calls "the conceit of scholars, who will have it that what they know is as old as the world" (*New Science*. par. 127).

In Vico's *New Science* human beings both think and imagine, yet thinking has never known fully what men thought they were thinking; their actions gave way to unintended consequences. Imagining also created worlds, yet what humans imagined is not exactly what things are.; at the same time without those imaginings understanding would not have been possible. In a sense we are limited to both our imaginings and our thinking, while both contribute to making the worlds and humans we are. Thus we need to develop both through education on autonomous grounds, and not make the one subservient to the other.

At a practical level Vico's program of education aims at making the student skilled in *topics,* rhetoric, or the skill of finding middle terms between two sides of a question, as against the modern Cartesians who wanted to teach the geometric method of philosophical criticism at the service of behavior. Life does not move by axioms, and education should take care to educate the faculties that created our human life the way we experience it. The *topics* should be the starting point for exercises to develop both imagination and understanding.

Today's state of education needs a Voltaire and also a criticism like *Candide*. The book appeared in 1759 as *Candide or Optimism,* and supposedly translated from the German by Dr. Ralph, with additions found in the pocket of the Doctor when he died at Minden. Of course the book was written by Voltaire and in it he gave us his testimony of what constitutes a good education ("cultivate the garden") and how to destroy through sarcasm the ideologies of the educators (Professor' Pangloss' [all tongue] belief that this was the best of all possible worlds). The book was so irreverent, so playful, so lethal in its sarcasm that the Great Council of Geneva almost at once after publication ordered it to be burned.

With misery upon misery, accident upon accident, pain upon pain Pangloss and *Candide* travel all over the world. Voltaire manages to include within his satire Leibniz's theodicy, Pope's optimism, religious abuses, monastic lack of chastity, class prejudices, political corruption, legal chicanery, judicial venality, the inhumanity of the penal code, the injustice of slavery, and the destructiveness of war. The book is a colossal exaggeration against all ideology and barbarism, and ends with the prayer, amidst all adversity that the education of the faculties is the only humane act left: "Let us therefore cultivate the garden."

Candide

CHAPTER I—HOW CANDIDE WAS BROUGHT UP IN A NOBLE CASTLE AND HOW HE WAS EXPELLED FROM THE SAME

In the castle of Baron Thunder-ten-tronckh in Westphalia[1] there lived a youth, endowed by Nature with the most gentle character. His face was the expression of his soul. His judgment was quite honest and he was extremely simpleminded; and this was the reason, I think, that he was named Candide. Old servants in the house suspected that he was the son of the Baron's sister and a decent honest gentleman of the neighborhood, whom this young lady would never marry because he could only prove seventy-one quarterings,[2] and the rest of his genealogical tree was lost, owing to the injuries of time.

The Baron was one of the most powerful lords in Westphalia, for his castle possessed a door and windows. His Great Hall was even decorated with a piece of tapestry. The dogs in his stable-yards formed a pack of hounds when necessary; his grooms were his huntsmen; the village curate was his Grand Almoner. They all called him "My Lord," and laughed heartily at his stories.

The Baroness weighed about three hundred and fifty pounds, was therefore greatly respected, and did the honors of the house with a dignity which rendered her still more respectable. Her daughter Cunegonde, aged seventeen, was rosy-cheeked, fresh, plump and tempting. The Baron's son appeared in every respect worthy of his father. The tutor Pangloss was the oracle of the house, and little Candide followed his lessons with all the candor of his age and character.

Pangloss taught metaphysico-theologo-cosmolonigology.[3] He proved admirably that there is no effect without a cause and that in this best of all possible worlds, My Lord the Baron's castle was the best of castles and his wife the best of all possible Baronesses.

1. **Westphalia** Section of Germany just east of Holland. In Voltair's day, it was a poor agricultural province through which he passed in 1750 on his way to the court of Frederick the Great.
2. **quarterings** These divisions on coats of arms are indications of the number of noble ancestors.
3. **cosmolonigology** The suggestion is that Pangloss ("all-tongue") is the teacher of abstract nonsense. Swift used a similar term for similar effect in *Gulliver's Travels*.

" 'Tis demonstrated," said he, "that things cannot be otherwise; for, since everything is made for an end, everything is necessarily for the best end. Obserse that noses were made to wear spectacles; and so we have spectacles. Legs were visibly instituted to be breeched, and we have breeches.[4] Stones were formed to be quarried and to build castles; and My Lord has a very noble castle; the greatest Baron in the province should have the best house; and as pigs were made to be eaten, we eat pork all the year round; consequently, those who have asserted that all is well[5] talk nonsense; they ought to have said that all is for the best."

Candide listened attentively and believed innocently; for he thought Mademoiselle Cunegonde extremely beautiful although he was never bold enough to tell her so. He decided that after the happiness of being born Baron of Thunder-ten-tronckh, the second degree of happiness was to be Mademoiselle Cunegonde; the third, to see her every day; and the fourth to listen to Doctor Pangloss, the greatest philosopher of the province and therefore of the whole world.

One day when Cunegonde was walking near the castle, in a little wood which was called The Park, she observed Doctor Pangloss in the bushes, giving a lesson in experimental physics to her mother's waiting maid, a very pretty and docile brunette. Mademoiselle Cunegonde had a great inclination for science and watched breathlessly the reiterated experiments she witnessed; she observed clearly the Doctor's sufficient reason, the effects and the causes, and returned home very much excited, pensive, filled with the desire of learning, reflecting that he might be hers.

On her way back to the castle she met Candide and blushed; Candide also blushed. She bade him good-morning in a hesitating voice; Candide replied without knowing what he was saying. Next day, when they left the table after dinner, Cunegonde and Candide found themselves behind a screen; Cunegonde dropped her handkerchief, Candide picked it up; she innocently held his hand; the young man innocently kissed the young lady's hand with remarkable vivacity, tenderness, and grace; their lips met, their eyes sparkled, their knees trembled, their hands wandered. Baron Thunder-ten-tronckh passed near the screen, and, observing this cause and effect, expelled Candide from the castle by kicking him in the backside frequently and hard. Cunegonde swooned; when she recovered her senses, the Baroness slapped her in the face; and all was in consternation in the noblest and most agreeable of all possible castles.

4. **breeches** Clear but ludicrous examples of what are called in philosophy "final causes," that is, ends of purposes which serve as causes of created things.
5. **all is well** See Introduction for Pope's phrasing.

CHAPTER II—WHAT HAPPENED TO CANDIDE AMONG THE BULGARIANS

Candide, expelled from the earthly paradise, wandered for a long time without knowing where he was going, weeping, turning up his eyes to Heaven, gazing back frequently at the noblest of castles which held the most beautiful of young Baronesses; he lay down to sleep supperless between two furrows in the open fields; it snowed heavily in large flakes. The next morning the shivering Candide, penniless, dying of cold and exhaustion, dragged himself towards the neighboring town, which was called Waldberghoff-trarbkdikdorff. He halted sadly at the door of an inn. Two men dressed in blue noticed him.

"Comrade," said one, "there's a well-built young man of the right height." They went up to Candide and very civilly invited him to dinner.

"Gentlemen," said Candide with charming modesty, "you do me a great honor, but I have no money to pay my share."

"Ah, sir," said one of the men in blue, "persons of your figure and merit never pay anything; are you not five feet five tall?"

"Yes, gentlemen," said he, bowing, "that is my height."

"Ah, sir, come to table; we will not only pay your expenses, we will never allow a man like you to be short of money; men were only made to help each other."

"You are in the right," said Candide, "that is what Doctor Pangloss was always telling me, and I see that everything is for the best."

They begged him to accept a few crowns, he took them and wished to give them an I O U; they refused to take it and all sat down to table. "Do you not love tenderly . . ."

"Oh, yes," said he. "I love Mademoiselle Cunegonde tenderly."

"No," said one of the gentlemen. "We were asking if you do not tenderly love the King of the Bulgarians."[1]

"Not a bit," said he, "for I have never seen him."

"What! He is the most charming of Kings, and you must drink his health."

"Oh, gladly, gentlemen." And he drank.

"That is sufficient," he was told. "You are now the support, the aid, the defender, the hero of the Bulgarians; your fortune is made and your glory assured."

They immediately put irons on his legs and took him to a regiment.[2] He was made to turn to the right and left, to raise the ramrod and return

---

1. **Bulgarians** Voltaire has his reasons to refer to Frederick the Great, King of Prussia, under this title.

2. **regiment** It was a common practice in England and on the continent to "press" young men into military service.

the ramrod, to take aim, to fire, to double up,[3] and he was given thirty strokes with a stick; the next day he drilled not quite so badly, and received only twenty strokes; the day after, he only had ten, and was looked on as a prodigy by his comrades.

Candide was completely mystified and could not make out how he was a hero. One fine spring day he thought he would take a walk, going straight ahead, in the belief that to use his legs as he pleased was a privilege of the human species as well as of animals. He had not gone two leagues when four other heroes, each six feet tall, fell upon him, bound him and dragged him back to a cell. He was asked by his judges whether he would rather be thrashed thirty-six times by the whole regiment or receive a dozen lead bullets at once in his brain. Although he protested that men's wills are free and that he wanted neither one nor the other, he had to make a choice; by virtue of that gift of God which is called *liberty*, he determined to run the gauntlet thirty-six times and actually did so twice. There were two thousand men in the regiment. That made four thousand strokes which laid bare the muscles and nerves from his neck to his backside. As they were about to proceed to a third turn, Candide, utterly exhausted, begged as a favor that they would be so kind as to smash his head; he obtained this favor; they bound his eyes and he was made to kneel down. At that moment the King of the Bulgarians came by and inquired the victim's crime; and as this King was possessed of a vast genius, he perceived from what he learned about Candide that he was a young metaphysician very ignorant in worldly matters, and therefore pardoned him with a clemency which will be praised in all newspapers and all ages. An honest surgeon healed Candide in three weeks with the ointments recommended by Dioscorides.[4] He had already regained a little skin and could walk when the King of the Bulgarians went to war with the King of the Abares.[5]

CHAPTER III—HOW CANDIDE ESCAPED FROM THE BULGARIANS AND WHAT BECAME OF HIM

Nothing could be smarter, more splendid, more brilliant, better drawn up than the two armies. Trumpets, fifes, hautboys, drums, cannons, formed a harmony such as has never been heard even in hell. The cannons first of all laid flat about six thousand men on each side; then the musketry removed from the best of worlds some nine or ten thousand blackguards who infested its surface. The bayonet also was the

3. **double up** Double-time.
4. **Dioscorides** Famous Greek doctor.
5. **Abares** The French-Austrian coalition, which fought against Frederick in the Seven Years' War.

sufficient reason for the death of some thousands of men. The whole might amount to thirty thousand souls. Candide, who trembled like a philosopher, hid himself as well as he could during this heroic butchery.

At last, while the two Kings each commanded a *Te Deum*[1] in his camp, Candide decided to go elsewhere to reason about effects and causes. He clambered over heaps of dead and dying men and reached a neighboring village, which was in ashes; it was an Abare village which the Bulgarians had burned in accordance with international law. Here, old men dazed with blows watched the dying agonies of their murdered wives who clutched their children to their bleeding breasts; there, disembowelled girls who had been made to satisfy the natural appetites of heroes gasped their last sighs; others, half-burned, begged to be put to death. Brains were scattered on the ground among dismembered arms and legs.

Candide fled to another village as fast as he could; it belonged to the Bulgarians, and Abarian heroes had treated it in the same way. Candide, stumbling over quivering limbs or across ruins, at last escaped from the theatre of war, carrying a little food in his knapsack, and never forgetting Mademoiselle Cunegonde. His provisions were all gone when he reached Holland; but, having heard that everyone in that country was rich and a Christian, he had no doubt at all but that he would be as well treated as he had been in the Baron's castle before he had been expelled on account of Mademoiselle Cunegonde's pretty eyes.

He asked an alms of several grave persons, who all replied that if he continued in that way he would be shut up in a house of correction to teach him how to live. He then addressed himself to a man who had been discoursing on charity in a large assembly for an hour on end. This orator, glancing at him askance, said: "What are you doing here? Are you for the good cause?"

"There is no effect without a cause," said Candide modestly. "Everything is necessarily linked up and arranged for the best. It was necessary that I should be expelled from the company of Mademoiselle Cunegonde, that I ran the gauntlet, and that I beg my bread until I can earn it; all this could not have happened differently."

"My friend," said the orator, "do you believe that the Pope is Anti-Christ?"

"I had never heard so before," said Candide, "but whether he is or isn't, I am starving."

"You don't deserve to eat," said the other. "Hence, rascal; hence, you wretch; and never come near me again."

The orator's wife thrust her head out of the window and seeing a man who did not believe that the Pope was Anti-Christ, she poured on

1. **Te Deum** A hymn of thanks to God for victory.

his head a full . . . O Heavens! To what excess religious zeal is carried by ladies!

A man who had not been baptized, an honest Anabaptist[2] named Jacques, saw the cruel and ignominious treatment of one of his brothers, a featherless two-legged creature with a soul; he took him home, cleaned him up, gave him bread and beer, presented him with two florins, and even offered to teach him to work at the manufacture of Persian stuffs which are made in Holland. Candide threw himself at the man's feet, exclaiming: "Doctor Pangloss was right in telling me that all is for the best in this world, for I am vastly more touched by your extreme generosity than by the harshness of the gentleman in the black cloak and his good lady."

The next day when he walked out he met a beggar covered with sores, dull-eyed, with the end of his nose fallen away, his mouth awry, his teeth black, who talked huskily, was tormented with a violent cough and spat out a tooth at every cough.

CHAPTER IV—HOW CANDIDE MET HIS OLD MASTER IN PHILOSOPHY, DOCTOR PANGLOSS, AND WHAT HAPPENED

Candide, moved even more by compassion than by horror, gave this horrible beggar the two florins he had received from the honest Anabaptist, Jacques. The phantom gazed fixedly at him, shed tears and threw its arms round his neck. Candide recoiled in terror.

"Alas!" said the wretch to the other wretch, "don't you recognise your dear Pangloss?"

"What do I hear? You, my dear master! You, in this horrible state! What misfortune has happened to you? Why are you no longer in the noblest of castles? What has become of Mademoiselle Cunegonde, the pearl of young ladies, the masterpiece of Nature?"

"I am exhausted," said Pangloss. Candide immediately took him to the Anabaptist's stable where he gave him a little bread to eat; and when Pangloss had recovered: "Well!" said he, "Cunegonde?"

"Dead," replied the other.

At this word Candide swooned; his friend restored him to his senses with a little bad vinegar which happened to be in the stable. Candide opened his eyes. "Cunegonde dead! Ah! best of worlds, where are you? But what illness did she die of? Was it because she saw me kicked out of her father's noble castle?"

"No," said Pangloss. "She was disembowelled by Bulgarian soldiers, after having been raped to the limit of possibility; they broke the Baron's head when he tried to defend her; the Baroness was cut to pieces; my

2. **Anabaptist** Member of a Protestant sect which opposed infant baptism.

poor pupil was treated exactly like his sister; and as to the castle, there is not one stone standing on another, not a barn, not a sheep, not a duck, not a tree; but we were well avenged, for the Abares did exactly the same to a neighboring barony which belonged to a Bulgarian Lord." At this, Candide swooned again; but, having recovered and having said all that he ought to say, he inquired the cause and effect, the sufficient reason which had reduced Pangloss to so piteous a state.

"Alas!" said Pangloss, "'tis love; love, the consoler of the human race, the preserver of the universe, the soul of all tender creatures, gentle love."

"Alas!" said Candide, "I am acquainted with this love, this so'vereign of hearts, this soul of our soul; it has never brought me anything but one kiss and twenty kicks in the backside. How could this beautiful cause produce in you so abominable an effect?"

Pangloss replied as follows: "My dear Candide! You remember Paquette, the maidservant of our august Baroness; in her arms I enjoyed the delights of Paradise which have produced the tortures of Hell by which you see I am devoured; she was infected and perhaps is dead. Paquette received this present from a most learned monk, who had it from the source; for he received it from an old countess, who had it from a cavalry captain, who owed it to a marchioness, who derived it from a page, who had received it from a Jesuit, who, when a novice, had it in a direct line from one of the companions of Christopher Columbus. For my part, I shall not give it to anyone, for I am dying."

"O Pangloss!" exclaimed Candide, "this is a strange genealogy! Wasn't the devil at the root of it?"

"Not at all," replied that great man. "It was something indispensable in this best of worlds, a necessary ingredient; for, if Columbus in an island of America had not caught this disease, which poisons the source of generation, and often indeed prevents generation, we should not have chocolate and cochineal[1]; it must also be noticed that hitherto in our continent this disease is peculiar to us, like theological disputes. The Turks, the Indians, the Persians, the Chinese, the Siamese and the Japanese are not yet familiar with it; but there is a sufficient reason why they in their turn should become familiar with it in a few centuries. Meanwhile, it has made marvellous progress among us, and especially in those large armies composed of honest, well-bred stipendiaries who decide the destiny of States; it may be asserted that when thirty thousand men fight a pitched battle against an equal number of troops, there are about twenty thousand with the pox on either side."

"Admirable!" said Candide. "But you must get cured."

---

1. **cochineal** A scarlet dye, prized in Europe, but an absurdly disproportionate advantage.

"How can I?" said Pangloss. "I haven't a sou, my friend, and in the whole extent of this globe, you cannot be bled or receive an enema without paying or without someone paying for you."

This last speech determined Candide; he went and threw himself at the feet of his charitable Anabaptist, Jacques, and drew so touching a picture of the state to which his friend was reduced that the good easy man did not hesitate to succor Pangloss; he had him cured at his own expense. In this cure Pangloss only lost one eye and one ear. He could write well and knew arithmetic perfectly. The Anabaptist made him his bookkeeper. At the end of two months he was compelled to go to Lisbon on business and took his two philosophers on the boat with him. Panglass explained to him how everything was for the best. Jacques was not of this opinion.

"Men," said he, "must have corrupted a nature a little, for they were not born wolves,[2] and they have become wolves. God did not give them twenty-four-pounder cannons or bayonets, and they have made bayonets and cannons to destroy each other. I might bring bankruptcies into the account and Justice which seizes the goods of bankrupts in order to deprive the creditors of them."

"It was all indispensable," replied the one-eyed doctor, "and private misfortunes make the public good, so that the more private misfortunes there are, the more everything is well."[3]

While he was reasoning, the air grew dark, the winds blew from the four quarters of the globe and the ship was attacked by the most horrible tempest in sight of the port of Lisbon.

CHAPTER V—STORM, SHIPWRECK, EARTHQUAKE, AND WHAT HAPPENED TO DR. PANGLOSS, TO CANDIDE AND THE ANABAPTIST JACQUES

Half the enfeebled passengers, suffering from that inconceivable anguish which the rolling of a ship causes in the nerves and in all the humors of bodies shaken in contrary directions, did not retain strength enough even to trouble about the danger. The other half screamed and prayed; the sails were torn, the masts broken, the vessel leaking. Those worked who could, no one cooperated, no one commanded. The Anabaptist tried to help the crew a little; he was on the main deck; a furious sailor struck him violently and stretched him on the deck; but the blow he delivered gave him so violent a shock that he fell head-first out of the ship. He remained hanging and clinging to part of the broken mast. The good Jacques ran to his aid, helped him to climb back, and from the

2. **wolves** A favorite contention of Jean-Jacques Rousseau, Voltair's contemporary.
3. **well** A further step in reducing philosophical optimism to absurdity.

effort he made was flung into the sea in full view of the sailor, who allowed him to drown without condescending even to look at him. Candide came up, saw his benefactor reappear for a moment and then be engulfed for ever. He tried to throw himself after him into the sea; he was prevented by the philosopher Pangloss, who proved to him that the Lisbon roads[1] had been expressly created for the Anabaptist to be drowned in them. While he was proving this *a priori*,[2] the vessel sank, and every one perished except Pangloss, Candide and the brutal sailor who had drowned the virtuous Anabaptist; the blackguard swam successfully to the shore and Pangloss and Candide were carried there on a plank.

When they had recovered a little, they walked toward Lisbon; they had a little money by the help of which they hoped to be saved from hunger after having escaped the storm. Weeping the death of their benefactor, they had scarcely set foot in the town when they felt the earth tremble under their feet; the sea rose in foaming masses in the port and smashed the ships which rode at anchor. Whirlwinds of flame and ashes covered the streets and squares; the houses collapsed, the roofs were thrown upon the foundations, and the foundations were scattered; thirty thousand inhabitants of every age and both sexes were crushed under the ruins. Whistling and swearing, the sailor said: "There'll be something to pick up here."

"What can be the sufficient reason for this phenomenon?" said Pangloss.

"It is the last day!"[3] cried Candide.

The sailor immediately ran among the debris, dared death to find money, found it, seized it, got drunk, and having slept off his wine, purchased the favors of the first woman of good will he met on the ruins of the houses and among the dead and dying. Pangloss, however, pulled him by the sleeve. "My friend," said he, "this is not well, you are disregarding universal reason, you choose the wrong time."

"Blood and 'ounds!" he retorted, "I am a sailor and I was born in Batavia; four times have I stamped on the crucifix during four voyages to Japan;[4] you have found the right man for your universal reason!"

Candide had been hurt by some falling stones; he lay in the street covered with debris. He said to Pangloss: "Alas! Get me a little wine and oil; I am dying."

"This earthquake is not a new thing," replied Pangloss. "The town of Lima felt the same shocks in America last year; similar causes produce

1. **roads** "Where ships may safely ride at anchor."
2. **a priori** The deductive method of argument which proceeds from preestablished principles, rather than from experience.
3. **last day** I.e., the Day of Judgment.
4. **Japan** A regulation imposed on merchants in an attempt to prevent commerce with Christians.

similar effects; there must certainly be a train of sulphur underground from Lima to Lisbon."

"Nothing is more probable," replied Candide; "but, for God's sake, a little oil and wine."

"What do you mean, probable?" replied the philosopher, "I maintain that it is proved."

Candide lost consciousness, and Pangloss brought him a little water from a neighboring fountain.

Next day they found a little food as they wandered among the ruins and regained a little strength. Afterwards they worked like others to help the inhabitants who had escaped death. Some citizens they had assisted gave them as good a dinner as could be expected in such a disaster; true, it was a dreary meal; the hosts watered their bread with their tears, but Pangloss consoled them by assuring them that things could not be otherwise. "For," said he, "all this is for the best; for, if there is a volcano at Lisbon, it cannot be anywhere else; for it is impossible that things should not be where they are; for all is well."

A little, dark man, a familiar of the Inquisition,[5] who sat beside him, politely took up the conversation, and said: "Apparently, you do not believe in original sin; for, if everything is for the best, there was neither fall nor punishment."[6]

"I most humbly beg your excellency's pardon," replied Pangloss still more politely, "for the fall of man and the curse necessarily entered into the best of all possible worlds."

"Then you do not believe in free will?" said the familiar.

"Your excellency will pardon me," said Pangloss; "free will can exist with absolute necessity; for it was necessary that we should be free; for in short, limited will . . ."

Pangloss was in the middle of his phrase when the familiar nodded to his armed attendant who was pouring out port or Oporto wine for him.

CHAPTER VI—HOW A SPLENDID AUTO-DA-FÉ WAS HELD TO PREVENT EARTHQUAKES, AND HOW CANDIDE WAS FLOGGED

After the earthquake which destroyed three-quarters of Lisbon, the wise men of that country could discover no more efficacious way of preventing a total ruin than by giving the people a splendid *auto-da-fé*.[1] It

5. **Inquisition** An officer of the Inquisition, or Holy Office, a tribunal which, from the thirteenth century to the eighteenth, attempted to stamp out heresy.

6. **punishment** The fall of man (*Genesis*, iii), with his subsequent redemption, is the orthodox Christian explanation of evil.

1. **auto-da-fé** "Act of faith"—the ceremony of burning heretics at the stake.

was decided by the university of Coimbre[1] that the sight of several persons being slowly burned in great ceremony is an infallible secret for preventing earthquakes. Consequently they had arrested a Biscayan convicted of having married his fellow-godmother, and two Portuguese who, when eating a chicken, had thrown away the bacon;[2] after dinner they came and bound Dr. Pangloss and his disciple Candide, one because he had spoken and the other because he had listened with an air of approbation; they were both carried separately to extremely cool apartments,[3] where there was never any discomfort from the sun; a week afterwards each was dressed in a sanbenito and their heads were ornamented with paper mitres; Candide's mitre and sanbenito[4] were painted with flames upside down and with devils who had neither tails nor claws; but Pangloss's devils had claws and tails, and his flames were upright.

Dressed in this manner they marched in procession and listened to a most pathetic sermon, followed by lovely plain song music. Candide was flogged in time to the music, while the singing went on; the Biscayan and the two men who had not wanted to eat the bacon were burned, and Pangloss was hanged, although this is not the custom. The very same day, the earth shook again with a terrible clamor.

Candide, terrified, dumbfounded, bewildered, covered with blood, quivering from head to foot, said to himself: "If this is the best of all possible worlds, what are the others? Let it pass that I was flogged, for I was flogged by the Bulgarians, but, O my dear Pangloss! The greatest of philosophers! Must I see you hanged without knowing why! O my dear Anabaptist! The best of men! Was it necessary that you should be drowned in port! O Mademoiselle Cunegonde! The pearl of women! Was it necessary that your belly should be slit!"

He was returning, scarcely able to support himself, preached at, flogged, absolved and blessed, when an old woman accosted him and said: "Courage, my son, follow me."

CHAPTER VII—HOW AN OLD WOMAN TOOK CARE OF CANDIDE AND HOW HE REGAINED THAT WHICH HE LOVED

Candide did not take courage, but he followed the old woman to a hovel; she gave him a pot of ointment to rub on, and left him food and drink; she pointed out a fairly clean bed; near the bed there was a suit of clothes. "Eat, drink, sleep," said she, "and may our Lady of Atocha, my

2. **Coimbre** Portuguese city north of Lisbon.
3. **bacon** Thus indicating that they were Jews.
4. **apartments** Ironical for "dank cells."
5. **sanbenito** Ceremonial frocks worn by condemned heretics. Voltaire's description is accurate.

Lord Saint Anthony of Padua and my Lord Saint James of Compostella take care of you; I shall come back tomorrow."

Candide, still amazed by all he had seen, by all he had suffered, and still more by the old woman's charity, tried to kiss her hand. " 'Tis not my hand you should kiss," said the old woman, "I shall come back tomorrow. Rub on the ointment, eat and sleep,"

In spite of all his misfortune, Candide ate and went to sleep. Next day the old woman brought him breakfast, examined his back and smeared him with another ointment; later she brought him dinner, and returned in the evening with supper. The next day she went through the same ceremony.

"Who are you?" Candide kept asking her. "Who has inspired you with so much kindness? How can I thank you?"

The good woman never made any reply; she returned in the evening without any supper. "Come with me," said she, "and do not speak a word."

She took him by the arm and walked into the country with him for about a quarter of a mile; they came to an isolated house, surrounded with gardens and canals. The old woman knocked at a little door. It was opened; she led Candide up a back stairway into a gilded apartment, left him on a brocaded sofa,[1] shut the door and went away. Candide thought he was dreaming, and felt that his whole life was a bad dream and the present moment an agreeable dream. The old woman soon reappeared; she was supporting with some difficulty a trembling woman of majestic stature, glittering with precious stones and covered with a veil.

"Remove the veil," said the old woman to Candide. The young man advanced and lifted the veil with a timid hand. What a moment! What a surprise! He thought he saw Mademoiselle Cunegonde, in fact he was looking at her, it was she herself. His strength failed him, he could not utter a word and fell at her feet. Cunegonde fell on the sofa. The old woman dosed them with distilled waters; they recovered their senses and began to speak: at first they uttered only broken words, questions and answers at cross purposes, sighs, tears, exclamations. The old woman advised them to make less noise and left them alone.

"What! Is it you?" said Candide. "You are alive, and I find you here in Portugal! Then you were not raped? Your belly was not slit, as the philosopher Pangloss assured me?"

"Yes, indeed," said the fair Cunegonde; "but those two accidents are not always fatal."

"But your father and mother were killed?"

" 'Tis only too true," said Cunegonde, weeping.

---

1. **sofa** Ladylike! Voltaire both uses and parodies the recognition scenes so frequent in tall tales of adventure.

"And your brother?"

"My brother was killed too."

"And why are you in Portugal? And how did you know I was here? And by what strange adventure have you brought me to this house?"

"I will tell you everything," replied the lady, "but first of all you must tell me everything that has happened to you since the innocent kiss you gave me and the kicks you received."

Candide obeyed with profound respect; and, although he was bewildered, although his voice was weak and trembling, although his back was still a little painful, he related in the most natural manner all he had endured since the moment of their separation. Cunegonde raised her eyes to heaven; she shed tears at the death of the good Anabaptist and Pangloss, after which she spoke as follows to Candide, who did not miss a word and devoured her with his eyes.

CHAPTER VIII—CUNEGONDE'S STORY

"I was fast asleep in bed when it pleased Heaven to send the Bulgarians to our noble castle of Thunder-ten-tronckh; they murdered my father and brother and cut my mother to pieces. A large Bulgarian six feet tall, seeing that I had swooned at the spectacle, began to rape me; this brought me to, I recovered my senses, I screamed, I struggled, I bit, I scratched. I tried to tear out the big Bulgarian's eyes, not knowing that what was happening in my father's castle was a matter of custom; the brute stabbed me with a knife in the left side where I still have the scar."

"Alas! I hope I shall see it," said the naïf Candide.

"You shall see it," said Cunegonde, "but let me go on."

"Go on," said Candide.

She took up the thread of her story as follows: "A Bulgarian captain came in, saw me covered with blood, and the soldier did not disturb himself. The captain was angry at the brute's lack of respect to him, and killed him on my body. Afterwards, he had me bandaged and took me to his billet as a prisoner of war. I washed the few shirts he had and did the cooking; I must admit he thought me very pretty; and I will not deny that he was very well built and that his skin was white and soft; otherwise he had little wit and little philosophy; it was plain that he had not been brought up by Dr. Pangloss. At the end of three months he lost all his money and got tired of me; he sold me to a Jew named Don Issachar, who traded in Holland and Portugal and had a passion for women. This Jew devoted himself to my person but he could not triumph over it; I resisted him better than the Bulgarian soldier; a lady of honor may be raped once, but it strengthens her virtue. In order to subdue me, the Jew brought me to this country house. Up till then I believed that there was nothing on earth so splendid as the castle of Thunder-ten-tronckh; I was undeceived.

"One day the Grand Inquisitor noticed me at Mass; he ogled me continually and sent a message that he wished to speak to me on secret affairs. I was taken to his palace; I informed him of my birth; he pointed out how much it was beneath my rank to belong to an Israelite. A proposition was made on his behalf to Don Issachar to give me up to His Lordship. Don Issachar, who is the court banker and a man of influence, would not agree. The Inquisitor threatened him with an *auto-da-fé*. At last the Jew was frightened and made a bargain whereby the house and I belong to both in common. The Jew has Mondays, Wednesdays and the Sabbath day, and the Inquisitor has the other days of the week. This arrangement has lasted for six months. It has not been without quarrels; for it has often been debated whether the night between Saturday and Sunday belonged to the old law or the new. For my part, I have hitherto resisted them both; and I think that is the reason why they still love me.

"At last My Lord the Inquisitor was pleased to arrange an *auto-da-fé* to remove the scourge of earthquakes and to intimidate Don Issachar. He honored me with an invitation. I had an excellent seat; and refreshments were served to the ladies between the Mass and the execution. I was indeed horror stricken when I saw the burning of the two Jews and the honest Biscayan who had married his fellow-godmother; but what was my surprise, my terror, my anguish, when I saw in a sanbenito and under a mitre a face which resembled Pangloss's! I rubbed my eyes, I looked carefully, I saw him hanged; and I fainted. I had scarcely recovered my senses when I saw you stripped naked; that was the height of horror, of consternation, of grief and despair. I will frankly tell you that your skin is even whiter and of a more perfect tint than that of my Bulgarian captain. This spectacle redoubled all the feelings which crushed and devoured me. I exclaimed, I tried to say: 'Stop, Barbarians!' but my voice failed and my cries would have been useless. When you had been well flogged, I said to myself: 'How does it happen that the charming Candide and the wise Pangloss are in Lisbon, the one to receive a hundred lashes and the other to be hanged, by order of My Lord the Inquisitor, whose darling I am? Pangloss deceived me cruelly when he said that all is for the best in the world.'

"I was agitated, distracted, sometimes beside myself and sometimes ready to die of faintness, and my head was filled with the massacre of my father, of my mother, of my brother, the insolence of my horrid Bulgarian soldier, the gash he gave, my slavery, my life as a kitchen wench, my Bulgarian captain, my horrid Don Issachar, my abominable Inquisitor, the hanging of Dr. Pangloss, that long plain song *miserere*[1]

1. **miserere**   The Latin chant: "Have mercy upon me, O God."

during which you were flogged, and above all the kiss I gave you behind the screen that day when I saw you for the last time. I praised God for bringing you back to me through so many trials, I ordered my old woman to take care of you and to bring you here as soon as she could. She has carried out my commission very well; I have enjoyed the inexpressible pleasure of seeing you again, of listening to you, and of speaking to you. You must be very hungry; I have a good appetite; let us begin by having supper."

Both sat down to supper; and after supper they returned to the handsome sofa we have already mentioned; they were still there when Signor Don Issachar, one of the masters of the house, arrived. It was the day of the Sabbath. He came to enjoy his rights and to express his tender love.

CHAPTER IX—WHAT HAPPENED TO CUNEGONDE, TO CANDIDE, TO THE GRAND INQUISITOR AND TO A JEW

This Issachar was the most choleric Hebrew who had been seen in Israel since the Babylonian captivity.[1] "What!" said he. "Bitch of a Galilean, isn't it enough to have the Inquisitor? Must this scoundrel share with me too?"

So saying, he drew a long dagger which he always carried and, thinking that his adversary was unarmed, threw himself upon Candide; but our good Westphalian had received an excellent sword from the old woman along with his suit of clothes. He drew his sword, and although he had a most gentle character, laid the Israelite stone-dead on the floor at the feet of the fair Cunegonde.

"Holy Virgin!" she exclaimed, "what will become of us? A man killed in my house! If the police come we are lost."

"If Pangloss had not been hanged," said Candide, "he would have given us good advice in this extremity, for he was a great philosopher. In default of him, let us consult the old woman."

She was extremely prudent and was beginning to give her advice when another little door opened. It was an hour after midnight, and Sunday was beginning. This day belonged to My Lord the Inquisitor. He came in and saw the flogged Candide sword in hand, a corpse lying on the ground, Cunegonde in terror, and the old woman giving advice. At this moment, here is what happened in Candide's soul and the manner of his reasoning: "If this holy man calls for help, he will infallibly have me burned; he might do as much to Cunegonde; he had me pitilessly lashed; he is my rival; I am in the mood to kill, there is no room for hesitation."

1. **captivity** The Jews were held in captivity by the Babylonians in the sixth century, B.C.

His reasoning was clear and swift; and, without giving the Inquisitor time to recover from his surprise, he pierced him through and through and cast him beside the Jew.

"Here's another," said Cunegonde, "there is no chance of mercy; we are excommunicated, our last hour has come. How does it happen that you, who were born so mild, should kill a Jew and a prelate in two minutes?"

"My dear young lady," replied Candide, "when a man is in love, jealous, and has been flogged by the Inquisition, he is beside himself."

The old woman than spoke up and said: "In the stable are three Andalusian horses, with their saddles and bridles; let the brave Candide prepare them; mademoiselle has moidores[2] and diamonds; let us mount quickly, although I can only sit on one buttock, and go to Cadiz; the weather is beautifully fine, and it is most pleasant to travel in the coolness of the night."

Candide immediately saddled the three horses. Cunegonde, the old woman and he rode thirty miles without stopping. While they were riding away, the Holy Hermandad[3] arrived at the house; My Lord was buried in a splendid church and Issachar was thrown into a sewer.

Candide, Cunegonde and the old woman had already reached the little town of Avacena in the midst of the mountains of the Sierra Morena; and they talked in their inn as follows.

CHAPTER X—HOW CANDIDE, CUNEGONDE AND THE OLD WOMAN ARRIVED AT CADIZ IN GREAT DISTRESS, AND HOW THEY EMBARKED

"Who can have stolen my pistoles[1] and my diamonds?" said Cunegonde, weeping. "How shall we live? What shall we do? Where shall we find Inquisitors and Jews to give me others?"

"Alas!" said the old woman, "I strongly suspect a reverend Franciscan father who slept in the same inn at Badajoz with us; Heaven forbid that I should judge rashly! But he twice came into our room and left long before we did."

"Alas!" said Candide, "the good Pangloss often proved to me that this world's goods are common to all men and that every one has an equal right to them. According to these principles the monk should have left

2. **moidores** Portuguese coin. As a slight concession to local color and realism, Voltaire invariably used the terms for money and food that were proper to the country concerned.

3. **Hermandad** Holy Brotherhood, an association formed in Spain to track down criminals.

1. **pistoles** Spanish gold coin.

us enough to continue our journey. Have you nothing left then, my fair Cunegonde?"

"Not a maravedi,"[2] said she. "What are we to do?" said Candide.

"Sell one of the horses," said the old woman. "I will ride postillion behind Mademoiselle Cunegonde, although I can only sit on one buttock, and we will get to Cadiz."

In the same hotel there was a Benedictine prior. He bought the horse very cheap.[3] Candide, Cunegonde and the old woman passed through Lucena, Chillas, Lebrixa, and at last reached Cadiz.[4] A fleet was there being equipped and troops were being raised to bring to reason the reverend Jesuit fathers of Paraguay,[5] who were accused of causing the revolt of one of their tribes against the kings of Spain and Portugal near the town of Sacramento. Candide, having served with the Bulgarians, went through the Bulgarian drill before the general of the little army with so much grace, celerity, skill, pride and agility,[6] that he was given the command of an infantry company. He was now a captain; he embarked with Mademoiselle Cunegonde, the old woman, two servants, and the two Andalusian horses which had belonged to the Grand Inquisitor of Portugal.

During the voyage they had many discussions about the philosophy of poor Pangloss. "We are going to a new world," said Candide, "and no doubt it is there that everything is for the best; for it must be admitted that one might lament a little over the physical and moral happenings in our own world."

"I love you with all my heart," said Cunegonde, "but my soul is still shocked by what I have seen and undergone."

"All will be well," replied Candide; "the sea in this new world already is better than the seas of our Europe; it is calmer and the winds are more constant. It is certainly the new world which is the best of all possible worlds."

"God grant it!" said Cunegonde, "but I have been so horribly unhappy in mine that my heart is nearly closed to hope."

"You complain," said the old woman to them. "Alas! you have not endured such misfortunes as mine."

Cunegonde almost laughed and thought it most amusing of the old woman to assert that she was more unfortunate. "Alas! my dear," said she, "unless you have been raped by two Bulgarians, stabbed twice in the belly, have had two castles destroyed, two fathers and mothers murdered

2. **maravedi** Copper coin of little value.
3. **cheap** Sudden change in point of view, for ironic effect.
4. **Cadiz** Seaport in southern Spain.
5. **Paraguay** This was no imaginary event. Voltaire had a financial interest in one of the ships, the *Pascal*.
6. **agility** The Prussian disciplinary drill was notoriously thorough.

before your eyes, and have seen two of your lovers flogged in an *auto-da-fé*, I do not see how you can surpass me; moreover, I was born a Baroness with seventy-two quarterings and I have been a kitchen wench."

"You do not know my birth," said the old woman, "and if I showed you my backside you would not talk as you do and you would suspend your judgment."

This speech aroused intense curiosity in the minds of Cunegonde and Candide. . . .

CHAPTER XVI—WHAT HAPPENED TO THE TWO TRAVELLERS WITH TWO GIRLS, TWO MONKEYS, AND THE SAVAGES CALLED OREILLONS

Candide and his valet were past the barriers before anybody in the camp knew of the death of the German Jesuit. The vigilant Cacambo had taken care to fill his saddlebag with bread, chocolate, ham, fruit, and several bottles of wine. On their Andalusian horses they plunged into an unknown country where they found no road. At last a beautiful plain traversed by streams met their eyes. Our two travellers put their horses to grass. Cacambo suggested to his master that they should eat and set the example.

"How can you expect me to eat ham," said Candide, "when I have killed the son of My Lord the Baron and find myself condemned never to see the fair Cunegonde again in my life? What is the use of prolonging my miserable days since I must drag them out far from her in remorse and despair! And what will the Journal de Trévoux[1] say?"

Speaking thus, he began to eat. The sun was setting. The two wanderers heard faint cries which seemed to be uttered by women. They could not tell whether these were cries of pain or of joy; but they rose hastily with that alarm and uneasiness caused by everything in an unknown country. These cries came from two completely naked girls who were running gently along the edge of the plain, while two monkeys pursued them and bit their buttocks. Candide was moved to pity; he had learned to shoot among the Bulgarians and could have brought down a nut from a tree without touching the leaves. He raised his double-barrelled Spanish gun, fired, and killed the two monkeys.

"God be praised, my dear Cacambo, I have delivered these two poor creatures from a great danger; if I committed a sin by killing an Inquisitor and a Jesuit, I have atoned for it by saving the lives of these two

---

1. **Trévoux** The celebrated Journal of the French Jesuits. Voltaire often satirized its editor.

girls. Perhaps they are young ladies of quality and this adventure may be of great advantage to us in this country."

He was going on, but his tongue clove to the roof of his mouth when he saw the two girls tenderly kissing the two monkeys, shedding tears on their bodies and filling the air with the most piteous cries.

"I did not expect so much human kindliness," he said at last to Cacambo, who replied: "You have performed a wonderful masterpiece; you have killed the two lovers of these young ladies."

"Their lovers! Can it be possible? You are jesting at me, Cacambo; how can I believe you?"

"My dear master," replied Cacambo, "you are always surprised by everything; why should you think it so strange that in some countries there should be monkeys who obtain ladies' favors? They are quarter men, as I am a quarter Spaniard."

"Alas!" replied Candide, "I remember to have heard Dr. Pangloss say that similar accidents occurred in the past and that these mixtures produce Aigypans, fauns and satyrs; that several eminent persons of antiquity have seen them; but I thought they were fables."[2]

"You ought now to be convinced that it is true," said Cacambo, "and you see how people behave when they have not received a proper education; the only thing I fear is that these ladies may get us into difficulty."

These wise reflections persuaded Candide to leave the plain and to plunge into the woods. He ate supper there with Cacambo and, after having cursed the Inquisitor of Portugal, the governor of Buenos Ayres and the Baron, they went to sleep on the moss. When they woke up they found they could not move; the reason was that during the night the Oreillons,[3] the inhabitants of the country, to whom they had been denounced by the two ladies, had bound them with ropes made of bark. They were surrounded by fifty naked Oreillons, armed with arrows, clubs and stone hatchets. Some were boiling a large cauldron, others were preparing spits and they were all shouting: "Here's a Jesuit, here's a Jesuit! We shall be revenged and have a good dinner: let us eat the Jesuit, let us eat the Jesuit!"

"I told you so, my dear master," said Cacambo sadly. "I knew those two girls would play us a dirty trick."

Candide perceived the cauldron and the spits and exclaimed: "We are certainly going to be roasted or boiled. Ah! What would Dr. Pangloss say

2. **fables** Voltaire had read these stories in a serious book on mythology by Abbé Banier.

3. **Oreillons** A tribe of Indians, so called because they distended their ears with ornaments.

4. **Jesuit** The translation should read: "Let us eat Jesuit." The Jesuits were expelled from France five years after *Candide*—but not because of *Candide*.

if he saw what the pure state of nature is? All is well, granted; but I confess it is very cruel to have lost Mademoiselle Cunegonde and to be spitted by the Oreillons."

Cacambo never lost his head. "Do not despair," he said to the wretched Candide. "I understand a little of their dialect and I will speak to them."

"Do not fail," said Candide, "to point out to them the dreadful inhumanity of cooking men and how very unchristian it is."

"Gentlemen," said Cacambo, "you mean to eat a Jesuit today? 'Tis a good deed; nothing could be more just than to treat one's enemies in this fashion.[5] Indeed the law of nature teaches us to kill our neighbor and this is how people behave all over the world. If we do not exert the right of eating our neighbor, it is because we have other means of making good cheer; but you have not the same resources as we, and it is certainly better to eat our enemies than to abandon the fruits of victory to ravens and crows. But, gentlemen, you would not wish to eat your friends. You believe you are about to place a Jesuit on the spit, and 'tis your defender, the enemy of your enemies you are about to roast. I was born in your country; the gentleman you see here is my master and, far from being a Jesuit, he has just killed a Jesuit and is wearing his clothes; which is the cause of your mistake. To verify what I say, take his gown, carry it to the first barrier of the kingdom of *Los Padres* and inquire whether my master has not killed a Jesuit officer. It will not take you long and you will have plenty of time to eat us if you find I have lied. But if I have told the truth, you are too well acquainted with the principles of public law, good morals and discipline, not to pardon us."

The Oreillons thought this a very reasonable speech; they deputed two of their notables to go with all diligence and find out the truth. The two deputies acquitted themselves of their task like intelligent men and soon returned with the good news. The Oreillons unbound their two prisoners, overwhelmed them with civilities, offered them girls, gave them refreshment, and accompanied them to the frontiers of their dominions, shouting joyfully: "He is not a Jesuit, he is not a Jesuit!"

Candide could not cease from wondering at the cause of his deliverance. "What a nation," said he. "What men! What manners! If I had not been so lucky as to stick my sword through the body of Mademoiselle Cunegonde's brother I should infallibly have been eaten. But, after all, there is something good in the pure state of nature, since these people, instead of eating me, offered me a thousand civilities as soon as they knew I was not a Jesuit."

5. **fashion** It was in fact a common practice among American Indians, a way of acquiring an enemy's valor.

CHAPTER XVII—ARRIVAL OF CANDIDE AND HIS VALET IN THE COUNTRY OF ELDORADO[1] AND WHAT THEY SAW THERE

When they reached the frontiers of the Oreillons, Cacambo said to Candide: "You see this hemisphere is no better than the other; take my advice, let us go back to Europe by the shortest road."

"How can we go back," said Candide, "and where can we go? If I go to my own country, the Bulgarians and the Abares are murdering everybody; if I return to Portugal I shall be burned; if we stay here, we run the risk of being spitted at any moment. But how can I make up my mind to leave that part of the world where Mademoiselle Cunegonde is living?"

"Let us go to Cayenne,"[2] said Cacambo, "we shall find Frenchmen there, for they go all over the world; they might help us. Perhaps God will have pity on us."

It was not easy to go to Cayenne. They knew roughly the direction to take, but mountains, rivers, precipices, brigands and savages were everywhere terrible obstacles. Their horses died of fatigue; their provisions were exhausted; for a whole month they lived on wild fruits and at last found themselves near a little river fringed with cocoanut-trees which supported their lives and their hopes.

Cacambo, who always gave advice as prudent as the old woman's, said to Candide: "We can go no farther, we have walked far enough; I can see an empty canoe in the bank, let us fill it with cocoanuts, get into the little boat and drift with the current; a river always leads to some inhabited place. If we do not find anything pleasant, we shall at least find something new."

"Come on then," said Candide, "and let us trust to Providence."

They drifted for some leagues between banks which were sometimes flowery, sometimes bare, sometimes flat, sometimes steep. The river continually became wider; finally it disappeared under an arch of frightful rocks which towered up to the very sky. The two travellers were bold enough to trust themselves to the current under this arch. The stream, narrowed between walls, carried them with horrible rapidity and noise. After twenty-four hours they saw daylight again; but their canoe was wrecked on reefs; they had to crawl from rock to rock for a whole league and at last they discovered an immense horizon, bordered by inaccessible mountains. The country was cultivated for pleasure as well as for necessity; everywhere the useful was agreeable. The roads were covered or

1. **Eldorado** A fabulous Land of Gold, in which even Sir Walter Raleigh once believed.
2. **Cayenne** Capital of Franch Guiana.

rather ornamented with carriages of brilliant material and shape, carrying men and women of singular beauty, who were rapidly drawn along by large red sheep whose swiftness surpassed that of the finest horses of Andalusia, Tetuan, and Mequinez.[3]

"This country," said Candide, "is better than Westphalia."

He landed with Cacambo near the first village he came to. Several children of the village, dressed in torn gold brocade, were playing quoits outside the village. Our two men from the other world amused themselves by looking on; their quoits were large round pieces, yellow, red and green which shone with peculiar lustre. The travellers were curious enough to pick up some of them; they were of gold, emeralds and rubies, the least of which would have been the greatest ornament in the Mogul's throne.

"No doubt," said Cacambo, "these children are the sons of the King of this country playing at quoits."

At that moment the village schoolmaster appeared to call them into school.

"This," said Candide, "is the tutor of the Royal Family."

The little beggars immediately left their game, abandoning their quoits and everything with which they had been playing. Candide picked them up, ran to the tutor, and presented them to him humbly, giving him to understand by signs that their Royal Highnesses had forgotten their gold and their previous stones. The village schoolmaster smiled, threw then on the ground, gazed for a moment at Candide's face with much surprise and continued on his way. The travellers did not fail to pick up the gold, the rubies and the emeralds.

"Where are we?" cried Candide. "The children of the King must be well brought up, since they are taught to despise gold and precious stones."

Cacambo was as much surrised as Candide. At last they reached the first house in the village, which was built like a European palace. There were crowds of people round the door and still more inside; very pleasant music could be heard and there was a delicious smell of cooking. Cacambo went up to the door and heard them speaking Peruvian; it was his maternal tongue, for everyone knows that Cacambo was born in a village of Tucuman where nothing else is spoken.

"I will act as your interpreter," he said to Candide, "this is an inn, let us enter."

Immediately two boys and two girls of the inn, dressed in cloth of gold, whose hair was bound up with ribbons, invited them to sit down to the table d'hôte. They served four soups each garnished with two parrots, a boiled condor which weighed two hundred pounds, two roast

---

3. **Mequinez** Tetuan and Mequinez are Moroccan towns.

monkeys of excellent flavor, three hundred colibris in one dish and six hundred hummingbirds in another, exquisite ragouts and delicious pastries, all in dishes of a sort of rock crystal. The boys and girls brought several sorts of drinks made of sugarcane. Most of the guests were merchants and coachmen, all extremely polite, who asked Cacambo a few questions with the most delicate discretion and answered his in a satisfactory manner.

When the meal was over, Cacambo, like Candide, thought he could pay the reckoning by throwing on the table two of the large pieces of gold he had picked up; the host and hostess laughed until they had to hold their sides. At last they recovered themselves.

"Gentlemen," said the host, "we perceive you are strangers; we are not accustomed to seeing them. Forgive us if we began to laugh when you offered us in payment the stones from our highways. No doubt you have none of the money of this country, but you do not need any to dine here. All the hotels established for the utility of commerce are paid for by the government. You have been ill entertained here because this is a poor village; but everywhere else you will be received as you deserve to be."

Cacambo explained to Candide all that the host had said, and Candide listened in the same admiration and disorder with which his friend Cacambo interpreted. "What can this country be," they said to each other, "which is unknown to the rest of the world and where all nature is so different from ours? Probably it is the country where everything is for the best; for there must be one country of that sort. And, in spite of what Dr. Pangloss said, I often noticed that everything went very ill in Westphalia."

CHAPTER XVIII—WHAT THEY SAW IN THE LAND OF ELDORADO

Cacambo informed the host of his curiosity, and the host said: "I am a very ignorant man and am all the better for it; but we have here an old man who has retired from the court and who is the most learned and most communicative man in the kingdom." And he at once took Cacambo to the old man. Candide now played only the second part and accompanied his valet. They entered a very simple house, for the door was only of silver and the panelling of the apartments in gold, but so tastefully carved that the richest decorations did not surpass it. The antechamber indeed was only encrusted with rubies and emeralds; but the order with which everything was arranged atoned for this extreme simplicity.

The old man received the two strangers on a sofa padded with colibri feathers, and presented them with drinks in diamond cups; after which he satisfied their curiosity in these words: "I am a hundred and seventy-two years old and I heard from my late father, the King's equerry, the astonishing revolutions of Peru of which he had been an eye-witness. The kingdom where we now are is the ancient country of the Incas, who most imprudently left it to conquer part of the world and were at last destroyed by the Spaniards. The princes of their family who remained in their native country had more wisdom; with the consent of the nation, they ordered that no inhabitants should ever leave our little kingdom, and this it is that has preserved our innocence and our felicity. The Spaniards had some vague knowledge of this country, which they called Eldorado, and about a hundred years ago an Englishman named Raleigh came very near to it; but, since we are surrounded by inaccessible rocks and precipices, we have hitherto been exempt from the rapacity of the nations of Europe who have an inconceivable lust for the pebbles and mud of our land and would kill us to the last man to get possession of them."

The conversation was long; it touched upon the form of the government, manners, women, public spectacles and the arts. Finally Candide, who was always interested in metaphysics, asked through Cacambo whether the country had a religion.

The old man blushed a little. "How can you doubt it?" said he. "Do you think we are ingrates?"

Cacambo humbly asked what was the religion of Eldorado.

The old man blushed again. "Can there be two religions?" said he. "We have, I think, the religion of every one else; we adore God from evening until morning."

"Do you adore only one God?" said Cacambo, who continued to act as the interpreter of Candide's doubts.

"Manifestly," said the old man, "there are not two or three or four. I must confess that the people of your world ask very extraordinary questions."

Candide continued to press the old man with questions; he wished to know how they prayed to God in Eldorado.

"We do not pray," said the good and respectable sage, "we have nothing to ask from him; he has given us everything necessary and we continually give him thanks."

Candide was curious to see the priests; and asked where they were.

The good old man smiled. "My friends," said he, "we are all priests; the King and all the heads of families solemnly sing praises every morning, accompanied by five or six thousand musicians."

"What! Have you no monks to teach, to dispute, to govern, to intrigue and to burn people who do not agree with them?"

"For that, we should have to become fools," said the old man; "here we are all of the same opinion and do not understand what you mean with your monks."

At all this Candide was in an ecstasy and said to himself: "This is very different from Westphalia and the castle of His Lordship the Baron; if our friend Pangloss had seen Eldorado, he would not have said that the castle of Thunder-ten-tronckh was the best of all that exists on the earth; certainly, a man should travel."

After this long conversation the good old man ordered a carriage to be harnessed with six sheep and gave the two travellers twelve of his servants to take them to court. "You will excuse me," he said, "if my age deprives me of the honor of accompanying you. The King will receive you in a manner which will not displease you and doubtless you will pardon the customs of the country if any of them disconcert you."

Candide and Cacambo entered the carriage; the six sheep galloped off and in less than four hours they reached the King's palace, which was situated at one end of the capital. The portal was two hundred and twenty feet high and a hundred feet wide; it is impossible to describe its material. Anyone can see the prodigious superiority it must have over the pebbles and sand we call *gold* and *gems*.

Twenty beautiful maidens of the guard received Candide and Cacambo as they alighted from the carriage, conducted them to the baths and dressed them in robes woven from the down of colibris; after which the principal male and female officers of the Crown led them to his Majesty's apartment through two files of a thousand musicians each, according to the usual custom. As they approached the throneroom, Cacambo asked one of the chief officers how they should behave in his Majesty's presence; whether they should fall on their knees or flat on their faces, whether they should put their hands on their heads or on their backsides; whether they should lick the dust of the throneroom; in a word, what was the ceremony?

"The custom," said the chief officer, "is to embrace the King and to kiss him on either cheek."

Candide and Cacambo threw their arms round his Majesty's neck; he received them with all imaginable favor and politely asked them to supper. Meanwhile they were carried to see the town, the public buildings rising to the very skies, the market-places ornamented with thousands of columns, the fountains of rose-water and of liquors distilled from sugarcane, which played continually in the public squares paved with precious stones which emitted a perfume like that of cloves and cinnamon.

Candide asked to see the law courts; he was told there were none, and that nobody ever went to law. He asked if there were prisons and was told there were none. He was still more surprised and pleased by the palace of sciences, where he saw a gallery two thousand feet long, filled with instruments of mathematics and physics.

After they had explored all the afternoon about a thousandth part of the town, they were taken back to the King. Candide sat down to table with his Majesty, his valet Cacambo and several ladies. Never was better cheer, and never was anyone wittier at supper than his Majesty. Cacambo explained the King's witty remarks to Candide and even when translated they still appeared witty. Among all the things which amazed Candide, this did not amaze him the least.

They enjoyed this hospitality for a month. Candide repeatedly said to Cacambo: "Once again, my friend, it is quite true that the castle where I was born cannot be compared with this country; but then Mademoiselle Cunegonde is not here and you probably have a mistress in Europe. If we remain here, we shall only be like everyone else; but if we return to our own world with only twelve sheep laden with Eldorado pebbles, we shall be richer than all the kings put together; we shall have no more Inquisitors to fear and we can easily regain Mademoiselle Cunegonde."

Cacambo agreed with this; it is so pleasant to be on the move, to show off before friends, to make a parade of the things seen on one's travels, that these two happy men resolved to be so no longer and to ask his Majesty's permission to depart.

"You are doing a very silly thing," said the King."I know my country is small; but when we are comfortable anywhere we should stay there; I certainly have not the right to detain foreigners, that is a tyranny which does not exist either in our manners or our laws; all men are free, leave when you please, but the way out is very difficult. It is impossible to ascend the rapid river by which you miraculously came here and which flows under arches of rock. The mountains which surround the whole of my kingdom are ten thousand feet high and are perpendicular like walls; they are more than ten leagues broad, and you can only get down from them by way of precipices. However, since you must go, I will give orders to the directors of machinery to make a machine which will carry you comfortably. When you have been taken to the other side of the mountains, nobody can proceed any farther with you; for my subjects have sworn never to pass this boundary and they are too wise to break their oath. Ask anything else of me you wish."

"We ask nothing of your Majesty," said Cacambo, "except a few sheep laden with provisions, pebbles and the mud of this country."

The King laughed. "I cannot understand," he said, "the taste you people of Europe have for our yellow mud; but take as much as you wish, and much good may it do you."

He immediately ordered his engineers to make a machine to hoist these two extraordinary men out of his kingdom. Three thousand learned scientists worked at it; it was ready in a fortnight and only cost about twenty million pounds sterling in the money of that country. Candide and Cacambo were placed on the machine; there were two large red sheep¹ saddled and bridled for them to ride on when they had passed the mountains, twenty sumpter sheep laden with provisions, thirty carrying presents of the most curious productions of the country and fifty laden with gold, precious stones and diamonds. The King embraced the two vagabonds tenderly. Their departure was a splendid sight and so was the ingenious manner in which they and their sheep were hoisted on to the top of the mountains. The scientists took leave of them after having landed them safely, and Candide's only desire and object was to go and present Mademoiselle Cunegonde with his sheep.

"We have sufficient to pay the governor of Buenos Ayres," said he, "if Mademoiselle Cunegonde can be bought. Let us go to Cayenne, and take ship, and then we will see what kingdom we will buy."

CHAPTER XIX—WHAT HAPPENED TO THEM AT SURINAM AND HOW CANDIDE MADE THE ACQUAINTANCE OF MARTIN

Our two travellers' first day was quite pleasant. They were encouraged by the idea of possessing more treasures than all Asia, Europe and Africa could collect. Candide in transport carved the name of Cunegonde on the trees. On the second day two of the sheep stuck in a marsh and were swallowed up with their loads; two other sheep died of fatigue a few days later; then seven or eight died of hunger in a desert; several days afterwards others fell off precipices. Finally, after they had travelled for a hundred days, they had only two sheep left.

Candide said to Cacambo: "My friend, you see how perishable are the riches of this world; nothing is steadfast but virtue and the happiness of seeing Mademoiselle Cunegonde again."

"I admit it," said Cacambo, "but we still have two sheep with more treasures than ever the King of Spain will have, and in the distance I see a town I suspect is Surinam,² which belongs to the Dutch. We are at the end of our troubles and the beginning of our happiness."

As they drew near the town they came upon a negro lying on the ground wearing only half his clothes, that is to say, a pair of blue cotton drawers; this poor man had no left leg and no right hand. "Good heavens!" said Candide to him in Dutch, "what are you doing there, my friend, in that horrible state?"

1. **sheep** Pack-sheep.

2. **Surinam** In Dutch Guiana.

"I am waiting for my master, the famous merchant Monsieur Vanderdendur."

"Was it Monsieur Vanderdenur," said Candide, "who treated you in that way?"

"Yes, sir," said the negro, "it is the custom. We are given a pair of cotton drawers twice a year as clothing. When we work in the sugar mills and the grindstone catches our fingers, they cut off the hand; when we try to run away, they cut off a leg. Both these things happened to me. This is the price paid for the sugar you eat in Europe. But when my mother sold me for ten patagons on the coast of Guinea, she said to me: 'My dear child, give thanks to our fetishes, always worship them, and they will make you happy; you have the honor to be a slave of our lords the white men and thereby you have made the fortune of your father and mother.' Alas! I do not know whether I made their fortune, but they certainly did not make mine. Dogs, monkeys and parrots are a thousand times less miserable than we are; the Dutch fetishes who converted me tell me that we are all of us, whites and blacks, the children of Adam. I am not a genealogist, but if these preachers tell the truth, we are all second cousins. Now, you will admit that no one could treat his relatives in a more horrible way."

"O Pangloss!" cried Candide. "This is an abomination you had not guessed; this is too much, in the end I shall have to renounce optimism."

"What is optimism?" said Cacambo.

"Alas!" said Candide, "it is the mania of maintaining that everything is well when we are wretched."[2] And he shed tears as he looked at his negro; and he entered Surinam weeping.

The first thing they inquired was whether there was any ship in the port which could be sent to Buenos Ayres. The person they addressed happened to be a Spanish captain, who offered to strike an honest bargain with them. He arranged to meet them at an inn. Candide and the faithful Cacambo went and waited for him with their two sheep. Candide, who blurted everything out, told the Spaniard all his adventures and confessed that he wanted to elope with Mademoiselle Cunegonde.

"I shall certainly not take you to Buenos Ayres," said the captain. "I should be hanged and you would, too. The fair Cunegonde is his Lordship's favorite mistress."

Candide was thunderstruck; he sobbed for a long time; then he took Cacambo aside. "My dear friend," said he, "this is what you must do. We have each of us in our pockets five or six millions worth of diamonds; you are more skilful than I am; go to Buenos Ayres and get

---

2. **wretched**   This is Voltaire's main point. Happiness in the abstract has no meaning for the suffering individual.

Mademoiselle Cunegonde. If the governor makes any difficulties give him a million; if he is still obstinate give him two; you have not killed an Inquisitor so they will not suspect you. I will fit out another ship, I will go and wait for you at Venice; it is a free country where there is nothing to fear from Bulgarians, Abares, Jews or Inquisitors."

Cacambo applauded this wise resolution; he was in despair at leaving a good master who had become his intimate friend; but the pleasure of being useful to him overcame the grief of leaving him. They embraced with tears. Candide urged him not to forget the good old woman. Cacambo set off that very same day; he was a very good man, this Cacambo.

Candide remained some time longer at Surinam waiting for another captain to take him to Italy with the two sheep he had left. He engaged servants and bought everything necessary for a long voyage. At last Monsieur Vanderdendur, the owner of a large ship, came to see him.

"How much do you want," he asked this man, "to take me straight to Venice with my servants, my baggage and these two sheep?"

The captain asked for ten thousand piastres. Candide did not hesitate. "Oh! Ho!" said the prudent Vanderdendur to himself, "this foreigner gives ten thousand piastres immediately! He must be very rich." He returned a moment afterwards and said he could not sail for less than twenty thousand.

"Very well, you shall have them," said Candide.

"Whew!" said the merchant to himself, "this man gives twenty thousand piastres as easily as ten thousand." He came back again, and said he could not take him to Venice for less than thirty thousand piastres.

"Then you shall have thirty thousand," replied Candide.

"Oho!" said the Dutch merchant to himself again, "thirty thousand piastres is nothing to this man; obviously the two sheep are laden with immense treasures; I will not insist any further; first let me make him pay the thirty thousand piastres, and then we will see."

Candide sold two little diamonds, the smaller of which was worth more than all the money the captain asked. He paid him in advance. The two sheep were taken on board. Candide followed in a little boat to join the ship which rode at anchor; the captain watched his time, set his sails and weighed anchor; the wind was favorable. Candide, bewildered and stupefied, soon lost sight of him. "Alas!" he cried, "this is a trick worthy of the old world."

He returned to shore, in grief; for he had lost enough to make the fortunes of twenty kings. He went to the Dutch judge; and, as he was rather disturbed, he knocked loudly at the door; he went in, related what had happened and talked a little louder than he ought to have done. The judge began by fining him ten thousand piastres for the noise he had made; he then listened patiently to him, promised to look into his affair as soon as the merchant returned, and charged him another ten thousand piastres for the expenses of the audience.

This behavior reduced Candide to despair; he had indeed endured misfortunes a thousand times more painful; but the calmness of the judge and of the captain who had robbed him, stirred up his bile and plunged him into a black melancholy. The malevolence of men revealed itself to his mind in all its ugliness; he entertained only gloomy ideas.

At last a French ship was about to leave for Bordeaux and, since he no longer had any sheep laden with diamonds to put on board, he hired a cabin at a reasonable price and announced throughout the town that he would give the passage, food and two thousand piastres to an honest man who would make the journey with him, on condition that his man was the most unfortunate and the most disgusted with his condition in the whole province. Such a crowd of applicants arrived that a fleet would not have contained them. Candide, wishing to choose among the most likely, picked out twenty persons who seemed reasonably sociable and who all claimed to deserve his preference. He collected them in a tavern and gave them supper, on condition that each took an oath to relate truthfully the story of his life, promising that he would choose the man who seemed to him the most deserving of pity and to have the most cause for being discontented with his condition, and that he would give the others a little money. The sitting lasted until four o'clock in the morning. As Candide listened to their adventures he remembered what the old woman had said on the voyage to Buenos Ayres and how she had wagered that there was nobody on the boat who had not experienced very great misfortunes. At each story which was told him, he thought of Pangloss.

"This Pangloss," said he, "would have some difficulty in supporting his system. I wish he were here. Certainly, if everything is well, it is only in Eldorado and not in the rest of the world."

He finally determined in favor of a poor man of letters who had worked ten years for the booksellers at Amsterdam. He judged that there was no occupation in the world which could more disgust a man.[3] This man of letters, who was also a good man, had been robbed by his wife, beaten by his son, and abandoned by his daughter, who had eloped with a Portuguese. He had just been deprived of a small post on which he depended and the preachers of Surinam were persecuting him because they thought he was a Socinian.[4] It must be admitted that the others were at least as unfortunate as he was; but Candide hoped that this

---

3. **man** Voltaire had had unhappy personal dealings with the Dutch publishers.
4. **Socinian** A sect resembling the Unitarians.

learned man would help to pass the time during the voyage. All his other rivals considered that Candide was doing them a great injustice; but he soothed them down by giving each of them a hundred piastres.

CHAPTER XXVIII—WHAT HAPPENED TO CANDIDE, TO CUNEGONDE, TO PANGLOSS, TO MARTIN, ETC.

"Pardon once more," said Candide to the Baron, "pardon me, reverend father, for having thrust my sword through your body."

"Let us say no more about it," said the Baron. "I admit I was a little too sharp; but since you wish to know how it was you saw me in a galley, I must tell you that after my wound was healed by the brother apothecary of the college, I was attacked and carried off by a Spanish raiding party; I was imprisoned in Buenos Ayres at the time when my sister had just left. I asked to return to the Vicar-General in Rome. I was ordered to Constantinople to act as almoner to the Ambassador of France. A week after I had taken up my office I met towards evening a very handsome young page of the Sultan. It was very hot; the young man wished to bathe; I took the opportunity to bathe also. I did not know that it was a most serious crime for a Christian to be found naked with a young Mahometan. A cadi sentenced me to a hundred strokes on the soles of my feet and condemned me to the galley. I do not think a more horrible injustice has ever been committed. But I should very much like to know why my sister is in the kitchen of a Transylvanian sovereign living in exile among the Turks."

"But, my dear Pangloss," said Candide, "how does it happen that I see you once more?"

"It is true," said Pangloss, "that you saw me hanged; and in the natural course of events I should have been burned.[1] But you remember, it poured with rain when they were going to roast me; the storm was so violent that they despaired of lighting the fire; I was hanged because they could do nothing better; a surgeon bought my body, carried me home and dissected me. He first made a crucial incision in me from the navel to the collarbone. Nobody could have been worse hanged than I was. The executioner of the holy Inquisition, who was a sub-deacon, was marvellously skilful in burning people, but he was not accustomed to hang them; the rope was wet and did not slide easily and it was knotted; in short, I still breathed. The crucial incision caused me to utter so loud a scream that the surgeon fell over backwards and, thinking he was dissecting the devil, fled away in terror and fell down the staircase in his flight. His wife ran in from another room at the noise; she saw me

1. **burned** But burning would not have served Voltaire's purposes.

stretched out on the table with my crucial incision; she was still more frightened than her husband, fled, and fell on top of him. When they had recovered themselves a little, I heard the surgeon's wife say to the surgeon: 'My dear, what were you thinking of, to dissect a heretic? Don't you know the devil always possesses them? I will go and get a priest at once to exorcise him.'

"At this I shuddered and collected the little strength I had left to shout: 'Have pity on me!' At last the Portuguese barber[2] grew bolder; he sewed up my skin; his wife even took care of me, and at the end of a fortnight I was able to walk again. The barber found me a situation and made me lackey to a Knight of Malta who was going to Venice; but, as my master had no money to pay me wages, I entered the service of a Venetian merchant and followed him to Constantinople.

"One day I took it into my head to enter a mosque; there was nobody there except an old Imam and a very pretty young devotee who was reciting her prayers; her breasts were entirely uncovered; between them she wore a bunch of tulips, roses, anemones, ranunculus, hyacinths and auriculas; she dropped her bunch of flowers; I picked it up and returned it to her with a most respectful alacrity. I was so long putting them back that the Imam grew angry and, seeing I was a Christian, called for help. I was taken to the cadi, who sentenced me to receive a hundred strokes on the soles of my feet and sent me to the galleys. I was chained on the same seat and in the same galley as My Lord the Baron. In this galley there were four young men from Marseilles, five Neapolitan priests and two monks from Corfu, who assured us that similar accidents occurred every day. His Lordship the Baron claimed that he had suffered a greater injustice than I; and I claimed that it was much more permissible to replace a bunch of flowers between a woman's breasts than to be naked with one of the Sultan's pages. We argued continually, and every day received twenty strokes of the bull's pizzle, when the chain of events of this universe led you to our galley and you ransomed us."

"Well! my dear Pangloss," said Candide, "when you were hanged, dissected, stunned with blows and made to row in the galleys, did you always think that everything was for the best in this world?"

"I am still of my first opinion," replied Pangloss, "for after all I am a philosopher; and it would be unbecoming for me to recant, since Leibnitz could not be in the wrong and pre-established harmony is the finest thing imaginable like the plenum and subtle matter."[3]

2. **barber** Like the Barber of Seville, he was also the surgeon.

3. **matter** According to Leibnitz, harmony between the spiritual and material worlds was pre-established by God. The plenum and subtle matter form part of the German philosopher's outmoded physics.

CHAPTER XXIX—HOW CANDIDE FOUND CUNEGONDE AND THE OLD WOMAN AGAIN

While Candide, the Baron, Pangloss, Martin and Cacambo were relating their adventures, reasoning upon contingent or non-contingent events of the universe, arguing about effects and causes, moral and physical evil, free will and necessity, and the consolation to be found in the Turkish galleys, they came to the house of the Transylvanian prince on the shores of Propontis.

The first objects which met their sight were Cunegonde and the old woman hanging out towels to dry on the line. At this sight the Baron grew pale. Candide, that tender lover, seeing his fair Cunegonde sunburned, blear-eyed, flat-breasted, with wrinkles round her eyes and red, chapped arms, recoiled three paces in horror, and then advanced from mere politeness. She embraced Candide and her brother. They embraced the old woman; Candide bought them both.

In the neighborhood was a little farm; the old woman suggested that Candide should buy it, until some better fate befell the group. Cunegonde did not know that she had become ugly, for nobody had told her so; she reminded Candide of his promises in so peremptory a tone that the good Candide dared not refuse her. He therefore informed the Baron that he was about to marry his sister.

"Never," said the Baron, "will I endure such baseness on her part and such insolence on yours; nobody shall ever reproach me with this infamy; my sister's children could never enter the chapters of Germany. No, my sister shall never marry anyone but a Baron of the Empire."

Cunegonde threw herself at his feet and bathed them in tears; but he was inflexible.

"Madman," said Candide, "I rescued you from the galleys, I paid your ransom and your sister's; she was washing dishes here, she is ugly, I am so kind as to make her my wife, and you pretend to oppose me! I should re-kill you if I listened to my anger."

"You may kill me again," said the Baron, "but you shall never marry my sister while I am alive."

CHAPTER XXX—CONCLUSION

At the bottom of his heart Candide had not the least wish to marry Cunegonde. But the Baron's extreme impertinence determined him to complete the marriage, and Cunegonde urged it so warmly that he could not retract. He consulted Pangloss, Martin and the faithful Cacambo.

1. **contingent** A contingent event is a possible but not inevitable eventuality.
2. **chapters** Knightly assemblies.

Pangloss wrote an excellent memorandum by which he proved that the Baron had no rights over his sister and that by all the laws of the empire she could make a left-handed marriage with Candide. Martin advised that the Baron should be thrown into the sea; Cacambo decided that he should be returned to the Levantine captain and sent back to the galleys, after which he would be returned by the first ship to the Vicar-General at Rome. This was thought to be very good advice; the old woman approved it; they said nothing to the sister; the plan was carried out with the aid of a little money and they had the pleasure of duping a Jesuit and punishing the pride of a German Baron.

It would be natural to suppose that when, after so many disasters, Candide was married to his mistress, and living with the philosopher Pangloss, the philosopher Martin, the prudent Cacambo and the old woman, having brought back so many diamonds from the country of the ancient Incas, he would lead the most pleasant life imaginable.[2] But he was so cheated by the Jews[3] that he had nothing left but his little farm; his wife, growing uglier every day, became shrewish and unendurable; the old woman was ailing and even more bad tempered than Cunegonde. Cacambo, who worked in the garden and then went to Constantinople to sell vegetables, was overworked and cursed his fate. Pangloss was in despair because he did not shine in some German university.

As for Martin, he was firmly convinced that people are equally uncomfortable everywhere; he accepted things patiently. Candide, Martin and Pangloss sometimes argued about metaphysics and morals. From the windows of the farm they often watched the ships going by, filled with effendis, pashas, and cadis, who were being exiled to Lemnos, to Mitylene and Erzerum. They saw other cadis, other pashas and other effendis coming back to take the place of the exiles and to be exiled in their turn. They saw the neatly impaled heats which were taken to the Sublime Porte.[4] These sights redoubled their discussions; and when they were not arguing, the boredom was so excessive that one day the old woman dared to say to them: "I should like to know which is worse, to be raped a hundred times by negro pirates, to have a buttock cut off, to run the gauntlet among the Bulgarians, to be whipped and flogged in an *auto-da-fé*, to be dissected, to row in a galley, in short, to endure all the miseries through which we have passed, or to remain here doing nothing?"

1. **marriage** A morganatic marriage, which does not give equality to the party of lower rank.
2. **imaginable** If this were an idle tale of adventure, the couple would have been left here, to "live happily ever afterwards."
3. **Jews** Voltaire suffered several severe financial losses through the bankruptcies of Jewish bankers.
4. **Porte** The Gate of the Turkish Sultan's palace, which was also the Palace of Justice.

"'Tis a great question," said Candide.

These remarks led to new reflections, and Martin especially concluded that man was born to live in the convulsions of distress or in the lethargy of boredom. Candide did not agree, but he asserted nothing. Pangloss confessed that he had always suffered horribly; but, having once maintained that everything was for the best, he had continued to maintain it without believing it.

One thing confirmed Martin in his detestable principles, made Candide hesitate more than ever, and embarrassed Pangloss. And it was this. One day there came to their farm Paquette and Friar Giroflée, who were in the most extreme misery; they had soon wasted their three thousand piastres, had left each other, made it up, quarrelled again, been put in prison, escaped, and finally Friar Giroflée had turned Turk. Paquette continued her occupation everywhere and now earned nothing by it.

"I foresaw," said Martin to Candide, "that your gifts would soon be wasted and would only make them the more miserable. You and Cacambo were once bloated with millions of piastres and you are no happier than Friar Giroflée and Paquette."

"Ah! Ha!" said Pangloss to Paquette, "so Heaven brings you back to us, my dear child? Do you know that you cost me the end of my nose, an eye and an ear! What a plight you are in! Ah! What a world this is!"

This new occurrence caused them to philosophise more than ever. In the neighborhood there lived a very famous Dervish, who was supposed to be the best philosopher in Turkey; they went to consult him; Pangloss was the spokesman and said: "Master, we have come to beg you to tell us why so strange an animal as man was ever created."

"What has it to do with you?" said the Dervish. "It is your business?"

"But reverend father," said Candide, "there is a horrible amount of evil in the world."

"What does it matter," said the Dervish, "whether there is evil or good? When his highness sends a ship[5] to Egypt, does he worry about the comfort or discomfort of the rats in the ship?"

"Then what should we do?" said Pangloss.

"Hold your tongue," said the Dervish.

"I flattered myself," said Pangloss, "that I should discuss with you effects and causes, this best of all possible worlds, the origin of evil, the nature of the soul and pre-established harmony."

At these words the Dervish slammed the door in their faces.

During this conversation the news went round that at Constantinople two viziers and the mufti had been strangled and several of their friends impaled. This catastrophe made a prodigious noise everywhere for

5. **ship** This pessimistic passage seems to limit severely the extent of Divine Providence. Compare the ending of the Book of Job.

several hours. As Pangloss, Candide and Martin were returning to their little farm, they came upon an old man who was taking the air under a bower of orange trees at his door. Pangloss, who was as curious as he was argumentative, asked him what was the name of the mufti who had just been strangled.

"I do not know," replied the old man. "I have never known the name of any mufti or of any vizier. I am entirely ignorant of the occurrence you mention; I presume that in general those who meddle with public affairs sometimes perish miserably and that they deserve it; but I never inquire what is going on in Constantinople; I content myself with sending there for sale the produce of the garden I cultivate."

Having spoken thus, he took the strangers into his house. His two daughters and his two sons presented them with several kinds of sherbert which they made themselves, caymac flavored with candied citron peel, oranges, lemons, limes, pineapples, dates, pistachios and Mocha coffee which had not been mixed with the bad coffee of Batavia and the Isles. After which this good Mussulman's two daughters perfumed the beards of Candide, Pangloss and Martin.

"You must have a vast and magnificent estate?" said Candide to the Turk.

"I have only twenty acres," replied the Turk. "I cultivate them with my children; and work keeps at bay three great evils: boredom, vice and need."

As Candide returned to his farm he reflected deeply on the Turk's remarks. He said to Pangloss and Martin: "That good old man seems to me to have chosen an existence preferable by far to that of the six kings with whom we had the honor to sup."

"Exalted rank," said Pangloss, "is very dangerous, according to the testimony of all philosophers; for Eglon, King of the Moabites, was murdered by Ehud; Absalom was hanged by the hair and pierced by three darts; King Nadab, son of Jeroboam, was killed by Baasha; King Elah by Zimri; Ahaziah by Jehu; Athaliah by Jehoiada; the Kings Jehoiakim, Jeconiah and Zedekiah were made slaves. You know in what manner died Crœsus, Astyages, Darius, Denys of Syracuse, Pyrrhus, Perseus, Hannibal, Jugurtha, Ariovistus, Cæsar, Pompey, Nero, Otho, Vitellius, Domitian, Richard II of England, Edward II, Henry VI, Richard III, Mary Stuart, Charles I, the three Henrys of France, the Emperor Henry IV. You know . . ."

"I also know," said Candide, "that we should cultivate our gardens."

"You are right," said Pangloss, "for, when man was placed in the

6. **need** This is the key to Voltaire's philosophy of life. *Candide* gives abundant examples of all three of these evils.

7. **slaves** To explain these Biblical references would be pedantry—which Voltaire is here satirizing.

Garden of Eden, he was placed there *ut operaretur eum,* to dress it and to keep it; which proves that man was not born for idleness."

"Let us work without theorizing,"[8]said Martin; "'tis the only way to make life endurable."

The whole small fraternity entered into this praiseworthy plan, and each started to make use of his talents. The little farm yielded well. Cunegonde was indeed very ugly, but she became an excellent pastry cook; Paquette embroidered; the old woman took care of the linen. Even Friar Giroflée performed some service; he was a very good carpenter and even became a man of honor; and Pangloss sometimes said to Candide: "All events are linked up in this best of all possible worlds; for, if you had not been expelled from the noble castle, by hard kicks in your backside for love of Mademoiselle Cunegonde, if you had not been clapped into the Inquisition, if you had not wandered about America on foot, if you had not stuck your sword in the Baron, if you had not lost all your sheep from the land of Eldorado, you would not be eating citrons and pistachios here."[9]

"'Tis well said," replied Candide, "but we must cultivate our gardens."

FOCUSING QUESTIONS

1. How does Vico understand imagination?

2. Why does Vico believe that imagination created the worlds of the ancients?

3. What is the difference between the metaphysics of imagination and the metaphysics of reason?

4. Why does Vico suggest that the *topics* should be the starting point of education?

5. What does Voltaire mean by the assertion that this is the best of all possible worlds?

6. Can ideology educate?

7. Why does Voltaire end his book with Candide making a plea to all of us to "cultivate the garden"?

8. Could you identify other ideologies in contemporary education that could be ridiculed the way Voltaire does in his Candide?

8. **theorizing** I.e., since men can never grasp the ultimate ends of life, let us make the best of it without worrying—an "optimistic" acceptance of life as it is.
9. **here** The final reduction of Pangloss's philosophy to the absurd.

SUGGESTIONS FOR OTHER PRESENTATIONS

Nietzsche,   *Beyond Good and Evil* and *On the Genealogy of Morals.*

SUPPLEMENTARY READINGS

Vico, Giambattista.   *The New Science of Giambattista. Vico.* Translated by Thomas
   Goddard Bergin and Max Harold Fisch. Ithaca, N.Y.: Cornell University
   Press, 1970.

————.*On The Study Methods of Our Time.* Elio Gianturco. Indianapolis: Bobbs-
   Merrill, 1965.

Voltaire.   *Candide.*

Durant, Will and Ariel.   "The Age of Voltaire." In *The Story of Civilization.* Vol. 9.
   New York: Simon and Schuster.

10

The Contemporary University: John Dewey, Ortega y Gasset

The selections from John Dewey are accompanied by an article "Marx, Dewey, and Maritain: The Role of Religion in Society," by Prof. Jude P. Dougherty. Students and faculty might be able to read Dewey from a broader perspective of the presuppositions under which contemporary orthodoxies militate. The consequences of our own unquestioned premises are enormous for our educational goals and bringing them out into the open is already aiding in that goal.

John Dewey (1859–1952) is the best catalyst of the American modern period and the most influential theorist of modern education. Born in Vermont, he studied philosophy at Johns Hopkins in 1884, but it was at the University of Chicago where he lectured that he started his deep influence on American education, from 1896 to 1904. The rest is our history of education.

In a course on the philosophy of education it would serve little purpose to be candid and to offer my own philosophical evaluation of Dewey's philosophy or of Dewey as a philosopher. What I usually do with my own students is to read Dewey aloud in class, a page at a time and ask the students for their own evaluation. A first reading of Dewey raises no disagreements. All, or almost all the students agree with him. Yes, education is for a democratic society; yes, education should be based on experience; yes, education should make us free; yes, education should be based on reason and not emotion; yes, education should ground emotion on rational experience—and so forth. Then, I ask for a group of volunteers and entrust them for an itemized definition of the words Dewey uses: freedom, democracy, experience, etc. The following session we read the pages from Dewey again. I have never seen people change their minds so quickly about the interpretation of a text. The students soon discover that every word Dewey uses to sell his program of education has a different meaning from the one they take to the reading of the text. They soon learn to read experience as the experience of objects, theories, etc., achieved through the scientific method, freedom as the freedom to choose this scientific method from among all other methods; democracy, as a whole people trained in the use of the scientific method, i.e., aesthetics, theories, and experiences gathered through or by the scientific method. In sum, the students feel repulsion at their own inability to read in the first place, and secondly, a sense of betrayal against one who uses their original meanings with an indoctrinating twist. The students are not very kind in their judgment of Dewey.

Dewey is the advocate of applying the open-ended philosophy of pragmatism to education: education educates if it solves social problems. But in so doing Dewey justified the presence of the social sciences in education and devalued philosophical criticism. It is at the hands of this philosophy that we witness an indiscriminate "appropriation of meaning" from words, institutions, and policies of the past, and see them re-defined to accommodate pragmatist goals. Knowledge in the hands of Dewey becomes an instrument to solve problems.

Dewey, no doubt, was afraid of the individualist emotionalism of dictators, like Hitler, in Europe. He envisioned American society as a unified society to solve its problems through the method of the sciences. He did not see clearly the consequences of such a narrow conception of science, nor of the instrumentality of knowledge, nor of the contradictions inherent in such concepts as democratic society (plural) and scientific method (singular), as experience (plural) and scientific experience (singular), as education (plurality of faculties and acts) and scientific method (singularity of method universally applied), etc.

Let the students, through their presentation and vocabulary re-definition make up their minds on this issue; after all, this is the philosophy most preeminently surrounding them. But, let the students read the original Dewey and avoid commentators.

The *instrumentality* of knowledge is the present activity of the universities. Answers are important, even when the questions are neither understood nor relevant. And pragmatism is not the only culprit. The social sciences are the dispensers of the new philosophy of instrumentalism of reason and they have found powerful allies in departments of the humanities such as comparative literature and philosophy. Critical theory, either in the fashion of Hegel or that of Marx uses the same instrumentalism and appropriation of meaning to carry out their labor of teaching. At their hands, tradition has been buried, the classics are named but only to bury them again, and ignorance of other possible acts and other possible reflective activities are absent in education. And the student cannot be blamed for knowing too well a lesson we teach day in and day out. As a result we have inflation of nominalism in education, substituting for the educational process of the past. Words are the currency of the classroom and appropriation of meaning is the sign of an educated student or professor. Words are, on the one hand, very important, but on the other, they are empty of content; they are cut off from things and truth, from tradition or context and are shown to exist only in a logical world of their own with no inherent meaning. Language becomes manipulated by theories of language, each more radical than the previous one, and all contribute to political and educational confusion which even the American broad-mindedness finds it difficult to deal with. Students are asked to pay attention only to theories, and theories and their names are all students need to learn and accept—not to join the elite of the educated, but the paradise of the therapy set: groups of individual experts clamoring for individual rights. Our present education is producing on a large scale what Ortega y Gasset called "the mass-man." These educated masses now occupy the seats of highest social power. The mass-man is anyone who does not value himself or herself by any particular criterion, and who says instead that he or she is just like everybody else. This ridiculous claim makes the mass-man feel reassured, smugly at ease. Thus he or she demands nothing of himself or herself. Living is for these people what they already are, with no effort toward perfection; thus Ortega calls them "buoys floating on the waves."

Ortega y Gasset classifies this phenomenon of the appearence of mass-man as the "triumph of hyperdemocracy," where the mass-man, in union with other mass-men, takes direct action without regard for tradition and even the law, imposing their own desires and taste by material pressure. Mass-man believes in rights, even the right to impose and lend force to notions deriving from its own platitudes. If the individuals who make up the mass thought of themselves as specifically qualified, we would have in our hands merely a case of personal error, not a matter of sociological subversion. The characteristic note of our educated masses is that of the mediocre soul, the commonplace mind, knowing itself to be mediocre, having the audacity to assert rights to itself to be mediocre, and going on to impose itself on others wherever it can. The mass-man crushed the different, the noble, the excellent, the individual, the select, the choice. Whoever is not like everybody else, who does not think and behave like everybody else, runs the risk of being eliminated socially or economically. In normal times "everybody" was the complex union of mass with special, divergent minorities. Today "everybody" means the mass, the masses, and only the masses. Masses who are only concerned with their own well-being simultaneously show no concern for the causes and reasons for that well-being. They are uninterested. They interpret cultural rights with the same attitude as they take the natural right to breathe, and with the same lack of effort, except to cry for individual rights. But they purposely forget the effort it took to create all those advantages and rights of our civilization. But how can we link the students to that past when we live only in the present, an actual present that has both lost its own shadow, and has no ghosts in its closets?

Ortega y Gasset (1883–1955) wrote his *The Revolt of the Masses* (1931) around the same time that Dewey was propounding his evangelical ideas about education. Both men should be presented together, for were Dewey's system of philosophy capable of becoming contextualized, namely using the method that the context allows and not universally the scientific method, then Ortega and Dewey would come very close together as the proponents of the most concrete policies on education.

Ortega y Gasset is not afraid to delve into the classics to solve modern problems, but rather than focus on ideas, or theories, he wants to recover the original *act* which they called philosophy and which solved the problems they faced:

> The Universe is not discovered by philosophy, [but rather] philosophy has been a series of trials during twenty-five centuries to deal with the universe through the mental procedure that is philosophy. In this experiment diverse ways of making that instrument function have been tried. Every new try takes advantage of the previous one. Above all it takes advantage of the errors and limitations of the previous ones. In this sense it is proper to talk of the history of philosophy as being the description of the progress of philosophizing. This progress may end up by being in the end that some day we may discover that not only this or that way of thinking philosophically was limited and therefore wrong, but in absolute terms, to philosophize, any kind of philosophizing, is a limitation, an insufficiency, an error, and that there will be a need to invent another way of intellectually facing the universe; a way different from any previous to philosophy and from philosophy itself.
>
> *Obras Completas*, Vol. 8, pp. 269–270, Madrid

For Ortega to philosophize is to be always at the origins, to be original. Only that our own origins, namely our own origins in Greece are ambivalent. On the one hand we have Parmenides, with his demand for the fullness of being, the image of absolute thought able to save the phenomena even if one needs to reduce all phenomena to the necessities of thought. On the other hand we have Heraclitus, a vision of constant mutation, a multiplicity of points of view, an everlasting interpretation, a radical scarcity. Between these two poles, the *poros* and *penia* of being, Ortega chose the middle path: culture, which is visible and fixed at the surface level of ideas, and which is hidden and original at the level of presuppositions. In this manner he kept education opened to the past in culture and the present in originality, tradition, and renewal, avoiding the Parmenidean dream of superficial and imperialistic unities.

> Whoever aspires to understand man—that eternal tramp, a thing essentially on the road—must throw overboard all immobile concepts and learn to think in ever-shifting terms.
>
> *Obras Completas*, Vol. 5, p. 650

This inner mobility is what makes Ortega's system of education open where others found only closures of method:

> If primitive humanity had not possessed this ability to inflame itself with far-off things in order to struggle against the obstacles it encountered close at hand, humanity would continue to be static.
>
> *Obras Completas,* Vol. 4, p. 314

This task, this everlasting project of recreation of culture, Ortega ascribes to a joint effort of philosophy and education:

> We need to discover a new technique of invention. . . . Each people, each epoch takes new selections form the general repertory of "human" objects, and inside each epoch and each people, the individual exercises the final modulation.
>
> *Obras Completas,* Vol. 3, pp. 291 and 500.

The selections from Ortega y Gasset included in this volume have the following purposes. The selections from *The Revolt of the Masses* are offered as an exercise in reflection, the critical distancing from the beliefs surrounding us, our ideas, and even our platitudes to see how they stand the light of reason. The selection from *Mission of the University* has the purpose of presenting a whole thought about the one thing no one talks about any more, has the University any mission? It will be an excellent opportunity for acquainting faculty and students with a comprehensive program of action and speculation about the university. Neither students or faculty need agree with Ortega's program of education, as this is not the objective. The main purpose is the actual confrontation with the project. A presentation in public of the ideal and the actual presence of the university the students face daily should be an educational experience no one present would forget easily.

Marx, Dewey, and Maritain: The Role of Religion in Society

Jude P. Dougherty

Almost before our eyes, in the brief span of a few decades since World War II, this nation, like much of the West, has become intellectually secularized with consequences for the social order. Lord Patrick Devlin,[1] writing in the early 1960s, speculated that if a society's laws are based on a particular worldview and that worldview collapses, the laws will themselves crumble.

We have seen this happen gradually in the United States as the universities, many of which were founded by religious organizations, became secular and contributed to the secularization of the nation. How that happened is too long a story to tell here, but its outlines are well known. Largely through court decisions and aided by the major media, our intellectual elites have been able to instantiate a set of laws and gain acceptance for a life-style that anyone with memories of a prewar period would regard as alien. From a Christian perspective on life, and from laws which protected that perspective, this nation has come to embrace a secular mentality and laws which foster an almost unrestrained hedonism.

Once with Sunday closing laws we publicly proclaimed the Sabbath; with laws against the sale of contraceptives, affirmed the procreative end of marriage; with laws against pornography, taught the meaningfulness of the sexual act; with laws against abortion, taught the sacredness of human life; and with stiff penalties for criminal activity from homicide to drug peddling, taught other uncontested values. Devlin has been proven correct by the course of events, as the presuppositions behind these laws were challenged by important segments of society and the laws gave way. The ethics of our current intellectual elites prevail, with tragic consequences for the people. It now takes two working people to support a home whose permanence is not assured as the divorce rate approaches 50 percent and where the reproductive rate is well below that required for population maintenance.

What went wrong? The answer is bound to be complex and there are many ways to view the period. By exploring two fundamental ideas of Western civilization, "democracy" and "religion," from three major alter-

1. Patrick Devlin, *The Enforcement of Morals* (London: Oxford University Press, 1965), 1–25.

native viewpoints which are all still eminently influential yet representative of the divergence between this and the previous period—those of Karl Marx, John Dewey, and Jacques Maritain—we will advance toward an answer. The selection of Marx needs no explanation, given his historical and contemporary global influence. Dewey represents the perspective of secular humanism that he not only helped define but promoted from its intellectual roots to an activist social program. Maritain represents a historically and religiously informed mind, and in the tradition of his fellow countryman de Tocqueville, finds a close connection between the practice of religion and the viability of a democracy. This is not meant to be a mere textual exercise. For if one focuses on the global situation and finds there a contest between two superpowers, the deciding factor is not apt to be the presence or absence of a market economy. One has to probe beneath economics. From that perspective one can see that what our dominant intellectuals believe is not remarkably different from Marx's beliefs. Among the three, Dewey and Marx are closer to each other intellectually than are Dewey and Maritain.

It is not by accident that the Soviet Union distrusts and suppresses all but subservient forms of religion. No matter how removed from its initial Marxist charter, it is still bound to an ideology that is suspicious of all intermediary institutions. Since the beginning of Bolshevik control, religion has not merely represented an alternative ideology; it has been an obstacle to the progress of state control. "Believers" within the jurisdiction of the Soviet Union know what to expect of their government; this is less true in the West. In most Western countries the prevailing relationship between the ecclesial and secular orders is thought to have been worked out long ago to the mutual benefit of both. But I am convinced this is false. There is, in fact, a wide chasm between the agnosticism of the intellectuals who determine policy and the religious beliefs of the populace. And the former seem steadily to increase their influence on the laws which prevail in most Western nations.

In a previous century we might have considered our generation as an ebb tide in the rise and fall of cultures, certain that matters would right themselves in the course of time. But with a formidable military foe to the East bent on subduing the West the situation is different. The West must take stock of its resources, material and spiritual. The basic question is, can a Western form of materialism, a liberal secularism, withstand the ideological assault of the East with which it does not differ in important respects? An examination of conscience is long overdue. We must attend to the wellsprings of our culture and to the role which religion has played in shaping that culture.

MARX'S CRITIQUE OF RELIGION

With respect to his views on religion, Marx was a product of the then current literature, greatly influenced by theologians and biblical scholars David Strauss and Bruno Bauer.[2] From Hegel he accepted the notion that religion was a comprehensive account of human existence, somewhat more refined and precise than the ambiguous conception allowable to the poet, but lacking the rigor and precision that only philosophy can provide. This perception of the quasi-poetic nature of religion was reinforced by Strauss and Bauer who showed Marx how to understand Biblical literature. In the 1830s and 1840s when this idea was relatively new, Strauss and Bauer convinced Marx that the Sacred Scriptures were simply a work of the human imagination. The message of the Scriptures is wholly metaphorical; it is merely an imaginative expression of men's moral ideas. Strauss and Bauer agreed with Hegel that God is only an imaginative way of looking at the Absolute. Accordingly, they were convinced that we must move beyond the traditional notion of God and recognize that religion is merely one way of portraying the relationship between man and his moral ideas—an imperfect way, Feuerbach would say, since religion puts moral ideas into a separate and distant realm. The task, says Feuerbach, is to recover the purely human meaning of religion. We have to bring religion back to its proper proportions as an expression of human moral aspirations.[3]

Marx was in strong agreement with Feuerbach's ideas. He declared,[4] "For Germany, the criticism of religion is in the main complete, and criticism of religion is the premise of all criticism." From now on the criticism of religion would be translated into criticism of politics and the social order. Marx meant that he accepted the current secular understanding of religion and did not wish to redo the work of Hegel, Strauss, Bauer, and Feuerbach. He thought it important, however, to add one

2. David Strauss (1808–1874) in his first major work, *Das Leben Jesu, kritisch bearbeitet* (2 vols. 1835–36; *The Life of Jesus, Critically Examined,* 1846), denied the historical value of the Christian Gospels as historical myths, unintentionally created, the embodiment of the primitive hopes of the early Christian community. Shortly before the end of his life, he published *Der alte und neue Glaube* (1872; the Old Earth and The New, 1873), in which he ventured to replace Christianity with a Darwinian-influenced "scientific materialism." Bauer (1808–1882) similarly concluded that the Gospels were a record not of history but of human fantasies. Marx, when a student in Berlin, enrolled in one of Bauer's courses on the prophet Isaiah.

3. Ludwig Feurbach, *Das Wesen des Christentums* (1841; The Essence of Christianity, 1854).

4. Karl Marx, "Contribution to the Critique of Hegel's Philosophy of Law: Introduction" Karl Marx and Friedrich Engels, *Collected Works* (New York: International Publishers, 1976), Vol. 3, 175.

note. Feuerbach had been extremely vague about the reason why men tend to project their ideas into the objective order or tend to personify them in God. Marx, taking his cue from Feuerbach, concluded that because of intolerable social conditions engendered by a capitalist economy, people were forced to project their moral ideal into an afterworld.

This addition gives a more precise meaning to Marx's concept of religion. In his essay on Hegel, Marx calls religion the theoretical counterpart of private property. He uses the phrase "the perverted consciousness of a perverted world." In the practical order we have the inhuman capitalist system which has resulted in the creation of the relief of religion in the theoretical order, or within our own reflection. Thus we have Marx's famous dictum, "[religion] is the opium of the people." The best way to break the habit of religious reference is not to attack it head-on but to attack the practical conditions that engender the religious ideal. The true abolition of religion will occur automatically as a by-product of changing economics and social structures. Eventually, religion will wither away as capitalism withers away. Marx wrote:

> To be radical is to grasp things by the root. But for man the root is man himself. . . . The criticism of religion ends with the doctrine that man is the supreme being for man. It ends therefore with the categorical imperative to overthrow all those conditions in which man is an abased, enslaved, abandoned, contemptible being.[6]

If man and his world are self-created, then man cannot and should not expect to be liberated from his sufferings by some superhuman force—good or evil—but must set about freeing himself. In other words, belief in self-creation implies that one must also accept the idea of self-emancipation. The proletariat, in liberating the whole of mankind, can liberate itself as a class. This is the foundation of Marx's socialism. The struggle for fulfillment demands a militant humanism, with a goal nothing less than the formation of a classless society. The goal is projected not merely for German society, but for mankind in general. Struggle is unavoidable. Marx is not hesitant to enlist hatred of the enemy in the name of love of neighbor: this is a contradiction only if one does not see beyond the surface. For Marx the humanist must approach the problem of love not abstractly but in a concrete way. He enjoins actions to frustrate and render harmless all those who, for the sake of their private interests, bar men's way to happiness. For in a society demarcated by class, they are enemies of mankind, whether their behavior is conscious or unconscious. Anyone who understands this must also realize that the enemies of brotherly love—enemies of the cause of humanity—

6. Marx, 182.

must be fought actively, and this is inseparably connected with feelings of hate. Love of mankind, far from excluding hatred of those who act objectively in the name of the oppressed, in fact presupposes it.

JOHN DEWEY'S THOUGHT

Another student of Hegel and Feuerbach, John Dewey, taught for half a century in three major universities and played a critical role in the training of public-school teachers. The longest part of Dewey's teaching career was spent at Columbia University, which once trained 95 percent of all superintendents of the U.S. public schools. Dewey transmitted his views to educators who wrote the manuals that were used in teachers' colleges throughout the country. The evangelical character of his philosophy, with its emphasis on utility, change, progress, and the future rather than the past caught on and became the standard American credo.

The core of Dewey's philosophy can be found in a small book he produced near the end of his teaching career, *A Common Faith.* Dewey opens the book with the observation that throughout history men have been divided into two camps over the question of religion.[7] The focal-point of this division is, in his view, "the supernatural."[8] Religionists maintain that no belief can be genuinely called religious which is not connected with the supernatural. Among believers there is a range of positions—from those of the Greek and Roman Churches who hold that their dogmatic and sacramental systems are the only sure means of access to the supernatural to the nondoctrinal theist or mild deist. Also in this spectrum are many Protestant persuasions which consider scripture and conscience to be adequate avenues to religious truth. Those who are opposed to religion believe that the advance of anthropological and psychological studies has adequately revealed the all too human sources of what has customarily been ascribed to the supernatural. The extremists in this group believe that with the elimination of the supernatural not only historical religions but everything of a religious nature must be dismissed.

Having appraised the situation, Dewey sets out to examine the root cause of the division among men over the issue of religion. He attempts to determine the reasons for the identification of the religious with the supernatural and the ensuing consequences. In so doing, he offers another conception of the nature of the religious experience, one that separates it from the supernatural and its derivations. Removing these, in his view, will enable genuinely religious human experience to develop

7. John Dewey, *A Common Faith* (New Haven: Yale University Press, 1934).
8. Dewey, *Faith*, 1.

freely on its own account. To this end, in the first of the three chapters comprising *A Common Faith,* Dewey introduces a distinction between the noun 'religion' and the adjective 'religious.'[9]This distinction provides a hermeneutical tool for salvaging that which is valid in "religious" experiences and freeing it from the encumbrances resulting from efforts of various historical religions to explain those experiences.[10]There is, in Dewey's estimation, a validity to what is globally designated as religious experience. Yet this can be had apart from historical religions, which have in fact hampered the full import of such experiences.[11]If this valid core can be brought to light, then men will stop thinking that they need religions to have religious experience.

Dewey acknowledges that religion plays a part in the lives of most men. When fully embraced, it can modify one's attitude to life in a significant and enduring way. In the face of adversity, religion can inspire a sense of peace and security; in a period of change, it can help one to adjust and adapt. Unifying the diverse elements of experience, it can produce a vision that entails a voluntary submission to reality, not in stoic acceptance of what cannot be changed but through an interior redirection of will and attitude.[12]

While Dewey does not deny that a religious attitude has these and many other benefits, he does deny that these effects are peculiar to religion. Religions claim to bring about a change in attitude, yet institutions use these attitudes to create established churches, thereby changing moral faith into speculative faith and dogma. Moral faith entails the conviction that some spiritual end should be supreme over one's conduct; speculative faith, by contrast, attributes existence to that end, objectifying it and making it a truth for the intellect. Moral faith subordinates itself to an end that asserts a rightful claim over one's desires and purposes. It is practical, not intellectual. And while it goes beyond evidence, it has only the authority of a freely admitted ideal, not that of a fact. Institutional religions take this attitude, give objective reality to what was a moral ideal, and present it as the final reality at the heart of everything that exists. Religion has no difficulty in doing this, for desire has a powerful influence on intellectual beliefs. Men tend to believe what they ardently desire to be the case. At any rate, it is always easier to believe that the ideal is already a fact than to strive to make it so.[13]

Dewey regards the ideal of moral faith as fundamentally more religious than its reification in formal religions, for the ideal points to possibilities, and all human endeavor is better motivated by faith in what

9. Dewey, *Faith*, 1.
10. Dewey, *Faith*, 2.
11. Dewey, *Faith*, 3.
12. Dewey, *Faith*, 16–17.
13. Dewey, *Faith*, 22.

is possible than by adherence to what is already actual. Furthermore, such an ideal can be denotive of activity on the natural level. It is consonant with nature and does not divorce us from it. He states, "Faith in the continued disclosing of truth through directed cooperative human endeavor is more religious in quality than is any faith in a completed revelation." Thus, nature and man's experience in it become both the source and object of the ideal that directs life. Any activity pursued on behalf of an ideal end is religious in nature. The essentially irreligious attitude is that which attributes human achievement and purpose to man in isolation from nature and his fellow men. To regard the religious act in this way is to avoid the antagonism between religion and modern science:

> The positive lesson is that religious qualities and values, if they are real at all, are not bound up with any single item of intellectual assent, not even that of the existence of the God of theism; and that under existing conditions, the religious function in experience can be emancipated only through surrender of the whole notion of special truths that are religious by their own nature, together with the idea of peculiar avenues of access to such truths. For were we to admit that there is but one method for ascertaining fact and truth—that conveyed by the word "scientific" in its most general and generous sense—no discovery in any branch of knowledge and inquiry could then disturb the faith that is religious.[14]

It is worth noting that Dewey takes leave of William James's pragmatic approach to religious belief. James had been willing to grant some validity and meaning to a belief that produced satisfactory results in the life of the believer. Dewey is more cautious. He asks whether James employs the pragmatic method to discover value in the consequences of some religious formula that has its logical content already fixed, or uses his pragmatic method to criticize, revise, and, ultimately, constitute the meaning of the formula.[15] Dewey is afraid lest some may understand pragmatism in the first sense and be disposed to attribute existential value to fixed dogmas that science has rendered untenable. If pragmatism is of any value in the religious sphere, its contribution is to replace faith in the supernatural order found in traditional religion with faith in the religious possibilities found in ordinary experience. There can be faith in intelligence, a devotion to the process by which truth is discovered, which would include a commitment both to science and to the worth and dignity of man. In this way, morality and religion will become an integral part of everyday living, emerging out of nature and renovating the nature out of which it has arisen.

14. Dewey, *Faith*, 32–33.
15. See also Dewey's *Essays in Experimental Logic* (Chicago: University of Chicago Press, 1916), 313.

The ideal ends to which we attach our faith are not shadowy and waver-
ing. They assume concrete form in our understanding of our relations to
one another and the values contained in these relations. We who now live
are parts of a humanity that has reacted with nature. The things in
civilization we most prize are not of ourselves. They exist by grace of the
doings and sufferings of the continuous human community in which we
are a link.[16]

Though Dewey's naturalism rules out a God who is responsible for
the creation and governance of the universe, he nevertheless attempts to
understand the concept 'God,' its origin and function. In this effort his
work is not unlike that of Feuerbach, though it is not certain that Dewey
ever read *The Essence of Christianity*. Putting the question to himself "Are
the ideals which move us genuinely ideal, or are they ideal only in
contrast with our present estate?" he replies that the answer to this
question determines the meaning of the word 'God.' For Dewey the word
'God' denotes the unity of all the ideal ends arousing us to desire and
action.[17]

According to Dewey, the origin of the traditional notion of God is
easy enough to explain. There has always been in human nature a
tendency to attribute prior existence to the objects of desire. Qualities
are discovered in nature; goods are grouped in experience. Physical and
psychological tendencies and activities are observed. These become en-
twined and united in human emotion and activity. It is not at all surprising that they should be thought to have a unified existence in their
perfect state apart from the conditions under which we find them in
experience.

To reseparate the various qualities may, indeed, be a difficult task, but
the benefits to be derived from such an effort are many. In the first
place, such a separation will free the religious attitude from tenets that
are daily becoming more dubious. Witness the doubt which discoveries
in geology and astronomy have cast on the doctrine of creation, the
findings in modern biology which have rendered ancient conceptions of
soul and body obsolete, and the explanations in psychology for what
were once understood to be supernatural phenomena.

There is another built-in difficulty with the search for a personal
God. Such an inquiry necessarily diverts man's attention and energy
away from ideal values and the conditions by which they may be promoted. To the extent that we argue about the existence of God, we
choose to spend valuable time on something from which no good can
come in preference to devoting that time to more fruitful enterprises.
History has shown that men have never fully used their powers to

16. Dewey, *Faith*, 87.
17. Dewey, *Faith*, 42.

advance the good life as long as they have waited upon some extrinsic power to remedy the situation for them. Such an attitude necessarily neglects the value intrinsic to the natural order. It leaves the world alone and seeks a solution for difficulty elsewhere. It substitutes personal prayer for cooperative effort.

If, on the other hand, we do not identify the ideal as a reified personal being, then this ideal may be thought of as being grounded in natural conditions. The ideal emerges as man's imagination idealizes existence with respect to the possibilities offered by thought and action.

> There are values, goods, actually realized upon a natural basis—the goods of human association, of art and knowledge. The idealizing imagination seizes upon the most precious things found in the climacteric moments of experience and projects them. We need no external criterion and guarantee for their goodness. They are had, they exist as good, and out of them we frame our ideal ends.[18]

It is also true that these ideals do in a sense exist. They direct our actions and exist in the conditions that prompt their fulfillment. With a new ideal end, a new vision emerges and familiar objects are seen in new relations as they serve that end. As these values and ideals are dwelt upon and tested by practice, they are purified and strengthened. The values become more definitive and coherent and so have greater effect upon present conditions.

Values and situations modify each other. We have neither ideals that are completely embodied in existence nor ideals that are merely rootless fancies. This active relation between the ideal and actual is what Dewey calls "God." By so conceiving God, he seeks to make man a citizen of earth and to restore him to the fatherland, in which he has his roots and his destiny.

This concept of God encompasses all the possibilities that nature exhibits. These possibilities beckon each and every man. They point to the possibility of a fuller and more perfect reality as a result of action aimed at bettering the natural situation. They are perceived by the imagination, clarified by the method of science, and tested and modified by experience. Thus reshaped and purified, they in turn shape and purify the activity which they inspire.

Criticizing the traditional idea of God, Dewey cannot see how a God who exists apart from the universe can in any way be a God for man. To direct man to believe in such a God is to dehumanize and denaturalize him. Dewey thought that even the Absolute Mind of Hegel, immanent in nature, denied the reality of the finite and the natural.

In Chapter III, the final chapter of *A Common Faith,* Dewey addresses

18. Dewey, *Faith,* 36.

what he calls "The Human Abode of the Religious Function." There he observes that the core of religion has generally been found in rites and ceremonies. But given the secular character of our present society, few persons can understand, without the use of imagination, what it means socially for a religion to permeate all the customs and activities of group life. Since the Renaissance there has been a shift in the social center of gravity from the sacred to the secular. Today the conditions under which people meet and act together are thoroughly secular. Interests and values are neither derived from nor related to the church. Religion is a matter of personal choice and not a matter of the social order.

But this is not to be regretted. When religion was grounded in the supernatural, a sharp line between the religious and the secular prevailed. In Dewey's view religion necessitates no such division; for when the religious function is emancipated from religion, the distinction between the sacred and the secular fades. Protestantism has rightly emphasized the fact that the relation of man to God is primarily an individual matter, a matter of personal choice and responsibility. Beliefs and rites that make the relation between man and God a collective and institutional affair erect barriers between the human soul and the divine spirit. When primacy is given to the direct relation of the conscience and will to God, religion is placed on its only real and solid foundation. Social change is better accomplished through the common effort of men and women than through any institutional effort. Contrary to a popular misperception, Dewey argues that the secularization of society has not been accompanied by increasing degeneration. Rather, it is the forces that are independent of organized religion that have worked to enhance human relations and have resulted in intellectual and aesthetic development. In fact, the churches have lagged behind in most social movements.

Dewey is convinced that a depreciation of natural social values results from a comparison with a supernatural source. "The objection to supernaturalism is that it stands in the way of an effective realization of the sweep and depth of the implications of natural human relations. It stands in the way of using the means that are in our power to make radical changes in these relations."[19]

Though Dewey discounts religion as the "only finally dependable source of motivation," he would, nevertheless, have the churches show a more active interest in social affairs. But they would have to do so on equal footing with other institutions. This participation would require their surrender of any claims to an exclusive and authoritative position. "Secular interests and activities have grown up outside of organized religions and are independent of their authority. The hold of these

19. Dewey, *Faith*, 80.

interests upon the thoughts and desires of men has cowed the social importance of organized religions into a corner and the area of this corner is decreasing." [20]

Dewey suggests that thoughtful persons should work to emancipate the religious quality of experience from the accretions that have grown up about it which limit its credibility and influence. Philosophers should develop and make explicit those principles and values inherent in civilization to which the race is heir, values that are inherent in the continuous human community of which the present generation is but a link. In these are contained all the elements for a religious faith that is not confined to sect, class, or race. "Such a faith has always been implicitly the common faith of mankind. It remains to make it explicit and militant." [21]

Democracy as understood by Dewey does not refer to a system of balloting. Nor is it a government with checks and balances intended to prevent the majority from running roughshod over the rights of a minority. Rather, it is a method for dissolving majorities and minorities; it is a way of conceptually resolving differences. The majority must give up its claim to truth, correctness, or rightness in the face of serious challenge. Numerical strength does not provide a warrant. Unrestrained legislation which favors one point of view is not justified by the fact that an overwhelming majority shares that viewpoint as long as a minority exists with different opinions.

Democracy calls for compromise—conceptually and practically. Between affirmation and negation lies the "truth." The truth is not simply expedient, nor is it to be anchored in a historically given constitution. A constitution is itself not strictly an immutable document; it must be interpreted in the light of contemporary circumstances. Appeals to a Christian past, to a Christian heritage, to a Christian rationale for our present law are not to be admitted. Problems have to be resolved in the present context. Our forebears have no hold on us. Like Marx, Dewey provides a purely naturalistic account of religion limited to a progressivist view of human nature and history.

JACQUES MARITAIN

The views of Jacques Maritain developed out of his study of Aristotle and Thomas Aquinas. In common with the Greeks, his emphasis is on moral virtue as a condition for the achievement of the commonwealth. As a philosopher he subscribes to a natural-law outlook; as a Christian he

20. Dewey, *Faith*, 83.
21. Dewey, *Faith*, 87.
22. Jacques Maritain, *Democracy and Education* (New York: The MacMillan Company, 1961), 88 ff.

believes in divine revelation. In *Man and the State*, a small work that includes his Walgreen lectures at the University of Chicago, Maritain makes an important distinction between "nation," "body politic," and "state."[23]

As Maritain defines it, a nation is something ethico-social. It is a natural structure, a community, and has its basis in regional, ethnic, linguistic, class, or religious affinities. It is not identical to a society. A society is deliberately brought into being as its members organize to achieve common ends. Maritain writes:

> An ethnic community, generally speaking, can be defined as a community of patterns of feeling rooted in the physical soil of the origin of the group as well as in the moral soil of history; it becomes a *nation* when this factual situation enters the sphere of self awareness . . . when the ethnic group *becomes conscious* of the fact that it constitutes a community of patterns of feeling . . . and possesses its own unity and individuality, its own will to endure its existence.[25]

On the basis of Maritain's language, it is obvious that the Ukrainian people are a nation but it is not so obvious that the United States is a nation.

Both the body politic and the state are societies, yet though the terms 'body politic' and 'state' are often used synonymously, they should be distinguished. They are related as a whole to its parts. The body politic is the whole. The primary condition for the existence of the body politic is a common sense of justice, though friendship may be said to be its life-giving element. A civic outlook requires a sense of devotion and mutual love as well as a sense of justice and law. These attitudes of mind and will develop as part of a heritage that is preserved by mediating or secondary institutions. Nothing matters more to the life and preservation of the body politic than the accumulated energy and historical continuity of the national community that it has caused to exist. Common inherited experience and moral and intellectual instinct are its basis. The political life as well as the very existence and prosperity of the body politic depend on the vitality of family, economic, cultural, educational, and religious life.

The state in Maritain's analysis is the part of the body politic that is concerned with the common welfare, the public order, and the administration of public affairs. It is the part that specializes in the interest of the whole. It is not comprised of men, but is rather a set of institutions combined into a unified machine. The goals of the state are imple-

23. Maritain, *Man and the State* (Chicago: University of Chicago Press, 1951).
24. Maritain, *Man*, 2 ff.
25. Maritain, *Man*, 5.
26. Maritain, *Man*, 11.

mented by experts or specialists in public order and welfare. It constitutes an impersonal, lasting superstructure. When functioning
properly, the state is rational and bound by law. As an instrument of the
body politic, the state is an agency entitled to use power and coercion.
Though the state is the superior part of society, it does not transcend its
members entirely; it exists for the sake of man. The state is neither a
whole, nor a person, nor does it hold rights. The common good of the
political society is the final aim of the state and comes before the state's
goal of the maintenance of the public order. The state overreaches its
mandate when it ascribes to itself a goal of simply self-preservation and
growth.

When the state identifies itself with the whole of political society and
takes upon itself the performance of tasks which normally pertain to
society or its organs, we have what Maritain calls the "paternalistic state."
From the political point of view, the state is at its best when it is most
restrained in seeking the common good. When it takes upon itself the
organizing, controlling, or managing of the economic, commercial, industrial, or cultural forms, it has transcended its skill and competence. If
the state attempts to become a boss or a manager in business or industry,
or a patron of art, or a leading spirit in the affairs of culture, science, and
philosophy, it betrays its nature.[27]

The state receives its authority from a community of people. The
people have a natural right to self-government. They exercise this right
when they establish a constitution, written or unwritten. The people are
the multitude of persons who unite under just laws by mutual friendship
for their common good. But the people not only constitute a body
politic; each has a spiritual soul and a supratemporal destiny. The people
are above the state; the state exists for the people.

Maritain takes pains to emphasize the primacy of the spiritual. From
the religious point of view, the common good the body politic implies an
intrinsic, though indirect, ordination to something which transcends it.
The state is under the command of no superior authority, but the order
of eternal life is superior to the order of temporal life. The two orders
need not create a conflict. From a secular perspective, the church is an
institution concerned with the spiritual life of the believer. "From the
point of view of the political common good, the activities of citizens as
members of the church have an impact on that common good." Thus the
church in one sense serves the body politic, but in another and important sense, transcends it.

The church and the body politic cannot live and develop in sheer
isolation from and ignorance of each other. The same person is simulta-

27. Maritain, *Man, 21*.
28. *Maritain, Man*, 152.

neously a member of the body politic and a member of a church. An absolute division is both impossible and absurd. There must be cooperation. But what form should the cooperation take? It is evident that we no longer live in a sacral age. If classical antiquity or medieval Christianity were characterized by a unity of faith and if that unity of faith were required for a political unity, such does not now seem to be the case. Religious plurality is a fact, and the modern situation seems to demonstrate that religious unity is not a prerequisite for political unity. Nor can the church wield authority over the state, calling emperors, kings, princes, or nations to account. Indeed, the opposite is frequently the case, with the church demanding freedom within the political order to develop her own institutions.

Maritain leaves unresolved the problem of moral unity of a people. While he cannot opt for the "common faith" described by John Dewey, a naturalistic credo that goes beyond the merely political, he is tempted by the "civic faith" delineated by his friend John Courtney Murray in *We Hold These Truths*.[29]But how are the wellsprings of conscience and civic faith to be maintained? Before his death Maritain was to see the breakdown of inherited morality discussed in the opening pages of this essay. A common Christian outlook on matters such as civic decorum, contraception, divorce, abortion, homosexuality, pornography, and capital punishment gave way. The morality commonly affirmed in the nineteenth century came to be widely denied. The denial has been translated into law, if not by legislation, then by the courts as they have interpreted the law.

Maritain recognizes that if religious institutions are to possess any authority, it will be through their moral influence as their teachings touch man's conscience. Still, this spiritual influence may be checked by an opposite course of action, chosen by other citizens. But Maritain believes that a free exchange of ideas, despite possible setbacks, is a surer way of attaining influence in the long run. The church is less likely to lose her independence. If the state were to be enlisted to implement ecclesiastical goals, it is likely that it would serve its own purposes first. History teaches us that the secular arm, always eager to exercise control, takes the initiative. Maritain proposes that the church should be free to educate and that she should be positioned to compete as an equal in the marketplace of ideas. He is conscious, however, that such may not be the case, even in his primary paradigm, the United States.

In the twentieth century, governments have taken upon themselves more and more of the role of an immense and tutelary power catering to all needs. In an age of limited government, before government began to play a role in ordering a vast range of social and economic activities, the

29. John Courtney Murray, *We Hold These Truths* (New York: Sheed and Ward, 1960).

doctrine of "strict separation" or of "a benevolent neutrality" that pro-
hibited the government from giving aid of any kind to religion may have
made some sense. But in an age of positive government, equating neutrality with a strict "no aid" position may be less tenable. The framers of
the Constitution expected religion to play a part in the established social
order and also assumed that the state would play a minimal role in
forming that order. In our own time, the question of how to treat
religious groups and interests has become a fundamentally different
one.

The issue is not clearly resolved. Maritain affirms, on the one hand,
that "freedom of inquiry, even at the risk of error, is the normal condition for men to access to truth, so that freedom to search for God in
their own way, for those who have been brought up in ignorance or semi-
ignorance of Him, is the normal condition in which to listen to the
message of the Gospel." Yet he is convinced that "willingly or unwillingly
States will be obliged to make a choice for or against the Gospel. They
will be shaped either by the totalitarian spirit or by the Christian
spirit."[31]

The West, symbolically at least, continues in many ways to reflect its
Christian heritage. Thus, the public acknowledgment of God's existence,
Maritain believes, is good and should be maintained. It is to be expected
that a public expression of common faith will assume the form of that
Christian confession to which history and the traditions of a people are
most vitally linked. The citizens who are unbelievers will have only to
realize that the body politic as a whole is just as free with regard to the
private expression of their nonreligious conviction.

If Maritain has a fault, it lies in his idealism, in his optimism that
goodwill and common sense will prevail and that public assessments of
the value of religion will result in conclusions similar to those reached by
him. He believes that these conclusions have been reached by reflective
men in every period of the history of the West. Maritain may also be
accused of an excessively optimistic view of the United States. He seemed
to ignore the fact that manifestations of religion vary and are not all
beneficent. If assessors of the value of religion are not of one mind as
they measure its contributions to the social order, the fault may lie in part
with the division and feebleness of religious witness and institutions
themselves. Religion seems more to follow than to lead, to sanction what
is rather than to encourage progress. But even if this sobering view is
more correct than Maritain's, the question needs to be posed, what
should the state's attitude toward religion be? If social observers are right
in decrying the loss of a common religious vision, then an assessment of

30. Maritain, *Man and the State*, 161–162.
31. Maritain, *Man*, 159.

this social fact ought to be made a public concern. For it cannot be assumed that religion's loss of cultural influence is a social good.

Maritain's contribution to the debate shows religion's indispensible function in society and the state's concomitant obligation to provide an impartial and unencumbered aid to insure enlightened internal development within religious bodies—development that makes a superior cultural contribution possible. Maritain's genius lies in his interpretation of a tradition that has its roots in the Gospels, yet has developed through twenty centuries in the West. It is a tradition that recognizes the two interrelated orders of church and state and the common social good that must prevail when inevitable tensions arise. While political contexts vary, man is by nature a citizen of two cities. Maritain in effect says that the best government recognizes this fact and impedes growth in neither domain.

IN THE BALANCE

Though Dewey, Marx, and Maritain do not represent a full spectrum of theological and social views, they do represent very different intellectual directions. Obviously, religion is more than a community of worshippers paying a commonly acknowledged debt to an unseen God. Religion carries within it its own intellectual tradition. The very awareness of God's existence presupposes some kind of consideration, be it metaphysical in the classical Greek sense or hermeneutical in the Hebraic manner. Included within those traditions are attitudes toward ritual and sacred art, from vestment, statuary, and architecture, to painting and music. Since revelation is given over time, religion entails a historical sense and a relationship to the past. As Dewey correctly saw, religion robs the present of its uniqueness, for both speculative and practical wisdom suggest that human nature has not changed since antiquity and that it will face familiar challenges in the future. No one who is acquainted with the Hebrew scriptures can believe in the unlimited perfectibility of man or society. And it will not do to give a Voltairean romantic interpretation to the sacred texts and rites of a people, regarding them all as poetic expressions of something that can be stated more accurately by philosophy. The religious mind holds that God is, and that certain things flow from that belief. A flat denial that such a belief can be true (no one purports to offer proof) is more than an intellectual sleight of hand. In the political realm, this denies the believer the full rights of citizenship as it refuses to take his views seriously.

While the ultimate debate may center on the existence of God, the immediate contest concerns the role of religion in society. Those who hold that the religious mind is mistaken are not likely to place much confidence in its role as a bearer of the culture. Marx and Dewey believed that the past would be overcome as men moved into a future shaped by technological progress. Both Dewey and Marx might have felt justified in excluding religion from education, but the cost of this position in modern society has been heavy. Not only are the great majority illiterate regarding religion but, conversely, religion is deprived of the aid of the best minds.

The people, cut off from the tradition which has produced their culture, grope for a source of enlightenment. Who would claim that the worldview once presented by Christianity has been adequately replaced by the secular mind that challenged it? Dewey's common faith has not replaced Christianity in any important respect, and no longer inspires popular confidence. The question is, Can European or Western civilization endure apart from its historic roots? Need the nonbeliever in order to feel secure insist that the heritage acknowledged by the great majority remain a dim and impotent intellectual force; or, is accommodation possible? Can the secular mind acknowledge the cultural and moral importance of the Western religious tradition and allow it to proceed unencumbered, or must it claim for itself exclusive control of the wellsprings of culture? These questions need to be addressed.

Experience and Education

John Dewey

Note: Experience and Education *was written by John Dewey about twenty years after his Democracy and Education (1916) had already been tested in the "laboratory school" for children connected with the University of Chicago. Dewey reformulated some of his ideas after his experience with the progressive schools and gave us in this book the most concise, simplest, and most readable account of his philosophy of education.*

Dewey studies in this book "traditional" and "progressive" education. The bases of traditional education were subjects or the cultural heritage, and the method regimentation and discipline; while the modern schooling advocates excessive individualism and a deceptive spontaneity which is taken as an index of freedom. Dewey proposes an education based on the scientific method, acquiring cumulative knowledge of meanings and values, these, however, being only data for critical study and intelligent living. Knowledge, thus, becomes the means for further study, leading to the study of the nature of problems, their age, conditions, and significance. Consequently education must employ progressive organization of subject matter so that in this manner the meaning and significance of the problem may be studied. Scientific study, thus understood, leads to and enlarges experience, if this experience rests on a continuity of significant knowledge and method to acquire it.

PREFACE

All social movements involve conflicts which are reflected intellectually in controversies. It would not be a sign of health if such an important social interest as education were not also an arena of struggles, practical and theoretical. But for theory, at least for the theory that forms a philosophy of education, the practical conflicts and the controversies that are conducted upon the level of these conflicts only set a problem. It is the business of an intelligent theory of education to ascertain the causes for the conflicts that exist and then, instead of taking one side or the other, to indicate a plan of operations proceeding from a level deeper and more inclusive than is represented by the practices and ideas of the contending parties.

This formulation of the business of the philosophy of education does not mean that the latter should attempt to bring about a compromise between opposed schools of thought, to find a *via media,* nor yet make an eclectic combination of points picked out hither and yon from all schools. It means the necessity of the introduction of a new order of conceptions leading to new modes of practice. It is for this reason that it is so difficult to develop a philosophy of education, the moment tradition and custom are departed from. It is for this reason that the conduct of schools, based upon a new order of conceptions, is so much more difficult than is the management of schools which walk in beaten paths. Hence, every movement in the direction of a new order of ideas and of activities directed by them calls out, sooner or later, a return to what appear to be simpler and more fundamental ideas and practices of the past—as is exemplified at present in education in the attempt to revive the principles of ancient Greece and of the middle ages.

It is in this context that I have suggested at the close of this little volume that those who are looking ahead to a new movement in education, adapted to the existing need for a new social order, should think in terms of Education itself rather than in terms of some 'ism about education, even such an 'ism as "progressivism." For in spite of itself any movement that thinks and acts in terms of an 'ism becomes so involved in reaction against other 'isms that it is unwittingly controlled by them. For it then forms its principles by reaction against them instead of by a comprehensive, constructive survey of actual needs, problems, and possibilities. Whatever value is possessed by the essay presented in this little volume resides in its attempt to call attention to the larger and deeper issues of Education so as to suggest their proper frame of reference.

CHAPTER 1—TRADITIONAL VS. PROGRESSIVE EDUCATION

Mankind likes to think in terms of extreme opposites. It is given to formulating its beliefs in terms of *Either-Ors,* between which it recognizes no intermediate possibilities. When forced to recognize that the extremes cannot be acted upon, it is still inclined to hold that they are all right in theory but that when it comes to practical matters circumstances compel us to compromise. Educational philosophy is no exception. The history of educational theory is marked by opposition between the idea that education is development from within and that it is formation from without; that it is based upon natural endowments and that education is a process of overcoming natural inclination and substituting in its place habits acquired under external pressure.

At present, the opposition, so far as practical affairs of the school are concerned, tends to take the form of contrast between traditional and progressive education. If the underlying ideas of the former are formulated broadly, without the qualifications required for accurate statement, they are found to be about as follows: The subject-matter of education consists of bodies of information and of skills that have been worked out in the past; therefore, the chief business of the school is to transmit them to the new generation. In the past, there have also been developed standards and rules of conduct; moral training consists in forming habits of action in conformity with these rules and standards. Finally, the general pattern of school organization (by which I mean the relations of pupils to one another and to the teachers) constitutes the school a kind of institution sharply marked off from other social institutions. Call up in imagination the ordinary schoolroom, its time-schedules, schemes of classification, of examination and promotion, of rules of order, and I think you will grasp what is meant by "pattern of organization." If then you contrast this scene with what goes on in the family, for example, you will appreciate what is meant by the school being a kind of institution sharply marked off from any other form of social organization.

The three characteristics just mentioned fix the aims and methods of instruction and discipline. The main purpose or objective is to prepare the young for future responsibilities and for success in life, by means of acquisition of the organized bodies of information and prepared forms of skill which comprehend the material of instruction. Since the subject-matter as well as standards of proper conduct are handed down from the past, the attitude of pupils must, upon the whole, be one of docility, receptivity, and obedience. Books, especially textbooks, are the chief representatives of the lore and wisdom of the past, while teachers are the organs through which pupils are brought into effective connection with the material. Teachers are the agents through which knowledge and skills are communicated and rules of conduct enforced.

I have not made this brief summary for the purpose of criticizing the underlying philosophy. The rise of what is called new education and progressive schools is of itself a product of discontent with traditional education. In effect it is a criticism of the latter. When the implied criticism is made explicit it reads somewhat as follows: The traditional scheme is, in essence, one of imposition from above and from outside. It imposes adult standards, subject-matter, and methods upon those who are only growing slowly toward maturity. The gap is so great that the required subject-matter, the methods of learning and of behaving are foreign to the existing capacities of the young. They are beyond the reach of the experience the young learners already possess. Consequently, they must be imposed; even though good teachers will use devices of art to cover up the imposition so as to relieve it of obviously brutal features.

But the gulf between the mature or adult products and the experience and abilities of the young is so wide that the very situation forbids much active participation by pupils in the development of what is taught. Theirs is to do—and learn, as it was the part of the six hundred to do and die. Learning here means acquisition of what already is incorporated in books and in the heads of the elders. Moreover, that which is taught is thought of as essentially static. It is taught as a finished product, with little regard either to the ways in which it was originally built up or to changes that will surely occur in the future. It is to a large extent the cultural product of societies that assumed the future would be much like the past, and yet it is used as educational food in a society where change is the rule, not the exception.

If one attempts to formulate the philosophy of education implicit in the practices of the new education, we may, I think, discover certain common principles amid the variety of progressive schools now existing. To imposition from above is opposed expression and cultivation of individuality; to external discipline is opposed free activity; to learning from texts and teachers, learning through experience; to acquisition of isolated skills and techniques by drill, is opposed acquisition of them as means of attaining ends which make direct vital appeal; to preparation for a more or less remote future is opposed making the most of the opportunities of present life; to static aims and materials is opposed acquaintance with a changing world.

Now, all principles by themselves are abstract. They become concrete only in the consequences which result from their application. Just because the principles set forth are so fundamental and far-reaching, everything depends upon the interpretation given them as they are put into practice in the school and the home. It is at this point that the reference made earlier to *Either-Or* philosophies becomes peculiarly pertinent. The general philosophy of the new education may be sound, and yet the difference in abstract principles will not decide the way in which the moral and intellectual preference involved shall be worked out in practice. There is always the danger in a new movement that in rejecting the aims and methods of that which it would supplant, it may develop its principles negatively rather than positively and constructively. Then it takes its clue in practice from that which is rejected instead of from the constructive development of its own philosophy.

I take it that the fundamental unity of the newer philosophy is found in the idea that there is an intimate and necessary relation between the processes of actual experience and education. If this be true, then a positive and constructive development of its own basic idea depends upon having a correct idea of experience. Take, for example, the question of organized subject-matter—which will be discussed in some detail later. The problem for progressive education is: What is the place and meaning of subject-matter and of organization *within* experience? How does subject-matter function? Is there anything inherent in experience which tends towards progressive organization of its contents? What results follow when the materials of experience are not progressively organized? A philosophy which proceeds on the basis of rejection, of sheer opposition, will neglect these questions. It will tend to suppose that because the old education was based on ready-made organization, therefore it suffices to reject the principle of organization *in toto,* instead of striving to discover what it means and how it is to be attained on the basis of experience. We might go through all the points of difference between the new and the old education and reach similar conclusions. When external control is rejected, the problem becomes that of finding the factors of control that are inherent within experience. When external authority is rejected, it does not follow that all authority should be rejected, but rather that there is need to search for a more effective source of authority. Because the older education imposed the knowledge, methods, and the rules of conduct of the mature person upon the young, it does not follow, except upon the basis of the extreme *Either-Or* philosophy, that the knowledge and skill of the mature person has no directive value for the experience of the immature. On the contrary, basing education upon personal experience may mean more multiplied and more intimate contacts between the mature and the immature than ever existed in the traditional school, and consequently more, rather than less, guidance by others. The problem, then, is: how these contacts can be established without violating the principle of learning through personal experience. The solution of this problem requires a well thought-out philosophy of the social factors that operate in the constitution of individual experience.

What is indicated in the foregoing remarks is that the general principles of the new education do not of themselves solve any of the problems of the actual or practical conduct and management of progressive schools. Rather, they set new problems which have to be worked out on the basis of a new philosophy of experience. The problems are not even recognized, to say nothing of being solved, when it is assumed that it suffices to reject the ideas and practices of the old education and then go to the opposite extreme. Yet I am sure that you will appreciate what is meant when I say that many of the newer schools tend to make little or nothing of organized subject-matter of study; to proceed as if any form of direction and guidance by adults were an invasion of individual freedom, and as if the idea that education should be concerned with the present and future meant that acquaintance with the past has little or no role to play in education. Without pressing these defects to the point of exaggeration, they at least illustrate what is meant by a theory and practice of education which proceeds negatively or by reaction against what has been current in education rather than by a positive and constructive development of purposes, methods, and subject-matter on the foundation of a theory of experience and its educational potentialities.

It is not too much to say that an educational philosophy which professes to be based on the idea of freedom may become as dogmatic as ever was the traditional education which is reacted against. For any theory and set of practices is dogmatic which is not based upon critical examination of its own underlying principles. Let us say that the new education emphasizes the freedom of the learner. Very well. A problem is now set. What does freedom mean and what are the conditions under which it is capable of realization? Let us say that the kind of external imposition which was so common in the traditional school limited rather than promoted the intellectual and moral development of the young. Again, very well. Recognition of this serious defect sets a problem. Just what is the role of the teacher and of books in promoting the educational development of the immature? Admit that traditional education employed as the subject-matter for study facts and ideas so bound up with the past as to give little help in dealing with the issues of the present and future. Very well. Now we have the problem of discovering the connection which actually exists *within* experience between the achievements of the past and the issues of the present. We have the problem of ascertaining how acquaintance with the past may be translated into a potent instrumentality for dealing effectively with the future. We may reject knowledge of the past as the *end* of education and thereby only emphasize its importance as a *means*. When we do that we have a problem that is new in the story of education: How shall the young become acquainted with the past in such a way that the acquaintance is a potent agent in appreciation of the living present?

CHAPTER 2—THE NEED OF A THEORY OF EXPERIENCE

In short, the point I am making is that rejection of the philosophy and practice of traditional education sets a new type of difficult educational problem for those who believe in the new type of education. We shall operate blindly and in confusion until we recognize this fact; until we thoroughly appreciate that departure from the old solves no problems. What is said in the following pages is, accordingly, intended to indicate some of the main problems with which the newer education is confronted and to suggest the main lines along which their solution is to be sought. I assume that amid all uncertainties there is one permanent frame of reference: namely, the organic connection between education and personal experience; or, that the new philosophy of education is committed to some kind of empirical and experimental philosophy. But experience and experiment are not self-explanatory ideas. Rather, their meaning is part of the problem to be explored. To know the meaning of empiricism we need to understand what experience is.

The belief that all genuine education comes about through experience does not mean that all experiences are genuinely or equally educative. Experience and education cannot be directly equated to each other. For some experiences are mis-educative. Any experience is mis-educative that has the effect of arresting or distorting the growth of further experience. An experience may be such as to engender callousness; it may produce lack of sensitivity and of responsiveness. Then the possibilities of having richer experience in the future are restricted. Again, a given experience may increase a person's automatic skill in a particular direction and yet tend to land him in a groove or rut; the effect again is to narrow the field of further experience. An experience may be immediately enjoyable and yet promote the formation of a slack and careless attitude; this attitude then operates to modify the quality of subsequent experiences so as to prevent a person from getting out of them what they have to give. Again, experiences may be so disconnected from one another that, while each is agreeable or even exciting in itself, they are not linked cumulatively to one another. Energy is then dissipated and a person becomes scatter-brained. Each experience may be lively, vivid, and "interesting," and yet their disconnectedness may artificially generate dispersive, disintegrated, centrifugal habits. The consequence of formation of such habits is inability to control future experiences. They are then taken, either by way of enjoyment or of discontent and revolt, just as they come. Under such circumstances, it is idle to talk of self-control.

Traditional education offers a plethora of examples of experiences of the kinds just mentioned. It is a great mistake to suppose, even tacitly, that the traditional schoolroom was not a place in which pupils had experiences. Yet this is tacitly assumed when progressive education as a plan of learning by experience is placed in sharp opposition to the old. The proper line of attack is that the experiences which were had, by pupils and teachers alike, were largely of a wrong kind. How many students, for example, were rendered callous to ideas, and how many lost the impetus to learn because of the way in which learning was experienced by them? How many acquired special skills by means of automatic drill so that their power of judgment and capacity to act intelligently in new situations was limited? How many came to associate the learning process with ennui and boredom? How many found what they did learn so foreign to the situations of life outside the school as to give them no power of control over the latter? How many came to associate books with dull drudgery, so that they were "conditioned" to all but flashy reading matter?

If I ask these questions, it is not for the sake of wholesale condemnation of the old education. It is for quite another purpose. It is to emphasize the fact, first, that young people in traditional schools do have experiences; and, secondly, that the trouble is not the absence of experiences, but their defective and wrong character—wrong and defective from the standpoint of connection with further experience. The positive side of this point is even more important in connection with progressive education. It is not enough to insist upon the necessity of experience, nor even of activity in experience. Everything depends upon the *quality* of the experience which is had. The quality of any experience has two aspects. There is an immediate aspect of agreeableness or disagreeableness, and there is its influence upon later experiences. The first is obvious and easy to judge. The *effect* of an experience is not borne on its face. It sets a problem to the educator. It is his business to arrange for the kind of experiences which, while they do not repel the student, but rather engage his activities are, nevertheless, more than immediately enjoyable since they promote having desirable future experiences. Just as no man lives or dies to himself, so no experience lives and dies to itself. Wholly independent of desire or intent, every experience lives on in further experiences. Hence the central problem of an education based upon experience is to select the kind of present experiences that live fruitfully and creatively in subsequent experiences.

Later, I shall discuss in more detail the principle of the continuity of experience or what may be called the experiential continuum. Here I wish simply to emphasize the importance of this principle for the philosophy of educative experience. A philosophy of education, like any theory, has to be stated in words, in symbols. But so far as it is more than verbal it is a plan for conducting education. Like any plan, it must be framed with reference to what is to be done and how it is to be done. The more definitely and sincerely it is held that education is a development within, by, and for experience, the more important it is that there shall be clear conceptions of what experience is. Unless experience is so conceived that the result is a plan for deciding upon subject-matter, upon methods of instruction and discipline, and upon material equipment and social organization of the school, it is wholly in the air. It is reduced to a form of words which may be emotionally stirring but for which any other set of words might equally well be substituted unless they indicate operations to be initiated and executed. Just because traditional education was a matter of routine in which the plans and programs were handed down from the past, it does not follow that progressive education is a matter of planless improvisation.

The traditional school could get along without any consistently developed philosophy of education. About all it required in that line was a set of abstract words like culture, discipline, our great cultural heritage, etc., actual guidance being derived not from them but from custom and established routines. Just because progressive schools cannot rely upon established traditions and institutional habits, they must either proceed more or less haphazardly or be directed by ideas which, when they are made articulate and coherent, form a philosophy of education. Revolt against the kind of organization characteristic of the traditional school constitutes a demand for a kind of organization based upon ideas. I think that only slight acquaintance with the history of education is needed to prove that educational reformers and innovators alone have felt the need for a philosophy of education. Those who adhered to the established system needed merely a few fine-sounding words to justify existing practices. The real work was done by habits which were so fixed as to be institutional. The lesson for progressive education is that it requires in an urgent degree, a degree more pressing than was incumbent upon former innovators, a philosophy of education based upon a philosophy of experience.

I remarked incidentally that the philosophy in question is, to paraphrase the saying of Lincoln about democracy, one of education of, by, and for experience. No one of these words, *of, by* or *for,* names anything which is self-evident. Each of them is a challenge to discover and put into operation a principle of order and organization which follows from understanding what educative experience signifies.

It is, accordingly, a much more difficult task to work out the kinds of materials, of methods, and of social relationships that are appropriate to the new education than is the case with traditional education. I think many of the difficulties experienced in the conduct of progressive schools and many of the criticisms leveled against them arise from this source. The difficulties are aggravated and the criticisms are increased when it is supposed that the new education is somehow easier than the old. This belief is, I imagine, more or less current. Perhaps it illustrates again the *Either-Or* philosophy, springing from the idea that about all which is required is *not* to do what is done in traditional schools.

I admit gladly that the new education is *simpler* in principle than the old. It is in harmony with principles of growth, while there is very much which is artificial in the old selection and arrangement of subjects and methods, and artificiality always leads to unnecessary complexity. But the easy and the simple are not identical. To discover what is really simple and to act upon the discovery is an exceedingly difficult task. After the artificial and complex is once institutionally established and ingrained in custom and routine, it is easier to walk in the paths that have been beaten than it is, after taking a new point of view, to work out what is practically involved in the new point of view. The old Ptolemaic astronomical system was more complicated with its cycles and epicycles than the Copernican system. But until organization of actual astronomical phenomena on the ground of the latter principle had been effected the easiest course was to follow the line of least resistance provided by the old intellectual habit. So we come back to the idea that a coherent *theory* of experience, affording positive direction to selection and organization of appropriate educational methods and materials, is required by the attempt to give new direction to the work of the schools. The process is a slow and arduous one. It is a matter of growth, and there are many obstacles which tend to obstruct growth and to deflect it into wrong lines.

I shall have something to say later about organization. All that is needed, perhaps, at this point is to say that we must escape from the tendency to think of organization in terms of the *kind* of organization, whether of content (or subject-matter), or of methods and social relations, that mark traditional education. I think that a good deal of the current opposition to the idea of organization is due to the fact that it is so hard to get away from the picture of the studies of the old school. The moment "organization" is mentioned imagination goes almost automatically to the kind of organization that is familiar, and in revolting against that we are led to shrink from the very idea of any organization. On the other hand, educational reactionaries, who are now gathering force, use the absence of adequate intellectual and moral organization in the newer type of school as proof not only of the need of organization, but to identify any and every kind of organization with that instituted before the rise of experimental science. Failure to develop a conception of organization upon the empirical and experimental basis gives reactionaries a too easy victory. But the fact that the empirical sciences now offer the best type of intellectual organization which can be found in any field shows that there is no reason why we, who call ourselves empiricists, should be "pushovers" in the matter of order and organization.

CHAPTER 3—CRITERIA OF EXPERIENCE

If there is any truth in what has been said about the need of forming a theory of experience in order that education may be intelligently conducted upon the basis of experience, it is clear that the next thing in order in this discussion is to present the principles that are most significant in framing this theory. I shall not, therefore, apologize for engaging in a certain amount of philosophical analysis, which otherwise might be out of place. I may, however, reassure you to some degree by saying that this analysis is not an end in itself but is engaged in for the sake of obtaining criteria to be applied later in discussion of a number of concrete and, to most persons, more interesting issues.

I have already mentioned what I called the category of continuity, or the experiential continuum. This principle is involved, as I pointed out, in every attempt to discriminate between experiences that are worth while educationally and those that are not. It may seem superfluous to argue that this discrimination is necessary not only in criticizing the traditional type of education but also in initiating and conducting a different type. Nevertheless, it is advisable to pursue for a little while the idea that it is necessary. One may safely assume, I suppose, that one thing which has recommended the progressive movement is that it seems more in accord with the democratic ideal to which our people is committed than do the procedures of the traditional school, since the latter have so much of the autocratic about them. Another thing which has contributed to its favorable reception is that its methods are humane in comparison with the harshness so often attending the policies of the traditional school.

The question I would raise concerns why we prefer democratic and humane arrangements to those which are autocratic and harsh. And by "why," I mean the *reason* for preferring them, not just the *causes* which lead us to the preference. One *cause* may be that we have been taught not only in the schools but by the press, the pulpit, the platform, and our laws and law-making bodies that democracy is the best of all social institutions. We may have so assimilated this idea from our surroundings that it has become an habitual part of our mental and moral make-up. But similar causes have led other persons in different surroundings to widely varying conclusions—to prefer fascism, for example. The cause for our preference is not the same thing as the reason why we *should* prefer it.

It is not my purpose here to go in detail into the reason. But I would ask a single question: Can we find any reason that does not ultimately come down to the belief that democratic social arrangements promote a better quality of human experience, one which is more widely accessible and enjoyed, than do non-democratic and anti-democratic forms of social life? Does not the principle of regard for individual freedom and for decency and kindliness of human relations come back in the end to the conviction that these things are tributary to a higher quality of experience on the part of a greater number than are methods of repression and coercion or force? Is it not the reason for our preference that we believe that mutual consultation and convictions reached through persuasion, make possible a better quality of experience than can otherwise be provided on any wide scale?

If the answer to these questions is in the affirmative (and personally I do not see how we can justify our preference for democracy and humanity on any other ground), the ultimate reason for hospitality to progressive education, because of its reliance upon and use of humane methods and its kinship to democracy, goes back to the fact that discrimination is made between the inherent values of different experiences. So I come back to the principle of continuity of experience as a criterion of discrimination.

At bottom, this principle rests upon the fact of habit, when *habit* is interpreted biologically. The basic characteristic of habit is that every experience enacted and undergone modifies the one who acts and undergoes, while this modification affects, whether we wish it or not, the quality of subsequent experiences. For it is a somewhat different person who enters into them. The principle of habit so understood obviously goes deeper than the ordinary conception of *a* habit as a more or less fixed way of doing things, although it includes the latter as one of its special cases. it covers the formation of attitudes, attitudes that are emotional and intellectual; it covers our basic sensitivities and ways of meeting and responding to all the conditions which we meet in living. From this point of view, the principle of continuity of experience means that every experience both takes up something from those which have gone before and modifies in some way the quality of those which come after. As the poet states it,

> . . .all experience is an arch wherethro'
> Gleams that untraveled world, whose margin fades
> For ever and for ever when I move.

So far, however, we have no ground for discrimination among experiences. For the principle is of universal application. There is *some* kind of continuity in every case. It is when we note the different forms in which continuity of experience operates that we get the basis of discriminating among experiences. I may illustrate what is meant by an objection which has been brought against an idea which I once put forth—namely, that the educative process can be identified with growth when that is understood in terms of the active participle, *growing*.

Growth, or growing as developing, not only physically but intellectually and morally, is one exemplification of the principle of continuity. The objection made is that growth might take many different directions: a man, for example, who starts out on a career of burglary may grow in that direction, and by practice may grow into a highly expert burglar. Hence it is argued that "growth" is not enough; we must also specify the direction in which growth takes place, the end towards which it tends. Before, however, we decide that the objection is conclusive we must analyze the case a little further.

That a man may grow in efficiency as a burglar, as a gangster, or as a corrupt politician, cannot be doubted. But from the standpoint of growth as education and education as growth the question is whether growth in this direction promotes or retards growth in general. Does this form of growth create conditions for further growth, or does it set up conditions that shut off the person who has grown in this particular direction from the occasions, stimuli, and opportunities for continuing growth in new directions? What is the effect of gorwth in a special direction upon the attitudes and habits which alone open up avenues for development in other lines? I shall leave you to answer these questions, saying simply that when and *only* when development in a particular line

conduces to continuing growth does it answer to the criterion of education as growing. For the conception is one that must find universal and
not specialized limited application.

I return now to the question of continuity as a criterion by which to
discriminate between experiences which are educative and those which
are mis-educative. As we have seen, there is some kind of continuity in
any case since every experience affects for better or worse the attitudes
which help decide the quality of further experiences, by setting up
certain preference and aversion, and making it easier or harder to act for
this or that end. Moreover, every experience influences in some degree
the objective conditions under which further experiences are had. For
example, a child who learns to speak has a new facility and new desire.
But he has also widened the external conditions of subsequent learning.
When he learns to read, he similarly opens up a new environment. If a
person decides to become a teacher, lawyer, physician, or stockbroker,
when he executes his intention he thereby necessarily determines to
some extent the environment in which he will act in the future. He has
rendered himself more sensitive and responsive to certain conditions,
and relatively immune to those things about him that would have been
stimuli if he had made another choice.

But, while the principle of continuity applies in some way in every
case, the quality of the present experience influences the *way* in which
the principle applies. We speak of spoiling a child and of the spoilt child.
The effect of over-indulging a child is a continuing one. It sets up an
attitude which operates as an automatic demand that persons and objects
cater to his desires and caprices in the future. It makes him seek the kind
of situation that will enable him to do what he feels like doing at the time.
It renders him averse to and comparatively incompetent in situations
which require effort and perseverance in overcoming obstacles. There is
no paradox in the fact that the principle of the continuity of experience
may operate so as to leave a person arrested on a low plane of development, in a way which limits later capacity for growth.

On the other hand, if an experience arouses curiosity, strengthens
initiative, and sets up desires and purpose that are sufficiently intense to
carry a person over dead places in the future, continuity works in a very
different way. Every experience is a moving force. Its value can be
judged only on the ground of what it moves toward and into. The
greater maturity of experience which should belong to the adult as
educator puts him in a position to evaluate each experience of the young
in a way in which the one having the less mature experience cannot do. It
is then the business of the educator to see in what direction an experience is heading. There is no point in his being more mature if, instead of
using his greater insight to help organize the conditions of the experience of the immature, he throws away his insight. Failure to take the

moving force of an experience into account so as to judge and direct it on
the ground of what it is moving into means disloyalty to the principle of
experience itself. The disloyalty operates in two directions. The educator
is false to the understanding that he should have obtained from his own
past experience. He is also unfaithful to the fact that all human experience is ultimately social: that it involves contact and communication. The
mature person, to put it in moral terms, has no right to withhold from
the young on given occasions whatever capacity for sympathetic understanding his own experience has given him.

No sooner, however, are such things said than there is a tendency to
react to the other extreme and take what has been said as a plea for some
sort of disguised imposition from outside. It is worth while, accordingly,
to say something about the way in which the adult can exercise the
wisdom his own wider experience gives him without imposing a merely
external control. On one side, it is his business to be on the alert to see
what attitudes and habitual tendencies are being created. In this direction he must, if he is an educator, be able to judge what attitudes are
actually conducive to continued growth and what are detrimental. He
must, in addition, have that sympathetic understanding of individuals as
individuals which gives him an idea of what is actually going on in the
minds of those who are learning. It is, among other things, the need for
these abilities on the part of the parent and teacher which makes a
system of education based upon living experience a more difficult affair
to conduct successfully than it is to follow the patterns of traditional
education.

But there is another aspect of the matter. Experience does not go on
simply inside a person. It does go on there, for it influences the formation of attitudes of desire and purpose. But this is not the whole of the
story. Every genuine experience has an active side which changes in some
degree the objective conditions under which experiences are had. The
difference between civilization and savagery, to take an example on a
large scale, is found in the degree in which previous experiences have
changed the objective conditions under which subsequent experiences
take place. The existence of roads, of means of rapid movement and
transportation, tools, implements, furniture, electric light and power are
illustrations. Destroy the external conditions of present civilized experience, and for a time our experience would relapse into that of barbaric
peoples.

In a word, we live from birth to death in a world of persons and
things which in large measure is what it is because of what has been done
and transmitted from previous human activities. When this fact is ignored, experience is treated as if it were something which goes on
exclusively inside an individual's body and mind. It ought not to be
necessary to say that experience does not occur in a vacuum. There are

sources outside an individual which give rise to experience. It is constantly fed from these springs. No one would question that a child in a slum tenement has a different experience from that of a child in a cultured home; that the country lad has a different kind of experience from the city boy, or a boy on the seashore one different from the lad who is brought up on inland prairies. Ordinarily we take such facts for granted as too commonplace to record. But when their educational import is recognized, they indicate the second way in which the educator can direct the experience of the young without engaging in imposition. A primary responsibility of educators is that they not only be aware of the general principle of the shaping of actual experience by environing conditions, but that they also recognize in the concrete what surroundings are conducive to having experiences that lead to growth. Above all, they should know how to utilize the surroundings, physical and social, that exist so as to extract from them all that they have to contribute to building up experiences that are worth while.

Traditional education did not have to face this problem; it could systematically dodge this responsibility. The school environment of desks, blackboards, and a small school yard, was supposed to suffice. There was no demand that the teacher should become intimately acquainted with the conditions of the local community, physical, historical, economic, occupational, etc., in order to utilize them as educational resources. A system of education based upon the necessary connection of education with experience must, on the contrary, if faithful to its principle, take these things constantly into account. This tax upon the educator is another reason why progressive education is more difficult to carry on than was ever the traditional system.

It is possible to frame schemes of education that pretty systematically subordinate objective conditions to those which reside in the individuals being educated. This happens whenever the place and function of the teacher, of books, of apparatus and equipment, of everything which represents the products of the more mature experience of elders, is systematically subordinated to the immediate inclinations and feelings of the young. Every theory which assumes that importance can be attached to these objective factors only at the expense of imposing external control and of limiting the freedom of individuals rests finally upon the notion that experience is truly experience only when objective conditions are subordinated to what goes on within the individuals having the experience.

I do not mean that it is supposed that objective conditions can be shut out. It is recognized that they must enter in: so much concession is made to the inescapable fact that we live in a world of things and persons. But I think that observation of what goes on in some families and some schools would disclose that some parents and some teachers are acting upon the idea of *subordinating* objective conditions to internal ones. In that case, it is assumed not only that the latter are primary, which in one sense they are, but that just as they temporarily exist they fix the whole educational process.

Let me illustrate from the case of an infant. The needs of a baby for food, rest, and activity are certainly primary and decisive in one respect. Nourishment must be provided; provision must be made for comfortable sleep, and so on. But these facts do not mean that a parent shall feed the baby at any time when the baby is cross or irritable, that there shall not be a program of regular hours of feeding and sleeping, etc. The wise mother takes account of the needs of the infant but not in a way which dispenses with her own responsibility for regulating the objective conditions under which the needs are satisfied. And if she is a wise mother in this respect, she draws upon past experiences of experts as well as her own for the light that these shed upon what experiences are in general most conducive to the normal development of infants. Instead of these conditions being subordinated to the immediate internal condition of the baby, they are definitely ordered so that a particular kind of *interaction* with these immediate internal states may be brought about.

The word "interaction," which has just been used, expresses the second chief principle for interpreting an experience in its educational function and force. It assigns equal rights to both factors in experience— objective and internal conditions. Any normal experience is an interplay of these two sets of conditions. Taken together, or in their interaction, they form what we call a *situation*. The trouble with traditional education was not that it emphasized the external conditions that enter into the control of the experiences but that it paid so little attention to the internal factors which also decide what kind of experience is had. It violated the principle of interaction from one side. But this violation is no reason why the new education should violate the principle from the other side—except upon the basis of the extreme *Either-Or* educational philosophy which has been mentioned.

The illustration drawn from the need for regulation of the objective conditions of a baby's development indicates first, that the parent has responsibility for arranging the conditions under which an infant's experience of food, sleep, etc., occurs, and, secondly, that the responsibility is fulfilled by utilizing the funded experience of the past, as this is represented, say, by the advice of competent physicians and others who have made a special study of normal physical growth. Does it limit the freedom of the mother when she uses the body of knowledge thus provided to regulate the objective conditions of nourishment and sleep? Or does the enlargement of her intelligence in fulfilling her parental function widen her freedom? Doubtless if a fetish were made of the advice and directions so that they came to be inflexible dictates to be followed under every possible condition, then restriction of freedom of both parent and child would occur. But this restriction would also be a limitation of the intelligence that is exercised in personal judgment.

In what respect does regulation of objective conditions limit the freedom of the baby? Some limitation is certainly placed upon its immediate movements and inclinations when it is put in its crib, at a time when it wants to continue playing, or does not get food at the moment it would like it, or when it isn't picked up and dandled when it cries for attention. Restriction also occurs when mother or nurse snatches a child away from an open fire into which it is about to fall. I shall have more to say later about freedom. Here it is enough to ask whether freedom is to be thought of and adjudged on the basis of relatively momentary incidents or whether its meaning is found in the continuity of developing experience.

The statement that individuals live in a world means, in the concrete, that they live in a series of situations. And when it is said that they live *in* these situations, the meaning of the word "in" is different from its meaning when it is said that pennies are "in" a pocket or paint is "in" a can. It means, once more, that interaction is going on between an individual and objects and other persons. The conceptions of *situation* and of *interaction* are inseparable from each other. An experience is always what it is because of a transaction taking place between an individual and what, at the time, constitutes his environment, whether the latter consists of persons with whom he is talking about some topic or event, the subject talked about being also a part of the situation; or the toys with which he is playing; the book he is reading (in which his environing conditions at the time may be England or ancient Greece or an imaginary region); or the materials of an experiment he is performing. The environment, in other words, is whatever conditions interact with personal needs, desires, purposes, and capacities to create the experience which is had. Even when a person builds a castle in the air he is interacting with the objects which he constructs in fancy.

The two principles of continuity and interaction are not separate from each other. They intercept and unite. They are, so to speak, the longitudinal and lateral aspects of experience. Different situations succeed one another. But because of the principle of continuity something is carried over from the earlier to the later ones. As an individual passes from one situation to another, his world, his environment, expands or contracts. He does not find himself living in another world but in a different part or aspect of one and the same world. What he has learned in the way of knowledge and skill in one situation becomes an instrument of understanding and dealing effectively with the situations which follow. The process goes on as long as life and learning continue. Otherwise the course of experience is disorderly, since the individual factor that enters into making an experience is split. A divided world, a world whose parts and aspects do not hang together, is at once a sign and a cause of a divided personality. When the splitting-up reaches a certain point we call the person insane. A fully integrated personality, on the other hand, exists only when successive experiences are integrated with one another. It can be built up only as a world of related objects is constructed.

Continuity and interaction in their active union with each other provide the measure of the educative significance and value of an experience. The immediate and direct concern of an educator is then with the situations in which interaction takes place. The individual, who enters as a factor into it, is what he is at a given time. It is the other factor, that of objective conditions, which lies to some extent within the possibility of regulation by the educator. As has already been noted, the phrase "objective conditions" covers a wide range. It includes what is done by the educator and the way in which it is done, not only words spoken but the tone of voice in which they are spoken. It includes equipment, books, apparatus, toys, and games played. It includes the materials with which an individual interacts, and, most important of all, the total *social* set-up of the situations in which a person is engaged.

When it is said that the objective conditions are those which are within the power of the educator to regulate, it is meant, of course, that his ability to influence directly the experience of others and thereby the education they obtain places upon him the duty of determining that environment which will interact with the existing capacities and needs of those taught to create a worth-while experience. The trouble with traditional education was not that educators took upon themselves the responsibility for providing an environment. The trouble was that they did not consider the other factor in creating an experience; namely, the powers and purposes of those taught. It was assumed that a certain set of conditions was intrinsically desirable, apart from its ability to evoke a certain quality of response in individuals. This lack of mutual adaptation made the process of teaching and learning accidental. Those to whom the provided conditions were suitable managed to learn. Others got on as best they could. Responsibility for selecting objective conditions carries with it, then, the responsibility for understanding the needs and capacities of the individuals who are learning at a given time. It is not enough that certain materials and methods have proved effective with other individuals at other times. There must be a reason for thinking that they will function in generating an experience that has educative quality with particular individuals at a particular time.

It is no reflection upon the nutritive quality of beefsteak that it is not fed to infants. It is not an invidious reflection upon trigonometry that we do not teach it in the first or fifth grade of school. It is not the subject *per se* that is educative or that is conducive to growth. There is no subject that is in and of itself, or without regard to the stage of growth attained by the learner, such that inherent educational value can be attributed to it. Failure to take into account adaptation to the needs and capacities of individuals was the source of the idea that certain subjects and certain methods are intrinsically cultural or intrinsically good for mental discipline. There is no such thing as educational value in the abstract. The notion that some subjects and methods and that acquaintance with certain facts and truths possess educational value in and of themselves is the reason why traditional education reduced the material of education so largely to a diet of predigested materials. According to this notion, it was enough to regulate the quantity and difficulty of the material provided, in a scheme of quantitative grading, from month to month and from year to year. Otherwise a pupil was expected to take it in the doses that were prescribed from without. If the pupil left it instead of taking it, if he engaged in physical truancy, or in the mental truancy of mind-wandering and finally built up an emotional revulsion against the subject, he was held to be at fault. No question was raised as to whether the trouble might not lie in the subject-matter or in the way in which it was offered. The principle of interaction makes it clear that failure of adaptation of material to needs and capacities of individuals may cause an experience to be non-educative quite as much as failure of an individual to adapt himself to the material.

The principle of continuity in its educational application means, nevertheless, that the future has to be taken into account at every stage of the educational process. This idea is easily misunderstood and is badly distorted in traditional education. Its assumption is, that by acquiring certain skills and by learning certain subjects which would be needed later (perhaps in college or perhaps in adult life) pupils are as a matter of course made ready for the needs and circumstances of the future. Now "preparation" is a treacherous idea. In a certain sense every experience should do something to prepare a person for later experiences of a deeper and more expansive quality. That is the very meaning of growth, continuity, reconstruction of experience. But it is a mistake to suppose that the mere acquisition of a certain amount of arithmetic, geography, history, etc., which is taught and studied because it may be useful at some time in the future, has this effect, and it is a mistake to suppose that acquisition of skills in reading and figuring will automatically constitute preparation for their right and effective use under conditions very unlike those in which they were acquired.

Almost everyone has had occasion to look back upon his school days and wonder what has become of the knowledge he was supposed to have amassed during his years of schooling, and why it is that the technical skills he acquired have to be learned over again in changed form in order to stand him in good stead. Indeed, he is lucky who does not find that in order to make progress, in order to go ahead intellectually, he does not have to unlearn much of what he learned in school. These questions cannot be disposed of by saying that the subjects were not actually learned, for they were learned at least sufficiently to enable a pupil to pass examinations in them. One trouble is that the subject-matter in question was learned in isolation; it was put, as it were, in a water-tight compartment. When the question is asked, then, what has become of it, where has it gone to, the right answer is that it is still there in the special compartment in which it was originally stowed away. If exactly the same conditions recurred as those under which it was acquired, it would also recur and be available. But it was segregated when it was acquired and hence is so disconnected from the rest of experience that it is not available under the actual conditions of life. It is contrary to the laws of experience that learning of this kind, no matter how thoroughly engrained at the time, should give genuine preparation.

Nor does failure in preparation end at this point. Perhaps the greatest of all pedagogical fallacies is the notion that a person learns only the particular thing he is studying at the time. Collateral learning in the way of formation of enduring attitudes, of likes and dislikes, may be and often is much more important than the spelling lesson or lesson in geography or history that is learned. For these attitudes are fundamentally what count in the future. The most important attitude that can be formed is that of desire to go on learning. If impetus in this direction is weakened instead of being intensified, something much more than mere lack of preparation takes place. The pupil is actually robbed of native capacities which otherwise would enable him to cope with the circumstances that he meets in the course of his life. We often see persons who have had little schooling and in whose case the absence of set schooling proves to be a positive asset. They have at least retained their native common sense and power of judgment, and its exercise in the actual conditions of living has given them the precious gift of ability to learn from the experiences they have. What avail is it to win prescribed amounts of information about geography and history, to win ability to read and write, if in the process the individual loses his own soul: loses his appreciation of things worth while, of the values to which these things are relative; if he loses desire to apply what he has learned and, above all, loses the ability to extract meaning from his future experiences as they occur?

What, then, is the true meaning of preparation in the educational scheme? In the first place, it means that a person, young or old, gets out of his present experience all that there is in it for him at the time in which he has it. When preparation is made the controlling end, then the potentialities of the present are sacrificed to a suppositious future. When this happens, the actual preparation for the future is missed or distorted. The ideal of using the present simply to get ready for the future contradicts itself. It omits, and even shuts out, the very conditions by which a person can be prepared for his future. We always live at the time we live and not at some other time, and only by extracting at each present time the full meaning of each present experience are we prepared for doing the same thing in the future. This is the only preparation which in the long run amounts to anything.

All this means that attentive care must be devoted to the conditions which give each present experience a worthwhile meaning. Instead of inferring that it doesn't make much difference what the present experience is as long as it is enjoyed, the conclusion is the exact opposite. Here is another matter where it is easy to react from one extreme to the other. Because traditional schools tended to sacrifice the present to a remote and more or less unknown future, therefore it comes to be believed that the educator has little responsibility for the kind of present experiences the young undergo. But the relation of the present and the future is not an *Either-Or* affair. The present affects the future anyway. The persons who should have some idea of the connection between the two are those who have achieved maturity. Accordingly, upon them devolves the responsibility for instituting the conditions for the kind of present experience which has a favorable effect upon the future. Education as growth or maturity should be an ever-present process.

CHAPTER 4—SOCIAL CONTROL

I have said that educational plans and projects, seeing education in terms of life-experience, are thereby committed to framing and adopting an intelligent theory or, if you please, philosophy of experience. Otherwise they are at the mercy of every intellectual breeze that happens to blow. I have tried to illustrate the need for such a theory by calling attention to two principles which are fundamental in the constitution of experience: the principles of interaction and of continuity. If, then, I am asked why I have spent so much time on expounding a rather abstract philosophy, it is because practical attempts to develop schools based upon the idea that education is found in life-experience are bound to exhibit inconsistencies and confusions unless they are guided by some conception of what experience is, and what marks off educative experience from non-educative and mis-educative experience. I now come to a group of actual educational questions the discussion of which will, I hope, provide topics and material that are more concrete than the discussion up to this point.

The two principles of continuity and interaction as criteria of the value of experience are so intimately connected that it is not easy to tell just what special educational problem to take up first. Even the convenient division into problems of subject-matter or studies and of methods of teaching and learning is likely to fail us in selection and organization of topics to discuss. Consequently, the beginning and sequence of topics is somewhat arbitrary. I shall commence, however, with the old question of individual freedom and social control and pass on to the questions that grow naturally out of it.

It is often well in considering educational problems to get a start by temporarily ignoring the school and thinking of other human situations. I take it that no one would deny that the ordinary good citizen is as a matter of fact subject to a great deal of social control and that a considerable part of this control is not felt to involve restriction of personal freedom. Even the theoretical anarchist, whose philosophy commits him to the idea that state or government control is an unmitigated evil, believes that with abolition of the political state other forms of social control would operate: indeed, his opposition to governmental regulation springs from his belief that other and to him more normal modes of control would operate with abolition of the state.

Without taking up this extreme position, let us note some examples of social control that operate in everyday life, and then look for the principle underlying them. Let us begin with the young people themselves. Children at recess or after school play games, from tag and one-old-cat to baseball and football. The games involve rules, and these rules order their conduct. The games do not go on haphazardly or by a succession of improvisations. Without rules there is no game. If disputes arise there is an umpire to appeal to, or discussion and a kind of arbitration are means to a decision; otherwise the game is broken up and comes to an end.

There are certain fairly obvious controlling features of such situations to which I want to call attention. The first is that the rules are a part of the game. They are not outside of it. No rules, then no game; different rules, then a different game. As long as the game goes on with a reasonable smoothness, the players do not feel that they are submitting to external imposition but that they are playing the game. In the second place an individual may at times feel that a decision isn't fair and he may even get angry. But he is not objecting to a rule but to what he claims is a violation of it, to some one-sided and unfair action. In the third place, the rules, and hence the conduct of the game, are fairly standardized. There are recognized ways of counting out, of selection of sides, as well as for positions to be taken, movements to be made, etc. These rules have the sanction of tradition and precedent. Those playing the game have seen, perhaps, professional matches and they want to emulate their elders. An element that is conventional is pretty strong. Usually, a group of youngsters change the rules by which they play only when the adult group to which they look for models have themselves made a change in the rules, while the change made by the elders is at least supposed to conduce to making the game more skillful or more interesting to spectators.

Now, the general conclusion I would draw is that control of individual actions is effected by the whole situation in which individuals are involved, in which they share and of which they are co-operative or interacting parts. For even in a competitive game there is a certain kind of participation, of sharing in a common experience. Stated the other way around, those who take part do not feel that they are bossed by an individual person or are being subjected to the will of some outside superior person. When violent disputes do arise, it is usually on the alleged ground that the umpire or some person on the other side is being unfair; in other words, that in such cases some individual is trying to impose his individual will on someone else.

It may seem to be putting too heavy a load upon a single case to argue that this instance illustrates the general principle of social control of individuals without the violation of freedom. But if the matter were followed out through a number of cases, I think the conclusion that this particular instance does illustrate a general principle would be justified. Games are generally competitive. If we took instances of co-operative activities in which all members of a group take part, as for example in well-ordered family life in which there is mutual confidence, the point would be even clearer. In all such cases it is not the will or desire of any one person which establishes order but the moving spirit of the whole group. The control is social, but individuals are parts of a community, not outside of it.

I do not mean by this that there are no occasions upon which the authority of, say, the parent does not have to intervene and exercise fairly direct control. But I do say that, in the first place, the number of these occasions is slight in comparison with the number of those in which the control is exercised by situations in which all take part. And what is even more important, the authority in question when exercised in a well-regulated household or other community group is not a manifestation of merely personal will; the parent or teacher exercises it as the representative and agent of the interests of the group as a whole. With respect to the first point, in a well-ordered school the main reliance for control of this and that individual is upon the activities carried on and upon the situations in which these activities are maintained. The teacher reduces to a minimum the occasions in which he or she has to exercise authority in a personal way. When it is necessary, in the second place, to speak and act firmly, it is done in behalf of the interest of the group, not as an exhibition of personal power. This makes the difference between action which is arbitrary and that which is just and fair.

Moreover, it is not necessary that the difference should be formulated in words, by either teacher or the young, in order to be felt in experience. The number of children who do not feel the difference (even if they cannot articulate it and reduce it to an intellectual principle) between action that is motivated by personal power and desire to dictate and action that is fair, because in the interest of all, is small. I should even be willing to say that upon the whole children are more sensitive to the signs and symptoms of this difference than are adults. Children learn the difference when playing with one another. They are willing, often too willing if anything, to take suggestions from one child and let him be a leader if his conduct adds to the experienced value of what they are doing, while they resent the attempt at dictation. Then they often withdraw and when asked why, say that it is because so-and-so "is too bossy."

I do not wish to refer to the traditional school in ways which set up a caricature in lieu of a picture. But I think it is fair to say that one reason the personal commands of the teacher so often played an undue role and a reason why the order which existed was so much a matter of sheer obedience to the will of an adult was because the situation almost forced it upon the teacher. The school was not a group or community held together by participation in common activities. Consequently, the normal, proper conditions of control were lacking. Their absence was made up for, and to a considerable extent had to be made up for, by the direct intervention of the teacher, who, as the saying went, "*kept* order." He kept it because order was in the teacher's keeping, instead of residing in the shared work being done.

The conclusion is that in what are called the new schools, the primary source of social control resides in the very nature of the work done as a social enterprise in which all individuals have an opportunity to contribute and to which all feel a responsibility. Most children are naturally "sociable." Isolation is even more irksome to them than to adults. A genuine community life has its ground in this natural sociability. But community life does not organize itself in an enduring way purely spontaneously. It requires thought and planning ahead. The educator is responsible for a knowledge of individuals and for a knowledge of subject-matter that will enable activities to be selected which lend themselves to social organization, an organization in which all individuals have an opportunity to contribute something, and in which the activities in which all participate are the chief carrier of control.

I am not romantic enough about the young to suppose that every pupil will respond or that any child of normally strong impulses will respond on every occasion. There are likely to be some who, when they come to school, are already victims of injurious conditions outside of the school and who have become so passive and unduly docile that they fail to contribute. There will be others who, because of previous experience, are bumptious and unruly and perhaps downright rebellious. But it is certain that the general principle of social control cannot be predicated upon such cases. It is also true that no general rule can be laid down for dealing with such cases. The teacher has to deal with them individually. They fall into general classes, but no two are exactly alike. The educator has to discover as best he or she can the causes for the recalcitrant attitudes. He or she cannot, if the educational process is to go on, make it a question of pitting one will against another in order to see which is strongest, nor yet allow the unruly and non-participating pupils to stand permanently in the way of the educative activities of others. Exclusion perhaps is the only available measure at a given juncture, but it is no solution. For it may strengthen the very causes which have brought about the undesirable anti-social attitude, such as desire for attention or to show off.

Exceptions rarely prove a rule or give a clue to what the rule should be. I would not, therefore, attach too much importance to these exceptional cases, although it is true at present that progressive schools are likely often to have more than their fair share of these cases, since parents may send children to such schools as a last resort. I do not think weakness in control when it is found in progressive schools arises in any event from these exceptional cases. It is much more likely to arise from failure to arrange in advance for the kind of work (by which I mean all kinds of activities engaged in) which will create situations that of themselves tend to exercise control over what this, that, and the other pupil does and how he does it. This failure most often goes back to lack of sufficiently thoughtful planning in advance. The causes for such lack are varied. The one which is peculiarly important to mention in this connection is the idea that such advance planning is unnecessary and even that it is inherently hostile to the legitimate freedom of those being instructed.

Now, of course, it is quite possible to have preparatory planning by the teacher done in such a rigid and intellectually inflexible fashion that it does result in adult imposition, which is none the less external because executed with tact and the semblance of respect for individual freedom. But this kind of planning does not follow inherently from the principle involved. I do not know what the greater maturity of the teacher and the teacher's greater knowledge of the world, of subject-matters and of individuals is for unless the teacher can arrange conditions that are conducive to community activity and to organization which exercises control over individual impulses by the mere fact that all are engaged in communal projects. Because the kind of advance planning heretofore engaged in has been so routine as to leave little room for the free play of individual thinking or for contributions due to distinctive individual experience, it does not follow that all planning must be rejected. On the contrary, there is incumbent upon the educator the duty of instituting a much more intelligent, and consequently more difficult, kind of planning. He must survey the capacities and needs of the particular set of individuals with whom he is dealing and must at the same time arrange the conditions which provide the subject-matter or content for experiences that satisfy these needs and develop these capacities. The planning must be flexible enough to permit free play for individuality of experience and yet firm enough to give direction towards continuous development of power.

The present occasion is a suitable one to say something about the province and office of the teacher. The principle that development of experience comes about through interaction means that education is essentially a social process. This quality is realized in the degree in which individuals form a community group. It is absurd to exclude the teacher from membership in the group. As the most mature member of the group he has a peculiar responsibility for the conduct of the interactions and intercommunications which are the very life of the group as a community. That children are individuals whose freedom should be respected while the more mature person should have no freedom as an individual is an idea too absurd to require refutation. The tendency to exclude the teacher from a positive and leading share in the direction of the activities of the community of which he is a member is another instance of reaction from one extreme to another. When pupils were a class rather than a social group, the teacher necessarily acted largely from the outside, not as a director of processes of exchange in which all had a share. When education is based upon experience and educative experience is seen to be a social process, the situation changes radically. The teacher loses the position of external boss or dictator but takes on that of leader of group activities.

In discussing the conduct of games as an example of normal social control, reference was made to the presence of a standardized conventional factor. The counterpart of this factor in school life is found in the question of manners, especially of good manners in the manifestations of politeness and courtesy. The more we know about customs in different parts of the world at different times in the history of mankind, the more we learn how much manners differ from place to place and time to time. This fact proves that there is a large conventional factor involved. But there is no group at any time or place which does not have some code of manners as, for example, with respect to proper ways of greeting other persons. The particular form a convention takes has nothing fixed and absolute about it. But the existence of some form of convention is not itself a convention. It is a uniform attendant of all social relationships. At the very least, it is the oil which prevents or reduces friction.

It is possible, of course, for these social forms to become, as we say, "mere formalities." They may become merely outward show with no meaning behind them. But the avoidance of empty ritualistic forms of social intercourse does not mean the rejection of every formal element. It rather indicates the need for development of forms of intercourse that are inherently appropriate to social situations. Visitors to some progressive schools are shocked by the lack of manners they come across. One who knows the situation better is aware that to some extent their absence is due to the eager interest of children to go on with what they are doing. In their eagerness they may, for example, bump into each other and into visitors with no word of apology. One might say that this condition is better than a display of merely external punctilio accompanying intellectual and emotional lack of interest in school work. But it also represents a failure in education, a failure to learn one of the most important lessons of life, that of mutual accommodation and adaptation. Education is going on in a one-sided way, for attitudes and habits are in process of formation that stand in the way of the future learning that springs from easy and ready contact and communication with others.

CHAPTER 5—THE NATURE OF FREEDOM

At the risk of repeating what has been often said by me I want to say something about the other side of the problem of social control, namely, the nature of freedom. The only freedom that is of enduring importance is freedom of intelligence, that is to say, freedom of observation and of judgment exercised in behalf of purposes that are intrinsically worth while. The commonest mistake made about freedom is, I think, to identify it with freedom of movement, or with the external or physical side of activity. Now, this external and physical side of activity cannot be separated from the internal side of activity; from freedom of thought, desire, and purpose. The limitation that was put upon outward action by the fixed arrangements of the typical traditional schoolroom, with its fixed rows of desks and its military regimen of pupils who were permitted to move only at certain fixed signals, put a great restriction upon intellectual and moral freedom. Strait-jacket and chain-gang procedures had to be done away with if there was to be a chance for growth of individuals in the intellectual springs of freedom without which there is no assurance of genuine and continued normal growth.

But the fact still remains that an increased measure of freedom of outer movement is a *means,* not an end. The educational problem is not solved when this aspect of freedom is obtained. Everything then depends, so far as education is concerned, upon what is done with this added liberty. What end does it serve? What consequences flow from it? Let me speak first of the advantages which reside potentially in increase of outward freedom. In the first place, without its existence it is practically impossible for a teacher to gain knowledge of the individuals with whom he is concerned. Enforced quiet and acquiescence prevent pupils from disclosing their real natures. They enforce artificial uniformity. They put seeming before being. They place a premium upon preserving the outward appearance of attention, decorum, and obedience. And everyone who is acquainted with schools in which this system prevailed well knows that thoughts, imaginations, desires, and sly activities ran their own unchecked course behind this façade. They were disclosed to the teacher only when some untoward act led to their detection. One has only to contrast this highly artificial situation with normal human relations outside the schoolroom, say in a well-conducted home, to appreciate how fatal it is to the teacher's acquaintance with and understanding of the individuals who are, supposedly, being educated. Yet without this insight there is only an accidental chance that the material of study and the methods used in instruction will so come home to an individual that his development of mind and character is actually directed. There is a vicious circle. Mechanical uniformity of studies and methods creates a kind of uniform immobility and this reacts to perpetuate uniformity of studies and of recitations, while behind this enforced uniformity individual tendencies operate in irregular and more or less forbidden ways.

The other important advantage of increased outward freedom is found in the very nature of the learning process. That the older methods set a premium upon passivity and receptivity has been pointed out. Physical quiescence puts a tremendous premium upon these traits. The only escape from them in the standardized school is an activity which is irregular and perhaps disobedient. There cannot be complete quietude in a laboratory or workshop. The non-social character of the traditional school is seen in the fact that it erected silence into one of its prime virtues. There is, of course, such a thing as intense intellectual activity without overt bodily activity. But capacity for such intellectual activity marks a comparatively late achievement when it is continued for a long period. There should be brief intervals of time for quiet reflection provided for even the young. But they are periods of genuine reflection only when they follow after times of more overt action and are used to organize what has been gained in periods of activity in which the hands and other parts of the body beside the brain are used. Freedom of movement is also important as a means of maintaining normal physical and mental health. We have still to learn from the example of the Greeks who saw clearly the relation between a sound body and a sound mind. But in all the respects mentioned freedom of outward action is a means to freedom of judgment and of power to carry deliberately chosen ends into execution. The amount of external freedom which is needed varies from individual to individual. It naturally tends to decrease with increasing maturity, though its complete absence prevents even a mature individual from having the contacts which will provide him with new materials upon which his intelligence may exercise itself. The amount and the quality of this kind of free activity as a means of growth is a problem that must engage the thought of the educator at every stage of development.

There can be no greater mistake, however, than to treat such freedom as an end in itself. It then tends to be destructive of the shared cooperative activities which are the normal source of order. But, on the other hand, it turns freedom which should be positive into something negative. For freedom from restriction, the negative side, is to be prized only as a means to a freedom which is power: power to frame purposes, to judge wisely, to evaluate desires by the consequences which will result from acting upon them; power to select and order means to carry chosen ends into operation.

Natural impulses and desires constitute in any case the starting point. But there is no intellectual growth without some reconstruction, some remaking, of impulses and desires in the form in which they first show themselves. This remaking involves inhibition of impulse in its first estate. The alternative to externally imposed inhibition is inhibition through an individual's own reflection and judgment. The old phrase "stop and think" is sound psychology. For thinking is stoppage of the immediate manifestation of impulse until that impulse has been brought into connection with other possible tendencies to action so that a more comprehensive and coherent plan of activity is formed. Some of the other tendencies to action lead to use of eye, ear, and hand to observe objective conditions; others result in recall of what has happened in the past. Thinking is thus a postponement of immediate action, while it effects internal control of impulse through a union of observation and memory, this union being the heart of reflection. What has been said explains the meaning of the well-worn phrase "self-control." The ideal aim of education is creation of power of self-control. But the mere removal of external control is no guarantee for the production of self-control. It is easy to jump out of the frying-pan into the fire. It is easy, in other words, to escape one form of external control only to find oneself in another and more dangerous form of external control. Impulses and desires that are not ordered by intelligence are under the control of accidental circumstances. It may be a loss rather than a gain to escape from the control of another person only to find one's conduct dictated by immediate whim and caprice; that is, at the mercy of impulses into whose formation intelligent judgment has not entered. A person whose conduct is controlled in this way has at most only the illusion of freedom. Actually he is directed by forces over which he has no command.

CHAPTER 6—THE MEANING OF PURPOSE

It is, then, a sound instinct which identifies freedom with power to frame purposes and to execute or carry into effect purposes so framed. Such freedom is in turn identical with self-control; for the formation of purposes and the organization of means to execute them are the work of intelligence. Plato once defined a slave as the person who executes the purposes of another, and, as has just been said, a person is also a slave who is enslaved to his own blind desires. There is, I think, no point in the philosophy of progressive education which is sounder than its emphasis upon the importance of the participation of the learner in the formation of the purposes which direct his activities in the learning process, just as there is no defect in traditional education greater than its failure to secure the active co-operation of the pupil in construction of the purposes involved in his studying. But the meaning of purposes and ends is not self-evident and self-explanatory. The more their educational importance is emphasized, the more important it is to understand what a purpose is; how it arises and how it functions in experience.

A genuine purpose always starts with an impulse. Obstruction of the immediate execution of an impulse converts it into a desire. Nevertheless neither impulse nor desire is itself a purpose. A purpose is an end-view. That is, it involves foresight of the consequences which will result from acting upon impulse. Foresight of consequences involves the operation of intelligence. It demands, in the first place, observation of objective conditions and circumstances. For impulse and desire produce consequences not by themselves alone but through their interaction or cooperation with surrounding conditions. The impulse for such a simple action as walking is executed only in active conjunction with the ground on which one stands. Under ordinary circumstances, we do not have to pay much attention to the ground. In a ticklish situation we have to observe very carefully just what the conditions are, as in climbing a steep and rough mountain where no trail has been laid out. Exercise of observation is, then, one condition of transformation of impulse into a purpose. As in the sign by a railway crossing, we have to stop, look, listen.

But observation alone is not enough. We have to understand the *significance* of what we see, hear, and touch. This significance consists of the consequences that will result when what is seen is acted upon. A baby may *see* the brightness of a flame and be attracted thereby to reach for it. The significance of the flame is then not its brightness but its power to burn, as the consequence that will result from touching it. We can be aware of consequences only because of previous experiences. In cases that are familiar because of many prior experiences we do not have to stop to remember just what those experiences were. A flame comes to signify light and heat without our having expressly to think of previous experiences of heat and burning. But in unfamiliar cases, we cannot tell just what the consequences of observed conditions will be unless we go over past experiences in our mind, unless we reflect upon them and by seeing what is similar in them to those now present, go on to form a judgment of what may be expected in the present situation.

The formation of purposes is, then, a rather complex intellectual operation. It involves (1) observation of surrounding conditions; (2) knowledge of what has happened in similar situations in the past, a knowledge obtained partly by recollection and partly from the information, advice, and warning of those who have had a wider experience; and (3) judgment which puts together what is observed and what is recalled to see what they signify. A purpose differs from an original impulse and desire through its translation into a plan and method of action based upon foresight of the consequences of acting under given observed conditions in a certain way. "If wishes were horses, beggars would ride." Desire for something may be intense. It may be so strong as to override estimation of the consequences that will follow acting upon it. Such occurrences do not provide the model for education. The crucial educational problem is that of procuring the postponement of immediate action upon desire until observation and judgment have intervened. Unless I am mistaken, this point is definitely relevant to the conduct of progressive schools. Overemphasis upon activity as an end, instead of upon *intelligent* activity, leads to identification of freedom with immediate execution of impulses and desires. This identification is justified by a confusion of impulse with purpose; although, as has just been said, there is no purpose unless overt action is postponed until there is foresight of the consequences of carrying the impulse into execution—a foresight that is impossible without observation, information, and judgment. Mere foresight, even if it takes the form of accurate prediction, is not, of course, enough. The intellectual anticipation, the idea of consequences, must blend with desire and impulse to acquire moving force. It then gives direction to what otherwise is blind, while desire gives ideas impetus and momentum. An idea then becomes a plan in and for an activity to be carried out. Suppose a man has a desire to secure a new home, say by building a house. No matter how strong his desire, it cannot be directly executed. The man must form an idea of what kind of house he wants, including the number and arrangement of rooms, etc. He has to draw a plan, and have blue prints and specifications made. All this might be an idle amusement for spare time unless he also took stock of his resources. He must consider the relation of his funds and available credit to the execution of the plan. He has to investigate available sites, their price, their nearness to his place of business, to a congenial neighborhood, to school facilities, and so on and so on. All of the things reckoned with: his ability to pay, size and needs of family, possible locations, etc., etc., are objective facts. They are no part of the original desire. But they have to be viewed and judged in order that a desire may be converted into a purpose and a purpose into a plan of action.

All of us have desires, all at least who have not become so pathological that they are completely apathetic. These desires are the ultimate moving springs of action. A professional businessman wishes to succeed in his career; a general wishes to win the battle; a parent to have a comfortable home for his family, and to educate his children, and so on indefinitely. The intensity of the desire measures the strength of the efforts that will be put forth. But the wishes are empty castles in the air unless they are translated into the means by which they may be realized. The question of *how soon* or of means takes the place of a projected imaginative end, and, since means are objective, they have to be studied and understood if a genuine purpose is to be formed.

Traditional education tended to ignore the importance of personal impulse and desire as moving springs. But this is no reason why progressive education should identify impulse and desire with purpose and thereby pass lightly over the need for careful observation, for wide range of information, and for judgment if students are to share in the formation of the purposes which activate them. In an *educational* scheme, the occurrence of a desire and impulse is not the final end. It is an occasion and a demand for the formation of a plan and method of activity. Such a plan, to repeat, can be formed only by study of conditions and by securing all relevant information.

The teacher's business is to see that the occasion is taken advantage of. Since freedom resides in the operations of intelligent observation and judgment by which a purpose is developed, guidance given by the teacher to the exercise of the pupils' intelligence is an aid to freedom, not a restriction upon it. Sometimes teachers seem to be afraid even to make suggestions to the members of a group as to what they should do. I have heard of cases in which children are surrounded with objects and materials and then left entirely to themselves, the teacher being loath to suggest even what might be done with the materials lest freedom be infringed upon. Why, then, even supply materials, since they are a source of some suggestion or other? But what is more important is that the suggestion upon which pupils act must in any case come from somewhere. It is impossible to understand why a suggestion from one who has a larger experience and a wider horizon should not be at least as valid as a suggestion arising from some more or less accidental source.

It is possible of course to abuse the office, and to force the activity of the young into channels which express the teacher's purpose rather than that of the pupils. But the way to avoid this danger is not for the adult to withdraw entirely. The way is, first, for the teacher to be intelligently aware of the capacities, needs, and past experiences of those under instruction, and, secondly, to allow the suggestion made to develop into a plan and project by means of the further suggestions contributed and organized into a whole by the members of the group. The plan, in other words, is a co-operative enterprise, not a dictation. The teacher's suggestion is not a mold for a cast-iron result but is a starting point to be developed into a plan through contributions from the experience of all engaged in the learning process. The development occurs through reciprocal give-and-take, the teacher taking but not being afraid also to give. The essential point is that the purpose grow and take shape through the process of social intelligence.

CHAPTER 7—PROGRESSIVE ORGANIZATION OF SUBJECT-MATTER

Allusion has been made in passing a number of times to objective conditions involved in experience and to their function in promoting or failing to promote the enriched growth of further experience. By implication, these objective conditions, whether those of observation, of memory, of information procured from others, or of imagination, have been identified with the subject-matter of study and learning; or, speaking more generally, with the stuff of the course of study. Nothing, however, has been said explicitly so far about subject-matter as such. That topic will now be discussed. One consideration stands out clearly when education is conceived in terms of experience. Anything which can be called a study, whether arithmetic, history, geography, or one of the natural sciences, must be derived from materials which at the outset fall within the scope of ordinary life-experience. In this respect the newer education contrasts sharply with procedures which start with facts and truths that are outside the range of the experience of those taught, and which, therefore, have the problem of discovering ways and means of bringing them within experience. Undoubtedly one chief cause for the great success of newer methods in early elementary education has been its observance of the contrary principle.

But finding the material for learning within experience is only the first step. The next step is the progressive development of what is already experienced into a fuller and richer and also more organized form, a form that gradually approximates that in which subject-matter is presented to the skilled, mature person. That this change is possible without departing from the organic connection of education with experience is shown by the fact that this change takes place outside of the school and apart from formal education. The infant, for example, begins with an environment of objects that is very restricted in space and time. That environment steadily expands by the momentum inherent in experience itself without aid from scholastic instruction. As the infant learns to reach, creep, walk, and talk, the intrinsic subject-matter of its experience widens and deepens. It comes into connection with new objects and events which call out new powers, while the exercise of these powers refines and enlarges the content of its experience. Life-space and life-durations are expanded. The environment, the world of experience, constantly grows larger and, so to speak, thicker. The educator who receives the child at the end of this period has to find ways for doing consciously and deliberately what "nature" accomplishes in the earlier years.

It is hardly necessary to insist upon the first of the two conditions which have been specified. It is a cardinal precept of the newer school of education that the beginning of instruction shall be made with the experience learners already have; that this experience and the capacities that have been developed during its course provide the starting point for all further learning. I am not so sure than the other condition, that of orderly development toward expansion and organization of subject-matter through growth of experience, receives as much attention. Yet the principle of continuity of educative experience requires that equal thought and attention be given to solution of this aspect of the educational problem. Undoubtedly this phase of the problem is more difficult than the other. Those who deal with the pre-school child, with the kindergarten child, and with the boy and girl of the early primary years do not have much difficulty in determining the range of past experience or in finding activities that connect in vital ways with it. With older children both factors of the problem offer increased difficulties to the educator. It is harder to find out the background of the experience of individuals and harder to find out just how the subject-matters already contained in that experience shall be directed so as to lead out to larger and better organized fields.

It is a mistake to suppose that the principle of the leading on of experience to something different is adequately satisfied simply by giving pupils some new experiences any more than it is by seeing to it that they have greater skill and ease in dealing with things with which they are already familiar. It is also essential that the new objects and events be related intellectually to those of earlier experiences, and this means that there be some advance made in conscious articulation of facts and ideas. It thus becomes the office of the educator to select those things within the range of existing experience that have the promise and potentiality of presenting new problems which by stimulating new ways of observation and judgment will expand the area of further experience. He must constantly regard what is already won not as a fixed possession but as an agency and instrumentality for opening new fields which make new demands upon existing powers of observation and of intelligent use of memory. Connectedness in growth must be his constant watchword.

The educator more than the member of any other profession is concerned to have a long look ahead. The physician may feel his job done when he has restored a patient to health. He has undoubtedly the obligation of advising him how to live so as to avoid similar troubles in the future. But, after all, the conduct of his life is his own affair, not the physician's; and what is more important for the present point is that as far as the physician does occupy himself with instruction and advice as to the future of his patient he takes upon himself the function of an educator. The lawyer is occupied with winning a suit for his client or getting the latter out of some complication into which he has got himself. If it goes behind the case presented to him he too becomes an educator. The educator by the very nature of his work is obliged to see his present work in terms of what it accomplishes, or fails to accomplish, for a future whose objects are linked with those of the present.

Here, again, the problem for the progressive educator is more difficult than for the teacher in the traditional school. The latter had indeed to look ahead. But unless his personality and enthusiasm took him beyond the limits that hedged in the traditional school, he could content himself with thinking of the next examination period or the promotion to the next class. He could envisage the future in terms of factors that lay within the requirements of the school system as that conventionally existed. There is incumbent upon the teacher who links education and actual experience together a more serious and a harder business. He must be aware of the potentialities for leading students into new fields which belong to experiences already had, and must use this knowledge as his criterion for selection and arrangement of the conditions that influence their present experience.

Because the studies of the traditional school consisted of subject-matter that was selected and arranged on the basis of the judgment of adults as to what would be useful for the young sometime in the future, the material to be learned was settled upon outside the present life-experience of the learner. In consequence, it had to do with the past; it was such as had proved useful to men in past ages. By reaction to an opposite extreme, as unfortunate as it was probably natural under the circumstances, the sound idea that education should derive its materials from present experience and should enable the learner to cope with the problems of the present and future has often been converted into the idea that progressive schools can to a very large extent ignore the past. If the present could be cut off from the past, this conclusion would be sound. But the achievements of the past provide the only means at command for understanding the present. Just as the individual has to draw in memory upon his own past to understand the conditions in which he individually finds himself, so the issues and problems of present *social* life are in such intimate and direct connection with the past that students cannot be prepared to understand either these problems or the best way of dealing with them without delving into their roots in the past. In other words, the sound principle that the objectives of learning are in the future and its immediate materials are in present experience can be carried into effect only in the degree that present experience is stretched, as it were, backward. It can expand into the future only as it is also enlarged to take in the past.

If time permitted, discussion of the political and economic issues which the present generation will be compelled to face in the future would render this general statement definite and concrete. The nature of the issues cannot be understood save as we know how they came about. The institutions and customs that exist in the present and that give rise to present social ills and dislocations did not arise overnight. They have a long history behind them. Attempt to deal with them simply on the basis of what is obvious in the present is bound to result in adoption of superficial measures which in the end will only render existing problems more acute and more difficult to solve. Policies framed simply upon the ground of knowledge of the present cut off from the past is the counterpart of heedless carelessness in individual conduct. The way out of scholastic systems that made the past an end in itself is to make acquaintance with the past a *means* of understanding the present. Until this problem is worked out, the present clash of educational ideas and practices will continue. On the one hand, there will be reactionaries that claim that the main, if not the sole, business of education is transmission of the cultural heritage. On the other hand, there will be those who hold that we should ignore the past and deal only with the present and future.

That up to the present time the weakest point in progressive schools is in the matter of selection and organization of intellectual subject-matter is, I think, inevitable under the circumstances. It is as inevitable as it is right and proper that they should break loose from the cut and dried material which formed the staple of the old education. In addition, the field of experience is very wide and it varies in its contents from place to place and from time to time. A single course of studies for all progressive schools is out of the question; it would mean abandoning the fundamental principle of connection with life-experiences. Moreover, progressive schools are new. They have had hardly more than a generation in which to develop. A certain amount of uncertainty and of laxity in choice and organization of subject-matter is, therefore, what was to be expected. It is no ground for fundamental criticism or complaint.

It is a ground for legitimate criticism, however, when the ongoing movement of progressive education fails to recognize that the problem of selection and organization of subject-matter for study and learning is fundamental. Improvisation that takes advantage of special occasions prevents teaching and learning from being stereotyped and dead. But the basic material of study cannot be picked up in a cursory manner. Occasions which are not and cannot be foreseen are bound to arise wherever there is intellectual freedom. They should be utilized. But there is a decided difference between using them in the development of a continuing line of activity and trusting to them to provide the chief material of learning.

Unless a given experience leads out into a field previously unfamiliar no problems arise, while problems are the stimulus to thinking. That the conditions found in present experience should be used as sources of problems is a characteristic which differentiates education based upon experience from traditional education. For in the latter, problems were set from outside. Nonetheless, growth depends upon the presence of difficulty to be overcome by the exercise of intelligence. Once more, it is part of the educator's responsibility to see equally to two things: First, that the problem grows out of the conditions of the experience being had in the present, and that it is within the range of the capacity of students; and, secondly, that it is such that it arouses in the learner an active quest for information and for production of new ideas. The new facts and new ideas thus obtained become the ground for further experiences in which new problems are presented. The process is a continuous spiral. The inescapable linkage of the present with the past is a principle whose application is not restricted to a study of history. Take natural science, for example. Contemporary social life is what it is in very large measure because of the results of application of physical science. The experience of every child and youth, in the country and the city, is what it is in its present actuality because of appliances which utilize electricity, heat, and chemical processes. A child does not eat a meal that does not involve in its preparation and assimilation chemical and physiological principles. He does not read by artificial light or take a ride in a motor car or on a train without coming into contact with operations and processes which science has engendered.

It is a sound educational principle that students should be introduced to scientific subject-matter and be initiated into its facts and laws through acquaintance with everyday social applications. Adherence to this method is not only the most direct avenue to understanding of science itself but as the pupils grow more mature it is also the surest road to the understanding of the economic and industrial problems of present society. For they are the products to a very large extent of the application of science in production and distribution of commodities and services, while the latter processes are the most important factor in determining the present relations of human beings and social groups to one another. It is absurd, then, to argue that processes similar to those studied in laboratories and institutes of research are not a part of the daily life-experience of the young and hence do not come within the scope of education based upon experience. That the immature cannot study scientific facts and principles in the way in which mature experts study them goes without saying. But this fact, instead of exempting the educator from responsibility for using present experiences so that learners may gradually be led, through extraction of facts and laws, to experience of a scientific order, sets one of his main problems.

For if it is true that existing experience in detail and also on a wide scale is what it is because of the application of science, first, to processes of production and distribution of goods and services, and then to the relations which human beings sustain socially to one another, it is impossible to obtain an understanding of present social forces (without which they cannot be mastered and directed) apart from an education which leads learners into knowledge of the very same facts and principles which in their final organization constitute the sciences. Nor does the importance of the principle that learners should be led to acquaintance with scientific subject-matter cease with the insight thereby given into present social issues. The methods of science also point the way to the measures and policies by means of which a better social order can be brought into existence. The applications of science which have produced in large measure the social conditions which now exist do not exhaust the possible field of their application. For so far science has been applied more or less casually and under the influence of ends, such as private advantage and power, which are a heritage from the institutions of a prescientific age.

We are told almost daily and from many sources that it is impossible for human beings to direct their common life intelligently. We are told, on one hand, that the complexity of human relations, domestic and international, and on the other hand, the fact that human beings are so largely creatures of emotion and habit, make impossible large-scale social planning and direction by intelligence. This view would be more credible if any systematic effort, beginning with early education and carried on through the continuous study and learning of the young, had ever been undertaken with a view to making the method of intelligence, exemplified in science, supreme in education. There is nothing in the inherent nature of habit that prevents intelligent method from becoming itself habitual; and there is nothing in the nature of emotion to prevent the development of intense emotional allegiance to the method.

The case of science is here employed as an illustration of progressive selection of subject-matter resident in present experience towards organization: an organization which is free, not externally imposed, because it is in accord with the growth of experience itself. The utilization of subject-matter found in the present life-experience of the learner towards science is perhaps the best illustration that can be found of the basic principle of using existing experience as the means of carrying learners on to a wider, more refined, and better organized environing world, physical and human, than is found in the experiences from which educative growth sets out. Hogben's recent work, *Mathematics for the Million,* shows how mathematics, if it is treated as a mirror of civilization and as a main agency in its progress, can contribute to the desired goal as surely as can the physical sciences. The underlying ideal in any case is that of progressive organization of knowledge. It is with reference to organization of knowledge that we are likely to find *Either-Or* philosophies most acutely active. In practice, if not in so many words, it is often held that since traditional education rested upon a conception of organization of knowledge that was almost completely contemptuous of living present experience, therefore education based upon living experience should be contemptuous of the organization of facts and ideas.

When a moment ago I called this organization an *ideal,* I meant, on the negative side, that the educator cannot start with knowledge already organized and proceed to ladle it out in doses. But as an ideal the active process of organizing facts and ideas is an ever-present educational process. No experience is educative that does not tend both to knowledge of more facts and entertaining of more ideas and to a better, a more orderly, arrangement of them. It is not true that organization is a principle foreign to experience. Otherwise experience would be so dispersive as to be chaotic. The experience of young children centers about persons and the home. Disturbance of the normal order of relationships in the family is now known by psychiatrists to be a fertile source of later mental and emotional troubles—a fact which testifies to the reality of this kind of organization. One of the great advances in early school education, in the kindergarten and early grades, is that it preserves the social and human center of the organization of experience, instead of the older violent shift of the center of gravity. But one of the outstanding problems of education, as of music, is modulation. In the case of education, modulation means movement from a social and human center toward a more objective intellectual scheme of organization, always bearing in mind, however, that intellectual organization is not an end in itself but is the means by which social relations, distinctively human ties and bonds, may be understood and more intelligently ordered.

When education is based in theory and practice upon experience, it goes without saying that the organized subject-matter of the adult and the specialist cannot provide the starting point. Nevertheless, it represents the goal toward which education should continuously move. It is hardly necessary to say that one of the most fundamental principles of the scientific organization of knowledge is the principle of cause-and-effect. The way in which this principle is grasped and formulated by the scientific specialist is certainly very different from the way in which it can be approached in the experience of the young. But neither the relation nor grasp of its meaning is foreign to the experience of even the young child. When a child two or three years of age learns not to approach a flame too closely and yet to draw near enough a stove to get its warmth he is grasping and using the causal relation. There is no intelligent activity that does not conform to the requirements of the relation, and it is intelligent in the degree in which it is not only conformed to but consciously borne in mind.

In the earlier forms of experience the causal relation does not offer itself in the abstract but in the form of the relation of means employed to ends attained; of the relation of means and consequences. Growth in judgment and understanding is essentially growth in ability to form purposes and to select and arrange means for their realization. The most elementary experiences of the young are filled with cases of the means-consequence relation. There is not a meal cooked nor a source of illumination employed that does not exemplify this relation. The trouble with education is not the absence of situations in which the causal relation is exemplified in the relation of means and consequences. Failure to utilize the situations so as to lead the learner on to grasp the relation in the given cases of experience is, however, only too common. The logician gives the names "analysis and synthesis" to the operations by which means are selected and organized in relation to a purpose.

This principle determines the ultimate foundation for the utilization of *activities* in school. Nothing can be more absurd educationally than to make a plea for a variety of active occupations in the school while decrying the need for progressive organization of information and ideas. Intelligent activity is distinguished from aimless activity by the fact that it involves selection of means—analysis—out of the variety of conditions that are present, and their arrangement—synthesis—to reach an intended aim or purpose. That the more immature the learner is, the simpler must be the ends held in view and the more rudimentary the means employed, is obvious. But the principle of organization of activity in terms of some perception of the relation of consequences to means applies even with the very young. Otherwise an activity ceases to be educative because it is blind. With increased maturity, the problem of interrelation of means becomes more urgent. In the degree in which intelligent observation is transferred from the relation of means to ends to the more complex question of the relation of means to one another, the idea of cause and effect becomes prominent and explicit. The final justification of shops, kitchens, and so on in the school is not just that they afford opportunity for activity, but that they provide opportunity for the *kind* of activity or for the acquisition of mechanical skills which leads students to attend to the relation of means and ends, and then to consideration of the way things interact with one another to produce definite effects. It is the same in principle as the ground for laboratories in scientific research.

Unless the problem of intellectual organization can be worked out on the ground of experience, reaction is sure to occur toward externally imposed methods of organization. There are signs of this reaction already in evidence. We are told that our schools, old and new, are failing in the main task. They do not develop, it is said, the capacity for critical discrimination and the ability to reason. The ability to think is smothered, we are told, by accumulation of miscellaneous ill-digested information, and by the attempt to acquire forms of skill which will be immediately useful in the business and commercial world. We are told that these evils spring from the influence of science and from the magnification of present requirements at the expense of the tested cultural heritage from the past. It is argued that science and its method must be subordinated; that we must return to the logic of ultimate first principles expressed in the logic of Aristotle and St. Thomas, in order that the young may have sure anchorage in their intellectual and moral life, and not be at the mercy of every passing breeze that blows.

If the method of science had ever been consistently and continuously applied throughout the day-by-day work of the school in all subjects, I should be more impressed by this emotional appeal than I am. I see at bottom but two alternatives between which education must choose if it is not to drift aimlessly. One of them is expressed by the attempt to induce educators to return to the intellectual methods and ideals that arose centuries before scientific method was developed. The appeal may be temporarily successful in a period when general insecurity, emotional and intellectual as well as economic, if rife. For under these conditions the desire to lean on fixed authority is active. Nevertheless, it is so out of touch with all the conditions of modern life that I believe it is folly to seek salvation in this direction. The other alternative is systematic utilization of scientific method as the pattern and ideal of intelligent exploration and exploitation of the potentialities inherent in experience.

The problem involved comes home with peculiar force to progressive schools. Failure to give constant attention to development of the intellectual content of experiences and to obtain ever-increasing organization of facts and ideas may in the end merely strengthen the tendency toward a reactionary return to intellectual and moral authoritarianism. The present is not the time nor place for a disquisition upon scientific method. But certain features of it are so closely connected with any educational scheme based upon experience that they should be noted.

In the first place, the experimental method of science attaches more importance, not less, to ideas as ideas than do other methods. There is no such thing as experiment in the scientific sense unless action is directed by some leading idea. The fact that the ideas employed are hypotheses, not final truths, is the reason why ideas are more jealously guarded and tested in science than anywhere else. The moment they are taken to be first truths in themselves there ceases to be any reason for scrupulous examination of them. As fixed truths they must be accepted and that is the end of the matter. But as hypotheses, they must be continuously tested and revised, a requirement that demands they be accurately formulated.

In the second place, ideas or hypotheses are tested by the consequences which they produce when they are acted upon. This fact means that the consequences of action must be carefully and discriminatingly observed. Activity that is not checked by observation of what follows from it may be temporarily enjoyed. But intellectually it leads nowhere. It does not provide knowledge about the situations in which action occurs nor does it lead to clarification and expansion of ideas.

In the third place, the method of intelligence manifested in the experimental method demands keeping track of ideas, activities, and observed consequences. Keeping track is a matter of reflective review and summarizing, in which there is both discrimination and record of the significant features of a developing experience. To reflect is to look back over what has been done so as to extract the net meanings which are the capital stock for intelligent dealing with further experiences. It is the heart of intellectual organization and of the disciplined mind.

I have been forced to speak in general and often abstract language. But what has been said is organically connected with the requirement that experiences in order to be educative must lead out into an expanding world of subject-matter, a subject-matter of facts or information and of ideas. This condition is satisfied only as the educator views teaching and learning as a continuous process of reconstruction of experience. This condition in turn can be satisfied only as the educator has a long look ahead, and views every present experience as a moving force in influencing what future experiences will be. I am aware that the emphasis I have placed upon scientific method may be misleading, for it may result only in calling up the special technique of laboratory research as that is conducted by specialists. But the meaning of the emphasis placed upon scientific method has little to do with specialized techniques. It means that scientific method is the only authentic means at our command for getting at the significance of our everyday experiences of the world in which we live. It means that scientific method provides a working pattern of the way in which and the conditions under which experiences are used to lead ever onward and outward. Adaptation of the method to individuals of various degrees of maturity is a problem for the educator, and the constant factors in the problem are the formation of ideas, acting upon ideas, observation of the conditions which result, and organization of facts and ideas for future use. Neither the ideas, nor the activities, nor the observations, nor the organization are the same for a person six years old as they are for one twelve or eighteen years old, to say nothing of the adult scientist. But at every level there is an expanding development of experience if experience is educative in effect. Consequently, whatever the level of experience, we have no choice but either to operate in accord with the pattern it provides or else to neglect the place of intelligence in the development and control of a living and moving experience.

CHAPTER 8—EXPERIENCE—THE MEANS AND GOAL OF EDUCATION

In what I have said I have taken for granted the soundness of the principle that education in order to accomplish its ends both for the individual learner and for society must be based upon experience—which is always the actual life-experience of some individual. I have not argued for the acceptance of this principle nor attempted to justify it. Conservatives as well as radicals in education are profoundly discontented with the present educational situation taken as a whole. There is at least this much agreement among intelligent persons of both schools of educational thought. The educational system must move one way or another, either backward to the intellectual and moral standards of a pre-scientific age or forward to ever greater utilization of scientific method in the development of the possibilities of growing, expanding experience. I have but endeavored to point out some of the conditions which must be satisfactorily fulfilled if education takes the latter course.

For I am so confident of the potentialities of education when it is treated as intelligently directed development of the possibilities inherent in ordinary experience that I do not feel it necessary to criticize here the other route nor to advance arguments in favor of taking the route of experience. The only ground for anticipating failure in taking this path resides to my mind in the danger that experience and the experimental method will not be adequately conceived. There is no discipline in the world so severe as the discipline of experience subjected to the test of intelligent development and direction. Hence the only ground I can see for even a temporary reaction against the standards, aims, and methods of the newer education is the failure of educators who professedly adopt them to be faithful to them in practice. As I have emphasized more than once, the road of the new education is not an easier one to follow than the old road but a more strenuous and difficult one. It will remain so until it has attained its majority and that attainment will require many years of serious co-operative work on the part of its adherents. The greatest danger that attends its future is, I believe, the idea that it is an easy way to follow, so easy that its course may be improvised, if not in an impromptu fashion, at least almost from day to day or from week to week. It is for this reason that instead of extolling its principles, I have confined myself to showing certain conditions which must be fulfilled if it is to have the successful career which by right belongs to it.

I have used frequently in what precedes the word "progressive" and "new" education. I do not wish to close, however, without recording my firm belief that the fundamental issue is not of new versus old education nor of progressive against traditional education but a question of what anything whatever must be to be worthy of the name *education*. I am not, I hope and believe, in favor of any ends or any methods simply because the name progressive may be applied to them. The basic question concerns the nature of education with no qualifying adjectives prefixed. What we want and need is education pure and simple, and we shall make surer and faster progress when we devote ourselves to finding out just what education is and what conditions have to be satisfied in order that education may be a reality and not a name or a slogan. It is for this reason alone that I have emphasized the need for a sound philosophy of experience.

The Revolt of the Masses

José Ortega y Gasset

1—THE COMING OF THE MASSES

There is one fact which, whether for good or ill, is of utmost importance in the public life of Europe at the present moment. This fact is the accession of the masses to complete social power. As the masses, by definition, neither should nor can direct their own personal existence, and still less rule society in general, this fact means that actually Europe is suffering from the greatest crisis that can afflict peoples, nations, and civilisation. Such a crisis has occurred more than once in history. Its characteristics and its consequences are well known. So also is its name. It is called the rebellion of the masses. In order to understand this formidable fact, it is important from the start to avoid giving to the words "rebellion," "masses," and "social power" a meaning exclusively or primarily political. Public life is not solely political, but equally, and even primarily, intellectual, moral, economic, religious; it comprises all our collective habits, including our fashions both of dress and of amusement.

Perhaps the best line of approach to this historical phenomenon may be found by turning our attention to a visual experience, stressing one aspect of our epoch which is plain to our very eyes. This fact is quite simple to enunciate, though not so to analyse. I shall call it the fact of agglomeration, of "plenitude." Towns are full of people, houses full of tenants, hotels full of guests, trains full of travellers, cafés full of customers, parks full of promenaders, consulting-rooms of famous doctors full of patients, theatres full of spectators, and beaches full of bathers. What previously was, in general, no problem, now begins to be an everyday one, namely, to find room.

That is all. Can there be any fact simpler, more patent, more constant in actual life? Let us now pierce the plain surface of this observation and we shall be surprised to see how there wells forth an unexpected spring in which the white light of day, of our actual day, is broken up into its rich chromatic content. What is it that we see, and the sight of which causes us so much surprise? We see the multitude, as such, in possession of the places and the instruments created by civilisation. The slightest reflection will then make us surprised at our own surprise. What about it? Is this not the ideal state of things? The theatre has seats to be occupied—in other words, so that the house may be full—and now they are overflowing; people anxious to use them are left standing outside. Though the fact be quite logical and natural, we cannot but recognise that this did not happen before and that now it does; consequently, there has been a change, an innovation, which justifies, at least for the first moment, our surprise.

To be surprised, to wonder, is to begin to understand. This is the sport, the luxury, special to the intellectual man. The gesture characteristic of his tribe consists in looking at the world with eyes wide open in wonder. Everything in the world is strange and marvellous to well-open eyes. This faculty of wonder is the delight refused to your football "fan," and, on the other hand, is the one which leads the intellectual man through life in the perpetual ecstasy of the visionary. His special attribute is the wonder of the eyes. Hence it was that the ancients gave Minerva her owl, the bird with ever-dazzled eyes.

Agglomeration, fullness, was not frequent before. Why then is it now? The components of the multitudes around us have not sprung from nothing. Approximately the same number of people existed fifteen years ago. Indeed, after the war it might seem natural that their number should be less. Nevertheless, it is here we come up against the first important point. The individuals who made up these multitudes existed, but not *qua* multitude. Scattered about the world in small groups, or solitary, they lived a life, to all appearances, divergent, dissociate, apart. Each individual or small group occupied a place, its own, in country, village, town, or quarter of the great city. Now, suddenly, they appear as an agglomeration, and looking in any direction our eyes meet with the multitudes. Not only in any direction, but precisely in the best places, the relatively refined creation of human culture, previously reserved to lesser groups, in a world, to minorities. The multitude has suddenly become visible, installing itself in the preferential positions in society. Before, if it existed, it passed unnoticed, occupying the background of the social stage; now it has advanced to the footlights and is the principal character. There are no longer protagonists; there is only the chorus.

The concept of the multitude is quantitative and visual. Without changing its nature, let us translate it into terms of sociology. We then meet with the notion of the "social mass." Society is always a dynamic unity of two component factors: minorities and masses. The minorities are individuals or groups of individuals which are specially qualified. The mass is the assemblage of persons not specially qualified. By masses, then, is not to be understood, solely or mainly, "the working masses." The mass is the average man. In this way what was mere quantity—the multitude—is converted into a qualitative determination: it becomes the common social quality, man as undifferentiated from other men, but as repeating in himself a generic type. What have we gained by this conversion of quantity into quality? Simply this: by means of the latter we understand the genesis of the former. It is evident to the verge of platitude that the normal formation of a multitude implies the coincidence of desires, ideas, ways of life, in the individuals who constitute it. It will be objected that this is just what happens with every social group, however select it may strive to be. This is true; but there is an essential difference. In those groups which are characterised by not being multitude and mass, the effective coincidence of its members is based on some desire, idea, or ideal, which of itself excludes the great number. To form a minority, of whatever kind, it is necessary beforehand that each member separate himself from the multitude for *special,* relatively personal, reasons. Their coincidence with the others who form the minority is, then, secondary, posterior to their having each adopted an attitude of singularity, and is consequently, to a large extent, a coincidence in not coinciding. There are cases in which this singularising character of the group appears in the light of day: those English groups, which style themselves "nonconformists," where we have the grouping together of those who agree only in their disagreement in regard to the limitless multitude. This coming together of the minority precisely in order to separate themselves from the majority is a necessary ingredient in the formation of every minority. Speaking of the limited public which listened to a musician of refinement, Mallarmé wittily says that this public by its presence in small numbers stressed the absence of the multitude.

Strictly speaking, the mass, as a psychological fact, can be defined without waiting for individuals to appear in mass formation. In the presence of one individual we can decide whether he is "mass" or not. The mass is all that which sets no value on itself—good or ill—based on specific grounds, but which feels itself "just like everybody," and nevertheless is not concerned about it; is, in fact, quite happy to feel itself as one with everybody else. Imagine a humble-minded man who, having tried to estimate his own worth on specific grounds—asking himself if he has any talent for this or that, if he excels in any direction—realises that he possesses no quality of excellence. Such a man will feel that he is mediocre and commonplace, ill-gifted, but will not feel himself "mass."

When one speaks of "select minorities" is is usual for the evil-minded to twist the sense of this expression, pretending to be unaware that the select man is not the petulant person who thinks himself superior to the rest, but the man who demands more of himself than the rest, even though he may not fulfil in his person those higher exigencies. For there is no doubt that the most radical division that it is possible to make of humanity is that which splits it into two classes of creatures: those who make great demands on themselves, piling up difficulties and duties; and those who demand nothing special of themselves, but for whom to live is to be every moment what they already are, without imposing on themselves any effort towards perfection; mere buoys that float on the waves.

The division of society into masses and select minorities is, then, not a division into social classes, but into classes of men, and cannot coincide with the hierarchic separation of "upper" and "lower" classes. It is, of course, plain that in these "upper" classes, when and as long as they really are so, there is much more likelihood of finding men who adopt the "great vehicle," whereas the "lower" classes normally comprise individuals of minus quality. But, strictly speaking, within both these social classes, there are to be found mass and genuine minority. As we shall see, a characteristic of our times is the predominance, even in groups traditionally selective, of the mass and the vulgar. Thus, in the intellectual life, which of its essence requires and presupposes qualification, one can note the progressive triumph of the pseudo-intellectual, unqualified, unqualifiable, and, by their very mental texture, disqualified. Similarly, in the surviving groups of the "nobility," male and female. On the other hand, it is not rare to find to-day amongst working men, who before might be taken as the best example of what we are calling "mass," nobly disciplined minds.

There exist, then, in society, operations, activities, and functions of the most diverse order, which are of their very nature special, and which consequently cannot be properly carried out without special gifts. For example: certain pleasures of an artistic and refined character, or again the functions of government and of political judgment in public affairs. Previously these special activities were exercised by qualified minorities, or at least by those who claimed such qualification. The mass asserted no right to intervene in them; they realised that if they wished to intervene they would necessarily have to acquire those special qualities and cease being mere mass. They recognised their place in a healthy dynamic social system.

If we now revert to the facts indicated at the start, they will appear clearly as the heralds of a changed attitude in the mass. They all indicate that the mass has decided to advance to the foreground of social life, to occupy the places, to use the instruments and to enjoy the pleasures hitherto reserved to the few. It is evident, for example, that the places were never intended for the multitude, for their dimensions are too limited, and the crowd is continuously overflowing; thus manifesting to our eyes and in the clearest manner the new phenomenon: the mass without ceasing to be mass, is supplanting the minorities.

No one, I believe, will regret that people are to-day enjoying themselves in greater measure and numbers than before, since they have now both the desire and the means of satisfying it. The evil lies in the fact that this decision taken by the masses to assume the activities proper to the minorities is not, and cannot be, manifested solely in the domain of pleasure, but that it is a general feature of our time. Thus—to anticipate what we shall see later—I believe that the political innovations of recent times signify nothing less than the political domination of the masses.

The old democracy was tempered by a generous dose of liberalism and of enthusiasm for law. By serving these principles the individual bound himself to maintain a severe discipline over himself. Under the shelter of liberal principles and the rule of law, minorities could live and act. Democracy and law—life in common under the law—were synonymous. To-day we are witnessing the triumphs of a hyperdemocracy in which the mass acts directly, outside the law, imposing its aspirations and its desires by means of material pressure. It is a false interpretation of the new situation to say that the mass has grown tired of politics and handed over the exercise of it to specialised persons. Quite the contrary. That was what happened previously; that was democracy. The mass took it for granted that after all, in spite of their defects and weaknesses, the minorities understood a little more of public problems than it did itself. Now, on the other hand, the mass believes that it has the right to impose and to give force of law to notions born in the café. I doubt whether there have been other periods of history in which the multitude has come to govern more directly than in our own. That is why I speak of hyperdemocracy.

The same thing is happening in other orders, particularly in the intellectual. I may be mistaken, but the present-day writer, when he takes his pen in hand to treat a subject which he has studied deeply, has to bear in mind that the average reader, who has never concerned himself with this subject, if he reads does so with the view, not of learning something from the writer, but rather, of pronouncing judgment on him when he is not in agreement with the commonplaces that the said reader carries in his head. If the individuals who make up the mass believed themselves specially qualified, it would be a case merely of personal error, not a sociological subversion. *The characteristic of the hour is that the commonplace mind, knowing itself to be commonplace, has the assurance to proclaim the rights of the commonplace and to impose them wherever it will.* As they say in the United States: "to be different is to be indecent." The mass crushes beneath it everything that is different, everything that is excellent, individual, qualified and select. Anybody who is not like everybody, who does not think like everybody, runs the risk of being eliminated. And it is clear, of course, that this "everybody" is not "everybody." "Everybody" was normally the complex unity of the mass and the divergent, specialised minorities. Nowadays, "everybody" is the mass alone. Here we have the formidable fact of our times, described without any concealment of the brutality of its features.

2—THE RISE OF THE HISTORIC LEVEL

Such, then, is the formidable fact of our times, described without any concealment of the brutality of its features. It is, furthermore, entirely new in the history of our modern civilisation. Never, in the course of its development, has anything similar happened. If we wish to find its like we shall have to take a leap outside our modern history and immerse ourselves in a world, a vital element, entirely different from our own; we shall have to penetrate the ancient world till we reach the hour of its decline. The history of the Roman Empire is also the history of the uprising of the Empire of the Masses, who absorb and annul the directing minorities and put themselves in their place. Then, also, is produced the phenomenon of agglomeration, of "the full." For that reason, as Spengler has very well observed, it was necessary, just as in our day, to construct enormous buildings. The epoch of the masses is the epoch of the colossal.[1] We are living, then, under the brutal empire of the masses. Just so; I have now twice called this empire "brutal," and have thus paid my tribute to the god of the commonplace. Now, ticket in hand, I can cheerfully enter into my subject, see the show from inside. Or perhaps it was thought that I was going to be satisfied with that description, possibly exact, but quite external; the mere features, the aspect under which this tremendous fact presents itself when looked at from the view-point of the past? If I were to leave the matter here and strangle off my present essay without more ado, the reader would be left thinking, and quite justly, that this fabulous uprising of the masses above the surface of history inspired me merely with a few petulant, disdainful words, a certain amount of hatred and a certain amount of disgust. This all the more in my case, when it is well known that I uphold a radically aristocratic interpretation of history. Radically, because I have never said that human society *ought* to be aristocratic, but a great deal more than that. What I have said, and still believe with ever-increasing conviction, is that human society *is* always, whether it will or no, aristocratic by its very essence, to the extreme that it is a society in the measure that it is aristocratic, and ceases to be such when it ceases to be aristocratic. Of course I am speaking now of society and not of the State. No one can imagine that, in the face of this fabulous seething of the masses, it is the aristocratic attitude to be satisfied with making a supercilious grimace, like a fine gentleman of Versailles. Versailles—the Versailles of the grimaces—does not represent aristocracy; quite the contrary, it is the death and dissolution of a magnificent aristocracy. For this reason, the only element of aristocracy left in such beings was the dignified grace with which their necks received the attentions of the guillotine; they accepted it as the tumour accepts the lancet. No; for anyone who has a sense of the real mission of aristocracies, the spectacle of the mass incites and enflames him, as the sight of virgin marble does the sculptor. Social aristoc-

1. The tragic thing about this process is that while these agglomerations were in formation there was beginning that depopulation of the countryside which was to result in an absolute decrease of the number of inhabitants in the Empire.

racy has no resemblance whatever to that tiny group which claims for itself alone the name of society, which calls itself "Society"; people who live by inviting or not inviting one another. Since everything in the world has its virtue and its mission, so within the vast world this small "smart world" has its own, but it is a very subordinate mission, not to be compared with the herculean task of genuine aristocracies. I should have no objection to discussing the meaning that lies in this smart world, to all appearance so meaningless, but our subject is now one of greater proportions. Of course, this self-same "distinguished society" goes with the times. Much food for thought was given me by a certain *jeune fille en fleur*, full of youth and modernity, a star of the first magnitude in the firmament of "smart" Madrid, when she said to me: "I can't stand a dance to which less than eight hundred people have been invited." Behind this phrase I perceived that the style of the masses is triumphant over the whole area of modern life, and imposes itself even in those sheltered corners which seemed reserved for the "happy few."

I reject equally, then, the interpretation of our times which does not lay clear the positive meaning hidden under the actual rule of the masses and that which accepts it blissfully, without a shudder of horror. Every destiny is dramatic, tragic in its deepest meaning. Whoever has not felt the danger of our times palpitating under his hand, has not really penetrated to the vitals of destiny, he has merely pricked its surface. The element of terror in the destiny of our time is furnished by the overwhelming and violent moral upheaval of the masses; imposing, invincible, and treacherous, as is destiny in every case. Whither is it leading us? Is it an absolute evil or a possible good? There it is, colossal, astride our times like a giant, a cosmic note of interrogation, always of uncertain shape, with something in it of the guillotine or the gallows, but also with something that strives to round itself into a triumphal arch.

The fact that we must submit to examination may be formulated under two headings: first, the masses are today exercising functions in social life which coincide with those which hitherto seemed reserved to minorities; and secondly, these masses have at the same time shown themselves indocile to the minorities—they do not obey them, follow them, or respect them; on the contrary, they push them aside and supplant them.

Let us analyse what comes under the first heading. By it I mean that the masses enjoy the pleasures and use the instruments invented by the select groups, and hitherto exclusively at the service of the latter. They feel appetites and needs which were previously looked upon as refinements, inasmuch as they were the patrimony of the few. Take a trivial example: in 1820 there cannot have been ten bathrooms in private houses in Paris (see the *Memoirs of the Comtesse de Boigne*). But furthermore, the masses to-day are acquainted with, and use with relative skill,

many of the technical accomplishments previously confined to specialised individuals. And this refers not only to the technique of material
objects, but, more important, to that of laws and society. In the XVIIIth
Century, certain minority groups discovered that every human being, by
the mere fact of birth, and without requiring any special qualification
whatsoever, possessed certain fundamental political rights, the so-called
rights of the man and the citizen; and further that, strictly speaking,
these rights, common to all, are the only ones that exist.

Every other right attached to special gifts was condemned as being a
privilege. This was at first a mere theory, the idea of a few men; then
those few began to put the idea into practice, to impose it and insist upon
it. Nevertheless, during the whole of the XIXth Century, the mass, while
gradually becoming enthusiastic for those rights as an ideal, did not feel
them as rights, did not exercise them or attempt to make them prevail,
but, in fact, under democratic legislation, continued to feel itself just as
under the old regime. The "people"—as it was then called—the "people"
had learned that it was sovereign, but did not believe it. To-day the ideal
has been changed into a reality; not only in legislation, which is the mere
framework of public life, but in the heart of every individual, whatever
his ideas may be, and even if he be a reactionary in his ideas, *that is to say,
even when he attacks and castigates institutions by which those rights are sanc-
tioned.* To my mind, anyone who does not realise this curious moral
situation of the masses can understand nothing of what is to-day beginning to happen in the world. The sovereignty of the unqualified individual, of the human being as such, generically, has now passed from being
a juridical idea or ideal to be a psychological state inherent in the average
man. And note this, that when what was before an ideal becomes a
component part of reality, it inevitably ceases to be an ideal. The prestige
and the magic that are attributes of the ideal are volatilised. The levelling
demands of a generous democratic inspiration have been changed from
aspirations and ideals into appetites and unconscious assumptions.

Now, the meaning of this proclamation of the rights of man was none
other than to lift human souls from their interior servitude and to
implant within them a certain consciousness of mastery and dignity. Was
it not this that it was hoped to do, namely, that the average man should
feel himself master, lord, and ruler of himself and of his life? Well, that is
now accomplished. Why, then, these complaints of the liberals, the
democrats, the progressives of thirty years ago? Or is it that, like children, they want something, but not the consequences of that something?
You want the ordinary man to be master. Well, do not be surprised if he
acts for himself, if he demands all forms of enjoyment, if he firmly
asserts his will, if he refuses all kinds of service, if he ceases to be docile to
anyone, if he considers his own person and his own leisure, if he is
careful as to dress: these are some of the attributes permanently attached

to the consciousness of mastership. To-day we find them taking up their abode in the ordinary man, in the mass.

The situation, then, is this: the life of the ordinary man is to-day made up of the same "vital repertory" which before characterised only the superior minorities. Now the average man represents the field over which the history of each period acts; he is to history what sea-level is to geography. If, therefore, to-day the mean-level lies at a point previously only reached by aristocracies, the signification of this is simply that the level of history has suddenly risen—after long subterraneous preparations, it is true—but now quite plainly to the eyes, suddenly, at a bound, in one generation. Human life taken as a whole has mounted higher. The soldier of to-day, we might say, has a good deal of the officer; the human army is now made up of officers. Enough to watch the energy, the determination, the ease with which each individual moves through life to-day, snatches at the passing pleasure, imposes his personal will.

Everything that is good and bad in the present and in the immediate future has its cause and root in the general rise of the historic level. But here an observation that had not previously occurred to us presents itself. This fact, that the ordinary level of life to-day is that of the former minorities, is a new fact in Europe, but in America the natural, the "constitutional" fact. To realise my point, let the reader consider the matter of consciousness of equality before the law. That psychological state of feeling lord and master of oneself and equal to anybody else, which in Europe only outstanding groups succeeded in acquiring, was in America since the XVIIIth Century (and therefore, practically speaking, always) the natural state of things. And a further coincidence, still more curious, is this: when this psychological condition of the ordinary man appeared in Europe, when the level of his existence rose, the tone and manners of European life in all orders suddenly took on a new appearance which caused many people to say: "Europe is becoming Americanised." Those who spoke in this way gave no further attention to the matter; they thought it was a question of a slight change of custom, a fashion, and, deceived by the look of things, attributed it to some influence or other of America on Europe. This, to my mind, is simply to trivialise a question which is much more subtle and pregnant with surprises. Gallantry here makes an attempt to suborn me into telling our brothers beyond the sea that, in fact, Europe has become Americanised, and that this is due to an influence of America on Europe. But no; truth comes into conflict with gallantry, and it must prevail. Europe has not been Americanised; it has received no great influence from America. Possibly both these things are beginning to happen just now; but they did not occur in the recent part of which the present is the flowering. There is floating around a bewildering mass of false ideas which blind the vision of both parties, Americans and Europeans. The triumph of the masses and the consequent magnificent uprising of the vital level have come about in Europe for internal reasons, after two centuries of education of the multitude towards progress and a parallel economic improvement in society. But it so happens that the result coincides with the most marked aspect of American life; and on account of this coincidence of the moral situation of the ordinary man in Europe and in America, it has come about that for the first time the European understands American life which was to him before an enigma and a mystery. There is no question, then, of an influence, which indeed would be a little strange, would be, in fact, a "refluence," but of something which is still less suspected, namely, of a levelling. It has always been obscurely seen by Europeans that the general level of life in America was higher than in the Old World. It was the intuition, strongly felt, if unanalysed, of this fact which gave rise to the idea, always accepted, never challenged, that the future lies with America. It will be understood that such an idea, widespread and deep-rooted, did not float down on the wind, as it is said that orchids grow rootless in the air. The basis of it was the realisation of a higher level of average existence in America, in contrast with a lower level in the select minorities there as compared with those of Europe. But history, like agriculture, draws its nourishment from the valleys and not from the heights, from the average social level and not from men of eminence.

We are living in a levelling period; there is a levelling of fortunes, of culture among the various social classes, of the sexes. Well, in the same way there is a levelling of continents, and as the European was formerly lower from a vital point of view, he has come out the gainer from this levelling. Consequently, from this standpoint, the uprising of the masses implies a fabulous increase of vital possibilities, quite the contrary of what we hear so often about the decadence of Europe. This is a confused and clumsy expression, in which it is not clear what is being referred to, whether it is the European states, or European culture, or what lies underneath all this, and is of infinitely greater importance, the vital activity of Europe.

Of European states and culture we shall have a word to say later on—though perhaps what we have already said is enough—but as regards the vitality, it is well to make clear from the start that we are in the presence of a gross error. Perhaps if I give it another turn, my statement may appear more convincing or less improbable; I say, then, that to-day the average Italian, Spaniard, or German is less differentiated in vital tone from the North American or the Argentine than he was thirty years ago. And this is a fact that the people of America ought not to forget . . .

5—A STATISTICAL FACT

This essay is an attempt to discover the diagnosis of our time, of our actual existence. We have indicated the first part of it, which may be resumed thus: our life as a programme of possibilities is magnificent, exuberant, superior to all others known to history. But by the very fact that its scope is greater, it has overflowed all the channels, principles, norms, ideals handed down by tradition. It is more life than all previous existence, and therefore all the more problematical. It can find no direction from the past.[1] It has to discover its own destiny.

But now we must complete the diagnosis. Life, which means primarily what is possible for us to be, is likewise, and for that very reason, a choice, from among these possibilities, of what we actually are going to be. Our circumstances—these possibilities—form the portion of life given us, imposed on us. This constitutes what we call the world. Life does not choose its own world, it finds itself, to start with, in a world determined and unchangeable: the world of the present. Our world is that portion of destiny which goes to make up our life. But this vital destiny is not a kind of mechanism. We are not launched into existence like a shot from a gun, with its trajectory absolutely predetermined. The destiny under which we fall when we come into this world—it is always *this* world, the actual one—consists in the exact contrary. Instead of imposing on us one trajectory, it imposes several, and consequently forces us to choose. Surprising condition, this, of our existence! To live is to feel ourselves *fatally* obliged to exercise our *liberty*, to decide what we are going to be in this world. Not for a single moment is our activity of decision allowed to rest. Even when in desperation we abandon ourselves to whatever may happen, we have decided not to decide.

It is, then, false to say that in life "circumstances decide." On the contrary, circumstances are the dilemma, constantly renewed, in presence of which we have to make our decision; what actually decides is our character. All this is equally valid for collective life. In it also there is, first, a horizon of possibilities, and then, a determination which chooses and decides on the effective form of collective existence. This determination has its origin in the character of society, or what comes to the same thing, of the type of men dominant in it. In our time it is the mass-man who dominates, it is he who decides. It will not do to say that this is what happened in the period of democracy, of universal suffrage. Under universal suffrage, the masses do not decide, their role consists in supporting the decision of one minority or other. It was these who presented their "programmes"—excellent word. Such programmes were, in fact, programmes of collective life. In them the masses were invited to accept a line of decision.

To-day something very different is happening. If we observe the public life of the countries where the triumph of the masses has made

1. We shall see, nevertheless, how it is possible to obtain from the past, if not positive orientation, certain negative counsel. The past will not tell us what we ought to do, but it will what we ought to avoid.

most advance—these are the Mediterranean countries—we are surprised to find that politically they are living from day to day. The phenomenon is an extraordinarily strange one. Public authority is in the hands of a representative of the masses. These are so powerful that they have wiped out all opposition. They are in possession of power in such an unassailable manner that it would be difficult to find in history examples of a Government so all-powerful as these are. And yet public authority—the Government—exists from hand to mouth, it does not offer itself as a frank solution for the future, it represents no clear announcement of the future, it does not stand out as the beginning of something whose development or evolution is conceivable. In short, it lives without any vital programme, any plan of existence. It does not know where it is going, because, strictly speaking, it has no fixed road, no predetermined trajectory before it. When such a public authority attempts to justify itself it makes no reference at all to the future. On the contrary, it shuts itself up in the present, and says with perfect sincerity: "I am an abnormal form of Government imposed by circumstances." Hence its activities are reduced to dodging the difficulties of the hour; not solving them, but escaping from them for the time being, employing any methods whatsoever, even at the cost of accumulating thereby still greater difficulties for the hour which follows. Such has public power always been when exercised directly by the masses: omnipotent and ephemeral. The mass-man is he whose life lacks any purpose, and simply goes drifting along. Consequently, though his possibilities and his powers be enormous, he constructs nothing. And it is this type of man who decides in our time. It will be well, then, that we analyse his character.

The key to this analysis is found when, returning to the starting-point of this essay, we ask ourselves: "Whence have come all these multitudes which nowadays fill to overflowing the stage of history?" Some years ago the eminent economist, Werner Sombart, laid stress on a very simple fact, which I am surprised is not present to every mind which meditates on contemporary events. This very simple fact is sufficient of itself to clarify our vision of the Europe of to-day, or if not sufficient, puts us on the road to enlightenment. The fact is this: from the time European history begins in the VIth Century up to the year 1800—that is, through the course of twelve centuries—Europe does not succeed in reaching a total population greater than 180 million inhabitants. Now, from 1800 to 1914—little more than a century—the population of Europe mounts from 180 to 460 millions! I take it that the contrast between these figures leaves no doubt as to the prolific qualities of the last century. In three generations it produces a gigantic mass of humanity which, launched like a torrent over the historic area, has inundated it. This fact, I repeat, should suffice to make us realise the triumph of the masses and all that is implied and announced by it. Furthermore, it should be added as the most concrete item to that rising of the level of existence which I have already indicated.

But at the same time this fact proves to us how unfounded is our admiration when we lay stress on the increase of new countries like the United States of America. We are astonished at this increase, which has reached to 100 millions in a century, when the really astonishing fact is the teeming fertility of Europe. Here we have another reason for correcting the deceptive notion of the Americanisation of Europe. Not even that characteristic which might seem specifically American—the rapidity of increase in population—is peculiarly such. Europe has increased in the last century much more than America. American has been formed from the overflow of Europe.

But although this fact ascertained by Werner Sombart is not as well known as it should be, the confused idea of a considerable population increase in Europe was widespread enough to render unnecessary insistence on it. In the figures cited, then, it is not the increase of population which interests me, but the fact that by the contrast with the previous figures the dizzy rapidity of the increase is brought into relief. This is the point of importance for us at the moment. For that rapidity means that heap after heap of human beings have been dumped on to the historic scene at such an accelerated rate, that it has been difficult to saturate them with traditional culture. And in fact, the average type of European at present possesses a soul, healthier and stronger it is true than those of the last century, but much more simple. Hence, at times he leaves the impression of a primitive man suddenly risen in the midst of a very old civilisation. In the schools, which were such a source of pride to the last century, it has been impossible to do more than instruct the masses in the technique of modern life; it has been found impossible to educate them. They have been given tools for an intenser form of existence, but no feeling for their great historic duties; they have been hurriedly inoculated with the pride and power of modern instruments, but not with their spirit. Hence they will have nothing to do with their spirit, and the new generations are getting ready to take over command of the world as if the world were a paradise without trace of former footsteps, without traditional and highly complex problems.

To the last century, then, falls the glory and the responsibility of having let loose upon the area of history the great multitudes. And this fact affords the most suitable view-point in order to judge that century with equity. There must have been something extraordinary, incomparable, in it when such harvests of human fruit were produced in its climate. Any preference for the principles which inspired other past ages is frivolous and ridiculous if one does not previously show proof of having realised this magnificent fact and attempted to digest it. The whole of history stands out as a gigantic laboratory in which all possible experiments have been made to obtain a formula of public life most favourable to the plant "man." And beyond all possible explaining away, we find ourselves face to face with the fact that, by submitting the seed of humanity to the treatment of two principles, liberal democracy and technical knowledge, in a single century the species in Europe has been triplicated.

Such an overwhelming fact forces us, unless we prefer not to use our reason, to draw these conclusions: first, that liberal democracy based on technical knowledge is the highest type of public life hitherto known; secondly, that that type may not be the best imaginable, but the one we imagine as superior to it must preserve the essence of those two principles; and thirdly, that to return to any forms of existence inferior to that of the XIXth Century is suicidal.

Once we recognise this with all the clearness that the clearness of the fact itself demands we must then rise up against the XIXth Century. If it is evident that there was in it something extraordinary and incomparable, it is no less so that it must have suffered from certain radical vices, certain constitutional defects, when it brought into being a caste of men—the mass-man in revolt—who are placing in imminent danger those very principles to which they owe their existence. If that human type continues to be master in Europe, thirty years will suffice to send our continent back to barbarism. Legislative and industrial technique will disappear with the same facility with which so many trade secrets have often disappeared.[1] The whole of life will be contracted. The actual abundance of possibilities will change into practical scarcity, a pitiful impotence, a real decadence. For the rebellion of the masses is one and the same thing with what Rathenau called "the vertical invasion of the barbarians." It is of great importance, then, to understand thoroughly this mass-man with his potentialities of the greatest good and the greatest evil.

6—THE DISSECTION OF THE MASS-MAN BEGINS

What is he like, this mass-man who to-day dominates public life, political and non-political, and why is he like it, that is, how has he been produced?

1. Herman Weyl, one of the greatest of present-day physicists, the companion and continuer of the work of Einstein, is in the habit, of saying in conversation that if ten or twelve specified individuals were to die suddenly, it is almost certain that the marvels of physics to-day would be lost for ever to humanity. A preparation of many centuries has been needed in order to accommodate the mental organ to the abstract complexity of physical theory. Any event might annihilate such prodigious human possibilities, which in addition are the basis of future technical development.

It will be well to answer both questions together, for they throw light on one another. The man who to-day is attempting to take the lead in European existence is very different from the man who directed the XIXth Century, but he was produced and prepared by the XIXth Century. Any keen mind of the years 1820, 1850, and 1880 could by simple *a priori* reasoning, foresee the gravity of the present historical situation, and in fact nothing is happening now which was not foreseen a hundred years ago. "The masses are advancing," said Hegel in apocalyptic fashion. "Without some new spiritual influence, our age, which is a revolutionary age, will produce a catastrophe," was the pronouncement of Comte. "I see the flood-tide of nihilism rising," shrieked Nietzsche from a crag of the Engadine. It is false to say that history cannot be foretold. Numberless times this has been done. If the future offered no opening to prophecy, it could not be understood when fulfilled in the present and on the point of falling back into the past. The idea that the historian is on the reverse side a prophet, sums up the whole philosophy of history. It is true that it is only possible to anticipate the general structure of the future, but that is all that we in truth understand of the past or of the present. Accordingly, if you want a good view of your own age, look at it from far off. From what distance? The answer is simple. Just far enough to prevent you seeing Cleopatra's nose.

What appearance did life present to that multitudinous man who in ever-increasing abundance the XIXth Century kept producing? To start with, an appearance of universal material ease. Never had the average man been able to solve his economic problem with greater facility. Whilst there was a proportionate decrease of great fortunes and life became harder for the individual worker, the middle classes found their economic horizon widened every day. Every day added a new luxury to their standard of life. Every day their position was more secure and more independent of another's will. What before would have been considered one of fortune's gifts, inspiring humble gratitude towards destiny, was converted into a right, not to be grateful for, but to be insisted on.

From 1900 on, the worker likewise begins to extend and assure his existence. Nevertheless, he has to struggle to obtain his end. He does not, like the middle class, find the benefit attentively served up to him by a society and a state which are a marvel of organisation. To this ease and security of economic conditions are to be added the physical ones, comfort and public order. Life runs on smooth rails, and there is no likelihood of anything violent or dangerous breaking in on it. Such a free, untrammelled situation was bound to instil into the depths of such souls an idea of existence which might be expressed in the witty and penetrating phrase of an old country like ours: "Wide is Castile." That is to say, in all its primary and decisive aspects, life presented itself to the new man as *exempt from restrictions*. The realisation of this fact and of its importance becomes immediate when we remember that such a freedom of existence was entirely lacking to the common men of the past. On the contrary, for them life was a burdensome destiny, economically and physically. From birth, existence meant to them an accumulation of impediments which they were obliged to suffer, without possible solution other than to adapt themselves to them, to settle down in the narrow space they left available.

But still more evident is the contrast of situations, if we pass from the material to the civil and moral. The average man, from the second half of the XIXth Century on, finds no social barriers raised against him. That is to say, that as regards the forms of public life he no longer finds himself from birth confronted with obstacles and limitations. There is nothing to force him to limit his existence. Here again, "Wide is Castile." There are no "estates" or "castes." There are no civil privileges. The ordinary man learns that all men are equal before the law.

Never in the course of history had man been placed in vital surroundings even remotely familiar to those set up by the conditions just mentioned. We are, in fact, confronted with a radical innovation in human destiny, implanted by the XIXth Century. A new stage has been mounted for human existence, new both in the physical and the social aspects. Three principles have made possible this new world: liberal democracy, scientific experiment, and industrialism. The two latter may be summed up in one word: technicism. Not one of those principles was invented by the XIXth Century; they proceed from the two previous centuries. The glory of the XIXth Century lies not in their discovery, but in their implantation. No one but recognises that fact. But it is not sufficient to recognise it in the abstract, it is necessary to realise its inevitable consequences.

The XIXth Century was of its essence revolutionary. This aspect is not to be looked for in the scenes of the barricades, which are mere incidents, but in the fact that it placed the average man—the great social mass—in conditions of life radically opposed to those by which he had always been surrounded. It turned his public existence upside down. Revolution is not the uprising against pre-existing order, but the setting up of a new order contradictory to the traditional one. Hence there is no exaggeration in saying that the man who is the product of the XIXth Century is, for the effects of public life, a man apart from all other men. The XVIIIth-Century man differs, of course, from the XVIIth-Century man, and this one in turn from his fellow of the XVIth Century, but they are all related, similar, even identical in essentials when confronted with this new man. For the "common" man of all periods "life" had principally meant limitation, obligation, dependence; in a word, pressure. Say oppression, if you like, provided it be understood not only in the juridical and social sense, but also in the cosmic. For it is this latter which has never been lacking up to a hundred years ago, the date at which starts the practically limitless expansion of scientific technique—physical and administrative. Previously, even for the rich and powerful, the world was a place of poverty, difficulty and danger. [1]

The world which surrounds the new man from his birth does not compel him to limit himself in any fashion, it sets up no veto in opposition to him; on the contrary, it incites his appetite, which in principle can increase indefinitely. Now it turns out—and this is most important—that this world of the XIXth and early XXth Centuries not only has the perfections and the completeness which it actually possesses, but furthermore suggests to those who dwell in it the radical assurance that to-morrow it will be still richer, ampler, more perfect, as if it enjoyed a spontaneous, inexhaustible power of increase. Even today, in spite of some signs which are making a tiny breach in that sturdy faith, even to-day, there are few men who doubt that motorcars will in five years' time be more comfortable and cheaper than to-day. They believe in this as they believe that the sun will rise in the morning. The metaphor is an exact one. For, in fact, the common man, finding himself in a world so excellent, technically and socially, believes that it has been produced by nature, and never thinks of the personal efforts of highly-endowed individuals which the creation of this new world presupposed. Still less will he admit the notion that all these facilities still require the support of certain difficult human virtues, the least failure of which would cause the rapid disappearance of the whole magnificent edifice.

This leads us to note down in our psychological chart of the mass-man of to-day two fundamental traits: the free expansion of his vital desires, and therefore, of his personality; and his radical ingratitude towards all that has made possible the ease of his existence. These traits together make up the well-known psychology of the spoilt child. And in fact it would entail no error to use this psychology as a "sight" through which to observe the soul of the masses of to-day. Heir to an ample and generous past—generous both in ideals and in activities—the new commonalty has been spoiled by the world around it. To spoil means to put no limit on caprice, to give one the impression that everything is permitted to him and that he has no obligations. The young child exposed to this regime has no experience of its own limits. By reason of the removal of all external restraint, all clashing with other things, he comes actually

1. However rich an individual might be in relation to his fellows, as the world in its totality was poor, the sphere of conveniences and commodities with which his wealth furnished him was very limited. The life of the average man to-day is easier, more convenient and safer than that of the most powerful of another age. What difference does it make to him not to be richer than others if the world is richer and furnishes him with magnificent roads, railways, telegraphs, hotels, personal safety and aspirin?

to believe that he is the only one that exists, and gets used to not considering others, especially not considering them as superior to himself. This feeling of another's superiority could only be instilled into him by someone who, being stronger than he is, should force him to give up some desire, to restrict himself, to restrain himself. He would then have learned this fundamental discipline: "Here I end and here begins another more powerful than I am. In the world, apparently, there are two people: I myself and another superior to me." The ordinary man of past times was daily taught this elemental wisdom by the world about him, because it was a world so rudely organised, that catastrophes were frequent, and there was nothing in it certain, abundant, stable. But the new masses find themselves in the presence of a prospect full of possibilities, and furthermore, quite secure, with everything ready to their hands, independent of any previous efforts on their part, just as we find the sun in the heavens without our hoisting it up on our shoulders. No human being thanks another for the air he breathes, for no one has produced the air for him; it belongs to the sum-total of what "is there," of which we say "it is natural," because it never fails. And these spoiled masses are unintelligent enough to believe that the material and social organisation, placed at their disposition like the air, is of the same origin, since apparently it never fails them, and is almost as perfect as the natural scheme of things.

My thesis, therefore, is this: the very perfection with which the XIXth Century gave an organisation to certain orders of existence has caused the masses benefited thereby to consider it, not as an organised, but as a natural system. Thus is explained and defined the absurd state of mind revealed by these masses; they are only concerned with their own well-being, and at the same time they remain alien to the cause of that well-being. As they do not see, behind the benefits of civilisation, marvels of invention and construction which can only be maintained by great effort and foresight, they imagine that their role is limited to demanding these benefits peremptorily, as if they were natural rights. In the disturbances caused by scarcity of food, the mob goes in search of bread, and the means it employs is generally to wreck the bakeries. This may serve as a symbol of the attitude adopted, on a greater and more complicated scale, by the masses of to-day towards the civilisation by which they are supported.

7—NOBLE LIFE AND COMMON LIFE, OR EFFORT AND INERTIA

To start with, we are what our world invites us to be, and the basic features of our soul are impressed upon it by the form of its surroundings as in a mould. Naturally, for our life is no other than our relations with the world around. The general aspect which it presents to us will form the general aspect of our own life. It is for this reason that I stress so much the observation that the world into which the masses of to-day have been born displays features radically new to history. Whereas in past times life for the average man meant finding all around him difficulties, dangers, want, limitations of his destiny, dependence, the new world appears as a sphere of practically limitless possibilities, safe, and independent of anyone. Based on this primary and lasting impression, the mind of every contemporary man will be formed, just as previous minds were formed on the opposite impression. For that basic impression becomes an interior voice which ceaselessly utters certain words in the depths of each individual, and tenaciously suggests to him a definition of life which is, at the same time, a moral imperative. And if the traditional sentiment whispered: "To live is to feel oneself limited, and therefore to have to count with that which limits us," the newest voice shouts: "To live is to meet with no limitation whatever and, consequently, to abandon oneself calmly to one's self. Practically nothing is impossible, nothing is dangerous, and, in principle, nobody is superior to anybody." This basic experience completely modifies the traditional, persistent structure of the mass-man. For the latter always felt himself, by his nature, confronted with material limitations and higher social powers. Such, in his eyes, was life. If he succeeded in improving his situation, if he climbed the social ladder, he attributed this to a piece of fortune which was favourable to him in particular. And if not to this, then to an enormous effort, of which he knew well what it had cost him. In both cases it was a question of an exception to the general character of life and the world; an exception which, as such, was due to some very special cause.

But the modern mass finds complete freedom as its natural, established condition, without any special cause for it. Nothing from outside incites it to recognise limits to itself and, consequently, to refer at all times to other authorities higher than itself. Until lately, the Chinese peasant believed that the welfare of his existence depended on the private virtues which the Emperor was pleased to possess. Therefore, his life was constantly related to this supreme authority on which it depended. *But the man we are now analysing accustoms himself not to appeal from his own to any authority outside him.* He is satisfied with himself exactly as he is. Ingenuously, without any need of being vain, as the most natural thing in the world, he will tend to consider and affirm as good everything he finds within himself: opinions, appetites, preferences, tastes. Why not, if, as we have seen, nothing and nobody force him to realise that he is a second-class man, subject to many limitations, incapable of creating or conserving that very organisation which gives his life the fullness and contentedness on which he bases this assertion of his personality?

The mass-man would never have accepted authority external to himself had not his surroundings violently forced him to do so. As to-day his surroundings do not so force him, the everlasting mass-man, true to his character, ceases to appeal to other authority and feels himself lord of his own existence. On the contrary the select man, the excellent man is urged, by interior necessity, to appeal from himself to some standard beyond himself, superior to himself, whose service he freely accepts. Let us recall that at the start we distinguished the excellent man from the common man by saying that the former is the one who makes great demands on himself, and the latter the one who makes no demands on himself, but contents himself with what he is, and is delighted with himself.[1] Contrary to what is usually thought, it is the man of excellence, and not the common man who lives in essential servitude. Life has no savour for him unless he makes it consist in service to something transcendental. Hence he does not look upon the necessity of serving as an oppression. When, by chance, such necessity is lacking, he grows restless and invents some new standard, more difficult, more exigent, with which to coerce himself. This is life lived as a discipline—the noble life. Nobility is defined by the demands it makes on us—by obligations, not by rights. *Noblesse oblige.* "To live as one likes in plebeian; the noble man aspires to order and law" (Goethe). The privileges of nobility are not in their origin concessions or favours; on the contrary, they are conquests. And their maintenance supposes, in principle, that the privileged individual is capable of reconquering them, at any moment, if it were necessary, and anyone were to dispute them.[2] Private rights or *privileges* are not, then, passive possession and mere enjoyment, but they represent the standard attained by personal effort. On the other hand, common rights, such as those "of the man and the citizen." are passive property, pure usufruct and benefit, the generous gift of fate which every man finds before him, and which answers to no effort whatever, unless it be that of breathing and avoiding insanity. I would say, then, that an impersonal right is held, a personal one is upheld.

It is annoying to see the degeneration suffered in ordinary speech by a word so inspiring as "nobility." For, by coming to mean for many people hereditary "noble blood," it is changed into something similar to common rights, into a static, passive quality which is received and trans-

1. That man is intellectually of the mass who, in face of any problem, is satisfied with thinking the first thing he finds in his head. On the contrary, the excellent man is he who contemns what he finds in his mind without previous effort, and only accepts as worthy of him what is still far above him and what requires a further effort in order to be reached.

2. Vide *España Invertebrada* (1922), p. 156.

mitted like something inert. But the strict sense, the *etymon* of the word nobility is essentially dynamic. Noble means the "well known," that is, known by everyone, famous, he who has made himself known by excelling the anonymous mass. It implies an unusual effort as the cause of his fame. Noble, then, is equivalent to effortful, excellent. The nobility or fame of the son is pure benefit. The son is known because the father made himself famous. He is known by reflection, and in fact, hereditary nobility has an indirect character, it is mirrored light, lunar nobility, something derived from the dead. The only thing left to it of living, authentic, dynamic is the impulse it stirs in the descendant to maintain the level of effort reached by the ancestor. Always, even in this altered sense, *noblesse oblige*. The original noble lays an obligation on himself, the noble heir receives the obligation with his inheritance, but in any case there is a certain contradiction in the passing-on of nobility from the first noble to his successors. The Chinese, more logical, invert the order of transmission; it is not the father who ennobles the son, but the son who, by acquiring noble rank, communicates it to his forebears, by his personal efforts bringing fame to his humble stock. Hence, when granting degrees of nobility, they are graduated by the number of previous generations which are honoured; there are those who ennoble only their fathers, and those who stretch back their fame to the fifth or tenth grandparent. The ancestors live by reason of the actual man, whose nobility is effective, active—in a word: *is* not *was*.[1]

"Nobility" does not appear as a formal expression until the Roman Empire, and then precisely in opposition to the hereditary nobles, then in decadence.

For me, then, nobility is synonymous with a life of effort, ever set on excelling oneself, in passing beyond what one is to what one sets up as a duty and an obligation. In this way the noble life stands opposed to the common or inert life, which reclines statically upon itself, condemned to perpetual immobility, unless an external force compels it to come out of itself. Hence we apply the term mass to this kind of man—not so much because of his multitude as because of his inertia.

As one advances in life, one realises more and more that the majority of men—and of women—are incapable of any other effort than that strictly imposed on them as a reaction to external compulsion. And for that reason, the few individuals we have come across who are capable of a spontaneous and joyous effort stand out isolated, monumentalised, so to speak, in our experience. These are the select men, the nobles, the only ones who are active and not merely reactive, for whom life is a

1. As in the foregoing it is only a matter of bringing the word "nobility" back to its original sense which excludes inheritance, this is not the place to study the fact that a "nobility of blood" makes its appearance so often in history. This question, then, is left untouched.

perpetual striving, an incessant course of training. Training = *askesis*. These are the ascetics.[1] This apparent digression should not cause surprise. In order to define the actual mass-man, who is as much "mass" as ever, but who wishes to supplant the "excellent," it has been necessary to contrast him with the two pure forms which are mingled in him: the normal mass and the genuine noble or man of effort.

Now we can advance more rapidly, because we are now in possession of what, to my thinking, is the key—the psychological equation—of the human type dominant to-day. All that follows is a consequence, a corollary, of that root-structure, which may be summed up thus: the world as organised by the XIXth Century, when automatically producing a new man, has infused into him formidable appetites and powerful means of every kind for satisfying them. These include the economic, the physical (hygiene, average health higher than any preceding age), the civil and the technical (by which I mean the enormous quantity of partial knowledge and practical efficiency possessed by the average man to-day and lacking to him in the past). After having supplied him with all these powers, the XIXth Century has abandoned him to himself, and the average man, following his natural disposition, has withdrawn into himself. Hence, we are in presence of a mass stronger than that of any preceding period, but differing from the traditional type in that it remains hermetically enclosed within itself, incapable of submitting to anything or anybody, believing itself self-sufficient—in a word, indocile.[2] If things go on as they are at present, it will be every day more noticeable in Europe—and by reflection, throughout the whole world—that the masses are incapable of submitting to direction of any kind. In the difficult times that are at hand for our continent, it is possible that, under a sudden affliction, they may for a moment have the good will to accept, in certain specially urgent matters, the direction of the superior minorities.

But even that good will will result in failure. For the basic texture of their soul is wrought of hermetism and indocility; they are from birth deficient in the faculty of giving attention to what is outside themselves, be it fact or person. They will wish to follow someone, and they will be unable. They will want to listen, and will discover they are deaf.

On the other hand, it is illusory to imagine that the mass-man of to-day, however superior his vital level may be compared with that of other times, will be able to control, by himself, the process of civilisation. I say process, and not progress. The simple process of preserving our present civilisation is supremely complex, and demands incalculably subtle

1. Vide "El Origen deportivo del Estado," in *El Espectador*, VII, recently published.
2. On the indocility of the masses, especially of the Spanish masses, I have already spoken in *España Invertebrada* (1922), and I refer the reader to what is there said.

powers. Ill-fitted to direct it is this average man who has learned to use much of the machinery of civilisation, but who is characterised by root-ignorance of the very principles of that civilisation.

I reiterate to the reader who has patiently followed me up to this point, the importance of not giving to the facts enunciated a primarily political significance. On the contrary, political activities, of all those in public life the most efficient and the most visible, are the final product of others more intimate, more impalpable. Hence, political indocility would not be so grave did it not proceed from a deeper, more decisive intellectual indocility. In consequence, until we have analysed this latter, the thesis of this essay will not stand out in its final clarity.

12—THE BARBARISM OF "SPECIALISATION"

My thesis was that XIXth-Century civilisation has automatically produced the mass-man. It will be well not to close the general exposition without analysing, in a particular case, the mechanism of that production. In this way, by taking concrete form, the thesis gains in persuasive force.

This civilisation of the XIXth Century, I said, may be summed up in the two great dimensions: liberal democracy and technicism. Let us take for the moment only the latter. Modern technicism springs from the union between capitalism and experimental science. Not all technicism is scientific. That which made the stone axe in the Chelian period was lacking in science, and yet a technique was created. China reached a high degree of technique without in the least suspecting the existence of physics. It is only modern European technique that has a scientific basis, from which it drives its specific character, its possibility of limitless progress. All other techniques—Mesopotamian, Egyptian, Greek, Roman, Oriental—reach up to a point of development beyond which they cannot proceed, and hardly do they reach it when they commence to display a lamentable retrogression.

This marvellous Western technique has made possible the proliferation of the European species. Recall the fact from which this essay took its departure and which, as I said, contains in germ all these present considerations. From the VIth Century to 1800, Europe never succeeds in reaching a population greater than 180 millions. From 1800 to 1914 it rises to more than 460 millions. The jump is unparalleled in our history. There can be no doubt that it is technicism—in combination with liberal democracy—which has engendered mass-man in the quantitative sense of the expression. But these pages have attempted to show that it is also responsible for the existence of mass-man in the qualitative and pejorative sense of the term.

By mass—as I pointed out at the start—is not to be specially understood the workers; it does not indicate a social class, but a kind of man to be found to-day in all social classes, who consequently represents our age, in which he is the predominant, ruling power. We are now about to find abundant evidence for this.

Who is it that exercises social power to-day? Who imposes the forms of his own mind on the period? Without a doubt, the man of the middle class. Which group, within that middle class, is considered the superior, the aristocracy of the present? Without a doubt, the technician: engineer, doctor, financier, teacher, and so on. Who, inside the group of technicians, represents it at its best and purest? Again, without a doubt, the man of science. If an astral personage were to visit Europe today and, for the purpose of forming judgment on it, inquire as to the type of man by which it would prefer to be judged, there is no doubt that Europe, pleasantly assured of a favourable judgment, would point to her men of science. Of course, our astral personage would not inquire for exceptional individuals, but would seek the generic type of "man of science," the high-point of European humanity.

And now it turns out that the actual scientific man is the prototype of the mass-man. Not by chance, not through the individual failings of each particular man of science, but because science itself—the root of our civilisation—automatically converts him into mass-man, makes of him a primitive, a modern barbarian. The fact is well known; it has made itself clear over and over again; but only when fitted into its place in the organism of this thesis does it take on its full meaning and its evident seriousness.

Experimental science is initiated towards the end of the XVIth Century (Galileo), it is definitely constituted at the close of the XVIIth (Newton), and it begins to develop in the middle of the XVIIIth. The development of anything is not the same as its constitution; it is subject to different conditions. Thus, the constitution of physics, the collective name of the experimental sciences, rendered necessary an effort towards unification. Such was the work of Newton and other men of his time. But the development of physics introduced a task opposite in character to unification. In order to progress, science demanded specialisation, not in herself, but in men of science. Science is not specialist. If it were, it would *ipso facto* cease to be true. Not even empirical science, taken in its integrity, can be true if separated from mathematics, from logic, from philosophy. But scientific work does, necessarily, require to be specialised.

It would be of great interest, and of greater utility than at first sight appears, to draw up the history of physical and biological sciences, indicating the process of increasing specialisation in the work of investigators. It would then be seen how, generation after generation, the scientist has been gradually restricted and confined into narrower fields of mental occupation. But this is not the important point that such a history would show, but rather the reverse side of the matter: how in each generation the scientist, through having to reduce the sphere of his labour, was progressively losing contact with other branches of science, with that integral interpretation of the universe which is the only thing deserving the names of science, culture, European civilisation.

Specialisation commences precisely at a period which gives to civilised man the title "encyclopaedic." The XIXth Century starts on its course under the direction of beings who lived "encyclopaedically," though their production has already some tinge of specialism. In the following generation, the balance is upset and specialism begins to dislodge integral culture from the individual scientist. When by 1890 a third generation assumes intellectual command in Europe we meet with a type of scientist unparalleled in history. He is one who, out of all that has to be known in order to be a man of judgment, is only acquainted with one science, and even of that one only knows the small corner in which he is an active investigator. He even proclaims it as a virtue that he takes no cognisance of what lies outside the narrow territory specially cultivated by himself, and gives the name of "dilettantism" to any curiosity for the general scheme of knowledge.

What happens is that, enclosed within the narrow limits of his visual field, he does actually succeed in discovering new facts and advancing the progress of the science which he hardly knows, and incidentally the encyclopedia of thought of which he is conscientiously ignorant. How has such a thing been possible, how is it still possible?. For it is necessary to insist upon this extraordinary but undeniable fact: experimental science has progressed thanks in great part to the work of men astoundingly mediocre, and even less than mediocre. That is to say, modern science, the root and symbol of our actual civilisation, finds a place for the intellectually commonplace man and allows him to work therein with success. The reason of this lies in what is at the same time the great advantage and the gravest peril of the new science, and of the civilisation directed and represented by it, namely, mechanisation. A fair amount of the things that have to be done in physics or in biology is mechanical work of the mind which can be done by anyone, or almost anyone. For the purpose of innumerable investigations it is possible to divide science into small sections, to enclose oneself in one of these, and to leave out of consideration all the rest. The solidity and exactitude of the methods allow of this temporary but quite real disarticulation of knowledge. The work is done under one of these methods as with a machine, and in order to obtain quite abundant results it is not even necessary to have rigorous notions of their meaning and foundations. In this way the majority of scientists help the general advance of science while shut up in the narrow cell of their laboratory, like the bee in the cell of its hive, or the turnspit in its wheel.

But this creates an extraordinarily strange type of man. The investigator who has discovered a new fact of Nature must necessarily experience a feeling of power and self-assurance. With a certain apparent justice he will look upon himself as "a man who knows." And in fact there is in him a portion of something which, added to many other portions not existing in him, does really constitute knowledge. This is the true inner nature of the specialist, who in the first years of this century has reached the wildest stage of exaggeration. The specialist "knows" very well his own tiny corner of the universe; he is radically ignorant of all the rest.

Here we have a precise example of this strange new man, whom I have attempted to define, from both of his two opposite aspects. I have said that he was a human product unparalleled in history. The specialist serves as a striking concrete example of the species, making clear to us the radical nature of the novelty. For, previously, men could be divided simply into the learned and the ignorant, those more or less the one, and those more or less the other. But your specialist cannot be brought in under either of these two categories. He is not learned, for he is formally ignorant of all that does not enter into his speciality; but neither is he ignorant, because he is "a scientist," and "knows" very well his own tiny portion of the universe. We shall have to say that he is a learned ignoramus, which is a very serious matter, as it implies that he is a person who is ignorant, not in the fashion of the ignorant man, but with all the petulance of one who is learned in his own special line.

And such in fact is the behaviour of the specialist. In politics, in art, in social usages, in the other sciences, he will adopt the attitude of primitive, ignorant man; but he will adopt them forcefully and with self-sufficiency, and will not admit of—this is the paradox—specialists in those matters. By specialising him, civilisation has made him hermetic and self-satisfied within his limitations; but this very inner feeling of dominance and worth will induce him to wish to predominate outside his speciality. The result is that even in this case, representing a maximum of qualification in man—specialisation—and therefore the thing most opposed to the mass-man, the result is that he will behave in almost all spheres of life as does the unqualified, the mass-man.

This is no mere wild statement. Anyone who wishes can observe the stupidity of thought, judgment, and action shown to-day in politics, art, religion, and the general problems of life and the world by the "men of science," and of course, behind them, the doctors, engineers, financiers, teachers, and so on. That state of "not listening," of not submitting to higher courts of appeal which I have repeatedly put forward as characteristic of the mass-man, reaches its height precisely in these partially qualified men. They symbolise, and to a great extent constitute, the actual domination of the masses, and their barbarism is the most immediate cause of European demoralisation. Furthermore, they afford the clearest, most striking example of how the civilisation of the last century, *abandoned to its own devices,* has brought about this rebirth of primitivism and barbarism.

The most immediate result of this *unbalanced* specialisation has been that to-day, when there are more "scientists" than ever, there are much less "cultured" men than, for example, about 1750. And the worst is that with these turnspits of science not even the real progress of science itself is assured. For science needs from time to time, as a necessary regulator of its own advance, a labour of reconstitution, and, as I have said, this demands an effort towards unification, which grows more and more difficult, involving, as it does, ever-vaster regions of the world of knowledge. Newton was able to found his system of physics without knowing much philosophy, but Einstein needed to saturate himself with Kant and Mach before he could reach his own keen synthesis. Kant and Mach— the names are mere symbols of the enormous mass of philosophic and psychological thought which has influenced Einstein—have served to *liberate* the mind of the latter and leave the way open for his innovation. But Einstein is not sufficient. Physics is entering on the gravest crisis of its history, and can only be saved by a new "Encyclopaedia" more systematic than the first.

The specialisation, then, that has made possible the progress of experimental science during a century, is approaching a stage where it can no longer continue its advance unless a new generation undertakes to provide it with a more powerful form of turnspit.

But if the specialist is ignorant of the inner philosophy of the science he cultivates, he is much more radically ignorant of the historical conditions requisite for its continuation; that is to say: how society and the heart of man are to be organised in order that there may continue to be investigators. The decrease in scientific vocations noted in recent years, to which I have alluded, is an anxious symptom for anyone who has a clear idea of what civilisation is, an idea generally lacking to the typical "scientist," the high-point of our present civilisation. He also believes that civilisation *is there* in just the same way as the earth's crust and the forest primeval. . .

15—WE ARRIVE AT THE REAL QUESTION

This is the question: Europe has been left without a moral code. It is not that the mass-man has thrown over an antiquated one in exchange for a new one, but that at the centre of his scheme of life there is precisely the aspiration to live without conforming to any moral code. Do not believe a word you hear from the young when they talk about the "new morality." I absolutely deny that there exists to-day in any corner of the Continent a group inspired by a new *ethos* which shows signs of being a moral code. When people talk of the "new morality" they are merely committing a new immorality and looking for a way of introducing contraband goods.[1] Hence it would be a piece of ingenuousness to accuse the man of to-day of his lack of moral code. The accusation would leave him cold, or rather, would flatter him. Immoralism has become a commonplace, and anybody and everybody boasts of practising it.

If we leave out of question, as has been done in this essay, all those groups which imply survivals from the past—Christians, Idealists, the old Liberals—there will not be found amongst all the representatives of the actual period, a single group whose attitude to life is not limited to believing that it has all the rights and none of the obligations. It is indifferent whether it disguises itself as reactionary or revolutionary; actively or passively, after one or two twists, its state of mind will consist, decisively, in ignoring all obligations, and in feeling itself, without the slightest notion why, possessed of unlimited rights. Whatever be the substance which takes possession of such a soul, it will produce the same result, and will change into a pretext for not conforming to any concrete purpose. If it appears as reactionary or anti-liberal it will be in order to affirm that the salvation of the State gives a right to level down all other standards, and to manhandle one's neighbour, above all if one's neighbour is an outstanding personality. But the same happens if it decides to act the revolutionary; the apparent enthusiasm for the manual worker, for the afflicted and for social justice, serves as a mask to facilitate the refusal of all obligations, such as courtesy, truthfulness and, above all, respect or esteem for superior individuals. I know of quite a few who have entered the ranks of some labour organisation or other merely in order to win for themselves the right to despise intelligence and to avoid paying it any tribute. As regards other kinds of Dictatorship, we have seen only too well how they flatter the mass-man, by trampling on everything that appeared to be above the common level.

This fighting-shy of every obligation partly explains the phenomenon, half ridiculous, half disgraceful, of the setting-up in our days of the platform of "youth" as youth. Perhaps there is no more grotesque spectacle offered by our times. In comic fashion people call themselves "young," because they have heard that youth has more rights than obligations, since it can put off the fulfilment of these latter to the Greek Kalends of maturity. The youth, as such, has always been considered

1. I do not suppose there are more than two dozen men scattered about the world who can recognise the springing up of what one day may be a new moral code. For that very reason, such men are the least representative of this actual time.

exempt from *doing* or *having done* actions of importance. He has always lived on credit. It was a sort of false right, half ironic, half affectionate, which the no-longer young conceded to their juniors. But the astounding thing at present is that these take it as an effective right precisely in order to claim for themselves all those other rights which only belong to the man who has already done something.

Though it may appear incredible, "youth" has become a *chantage;* we are in truth living in a time when this adopts two complementary attitudes, violence and caricature. One way or the other, the purpose is always the same; that the inferior, the man of the crowd, may feel himself exempt from all submission to superiors.

It will not do, then, to dignify the actual crisis by presenting it as the conflict between two moralities, two civilisations, one in decay, the other at its dawn. The mass-man is simply without morality, which is always, in essence, a sentiment of submission to something, a consciousness of service and obligation. But perhaps it is a mistake to say "simply." For it is not merely a question of this type of creature doing without morality. No, we must not make his task too easy. Morality cannot be eliminated without more ado. What, by a word lacking even in grammar, is called *amorality* is a thing that does not exist. If you are unwilling to submit to any norm, you have, *nolens volens,* to submit to the norm of denying all morality, and this is not amoral, but immoral. It is a negative morality which preserves the empty form of the other. How has it been possible to believe in the amorality of life? Doubtless, because all modern culture and civilisation tend to that conviction. Europe is now reaping the painful results of her spiritual conduct. She has adopted blindly a culture which is magnificent, but has no roots.

In this essay an attempt has been made to sketch a certain type of European, mainly by analysing his behaviour as regards the very civilisation into which he was born. This had to be done because that individual does not represent a new civilisation struggling with a previous one, but a mere negation. Hence it did not serve our purpose to mix up the portrayal of his mind with the great question: What are the radical defects from which modern European culture suffers? For it is evident that in the long run the form of humanity dominant at the present day has its origin in these defects.

This great question must remain outside these pages. Its treatment would require of us to unfold in detail the doctrine of human existence which, like a *leitmotiv,* is interwoven, insinuated, whispered in them. Perhaps, before long, it may be cried aloud.

Mission of the University

José Ortega y Gasset

The Federación Universitaria Escolar of Madrid asked me to give a lecture on some topic related to the reform of higher education. The very poor acoustics of the Paraninfo, however, and my poor health at the time, prevented me from developing adequately the theme of my lecture. This circumstance prompted me afterward to rewrite somewhat more amply the notes I had taken with me to the Paraninfo. And here you have the result. It will be seen that except for an introduction, which the student mind of that time made necessary, I have kept rigorously to what I consider the crucial question. I was anxious to advance this question for discussion, and the pages which follow make no pretense of being anything more than the material for an extensive debate. Accordingly, I have set down my ideas with exaggerated sharpness and simplicity.

In no respect do I flatter myself that I have treated the theme of higher education with any sort of adequacy. The present essay is to be considered only as an anticipation of some future course on the Idea of the University. A definitive study calls first of all for a clear description of the essential characteristics of our age and an accurate diagnosis of the rising generation.

CHAPTER I—A TEMPERED SPIRIT OF REFORM

The Federation of University Students asked me to come here and speak to you on the reform of education.[1] Now I loathe speaking in public, to such an extent that I have managed to do so very few times in my life. Yet this time, without a moment's hesitation, I let myself be corralled by the students. Which shows with what enthusiasm I have come here. In fact, I come with great enthusiasm, but with small faith. For it is clear that these are two different things. Man would be badly off, indeed, if he were incapable of enthusiasm except for the things in which he has faith! Humanity would still be pursuing its existence in a hole in the ground; for everything that has made it possible to emerge from the cave and the primeval jungle appeared in its first hour as a highly dubious undertaking. Nevertheless, man has been able to grow enthusiastic over his vision of these unconvincing enterprises. He has put

1. EDITOR'S NOTE: Mrs. Helene Weyl dates this address "late in the autumn, or more likely, in the early winter of 1930." The present book, which was published soon after the lecture, bears the date of 1930, and speaks of the *Rebelión de las Masas* as "recientemente publicado." The first edition of the *Rebelión*, though dated 1929, has a colophon stating that the printing was finished August 26, 1930.

himself to work for the sake of an idea, seeking by magnificent exertions to arrive at the incredible. And in the end, he has arrived there. Beyond all doubt it is one of the vital sources of man's power, to be thus able to kindle enthusiasm from the mere glimmer of something improbable, difficult, remote. The other sort of enthusiasm, cradled comfortably by faith, is hardly worthy of the name, because it is sure of its success from the outset. Little is to be expected from the man who exerts himself only when he has the certainty of being recompensed in the end! I remember having written in 1916 that the Germans would lose the war, because they had entered it too sure of victory: their mind was wholly on the conquering, and not simply on fighting. One must go into any kind of struggle prepared for anything, including calamity and defeat. For these, as much as victory, are masks life can put on in a moment. Every day the conviction forces itself on me with new clarity, that too much security demoralizes men more than anything else. Because they came to feel too secure, all the aristocracies of history have fallen into irreparable degeneracy. And one of the ailments of the present time, particularly of the rising generation, is that the modern man, thanks to technological progress and social organization, is inclined to feel sure of too many things about his life.[2]

Do not be surprised therefore that I come before you, according to an old peculiarity of human nature, with more enthusiasm than faith. But why do I have so little faith? Let me tell you. It is now close to twenty-five years since I wrote my first articles on the reform of the Spanish state in general and the university in particular—articles which won me the friendship of don Francisco Giner de los Ríos. In those days, you could count on your fingers all the people in Spain who admitted the necessity of reforming either the state or the university. Anyone who dared speak of reform, or even insinuate that it was appropriate, was *ipso facto* declared a madman and an outlaw. He was cast off on a tangent from the circle of normal Spanish society, regardless of who he might be, and condemned to a marginal existence, as if reform were leprosy. Do not think that this hostility toward the slightest suspicion of reform arose because the reformers were a radical lot, a menace to society, etc., etc. Not at all. The most moderate of men would have been ostracized for the mention of reform. Such was the case of Antonio Maura, who had been raised to the height of power by the conservatives themselves. Convinced that even the most conservative point of view required changes in the organization of the state, Maura found himself suddenly relegated to the periphery of the national life. His attempt at reform was crushed by a witticism in vogue at the time, comparing him to a rural policeman in a china shop. Two things escaped the wits who bandied this joke about—

2. AUTHOR'S NOTE: On this matter see my recent book *The Revolt of the Masses*.

one, that in a few years their china shop was to be invaded by the whole police force on horseback; and the other, that they revealed a stubborn determination on their own part to preserve a *status quo* which had about it, indeed, all the frailty of chinaware.

I cite this notorious example to indicate the general, hidebound obstinacy which opposed the reform of anything then in power in Spain, including the state and the university. Those of us who advocated change and proposed to revise antiquated forms were called again and again "enemies of the University." For supporting new institutions like the *Residencia de Estudiantes,* which was created precisely to promote the welfare of the university by stimulating the ferment of thought, we were dubbed the university's official enemies. Today, of course, those who reviled the loudest are just the people who hasten to imitate the *Residencia de Estudiantes.* In this they deserve nothing but praise. But at the same time it is only fair to recall that, for many years, gibes and insults were the portion of those who felt some honest concern for the Spanish university and were determined that it should not continue indefinitely to be the sad, inert, spiritless thing it then was. For candor obliges one to observe that our university today is decidedly different from what it was, though it is still far from what it ought to be, and can be.

At present, throughout all our national life, the constellations have changed. Hard-fisted facts have come to silence the carping mouths and convince the slowest among us that government and university alike need reform: it is not a question of desiring reform or not; it is imperative that we make an effort, because neither of these institutions is working. They are machines worn out by the wear and tear of use and abuse.

Today we are not alone. Many people desire the transformation of the Spanish body politic, and those who do not are resigned to bear with it, somehow or other. Certainly the moment is full of opportunity. You do not appreciate, young people, what good fortune you have had: you have come into life at a magnificent juncture in the destinies of Spain— when the horizon lies open, and many, many great things are going to be possible, among them a new state and a new university. It would be difficult to be more optimistic than I am concerning the interpretation to be put on the current situation of the country. Events which nearly everyone has viewed with alarm seem to me to be ironical masks, under whose evil appearance are hidden really favorable developments. Certainly the moment is full of opportunity; you have come at the dawn of an illustrious era. A people dormant for centuries is beginning to stir, with those sleepy, jerking motions of a person about to awake and rise to his feet. The moment can be happily described by that very expressive line of poetry, in which the venerable poem of the Cid relates the dawning of a day:

Apriessa cantan los gallos e quieren crebrar albores . . .[3]

Then has not the moment arrived for joining a new faith with the old enthusiasm? To this I must answer, provisionally, "No, . . . not yet." In my optimism, it strikes me as clear and definite that the horizon which lies open before the Spaniard of today is a magnificent one. Now the horizon is a symbol of possibilities, presenting themselves before our human life. And this life of ours, in its turn, is a process of converting these possibilities into actual realities. Here is the point where my optimism falters, and my faith fails me. For in history—in life—possibilities do not become realities of their own accord; someone, with his hands and his brain, with his labor and his self-sacrifice, must make realities of them. History and life, for this reason, are a perpetual *creating*. Our life is not given to us ready-made: in a fundamental sense it is, precisely, what we are constantly and continuously making of ourselves. The process is going on at every instant. Nothing is ours outright, as a gift; we have to perform for ourselves even those of our actions which seem most passive. The humble Sancho Panza kept suggesting this on all occasions, by repeating his proverb: "If they give you the cow, you have to carry the rope." All we are given is possibilities—to make ourselves one thing or another. At this instant, for example, you are engaged in listening: decidedly no easy occupation, as you can tell from the fact that if you relax your attention the least bit, your listening will sink into mere hearing; or a bit more, and your fugitive attention would fail to register the boom of a cannon.

I say, then, that the circumstances offer a magnificent opportunity for a thorough reform of the Spanish state and university. But the reform of the one and of the other waits to be done *by someone*. Is there such a one in Spain today? By that I do not mean an individual, of course, one of those mythical creatures usually referred to, by a misapprehension, as a Great Man. History is not made by one man—however great he may be. History is like a sonnet; nor is it a game of solitaire. It is made by many people: by groups of people endowed, collectively, with the necessary qualities.

Since I have come here today with the intention of talking to you in absolute sincerity; since, out of loyalty to myself, I am resolved to say my say without mincing words, I cannot disguise my grave doubt that there exists, on this day, any group capable of achieving the reform of the state, or to limit ourselves to the present theme, the reform of the university. I say on this day—this fleeting day on which I am speaking. Within a dozen days, or weeks, this group *can* exist and I hope it will.

3. *"Abruptly, cocks begin to crow, the light of dawn is about to break" (Poema de mio Cid*, line 235).

Nothing prevents it from being brought together and organized: if I stress so emphatically that we lack such a group today, it is with the sole purpose of contributing to its realization tomorrow.

But you will say: "How can you doubt that a group exists, capable of effecting the reform? Once it is admitted that a thing is feasible, all that is necessary is the will to do it. And here are we, fairly clamoring for the reform of the university. There can be no doubt whether the group exists."

Certainly, certainly. To accomplish a thing which is possible, all you need is the will to do it. But everything depends on how fully the sense of this easy word is understood. It is easy to say and even to think that you are resolved upon something; but it is extremely difficult to be resolved in the true sense.

For this means resolving upon all the things which are necessary as intermediate steps; its means, for one thing, providing ourselves with the qualities that are requisite for the undertaking. Anything short of this is no real resolution, it is simply wishing. You rinse your imagination in the idea, you work yourself into a voluptuous excitement over it, and you spend your force in a vague effervescence of enthusiasm. In his *Philosophy of Universal History*, Hegel asserts that passion, without doubt, is responsible for all the significant accomplishments in history; but—he qualifies—*cool passion*. When passion is simply a frenzy of turbulent emotion, it is of no use at all. Anyone could be passionate, that way. But it is not so easy to maintain that sort of fire which is both critical and creative, that incandescence so supplied with thermal energy that it will not be cooled when the two coldest things in the world come to lodge within it: cool logic and an iron will. The vulgar, false, impotent sort of passion shrinks in terror from the proximity of reflective thought, for it senses that at such a chilly contact it will be frozen out of existence. Hence the symptom of high creative passion is that it seeks to complete itself by uniting with the cooler virtues; that it admits of reflective criticism, without losing its creative energy. It is fire supported with the constancy of clear understanding and a calm will.

This kind of resolute, clear-seeing will is what I do not find today, even at a formative stage, in any group of Spaniards—including yourselves. And without it, we shall await in vain the execution of a reform, a work of construction and creation.

The root of Spain's troubles, whether in the state or the university, may be given the most various names; but if you seek the very tip of the root, out of which all the rest arises and emerges, you encounter a fact which only one word can adequately describe: slovenliness.[4] It penetrates

4. EDITOR'S NOTE: One would like a slightly milder word to render *la chabacanería*.

our whole national life from top to bottom, directing, inspiring its actions. The state is slovenly in its dealings with the citizen, permitting him, on occasion, to evade compliance with its laws; or vice versa, the state itself applies the laws fraudulently and makes them a means of deceiving the citizen. Some day the story will be told, for instance, of what the government did on the authority of that famous law passed during the emergencies of the World War, called the "Law of Subsistencies." Things you would consider a far cry from any question of subsistence were perpetrated under the title of this law. Everyone knows what use the governors of provinces have made, for decades, of the Law of Associations. Just ask about that for yourselves, among the labor unions in the provinces. But it is not my intention now to present pathetic cases of this shabby deportment of the state. I am not here to talk politics, and moreover if I were, I should not be pathetic about it. My purpose is to make clear to you what constitutes this fundamental ailment of Spain and the Spaniard, which I call slovenliness. For there is no use to rant and declaim, after the fashion of public orations, that this conduct of the government is a crime, an intolerable abuse, a betrayal of public trust. It is all that, of course; but so meanly, so stupidly, so habitually—so far from any compensating profit to the government—that one feels ashamed to call it crime. To tell the truth, while it is crime in the juridical sense, it is not crime as a psychological fact—as a historical reality. Crime is something violent and terrible, and in this regard, respectable: this is no crime, but something inferior to crime. It is, in a word, slovenliness, the lack of all decorum, of all self-respect, of all decency in the state's manner of performing its peculiarly delicate function.

I do not mean by this that in Spain crimes are not committed. But I do deny that crimes are the bulk, or the worst, of Spain's trouble. For crimes, when they are really that, provoke a reaction, before very long, to cure the ailment. Slovenliness on the contrary grows accustomed to its own presence; it finds itself pleasantly comfortable, and tends to spread and perpetuate itself. Thus it permeates everything in Spain, from the state and its official acts, to the life of the family and the very grimace of the individual. In our university faculty meetings, the atmosphere is heavy with this slovenliness; and to walk through these halls, even on ordinary days, and hear the hullabaloo and see the gesticulations of you students, is to breathe an atmosphere so thick with slovenliness that it chokes.[5]

But the full meaning of a concept never becomes clear until it is confronted with its opposite, as for example up and down, more and less, etc. Every idea has its antagonist; in the combat between the two,

5. AUTHOR'S NOTE: For a number of years I have had to find a room outside the university buildings, because the habitual shouting of our precious students, standing around in the halls, makes it impossible to hear oneself talk in the classrooms.

their profile is delineated. What is the opposite of slovenliness? I shall use a word with which you are very familiar, since it belongs to the vocabulary of sports. The opposite of slovenliness is *to be in form*. You people well know the tremendous difference there is between an athlete when he is *in form,* and the same man when he is out of form. The difference in what he is able to do is every bit as striking as if he were two entirely different people. But this *form* is a thing that has to be acquired. In order to achieve it, the individual must first go off by himself and concentrate upon his own development: he has to go into training, and give up many things, in the determination to surpass himself, to be more alert, tense, supple. There is nothing that is indifferent to him, for every little thing either is favorable to his form, or else pulls it down, and with this in mind he goes out for one thing and avoids the other. Briefly, to be in form means never indulging in any dissipation whatever. And that indulgence of oneself—your "let it go anyhow," "it's all the same," "a bit more or less" "what of it?"—that is slovenliness.

Just as individuals, groups too may be in form or out of form, and it is evident in history that the only groups which have ever done anything are those which have achieved *form:* compact, perfectly organized groups, in which every member knows that the others will not fail him at the crucial point, so that the whole body may move swiftly in any direction without losing its balance or losing its head—as the abbé Fernando Galiani said of the Order of the Jesuits in the eighteenth century, when that Order was in form, "It is a sword with its hilt in Rome and its point everywhere." But a group does not acquire this *form* unless it has disciplined itself, and continues to discipline itself; unless it sees with perfect clarity what it proposes to do. And it cannot see clearly unless the purpose it sees is clear, well thought out, cogent, and as complete as the situation warrants.

All this is what I was referring to earlier. I doubt, then, that there exists in Spain, at the present moment, a group which is *in form* for the reforming of the state or of the university. And if it is not *in form,* all that may be attempted without the necessary qualities will come to nothing. It is obvious, in as much as slovenliness is the root of the evil, that a reform which is slovenly itself will not mend matters appreciably. You have seen for yourselves a petulant effort to reform the country, on the part of a group of people who had not given a moment's thought to the question of first providing themselves with the minimum of necessary equipment. Such has been the Dictatorship.[6] All it has achieved, despite the extraordinary opportunity that offered itself, has been to carry our national slovenliness to the point of madness.

6. EDITOR'S NOTE: The dictatorship had begun under Primo de Rivera in 1923, and was to last until the establishment of the Republic in 1931.

Let it be understood that I have not come here to advise you against taking part in the public affairs of Spain, or against petitioning, and even insisting upon, the reform of the university. On the contrary: I urge you to do all this; but do it seriously—do it *in form*. Otherwise, the future can be told now, with perfect assurance. If you attempt to take a part in public life without the proper preparation, this is what will happen. Since activity in public affairs means trying to influence the great mass of the public, and you are not a powerful, articulated body but merely a little formless mass, then the mechanics of history, identical at this point with the laws of physics, will simply follow its inexorable course. The larger mass will crush the smaller.

To exert influence upon a mass, you must be something other than a mass yourselves: a live force, or in other words, a group *in form*.

If I could see in you the determination to put yourselves in form—ah!—then, my friends, I should not be afflicted with this deficiency of faith.

I should believe it all to be possible, indeed, imminent. Contrary to a general belief, history may advance by jumps, and not always by gradual change. It was the characteristic error of the past century to count upon gradual evolution, and to presume that every whole achievement in history was produced by means of a very gradual preparation. It was a surprise when facts showed, clearly and undeniably, that in biology and in the spiritual world alike, spontaneous realities could emerge suddenly and in a sense without preparation.

To cite a symbolic case, let me recall to you how stupefied the historians were in the last century, when the fact was established that the highest, classical civilization of the Egyptians—the marvelous culture of the Pyramids—was without predecessors. It caused great astonishment to find that this most exquisite flourishing in the whole course of the Nile valley civilization appeared at the threshold of history—at the dawn of historic times. It had been supposed that excavation would reveal, under the land of the Pyramids, some vestiges of a less perfect culture, in progress toward that mature perfection. Great was the surprise when the archaeologists struck the remains, almost immediately under the pyramids, of a neolithic civilization. Which is to say that almost without transition, man had advanced from the chipped stone to the classic stone.[7]

No; history proceeds very often by jumps. These jumps, in which tremendous distances may be covered, are called generations. A generation *in form* can accomplish what centuries failed to achieve without form. And there, my young friends, lies a challenge.

7. EDITOR'S NOTE: Though later evidence indicates a longer and more significant epoch of transition, the case still illustrates the possibility of rapid social evolution.

CHAPTER II—THE FUNDAMENTAL QUESTION

[1] The reform of higher education cannot be limited, nor can even its main features be limited, to the correction of abuses. Reform is always the creation of new usages. Abuses are always of minor importance. For either they are abuses in the most natural sense of the word, namely, isolated, infrequent cases of departure from usage; or else they are so frequent and customary, so persistent and so generally tolerated, that they are no longer to be called abuses. In the first case, they will presumably be corrected automatically; in the second case, it would be futile to correct them, for their frequency and acceptance indicate that they are not exceptions to a rule, but manifestations of usages which are bad. It is something in the usage, the policy, and not the breach of it, which needs our attention.

Any reform movement which is limited to correcting slovenly or slipshod abuses in our university will lead inevitably to a reform which is equally slovenly.

What matters is usage. I can go further: a clear symptom that the usages constituting an institution are sound is the ability to withstand a good dose of abuses without serious harm, as a healthy man bears up under stress that would break a weakling. But an institution cannot be built of wholesome usage, until its precise mission has been determined. An institution is a machine in that its whole structure and functioning must be devised in view of the service it is expected to perform. In other words, the root of university reform is a complete formulation of its purpose. Any alteration, or touching up, or adjustment about this house of ours, unless it starts by reviewing the problem of its mission—clearly, decisively, truthfully—will be love's labors lost.

Through their failure to do this, all the improvements attempted hitherto, motivated in some cases by excellent intentions, including the projects worked out some years ago by the university faculty itself, have inevitably come to nought. They will never achieve the one thing which is both sufficient and requisite for any being—individual or collective— to live to the full of its powers: namely, that its life be the true, authentic fulfillment of its powers, and not some falsification of this inexorable destiny, imposed upon it by our stubborn and arbitrary preferences. The best attempts of the last fifteen years—not to speak of the worst— instead of putting the question squarely, "What is a university for, and what must it consequently be?" have done the thing that was easiest and most sterile. They have looked about to see what is done in the universities of other peoples.

1. EDITOR'S NOTE: The first three paragraphs of Chapter II have here been omitted. In them Ortega recapitulates Chapter I, and complains of the hall in which he had read that chapter. This is the only omission made in the present translation.

I do not criticize our informing ourselves by observing an exemplary neighbor; on the contrary, that is necessary. But such observation cannot excuse us from the labor of determining our destiny for ourselves. By this I do not mean any quest after "racial purity" and all that nonsense. Even if we were all—men or nations—identical with one another, imitation would still be fatal. For in imitating, we evade that creative exertion of laboring at a problem, from which we can learn the real nature, including the limits and the defects, of the solution we borrow. There is no question here of "racial purity," which is, in Spain anyway, as common as the hayseeds. It is immaterial whether we come to the same conclusions and the same forms as other countries; what matters is that we arrive by our own legs, after a personal combat with the fundamental question at issue.

The reasoning of our best attempts so far has been fallacious: British life has been, and is, a marvel; *therefore* the British secondary schools must be exemplary, *since* out of them British life has grown. German science is prodigious; therefore the German university is a model institution, *because* it engendered the prodigy. So let us imitate the British secondary schools and the German higher education.

The error stems directly from the nineteenth century as a whole. The English rout Napoleon I: "The battle of Waterloo was won on the playing fields of Eton." Bismarck crushes Napoleon III: "The war of 1870 is the victory of the Prussian schoolmaster and the German professor."

These clichés rest upon a fundamental error which we shall simply have to get out of our heads. It consists in supposing that nations are great *because* their schools are good—elementary, secondary, or higher. It is the residue of a pious "idealism" of the past century. It ascribes to the school a force which it neither has nor can have. That century, in order to feel enthusiasm for a thing, or even just to esteem it especially, found it necessary to exaggerate the thing to heroic proportions. Certainly *when* a nation is great, so will be its schools. There is no great nation without great schools. But the same holds for its religion, it statesmanship, its economy, and a thousand other things. A nation's greatness is the integration of many elements. If a people is bad politically, it is vain to expect anything at all of the most perfect school system. In such a case schools are for the few, who live apart and estranged from the rest of the country. Perhaps some day these educated few may influence the collective life of their country, and succeed in improving the whole national school system.

Principle of education: the school, when it is truly a functional organ of the nation, depends far more on the atmosphere of national culture in which it is immersed than it does on the pedagogical atmosphere created artificially within it. A condition of equilibrium between this inward and outward pressure is essential to produce a good school.

Consequence: even granting that English secondary education and German higher education are perfect, they would not be transferable, for the institutions are only a part of a larger entity. Their being, in its totality, is nothing less than the whole nation which created and maintains them.

Furthermore, the short-circuited reasoning I have described prevented its victims from looking squarely at these model schools and seeing what they are within themselves, purely as institutional structures. The framework was confused with the ambient air of English life, or German thought. Now in as much as neither English life nor German thought can be transported here but, at best, only the disengaged institutional structures, it is quite important that we see what these actually are, apart from those virtues which enveloped and pervaded them in their native countries.

Then one sees that the German university is, as an institution, a rather deplorable object. If German science had been dependent for its nourishment on the forces of the university, as an institution, that science would be of very small account. Fortunately an atmosphere of free inquiry has combined with the German's natural talent and disposition for science to outweigh the glaring imperfections of the German university. I am not well acquainted with English secondary education; but what I can discern of it leads me to think that there too the institutional structure is very defective.

But there is no need of my personal opinions. It is a fact, that secondary education in England and the university in Germany are undergoing a crisis. Fundamental criticism of the latter by the first Prussian Minister of Education since the founding of the Republic: Becker. The discussion which has ensued.[2]

Because, they have been willing to imitate and to evade thinking through the questions for themselves, our best professors live in all respects in a spirit fifteen or twenty years behind the times, except that they are up to date in the details of their fields. And this is the tragic lag behindhand, which is the fate of people who try to save themselves the effort of being authentic and forming their own convictions. The number of years comprising this lag is not a matter of chance. All the creation of history—in science, in politics—arises out of a certain pervading state of mind, or "spirit of the times." This state of mind changes at rhythmic intervals: the interval of the generation.[3]Out of the spirit of a generation come ideas, evaluations, and so on. The person who imitates

2. EDITOR'S NOTE: See p. 44 and note. For the explanation of Ortega's unfinished sentences see his dedication, p. 9.

3. EDITOR'S NOTE: Ortega has elaborated "The Concept of the Generation" in *The Modern Theme*, Chapter I and ff. For the background of the concept, see the résumé and brief bibliography in Christian Sénéchal, *Les grands courants de la littérature française contemporaine*, Paris: Malfère (1933), pp. 419–421; the introduction of Bopp and Paulhan to

these must wait until they have been formulated; or in other words, until the preceding generation has finished its work. Then he adopts its principles, at the time when they are beginning to decline, and a new generation is already making its reform, inaugurating the regime of a new spirit. Each generation struggles for fifteen years to establish itself, and its synthesis holds together another fifteen years—inevitable anachronism of an imitative, unauthentic people.

Let us look abroad for information. But not for a model.

There is no evading the fundamental question, then: What is the mission of the university?

To determine what the mission of the university is, let us try first to define what the university actually means today, in Spain and elsewhere. Whatever may be the differences in status, all the universities of Europe have some general characteristics in common.[4]

Albert Thibaudet, *Histoire de la littérature française de 1789 à nos jours,* Paris: Stock (1937); and also Sainte-Beuve's observation concerning individual literary production, in *Nouveaux lundis,* III, art. "Chateaubriand," part II (1862): "Quinze ans d'ordinaire font une carrière; il est donné à quelques-uns de la doubler, d'en recommencer ou même d'en remplir une seconde."

4. AUTHOR'S NOTE: It is usual, for example, to exaggerate the differences between the English and continental universities, neglecting the fact that the greatest differences are to be laid not to the universities themselves, but to the very extraordinary English character. What should be compared between countries is the tendencies which mark the evolution of their universities—not the degree, naturally variable, in which the tendencies have progressed. Thus, the conservatism of the English has caused them to maintain appearances, in their higher institutions, which they recognize themselves to be irrelevant, and which, indeed, they value as mere fictions quite incidental to the vital reality of British university life. It would seem ridiculous for someone to presume to limit the free will of the Englishman, and censure him for indulging, if he could and wanted to, in the luxury of consciously perpetuating these fictions. But it would be just as naive to take these figments seriously, and suppose that the Englishman deludes himself about their fictitious character. The studies I have read on the English university fall invariably into the subtle snare of English irony. They fail to notice that if England preserves the nonprofessional *aspect* of the university, like the wig of the magistrate, it is not through any obstinate belief that these are actualities, but precisely *because* they are antiquated and superfluous. Otherwise they could not provide the luxury, the diversion, the occasion for awe, and other values which the Englishman seeks in these mere appearances. Beneath the quaint peruke, the justice is modern to the minute; and beneath its nonprofessional aspect, the English university has become, in the last forty years, as professionalized as any other.

It is likewise not of the slightest importance for our central theme—the mission of the university—that the English universities are not institutions of the state. While this fact is of great importance for the life and history of the English people, it does not prevent their university from functioning essentially in the same way as the state-maintained universities of the continent. In the last analysis it would turn out that even in England the universities are institutions of the state; only the Englishman has an entirely different conception of the state from the continental idea of it. To sum up the point I wish to make: first, the enormous differences which exist between the universities of the various nations are not so much concerned with the universities proper as with the nations themselves; and second, the most striking fact in the last forty years is a convergent movement of all the universities of Europe that is tending to make them all homogeneous.

We meet the fact, first of all, that the university is the institution in which higher education is imparted to almost all those who receive any. "Almost," because there are also the specialized schools, whose separate existence gives rise to a problem likewise separate. Having made this exception, we may lay it aside and work with the practical generalization, that the people who receive higher education receive it in the university. But then we find ourselves face to face with another limitation more important than that of the specialized schools. All those who receive higher education are not all those who could and should receive it; they are only the children of the well-to-do classes. The university represents a privilege difficult to justify or defend. Theme: the working class in the university—a theme as yet intact. For two reasons. First, if one believes it is right, as I do, to offer the knowledge of the university to the working man, it is because one considers this knowledge valuable and desirable. The problem of universalizing the university rests upon the previous determination of what the higher learning and instruction are to be. And second, the process of making the university accessible to the working man is only in small part the concern of the university; it is almost wholly the business of the state. Only a great reform of our state will make our university effective. Failure of all the attempts made so far, such as "university extension," etc.[5]

The important thing at this point is to bear well in mind that all the people who receive higher education receive it in the university. If a greater number should receive it tomorrow than at present, so much the better for the force of the argument which follows.

Of what does this higher instruction consist, which is offered in the university to the vast legion of youth? It consists of two things:

(A) The teaching of the learned professions.

(B) Scientific research and the preparation of future investigators.

The university teaches people to be doctors, pharmacists, lawyers, judges, economists, public servants, teachers of the sciences and the humanities in secondary schools, and so on.

In the second place, science itself is cultivated in the university, through research and the transmission of its methods. In Spain, this function of creative science, and of creating scientists, is at a minimum; not by reason of any defect of the university, nor because the university

5. EDITOR'S NOTE: It should be noted that after half a century of growth, university extension in the United Statets has become an important agency for the training of people who must meanwhile earn their living. The cultural education of the working man is still admittedly deficient; but this is due rather to our poor understanding of the objective than to a lack of well-intentioned agencies. Organizations and institutions interested in the education of the working man are too numerous to need mention. Among the oldest are the British "Workers Educational Association," and Ruskin College in Oxford (founded 1899). For the explanation of Ortega's unfinished sentences see his dedication, p. 9.

considers that such activities are not its mission, but on account of the notorious lack of scientific callings and aptitude for research which marks our race. No doubt if science were abundantly carried on in Spain, it would be in the university by preference, as is more or less the case in the other countries. Let this point serve as an example, and save us the repetition of the same principle at every step: the obstinate backwardness of Spain in intellectual activity entails the result that we find here in a state of germination or mere tendency what appears elsewhere in its full development. For the purpose of stating the university problem in its basic form, these differences of degree are immaterial. It is sufficient that all the reforms of recent years clearly evince the intention to increase the research activities of our universities and the training of scientists: in short, to orient the entire institution in this direction. Commonplace and deceptive objections may be advanced on the other side. It is, however, notorious that our best professors, those who have the most influence in the course of the attempted reforms, believe that our university should vie with the foreign universities. And that is enough.

The higher education consists, then, of professionalism and research. Without attacking the subject now, let us note in passing that it is surprising to find two such disparate tasks joined, fused together. For there can be no doubt about this: to be a lawyer, a judge, a doctor, a druggist, a teacher of Latin or history in a secondary school, is very different from being a jurist, a physiologist, a biochemist, a philologist, etc. The former are engaged in practical professions; the latter in purely scientific occupations. Furthermore, society needs many doctors, pharamacists, teachers; but it needs only a restricted number of scientists.[6] If we really needed many of these it would be a catastrophe, since a true calling for science is extremely rare. It is surprising, then, to find mixed together the professional instruction which is for all, and research which is for a very few. But let us put this matter aside for a few moments. Is the higher education nothing more than professionalism and research? At first sight we discover nothing else. But, if we scrutinize the programs of instruction more closely, we discover that the student is nearly always required, apart from his professional apprenticeship and his research, to take some courses of a general character—philosophy, history.

It takes no great acumen to recognize in this requirement the last, miserable residue to something more imposing and more meaningful. The symptom that something is a residue—whether in biology or in history—is that we do not perceive why it is with us. In its present form, it serves no end at all; one must trace it back to some other age of its

6. AUTHOR'S NOTE: This number needs to be greater than has been attained at present; but even so, incomparably smaller than the number in the other professions.

evolution in order to find whole and active what exists today only as a residual stump.[7] The justification which is advanced today, in support of that ancient precept of higher education, is rather vague. The student ought, it is said, to receive something of "general culture."

"General culture." The absurdity of the term, its Philistinism, betrays its insincerity. "Culture," referring to the human mind and not to stock or crops, cannot be anything else but general. There is no being "cultured" in physics or mathematics. That would mean simply to be *learned* in a particular subject. The usage of the expression "general culture" shows an underlying notion that the student ought to be given some ornamental knowledge, which in some way is to educate his moral character or his intellect. For so vague a purpose, one discipline is as good as another, among those that are more or less indefinite and not so technical—like philosophy, or history, or sociology!

But the fact is that if we go back to the medieval epoch in which the university was created, we see clearly that the relic before us is the humble remains of what then constituted higher education, proper and entire.

The medieval university does no research.[8] It is very little concerned with professions. All is *"general culture"*—theology, philosophy, "arts." [9]

But what is called "general culture" today was something very different for the Middle Ages. It was not an ornament for the mind or a training of the character. It was, on the contrary, the system of ideas, concerning the world and humanity, which the man of that time possessed. It was, consequently, the repertory of convictions which became the effective guide of his existence.

Life is a chaos, a tangled and confused jungle in which man is lost. But his mind reacts against the sensation of bewilderment: he labors to find "roads," "ways" through the woods,[10] in the form of clear, firm ideas

---

7. AUTHOR'S NOTE: Imagine for a moment the conditions of primitive life. One of its constant characteristics is the lack of personal security. It is perilous for two persons to approach each other, for everyone goes about armed. Hence this act has to be safeguarded by customs and ceremonies which give assurance that weapons have been left behind, and that the hand is not going to reach suddenly for one that is hidden. For this purpose, the best procedure is for each man, upon approaching, to grasp the hand of the other—the killing hand, which is normally the right hand. Such is the origin and purpose of our salute by shaking hands, which in the present times, remote from the type of life, is an incomprehensible relic.

8. AUTHOR'S NOTE: Which does not mean that no research was done in the Middle Ages.

9. EDITOR'S NOTE: The exaggeration here does not essentially damage Sr. Ortega's thesis that the modern university should teach a kind of "culture" which this reference to the Middle Ages helps to describe.

10. AUTHOR'S NOTE: Whence there arises at the beginning of all cultures a term expressing "road" in this sense: the *odos* and *methods* of the Greeks, the *tao* and *te* of the Chinese, the *path* and *vehicle* of India.

concerning the universe, positive convictions about the nature of things. The ensemble, or system, of these ideas, is culture in the true sense of the term; it is precisely the opposite of external ornament. Culture is what saves human life from being a mere disaster; it is what enables man to live a life which is something above meaningless tragedy or inward disgrace.

We cannot live on the human level without ideas. Upon them depends what we do. Living is nothing more nor less than doing one thing instead of another. Hence the oldest book of India: "Our acts follow our thoughts as the wheel of the cart follows the hoof of the ox." In this sense—which by itself implies no intellectualistic doctrine—we *are* our ideas.[11]

Gideon, in this case exceptionally profound, would make it clear that man is always born into a specific period. That is, he is called to live his life at some definite stage in the unfolding of human destinies. A man belongs to a generation; he is of one substance with it. And each generation takes its place not in some chance location, but directly and squarely upon the preceding one. This comes to mean that man lives, perforce, at *the level of his time,* and more particularly, at *the level of the ideas of his time.*[12]

Culture is the *vital* system of ideas of a period. It makes not a particle of difference whether these ideas, or convictions, lie partly or wholly in the province of science. Culture is not science. It is characteristic of our present culture that a great part of its content proceeds out of science; but in other cultures this has not been the case, nor is it decreed anywhere that in ours it will always be so to the same degree as at present.

Compared with the medieval university, the contemporary university has developed the mere seed of professional instruction into an enormous activity; it has added the function of research; and it has abandoned almost entirely the teaching or transmission of culture.

It is evident that the change has been pernicious. Europe today is taking its sinister consequences. The convulsive situation in Europe at the present moment is due to the fact that the average Englishman, the average Frenchman, the average German are *uncultured:* they are ignorant of the essential system of ideas concerning the world and man, which belong to our time. This average person is the new barbarian, a laggard behind the contemporary civilization archaic and primitive in contrast with his problems, which are grimly, relentlessly modern.[13]This

11. AUTHOR'S NOTE: Our ideas, or convictions may well be unintellectualistic, as mine are, and in general, the ideas of our age.

12. AUTHOR'S NOTE: For the concept of "the height of the times," see *The Revolt of the Masses.*

13. AUTHOR'S NOTE: The analysis of this serious situation is presented in *The Revolt of the Masses.*

new barbarian is above all the professional man, more learned than ever before, but at the same time more uncultured—the engineer, the physician, the lawyer, the scientist.

The blame for this unpredicted barbarity, this radical and tragic anachronism, rests primarily with the pretentious nineteenth-century university of all countries. If this institution should by chance be torn to bits in the frenzy of a barbarous revolution, it would not have the feeblest reason to complain. When one has examined the matter, he must needs come to the conclusion that the guilt of the universities is not compensated for by the prodigious and brilliant service which they have undeniably rendered to science. Let us not be the dupes of science. For if science is the grandest creation of man, it is made possible, after all, by human life. A crime perpetrated against the fundamental conditions of human life cannot be atoned for through science.

The harm is so ingrained that I shall barely be understood by the generation anterior to the one I am addressing.

In the book of a Chinese thinker who lived in the fourth century B.C., Chuang-tsu, certain symbolic characters are conversing together, and one of them, called the God of the Northern Sea, asks, "How shall I talk of the sea to the frog, if he has never left his pond? How shall I talk of the frost to the bird of the summer land, if it has never left the land of its birth? How shall I talk of life with the sage, if he is the prisoner of his doctrine?"

Society needs good professional men—judges, doctors, engineers— and therefore the university is prepared to furnish professional training. But society needs before this, and more than this, to be assured that the capacity is developed for another kind of profession, the profession of governing. In every society someone governs, whether a group or a class, few people or many. By "governing" I mean not so much the legal exercise of authority as a diffuse pressure, or influence, exerted upon the body politic. Today, the societies in Europe are governed by the bourgeois classes, whose majority is composed of professional men. It is of the first importance to these societies, therefore, that these professional people, aside from their several professions, possess the power to make their lives a vital influence, in harmony with the height of their times. Hence it is imperative to set up once more, in the university, the teaching of the culture, the system of vital ideas, which the age has attained. This is the basic function of the university. This is what the university must be, above all else.

If the working man should become the governing man tomorrow, the problem remains the same: he must govern in accordance with the height of the times—otherwise his regime will be supplanted.[14]

14. AUTHOR'S NOTE: Since in actual practice the working man does govern, sharing that function with the middle class, it is urgent that the university education be extended to him.

When one considers that the European countries have deemed it admissible to grant professional titles and prestige to magistrates and doctors without making sure that these men have a clear idea, for example, of the physical conception we now have of the world, and an equally clear idea of the character and limitations of the marvelous science by which that concept has been attained—we need not be surprised that affairs have come to such a pass in Europe. At a juncture like this, let us not bandy aobut fine phrases. The vague desire for a vague culture, I repeat, will lead us nowhere. Physics, and its method, is one of the great essential instruments of the modern mind. Into that science have gone four centuries of intellectual discipline, and its doctrine is intimately connected with the cultured man's concept of God and society, of matter and that which is not matter, together with all the other essentials for an enlightened life. Of course, one can do without that science and be neither disgraced nor condemned—in certain situations: if one is a humble shepherd in the hills, or a serf attached to the soil, or a manual laborer enslaved to the machine. But the gentleman who professes to be a doctor, or magistrate, or general, or philologist, or bishop—that is, a person who belongs to the directive class of society—if he is ignorant of what the physical cosmos is today for the European man, is a perfect barbarian, however well he may know his laws, or his medicines, or his Holy Fathers. And I should say the same of the person who has not a decently coherent picture of the great movements of history which have brought Humanity to its present parting of ways (for ours is a day of crucial situations). And I should say the same again of the person who has no definite idea of how speculative philosophy conceives today its perpetual essay to formulate a plan of the universe; or how biology endeavors to interpret the fundamental facts of organic life.

For the moment, let us not obscure this simple, evident proposition, by raising the question of how a lawyer, without preparation in higher mathematics, can understand the idea of twentieth-century physics. We shall deal with that question later. For now, let us simply admit into our minds, as we must, the light which proceeds from this observation. The man who does not possess the concept of physics (not the science of physics proper, but the vital idea of the world which it has created), and the concept afforded by history and by biology, and the scheme of speculative philosophy, is not an educated man. Unless he should happen to be endowed with exceptional qualities, it is extremely unlikely that such a man will be, in the fullest sense, a good doctor, a good judge, or a good technical expert. But it is certain that all the other things he does in life, including parts of his profession itself which transcend its proper academic boundaries, will turn out unfortunately. His political ideas and actions will be inept; his affairs of the heart, beginning with the type of woman he will prefer, will be crude and ridiculous; he will bring to his family life an atmosphere of unreality and cramped narrowness, which will warp the upbringing of his children; and outside, with his friends, he will emit thoughts that are monstrosities, and opinions that are a torrent of drivel and bluff.

There is no other way: to move with assurance in the tangle of life, one must be cultivated, one must know the topography—the "ways" and "methods." One must have an idea of the time and place in which he lives: in a word, the "culture" of the age. Now then, this culture is either received, or else it is invented. He who exposes himself to the labor of inventing it for himself, accomplishing alone what thirty centuries of humanity have already accomplished, is the only man who has the right to deny the proposition that the university must undertake to impart culture. But the unfortunate truth is that this lone person, who could oppose my thesis, would have to be a madman!

Civilization has had to await the beginning of the twentieth century, to see the astounding spectacle of how brutal, how stupid, and yet how aggressive is the man learned in one thing and fundamentally ignorant of all else. Professionalism and specialism, through insufficient counter-balancing, have smashed the European man in pieces; and he is consequently missing at all the points where he claims to be, and is badly needed. The engineer possesses engineering; but that is just one piece, one dimension of the European man: the whole man is not to be found in this fragment called "engineer." And so in the rest of the cases. When one says that "Europe is broken in pieces," thinking to use a baroque and exaggerated expression, he says more truth than he suspects. Indeed, the crumbling away of Europe which we are witnessing is the result of the invisible fragmentation that the European man has progressively undergone.[16]

The great task immediately before us is something like a jigsaw puzzle: we have to reassemble out of scattered pieces—*disiecta membra*—a complete living organism, the European man. What we must achieve is that every individual, or (not to be Utopian) many individuals, should each succeed in constituting the type of the whole man in its entirety. What force can bring this about, if it is not the university?

Then there are no two ways about it. The university must add this other function, huge as it is, to the list of those it already attempts to accomplish.

For that matter, outside Spain a movement is making itself felt with great vigor, to orient higher education toward the teaching of culture, or

15. AUTHOR'S NOTE: See the chapter entitled "The barbarism of specialization" in *The Revolt of the Masses*.

16. AUTHOR'S NOTE: The statement is true to such a point that it cannot only be made thus vaguely, but it can be developed by enumerating the precise phases of the progressive fragmentation, in the three generations of the past century and the first generation of the twentieth.

the transmission to the newer generation of the system of ideas concerning the world and man which has reached its maturity with the passing generation.

We come to the conclusion therefore that the university's teaching comprises these three functions:

    I. The transmission of culture.
    II. The teaching of the professions.
    III. Scientific research and the training of new scientists.

Have we thus answered our question, What is the mission of the university? By no means: we have only massed together what the university of today believes to be its business, and one thing which, in our judgment, it is not doing but must do. We have prepared the question; no more than that.

It seems to me unnecessary, or at least incidental, to debate as did the philosopher Scheler and the Minister of Education Becker, a few years ago, over the question whether these functions are to be performed by a single institution or by various institutions. It is vain because in the end all these functions would unite in the person of the student: they would all eventually come to gravitate around his adolescent years, as a common center.[17]

The question is different. It is this: Even when instruction is limited, as at present, to professional matter and the methods of science, the result is a fabulous profusion of studies. It is impossible even for the better than ordinary student to come anywhere near real success in learning what the university professes to teach him. But institutions exist—they are necessary and they have meaning—because the ordinary man exists. If there were none but extraordinary creatures, it is very probable that there would be no institutions, either educational or political.[18] It is therefore necesssary to consider any institution with reference to the man of ordinary endowment. For him it is made, and he must be its unit of measure.

Let us suppose for a moment that in the university, as it is, we find nothing which deserves to be called an abuse. Everything is running smoothly and properly according to what the university professes itself to be. Very well: even then I should say the university of today is an abuse in itself, because it is, in itself, a falsehood.

---

17. EDITOR'S NOTE: See especially Carl Heinrich Becker (by error "Beeker" in the Spanish editions), *Gedanken zur Hochschulreform*, Leipzig: Quelle u. Meyer, 1919; and Max Scheler, *"Innere Widersprüche der deutschen Universitäten," Westdeutsche Wochenschrift* 1, 32: 493–495; 33: 511–512; 34: 524–527; 35: 539–541; 36: 551–553.

18. AUTHOR'S NOTE: Anarchy is logical when it declares all institutions to be useless and thus pernicious, for it starts with the postulate that every man is extraordinary by birth—i.e. good, prudent, intelligent, and just.

It is so thoroughly impossible for the ordinary student to master what the university tries to teach him, that it has become a part of university life to accept the failure. In other words, it is taken for granted as a regular thing, that what the university attempts to be is a delusion. We accept the falsity of the university's inward life—its very essence is composed of its own falsification. This is the root of the whole trouble (as it always is in life, individual or collective). The original sin stems from the pretension to be other than one's true self. It is our privilege to *try* to be whatever we wish; but it is vicious to pretend to be what we are not, and to delude ourselves by growing habituated to a radically false idea of what we are. When the habitual behavior of a man or an institution is false, the next step is complete demoralization. And thence to degeneracy, for it is not possible for anyone to submit to the falsification of his nature without losing his self-respect.

That is why Leonardo da Vinci said: "Chi non può quel che vuol, quel che può voglia"—"Who cannot what he will, let him will what he can."

This maxim of Leonardo's must guide from the beginning any real reform of the university. Only a firm resolution to be genuine will bear fruit. And not only the life of the university, but the whole new life must be fashioned by artisans whose first thought is *authenticity*. (Note this, Younger Generation. Otherwise, you are lost. In fact you show signs of being lost already.)

An institution, then, which feigns to give and to require what it cannot, is false and demoralized. Yet this principle of deceit is to be found throughout the whole plan and structure of the present university.

The conclusion seems to me inescapable, that we must turn the present university upside down, so to speak, and stand it upon precisely the opposite principle. Instead of teaching what *ought* to be taught, according to some Utopian desire, we must teach only what *can* be taught; that is, *what can be learned.*

I shall attempt to develop the implications of this formula.

The problem extends in reality quite beyond the subject of higher education. It involves the capital question of education at all levels.

What has been the great historic advance in pedagogy? Beyond doubt, the turn it has taken under the inspiration of Rousseau, Pestalozzi, Froebel, and German idealism, amounting to a revolutionary avowal of the obvious. In education there are three elemental factors: what is taught (knowledge, wisdom), and the teacher and the learner. Yet with peculiar blindness, education had centered about knowledge and the teacher. The learner was no factor in pedagogy. The innovation of Rousseau and his successors was simply to shift the center of gravity of the science from knowledge and the teacher to the learner, recognizing that it is the learner and his characteristics which alone can guide us in our effort to make something organic of education. Knowledge and research have their own structure, which is not applicable to that other activity proposing to impart knowledge. The principle of pedagogy is entirely different from that on which culture and science are built.

But we must go a step further. Rather than lose ourselves in a minute study of the learner's characteristics as a child, as a youth, etc., we are constrained to limit the subject for our present purpose, and consider the child and the youth from a more modest point of view, which is more precise: namely, as a student and apprentice. Then we strike upon the fact that it is not the child as a child, or the youth because of his youth, that obliges us to ply this special profession we call "teaching." It is something far less complicated, and in fact, very definite and simple.

Let me explain.

CHAPTER III—THE PRINCIPLE OF ECONOMY IN EDUCATION

The science of political economy emerged from the war in much the same shattered state as did the economies of the belligerent nations. There was nothing to do but set about reconstructing this whole body of knowledge from the ground up. Such adventures are as a rule beneficial in the life of a science, for they force it to seek a more solid basis than has been in use, a more general and fundamental principle. And in fact at the present time, political economy is arising from its ruins, for a reason so obvious that it is embarrassing to mention. To wit: that economic *science* necessarily responds to the fundamental principle underlying the economic *activity* of man. Why is it that mankind engages in economic occupations, producing, managing, bartering, saving, appraising, etc.? For one astonishing reason, and that alone: because many of the things man desires and requires are not to be had in unlimited abundance. If all we need existed in plenty and to spare, it would never have occurred to men to fatigue themselves with economic exertion. Air, for example, does not usually give rise to activity we could call economic. Yet as soon as air becomes scarce in some way or other, it immediately occasions economic activity. For example children in a schoolroom need a certain amount of air. If the room is small there is a scarcity of air; hence an economic problem, ending in an enlarged school which is accordingly more expensive.

Again, even though our planet is rolling in air, so to speak, its air is not all of the same quality. "Pure air" is to be had only at certain places, at certain altitudes, under specific conditions of climate. "Pure air" is scarce. And that simple fact provokes an intense economic activity among the Swiss—hotels, sanitariums—converting this scarce raw material into health, at so much per day.

This is all astonishingly simple, I repeat; but it is undeniably true. Scarcity is the basis of economic activity, and indeed the Swedish economist Cassel, some years ago, revised the science of economics by taking as a point of departure the *principle of scarcity*.[1]Einstein has remarked many times that "if perpetual motion existed, there would be no such thing as physics." Similarly, we may be sure that in Elysium there is no economic activity, and consequently no science of economics.

I am persuaded that an analogous situation has its effect in education. Why does pedagogical activity exist at all? Why is it an occupation and a preoccupation of man? To these questions the romantics gave most brilliant, moving, and transcendental answers, in which they drew upon all things human and a good portion of the divine. For their taste, it was always necessary to obscure the bare nature of things with festoons of ornamental foliage, and a touch of melodrama. We, on the contrary— am I not right, young people?—we are content to accept things for what they are (at least for the time being), and nothing more. We like their bareness. We do not mind cold and inclemency. We know that life is hard, and will be hard. We accept the rigor of it; we do not try to sophisticate destiny. Because life is hard, it does not seem to us any the less magnificent. On the contrary, if it is hard it is also solid and sturdy. Above all, it is free of any hypocrisy. We value openness in our dealings with things. We like to strip things bare, and when they are thus denuded, to wash them clean as we examine them, and see what they are *in puris naturalibus*.

Man is occupied and preoccupied with education for a reason which is simple, bald, and devoid of glamour: in order to live with assurance and freedom and efficiency, it is necessary to know an enormous number of things, and the child or youth has an extremely limited capacity for learning. That is the reason. If childhood and youth lasted a century apiece, or if the child and the adolescent possessed intelligence and the power of attention practically without limit, the teaching activity would never exist. Even if those appealing, transcendental reasons had never operated at all, mankind would have had to develop that variety of the species known as the teacher.

Scarcity of the capacity to learn is the cardinal principle of education. It is necessary to provide for teaching precisely in proportion as the learner is unable to learn.

Is it not a too striking coincidence that the ferment in education erupted toward the middle of the eighteenth century, and has continued to increase up to the present? Why did this not happen sooner? The explanation is simple: it was precisely at that time that the first great

1. AUTHOR'S NOTE: See Gustavo Cassel, *Theoretische Sozialœkonomie*, 1921, pp. 3 ff. In part this amounts to a return to some positions of classic economics, as opposed to the economics of the last sixty years.

flowering of modern culture ripened for harvest. In a short time, the treasure of active human knowledge became enlarged by a tremendous increment. Life was entering into the full swing of the new capitalism, which recent inventions had made possible: life was consequently assuming a new and appalling complexity, and it was exacting a greater and greater equipment of technics. Accordingly, along with the necessity for learning a quantity of things quite beyond the capacity to learn, pedagogy was promptly intensified and expanded to meet the need.

In primitive epochs, on the other hand, there is scarcely such a thing as education? Why should there be, if there is scarcely any need for it—if the capacity to learn is far ahead of the material to be assimilated? The capacity is in excess. There are but a few branches of knowledge, certain magic formulas and rituals for fabricating the most difficult instruments, like the canoe, or for curing illness and casting out devils. This is all the subject matter there is. Since it is so scant, anyone could learn it without applying himself with any special effort. Hence there arises a peculiar situation, which corroborates my thesis in the most unexpected fashion. The fact is that education appears among primitive peoples in an inverted form: The vocation of teaching is actually one of concealing. The sacred formulas are conserved as secrets, and passed on esoterically to a chosen few. Outsiders would learn them all too readily. Whence the universal phenomenon of secret rites.

The phenomenon is so persistent that it reappears at any level of civilization, when there arises a particularly novel variety of knowledge, superior in kind to all that has been previously known. Since the new and enviable knowledge exists at first only in small quantity, it is a valuable kind of property, to be imparted only in jealous secrecy. Thus it happened with the Pythagorean school's philosophy of precision, and even with so enlightened a philosopher as Plato. For we have his famous seventh epistle, written with the purpose of protesting against the accusation that he had taught his philosophy to Dionysius of Syracuse, as if that were a heinous crime. All primitive education, in which there is little to teach, is esoteric and secretive; in that respect it is the antithesis of education as we conceive it in our day.

Education comes into being, then, when the knowledge which has to be acquired is out of proportion to the capacity to learn. Today, more than ever before, the profusion of cultural and technical possessions is such that it threatens to bring a catastrophe upon mankind, in as much as every generation is finding it more nearly impossible to assimilate it.

2. EDITOR'S NOTE: The primitive cultures we are able to observe do of course transmit to their youth considerable knowledge of zoology and anatomy, botany, social usage and even philosophy of the differences in tribal cultures. But the point remains valid, that primitive cultures are not confronted with the problem of an unmanageable quantity of important knowledge.

It is urgent therefore that we base our science of teaching, its methods and institutions, upon the plain, humble principle that the child or the youth who is to be the learner cannot learn all we should like him to know—the principle of economy in education.

Since it could not be otherwise, this rule has always been in operation where there has been pedagogical activity; but only because it could not be helped, and hence in a restricted degree. It has never been set up as a principle, perhaps because at first sight it is not dramatic—it does not talk of imposing transcendentals.

The university of today, outside Spain even more than within, is a tropical underbrush of subject matters. If to this we add what we have deemed imperative—the teaching of culture—the verdure threatens to hide the horizon altogether: the horizon of youth which needs to be clear and open, in order that it may expose to view the beckoning glow afar off. There is no remedy but to rise up against this turgid overgrowth and use the principle of economy like a hatchet. First of all, a thorough pruning.

The principle of economy not only implies that it is necessary to economize in the subject matter to be offered. It has a further implication: that the organization of higher education, the construction of the university, must be based upon the student, and not upon the professor or upon knowledge. The university must be the projection of the student to the scale of an institution. And his two dimensions are, first, what he is—a being of limited learning capacity—and second, what he needs to know in order to live his life.

(The present student movement comprises many ingredients. Out of the conventional ten parts, seven are made up of pure buffoonery. But the other three are absolutely reasonable and more than justify the whole student agitation. One is the political unrest of the country: the soul of the nation is perturbed. The second is a series of real though incredible abuses on the part of a few professors. And the third, which is the most important and decisive, influences the students without their realizing it. It is the fact that neither they nor anybody in particular, but the times themselves, the present circumstances in education throughout the world, are forcing the university to center itself once more on the student—to *be* the student, and not the professor, as it was in the heyday of its greatness.[3] The tendencies of the times press on inevitably, though mankind, impelled as it is by them, may be unaware of their presence, and quite unable to define them or give them a name. The students should eliminate the discreditable parts of their activity

3. EDITOR'S NOTE: This is true of both the Parisian and the Bolognese families of the medieval university. While Paris is said to have had a "magisterial constitution," as opposed to the "student constitution" of the other family, yet even at Paris the students, through their organization in "nations," had a responsible part in the maintenance of discipline and morale.

and emphasize these three, especially the last, for in these they are entirely right.[4])

We must begin, therefore, with the ordinary student, and take as the nucleus of the institution, as its central and basic portion, *exclusively* the subject matters which can be required with absolute stringency, i.e. those a good ordinary student can really learn.

This, I repeat, is what the university should be, at its very base. Presently we shall see that the university must be, in addition, several other things which are no less important. But what is important at this point is not to confuse things: it is to separate carefully from one another the various functions and organs of that imposing institution, the university.

How are we to determine the body of subjects which are to constitute the torso or *minimum* of the curriculum? By submitting the present conglomeration to two tests:

1. We must pick out that which appears as strictly necessary for the life of the man who is now a student. Life, with its inexorable requirements, is the criterion that should guide this first stroke of the pruning knife.

2. What remains, having been judged strictly necessary, must be further reduced to what the student can really learn with thoroughness and understanding.

It is not enough that this or that is necessary. When we least expect, the necessary suddenly passes beyond the capabilities of the student. It would be fantastic on our part to rant and rave that it is necessary. Only so much must be taught as can truly be learned. On this point we must be unshakable, though the line of action which issues from it is drastic.

CHAPTER IV—WHAT THE UNIVERSITY MUST BE PRIMARILY: THE UNIVERSITY; PROFESSION AND SCIENCE

By applying the principles we have discussed, we come to the following propositions:

(A) The university consists, primarily and basically, of the higher education which the ordinary man should receive.

---

4. AUTHOR'S NOTE: The concept that the university *is* the student is to be carried out even to the point of affecting its material organization. It is absurd to consider the university, as it has been considered hitherto, the professor's house in which he receives pupils. Rather the contrary: put the students in charge of the house, and let the student body constitute the torso of the institution, complemented by the faculties of professors. The maintenance of discipline through beadles gives rise to shameful squabbles, and organizes the students into a rebellious horde. The students are not to blame, but the institution, which is badly planned. The students themselves, properly organized for the purpose, should direct the internal ordering of the university, determine the decorum of usages and manners, impose disciplinary measures, and feel responsible for the morale.

(B) It is necessary to make of this ordinary man, first of all, a cultured person: to put him at the height of the times. It follows then, that the primary function of the university is to teach the great cultural disciplines, namely:

1. The physical scheme of the world (Physics).
2. The fundamental themes of organic life (Biology).
3. The historical process of the human species (History).
4. The structure and functioning of social life (Sociology).
5. The plan of the universe (Philosophy).

(C) It is necessary to make the ordinary man a good professional. Besides his apprenticeship to culture, the university will teach him, by the most economical, direct and efficacious procedures intellect can devise, to be a good doctor, a good judge, a good teacher of mathematics or of history. The specific character of this professional teaching must be set aside, however, for fuller discussion.

(D) There is no cogent reason why the ordinary man needs or ought to be a scientist. Scandalous consequence: science in the true sense, i.e. scientific investigation, does not belong in any direct, constituent capacity among the primary functions of the university. It is something independent. In what sense the university is inseparable from science, and must be in addition a place of scientific research, is a question we shall treat further on.

No doubt this heretical opinion will call down on itself the deluge of inanities which always threatens from the horizon, like a cloud with teeming paunch. I realize that there are serious objections against this thesis of mine; but before these are advanced, we shall see erupting that volcano of commonplaces which every man becomes when he speaks on a question he has not thought out beforehand.

The plan of a university which I am expounding requires that you indulgently dispose your mind to distinguish three things, each quite different from the others: namely science, culture, and learned profession. You must renounce that restful light in which all cats are gray.

First let us differentiate between profession and science. Science is not just whatever you will. Obviously, it is not science to buy yourself a microscope or to throw together a laboratory. But *neither is it science to expound, or learn, the content of a science.* In its proper and authentic sense, science is exclusively investigation: the setting up of problems, working at them, and arriving at their solution. From the moment a solution is reached, all that may subsequently be done with the solution is not science.[1] And that is why it is not science to learn or teach a science, or to

---

1. AUTHOR'S NOTE: Except to question it afresh, to convert it back to a problem by criticizing it, and hence to repeat the cycle of scientific investigation.

apply and appropriate science. It may well be best—with what reservations, we shall presently see—for the man entrusted with the teaching of a science to be a scientist at the same time. But that is not absolutely necessary, and as a matter of fact there have been and are prodigious teachers of the sciences who are not investigators, i.e. scientists. It is sufficient that they *know* their science. But to know is not to investigate. To investigate is to discover a truth, or inversely, to demonstrate an error. To know means to assimilate a truth into one's consciousness, to possess a fact after it has been attained and secured.

At the beginnings of science, in Greece, when there was yet little science to be had ready made, men hardly ran the same risk of confusing it with things which are not science. The words they used to designate science exposed its identity with inquiry, creative work, investigation. Even the contemporaries of Plato and Aristotle lacked any term to match exactly—including its equivocalness—the modern word "science." They spoke of *historía, exétasis, philosophía,* which mean, with one nuance or another, "a learning by inquiry," "a searching out," and "a systematic treatment of a subject, or scientific investigation"—but not "possession of knowledge." The name *philo-sophía* arose, comparatively late, from the effort to distinguish from the usual learning that novel activity which was not to *be learned,* but to *seek* knowledge.[2]

Science is one of the most sublime pursuits and achievements of mankind: more sublime than the university itself, conceived as an educational institution. For science is creation, and teaching aims only to convey what has been created, to digest it and to induce learners to digest it. Science is carried on upon so high a plane that it is necessarily an extremely delicate process. Whether we like it or not, science excludes the ordinary man. It involves a calling most infrequent, and remote from the ordinary run of the human species. The scientist is the monk of modern times.

To pretend that the normal student is a scientist is at once a ridiculous pretension, which could scarcely have been contracted (pretensions are contracted, like colds and other inflammations) but for that vice of utopianism, the bane of the generation just preceding ours. But furthermore it is not desirable, even under ideal circumstances, that the ordinary man should be a scientist. If science is one of the highest of human pursuits, it is not the only one. There are others of equal dignity, and there is no reason to sacrifice these, dedicating all humanity to science. The sublimity, moreover, belongs to science itself and not to the man of science. His career is a mode of existence quite as limited and narrow as another; in fact more so than some of you could imagine. Here I cannot

---

2. AUTHOR'S NOTE: The term *epistéme* correspnds better to the bundle of meanings included in our words "knowledge" and "understanding." For the astonishment occasioned by the novel term *philosophía,* see Cicero, *Tusculan Disputations,* V, 3.

embark on an analysis of what it means to be a scientist. Nor do I wish to. It would be out of place, and besides, some of what I should say might appear noisome. Returning then to the essential matter, let me observe that up to our time at least, the *real* scientist, considered as a person, has been with notorious frequency a visionary and a freak, when he has not been absolutely demented. The real marvel, the precious thing, is what this very limited person succeeds in isolating: the pearl, not the oyster that secreted it. It is futile to idealize the scientist and hold him up as the model for all men to imitate, without taking into account the complex circumstances—miraculous, some of them, and some of them quite unfathomable—which are wont to enter into the making of a scientist.[3]

The teaching of the professions and the search for truth *must* be separated. They must be clearly distinguished one from the other, both in the minds of the professors and in the minds of the students. For their present confusion is an impediment to science. Granted, the apprenticeship to some professions includes as a very important element the mastery of the systematized content of numerous sciences; but this content is the end result of investigation, and not the investigation itself. As a general principle, the normal student is not an apprentice to science. The physician is learning to effect cures, and as a physician he need not go beyond that. For his purpose, he needs to know the system of physiology current in his day, but he need not be, and in fact cannot be expected to be, a trained physiologist. Why do we persist in expecting the impossible? I cannot understand. I am only disgusted by this itching to delude oneself—"you *have* to have your illusions"—this everlasting delusion of grandeur, this die-hard utopianism of persuading ourselves that we are achieving what we are not. Utopianism results in a pedagogy of self-abuse.

It is the virtue of the child to think in terms of wishes, it is the child's role to make believe. But the virtue of the grown man is to will, and his role is to do and achieve. Now we can achieve things only by concentrating our energy: by limiting ourselves. And in this limiting of ourselves lies the truth and the authenticity of our life. Indeed, all life is destiny: if our existence were unlimited in duration and in the forms it could assume, there would be no "destiny."[4] The authentic life, young people,

3. AUTHOR'S NOTE: It is notorious for example how readily scientists have always acquiesced in tyrannical governments. This is no cause for disappointment, nor can it be considered a liability to society. The cause of it lies in the very nature of the scientist, and is perfectly respectable.

4. EDITOR'S NOTE: Ortega's term "destino" presents much the same difficulty as Aristotle's two terms δυναμιζ and ενεργεια, for which English translators have found no satisfying translation. The organism is conceived as being endowed with a specific *potentiality*, whose *realization* constitutes the organism's proper life. The term "destiny," as well as another, will take on the intended meaning as the essay proceeds.

consists in cheerfully accepting an inexorable destiny—a limitation we cannot alter. It is this state of mind which the mystics, following a profound intuition, used to call "the state of grace." He who has once honestly accepted his destiny, his own limitations, is imperturbable. *"Impavidum ferient ruinae."*

If a man has the calling to be a physician and nothing more, let him not dabble in science. He will but turn science into mediocrity. It is enough, in fact it is everything, that he is a good physician. The same holds in my opinion for the man who is a good professor of history in a secondary school. Is it not a mistake to confuse him in college by making him think he is going to be an historian? What do you gain? You force him to consume his time in a fragmentary study of techniques necessary to the research of the historian, but irrelevant to the teaching of history. You excuse him from that other task of achieving a clear, organized, comprehensible idea of the general body of human history, which it is his mission to teach.[5]

The trend toward a university dominated by "inquiry" has been disastrous. It has led to the elimination of the prime concern: culture. It has deflected attention from the problem of how best to train future professionals for their professions.

The medical schools aspire to teach physiology and chemistry complete to the nth degree; but perhaps in no medical school the world over is there anyone seriously occupied with thinking out what it really means to be a good physician, what the ideal type should be for our times. The profession, which after culture is the most urgent concern, is entrusted largely to the kindness of Providence. But the harm of our confused procedure has worked both ways. Science too has suffered by our wishful attempt to bring it into line alongside the professions.

Pedantry and the want of reflection have been large causes in bringing on the "scientism" which afflicts the university. In Spain, both these deplorable forces are coming to be a serious nuisance. Any nincompoop that has been six months in a school or a laboratory in Germany or North America, any parrot that has made a third rate scientific discovery, comes back a *nouveau riche* of science. Without having reflected a quarter of an hour on the mission of the university, he propounds the most pedantic and ridiculous reforms. Moreover he is incapable of teaching his own courses, for he has no grasp of the discipline as a whole.

We must therefore shake science off the tree of the professions, and retain only the portion of science which is strictly necessary, in order to

---

5. AUTHOR'S NOTE: It is obvious that he must learn what composes the techniques by which history is obtained. But this does not mean that he must become an adept, himself, in these techniques.

attend to the professions themselves, whose teaching, today, runs quite wild. At this step everything is still to be begun.[6]

Logical organization and ingenious teaching will make it possible to teach the professions much more efficiently and with greater breadth, with less time and effort than at present.

But now let us proceed to that other distinction, between science and culture.

CHAPTER V—CULTURE AND SCIENCE

If we review in substance the distinction between profession and science, we find ourselves in possession of a few clear ideas. For example, medicine is not a science but a profession, a matter of practice. Hence it represents a point of view distinct from that of science. It proposes as its object to restore and maintain health in the human species. To this end, it appropriates what it finds useful: it goes to science and takes whatever results of research it considers efficacious; but it leaves all the rest. It leaves particularly what is most characteristic of science: the cultivation of the problematic and doubtful. This would suffice to differentiate radically between medicine and science. Science consists in an urge to solve problems; the more it is engaged in this occupation, the more purely it accomplishes its mission. But medicine exists for the purpose of applying solutions. If they happen to be scientific, so much the better. But they are not necessarily so. They may have grown out of some millennial experience which science has not yet explained or even confirmed.

In the last fifty years, medicine has allowed itself to be swept off its feet by science, it has neglected its own mission and failed to assert properly its own professional point of view.[1] Medicine has committed the besetting sin of that whole period: namely, to look askance at destiny and strain to be something else—in this case, pure science.

Let us make no mistake about it. Science, upon entering into a profession, must be detached from its place in pure science, to be organized upon a new center and a new principle, as professional tech-

---

6. AUTHOR'S NOTE: The basic idea, the prototype of each profession—what it means to be a doctor, judge, lawyer, professor, etc.—is not at present delineated in the popular mind, nor does anyone devote himself to studying and formulating such an idea.

1. AUTHOR'S NOTE: On the other hand, when medicine has devoted itself to its proper function of curing, its work has proved most fruitful for science. Contemporary physiology was launched on its career, early in the last century, not by scientists but by the physicians, who turned aside from the scholasticism that had reigned over eighteenth century biology (taxonomy, anatomism, etc.) to meet their urgent mission with pragmatic theories. See Emanuel Radl, *Geschichte der biologischen Theorien*, vol. II (1909), a book which seems the more admirable with the passing of time.

nics. And if this is true, it must certainly have an effect on the teaching of the professions.

Something similar is to be said of the relations between culture and science. The difference between them seems to me clear enough. Yet I should like not only to leave the concept of culture very definite in the mind of the reader but also to show what basis it has. First, the reader must go to the trouble of scrutinizing and reflecting upon the following résumé—which will not be easy: culture is the system of vital ideas which each age possesses; better yet, it is the system of ideas *by* which the age lives. There is no denying the fact that man invariably lives according to some definite ideas which constitute the very foundation of his way of life. These ideas which I have called "vital," meaning ideas by which an age conducts its life, are no more nor less than the repertory of our *active* convictions as to the nature of our world and our fellow creatures, convictions as to the hierarchy of the values of things—which are more to be esteemed, and which less.[2]

It is not in our hands, whether to possess such a repertory of convictions or not. It is a matter of inescapable necessity, an ingredient essential to every human life, of whatever sort it may be. The reality we are wont to refer to as "human life," your life and the next fellow's, is something quite remote from biology, the science of organisms. Biology, like any other science, is no more than one occupation to which some men devote their "life." The basic and truest meaning of the word *life* is not biological but biographical: and that is the meaning it has always had in the language of the people. It means the totality of what we do and what we are—that formidable business, which every man must exercise on his own, of maintaining a place in the scheme of things and steering a course among the beings of the world. "To live is, in fact, to have dealing with the world: to address oneself to it, exert oneself in it, and occupy oneself with it."[3] If these actions and occupations which compose our living were produced in us mechanically, the result would not be human life. The automaton does not *live*. The whole difficulty of the matter is that life is not given us ready made. Like it or not, we must go along from instant to instant, deciding for ourselves. At each moment it is necessary to make up our minds what we are going to do next: the life of man is an ever recurrent problem. In order to decide at one instant what he is going to do or to be at the next, man is compelled to form a plan of some sort, however simple or puerile it may be. It is not that he *ought* to make a plan. There is simply no possible life, sublime or mean, wise or

2. EDITOR'S NOTE: Cf. Ortega's *The Modern Theme*, p. 75: "Culture is merely a special direction which we give to the cultivation of our animal potencies."

3. AUTHOR'S NOTE: I have borrowed this formula from my essay *El Estado, la juventud y el carnaval*, published in *La Nación*, of Buenos Aires, December 1924, and reprinted in *El Espectador* (VII).

stupid, which is not essentially characterized by its proceeding with reference to some plan.[4] Even to abandon our life to chance, in a moment of despair, is to make a plan. Every human being, perforce, picks his way through life. Or what comes to the same, as he decides upon each act he performs, he does so *because* that act "seems best," given the circumstances. This is tantamount to saying that every life is obliged, willy-nilly, to justify itself in its own eyes. Self-justification is a constituent part of our life. We refer to one and the same fact, whether we say that "to live is to conduct oneself according to a plan," or that "life is a continuous justification to oneself." But this plan or justification implies that we have acquired some "idea" of the world and the things in it, and also of our potential acts which have bearing upon it. In short, man cannot live without reacting to his environment with some rudimentary concept of it. He is forced to make an intellectual interpretation of the world about him, and of his conduct in it. This interpretation is the repertory of ideas or convictions to which I have referred, and which, as it is now perfectly evident, cannot be lacking in any human life whatsoever.[5]

The vast majority of these convictions or ideas are not fabricated by the individual, Crusoe-wise, but simply received by him from his historical environment—his times. Naturally, any age presents very disparate systems of convictions. Some are a drossy residue of other times. But there is always a system of live ideas which represents the superior level of the age, a system which is essentially characteristic of its times; and this system is the culture of the age. He who lives at a lower level, on archaic ideas, condemns himself to a lower life, more difficult, toilsome, unrefined. This is the plight of backward peoples—or individuals. They ride through life in an ox-cart while others speed by them in automobiles. Their concept of the world wants truth, it wants richness, and it wants acumen. The man who lives on a plane beneath the enlightened level of his time is condemned, relatively, to the life of an infra-man.

In our age, the content of culture comes largely from science. But our discussion suffices to indicate that culture is not science. The content of culture, though it is being made in the field of science more than elsewhere, is not scientific fact but rather a vital faith, a conviction

---

4. AUTHOR'S NOTE: The sublimity or meanness of a life, its wisdom or stupidity is, precisely, its plan. Obviously our plan does not remain the same for life; it may vary continually. The essential fact is that life and plan are inseparable.

5. AUTHOR'S NOTE: It is easy to see that when an element of our life so fundamental as this self-justification functions irregularly, the ailment which ensues is grave. Such is the case with the curious type of man I have studied in *The Revolt the Masses*. But the first edition of that book is incomplete. A prolonged illness prevented me from finishing it. In the later editions [not yet appeared, Oct. 1944—ED.] I am adding the third part of the study, analyzing more in detail this formidable problem of "justification," and thus adding the finishing touch to that book's investigation into this very prevalent phenomenon.

characteristic of our times. Five hundred years ago, faith was reposed in ecclesiastical councils, and the content of culture emanated in large part from them.

Culture does with science, therefore, the same thing the profession does. It borrows from science what is vitally necessary for the interpretation of our existence. There are entire portions of science which are not culture, but pure scientific technique. And vice versa, culture requires that we possess a complete concept of the world and of man; it is not for culture to stop, with science, at the point where the methods of absolute theoretic rigor happen to end. Life cannot wait until the sciences may have explained the universe scientifically. We cannot put off living until we are ready. The most salient characteristic of life is its coerciveness: it is always urgent, "here and now" without any possible postponement. Life is fired at us point-blank. And culture, which is but its interpretation, cannot wait any more than can life itself.

This sharpens the distinction between culture and the sciences. Science is not something by which we live. If the physicist had to live by the ideas of his science, you may rest assured that he would not be so finicky as to wait for some other investigator to complete his research a century or so later. He would renounce the hope of a complete scientific solution, and fill in, with approximate or probable anticipations, what the rigorous corpus of physical doctrine lacks at present, and in part, always will lack.

The internal conduct of science is not a *vital* concern; that of culture is. Science is indifferent to the exigencies of our life, and follows its own necessities. Accordingly, science grows constantly more diversified and specialized without limit, and is never completed. But culture is subservient to our life here and now, and is required to be, at every instant, a complete, unified, coherent system—the plan of life, the path leading through the forest of existence.

That metaphor of ideas as paths or roads (*méthodoi*) is as old as culture itself. Its origin is evident. When we find ourselves in a perplexing, confused situation, it is as though we stood before a dense forest, through whose tangles we cannot advance without being lost. Someone explains the situation, with a happy idea, and we experience a sudden illumination—the "light" of understanding. The thicket immediately appears ordered, and the lines of its structure seem like paths opening through it. Hence the term *method* is regularly associated with that of enlightenment, illumination, *Aufklärung*. What we call today "a cultured man" was called more than a century ago "an enlightened man," i.e. a man who sees the paths of life in a clear light.

Let us cast away once for all those vague notions of enlightenment and culture, which make them appear as some sort of ornamental accessory for the life of leisure. There could not be a falser misrepresentation. Culture is an indispensable element of life, a dimension of our existence, as much a part of man as his hands. True, there is such a thing as man without hands; but that is no longer simply man: it is man crippled. The same is to be said of life without culture, only in a much more fundamental sense. It is a life crippled, wrecked, false. The man who fails to live at the height of his times is living beneath what would constitute his right life. Or in other words, he is swindling himself out of his own life

We are passing at present, despite certain appearances and presumptions, through an age of terrific *un-culture*. Never perhaps has the ordinary man been so far below his times and what they demand of him. Never has the civilized world so abounded in falsified, cheated lives. Almost nobody is poised squarely upon his proper and authentic place in life. Man is habituated to living on subterfuges with which he deceives himself, conjuring up around him a very simple and arbitrary world, in spite of the admonitions of an active conscience which forces him to observe that his real world, the world that corresponds to the whole of actuality, is one of enormous complexity and grim urgency. But he is afraid—our ordinary man is timorous at heart, with all his brave gesticulations—he is afraid to admit this real world, which would make great demands on him. He prefers to falsify his life, and keep it sealed up in the cocoon of his fictitious, oversimplified concept of the world.[6]

Hence the historic importance of restoring to the university its cardinal function of "enlightenment," the task of imparting the full culture of the time and revealing to mankind, with clarity and truthfulness, that gigantic world of today in which the life of the individual must be articulated, if it is to be authentic.

Personally, I should make a Faculty of Culture the nucleus of the university and of the whole higher learning.[7] I have already sketched the outline of its disciplines. Each of these, it will be remembered, bears two names: for example "The physical scheme of the world (Physics)." This

6. AUTHOR'S NOTE: On this subject in general see *The Revolt of the Masses* in its next edition [not yet published, Oct. 1944—ED.], where I deal more in detail with the specific ways in which the people of today are falsifying their lives: for example, the naive belief that "you have to be arbitrary," from which has issued in politics the lie of Fascism, and in letters and philosophy, the young Spanish "intellectual" of recent years.

7. EDITOR'S NOTE: The form of this proposal has been objected to by readers of the manuscript, on the ground that it gives too much responsibility and too much power to one group. The American college or university might better seek to solve the administrative problem through a committee representative of the whole faculty, serving as the spearhead for the reform yet democratically stimulating and coordinating the initiative arising from all parts of the institution. Another committee of the whole faculty might be made responsible to improve the conditions for research; and each professional department might appoint a committee of appropriate academic and community representatives to examine how the occupational training can be oriented toward a richer service to society.

dual designation is intended to suggest the difference between a cultural discipline, vitally related to life, and the corresponding science by which it is nurtured. The "Faculty" of Culture would not expound physics as the science is presented to a student intending to devote his life to physico-mathematical research. The physics in culture is the rigorously derived synthesis of ideas about the nature and functioning of the physical cosmos, as these ideas have emerged from the physical research so far completed. In addition, this discipline will analyze the means of acquiring knowledge, by which the physicist has achieved his marvelous construction; it will therefore be necessary to expound the principles of physics, and to trace, briefly but scrupulously, the course of their historical evolution. This last element of the course will enable the student to visualize what the "world" was, in which man lived a generation or a century or a thousand years ago; and by contrast, he will be able to realize and appreciate the peculiarities of our "world" of today.

This is the time to answer an objection which arose at the beginning of my essay, and was postponed. How—it is asked—can the present day concept of matter be made intelligible to anyone who is not versed in higher mathematics? Every day, mathematical method makes some new advance at the very base of physical science.

I should like the reader to consider the tragedy without escape which would confront humanity if the view implied here were correct. Either everyone would be obliged to be a thorough physicist, devoting himself, dedicating his life,[8] to research in order not to live inept and devoid of insight into the world we live in; or else most of us must resign ourselves to an existence which, in one of its dimensions, is doomed to stupidity. The physicist would be for the man in the street like some being endowed with a magical, hieratical knowledge. Both of these solutions would be—among other things—ridiculous.

But fortunately there is no such dilemma. In the first place, the doctrine I am defending calls for a thorough rationalizing of the methods of instruction, from the primary grades to the university. Precisely by recognizing science to be a thing apart, we pave the way to the segregating of its cultural elements so that these may be made assimilable. The "principle of economy in education" is not satisfied by extruding disciplines the student cannot learn; it requires economy in the teaching of what remains to be taught. Economy in these two respects would add a new margin to the learning capacity of the student, so that he could actually learn more than at present.[9] I believe, then, that in time to come

8. AUTHOR'S NOTE: It is to be noted that any dedicating of oneself, if it is real, means the dedication of one's life and nothing less.

9. AUTHOR'S NOTE: Precisely because of the efficiency in the teaching, a greater power to learn is called into action.

no student will arrive at the university without being already acquainted with the mathematics of physics, sufficiently at least to be capable of understanding its formulas.

Mathematicians exaggerate a bit the difficulties of their subject. It is an extensive one but, after all, it is always expressible in definite terms to anyone who "knows beans." If it appears so incomprehensible today, it is because the necessary energy has not been applied to the simplifying of its teaching. This affords me an opportunity to proclaim for the first time, and with due solemnity, that if we fail to cultivate this sort of intellectual effort—effort addressed not to descriptive analysis, after the usual manner of research, but to the task of simplifying, and synthesizing the quintessence of science, without sacrifice of its quality or substantialness—then the future of science itself will be disastrous.

It is imperative that the present dispersion and complication of scientific labors be counterbalanced by the complementary kind of scientific activity, striving toward the concentration and consolidation of knowledge. We need to develop a special type of talent, for the specific function of synthesizing. The destiny of science is at stake.

But, in the second place, I deny roundly that in order to grasp the fundamental ideas—the principles, the methods of procedure, the end results—of any science which has fundamental ideas to offer, the student must necessarily have had formal training and become familiar with its techniques. The truth is quite otherwise. When a science, in its internal development, proceeds toward ideas which require technical familiarity in order to be understood, then its ideas are losing their fundamental character to become instruments subordinate to the science, rather than its substance proper. The mastery of higher mathematics is essential for *making* the science but not for understanding its import for human life.

It happens, at once luckily and unluckily, that the nation which stands gloriously and indisputably in the van of science is Germany. The German, in addition to his prodigious talent and inclination for science, has a congenital weakness which it would be extremely hard to extirpate: he is a *nativitate* pedantic and impervious of mind. This fact has brought it about that not a few sides of our present-day science are not really science, but only pedantic detail, all too easily and credulously gathered together. One of the tasks Europe needs to perform with dispatch is to rid contemporary science of its purely German excrescences, its rituals and mere whims, in order to save its essential parts uncontaminated.[11]

10. AUTHOR'S NOTE: In the last analysis, mathematics is wholly instrumental in character, not fundamental or substantial in itself—just as is that branch of science which studies the microscope.

11. AUTHOR'S NOTE: Do not forget, in seeking to grasp the implications of this opinion, that the writer of it owes to Germany four fifths of his intellectual possessions. I am more conscious today than ever before of the indisputable, towering preeminence of German science. The question alluded to has nothing to do with this.

Europe cannot be saved without a return to intellectual discipline, and this discipline needs to be more rigorous than those which have been used or abused in other times. No one must be allowed to escape. Not even the man of science. Today this personage conserves not a little of feudal violence, egotism and arrogance, vanity and pontification.

There is need to humanize the scientist, who rebelled, about the middle of the last century, and to his shame let himself be contaminated by the gospel of insubordination which has been thenceforth the great vulgarity and the great falsity of the age.[12] The man of science can no longer afford to be what he now is with lamentable frequency—a barbarian knowing much of one thing. Fortunately the principal figures in the present generation of scientists have felt impelled by the internal necessities of their sciences to balance their specialization with a symmetrical culture. The rest will follow in their steps as sheep follow the leading ram.

From all quarters the need presses upon us for a new integration of knowledge, which today lies in pieces scattered over the world. But the labor of this undertaking is enormous; it is not to be thought of while there exists no methodology of higher education even comparable to what we have for the preceding levels of education. At present we lack completely a pedagogy of the university—though this statement seems untrue at first.

It has come to be an imminent problem, one which mankind can no longer evade, to invent a technique adequate to cope with the accumulation of knowledge now in our possession. Unless some practicable way is found to master this exuberant growth, man will eventually become its victim. On top of the primitive forest of life we would only add the forest of science, whose intention was to simplify the first. If science has brought order into life we shall now have to put science in order, organize it—seeing that it is impossible to regiment science—for the sake of its healthy perpetuation. To this end we must vitalize science: that is, we must provide it with a form compatible with the human life by which and for which it was made in the first place. Otherwise—for there is no use to entrench ourselves behind a vague optimism—otherwise science will cease to function; mankind will lose interest in it.

And so you see that by thinking over what is the mission of the university, by seeking to discover the consequent character of its cultural disciplines (viz. systematic and synthetic), we come out upon a vast horizon that spreads quite beyond the field of pedagogy, and engages us

12. AUTHOR'S NOTE: The great task of the present age, in the field of morality, is to convince common men (uncommon men never fall into the snare) of the inane foolishness which envelops this urge to revolt, and make them see the cheap facility, the meanness of it; even though we may freely admit that most of the things revolted against deserve to be buried away. The only true revolt is creation—the revolt against nothingness. Lucifer is the patron saint of mere negativistic revolt.

to see in the institution of higher learning an agent for the salvation of science itself.

The need to create sound syntheses and systematizations of knowledge, to be taught in the "Faculty of Culture," will call out a kind of scientific genius which hitherto has existed only as an aberration: the genius for integration. Of necessity this means specialization, as all creative effort inevitably does; but this time, the man will be specializing in the construction of a whole. The momentum which impels investigation to dissociate indefinitely into particular problems, the pulverization of research, makes necessary a compensative control—as in any healthy organism—which is to be furnished by a force pulling in the opposite direction, constraining centrifugal science in a wholesome organization.

Men endowed with this genius come nearer being good professors than those who are submerged in their research. One of the evils attending the confusion of the university with science has been the awarding of professorships, in keeping with the mania of the times, to research workers who are nearly always very poor professors, and regard their teaching as time stolen away from their work in the laboratory or the archives. This was brought home to me by experience, during my years of study in Germany. I have lived close to a good number of the foremost scientists of our time, yet I have not found among them a single good teacher—just so that no one will come and tell me that the German university, as an institution, is a model![13]

CHAPTER VI—WHAT THE UNIVERSITY MUST BE "IN ADDITION"

The "principle of economy," which amounts to the determination to see things as they are and not as a Utopian illusion, has led us to define the primary mission of the university in this wise:

1. University, in the strict sense, is to mean that institution which teaches the ordinary student to be a cultured person and a good member of a profession.
2. The university will not tolerate in its program any false pretense: it will profess to require of the student only what actually can be required of him.
3. It will consequently avoid causing the ordinary student to waste part of his time in pretending that he is going to be a scientist. To

13. AUTHOR'S NOTE: Which does not mean that none exist; but it does indicate that the combination does not occur with any dependable frequency.

this end, scientific investigation proper is to be eliminated from the core or minimum of the university.

4. The cultural disciplines and the professional studies will be offered in a rationalized form based on the best pedagogy—systematic, synthetic, and complete—and not in the form which science would prefer, if it were left to itself: special problems, "samples" of science, and experimentation.

5. The selection of professors will depend not on their rank as investigators but on their talent for synthesis and their gift for teaching.

6. When the student's apprenticeship has been reduced to the minimum, both quantitatively and qualitatively, the university will be inflexible in its requirement of him.

This ascetic frugality of pretensions, this severe loyalty in recognizing the limits of the attainable, will, in my belief, procure what is the university's most fundamental need: the need that its institutional life correspond squarely to its proper functions and true limits, in order that its life may be genuine and sincere in its inmost dealings. I have already proposed that the new life should take as its point of departure this simple recognition of the destiny of the individual or of the institution. All else that we may subsequently wish to make of ourselves, or of private institutions or the state, will take root and come to fruition only if we have planted its seed in the rich soil of a nature resigned to be, first of all, the essential minimum which corresponds to its destiny. Europe is sick because its people profess to stand upon a precarious tenth rung in life, without having taken the trouble first to secure a footing on the elemental one, two, three. Destiny is the only bedrock on which human life and all its aspirations can stand. Life on any other basis is false. It has no authentic personality, it is something up in the air. It lacks a local habitation and a name.

Now we can open our minds without fear or reservation, to consider all that the university should be "in addition."

Indeed, the university, such as we have defined it for the nonce, cannot be that alone. And now is the proper time for us to recognize, in all its breadth and depth, the role science must play in the physiology of the university, or rather let us say its psychology, for the university is better to be compared with a spirit than a body.

In the first place, we have seen that culture and profession are not science, but are largely nourished by science. Without science, the destiny of the European man would be an impossibility. The European man represents, in the panorama of history, the being resolved to live according to his intellect; and science is but intellect "in form." Is it perchance a mere accident that only Europe has possessed universities, among so many peoples? The university *is* the intellect, it *is* science, erected into an institution. And this institutionalizing of intellect is the originality of Europe compared with other races, other lands, and other ages. It signifies the peculiar resolution adopted by the European man, to live according to the dictates of his intelligence. Others have chosen to live according to other faculties. Remember the marvelous laconisms in which Hegel sums up universal history, like an alchemist reducing tons of carbon to a few diamonds: Persia, land of Light! (referring to mystical religion); Greece, land of Grace! India, land of Dream! Rome, land of Empire![1]

Europe is the intelligence. A wonderful power: it is the only power which perceives its own limitations—and thereby it proves how intelligent it is! This power which is its own restraint finds in science the scope for its full grandeur.

If culture and the professions were to be isolated in the university and have no contact with the incessant ferment of science, of investigation of all sorts, it would not be long before they would be overtaken by the creeping paralysis of scholasticism. Around the central part of the university, the sciences must pitch their camps—their laboratories and seminars and discussion centers. The sciences are the soil out of which the higher learning grows and from which it draws its sustenance. Accordingly its roots must reach out to the laboratories of every sort and tap them for the nourishment they can provide. All normal university students will come and go between the university and these outlying camps of the sciences, where they will find courses conceived from an exclusively scientific point of view, on all things human and divine. Of the professors, those who are more amply gifted will be investigators as well, and the others, who are purely teachers, will work none the less in closest contact with science, under its criticism and the influence of its ferment and stimulation. What is inadmissible is the confusion of the central portion of the university with the zone of research surrounding its borders. The university and the laboratory are distinct, correlative organs in a complete physiology. The essential difference between them is that only the university proper is to be characterized as an institution. Science is an activity too sublime and subtle to be organized in an institution. Science is neither to be coerced nor regimented. Hence it is harmful, both for the higher learning and for investigation, to attempt to fuse them into one instead of letting them work hand in hand in an exchange of influence as free and spontaneous as it is intense.

Thus the university is distinct from science yet inseparable from it. I should say myself, "The university *is* science *in addition*."

1. AUTHOR'S NOTE: Hegel, *Lectures on the Philosophy of History* (translated from the third German edition by J. Sibree, London, 1861: see pp. xxix ff.).

Not, however, the simple "addition" of an increment set down in merely external proximity to the institution. Quite the contrary.—And now we may make the point without fear of misunderstanding. The university must *be* science before it can be a university. An atmosphere charged with enthusiasm, the exertion of science, is the presupposition at the base of the university's existence. Precisely because the institution cannot be composed of science—the unrestricted creation of exact knowledge—it requires the spirit of science to animate its institutional life. Unless this spirit is presupposed, all that has been said in the present essay has no sense. Science is the dignity of the university—and more, for life is possible without dignity: it is the soul of the institution, the principle which gives it the breath of life and saves it from being an automaton. This is the sense in which the university "is science, in addition."

But it is still more.[2] Not only does it need perpetual contact with science, on pain of atrophy, it needs contact, likewise, with the public life, with historical reality, with the present, which is essentially a whole to be dealt with only in its totality, not after amputations *ad usum Delphini*. The university must be open to the whole reality of its time. It must be in the midst of real life, and saturated with it.

And all this not only because it suits the purpose of the university to live in the quickening atmosphere of historical reality. Conversely as well, the life of the people needs acutely to have the university participate, *as the university*, in its affairs.

On this point there is much I should like to say. But to be brief, let me simply allude to the fact that in the collective life of society today there is no other "spiritual power" than the press. The corporate life, which is the real life of history,[3] needs always to be directed, whether we like the idea or not. Of itself it has no form, no eyes to see with, no guiding sense of direction. Now then, in our times, the ancient "spiritual powers" have disappeared: the Church because it has abandoned the present (whereas the life of the people is ever a decidedly current affair); and the state because with the triumph of democracy, it has given up governing the life of the people to be governed instead by their opinion. In this

2. AUTHOR'S NOTE: I have deliberately refrained in this essay from even naming the topic of moral education in the university, in order to devote undivided attention to the problem of intellectual content.

3. EDITOR'S NOTE: Sr. Ortega has discussed this concept—that "cultures are organisms and are the true subjects for history"—in *Las Atlántidas* (Madrid, 1924), especially p. xxiv, and in the foreword which he wrote for the Spanish edition of Spengler's *Decline of the West*. Sr. Ortega mentions that he had arrived at the concept independently of Spengler. For a discussion of the difficulties that have since discredited the conception of a society as an organism, see Melvin Rader, *No Compromise* (Macmillan, 1939), pp. 239 ff. and 306 ff. See also the essays of Ortega assembled by Mrs. Helen Weyl in *Toward a Philosophy of History*, New York: W. W. Norton, 1941.

situation, the public life has devolved into the hands of the only spiritual force which necessarily concerns itself with current affairs—the press.

I should not wish to throw too many stones at the journalists; among other motives, there is the consideration that I may be nothing more than a journalist myself. But it is futile to shut our eyes to the obvious fact that spiritual realities differ in worth. They compose a hierarchy of values, and in this hierarchy, journalism occupies an inferior place. It has come to pass that today no pressure and no authority make themselves felt in the public consciousness, save on the very low spiritual plane adopted by the emanations of the press. So low a plane it is that not infrequently the press falls quite short of being a spiritual power, and is rather the opposite force. By the default of other powers, the responsibility for nourishing and guiding the public soul has fallen to the journalist, who not only is one of the least cultured types in contemporary society but who moreover—for reasons I hope may prove to have been merely transitory—admits into his profession the frustrated pseudo-intellectuals, full of resentment and hatred toward what is truly spiritual. Furthermore the journalist's profession leads him to understand by the reality of the times that which creates a passing sensation, regardless of what it is, without any heed for perspective or architecture. Real life is, certainly, purely of the present; but the journalist deforms this truism when he reduces the present to the momentary, and the momentary to the sensational. The result is that, in the public consciousness today, the image of the world appears exactly upside down. The space devoted to people and affairs in the press is inversely proportionate to their substantial and enduring importance; what stands out in the columns of the newspapers and magazines is what will be a "success" and bring notoriety. Were the periodicals to be freed from motives that are often unspeakable; were the dailies kept chastely aloof from any influence of money in their opinions—the press would still, of itself, forsake its proper mission and paint the world inside out. Not a little of the grotesque and general upset of our age—(for Europe has been going along for some time now with her head on the ground and her plebeian feet waving in the air)—is the result of this unchallenged sway of the press as sole "spiritual power."

It is a question of life and death for Europe to put this ridiculous situation to rights. And if this is to be done the university must intervene, *as* the university, in current affairs, treating the great themes of the day from its own point of view: cultural, professional, and scientific.[4] Thus it will not be an institution exclusively for students, a retreat *ad usum*

4. AUTHOR'S NOTE: It is inconceivable, for example, that in the face of a problem such as that of foreign exchange, which now preoccupies Spain, the university should not be offering the serious public a course on this difficult economic question.

Delphini. In the thick of life's urgencies and its passions, the university must assert itself as a major "spiritual power," higher than the press, standing for serenity in the midst of frenzy, for seriousness and the grasp of intellect in the face of frivolity and unashamed stupidity.

Then the university, once again, will come to be what it was in its grand hour: an uplifting principle in the history of the western world.

FOCUSING QUESTIONS

1. What does Dewey mean by freedom, democracy, and experience?
2. What is scientific method?
3. What is the difference between the method of the sciences and scientism?
4. What is progressive education?
5. What is pragmatism?
6. Is there a conflict in Dewey between individual and society?
7. Is it sufficient to educate the student to become a social being?
8. What is the instrumentalism of knowledge?
9. Who is a mass-man?
10. Is a mass-man self-made or educated?
11. Does the university have a mission?
12. How much science should the undergraduate curriculum include?
13. How many laboratory hours should the undergraduate curriculum include?
14. What is the difference between natural rights and cultural rights?
15. Who is an educated person according to Dewey? To Ortega?
16. What is the relation between education and decision making?
17. Are cognitive skills sufficient for decision making?
18. If not then how can we educate for decision making?
19. Are we educating mass-men (mass-women) or are they the product of education?
20. What is the relation between the "expert" and the mass-man?

SUPPLEMENTARY READINGS

Dewey, John.　*A Common Faith*. New Haven, Conn.: Yale University Press, 1934.

————.　*Human Nature and Conduct*. New York: Modern Library, 1957.

————.　*The Sources of a Science of Education*. Liveright. New York, 1929.

————.　*Democracy and Education*. Carbondale, Ill.: Southern Illinois University Press, 1980.

————.　*Freedom and Culture*.

Ortega y Gasset.　*Obras Completas*, Vol. 12. Madrid: Revista de Occidente, 1946.

————.　*The Revolt of the Masses*. Translated by Anthony Kerrigan. Notre Dame, Ind.: University of Notre Dame Press, 1958.

————.　*Meditation on Quixote*. New York: Norton, 1961.

————.　*Some Lesson in Metaphysics*. Translated by Mildred Adams. New York: Norton, 1969.

————.　*What is Philosophy?* Translated by Mildred Adams. New York: Norton, 1960.

————.　*Man and Crisis*, 1958.

PART THREE

Our Resources

11

Socrates, Plato, the Poets

The thesis we have been developing in this volume may be summarized in this manner: as a culture we have been standing on theory, and our system of higher education has been a very successful effort at making theory our only habit of mind. The fact that historically we were able to develop different habits of mind is not as significant as the fact that our institutions shared a concerted effort to make theory the basis of our Western way of life.

In practice this formulation may be translated as establishing the fact that we in the West are people of principles, but we lack origins. Principles are discoverable through cognitive operations, origins through imaginative ones. An educational system that does not place cognitive skills in the foreground of the imaginative ones is bound to create in the willing or unwilling subject a disembodied condition resembling more the life of ghosts than that of people in the flesh. We claim to be people, all equally disembodied with hardly any background differences, for backgrounds do not count, and thus we find ourselves speaking as if we were 'human beings,' ethereal beings attached to external machines and to our body machine, disembodied from internal and external gods, from internal and external experiences that cannot be mediated by thought, opinion, or belief. From within the habit of theory we feel our own desensitization from the world and try to escape through those magical trips we inject into ourselves. Every man, woman, and child is an island, a ghostly island, true especially of the more educated. No one can expect from generations brought up in this habitual theorizing to be suddenly sensitized to a new habit of thought and thus to prolong the agony of ghosts, and we rightly blame education.

It was our propensity to theorize that blurred the lines separating foreground (the world) and background (the native gods, the native imaginings of the culture), and separating interiority and exteriority within humans. We assigned interiority to thought and the rest of the world we called exterior. What we did not include in this division we branded private, fantasy, imagining, cultural gods, religion. And since we had no other mediation between us and the world to make decisions on the world we were forced to act on opinion, my opinion as good as anybody's. There is no way any human may have enough knowledge in this context, to make a sound decision, one without room for doubt. Relativism, scattered individualism, is the natural outcome. Our habits are our decision makers, and if we educate insufficient habits we will get back insufficient decisions. We also inculcate confusion and the lack of decision, the lack of will. Cognitive skills develop no will at all, except the individual will of self-gratification. Imagining, feelings, and body go hand in hand. Principles, cognitive skills, and brain go also hand in hand. To try to substitute one for the other will never work; to educate one over the other will not work either. Education should be based on developing those and any other faculties we might have accumulated as a species to the fullest.

There is nothing more pathetic than to enter a classroom in the humanities and listen to a professor dispensing information to students as if with the information they were not also simultaneously carving an inner habit of theory making, thus damning the students to a world of ghosts. Focusing is an internal act which if repeated enough times becomes a habit in the student, regardless of the quality and quantity of information we impart to them. The habit of focusing, the acts of focusing, the rewards of focusing, the repetition of what it is being focused upon, this is the education we in fact impart. And this education has turned out to be insufficient. We have precedents in history of this shortsighted type of education.

Writing and living in the fourth century A.D., Augustine of Hippo (St. Augustine) identified his ultimate quest in life as being identical with the ultimate form of the desire of his soul: *"desiderium beatitudinis"* (desire for happiness). But the lover of Latin and Roman rhetoric soon translated this desire of the soul for the desire of the brain: *"desiderium essendi"* (the desire to be). And thus he entered philosophy the way one enters religion, for the soul's salvation, as narrated in his *De Vera Religione* and *Dialogues*. But his theoretical mind soon played tricks upon him. The God of Being became in his hands the "being of God," the God who became man becomes "the Man God," and from faith he descends into understanding of faith and finally he is content with an intellectual intuition. Regardless of what other virtues Augustine is praised for, his intellectual foundations for the highest human acts have a blinding reductionism on the human soul that is still present in our habits. At his hands religion remains an opaque hybrid text, a form of reflection joined with prayer, of thinking and salvation unified in a common social project of transformation, a mixture of reason and individual will, of thought and tears, intellection and occultism as a result of his own particular habit of thought inherited from the so called Neoplatonists. No revelation here, no imagination either, simply the pathos of an insufficient education. He identified so closely any form of transcendence with his own mortal faculties that his own hope of immortality becomes a hopeless project once it is realized that the conditions for that kind of knowledge (of immortality) disappear with death through the disintegration of those same faculties and the conditions for their operation. Augustine's agonistic quest for happiness is similar to the one our students share, and so is the outcome, except that our students lack the brute force of Augustine's faith and his dedication. They also labor under several more layers of theory and abstraction than he did, and the history of humanity has never been able to put so many specialists on theory to work more systematically and with greater dedication than the university professors do today on the students under their care.

Our students, the natives, the immigrants, the foreigners, are not the unextended rational substances of Descartes, nor the *tabulae rasae* (empty blackboards) of Locke, nor the association matrices of Hume, nor the passive reinforcement-driven animals of Skinner, nor the genetically hard-wired robots of the sociobiologists. They all share in a total image of the origin, which though hidden as a model, reappears as a paradigmatic image in the collectivity that gives birth and sensation and articulates itself as different cultures. These cultural paradigms appear *distributively* in each life individually as the embodiment of a cultural primordial image. The manifestation of these paradigmatic images is what makes possible, collectively and individually, the decisions in the environment and those of individuals about their own lives and their lives with others. Individuals are sensitized through those original images and methodologically transform their lives into decisions about, for, or against the environment. It is against this background of the original image that experience accumulates as memory, that the intellect is impregnated with those memories, and that the will is trained to act in accordance with those original memories. If, through education, we either bury or indoctrinate students to foreign skills (and most of our classical physics habits are foreign to them) we are not really dealing with education, but with obfuscation.

Is there a way out? Is there an educational alternative that would be possible to put into practice without destroying the achievements of the present system? In short, have we exhausted our cultural inheritance?

My claim is a simple one: Plato's project of education, in fact our cultural inheritance from the Greeks, the habits of mind of the Greeks, have never entered our educational system. It is true we have used their names and some of their theories, but none of their habits of mind. And this is our future in education.

I would like to share a personal experience. I write both philosophy and poetry. Each of these acts differs from the other, and on completing each I find myself in two different worlds. The writing of philosophy in different styles is my own need for clarity—clarity at a distance, clarity of the journey behind me. And the conclusion of the writing is always the same: distance. The truth leaves me absolutely cold. My senses have been emptied of sensation: the world, my friends, my family have practically died in the performance of that act. The only sensation is the act of writing, not the theories, not even the clarity. I find myself recalling everyone in the middle of the night so I may go to bed in human company.

Not so writing poetry. Sensitization follows the image from

the fingertips to the ground. The image becomes a total "holo-gram" of sensation, each part containing the image, the total image appearing in each part. Writing poetry does not allow for distance: everyone is immediately present when there is no one around. If then I need distance to go to sleep I do philosophy.

As I already mentioned in the early chapters of this volume, it was Nietzsche who first claimed that the history of philosophy was a concerted effort to dethrone Plato, and his reading of that history was fairly accurate. Plato was not interested, as is commonly held, in describing an ideal society of perfect men; his project is more practical; his project is remedial, for the education of the young within societies that are going to be always imperfect, as Plato confesses in *Republic* 473b. He proposes a sort of medicine to be administered through education for the political betterment of the *polis*. The key point, however, comes down to this. How are the young men and women of a society going to recognize sickness in a society? Where is the social model, the model of the city, the polis, for them to be able to recognize the sickness? And where is the medicine? In the cities? In the out-there world? Obviously not; they are all imperfect and sick. Where, then? In the cities he builds? As Tennyson proclaimed in "Camelot:"

the city is built
to music, therefore never built.
And, therefore, built for ever.

The only model to be found is within the soul of the student. It is to be found within, a soul carved by the plurality of acts a soul needs to develop to cover all the acts socially required, acts performed repeatedly in view of their own perfection, for their own sake, for the approximation to the same and the like, for the taste of the Good. No judgment can be made, no decision taken if that taste, internally felt in the performance of perfect acts has not been acquired. Do not look for a perfect, desensitized theory in order to decide. Decision implies the aesthetic feeling; if this is lacking, then we are making shots in the dark.

There is no more compelling figure than Socrates moving about during the first five books of the *Republic* forcing others to define justice, to come to the conclusion that theoretical definitions are not sufficient. Justice must be seen, tasted internally, for one to be able to recognize it or be aware of its absence in the public domain. Socrates never taught imparting information. He shaped his audience through act upon act to force them into an internal activity as close as it could be brought to the act of seeing and tasting. Socrates moved acts, never resting on definitions, all of which he finds incomplete. Unless the dead come back from the tomb and join the living in felt conversation, there is no end to the dialogue. The soul must be exercised to make itself just, to be educated. The technologies of seeing must be set in motion when the sun is setting in Athens so that they spend the night seeing, or trying to see justice. In the end whatever has been learned must be forgotten to find that person able to teach how, out of the possible, one may by habit choose the best. But how can one choose the best, if one does not have a taste for the best, or even the good?

The Greeks, Plato in particular, have left us little of the theoretical values the Romans thought so important; imitation, biography, family, nation, fatherland, national origin. They modeled their education on the religious practices of the mystery religions and insisted that a good education is an education that can measure the outside world by the perfection of the internal acts performed, or the proximity of the internal acts to existing hidden models, as the same and the like. A genealogy of perfection could thus be established to accept or discredit those internal acts in view of the public results. The cause is in the effect. And so that the effect be really effective those acts must be kept in constant exercise.

But we dislike pagan rites, and therefore translate Plato theoretically as if he were a Roman. And we dislike religion in education, and therefore Plato should be rational, and he had to be joking when he started the dialogues after a religious festival or as a comment on the practices of the mysteries.

The literature of Greece is filled with names, but each name is the brand of an act. Athena, Poseidon, Zeus, Alcyone, Hermes, Alope, Eros, Aphrodite, Apollo, Leto, Arachne, Argonauts, Ge, Dionysus, Persephone, Minotaur, Narcissus, Venus, Python, Zelus and his brothers Cratus, Bia, and sister Nike. All these and many more are not just names; any Greek could recognize their faces by looking in the soul and seeing the acts emanating from it. The Greek pantheon was seeable because the Greeks recognize the acts of their souls. One was the reflection of the other, one felt like the other, one was the model of the other. To be a Greek was to live and act in that company. The soul remembered itself in the feeling of the names, and recreated itself through an effacement of self-interest to become the same and the like of those original acts. And the gods were as much at hand in the skies as in the gymnasium; in the seas as much as in the fields; in the city as much as at home. There is no corner of Greek life that is not reached by the taste of gods, heroes, or those spiritual creatures of the Greek background. They are the feeling and the measure of the foreground, of the public life, of their own presence among mortals.

What Plato leaves to us in his divided line is the synthesis of these internal acts the Greeks were so familiar with, and the *Republic* is the education of the young into those acts that will keep alive for them and the community not only the gods but also the original acts of the heroes and the dead: chaos and cosmos simultaneously, Plato's way of recollection is an invitation to keep the acts of decision making in any context bathed with the feeling of the origin. Decision making cannot be only theoretically based; it needs a tactile soul familiar with the taste of the good so that decisions are good decisions. All decision, therefore, has to be grounded on the original background so that horizons already present may be newly articulated. And it is against this native background that Plato makes imagining the central, or deepest background of the training of the young. Plato's imagining is always a creation out of nothing, not borrowed from objects already made, but truly original, out of the past, out of the dead as in the narrative of Er in the *Republic*. Plato's imagining is fully determinative: it cannot stand ambiguity. We can only make good decisions on our learned ability to read the signs coming to us in the re-creation of the past, and this type of information does not tolerate doubt. Plato's imagining flourishes in a community of several readers, or community of embodied subjects—people familiar with the gods and their signs, for it is only in a community like this, a community of embodied subjects linked by a common background of aesthetic feeling and practice, that the materiality of the body and the biases of sensuality are overcome. Plato's imagining is innovative; it renews human sensation and this was as much the primary goal of the mystery religions as that of the practicing mystics of other religions. The human nervous system seems to be designed with an enormous capacity to register differences; that is, it becomes what it is through repetitions that become biological habits. The nervous system is the acknowledged presence of these habits tending to ignore the expected and responding more excitedly to new and unexpected stimuli. For this reason there is the continuous striving of the human body, always more intrigued by the odd than by the expected, more inspired by movement and change, contrasts and borderlines, than by any other characteristics of time and space. The practice of the mystics and those of the mystery religions put these simple truths into systems of practice. Plato's imagining is also synthetic. It creates unions, holographic marks, even in the absence of such marks. Silence is turned, in imagining, into a sign of decision making. Imagining is primarily built on internal acts and their continuous activity. It builds scenarios to be tested, and painfully rebuilds them when they prove false. All human faculties are involved in this activity of imagining, as much organs of action as they are of knowledge. The knowledge of imagining spreads to all human organs, faculties, and sinews in an inverse relation to the knowledge of cognitive skills. Imagining, in Plato's line, proceeds by gathering knowledge hierarchically. Simpler operations of motor organs inform higher cells with more complex operations and even more complex and decipherable stimuli. What Plato calls the technologies of the visible are just the education of the steps mentioned above and their exercise. For imagining is primarily a social function. Arousal, orientation, attention, motivation, transmission, and reading of signs are primarily social actions within social and cultural contexts. Successful imagining is identifiable only as social transformation. Look at Homer, Plato would ask through Socrates, what did he leave us? Imitation, and the burying of the dead. But look at Pythagoras, he left us a community and therefore he was good.

Educators, those dealing with students in a classroom, seem to be unaware of a very simple fact. Concepts, words, theories, and language are not simple tools they may pick up and hand over to students to hammer some innocent nails. Concepts, words, theories, and language are the technologies through which we reach the internal and external worlds around or within us. They are our *human extensions*. With them and through them we make decisions. Our insistence on exteriority and instrumentality has obscured the fact that we are dealing here with detachable organs the students may or may not develop to function in the world, their outside or their inside. If we only teach external technologies, that is, cognitive skills, external technologies will become internalized as the software of inner mechanisms in humans. Eventually software may become hardware and form a cultural loop, the way printing did with reading in our culture and subsequently in all others. Through external technologies, taught on the exclusive basis they are taught these days, men and women are displaced as the bearers of thought, imagination, and all other mental operations; men and women are being displaced by the machine, which by now not only thinks, counts, or imagines, but in certain cases even decides for humans. For example, a hormone made through genetic engineering brings science and technology so close that they are indistinguishable. Learning how a protein can be made by bacteria (science) and the production of a functional hormone (technology) were realized simultaneously. Science and technology are in this case inseparable. How can technology not escape detection when it masquerades as science? Who are the supervisors? If humans are deprived of the legitimate operations that identify them as humans, especially their will, what kind of humans are we educating? Inner technologies are linked to the human will. To the degree that we succeed in making our machines imagine or think, to that same degree we deprive our students of those exercises. And the problem is not obviously the machine. The problem is our selection of exercises for the classroom.

It is obvious even to the most biased reader that Plato's divided line and project of education is for the sake of training leaders to make just decisions that would affect all with equal justice. Education is not a theoretical game. From the bottom of the divided line borrowed images, opinions, objects of art and science, to the top imagining, the student is supposed to keep in constant exercise all these acts. Education is concerned with the quality of those acts. The quality of this performance consists in directing the will to select or sort out, those acts capable of being remembered and therefore executed. Thus the divisions of the acts are a lead to select those that are to be found in the quality itself of the act performed, not in the external properties of objects and their external relations. Divisions are made for their inner genealogy to separate the pure from the impure. And this selection leads to the model, not of object, but of acts. Acts, the same and like, as the invisible originals, the *eidos,* the idea, which in Greek means not theory but visible images, or images that can be made visible.

The classroom is the best place for students to practice the plurality of these acts and also to taste the feeling of the good as opposed to the bad performance. The audience, the student peers, know what it is they are seeing. And there is no better reminder and memory than the taste of success in a public presentation, after the students themselves have fought individually to form a community capable of making visible what up to the performance is only a theoretical possibility. This type of knowledge builds experience, is circled by experience and aesthetic feeling, and is the builder of memory and communities. It is the type of knowledge the Greeks left us as a model of educating our plural inner acts. It is also in our American plural society the type of performance through which cultures, backgrounds from the students themselves, may be articulated.

I wish to remind all our educators so biased in favor of cognitive skills to pay attention to Kant's own warning about the use of concepts. Talking of Plato's and his own classical physics project, he said:

> Plato made use of the expression "idea" is such a way as quite evidently to have meant by it something which not only can never be borrowed from the senses but far surpasses even the concepts of the understanding. . . . For Plato, ideas are archetypes of the things themselves, and not in the manner of categories, merely keys to possible experiences. In this view they have issued from the highest reason, and from that source have come to be shared in by human reason.

And he continues clarifying his own project by showing the reduction of mental life by the way he uses the set of concepts of pure reason:

> The absolute whole of all appearance . . . is only an idea. Since we can never represent it in images, it remains a problem to which there is no solution. *Critique,* A 327–328, B 384.

We should read the above quote from Kant every time we enter the classroom, and warn the students.

Or we could remind everyone of the consequences of living in the *simulacrum* without any regard for models or even the existence of such models. But all this might sound too theoretical. It might be easier to read to the students and faculty alike the consequences of *hubris,* the use of a knowledge not our own, in the myth of Daedalus and Icarus. Daedalus, the father, could escape the labyrinth for he knew how to make wings. And he made them of wax so that father and son Icarus could escape. But the son, who knew nothing about making wings, and who did not even listen to his father's instructions as to how to use them, became possessed by *hubris* and flew too close to the sun, and the wings melted and Icarus fell dead to the sea. Even when we hold in our hands the most powerful technologies, do we have any *idea,* in the Platonic sense, of how they should be used? Has anyone tasted the good with enough confidence to make decisions for the rest of us, with equal justice for all? We may have wings, but do we know where the sun is so that we do not fly too close?

We need to bring in the technologies of the visible and make them part of our education.

Note: Plato should be read after the students are acquainted with Greek mythology. *The Meridian Handbook of Classical Mythology* by Edward Tripp, New American Library, 1970, is the best summary.

The translations of the *Republic* are mostly from the Latin version by Marsilio Ficino (Florence, 1483–84) with partial use of Jowett and Shorey. Their translations, however, leave many gaps. I recommend John Bremer's *On Plato's Polity,* The Institute of Philosophy, P.O. Box 56201, Houston, Texas 77256, 1984.

John Bremer's essay in the selections "On Translation" speaks for itself and is an eye opener for the students.

The selections from Plato's *Republic* are Book I, and parts of V to X.

This part of the class presentations may be expanded with presentations on poetry, either from the Greeks, or modern poets like Rilke, Juan Ramón Jiménez, and others.

One of the most important class presentations is that of the education of women and modern education. As a contrast to

modern tendencies it would be interesting to make presentations on St. Teresa de Avila with readings from her life and the
biography by Victoria Lincoln, *Teresa: A Woman*, SUNY Press,
1985. The presentation of other cultures and their interpretation is also a must. My choice is the *Bhagavad Gítá*. This Hindu
scripture shows the conflict between fantasy and imagining and
the text shows how the technologies of imagining move on
memories. See my *Avatára: The Humanization of Philosophy
through the Bhagavad Gítá*, Nicolas Hays, Main, 1976.

On how images are made out of nothing and the practice of
the mystics repeating Plato, see my *Powers of Imagining: Ignatius
de Loyola*, SUNY Press, Albany, 1986.

Contrary to tradition, Western philosophy is not a footnote
to Plato, but rather Plato is a footnote to earlier traditions and
habits of mind.

Translating Plato: Some Reflections on Rhetoric

John Bremer*

The ancient liberal art of rhetoric was understood in many ways—in almost as many ways as there were rhetoricians. Its meaning changed and developed as its social function changed, and there is an intellectual history to be written connecting Homer's description of "winged words" with Aristotle's definition of rhetoric.

Aristotle defines the art of rhetoric as "the power of seeing in each [case] the possible means of persuasion." This is avowedly an ability, a faculty, a *dunamis,* a power of the rhetorician, but it is not the exercise of that power. Conversely, when Homer speaks of "winged words," he focuses attention on the exercised power, not, however, of the speaker, but of the words themselves. Although different Homeric speakers have different ways of winging the words, ultimately it is the words themselves that are winged.

Nobody supposes that Homer was specifically concerned with an art of rhetoric, as Aristotle clearly was, but his descriptions of speech and of speeches are very illuminating. The words are "winged" because they traverse space—the distance between speaker and hearer—and they do so with speed, force, and accuracy. Initially, the metaphor is derived from birds which, like the words, are winged or feathered and which naturally fly in a purposeful manner. Birds naturally wing their way, but it is *their* way which they pursue, moved by an internal principle of motion, their nature. Similarly, the words, once released by the speaker or once they have escaped from the speaker, take on a natural power of their own. They move with force and direction; they are vectors.

The metaphor is transformed, however, by the technology of war. Birds have a natural power to fly—they are winged or feathered—but the arrow, too, is winged and feathered, and it, too, flies. "Winged words," as a metaphorical phrase, becomes more directive, more menacing, more penetrating, and more hostile. The natural power of the feathers becomes a stabilizing device for a pointed shaft. The power of winging comes from the bow and the bowman, and the natural power inherent in the feathers is diminished into a supplementary means.

Moreover, birds fly naturally, by nature, and the wings and feathers are natural parts of the bird. They share in the ends or purposes that the

*Mr. Bremer is director of the Institute of Philosophy, Murrell's Inlet, South Carolina.

bird, as a whole, serves. The sharing means that they are improved or benefited by accomplishment of those purposes. Arrows fly artificially, by artifice, and the wings and feathers are artificial parts of the arrow which has no purpose of its own. Nor are the wings and feathers improved or benefited; they serve merely as instruments of use. They are pure means, simple technology.

The metaphor which accompanies the winging bird and the flying arrow has to do with the aim, with their direction and destination. The resting place after travel is home, whether for bird or arrow. Birds seek their nests, and arrows their marks—both are lodged. Homing pigeons return on their own, but weapons are thrust home. The home that the bird seeks, its nest, is a sanctuary, a place for rest and recuperation, for peace, for quietude, and for sleep. It is a haven for re-creating, for reconstructing, so that the natural life may continue. The home sought by the arrow is in the vitals of the quarry, there to deal death and destruction that the natural life of another may end.[1]

Homer is too wise to explicate the full meaning of "winged words," partly because he knows that winged words can be either birds or arrows. After all, he is a rhapsode whose material is composed of the souls of his audience and whose form is to be found in the words that he chants. In some way, his words, recounted by himself or by one of the Homeridae, must find their home in the souls of his audience. If they do not, he will have failed.

Homer is like Apollo—he shoots from afar. But his winged words are arrows directed at his audience, they are not birds simply flying to their own proper home. A rhapsode cannot merely send out his words and let them nest where they will; his success depends upon the words lodging in his audience, and not just in one or two members of that audience. He needs his words to find a home, to be at home, in the greatest possible number of his audience. Plato has the rhapsode Ion tell us this: "For at every performance I look down from the stage at them, now weeping, now glaring fiercely, and now amazed, according to what is said. I must pay a great deal of attention to them, for if I make them weep, I myself will get paid and will laugh, but if I make them laugh, I will lose money and will weep myself."

It is not without significance that in the *Ion* the first example quoted from Homer is of "Odysseus leaping onto the threshold, making himself known to the suitors, and emptying out the arrows at his feet." Nor should we ignore the fact that at the end of the dialogue, Ion maintains

---

1. Interestingly, the word *quarrel* has a double etymology, the one meaning a dispute, the other meaning a square-headed arrow for a crossbow. Of equal interest, the word *quarry*, also called "game"—something to be played at or with—is at the same time honored by its other meaning, "spirited." Our phrase "a good sport" continues in the same vein.

that the art of the rhapsode and the art of the general are the same. It is not an unintelligible metaphor to say that Ion thinks he must capture his audience, that he must overpower or even conquer them. He plays with them, they are his game.

However, Ion's domination of his audience is clearly temporary. He must take them over so that they feel what he wants them to feel, but he must also release them after the performance. The release is signaled by his payment—the audience then goes away saying, as it were, "That was a good show." It *was* a good show. They are free from it in the present. They may have been captured or captivated, but they did not suffer or die; they are now alive and free. The rhapsode, Ion, is also released—he has no wish to be burdened with the continuing responsibility for the life of his audience.

Apollo is the archer-god, he-who-strikes-from-afar, and his arrows are deadly. But he is also the god of the *logos,* of oracles, of healing, of music and song, and of the founding of cities. The dual-aspected Apollo has a counterpart in the dual aspects of speech.

GOALS OF RHETORIC

There are two rhetorics. The rhetoric of words as natural, seeking their proper resting place, and of words as artificial, seeking to take or to take over life. There is a rhetoric of life and a rhetoric of death, a rhetoric of liberation and a rhetoric of domination, a rhetoric of salvation and a rhetoric of damnation, a rhetoric of growth and a rhetoric of decay.

The two rhetorics are easily distinguished. The second, more common rhetoric of death, domination, damnation, and decay always has as its object something external to the hearer. Its purpose is to get the hearer to do, say, or be something that he is not—to change the hearer in accordance with some external object or form. Its purpose is to get someone to buy a particular make of car, to lobby or agitate, to approve or endorse someone or something, or to be angry about this or pleased about that. This is the rhetoric that is concerned with persuading someone of something, the persuasion of advertising in all its forms.

The other rhetoric, that of life, liberation, salvation, and growth has no external object about which the hearer must be persuaded. Its purpose is only to persuade the soul of the hearer to persuade itself, to discover and to be true to its own nature.

The character of that form of persuasion that we call "teaching" becomes clearer in its conventional duplicity. On the one hand, teaching means telling, conveying, instructing, and informing somebody who does not know what he ought to know, even though he may not know that he does not know it. The best virtues of the teacher dedicated to this kind of teaching are clarity, orderliness, precision, and direction—virtues primarily connected with the way in which subject matter is held and presented. The image Plato presented still holds. It is as if knowledge runs from full to empty, from the teacher who knows to the student who is ignorant (at least of that which the teacher teaches). There is an imbalance, an inequality between teacher and student that is measured by the knowledge that the teacher possesses and that the student does not. The teaching virtues are predicated on the assumption that the teacher knows his subject and has possession of the truth: It is the possession of truth that justifies the inequality between teacher and student. It is also possession of truth that justifies the authority of the teacher, for he is, after all, the author of the student's knowledge.

In this view of teaching, the best virtue of the student is being receptive and docile, accepting of the teacher's authority, and grateful for his willingness to teach the truth he possesses. The teacher's winged words are arrows—directed with precision at the ignorance of the student. If they hit their mark, they bring with them the knowledge of the teacher to the putative benefit of the student.

On the other hand, it is possible to see teaching as a very different kind of persuasion. It is, perhaps, more like an exhortation, an encouragement, than a persuasion in the usual sense, for the simple reason that it is intrinsically valuable and its worth does not depend on the content that is transferred. The teacher is not a purveyor or conveyer of information, knowledge, or truth—not that such things may not be useful, but they are not the characteristics of a teacher. This second kind of teaching has as its aim the encouragement of the student's soul to discover by itself whatever lies within it. The purpose is not to make up for the deficiency of the soul by telling it what it needs to know, but to encourage, to put courage into the student so that he will find what he needs to know within himself.

The well-known Socratic ignorance is ironical because he claims, at the same time and in the same set of Greek letters in the *Apology*, that he knew that he did not know, that he knew *that which* he did not know, and that he knew *because* he did not know. What he needed was already within him—in some sense. The Platonic view of knowledge as recollection, as *anamnesis*, only says again that what we need to know is generated from that which is within us. In the *Meno*, the famous episode with the slave makes manifest the internal power of the soul to search and see the rightness of things. This dialogue has led one commentator to remark that you could teach Meno's slave geometry, but you could not teach the sons of Pericles virtue. In a sense, this is true, but there is hidden shift in the meaning of "teach." The dialogue shows that geometry, an apt subject for exposition and for teaching of the first kind, may also be taught by "putting questions in the right way" (as Cebes has it in the

Phaedo), that is, by the second kind of teaching. It also shows that virtue can never be taught by the first kind of instruction—the kind that the unfortunate sons of Pericles experienced. It is a contradiction to suppose that the freedom and self-control required in virtue can be structured into the soul from without that they could find their origin outside of ourselves.

Socrates is a teacher of the second kind—although he claims to teach no one and only to ask questions. I am content to allow him his own formulation but must insist that he does admit to encouraging and exhorting the citizens of Athens to care more for virtue than for wealth. He is a persuader of the citizens, and especially of the young men—but, in the conventional sense, there is no content to the persuasion.

Socrates' winged words are not arrows. He has no target audience—he will talk with anyone who will play question and answer with him. He seeks to let those he talks with display themselves both to themselves and to others—for often, like Thrasymachus, they "have a fine answer ready," but sometimes they discover unexpected beauty in themselves, as did Charmides and Theatetus. Socrates does not try to tell or inform people of what they should think, believe, or say. That is their business, not his. If, in spite of his protestations, he is a teacher, his business is with the souls of his students, of those who talk with him, and even of those who just listen to him talk with others. The teacher, like the lover, must know about the soul.

Meno's soul is stuck with the glue of sophistic argument. Even his name punningly tells us that he will not move as the Greek word *menein* means to remain or stay. The task of Socrates is to get his soul to move. If he can do that, with Meno or with anyone, then the soul will find its own proper direction. It will seek for whatever truth there is, whatever truth it needs. That is the easy part. The hard part, the part in which we all need assistance, is helping the soul to move and, having moved, to keep moving. That is the true business of the teacher, of the teacher whose winged words are not arrows but birds seeking their proper home and lodgment in the human soul. Socrates cannot control whose soul will be open to his words and those of the people he speaks with; the words, like birds, can be set free but where they will alight, where they will nest, and who will give them sanctuary cannot be known.

If Socratic teaching is of this second kind, then the conduct of Socrates in the dialogues becomes more intelligible. His purpose is simply to help souls to move—to help them order themselves inwardly. His prayer at the end of the *Phaedrus,* the dialogue dedicated to love and rhetoric, is most apt:

> Beloved Pan, and all you other gods of this place, grant that I become beautiful within, and that such outward things as I have be friendly with me inwardly."

The relation between what is within and what is without is clear. Primacy is to the inward ordering of the soul: outward possessions must conform themselves to that inner order.

The purpose of love or friendship, purpose in the sense of its business, its work, is to assist in the right ordering of the soul. The greatest external sign of love, the greatest work of love, is to encourage, exhort, persuade the beloved to pay attention to the ordering of the soul, to what in the *Republic* is called justice. But the lover's persuasion is not simply based in words, it must be based ultimately in the life of the lover himself. The final way to encourage the beloved to attend to his soul's ordering is, of course, for the lover to attend to his own soul's ordering. As Socrates knew, this is a full-time job. To quote from an altogether different era:

> He who would not be slothful,
> Let him love.

This lofty conception of the lover's task and of its role in his own improvement, in his own growth in virtue, has its matter-of-fact counterpart in Aristotle's technical treatise on rhetoric:

> Persuasion is achieved by the speaker's personal character when the speech is so spoken as to make us think him credible. We believe good men more fully and more readily than others: this is true generally whatever the question is, and absolutely true where exact certainty is impossible and opinions are divided. This kind of persuasion, like the others, should be achieved by what the speaker says, not by what people think of his character before he begins to speak. It is not true, as some writers assume in their treatises on rhetoric, that the personal goodness revealed by the speaker contributes nothing to his power of persuasion; on the contrary, his character may almost be called the most effective means of persuasion he possesses (Book 1.2.3).

This is technical in the sense that it totally ignores the ultimate moral questions involved in persuasion and addresses only the efficacy of the means. Who should be persuaded, of what things, by whom, and on what occasions is not the concern of a technician. His moral character may well be the most effective means of persuasion that the speaker possesses, but the term "moral character" means the character of the speaker as it is perceived by the audience on a specific occasion. This perception is subject to some measure of control by the speaker himself because he can, to some extent, adopt the character that seems appropriate to the situation, the character that promises to work most effectively to his advantage. He presents himself in a certain way.

Socrates the rhetorician is not above giving himself a "moral character" or, at least, an "intellectual character," which amounts to the same thing for him. He will change, adapt, modify, falsify, or simply repeat words; he will remember or misremember or forget beliefs; he will quote, interpret, apply, and extrapolate from received opinion; he will treat seriously or comically views of other thinkers, present or not; he will even tell the truth, as he sees it, on occasion. What saves him from moral obloquy is the simple but unmistakable fact that he reaps no advantage, at least no personal, private advantage, nothing that anyone else would consider an advantage.

The aim of Socrates is to help the soul to move, be it the soul of Glaucon, Phaedrus, Simmias and Cebes, even of Callicles. It makes no difference. Once a soul starts to move it will find its proper direction and proceed toward its own right ordering. It is not necessary for Socrates— or for any teacher—to know what that right order is. It would be arrogant to presume that knowledge. The right order and the right ordering of the soul is the business of each and every soul; if a soul can be helped to move, or to move more forcefully or more directly, then the work of the teacher is being accomplished. Nothing more is necessary.

The teacher, Socrates, gains no advantage. He is not richer or more powerful politically, he is not more honored or higher in the social scale, he is not better able "to help friends and harm enemies" in the manner of Polemarchus, he gains nothing of the conventional goods that others seek or admire. All he gets is everything that matters: the continued exercise of his own soul in its search for and maintenance of its right order and the continuing companionship of others. That is all, and it is everything.

As Socrates admits in the *Phaedrus,* he never leaves Athens:

> I am a lover of learning, and trees and open country will not teach me anything, whereas men in the city do.

The soul learns from and with other souls.

Socratic rhetoric and Socratic teaching are directed toward helping the soul discover its own proper order. It does not claim to know what that order is, although in the Platonic dialogues the soul's elements, or powers, that need ordering are sketched and the possible orderings or relationships between the parts are indicated. But to have a sketch (or even a full-blown theory) is not to have an ordered soul. If Socrates has some idea of the nature of the soul and its parts, that does not give him the power to bring about the right ordering in anyone else. The right ordering is a continuing process for each of us.

Socratic persuasion, or Socratic teaching, (indeed, all true teaching), has to do with the soul's discovery (or rediscovery) of its own proper order in the process of achieving that order. Thus education and philosophy are intimately linked in a therapeutic endeavor to cure the soul of its disorder. The curious nature of the soul as that which moves itself becomes apparent in this endeavor, for the soul will find its proper peace in the realization of its own order. It will recognize the rightness of the order, and by that recognition it will know what is rightly ordered. The knowing and the being will be one and the same. No external criterion is necessary.

The most obvious metaphor for this activity is drawn from music. The classical Greek language was itself music. It varied in pitch even in ordinary discourse, and so had a powerful musical dimension. When it was changed by rhapsodes or sung by minstrels, the music, coupled with the meter or measure, must have strongly affected the soul. In addition, the musical search for measure and harmony affords exactly the kind of conception and language (or rhetoric) needed to describe the right ordering of the soul. It is not just a happy accident that in the *Republic* Plato speaks of moderation or temperance as stretching "from top to bottom of the whole scale" of the city, so that everybody sings the same song together. And finally, of course, music by its very nature is the quintessence of rhetoric in that it sets out to persuade us of nothing but itself.

That Socrates and Plato understood this relationship between philosophy and music cannot be doubted. To offer but one example from the *Phaedo,* consider Socrates' discussion of his dream whilst in prison. He dreamed there, as he had dreamed periodically throughout his life, of a figure who came and said, "Socrates, work and make music." Previously, he had assumed that the figure was encouraging him to do what he was already doing; for, he says, "philosophy was my work, and philosophy is the highest music." In case he had misunderstood the meaning of the figure, Socrates decided to compose a hymn *(prooimion)* to Apollo, whose festival had postponed his death for a few days, and then to set Aesop's fables to music. The *Phaedo* is a dialogue for the Pythagoreans, as is well known, for the identification of music and philosophy originated with Pythagoras.

The music of the Greek language, with all its inherent charm, and enhanced in the dialogues by Plato's genius, has an additional component, in the meaning of the winged words. That Socratic rhetoric is powerfully persuasive is clear (it seems to have persuaded Plato, although not Alcibiades). Yet the function of the words as words with meaning and not just as the bearers of musical melodies requires some consideration.

WORDS AS IMAGES

We would normally assume that winged words are specific words carrying a specific meaning. But, contrary to Aristotle, Platonic words are not univocal, they do not have one identifiable specific meaning or definition. In a certain sense, they have no definition at all, in that they do not have clearly prescribed limits. The Greek for definition is *horos*, the same word used for boundary, and for Plato the meaning of a word is like a zone or a region. Although in the context of a particular conversation some things clearly fall within the zone and other things equally clearly fall outside of it, there are some things that seem both to belong and not to belong.

This may seem a vague view of language, more suitable perhaps for the thought factory of Aristophanes' *Clouds*, but properly speaking it is a view of language as vague. This view is connected with the Platonic notion of images, of things that are not what they are. It does have a certain vagueness about it, but that is because words are images, and any attempt to give words a constant precision would give a totally false impression of what they referred to: Images are signed by words that, in their turn, are also images. Only the Platonic ideas or forms are really what they are, and they are beyond discourse.

In my library there is, I tell you a statue of Socrates. Calling it a statue is only a way of saying that it is an image. It is, in fact, if not in truth, a resin composition made from a mold—at least two more stages removed from the original—which, in turn, was made from a Roman copy of a Greek original dating from the third century B.C., which means at least two more stages of imaging. Moreover, the Roman copy was a miniature of what seems to have been a life-size statue, and it is not clear how many stages of imagining that entailed. The life-size original could not have been carved from life, so the relation of the statue to the original Socrates is problematical at best. In any case it involves a number of further stages of imaging. Since the statue suits my library so well, I have decided to photograph it and circulate a photocopy of the photograph among my associates, the Friends of the Forms. Some of them, in turn, photocopy the photocopy and show their colleagues. I shall not pretend to be able to count the number of imaging stages that will have been gone through. I do know that each stage of the imaging process reduces the definition of the statue and that if the process continues, it will be impossible to identify the image, without the use of a title or label. Even with a label, credulity might well be strained. During the process, someone might decide that the image is getting blurred and attempt to give it a better definition. Whether it is a better definition of Socrates or just a better definition would be moot.

A word is like that. A word has and ought to have a certain indistinctness, room for the meaning to move around in. Every word ought to have an indefinition as well as a definition, since it must have an indefiniteness. The indefiniteness, however, is not necessarily a disadvantage, and we should not, out of impatience or frustration, seek to make our words totally clear and distinct. Without producing an extended argument to support this view, the value of flexible word meanings can be seen in the various understandings poetry expresses with its multiple meanings and types of ambiguity.

The view here under consideration is that, again contrary to Aristotle, all language is metaphorical. Or that all language is poetic. Everybody knows that metaphors are like mathematical proportions, or series of ratios, with some of the terms suppressed. They derive their effectiveness as our knowledge of one set of things, or of one universe, is used to extend our knowledge of another set of things, or of another universe.

For example, everybody in ancient Athens knew the story of Theseus and the Minotaur, and yet, in the *Phaedo,* Plato is at great pains to remind them (and us) of its details. It seems an act of supererogation until it becomes clear to us that the story being told again is about Socrates and the fourteen named people who were with him on his last day. The number fourteen is the giveaway, simply because they must be the seven youths and seven maidens, the famous "seven pairs," who were sent as the Athenian tribute to Minos. The story of Theseus is a metaphor for the story of Socrates, and if we read the dialogue with this in mind, doubtless we shall seek to identify the Minotaur that Socrates killed. The story will help us, in our turn, to slay the same monster. The metaphor is undoubtedly there, but explicit verbal reference to it is suppressed, and it is left to us to see the connection.

There is not a total and explicit one-to-one correspondence between the parts of the metaphor and the elements of that which the metaphor represents. There is an overlap of boundaries, as it were. It must also be borne in mind that if Theseus is a metaphor of Socrates, Socrates is equally a metaphor of Theseus. The process is not clear and distinct, however, and it makes a demand upon the hearer or reader by making him supply the connections. That effort requires a greater investment of one's energy and a consequent greater commitment to the result, an educational outcome which is not minor.

The insistence upon language as metaphor, with its advantage of vividness and vitality and its disadvantage of possible blurred vision and imprecision, draws attention to the fact that in language one thing stands for another, although we have to be careful about the sense of "thing." Language is a sign system, and Plato is constantly drawing attention to the relation between the sign and what it signifies. This is also the concern of the rhapsode and of the rhetorician but in a somewhat different manner.

In the dialogue *Ion,* Socrates challenges Ion to say who will understand better the chariot race instructions in Book 23 of *The Iliad,* the rhapsode or the charioteer. The answer cannot be doubted in the context nor can the sense of Socrates' challenge. For the charioteer, the instructions from Nestor to his son have to be related to the actual role of language in philosophical investigation as Plato understands it. The truth about things is somehow lurking in the language ordinary people use, and truth is accessible to those people because they share in the language.

Words as spoken, language as used, are then somehow the home of truth. It is the realm in which both particulars and ideas coexist.

There is, however, another kind of sharing, another kind of participation, which takes place in the realm of language—that of human sharing. As we say, language is a medium of communication, a substratum for having or being in common. Socrates shares his quest, his second journey, with anyone and everyone, whether they initially will it or not. It has already been reported that, as a lover of learning, Socrates will not leave the city, for men teach him and the countryside does not. The philosophical quest of Socrates (and, of course, of Plato) takes place between two pairs of poles, between particular things and the ideas, and between Socrates the philosopher, and another man, a friend such as Glaucon or an opponent such as Protagoras. If the *Republic* needed a motto, it would not be inappropriate to take (from St. 424) "the things of friends are common," "friends share," *(koina ta philon)*, and it is not accidental that it is precisely this proverb that is used to identify the best city in the *Laws* (St. 739c).

The realm of words, of the logos, provides a local habitation for the ideas and for human souls. It could almost be said that it is the matrix out of which being and knowing—and better men—are generated. This gives to the world of the logos a status far different from that which it holds in the operations of the poets and rhapsodes. For the philosophers, words are the means of access to the intelligible world, to the realm of ideas that somewhat like Homeric gods "stand, hidden in air," and the means of access to other human beings. For the poets and rhapsodes, words are tools to be used and laid aside at will; for the philosophers, the logos is a nurturing habitat supporting an inquiring and self-examining life. For the poets and rhapsodes, the value of words is extrinsic, derived from their utility in stirring the souls of men; for the philosophers, the value of the logos is intrinsic, for it is self-subsisting and connects the human with the divine, and one human with another.

Words are not feelings, yet the rhapsode uses them to arouse the feelings he chooses in others. Words are not ideas; yet the philosopher uses them to arouse in others the ideas he himself has (and possibly those he does not have incidentally). How is this possible? How can this action at a distance come about?

Feelings and ideas are not transmitted directly, but somehow words can bring about the feelings and ideas of one person in the soul of another. That seems to be clear, yet the explanation is not obvious. The poet and the rhapsode do not need, for their purposes, to seek any

conduct of a chariot race. In the process of turning the corner of the course, is the advice good or not; if followed, will it ensure a safe, tight, and fast turn? For Ion, the instructions have to be related, not to the chariot race (in which he is not competing), but to the effects they have upon the audience (for whose approval he is competing). In the simplest terms possible, do they sound good? Now since some members of the audience will know something about charioteering, the instructions, as written by the poet and as chanted by the rhapsode, must not be contrary to what a skilled charioteer would do, yet they need not say all that he will do. The test for the congruence of the instructions with what a charioteer would do is mainly negative; nobody expects or wants a complete and exact treatise on charioteering.

Socrates is well aware that the true subject matter of Ion and the other rhapsodes and of Homer himself is the soul of man. He is well aware because, as a teacher, he shares the same subject matter. That is also the reason for his criticism of the poets in the *Republic*. The poets and the rhapsodes appear to be talking about one set of things, but they are really dealing with another set of things—"no small matter, but how a man should live." It is not so much that they are dealing in images, for Socrates himself deals in images. And it is not that the images are ill-founded because they write and speak, for example, about medical matters without medical training. It is really that they are not aware of or do not accept the responsibility for the fact that their business is to affect the human soul.

The rhapsodes and rhetoricians see language as a sign system, but the words are signs of power to arouse the soul; they are not signs of what they name, of what they would normally be thought to signify, of their meaning. This is philosophically and educationally objectionable because it has no vision of the right ordering of the soul, it has no concern with justice. In fact, Ion's success, in his own terms, depends precisely upon the disordering of the soul. In the dialogue which is effectively his obituary notice, the following exchange occurs:

> **Ion:** How clear your proof is to me, Socrates. I will tell you and hide nothing. Whenever I recite something pitiful, my eyes are filled with tears, and whenever I recite something fearful or horrible, my hair stands on end with fright and my heart throbs.
>
> **Socrates:** Well then, Ion, are we to say that such a man is in his right mind who, being dressed up in gorgeous garments and golden wreaths, bursts into tears at festivals and feasts, although he has lost none of his finery, or who, while standing among more than twenty thousand friendly people, is terrified, although no one is robbing or injuring him?

Ion has certainly told all and has hidden nothing. There is no sense here that he deliberately makes tears come to his eyes or his hair to stand on end in order to affect the audience. He himself really is affected, which is only another way of saying that he is not in his right mind. But the effects upon himself, contrived or not, are an indication to the audience as to how they should feel, what effects they should suffer on hearing the rhapsode's chant. The rhapsode acts as a leader—which partly explains Ion's claim that the rhapsode's art and the general's art are the same. Payment by the members of the audience (or by the judges of a contest on their behalf) is their acknowledgement that the rhapsode has been their general.

The ultimate subject matter of both Socrates and the rhapsodes is the soul, but the proximate subject matter is language, the words. The purpose for Socrates is to encourage the soul to "work itself and make music," that is to bring about the right ordering, the harmony, of the parts of the soul. Words must be attended to simply because they are a most powerful means by which this harmony can be encouraged. The purpose for Ion, for all rhapsodes and poets in fact, is not to let the soul of each audience member make its own music, but to let the words strike the soul as an instrument, just as the plectrum strikes the lyre, so as to bring forth the music already written by the poet. Paying the rhapsode is only a continuation of the same pattern—it expresses gratitude for having been made a fine instrument, a gratitude that the rhapsode is pleased, graciously pleased, to accept. It also marks the termination of the audience as instrument; the performance is now over.

Thus for Socrates and for Ion, for the philosopher and for the rhapsode, there are two matters in common, the soul and words. The topics are common but the ways and purposes of understanding are different. For the rhapsode, the words are winged toward a particular part of the soul, to this feeling or that, to arouse and give the feeling a kind of life of its own, independent of the whole soul and of the person and independent of any circumstance that might cause such a feeling in ordinary life. The subject matter of the words, their meaning and reference, what they signify, is truly incidental and all that is necessary is to observe some simple rules. Words about death are not usually capable of arousing laughter, and words of buffoons are not usually capable of causing grief. But even these simple rules are not inflexible and, with special care, may be violated in order to achieve a greater triumph by the surprising arousal of an unexpected feeling. Otherwise, words are used as necessary to arouse, restrain, or fulfill a feeling, or become, as the archsophist Pooh-Bah says, "Merely corroborative detail, intended to give artistic verisimilitude to an otherwise bald and unconvincing narrative."

For Socrates, for Plato, and, indeed, for Aristotle, language is not a useful tool or a mere means to provide corroborative detail, it is the realm between sensible things and ideas, the connecting kingdom between particulars and universals. It is the world in which meaning is

most readily accessible to us. To understand, go first to the w name and describe and discuss what you seek to understand is commonly said, for somewhere in what is commonly s received opinions, what is sought is to be found. Socrates, in passage of his intellectual biography in the *Phaedo*, reports tur "second sailing." He had heard someone reading from a book agoras in which the philosopher claimed that intelligence *(nou* everything. Socrates understood this to mean that explanatic given in accordance with the good, that explanations would stat was better for things to be the way they are rather than some oth He was, however, disappointed on reading the books of Anaxago no use was made of the good but, rather, the explanations were in of "air and aether and water and many other absurdities." Socrates to share with Cebes his second sailing, his second attempt, his use of when the wind had failed him. Although the Greek phrase *deuteros* meant, in part, a second best simply because no one would prefer ro over wind-power, there is a certain advantage in Socrates' second saili Its accomplishments result from his own efforts and remain in his o power.

This second sailing consists in turning away from a deducti method, from the good, or from intelligence, as Anaxagoras ha seemingly and falsely promised, and away from mechanical explanation in terms of "bones and sinews," to take refuge in *logoi*, in words, in language. Socrates no longer investigates the things themselves but rather their truth. It is the truth that connects the rational part of the soul with what can be known. It is truth that makes possible both the intellect's power to know and, simultaneously, the intelligibility of what is knowable.

Socrates shares questions and answers with others, and it is in these shared, common words that he searches for the truth of things. He lays down in words the most reliable, the strongest statement he can about what he seeks to understand. Other statements that harmonize with this are taken to be true, and those that do not harmonize are taken to be false. This method leads to what are known as the Ideas or the Forms *(eide)* and Socrates reverts to those "much babbled about" words in which it is taken for granted that there is something "beautiful by itself" and so forth. Something is beautiful because it shares or partakes in this "beautiful itself by itself"—and this is the paradigm for all statements about cause.

THE REDISCOVERY OF TRUTH

It is not necessary here to give a full account of the forms and of Socrates' second sailing. What is necessary, however, is to note the crucial

explanation. There is enough empirical evidence to show that it happens and enough experience to provide a wide range of practical instances for them to draw on in working with their audiences. The philosopher is not and should not be so easily satisfied. The explanation of how Socrates' idea can become Glaucon's idea is worth understanding in itself, and it may well be helpful in understanding how a particular beautiful thing participates in the idea of "beauty itself by itself." There are some obvious differences. The most notable is that there can be an equality— or a sameness—between Socrates' idea and that of Glaucon, whereas there is no equality between the image and the idea, although there is an interdependence. The image's existence is its participation in one or more of the ideas. But there is the added fact that the ideas are shared among men, not as possessions, for the idea does not belong to Socrates or to Glaucon, but as that which makes Socrates and Glaucon, and us, a community. Moreover, this community endures through time for, in a sense, the ideas become the soul. The rhapsode may well have all his hearers weeping at the same time but they are not a community, they are an aggregate, a regiment. And after the performance is over, all they have in common is the memory that they wept at the same time as twenty-thousand others, under the sway of their general-rhapsode, Ion.

The interest in words common to rhetoricians, the rhapsodes, and the philosophers is vastly different for each in its grounding. The interest in the soul is also common, but the reason for that interest is also different. For all three, the words, which are readily available, sensible sounds, give access to that which is hidden, the soul. But the soul is conceived differently and access to it is sought for very different reasons.

The rhetorician's interest in the soul extends only so far as is necessary for him to affect it. That is why in the *Gorgias* Socrates calls rhetoric, as practiced by Gorgias, "a flattery." The purpose of Gorgias, as rhetorician, is simply to make the soul feel good and he does that, by and large, simply by making the soul feel. In a certain sense, to have any feeling aroused (even an unpleasant feeling) makes us "feel good" for it reassures us of our being alive. Even if the feeling aroused is unpleasant in itself, we can enjoy just being able to feel; we can enjoy the feeling of being secure in the knowledge that there is no external or objective reality causing the feeling—our safety is not imperiled; and we can enjoy our dependence upon the rhetorician who will relieve us of our anxiety when we have reached (or before we have reached, in the case of less skillful speakers) our limit of endurance. The fundamental mechanism of the rhetoricians is the controlled causing and relaxing of tension.

The rhetoric of Socrates and Plato differs from that of the rhetoricians in that it does not aim to make the soul "feel good" but to help the soul "be good."

Neither Socrates nor Gorgias, neither Plato nor Isocrates, can be effective in their various uses of words unless those words are, in some sense, "at home" in the soul. The rhetorician and rhapsode do not care that the soul welcomes the logos, they simply use it to their own advantage. The philosopher not only cares, he sees it as a sign of never-ending hope, of an always-possible conversion. He sends words out into the air—carefully chosen words, sent in a carefully chosen manner (for he has a repertoire of "winging" styles to choose from). They are addressed, quite often, to a particular person (such as Glaucon or Callicles) but always labeled "to whom it may concern."

When Socrates talks with Glaucon, he does so in the presence of others. But when Plato writes a dialogue in which Socrates talks with Glaucon, he does so in the presence of us all. We all become hearers—if we are "concerned." The rhetorical problem Plato faced was quite clear to him, and he draws attention to it in the *Phaedrus* (St. 275):

> **Socrates:** You know, Phaedrus, that's the strange thing about writing, which makes it truly analogous to painting. The painter's products stand before us as though they were alive: but if you question them, they maintain a most majestic silence. It is the same with written words: they seem to talk to you as though they were intelligent, but if you ask them anything about what they say, from a desire to be instructed, they go on telling you just the same thing forever. And once a thing is put in writing, the composition, whatever it may be, drifts all over the place, getting into the hands not only of those who understand it, but equally of those who have no business with it; it doesn't know how to address the right people, and not address the wrong. And when it is ill-treated and unfairly abused it always needs its parent to come to its help, being unable to defend or help itself.

There is another kind of discourse, Plato writes, that does not have this disadvantage:

> The sort that goes together with knowledge, and is written in the soul of the learner: that can defend itself, and knows to whom it should speak and to whom it should say nothing.
>
> **Phaedrus:** You mean no dead discourse, but the living word, the original of which the written discourse may fairly be called a kind of image.

The writing of dialogues seems to be the form Plato chooses to minimize the problems both of fixity of written words and of inappropriate audiences. The dialogues imitate most closely the spoken and living word, like a mime of Sophron, as Aristotle remarks. But since they imitate ordinary conversation (sometimes about very extraordinary things), there is no formal announcement of a conclusion, although the discussions reach various stages just as they do in ordinary life. Although

Socrates (or his interlocutor) sometimes draws a comparison between the conversation and a trial, there is no defendent, no prosecutor, no evidence, no jury, and no verdict except within the soul of the hearers. Each hearer does as he sees fit. There is no charge from the judge to render a verdict, no arrows of winged words. Each decides for himself whether he wants to decide, and if he does want to make a decision, he does so on his own accord.

Some do not see that they need to make a decision. They have heard, been amused, intrigued, refreshed, frustrated, annoyed, or placated, each to his own. They can pass on their way, without even hearing the conversation to its end. Presumably, this freedom to stay and listen or not is one of the ways of guaranteeing that the words only reach those who are willing to hear them, those who will know how to let the words do their work of the soul.

It seems that those who paid attention, those to whom the conversations of Socrates made a difference, were either very constructive in their own way, such as Plato and Xenophon, or highly destructive, such as Alcibiades and Charmides. They were all, in some sense, powerful. Of those who were impassioned by the dialogues, it seems that some approved of Socrates and some did not—and with great vehemence in either case. Those who disapproved most strongly were people like Anytus—a not very attractive character in the dialogues—but a man with great ambition and not inconsiderable talent. Presumably, he saw Socrates as a rival, but not for political office; rather, Anytus saw that Socrates exemplified a way of life in which the goods that Anytus could offer had no value. In fact, he accuses Socrates of "corrupting the youth," which must mean changing their values. That would be much more disturbing to Anytus than a mere competitor for political office. When Socrates says in the *Gorgias* that he is the only true politician, the Anytuses of this world get the message.

For Aristotle, politics is, of course, the architectonic art. That is, it rules all the other arts. It claims by the exercise of its lawful authority to oversee all that goes on in the city. It has, at one level, all the other arts as its subject matter. But this is equally claimed by both rhetoric and dialectic, both of which claim the right and power to deal with all subject matters. Socrates is, perhaps, the most flagrant example of all the "wise men" because he not only assumes that he can talk about anything with anyone, but even insists on doing it with those who are supposedly most expert in the field. And even if the experts, as named in the Platonic dialogues, had been dead for many years, the dialogues themselves bring into question the authority of all who, like Ion, claim or can be expected to have expertise.

The dialogue *Laches,* for example, contains Socrates' discussion of courage with Gens. Laches and Nicias, the former noted for action, the latter for thought and words. The dramatic date of the dialogue is about 420 B.C. At that time Laches had established a reputation as a good soldier, having assisted in the capture of Messenia, but he had been overshadowed (as Alcibiades reports in the *Symposium*) by Socrates who had shown more courage at the retreat from Delium in 424, a fact for which Laches admired him. Nicias had a better reputation, but more as a politician than as a general, and in 421 he had negotiated the so-called Peace of Nicias with Sparta. The dialogue itself must have been written and publicly read around 390, after Nicias, by his superstition and indecision, had destroyed the Athenian force sent to Syracuse, in 415, and himself with it. Laches had been killed at the battle of Mantinaea, in 418, which the Spartans had won simply because of their own courage. It could not have been comfortable being an Athenian general at that time, witness the careers of Conon and Iphicrates. But to have the supposed characteristic of a soldier and a general (courage) publicly discussed in a way that showed the limitations of understanding of past generals must have given pause to current officeholders and ambitious future candidates.

Plato has Socrates invite the opinions of experts (publicly known or self-proclaimed) on the subjects he discusses. Laches and Nicias speak on courage, Gorgias on rhetoric, Callicles on power, Protagoras on the teachability of virtue, Meno on virtue itself, Agathon on love, and so forth. Presumably, the historical figures in the dialogue represent views that they actually held in life, or that were consistent with those that they held in life. But Plato goes further than letting or requiring historical figures to represent philosophical positions in a manner which may or may not be historically exact. He requires that the subject matter of the dialogue be exemplified in the dramatic action of the dialogue itself.

RHETORIC, PERSUASION, AND TRANSLATION

If rhetoric is seen as an art of persuasion, that means that it is an art that transmits a thought, feeling, or motive for action from one person to another. To say that it involves a transmission may beg too many questions, although it is a popular way of speaking. The process of rhetoric may be the arousal in one person of what is in another, but even then the word "in" requires a first and elementary distinction. The matter of persuasion may be "in" the persuader as something of which he himself is already persuaded, but it may be "in" him as something which he wants others to believe although it is and remains external to him. The persuaded must take "in" the thought or motive for action so that he acts upon it, if the persuader is to be successful and the persuasion is to take place.

This means that, in one aspect, rhetoric is the art of transmission or, loosely, of communication. It is the art by which thought, feeling, and desire are brought into being in another. Whether that is a transmittal remains an open question, but in any case, words are a significant element in the operation.

In Plato, words are images of ideas, but it is equally true that actions are images of the soul. One would look for some kind of conguity between words and deeds, between words and ideas, and also between ideas and actions. If they are not congruent, then integrity of the soul is missing. In the dialogues, as in life, we hear people speak, we see them act, and we note the congruences and the discrepancies. We are affected by the degree of congruity. A speaker's impact is influenced by the degree of congruity he manifests. If Laches had been a coward (which he was not), our opinion of his views on courage would be different. If Nicias had not been so indecisive, we might have respected his views more. As it is, we look for continuity between ideas, words, and deeds—and it does not matter in which we begin or how we choose to begin. The dialogue named after Meno begins with a question, a multiple choice question, that he puts to Socrates:

> Can you tell me, Socrates, is virtue something that can be taught? And if it's not taught, is it acquired by practice? And if neither by practice, nor by learning, does it come to men by nature, or in some other way?

Looked at as words, the question offers five possible answers and the rigid structuring of Meno's mind requires him to suppose that only one answer is correct. The dialogue shows, with incredible wit, that they are all correct and that none of them are correct. But the opening question reveals something more. The questioning of someone is an action, and Meno's questioning of Socrates is a revealing action. Although, as we learn later in the dialogue, Meno and Socrates had seen each other and talked on the previous day, there is no gentle word of greeting from Meno. He is arrogant and ill-mannered. His question is abrupt, peremptory, and controlling, and the character of Meno begins to be revealed as the opening question reflects in part in the soul of Meno. The haughty and demanding manner leaves no doubt as to how Meno thinks virtue is acquired and—more importantly—what it is.

It is best, perhaps, to use a well-established Platonic word to designate this whole activity. The ideas of courage or virtue or whatever are *imitated* by words and by actions. We inhabit a world of *mimesis*.

When Shakespeare's King Henry V urges his men to "imitate the actions of a tiger," he does not expect them to go around on all fours, swishing their tails and growling. Nor does he expect them to conform to Old Possum's Growltiger:

His manners and appearance did not calculate to please;
His coat was torn and seedy, he was baggy at the knees;
One ear was somewhat missing, no need to tell you why,
And he scowled upon a hostile world from one forbidding eye.

Harry expects his men to be fierce. The imitation is of the idea of the
tiger, as it were, or of the moral virtue of the tiger, not of its appearance.
Although we can make fun in

Tiger, tiger, my mistake,
I thought that you were William Blake,

the truth is that the well-known poem takes the tiger as an access to the
Creator, of whom it is an imitation. It asks:

What immortal hand or eye
Could frame thy fearful symmetry?

But the imitator is not easily known by the imitation:

Did He smile His work to see?
Did He who made the lamb make thee?

Rhetoric is the art of using one set of things to stand for another set
of things; it is, in fact, the art of translation. Persuasion, the conventional
and commonsense view of rhetoric, is clearly a special case of translation.
The opinions in the persuader are translated into another who, if the
translation is successful, becomes the persuaded.

The word "translation" itself is etymologically derived from that
highly irregular Latin verb *fero,* I carry, with the highly regular preposi-
tion *trans,* across—as is the word *transfer.* Although we use the word
translate, it is by no means clear that the word should be taken literally. It
is clear that the opinions in one mind can come into being in the mind of
another and that winged words have been involved; it is not so clear that
the opinion has been "transferred" or "carried across." How it got across,
or, to use the colloquialism, how it was put across, is another question.

The activity of translating from one language into another—in the
case of the Platonic dialogues from classical Greek into modern American English—is not different in kind from the activity of Socrates
talking with Glaucon, of our talking with one another. As has been
observed many times, communication is strictly impossible, but it takes
place. Talking with one another, we suppose that what the words mean
to us is the same as what the words mean to others. A little reflection
might prompt us to add "more or less," but we assume that we mean the

same things "by and large," that there is enough overlap of our meaning with theirs to make communication possible. That still leaves the puzzling question as to how that more-or-less same meaning is aroused by the word. And yet, for various reasons, we change the words we use to express our meanings in the light of circumstances, in the light of our audience, in the light of the subject matter, and in the light of the time we have.

THE ARCHITECTURE OF THE DIALOGUE

The rhetorician must be able to speak briefly or at length, just as he must be able to speak on happy or unhappy occasions, to small or to large audiences, and upon this subject or that.

In writing the dialogues, Plato must have been acutely aware of their length. The word *length* is somewhat misleading to us since it implies a space or a distance in space. In fact, the dialogues were read aloud, as were all writings in the ancient world, and therefore it would be truer to say that Plato must have been acutely aware of the time each took to read aloud or to recite.

What elements would go into determining the length? It is hard to say, partly because we do not know in what circumstances Plato expected his dialogues to be read. Nor do we know how available they were to people outside the immediate circle of the Academy. If their circulation were somewhat restricted, then Plato could have controlled the circumstances in which they were heard. They might have been ceremonially recited on specific occasions, so that the audience, whatever its composition, might have known, in advance, how much time was needed for a total reading.

The connection of the dialogues with time is important. Indeed, some of the dialogues tell the day on which they were dramatically recited. That is, we are informed of the date of the dramatic conversation. It does not follow that the dialogues would be read only on the day of their dramatic date, but it is curious that Plato often indicates the day of the year the conversation took place.

The conversation of the *Laws*, for example, is quite explicitly stated to have begun at dawn on the day of the summer solstice, more or less June 21. The *Republic* (or *Polity* as I prefer to call it) reports a conversation "yesterday" in the Piraeus on the feast of Bendis, reputedly 19 Thargeliōn, or about June 5. The *Apology* occurs on or about 7 Mounichiōn, (April 23), the *Crito* on 6 Thargeliōn (May 24), the *Phaedo* on 8 Thargeliōn (May 30), and so forth.

Even if the dialogues were recounted, originally, on their dramatic dates in some annual cycle of ceremonial readings, it would be hard to know how to translate that into a meaning for the modern student of

Plato. What is even harder to deal with is the fact that the modern Platonist will read the dialogues to himself silently, while Plato clearly wrote them to be heard. The rhetoric of writing to be read silently is different from the rhetoric of writing to be heard. Nobody thinks that looking at the musical score of a Bach cantata is the same as hearing the cantata performed.

Reading aloud and hearing what is read are more public activities than reading to oneself. Because of its public character, reading aloud creates a more extreme response; it is hard to ignore what is said, and it is equally hard to evade responsibility for one's response to what is said. This is especially true among a group of friends, for friends share.

It should also be noted that reading aloud demands a slower and more measured pace than reading silently, and the text has a better chance of being true to itself. When we read to ourselves, silently, we can easily take great liberties with the text.

Little attention has been paid to the dramatic dates of the dialogues, but it is possible that they are related to the cycle of the year and that where they come in that cycle is an element of their meaning. The relation between Socrates and Theseus has already been alluded to, but that connection was only possible because of the religious festival's date in the civil year. The *Laws* begins when the sun is at its highest point in the sky, when it is at its most powerful, or, if you prefer it, at the beginning of its decline, on the day reputed to be the birthday of Zeus. The *Timaeus* (which is *not* a successor to the *Polity*) takes place at the annual festival of the Lesser Panathenaea, which had a fixed date, although modern opinions differ as to what it was. The Greater Panathenaea, which took place every four years, was held between 23 and 30 Hecatombaion; some scholars suppose that the lesser festival took place at the same time, but others, following Proclus, put it in the month of Thargeliōn. What matters is that Plato knew when the festival was held.

The other temporal aspect of the dialogues is the duration of their reading, the length of time taken for their recounting. Is this determined by the subject under discussion? The *Symposium,* the dialogue on love, has 36,000 syllables and takes two hours and twenty-four minutes to read aloud, in the style of Plato. What does 36,000 have to do with love? The *Politicus* or *Statesman* also has 36,000 syllables. Is that connected with the length of the Great Year that, we are assured, was 36,000 regular years? The *Phaedo* has 45,000 syllables and takes exactly three hours to read. Why? What does that have to do with Theseus and Socrates, with the immortality of the soul? The *Meno* has 19,600 syllables and takes one hour and eighteen minutes to read aloud. What does that have to do with virtue and "how it comes"? It clearly has something to do with a square, the dialogue's well-used geometrical example, since the square root of 19,600 is 140, which in turn is the diagonal of the square with a side of 100. Is the dialogue constructed on the basis of a geometrical diagram? And if so, how should the translator deal with it?

Any translator of the dialogues must understand that they have a musical and metrical structure as well as a verbal content. The words may signify ideas, but those ideas are to be understood in relation to the mathematical structures provided by the nonverbal aspects of the dialogue. Every dialogue and speech has a rhythm, a metrical pattern, which contributes to its meaning. And every dialogue has a definite length of time for its reading. To disregard these aspects is to falsify Plato.

One of the universally acknowledged key passages in all of Plato is the discussion of the divisions of and relations between the sensible and the intelligible worlds, contained in what is called The Divided Line (*Polity*, end of Book 6). This images the structure of being and knowing and the connection of both to the idea of the good or, simply, to the good, which is beyond being and knowing. The Divided Line obviously divides the dialogue, and it does so in the ratio of eight to five. What does this mean? It would not be unreasonable to assume that the Divided Line, since it claims to image all knowing and all being, suggests a way of understanding all of the dialogues, including the *Polity* itself. Should a translator try to preserve the relative lengths of various Greek passages? If he does not there is no question but that something will be lost.

What gets lost is the architecture, as it were, of the dialogue, the geometrical and arithmetical structure within which the words are formed. Thus use of such architecture is well attested throughout the ages; a simple and straightforward example is contained in Dante's *Divine Comedy.* First, it has, in all, one hundred cantos. Second, after an introductory first canto, each of the three parts of the work, the *Inferno, Purgatorio,* and *Paradiso,* has thirty-three cantos. Moreover, each part ends with what has been called "the sweet and hopeful word *stelle.*"

That this structure is deliberate and conscious could scarcely be doubted, but the effect of such ordering can easily be ignored or underestimated. Metrical patterns have rhetorical effects. They also affect the memory. There was a time in the ancient world when all public utterances by leaders were made in verse, which meant that commands tended to be remembered and repeated. Especially in Plato, the metrical structuring cannot be dismissed as a mere "artistic device" or even as a "Platonic idiosyncrasy"; the metrical or numerical arrangements not only aided the retention of the meaning but were themselves part of the meaning.

The meter itself and the repeating metrical patterns of the syllables and their duration through time must have grown out of the rhythms of the body and of the soul. If they had not, then they would not have endured as they did. The rhythms of writings that last must in some way imitate or accord with the rhythms of the combined body and soul. We are told on the authority of the learned medical man Galen, who was himself following Herophilus, that there is a similarity between the systolic and diastolic beats of the pulse and the arsis and thesis of the two-beat metrical foot called the iamb. No one has ever lived removed from the continuing iambic di-dum, di-dum, di-dum of the heartbeat. It would not, therefore, be surprising if we responded to rhythmical sound, if we felt "at home" and comfortable in a properly pulsating universe, in a patterned universe of discourse.

The importance of rhythmical speech has always been appreciated by rhetoricians, and audiences have always enjoyed measured cadences. The reason must be that, in some way, the rhythms of speech are the rhythms of the soul, which is not really surprising since speech comes from the soul.

Perhaps "resonate" would be a better word than "translate" to name the process by which thoughts and feelings in one person are aroused in another person. What the rhapsode counted upon was the natural or current vibrations of the human soul. If his own vibrations could be made to correspond with those of his audience, then he could really increase the amplitude of their vibrations. They would feel more acutely, more keenly.

Every physical object has its own free vibrations, and if a sound can be made with the same period, it will resonate. Something analogous to that happens with the soul. It would be interesting to establish a connection between this and the resonance theory of hearing.

Plato seems to have had a view that could be characterized as a rhetoric of resonance. The soul has a natural, free period of vibration, although this gets distorted by being near things with different periods, or things with no detectable period at all (or near people with disordered souls). The task of the teacher, whether Socrates or Plato or somebody else, is to help the soul recover its free period of vibration and to strengthen it, to resonate. It would not be hard to connect this view with the notion of love in the Phaedrus and the causes for the sprouting of the soul's wings.

Whatever the appropriate metaphor, it seems to be a fact that the soul responds to meter, to rhythm, to periodicity, and it does this without necessarily being aware that it is doing so. If asked, most people would readily admit that music they had heard was measured, that it had sections or divisions within it, and that these divisions were marked off in some way. If further inquiry were made about the nature of those divisions and the way in which they were marked off, most people would admit that they could not answer. But the measures of the music would still have had their effect.

This dimension or aspect of Platonic and Socratic rhetoric is, on occasions, referred to by the term "charm," *epadein*. The Greek word in its verbal form means to sing to or to sing over, to soothe or to charm in order to heal. The word and its cognates appear about forty-five times in the whole Platonic corpus, about a third of them in the dialogue *Charmides* (whose name is related to *xarma*, delight), which takes place the day after Socrates returns from the campaign at Potidaea in 431/430. A characteristic use is found in the *Phaedo* where Simmias and Cebes wish to be rid of their Minotaur, the fear of death; Socrates does not say that he can argue it away, as they ask, but suggests that they say charms over it every day until it vanishes. In the *Polity*, St. 608, our childish love of poetry is to be charmed away by the argument, so that we do not take poetry seriously, as if it were connected with truth.

The soul can be charmed by incantations, and it can be healed and soothed by songs. The inescapable conclusion seems to be that it is the musical and poetic dimensions of the charms, not the intellectual content of the words, that produce the desired result. The soul responds to the metrical music, not to the meaning of the winged words. The reason for this must be that, for Plato, the soul has a numerical structure, and it is not for nothing that it was said that music is the number of the soul.

That the dialogues are charming, in the more vague modern sense, is without doubt. People still read them, even when they cannot say quite why they are doing it. Praise is heaped upon the *Polity*, for example, by translators and commentators for its unity and completeness, although none of them have ever successfully stated the principle of that unity—in fact, some of them have proceeded to deny it. Although there are many wise things said in the dialogues, they do not seem to be read primarily for those wise sayings. Again, many translators treat the dialogues as if they contained information and doctrine that needed to be conveyed to the modern, non-Greek-speaking world—but usually with the proviso that they are only the historical record of Plato's thought. They should not affect us.

The academic world usually treats the original Academic as if he were an object to be viewed and, perhaps, admired, but not followed. He can be explicated but not understood, he can be almost anything except the one thing that he strove to be—a teacher. We can learn about Plato, but we steadfastly refuse to allow him to affect us. The dialogues, however, have a seductive way, even in the most contorted translations, of still carrying the music which will help the soul to start on its long journey to the back or outside of the world where, in the *Phaedrus* it can see all that is real.

Some translators, unconsciously no doubt, seem to work on the assumption that Plato is a manufacturer with a salesman called Socrates.

The translator's task is, first, to identify Plato's product, what he is selling, and, second, to let his salesman speak as aggressively or as rudely as the translator thinks necessary to affect the translator's audience.

Other translators (usually British) go further along this road by insisting that their translation is "the way we would say this sort of thing these days." This is not helpful because Plato is precise and does not deal in "this sort of thing," and in any case, modern intellectual life is not famous for its Socratic conversations.

Yet other translators assume that the truth that they have is the truth that Plato had, or would have had if he had lived now, and translate him to conform to their own understanding. This is either a way of self-congratulation or else a gratuitous act of mistaken kindness.

That the Platonic dialogues have lasted for 2,300 years or more is amazing. No doubt they will last for at least another 2,300 years, or as long as people can read and discuss the meaning of human life. The history of the physical preservation of the texts is not necessarily related to the content of those texts, but once the contents were known people have always been found to preserve and transmit them. The genius of Plato is the cause of this. The dialogues have, for thoughtful people, an almost irresistible attraction. Part of this attraction is connected with the piety and awe that Plato obviously felt toward Socrates; that a man could say, as Plato does, that he has written nothing of his own, that the writings attributed to him are those of a Socrates made young and beautiful, is simply breath-taking. Another part of this attraction is the absolute freedom, modesty, and self-restraint with which Plato acknowledges the greatness of Socrates—"Such was the end . . . of our friend, who, we may say, among the men of that time whom we knew, was the best, the wisest and the most just." Here is the affection and respect between equals. Then there is the character of Socrates himself—true to his name which means "safe power."

The characters who converse with Socrates also play their roles in the enchantment. They are live people, they are like our friends, or our colleagues, or our relations. They are like us. And the discussions themselves seem to lay out all the possible points of view about the subject, and we can find within them, somewhere or other, our favorite and most cherished opinion. We may find it but having found it, we sometimes lose it. And yet we do not feel that the dialogue has done us violence, it has done us no injury.

The rhetoric of resonance is practiced by both Plato and Socrates and we respond. We do not feel any injury because the dialogue has only helped us to persuade ourselves of something we already, in some sense, knew. We have been free to learn and the dialogue has reminded us of our own soul's structure.

The dialogues imitate—are examples of *mimesis*—and what they imitate is the human soul in the act of considering the meaning of itself, in relation to some particular aspect of itself. Or, to put it more simply, the dialogues are all examples of *metempsychosis*.

The translator has to deal with the same transmigration of souls and it is easier to say what not to do than what needs to be done. What is not needed is embellishment and attention to what some translators call "style." The dialogues do not need to be "improved" or "made palatable to current taste," they do not need to be dressed in "modern" idiom. Good standard American English is fine, and when Plato uses the same word again and again, it is better to translate it in the same way each time. We should not seek "variety" or "novelty." The discussion of how a man should live is not to be sought in an amusement arcade or anywhere else where novelty is at a premium. The soul does not need sequins in order to discover its proper beauty, and it should be left alone to do its own proper work.

Plato was known, and rightly known, in antiquity as a master of style. He knew what he wanted to say and how he wanted to say it—the how and the what were inseparable for him. He understood how to affect the soul because he had a very rare and precious respect for it. He did not try to master it in anyone else, he did not try to use it. His dialogues all conform to the numbers of the soul.

It seems strange to say, after all that, how relatively unimportant the knowledge of classical Greek is to a translator. Of course it is important. But if the translator is convinced that Plato was really a Christian-Hegelian or a totalitarian or a frustrated homosexual or a university pedant, there is no knowledge of Greek that will ever rescue him from disaster. And if the translator sees the dialogues as a substitute for his own writing, as a means to achieve tenure through another publication, as an opportunity for adding never-ending footnotes that unerringly and asymptotically approach irrelevance, in short, as a means of personal aggrandizement, there is no antidote to be found in the mastery of Attic Greek.

Perhaps the best model is to be found in Plato himself. After all, he translated Socrates. While it is true that they both spoke the same language, Plato's task of translation was harder than that of any modern would-be translator of the texts, for he translated the spoken word of Socrates into the written word—not of Plato, but of the dialogues. The living word written in the soul was translated into a living written discourse that had and still has the power to fill us with the love of learning.

It is usually assumed that Plato's disavowal of writing anything and the attribution of those works called his to a Socrates made young and beautiful is merely a gracious—or evasive—modesty. Perhaps we should begin to take him seriously.

The Republic

Plato

BOOK I

PERSONS OF THE DIALOGUE

SOCRATES, *who is the narrator*	CEPHALUS
GLAUCON	THRASYMACHUS
ADEIMANTUS	CLEITOPHON
POLEMARCHUS	

And others who are mute auditors.

The scene is laid in the house of Cephalus at the Piraeus; and the whole dialogue is narrated by Socrates the day after it actually took place to Timaeus, Hermocrates,Critias, and a nameless person, who are introduced in the Timaeus.

I went down yesterday to the Piraeus with Glaucon the son of Ariston, that I might offer up my prayers to the goddess;[1] and also because I wanted to see in what manner they would celebrate the festival, which was a new thing. I was delighted with the procession of the inhabitants; but that of the Thracians was equally, if not more, beautiful. When we had finished our prayers and viewed the spectacle, we turned in the direction of the city; and at that instant Polemarchus the son of Cephalus chanced to catch sight of us from a distance as we were starting on our way home, and told his servant to run and bid us wait for him. The servant took hold of me by the cloak behind, and said: Polemarchus desires you to wait.

I turned round, and asked him where his master was.

There he is, said the youth, coming after you, if you will only wait.

Certainly we will, said Glaucon; and in a few minutes Polemarchus appeared, and with him Adeimantus, Glaucon's brother, Niceratus the son of Nicias, and several others who had been at the procession.

Polemarchus said to me: I perceive, Socrates, that you and your companion are already on your way to the city.

You are not far wrong, I said.

But do you see, he rejoined, how many we are?

Of course.

1. Bendis, the Thracian Artemis.

And are you stronger than all these? for if not, you will have to remain where you are.

May there not be the alternative, I said, that we may persuade you to let us go?

But can you persuade us, if we refuse to listen to you? he said.

Certainly not, replied Glaucon.

Then we are not going to listen; of that you may be assured.

Adeimantus added: Has no one told you of the torch-race on horseback in honor of the goddess which will take place in the evening?

With horses! I replied: That is a novelty. Will horsemen carry torches and pass them one to another during the race?

Yes, said Polemarchus, and not only so, but a festival will be celebrated at night, which you certainly ought to see. Let us rise soon after supper and see this festival; there will be a gathering of young men, and we will have a good talk. Stay then, and do not be perverse.

Glaucon said: I suppose, since you insist, that we must.

Very good, I replied.

Accordingly we went with Polemarchus to his house; and there we found his brothers Lysias and Euthydemus, and with them Thrasymachus the Chalcedonian, Charmantides the Paeanian, and Cleitophon the son of Aristonymus. There too was Cephalus the father of Polemarchus, whom I had not seen for a long time, and I thought him very much aged. He was seated on a cushioned chair, and had a garland on his head, for he had been sacrificing in the court; and there were some other chairs in the room arranged in a semicircle, upon which we sat down by him. He saluted me eagerly, and then he said:—

You don't come to see me, Socrates, as often as you ought: If I were still able to go and see you I would not ask you to come to me. But at my age I can hardly get to the city, and therefore you should come oftener to the Piraeus. For let me tell you, that the more the pleasures of the body fade away, the greater to me is the pleasure and charm of conversation. Do not then deny my request, but make our house your resort and keep company with these young men; we are old friends, and you will be quite at home with us.

I replied: There is nothing which for my part I like better, Cephalus, than conversing with aged men; for I regard them as travellers who have gone a journey which I too may have to go, and of whom I ought to inquire, whether the way is smooth and easy, or rugged and difficult. And this is a question which I should like to ask of you who have arrived at that time which the poets call the "threshold of old age"—Is life harder towards the end, or what report do you give of it?

I will tell you, Socrates, he said, what my own feeling is. Men of my age flock together; we are birds of a feather, as the old proverb says; and at our meetings the tale of my acquaintance commonly is—I can not eat,

I can not drink; the pleasures of youth and love are fled away: there was a good time once, but now that is gone, and life is no longer life. Some complain of the slights which are put upon them by relations, and they will tell you sadly of how many evils their old age is the cause. But to me, Socrates, these complainers seem to blame that which is not really in fault. For if old age were the cause, I too being old, and every other old man, would have felt as they do. But this is not my own experience, nor that of others whom I have known. How well I remember the aged poet Sophocles, when in answer to the question, How does love suit with age, Sophocles,—are you still the man you were? Peace, he replied; most gladly have I escaped the thing of which you speak; I feel as if I had escaped from a mad and furious master. His words have often occurred to my mind since, and they seem as good to me now as at the itme when he uttered them. For certainly old age has a great sense of calm and freedom; when the passions relax their hold, then, as Sophocles says, we are freed from the grasp not of one mad master only, but of many. The truth is, Socrates, that these regrets, and also the complaints about relations, are to be attributed to the same cause, which is not old age, but men's characters and tempers; for he who is of a calm and happy nature will hardly feel the pressure of age, but to him who is of an opposite disposition youth and age are equally a burden.

I listened in admiration, and wanting to draw him out, that he might go on—Yes, Cephalus, I said; but I rather suspect that people in general are not convinced by you when you speak thus; they think that old age sits lightly upon you, not because of your happy disposition, but because you are rich, and wealth is well known to be a great comforter.

You are right, he replied; they are not convinced: and there is something in what they say; not, however, so much as they imagine. I might answer them as Themistocles answered the Seriphian who was abusing him and saying that he was famous, not for his own merits but because he was an Athenian: "If you had been a native of my country or I of yours, neither of us would have been famous." And to those who are not rich and are impatient of old age, the same reply may be made; for to the good poor man old age can not be a light burden, nor can a bad rich man ever have peace with himself.

May I ask, Cephalus, whether your fortune was for the most part inherited or acquired by you?

Acquired! Socrates; do you want to know how much I acquired? In the art of making money I have been midway between my father and grandfather: for my grandfather, whose name I bear, doubled and trebled the value of his patrimony, that which he inherited being much what I possess now; but my father Lysanias reduced the property below what it is at present: and I shall be satisfied if I leave to these my sons not less but a little more than I received.

That was why I asked you the question, I replied, because I see that you are indifferent about money, which is a characteristic rather of those who have inherited their fortunes than of those who have acquired them; the makers of fortunes have a second love of money as a creation of their own, resembling the affection of authors for their own poems, or of parents for their children, besides that natural love of it for the sake of use and profit which is common to them and all men. And hence they are very bad company, for they can talk about nothing but the praises of wealth.

That is true, he said.

Yes, that is very true, but may I ask another question?—What do you consider to be the greatest blessing which you have reaped from your wealth?

One, he said, of which I could not expect easily to convince others. For let me tell you, Socrates, that when a man thinks himself to be near death, fears and cares enter into his mind which he never had before; the tales of a world below and the punishment which is exacted there of deeds done here were once a laughing matter to him, but now he is tormented with the thought that they may be true: either from the weakness of age, or because he is now drawing nearer to that other place, he has a clearer view of these things; suspicions and alarms crowd thickly upon him, and he begins to reflect and consider what wrongs he has done to others. And when he finds that the sum of his transgressions is great he will many a time like a child start up in his sleep for fear, and he is filled with dark forebodings. But to him who is conscious of no sin, sweet hope, as Pindar charmingly says, is the kind nurse of his age:

"Hope," he says, "cherishes the soul of him who lives in justice and holiness, and is the nurse of his age and the companion of his journey;—hope which is mightiest to sway the restless soul of man."

How admirable are his words! And the great blessings of riches, I do not say to every man, but to a good man, is, that he has had no occasion to deceive or to defraud others, either intentionally or unintentionally; and when he departs to the world below he is not in any apprehension about offerings due to the gods or debts which he owes to men. Now to this peace of mind the possession of wealth greatly contributes; and therefore I say, that, setting one thing against another, of the many advantages which wealth has to give, to a man of sense this is in my opinion the greatest.

Well said, Cephalus, I replied; but as concerning justice, what is it?—to speak the truth and to pay your debts—no more than this? And even to this are there not exceptions? Suppose that a friend when in his right mind has deposited arms with me and he asks for them when he is not in his right mind, ought I to give them back to him? No one would say that I ought or that I should be right in doing so, any more than they would say that I ought always to speak the truth to one who is in his condition.

You are quite right, he replied.

But then, I said, speaking the truth and paying your debts is not a correct definition of justice.

Quite correct, Socrates, if Simonides is to be believed, said Polemarchus interposing.

I fear, said Cephalus, that I must go now, for I have to look after the sacrifices, and I hand over the argument to Polemarchus and the company.

Is not Polemarchus your heir? I said.

To be sure, he answered, and went away laughing to the sacrifices.

Tell me then, O thou heir of the argument, what did Simonides say, and according to you truly say, about justice?

He said that the repayment of a debt is just, and in saying so he appears to me to be right.

I should be sorry to doubt the word of such a wise and inspired man, but his meaning, though probably clear to you, is the reverse of clear to me. For he certainly does not mean, as we were just now saying, that I ought to return a deposit of arms or of anything else to one who asks for it when he is not in his right senses; and yet a deposit can not be denied to be a debt.

True.

Then when the person who asks me is not in his right mind I am by no means to make the return?

Certainly not.

When Simonides said that the repayment of a debt was justice, he did not mean to include that case?

Certainly not; for he thinks that a friend ought always to do good to a friend and never evil.

You mean that the return of a deposit of gold which is to the injury of the receiver, if the two parties are friends, is not the repayment of a debt,—that is what you would imagine him to say?

Yes.

And are enemies also to receive what we owe to them?

To be sure, he said, they are to receive what we owe them, and an enemy, as I take it, owes to an enemy that which is due or proper to him—that is to say, evil.

Simonides, then, after the manner of poets, would seem to have spoken darkly of the nature of justice; for he really meant to say that justice is the giving to each man what is proper to him, and this he termed a debt.

That must have been his meaning, he said.

By heaven! I replied; and if we asked him what due or proper thing is given by medicine, and to whom, what answer do you think that he would make to us?

He would surely reply that medicine gives drugs and meat and drink to human bodies.

And what due or proper thing is given by cookery, and to what?

Seasoning to food.

And what is that which justice gives, and to whom?

If, Socrates, we are to be guided at all by the analogy of the preceding instances, then justice is the art which gives good to friends and evil to enemies.

That is his meaning then?

I think so.

And who is best able to do good to his friends and evil to his enemies in time of sickness?

The physician.

Or when they are on a voyage, amid the perils of the sea?

The pilot.

And in what sort of actions or with a view to what result is the just man most able to do harm to his enemy and good to his friend?

In going to war against the one and in making alliances with the other.

But when a man is well, my dear Polemarchus, there is no need of a physician?

No.

And he who is not on a voyage has no need of a pilot?

No.

Then in time of peace justice will be of no use?

I am very far from thinking so.

You think that justice may be of use in peace as well as in war?

Yes.

Like husbandry for the acquisition of corn?

Yes.

Or like shoemaking for the acquisition of shoes,—that is what you mean?

Yes.

And what similar use or power of acquisition has justice in time of peace?

In contracts, Socrates, justice is of use.

And by contracts you mean partnerships?

Exactly.

But is the just man or the skilful player a more useful and better partner at a game of draughts?

The skilful player.

And in the laying of bricks and stones is the just man a more useful or better partner than the builder?

Quite the reverse.

Then in what sort of partnership is the just man a better partner than the harp-player, as in playing the harp the harp-player is certainly a better partner than the just man?

In a money partnership.

Yes, Polemarchus, but surely not in the use of money; for you do not want a just man to be your counsellor in the purchase or sale of a horse; a man who is knowing about horses would be better for that, would he not?

Certainly.

And when you want to buy a ship, the shipwright or the pilot would be better?

True.

Then what is that joint use of silver or gold in which the just man is to be preferred?

When you want a deposit to be kept safely.

You mean when money is not wanted, but allowed to lie?

Precisely.

That is to say, justice is useful when money is useless?

That is the inference.

And when you want to keep a pruning-hook safe, then justice is useful to the individual and to the state; but when you want to use it, then the art of the vine-dresser?

Clearly.

And when you want to keep a shield or a lyre, and not to use them, you would say that justice is useful; but when you want to use them, then the art of the soldier or of the musician?

Certainly.

And so of all other things;—justice is useful when they are useless, and useless when they are useful?

That is the inference.

Then justice is not good for much. But let us consider this further point: Is not he who can best strike a blow in a boxing match or in any kind of fighting best able to ward off a blow?

Certainly.

And he who is most skilful in preventing or escaping[2] from a disease is best able to create one?

True.

And he is the best guard of a camp who is best able to steal a march upon the enemy?

Certainly.

2. Reading φυλαξασθαι και λαθειν, ουτοζ, κτλ.

Then he who is a good keeper of anything is also a good thief?

That, I suppose, is to be inferred.

Then if the just man is good at keeping money, he is good at stealing it?

That is implied in the argument.

Then after all the just man has turned out to be a thief.

And this is a lesson which I suspect you must have learned out of Homer; for he, speaking of Autolycus, the maternal grandfather of Odysseus, who is a favorite of his, affirms that

He was excellent above all men in theft and perjury.

And so, you and Homer and Simonides are agreed that justice is an art of theft; to be practised however "for the good of friends and for the harm of enemies,"—that was what you were saying?

No, certainly not that, although I do not now know what I did say; but I still stand by the latter words.

Well, there is another question: By friends and enemies do we mean those who are so really, or only in seeming?

Surely, he said, a man may be expected to love those whom he thinks good, and to hate those whom he thinks evil.

Yes, but do not persons often err about good and evil: many who are not good seem to be so, and conversely?

That is true.

Then to them the good will be enemies and the evil will be their friends?

True.

And in that case they will be right in doing good to the evil and evil to the good?

Clearly.

But the good are just and would not do an injustice?

True.

Then according to your argument it is just to injure those who do no wrong?

Nay, Socrates; the doctrine is immoral.

Then I suppose that we ought to do good to the just and harm to the unjust?

I like that better.

But see the consequence:—Many a man who is ignorant of human nature has friends who are bad friends, and in that case he ought to do harm to them; and he has good enemies whom he ought to benefit; but, if so, we shall be saying the very opposite of that which we affirmed to be the meaning of Simonides.

Very true, he said; and I think that we had better correct an error into which we seem to have fallen in the use of the words "friend" and "enemy."

What was the error, Polemarchus? I asked.

We assumed that he is a friend who seems to be or who is thought good.

And how is the error to be corrected?

We should rather say that he is a friend who is, as well as seems, good; and that he who seems only, and is not good, only seems to be and is not a friend; and of an enemy the same may be said.

You would argue that the good are our friends and the bad our enemies?

Yes.

And instead of saying simply as we did at first, that it is just to do good to our friends and harm to our enemies, we should further say: It is just to do good to our friends when they are good and harm to our enemies when they are evil?

Yes, that appears to me to be the truth.

But ought the just to injure any one at all?

Undoubtedly he ought to injure those who are both wicked and his enemies.

When horses are injured, are they improved or deteriorated?

The latter.

Deteriorated, that is to say, in the good qualities of horses, not of dogs?

Yes, of horses.

And dogs are deteriorated in the good qualities of dogs, and not of horses?

Of course.

And will not men who are injured be deteriorated in that which is the proper virtue of man?

Certainly.

And that human virtue is justice?

To be sure.

Then men who are injured are of necessity made unjust?

That is the result.

But can the musician by his art make men unmusical?

Certainly not.

Or the horseman by his art make them bad horsemen?

Impossible.

And can the just by justice make men unjust, or speaking generally, can the good by virtue make them bad?

Assuredly not.

Any more than heat can produce cold?

It cannot.

Or drought moisture?

Clearly not.

Nor can the good harm any one?

Impossible.

And the just is the good?

Certainly.

Then to injure a friend or any one else is not the act of a just man, but of the opposite, who is the unjust?

I think that what you say is quite true, Socrates.

Then if a man says that justice consists in the repayment of debts, and that good is the debt which a just man owes to his friends, and evil the debt which he owes to his enemies,—to say this is not wise; for it is not true, if, as has been clearly shown, the injuring of another can be in no case just.

I agree with you. said Polemarchus.

Then you and I are prepared to take up arms against any one who attributes such a saying to Simonides or Bias or Pittacus, or any other wise man or seer?

I am quite ready to do battle at your side, he said.

Shall I tell you whose I believe the saying to be?

Whose?

I believe that Periander or Perdiccas or Xerxes or Ismenias the Theban, or some other rich and mighty man, who had a great opinion of his own power, was the first to say that justice is "doing good to your friends and harm to your enemies."

Most true, he said.

Yes, I said; but if this definition of justice also breaks down, what other can be offered?

Several times in the course of the discussion Thrasymachus had made an attempt to get the argument into his own hands, and had been put down by the rest of the company, who wanted to hear the end. But when Polemarchus and I had done speaking and there was a pause, he could no longer hold his peace; and, gathering himself up, he came at us like a wild beast, seeking to devour us. We were quite panic-stricken at the sight of him.

He roared out to the whole company: What folly, Socrates, has taken possession of you all? And why, sillybillies, do you knock under to one another? I say that if you want really to know what justice is, you should not only ask but answer, and you should not seek honor to yourself from the refutation of an opponent, but have your own answer; for there is many a one who can ask and can not answer. And now I will not have you say that justice is duty or advantage or profit or gain or interest, for this sort of nonsense will not do for me; I must have clearness and accuracy.

I was panic-stricken at his words, and could not look at him without trembling. Indeed I believe that if I had not fixed my eye upon him, I should have been stuck dumb: but when I saw his fury rising, I looked at him first, and was therefore able to reply to him.

Thrasymachus, I said, with a quiver, don't be hard upon us. Polemarchus and I may have been guilty of a little mistake in the argument, but I can assure you that the error was not intentional. If we were seeking for a piece of gold, you would not imagine that we were "knocking under to one another," and so losing our chance of finding it. And why, when we are seeking for justice, a thing more precious than many pieces of gold, do you say that we are weakly yielding to one another and not doing our utmost to get at the truth? Nay, my good friend, we are most willing and anxious to do so, but the fact is that we can not. And if so, you people who know all things should pity us and not be angry with us.

How characteristic of Socrates! he replied, with a bitter laugh;—that's your ironical style! Did I not foresee—have I not already told you, that whatever he was asked he would refuse to answer, and try irony or any other shuffle, in order that he might avoid answering?

You are a philosopher, Thrasymachus, I replied, and well know that if you ask a person what numbers make up twelve, taking care to prohibit him whom you ask from answering twice six, or three times four, or six times two, or four times three, "for this sort of nonsense will not do for me,"—then obviously, if that is your way of putting the question, no one can answer you. But suppose that he were to retort, "Thrasymachus, what do you mean? If one of these numbers which you interdict be the true answer to the question, am I falsely to say some other number which is not the right one?—is that your meaning?"—How would you answer him?

Just as if the two cases were at all alike! he said.

Why should they not be? I replied; and even if they are not, but only appear to be so to the person who is asked, ought he not to say what he thinks, whether you and I forbid him or not?

I presume then that you are going to make one of the interdicted answers?

I dare say that I may, notwithstanding the danger, if upon reflection I approve of any of them.

But what if I give you an answer about justice other and better, he said, than any of these? What do you deserve to have done to you?

Done to me!—as becomes the ignorant, I must learn from the wise—that is what I deserve to have done to me.

What, and no payment! a pleasant notion!

I will pay when I have the money, I replied.

But you have, Socrates, said Glaucon: and you, Thrasymachus, need be under no anxiety about money, for we will all make a contribution for Socrates.

Yes, he replied, and then Socrates will do as he always does—refuse to answer himself, but take and pull to pieces the answer of some one else.

Why, my good friend, I said, how can any one answer who knows and says that he knows, just nothing; and who, even if he has some faint notions of his own, is told by a man of authority not to utter them? The natural thing is, that the speaker should be some one like yourself who professes to know and can tell what he knows. Will you then kindly answer, for the edification of the company and of myself?

Glaucon and the rest of the company joined in my request, and Thrasymachus, as any one might see, was in reality eager to speak; for he thought that he had an excellent answer, and would distinguish himself. But at first he affected to insist on my answering; at length he consented to begin. Behold, he said, the wisdom of Socrates; he refuses to teach himself, and goes about learning of others, to whom he never even says Thank you.

That I learn of others, I replied, is quite true; but that I am ungrateful I wholly deny. Money I have none, and therefore I pay in praise, which is all I have; and how ready I am to praise any one who appears to me to speak well you will very soon find out when you answer; for I expect that you will answer well.

Listen, then, he said; I proclaim that justice is nothing else than the interest of the stronger. And now why do you not praise me? But of course you won't.

Let me first understand you, I replied. Justice, as you say, is the interest of the stronger. What, Thrasymachus, is the meaning of this? You can not mean to say that because Polydamas, the pancratiast, is stronger than we are, and finds the eating of beef conducive to his bodily strength, that to eat beef is therefore equally for our good who are weaker than he is, and right and just for us?

That's abominable of you, Socrates; you take the words in the sense which is most damaging to the argument.

Not at all, my good sir, I said; I am trying to understand them; and I wish that you would be a little clearer.

Well, he said, have you never heard that forms of government differ; there are tyrannies, and there are democracies, and there are aristocracies?

Yes, I know.

And the government is the ruling power in each state?

Certainly.

And the different forms of government make laws democratical, aristocratical, tyrannical, with a view to their several interests; and these laws, which are made by them for their own interests, are the justice which they deliver to their subjects, and him who transgresses them they punish as a breaker of the law, and unjust. And that is what I mean when I say that in all states there is the same principle of justice, which is the interest of the government; and as the government must be supposed to have power, the only reasonable conclusion is, that everywhere there is one principle of justice, which is the interest of the stronger.

Now I understand you, I said; and whether you are right or not I will try to discover. But let me remark, that in defining justice you have yourself used the word "interest" which you forbade me to use. It is true, however, that in your definition the words "of the stronger" are added.

A small addition, you must allow, he said.

Great or small, never mind about that: we must first inquire whether what you are saying is the truth. Now we are both agreed that justice is interest of some sort, but you go on to say "of the stronger;" about this addition I am not so sure, and must therefore consider further.

Proceed.

I will; and first tell me, Do you admit that it is just for subjects to obey their rulers?

I do.

But are the rulers of states absolutely infallible, or are they sometimes liable to err?

To be sure, he replied, they are liable to err.

Then in making their laws they may sometimes make them rightly, and sometimes not?

True.

When they make them rightly, they make them agreeably to their interest; when they are mistaken, contrary to their interest; you admit that?

Yes.

And the laws which they make must be obeyed by their subjects,— and that is what you call justice?

Doubtless.

Then justice, according to your argument, is not only obedience to the interest of the stronger but the reverse?

What is that you are saying? he asked.

I am only repeating what you are saying, I believe. But let us consider: Have we not admitted that the rulers may be mistaken about their own interest in what they command, and also that to obey them is justice? Has not that been admitted?

Yes.

Then you must also have acknowledged justice not to be for the interest of the stronger, when the rulers unintentionally command things to be done which are to their own injury. For if, as you say, justice is the obedience which the subject renders to their commands, in that case, O wisest of men, is there any escape from the conclusion that the weaker are commanded to do, not what is for the interest, but what is for the injury of the stronger?

Nothing can be clearer, Socrates, said Polemarchus.

Yes, said Cleitophon, interposing, if you are allowed to be his witness.

But there is no need of any witness, said Polemarchus, for Thrasymachus himself acknowledges that rulers may sometimes command what is not for their own interest, and that for subjects to obey them is justice.

Yes, Polemarchus,—Thrasymachus said that for subjects to do what was commanded by their rulers is just.

Yes, Cleitophon, but he also said that justice is the interest of the stronger, and, while admitting both these propositions, he further acknowledged that the stronger may command the weaker who are his subjects to do what is not for his own interest; whence follows that justice is the injury quite as much as the interest of the stronger.

But, said Cleitophon, he meant by the interest of the stronger what the stronger thought to be his interest,—this was what the weaker had to do; and this was affirmed by him to be justice.

Those were not his words, rejoined Polemarchus.

Never mind, I replied, if he now says that they are, let us accept his statement. Tell me, Thrasymachus, I said, did you mean by justice what the stronger thought to be his interest, whether really so or not?

Certainly not, he said. Do you suppose that I call him who is mistaken the stronger at the time when he is mistaken?

Yes, I said, my impression was that you did so, when you admitted that the ruler was not infallible but might be sometimes mistaken.

You argue like an informer, Socrates. Do you mean, for example, that he who is mistaken about the sick is a physician in that he is mistaken? or that he who errs in arithmetic or grammar is an arithmetician or grammarian at the time when he is making the mistake, in respect of the mistake? True, we say that the physician or arithmetician or grammarian has made a mistake, but this is only a way of speaking; for the fact is that neither the grammarian nor any other person of skill ever makes a mistake in so far as he is what his name implies; they none of them err unless their skill fails them, and then they cease to be skilled artists. No artist or sage or ruler errs at the time when he is what his name implies; though he is commonly said to err, and I adopted the common mode of speaking. But to be perfectly accurate, since you are such a lover of accuracy, we should say that the ruler, in so far as he is ruler, is unerring, and, being unerring, always commands that which is for his own interest; and the subject is required to execute his commands; and therefore, as I said at first and now repeat, justice is the interest of the stronger.

Indeed, Thrasymachus, and do I really appear to you to argue like an informer?

Certainly, he replied.

And do you suppose that I ask these questions with any design of injuring you in the argument?

Nay, he replied, "suppose" is not the word—I know it; but you will be found out, and by sheer force of argument you will never prevail.

I shall not make the attempt, my dear man; but to avoid any misunderstanding occurring between us in the future, let me ask, in what sense do you speak of a ruler or stronger whose interest, as you were saying, he being the superior, it is just that the inferior should execute—is he a ruler in the popular or in the strict sense of the term?

In the strictest of all senses, he said. And now cheat and play the informer if you can; I ask no quarter at your hands. But you never will be able, never.

And do you imagine, I said, that I am such a madman as to try and cheat Thrasymachus? I might as well shave a lion.

Why, he said, you made the attempt a minute ago, and you failed.

Enough, I said, of these civilities. It will be better that I should ask you a question: Is the physician, taken in that strict sense of which you are speaking, a healer of the sick or a maker of money? And remember that I am now speaking of the true physician.

A healer of the sick, he replied.

And the pilot—that is to say, the true pilot—is he a captain of sailors or a mere sailor?

A captain of sailors.

The circumstance that he sails in the ship is not to be taken into account; neither is he to be called a sailor; the name pilot by which he is distinguished has nothing to do with sailing, but is significant of his skill and of his authority over the sailors.

Very true, he said.

Now, I said, every art has an interest?

Certainly.

For which the art has to consider and provide?

Yes, that is the aim of art.

And the interest of any art is the perfection of it—this and nothing else?

What do you mean?

I mean what I may illustrate negatively by the example of the body. Suppose you were to ask me whether the body is self-sufficing or has wants, I should reply: Certainly the body has wants; for the body may be ill and require to be cured, and has therefore interests to which the art of medicine ministers; and this is the origin and intention of medicine, as you will acknowledge. Am I not right?

Quite right, he replied.

But is the art of medicine or any other art faulty or deficient in any quality in the same way that the eye may be deficient in sight or the ear fail of hearing, and therefore requires another art to provide for the interests of seeing and hearing—has art in itself, I say, any similar liability to fault or defect, and does every art require another supplementary art to provide for its interests, and that another and another without end? Or have the arts to look only after their own interests? Or have they no need either of themselves or of another?—having no faults or defects, they have no need to correct them, either by the exercise of their own art or any other; they have only to consider the interest of their subject-matter. For every art remains pure and faultless while remaining true—that is to say, while perfect and unimpaired. Take the words in your precise sense, and tell me whether I am not right.

Yes, clearly.

Then medicine does not consider the interest of medicine, but the interest of the body?

True, he said.

Nor does the art of horsemanship consider the interests of the art of horsemanship, but the interests of the horse; neither do any other arts care for themselves, for they have no needs; they care only for that which is the subject of their art?

True, he said.

But surely, Thrasymachus, the arts are the superiors and rulers of their own subjects?

To this he assented with a good deal of reluctance.

Then, I said, no science or art considers or enjoins the interest of the stronger or superior, but only the interest of the subject and weaker?

He made an attempt to contest this proposition also, but finally acquiesced.

Then, I continued, no physician, in so far as he is a physician, considers his own good in what he prescribes, but the good of his patient; for the true physician is also a ruler having the human body as a subject, and is not a mere money-maker; that has been admitted?

Yes.

And the pilot likewise, in the strict sense of the term, is a ruler of sailors and not a mere sailor.

That has been admitted.

And such a pilot and ruler will provide and prescribe for the interest of the sailor who is under him, and not for his own or the ruler's interest?

He gave a reluctant "Yes."

Then, I said, Thrasymachus, there is no one in any rule who, in so far as he is a ruler, considers or enjoins what is for his own interest, but always what is for the interest of his subject or suitable to his art; to that he looks, and that alone he considers in everything which he says and does.

When we had got to this point in the argument, and every one saw that the definition of justice had been completely upset, Thrasymachus, instead of replying to me, said: Tell me, Socrates, have you got a nurse?

Why do you ask such a question, I said, when you ought rather to be answering?

Because she leaves you to snivel, and never wipes your nose: she has not even taught you to know the shepherd from the sheep.

What makes you say that? I replied.

Because you fancy that the shepherd or neatherd fattens or tends the sheep or oxen with a view to their own good and not to the good of himself or his master; and you further imagine that the rulers of states, if they are true rulers, never think of their subjects as sheep, and that they are not studying their own advantage day and night. Oh, no; and so entirely astray are you in your ideas about the just and unjust as not even to know that justice and the just are in reality another's good; that is to say, the interest of the ruler and stronger, and the loss of the subject and servant; and injustice the opposite; for the unjust is lord over the truly simple and just: he is the stronger, and his subjects do what is for his interest, and minister to his happiness, which is very far from being their own. Consider further, most foolish Socrates, that the just is always a loser in comparison with the unjust. First of all, in private contracts: wherever the unjust is the partner of the just you will find that, when the partnership is dissolved, the unjust man has always more and the just less. Secondly, in their dealings with the State: when there is an income-tax, the just man will pay more and the unjust less on the same amount of income; and when there is anything to be received the one gains nothing and the other much. Observe also what happens when they take an office; there is the just man neglecting his affairs and perhaps suffering other losses, and getting nothing out of the public, because he is just; moreover he is hated by his friends and acquaintances for refusing to serve them in unlawful ways. But all this is reversed in the case of the unjust man. I am speaking, as before, of injustice on a large scale in which the advantage of the unjust is most apparent; and my meaning will be most clearly seen if we turn to that highest form of injustice in which the criminal is the happiest of men, and the sufferers or those who refuse to do injustice are the most miserable—that is to say tyranny, which by fraud and force takes away the property of others, not little by little but wholesale; comprehending in one, things sacred as well as profane, private and public; for which acts of wrong, if he were detected perpetrating any of them singly, he would be punished and incur great disgrace—they who do such wrong in particular cases are called robbers of temples, and man-stealers and burglars and swindlers and thieves. But when a man besides taking away the money of the citizens has made slaves of them, then, instead of these names of reproach, he is termed happy and blessed, not only by the citizens but by all who hear of his having achieved the consummation of injustice. For mankind censure injustice, fearing that they may be victims of it and not because they shrink from committing it. And thus, as I have shown, Socrates, injustice, when on a sufficient scale, has more strength and freedom and mastery than justice; and, as I said at first, justice is the interest of the stronger, whereas injustice is a man's own profit and interest.

Thrasymachus, when he had thus spoken, having, like a bath-man, deluged our ears with his words, had a mind to go away. But the company would not let him; they insisted that he should remain and defend his position; and I myself added my own humble request that he would not leave us. Thrasymachus, I said to him, excellent man, how suggestive are your remarks! And are you going to run away before you have fairly taught or learned whether they are true or not? Is the attempt to determine the way of man's life so small a matter in your eyes—to determine how life may be passed by each one of us to the greatest advantage?

And do I differ from you, he said, as to the importance of the inquiry?

You appear rather, I replied, to have no care or thought about us, Thrasymachus—whether we live better or worse from not knowing what you say you know, is to you a matter of indifference. Prithee, friend, do not keep your knowledge to yourself; we are a large party; and any benefit which you confer upon us will be amply rewarded. For my own part I openly declare that I am not convinced, and that I do not believe injustice to be more gainful than justice, even if uncontrolled and allowed to have free play. For, granting that there may be an unjust man who is able to commit injustice either by fraud or force, still this does not convince me of the superior advantage of injustice, and there may be others who are in the same predicament with myself. Perhaps we may be wrong; if so, you in your wisdom should convince us that we are mistaken in preferring justice to injustice.

And how am I to convince you, he said, if you are not already convinced by what I have just said; what more can I do for you? Would you have me put the proof bodily into your souls?

Heaven forbid! I said; I would only ask you to be consistent; or, if you change, change openly and let there be no deception. For I must remark, Thrasymachus, if you will recall what was previously said, that although you began by defining the true physician in an exact sense, you did not observe a like exactness when speaking of the shepherd; you thought that the shepherd as a shepherd tends the sheep not with a view to their own good, but like a mere diner or banqueter with a view to the pleasures of the table; or, again, as a trader for sale in the market, and not as a shepherd. Yet surely the art of the shepherd is concerned only with the good of his subjects; he has only to provide the best for them, since the perfection of the art is already ensured whenever all the requirements of it are satisfied. And that was what I was saying just now about the ruler. I conceived that the art of the ruler, considered as ruler, whether in a state or in private life, could only regard the good of his flock or subjects; whereas you seem to think that the rulers in states, that is to say, the true rulers, like being in authority.

Think! Nay, I am sure of it.

Then why in the case of lesser offices do men never take them willingly without payment, unless under the idea that they govern for the advantage not of themselves but of others? Let me ask you a question: Are not the several arts different, by reason of their each having a separate function? And, my dear illustrious friend, do say what you think, that we may make a little progress.

Yes, that is the difference, he replied.

And each art gives us a particular good and not merely a general one—medicine, for example, gives us health; navigation, safety at sea, and so on?

Yes, he said.

And the art of payment has the special function of giving pay: but we do not confuse this with other arts, any more than the art of the pilot is to be confused with the art of medicine, because the health of the pilot may be improved by a sea voyage. You would not be inclined to say, would you, that navigation is the art of medicine, at least if we are to adopt your exact use of language?

Certainly not.

Or because a man is in good health when he receives pay you would not say that the art of payment is medicine?

I should not.

Nor would you say that medicine is the art of receiving pay because a man takes fees when he is engaged in healing?

Certainly not.

And we have admitted, I said, that the good of each art is specially confined to the art?

Yes.

Then, if there be any good which all artists have in common, that is to be attributed to something of which they all have the common use?

True, he replied.

And when the artist is benefited by receiving pay the advantage is gained by an additional use of the art of pay, which is not the art professed by him?

He gave a reluctant assent to this.

Then the pay is not derived by the several artists from their respective arts. But the truth is, that while the art of medicine gives health, and the art of the builder builds a house, another art attends them which is the art of pay. The various arts may be doing their own business and benefiting that over which they preside, but would the artist receive any benefit from his art unless he were paid as well?

I suppose not.

But does he therefore confer no benefit when he works for nothing? Certainly, he confers a benefit.

Then now, Thrasymachus, there is no longer any doubt that neither arts nor governments provide for their own interests; but, as we were before saying, they rule and provide for the interests of their subjects who are the weaker and not the stronger—to their good they attend and not to the good of the superior. And this is the reason, my dear Thrasymachus, why, as I was just now saying, no one is willing to govern; because no one likes to take in hand the reformation of evils which are not his concern without remuneration. For, in the execution of his work, and in giving his orders to another, the true artist does not regard his own interest, but always that of his subjects; and therefore in order that rulers may be willing to rule, they must be paid in one of three modes of payment, money or honor, or a penalty for refusing.

What do you mean, Socrates? said Glaucon. The first two modes of payment are intelligible enough, but what the penalty is I do not understand, or how a penalty can be a payment.

You mean that you do not understand the nature of this payment which to the best men is the great inducement to rule? Of course you know that ambition and avarice are held to be, as indeed they are, a disgrace?

Very true.

And for this reason, I said, money and honor have no attraction for them; good men do not wish to be openly demanding payment for governing and so to get the name of hirelings, nor by secretly helping themselves out of the public revenues to get the name of thieves. And not being ambitious they do not care about honor. Wherefore necessity must be laid upon them, and they must be induced to serve from the fear of punishment. And this, as I imagine, is the reason why the forwardness to take office, instead of waiting to be compelled, has been deemed dishonorable. Now the worst part of the punishment is that he who refuses to rule is liable to be ruled by one who is worse than himself. And the fear of this, as I conceive, induces the good to take office, not because they would, but because they can not help—not under the idea that they are going to have any benefit or enjoyment themselves, but as a necessity, and because they are not able to commit the task of ruling to any one who is better than themselves, or indeed as good. For there is reason to think that if a city were composed entirely of good men, then to avoid office would be as much an object of contention as to obtain office is at present; then we should have plain proof that the true ruler is not meant by nature to regard his own interest, but that of his subjects; and every one who knew this would choose rather to receive a benefit from another than to have the trouble of conferring one. So far am I from agreeing with Thrasymachus that justice is the interest of the stronger. This latter question need not be further discussed at present; but when Thrasymachus says that the life of the unjust is more advantageous than that of the just, his new statement appears to me to be of a far more serious character. Which of us has spoken truly? And which sort of life, Glaucon, do you prefer?

I for my part deem the life of the just to be the more advantageous, he answered.

Did you hear all the advantages of the unjust which Thrasymachus was rehearsing?

Yes, I heard him, he replied, but he has not convinced me.

Then shall we try to find some way of convincing him, if we can, that he is saying what is not true?

Most certainly, he replied.

If, I said, he makes a set speech and we make another recounting all the advantages of being just, and he answers and we rejoin, there must be a numbering and measuring of the goods which are claimed on either side, and in the end we shall want judges to decide; but if we proceed in our inquiry as we lately did, by making admissions to one another, we shall unite the offices of judge and advocate in our own persons.

Very good, he said.

And which method do I understand you to prefer? I said.

That which you propose.

Well, then, Thrasymachus, I said, suppose you begin at the beginning and answer me. You say that perfect injustice is more gainful than perfect justice?

Yes, that is what I say, and I have given you my reasons.

And what is your view about them? Would you call one of them virtue and the other vice?

Certainly.

I suppose that you would call justice virtue and injustice vice?

What a charming notion! So likely too, seeing that I affirm injustice to be profitable and justice not.

What else then would you say?

The opposite, he replied.

And would you call justice vice?

No, I would rather say sublime simplicity.

Then would you call injustice malignity?

No; I would rather say discretion.

And do the unjust appear to you to be wise and good?

Yes, he said; at any rate those of them who are able to be perfectly unjust, and who have the power of subduing states and nations; but perhaps you imagine me to be talking of cutpurses. Even this profession if undetected has advantages, though they are not to be compared with those of which I was just now speaking.

I do not think that I misapprehend your meaning, Thrasymachus, I replied; but still I can not hear without amazement that you class injustice with wisdom and virtue, and justice with the opposite.

Certainly, I do so class them.

Now, I said, you are on more substantial and almost unanswerable ground; for if the injustice which you were maintaining to be profitable had been admitted by you as by others to be vice and deformity, an answer might have been given to you on received principles; but now I perceive that you will call injustice honorable and strong, and to the unjust you will attribute all the qualities which were attributed by us before to the just, seeing that you do not hesitate to rank injustice with wisdom and virtue.

You have guessed most infallibly, he replied.

Then I certainly ought not to shrink from going through with the argument so long as I have reason to think that you, Thrasymachus, are speaking your real mind; for I do believe that your are now in earnest and are not amusing yourself at our expense.

I may be in earnest or not, but what is that to you?—to refute the argument is your business.

Very true, I said; that is what I have to do: But will you be so good as answer yet one more question? Does the just man try to gain any advantage over the just?

Far otherwise; if he did he would not be the simple amusing creature which he is.

And would he try to go beyond just action?

He would not.

And how would he regard the attempt to gain an advantage over the unjust; would that be considered by him as just or unjust?

He would think it just, and would try to gain the advantage; but he would not be able.

Whether he would or would not be able, I said, is not to the point. My question is only whether the just man, while refusing to have more than another just man, would wish and claim to have more than the unjust?

Yes, he would.

And what of the unjust—does he claim to have more than the just man and to do more than is just?

Of course, he said, for he claims to have more than all men.

And the unjust man will strive and struggle to obtain more than the unjust man or action, in order that he may have more than all?

True.

We may put the matter thus, I said—the just does not desire more than his like but more than his unlike, whereas the unjust desires more than both his like and his unlike?

Nothing, he said, can be better than that statement.

And the unjust is good and wise, and the just is neither?

Good again, he said.

And is not the unjust like the wise and good and the just unlike them?

Of course, he said, he who is of a certain nature, is like those who are of a certain nature; he who is not, not.

Each of them, I said, is such as his like is?

Certainly, he replied.

Very good, Thrasymachus, I said; and now to take the case of the arts: you would admit that one man is a musician and another not a musician?

Yes.

And which is wise and which is foolish?

Clearly the musician is wise, and he who is not a musician is foolish.

And he is good in as far as he is wise, and bad in as far as he is foolish?

Yes.

And you would say the same sort of thing of the physician?

Yes.

And do you think, my excellent friend, that a musician when he adjusts the lyre would desire or claim to exceed or go beyond a musician in the tightening and loosening the strings?

I do not think that he would.

But he would claim to exceed the non-musician?

Of course.

And what would you say of the physician? In prescribing meats and drinks would he wish to go beyond another physician or beyond the practice of medicine?

He would not.

But he would wish to go beyond the non-physician?

Yes.

And about knowledge and ignorance in general; see whether you think that any man who has knowledge ever would wish to have the choice of saying or doing more than another man who has knowledge. Would he not rather say or do the same as his like in the same case?

That, I suppose, can hardly be denied.

And what of the ignorant? would he not desire to have more than either the knowing or the ignorant?

I dare say.

And the knowing is wise?

Yes.

And the wise is good?

True.

Then the wise and good will not desire to gain more than his like, but more than his unlike and opposite?

I suppose so.

Whereas the bad and ignorant will desire to gain more than both?

Yes.

But did we not say, Thrasymachus, that the unjust goes beyond both his like and unlike? Were not these your words?

They were.

And you also said that the just will not go beyond his like but his unlike?

Yes.

Then the just is like the wise and good, and the unjust like the evil and ignorant?

That is the inference.

And each of them is such as his like is?

That was admitted.

Then the just has turned out to be wise and good and the unjust evil and ignorant.

Thrasymachus made all these admissions, not fluently, as I repeat them, but with extreme reluctance; it was a hot summer's day, and the perspiration poured from him in torrents; and then I saw what I had never seen before, Thrasymachus blushing. As we were now agreed that justice was virtue and wisdom, and injustice vice and ignorance, I proceeded to another point:

Well, I said, Thrasymachus, that matter is now settled; but were we not also saying that injustice had strength; do you remember?

Yes, I remember, he said, but do not suppose that I approve of what you are saying or have no answer; if however I were to answer, you would be quite certain to accuse me of haranguing; therefore either permit me to have my say out, or if you would rather ask, do so, and I will answer "Very good," as they say to story-telling old women, and will nod "Yes" and "No."

Certainly not, I said, if contrary to your real opinion.

Yes, he said, I will, to please you, since you will not let me speak. What else would you have?

Nothing in the world, I said; and if you are so disposed I will ask and you shall answer.

Proceed.

Then I will repeat the question which I asked before, in order that

our examination of the relative nature of justice and injustice may be
carried on regularly. A statement was made that injustice is stronger and
more powerful than justice, but now justice, having been identified with
wisdom and virtue, is easily shown to be stronger than injustice, if
injustice is ignorance; this can no longer be questioned by any one. But I
want to view the matter, Thrasymachus, in a different way: You would
not deny that a state may be unjust and may be unjustly attempting to
enslave other states, or may have already enslaved them, and may be
holding many of them in subjection?

True, he replied; and I will add that the best and most perfectly
unjust state will be most likely to do so.

I know, I said, that such was your position; but what I would further
consider is, whether this power which is possessed by the superior state
can exist or be exercised without justice or only with justice.

If you are right in your view, and justice is wisdom, then only with
justice; but if I am right, then without justice.

I am delighted, Thrasymachus, to see you not only nodding assent
and dissent, but making answers which are quite excellent.

That is out of civility to you, he replied.

You are very kind, I said; and would you have the goodness also to
inform me, whether you think that a state, or an army, or a band of
robbers and thieves, or any other gang of evildoers could act at all if they
injured one another?

No indeed, he said, they could not.

But if they abstained from injuring one another, then they might act
together better?

Yes.

And this is because injustice creates divisions and hatreds and fighting, and justice imparts harmony and friendship; is not that true,
Thrasymachus?

I agree, he said, because I do not wish to quarrel with you.

How good of you, I said; but I should like to know also whether
injustice, having his tendency to arouse hatred, wherever existing,
among slaves or among freemen, will not make them hate one another
and set them at variance and render them incapable of common action?

Certainly.

And even if injustice be found in two only, will they not quarrel and
fight, and become enemies to one another and to the just?

They will.

And suppose injustice abiding in a single person, would your wisdom
say that she loses or that she retains her natural power?

Let us assume that she retains her power.

Yet is not the power which injustice exercises of such a nature that
wherever she takes up her abode, whether in a city, in an army, in a

family, or in any other body, that body is, to begin with, rendered incapable of united action by reason of sedition and distraction; and does it not become its own enemy and at variance with all that opposes it, and with the just? Is not this the case?

Yes, certainly.

And is not injustice equally fatal when existing in a single person; in the first place rendering him incapable of action because he is not at unity with himself, and in the second place making him an enemy to himself and the just? Is not that true, Thrasymachus?

Yes.

And O my friend, I said, surely the gods are just?

Granted that they are.

But if so, the unjust will be the enemy of the gods, and the just will be their friends?

Feast away in triumph, and take your fill of the argument; I will not oppose you, lest I should displease the company.

Well then, proceed with your answers, and let me have the remainder of my repast. For we have already shown that the just are clearly wiser and better and abler than the unjust, and that the unjust are incapable of common action; nay more, that to speak as we did of men who are evil acting at any time vigorously together, is not strictly true, for if they had been perfectly evil, they would have laid hands upon one another; but it is evident that there must have been some remnant of justice in them, which enabled them to combine; if there had not been they would have injured one another as well as their victims; they were but half-villains in their enterprises; for had they been whole villains, and utterly unjust, they would have been utterly incapable of action. That, as I believe, is the truth of the matter, and not what you said at first. But whether the just have a better and happier life than the unjust is a further question which we also proposed to consider. I think that they have, and for the reasons which I have given; but still I should like to examine further, for no light matter is at stake, nothing less than the rule of human life.

Proceed.

I will proceed by asking a question: Would you not say that a horse has some end?

I should.

And the end or use of a horse or of anything would be that which could not be accomplished, or not so well accomplished, by any other thing?

I do not understand, he said.

Let me explain: Can you see, except with the eye?

Certainly not.

Or hear, except with the ear?

No.

These then may be truly said to be the ends of these organs?

They may.

But you can cut off a vine-branch with a dagger or with a chisel, and in many other ways?

Of course.

And yet not so well as with a pruning-hook made for the purpose?

True.

May we not say that this is the end of a pruning-hook?

We may.

Then now I think you will have no difficulty in understanding my meaning when I asked the question whether the end of anything would be that which could not be accomplished, or not so well accomplished, by any other thing?

I understand your meaning, he said, and assent.

And that to which an end is appointed has also an excellence? Need I ask again whether the eye has an end?

It has.

And has not the eye an excellence?

Yes.

And the ear has an end and an excellence also?

True.

And the same is true of all other things; they have each of them an end and a special excellence?

That is so.

Well, and can the eyes fulfil their end if they are wanting in their own proper excellence and have a defect instead?

How can they, he said, if they are blind and can not see?

You mean to say, if they have lost their proper excellence, which is sight, but I have not arrived at that point yet. I would rather ask the question more generally, and only inquire whether the things which fulfil their ends fulfil them by their own proper excellence, and fail of fulfilling them by their own defect?

Certainly, he replied.

I might say the same of the ears; when deprived of their own proper excellence they can not fulfil their end?

True.

And the same observation will apply to all other things?

I agree.

Well; and has not the soul an end which nothing else can fulfil? for example, to superintend and command and deliberate and the like. Are not these functions proper to the soul, and can they rightly be assigned to any other?

To no other.

And is not life to be reckoned among the ends of the soul?

Assuredly, he said.

And has not the soul an excellence also?

Yes.

And can she or can she not fulfil her own ends when deprived of that excellence?

She can not.

Then an evil soul must necessarily be an evil ruler and superintendent, and the good soul a good ruler?

Yes, necesssarily.

And we have admitted that justice is the excellence of the soul, and injustice the defect of the soul?

That has been admitted.

Then the just soul and the just man will live well, and the unjust man will live ill?

That is what your argument proves.

And he who lives well is blessed and happy, and he who lives ill the reverse of happy?

Certainly.

Then the just is happy, and the unjust miserable?

So be it.

But happiness and not misery is profitable.

Of course.

Then, my blessed Thrasymachus, injustice can never be more profitable than justice.

Let this, Socrates, he said, be your entertainment at the Bendidea.

For which I am indebted to you, I said, now that you have grown gentle towards me and have left off scolding. Nevertheless, I have not been well entertained; but that was my own fault and not yours. As an epicure snatches a taste of every dish which is successively brought to table, he not having allowed himself time to enjoy the one before, so have I gone from one subject to another without having discovered what I sought at first, the nature of justice. I left that inquiry and turned away to consider whether justice is virtue and wisdom or evil and folly; and when there arose a further question about the comparative advantages of justice and injustice, I could not refrain from passing on to that. And the result of the whole discussion has been that I know nothing at all. For I know not what justice is, and therefore I am not likely to know whether it is or is not a virtue, nor can I say whether the just man is happy or unhappy. . . .

BOOK V

I said: *Until philosophers are kings, or the kings and princes of this world have the spirit and power of philosophy, and political greatness and wisdom meet in one, and those commoner natures who pursue either to the exclusion of the other are compelled to stand aside, cities will never have rest from their evils,—no, nor the human race, as I believe—and then only will this our State have a possibility of life and behold the light of day.* Such was the thought, my dear Glaucon, which I would fain have uttered if it had not seemed too extravagant; for to be convinced that in no other State can there be happiness private or public is indeed a hard thing.

Socrates, what do you mean? I would have you consider that the word which you have uttered is one at which numerous persons, and very respectable persons too, in a figure pulling off their coats all in a moment, and seizing any weapon that comes to hand, will run at you might and main, before you know where you are, intending to do heaven knows what; and if you don't prepare an answer, and put yourself in motion, you will be "pared by their fine wits," and no mistake.

You got me into the scrape, I said.

And I was quite right; however, I will do all I can to get you out of it; but I can only give you good-will and good advice, and, perhaps, I may be able to fit answers to your questions better than another—that is all. And now, having such an auxiliary, you must do your best to show the unbelievers that you are right.

I ought to try, I said, since you offer me such invaluable assistance. And I think that, if there is to be a chance of our escaping, we must explain to them whom we mean when we say that philosophers are to rule in the State; then we shall be able to defend ourselves: There will be discovered to be some natures who ought to study philosophy and to be leaders in the State; and others who are not born to be philosophers, and are meant to be followers rather than leaders.

Then now for a definition, he said.

Follow me, I said, and I hope that I may in some way or other be able to give you a satisfactory explanation.

Proceed.

I dare say that you remember, and therefore I need not remind you, that a lover, if he is worthy of the name, ought to show his love, not to some one part of that which he loves, but to the whole.

I really do not understand, and therefore beg of you to assist my memory.

Another person, I said, might fairly reply as you do; but a man of pleasure like yourself ought to know that all who are in the flower of youth do somehow or other raise a pang or emotion in a lover's breast, and are thought by him to be worthy of his affectionate regards. Is not this a way which you have with the fair: one has a snub nose, and you praise his charming face; the hook-nose of another has, you say, a royal look; while he who is neither snub nor hooked has the grace of regularity: the dark visage is manly, the fair are children of the gods; and as to the sweet "honey pale," as they are called, what is the very name but the invention of a lover who talks in diminutives, and is not averse to paleness if appearing on the cheek of youth? In a word, there is no excuse which you will not make, and nothing which you will not say, in order not to lose a single flower that blooms in the springtime of youth.

If you make me an authority in matters of love, for the sake of the argument, I assent.

And what do you say of lovers of wine? Do you not see them doing the same? They are glad of any pretext of drinking any wine.

Very good.

And the same is true of ambitious men; if they can not command an army, they are willing to command a file; and if they can not be honored by really great and important persons, they are glad to be honored by lesser and meaner people,—but honor of some kind they must have.

Exactly.

Once more let me ask: Does he who desires any class of goods, desire the whole class or a part only?

The whole.

And may we not say of the philosopher that he is a lover, not of a part of wisdom only, but of the whole?

Yes, of the whole.

And he who dislikes learning, especially in youth, when he has no power of judging what is good and what is not, such an one we maintain not to be a philosopher or a lover of knowledge, just as he who refuses his food is not hungry, and may be said to have a bad appetite and not a good one?

Very true, he said.

Whereas he who has a taste for every sort of knowledge and who is curious to learn and is never satisfied, may be justly termed a philosopher? Am I not right?

Glaucon said: If curiosity makes a philosopher, you will find many a strange being will have a title to the name. All the lovers of sights have a delight in learning, and must therefore be included. Musical amateurs, too, are a folk strangely out of place among philosophers, for they are the last persons in the world who would come to anything like a philosophical discussion, if they could help, while they run about at the Dionysiac festivals as if they had let out their ears to hear every chorus; whether the performance is in town or country—that makes no difference—they are there. Now are we to maintain that all these and any who have similar tastes, as well as the professors of quite minor arts, are philosophers?

Certainly not, I replied; they are only an imitation.

He said: Who then are the true philosophers?

Those, I said, who are lovers of the vision of truth.

That is also good, he said; but I should like to know what you mean?

To another, I replied, I might have a difficulty in explaining; but I am sure that you will admit a proposition which I am about to make.

What is the proposition?

That since beauty is the opposite of ugliness, they are two?

Certainly.

And inasmuch as they are two, each of them is one?

True again.

And of just and unjust, good and evil, and of every other class, the same remark holds; taken singly, each of them is one; but from the various combinations of them with actions and things and with one another, they are seen in all sorts of lights and appear many?

Very true.

And this is the distinction which I draw between the sight-loving, art-loving, practical class and those of whom I am speaking, and who are alone worthy of the name of philosophers.

How do you distinguish them? he said.

The lovers of sounds and sights, I replied, are, as I conceive, fond of fine tones and colors and forms and all the artificial products that are made out of them, but their mind is incapable of seeing or loving absolute beauty.

True, he replied.

Few are they who are able to attain to the sight of this.

Very true.

And he who, having a sense of beautiful things has no sense of absolute beauty, or who, if another lead him to a knowledge of that beauty is unable to follow—of such an one I ask, Is he awake or in a dream only? Reflect: is not the dreamer, sleeping or waking, one who likens dissimilar things, who puts the copy in the place of the real object?

I should certainly say that such an one was dreaming.

But take the case of the other, who recognizes the existence of absolute beauty and is able to distinguish the idea from the objects which participate in the idea, neither putting the objects in the place of the idea nor the idea in the place of the objects—is he a dreamer, or is he awake?

He is wide awake.

And may we not say that the mind of the one who knows has knowledge, and that the mind of the other, who opines only, has opinion?

Certainly.

But suppose that the latter should quarrel with us and dispute our statement, can we administer any soothing cordial or advice to him, without revealing to him that there is sad disorder in his wits?

We must certainly offer him some good advice, he replied.

Come, then, and let us think of something to say to him. Shall we begin by assuring him that he is welcome to any knowledge which he may have, and that we are rejoiced at his having it? But we should like to ask him a question: Does he who has knowledge know something or nothing? (You must answer for him.)

I answer that he knows something.

Something that is or is not?

Something that is; for how can that which is not ever be known?

And are we assured, after looking at the matter from many points of view, that absolute being is or may be absolutely known, but that the utterly non-existent is utterly unknown?

Nothing can be more certain.

Good. But if there be anything which is of such a nature as to be and not to be, that will have a place intermediate between pure being and the absolute negation of being?

Yes, between them.

And, as knowledge corresponded to being and ignorance of necessity to not-being, for that intermediate between being and not-being there has to be discovered a corresponding intermediate between ignorance and knowledge, if there be such?

Certainly.

Do we admit the existence of opinion?

Undoubtedly.

As being the same with knowledge, or another faculty?

Another faculty.

Then opinion and knowledge have to do with different kinds of matter corresponding to this difference of faculties?

Yes.

And knowledge is relative to being and knows being. But before I proceed further I will make a division.

What division?

I will begin by placing faculties in a class by themselves: they are powers in us, and in all other things, by which we do as we do. Sight and hearing, for example, I should call faculties. Have I clearly explained the class which I mean?

Yes, I quite understand.

Then let me tell you my view about them. I do not see them, and therefore the distinctions of figure, color, and the like, which enable me to discern the differences of some things, do not apply to them. In speaking of a faculty I think only of its sphere and its result; and that which has the same sphere and the same result I call the same faculty, but that which has another sphere and another result I call different. Would that be your way of speaking?

Yes.

And will you be so very good as to answer one more question? Would you say that knowledge is a faculty, or in what class would you place it?

Certainly knowledge is a faculty, and the mightiest of all faculties.

And is opinion also a faculty?

Certainly, he said: for opinion is that with which we are able to form an opinion.

And yet you were acknowledging a little while ago that knowledge is not the same as opinion?

Why, yes, he said; how can any reasonable being ever identify that which is infallible with that which errs?

An excellent answer, proving, I said, that we are quite conscious of a distinction between them.

Yes.

Then knowledge and opinion having distinct powers have also distinct spheres or subject-matters?

That is certain.

Being is the sphere or subject-matter of knowledge, and knowledge is to know the nature of being?

Yes.

And opinion is to have an opinion?

Yes.

And do we know what we opine? or is the subject-matter of opinion the same as the subject-matter of knowledge?

Nay, he replied, that has been already disproven; if difference in faculty implies difference in the sphere or subject-matter, and if, as we were saying, opinion and knowledge are distinct faculties, then the sphere of knowledge and of opinion can not be the same.

Then if being is the subject-matter of knowledge, something else must be the subject-matter of opinion?

Yes, something else.

Well then, is not-being the subject-matter of opinion? or, rather, how can there be an opinion at all about not-being? Reflect: when a man has an opinion, has he not an opinion about something? Can he have an opinion which is an opinion about nothing?

Impossible.

He who has an opinion has an opinion about some one thing?

Yes.

And not-being is not one thing but, properly speaking, nothing?

True.

Of not-being, ignorance was assumed to be the necessary correlative; of being, knowledge?

True, he said.

Then opinion is not concerned either with being or with not-being?

Not with either.

And can therefore neither be ignorance nor knowledge?

That seems to be true.

But is opinion to be sought without and beyond either of them, in a greater clearness than knowledge, or in a greater darkness than ignorance?

In neither.

Then I suppose that opinion appears to you to be darker than knowledge, but lighter than ignorance?

Both; and in no small degree.

And also to be within and between them?

Yes.

Then you would infer that opinion is intermediate?

No question.

But were we not saying before, that if anything appeared to be of a sort which is and is not at the same time, that sort of thing would appear also to lie in the interval between pure being and absolute not-being; and that the corresponding faculty is neither knowledge nor ignorance, but will not be found in the interval between them?

True.

And in that interval there has now been discovered something which we call opinion?

There has.

Then what remains to be discovered is the object which partakes equally of the nature of being and not-being, and can not rightly be termed either, pure and simple; this unknown term, when discovered, we may truly call the subject of opinion, and assign each to their proper faculty,—the extremes to the faculties of the extremes and the mean to the faculty of the mean.

True.

This being premised, I would ask the gentleman who is of opinion that there is no absolute or unchangeable idea of beauty—in whose opinion the beautiful is the manifold—he, I say, your lover of beautiful sights, who can not bear to be told that the beautiful is one, and the just is one, or that anything is one—to him I would appeal, saying, Will you be so very kind, sir, as to tell us whether, of all these beautiful things, there is one which will not be found ugly; or of the just, which will not be found unjust; or of the holy, which will not also be unholy?

No, he replied; the beautiful will in some point of view be found ugly; and the same is true of the rest.

And may not the many which are doubles be also halves?—doubles, that is, of one thing, and halves of another?

Quite true.

And things great and small, heavy and light, as they are termed, will not be denoted by these any more than by the opposite names?

True; both these and the opposite names will always attach to all of them.

And can any one of those many things which are called by particular names be said to be this rather than not to be this?

He replied: They are like the punning riddles which are asked at feasts or the children's puzzle about the eunuch aiming at the bag, with what he hit him, as they say in the puzzle, and upon what the bat was sitting. The individual objects of which I am speaking are also a riddle, and have a double sense: nor can you fix them in your mind, either as being or not-being, or both, or neither.

Then what will you do with them? I said. Can they have a better place than between being and not-being? For they are clearly not in greater darkness or negation than not-being, or more full of light and existence than being.

That is quite true, he said.

Thus then we seem to have discovered that the many ideas which the multitude entertain about the beautiful and about all other things are tossing about in some region which is half-way between pure being and pure not-being?

We have.

Yes; and we had before agreed that anything of this kind which we might find was to be described as matter of opinion, and not as matter of knowledge; being the intermediate flux which is caught and detained by the intermediate faculty.

Quite true.

Then those who see the many beautiful, and who yet neither see absolute beauty, nor can follow any guide who points the way thither; who see the many just, and not absolute justice, and the like,—such persons may be said to have opinion but not knowledge?

That is certain.

But those who see the absolute and eternal and immutable may be said to know, and not to have opinion only?

Neither can that be denied.

The one love and embrace the subjects of knowledge, the other those of opinion? The latter are the same, as I dare say you will remember, who listened to sweet sounds and gazed upon fair colors, but would not tolerate the existence of absolute beauty.

Yes, I remember.

Shall we then be guilty of any impropriety in calling them lovers of opinion rather than lovers of wisdom, and will they be very angry with us for thus describing them?

I shall tell them not to be angry; no man should be angry at what is true.

But those who love the truth in each thing are to be called lovers of wisdom and not lovers of opinion.

Assuredly. . . .

BOOK VI

You have to imagine, then, that there are two ruling powers, and that one of them is set over the intellectual world, the other over the visible. I do not say heaven, lest you should fancy that I am playing upon the name (ουρανοζ, ορατοζ). May I suppose that you have this distinction of the visible and intelligible fixed in your mind?

I have.

Now take a line which has been cut into two unequal[13] parts, and divide each of them again in the same proportion, and suppose the two main divisions to answer, one to the visible and the other to the intelligible, and then compare the subdivisions in respect of their clearness and want of clearness, and you will find that the first section in the sphere of the visible consists of images. And by images I mean, in the first place, shadows, and in the second place, reflections in water and in solid, smooth and polished bodies and the like: Do you understand?

Yes, I understand.

Imagine, now, the other section, of which this is only the resemblance, to include the animals which we see, and everything that grows or is made.

Very good.

Would you not admit that both the sections of this division have different degrees of truth, and that the copy is to the original as the sphere of opinion is to the sphere of knowledge?

Most undoubtedly.

Next proceed to consider the manner in which the sphere of the intellectual is to be divided.

In what manner?

Thus:—There are two subdivisions, in the lower of which the soul uses the figures given by the former division as images; the inquiry can only be hypothetical, and instead of going upwards to a principle descends to the other end; in the higher of the two, the soul passes out of hypotheses, and goes up to a principle which is above hypotheses, making no use of images[14] as in the former case, but proceeding only in and through the ideas themselves.

13. Reading ανισα.
14. Reading ωνπερ εκεινο εικονων

I do not quite understand your meaning, he said.

Then I will try again; you will understand me better when I have made some preliminary remarks. You are aware that students of geometry, arithmetic, and the kindred sciences assume the odd and the even and the figures and three kinds of angles and the like in their several branches of science; these are their hypotheses, which they and everybody are supposed to know, and therefore they do not deign to give any account of them either to themselves or others; but they begin with them, and go on until they arrive at last, and in a consistent manner, at their conclusion?

Yes, he said, I know.

And do you not know also that although they make use of the visible forms and reason about them, they are thinking not of these, but of the ideals which they resemble; not of the figures which they draw, but of the absolute square and the absolute diameter, and so on—the forms which they draw or make, and which have shadows and reflections in water of their own, are converted by them into images, but they are really seeking to behold the things themselves, which can only be seen with the eye of the mind?

That is true.

And of this I spoke as the intelligible, although in the search after it the soul is compelled to use hypotheses; not ascending to a first principle, because she is unable to rise above the region of hypothesis, but employing the objects of which the shadows below are resemblances in their turn as images, they having in relation to the shadows and reflections of them a greater distinctness, and therefore a higher value.

I understand, he said, that you are speaking of the province of geometry and the sister arts.

And when I speak of the other division of the intelligible, you will understand me to speak of that other sort of knowledge which reason herself attains by the power of dialectic, using the hypotheses not as first principles, but only as hypotheses—that is to say, as steps and points of departure into a world which is above hypotheses, in order that she may soar beyond them to the first principle of the whole; and clinging to this and then to that which depends on this, by successive steps she descends again without the aid of any sensible object, from ideas, through ideas, and in ideas she ends.

I understand you, he replied; not perfectly, for you seem to me to be describing a task which is really tremendous; but, at any rate, I understand you to say that knowledge and being, which the science of dialectic contemplates, are clearer than the notions of the arts, as they are termed, which proceed from hypotheses only: these are also contemplated by the understanding, and not by the senses: yet, because they start from hypotheses and do not ascend to a principle, those who contemplate them appear to you not to exercise the higher reason upon them, although when a first principle is added to them they are cognizable by the higher reason. And the habit which is concerned with geometry and the cognate sciences I suppose that you would term understanding and not reason, as being intermediate between opinion and reason.

You have quite conceived my meaning, I said; and now, corresponding to these four divisions, let there be four faculties in the soul—reason answering to the highest, understanding to the second, faith (or conviction) to the third, and perception of shadows to the last—and let there be a scale of them, and let us suppose that the several faculties have clearness in the same degree that their objects have truth.

I understand, he replied, and give my assent, and accept your arrangement.

BOOK VII

And now, I said, let me show in a figure how far our nature is enlightened or unenlightened:—Behold! human beings living in an underground den, which has a mouth open towards the light and reaching all along the den; here they have been from their childhood, and have their legs and necks chained so that they can not move, and can only see before them, being prevented by the chains from turning round their heads. Above and behind them a fire is blazing at a distance, and between the fire and the prisoners there is a raised way; and you will see, if you look, a low wall built along the way, like the screen which marionette players have in front of them, over which they show the puppets.

I see.

And do you see, I said, men passing along the wall carrying all sorts of vessels, and statues and figures of animals made of wood and stone and various materials, which appear over the wall? Some of them are talking, others silent.

You have shown me a strange image, and they are strange prisoners.

Like ourselves, I replied; and they see only their own shadows, or the shadows of one another, which the fire throws on the opposite wall of the cave?

True, he said; how could they see anything but the shadows if they were never allowed to move their heads?

And of the objects which are being carried in like manner they would only see the shadows?

Yes, he said.

And if they were able to converse with one another, would they not suppose that they were naming what was actually before them?[1]

1. Reading παρόντα

Very true.

And suppose further that the prison had an echo which came from the other side, would they not be sure to fancy when one of the passers-by spoke that the voice which they heard came from the passing shadow?

No question, he replied.

To them, I said, the truth would be literally nothing but the shadows of the images.

That is certain.

And now look again, and see what will naturally follow if the prisoners are released and disabused of their error. At first, when any of them is liberated and compelled suddenly to stand up and turn his neck round and walk and look towards the light, he will suffer sharp pains; the glare will distress him, and he will be unable to see the realities of which in his former state he had seen the shadows; and then conceive some one saying to him, that what he saw before was an illusion, but that now, when he is approaching nearer to being and his eye is turned towards more real existence, he has a clearer vision,—what will be his reply? And you may further imagine that his instructor is pointing to the objects as they pass and requiring him to name them,—will he not be perplexed? Will he not fancy that the shadows which he formely saw are truer than the objects which are now shown to him?

Far truer.

And if he is compelled to look straight at the light, will he not have a pain in his eyes which will make him turn away to take refuge in the objects of vision which he can see, and which he will conceive to be in reality clearer than the things which are now being shown to him?

True, he said.

And suppose once more, that he is reluctantly dragged up a steep and rugged ascent, and held fast until he is forced into the presence of the sun himself, is he not likely to be pained an irritated? When he approaches the light his eyes will be dazzled, and he will not be able to see anything at all of what are now called realities.

Not all in a moment, he said.

He will require to grow accustomed to the sight of the upper world. And first he will see the shadows best, next the reflections of men and other objects in the water, and then the objects themselves; then he will gaze upon the light of the moon and the stars and the spangled heaven; and he will see the sky and the stars by night better than the sun or the light of the sun by day?

Certainly.

Last of all he will be able to see the sun, and not mere reflections of him in the water, but he will see him in his own proper place, and not in another; and he will contemplate him as he is.

Certainly.

He will then proceed to argue that this is he who gives the season and the years, and is the guardian of all that is in the visible world, and in a certain way the cause of all things which he and his fellows have been accustomed to behold?

Clearly, he said, he would first see the sun and then reason about him.

And when he remembered his old habitation, and the wisdom of the den and his fellow-prisoners, do you not suppose that he would felicitate himself on the change, and pity them?

Certainly, he would.

And if they were in the habit of conferring honors among themselves on those who were quickest to observe the passing shadows and to remark which of them went before, and which followed after, and which were together; and who were therefore best able to draw conclusions as to the future, do you think that he would care for such honors and glories, or envy the possessors of them? Would he not say with Homer,

"Better to be the poor servant of a poor master,"

and to endure anything, rather than think as they do and live after their manner?

Yes, he said, I think that he would rather suffer anything than entertain these false notions and live in this miserable manner.

Imagine once more, I said, such an one coming suddenly out of the sun to be replaced in his old situation; would he not be certain to have his eyes full of darkness?

To be sure, he said.

And if there were a contest, and he had to compete in measuring the shadows with the prisoners who had never moved out of the den, while his sight was still weak, and before his eyes had become steady (and the time whihc would be needed to acquire this new habit of sight might be very considerable), would he not be ridiculous? Men would say of him that up he went and down he came without his eyes; and that it was better not even to think of ascending; and if any one tried to loose another and lead him up to the light, let them only catch the offender, and they would put him to death.

No question, he said.

This entire allegory, I said, you may now append, dear Glaucon, to the previous argument; the prison-house is the world of sight, the light of the fire is the sun, and you will not misapprehend me if you interpret the journey upwards to be the ascent of the soul into the intellectual world according to my poor belief, which, at your desire, I have expressed—whether rightly or wrongly God knows. But, whether true or false, my opinion is that in the world of knowledge the idea of good appears last of all, and is seen only with an effort; and, when seen, is also inferred to be the universal author of all things beautiful and right, parent of light and of the lord of light in this visible world, and the immediate source of reason and truth in the intellectual; and that this is the power upon which he who would act rationally either in public or private life must have his eye fixed.

I agree, he said, as far as I am able to understand you.

Moreover, I said, you must not wonder that those who attain to this beatific vision are unwilling to descend to human affairs; for their souls are ever hastening into the upper world where they desire to dwell; which desire of theirs is very natural, if our allegory may be trusted.

Yes, very natural.

And is there anything surprising in one who passes from divine contemplations to the evil state of man, misbehaving himself in a ridiculous manner; if, while his eyes are blinking and before he has become accustomed to the surrounding darkness, he is compelled to fight in courts of law, or in other places, about the images or the shadows of images of justice, and is endeavoring to meet the conceptions of those who have never yet seen absolute justice?

Anything but surprising, he replied.

Any one who has common sense will remember that the bewilderments of the eyes are of two kinds, and arise from two causes, either from coming out of the light or from going into the light, which is true of the mind's eye, quite as much as of the bodily eye; and he who remembers this when he sees any one whose vision is perplexed and weak, will not be too ready to laugh; he will first ask whether that soul of man has come out of the brighter life, and is unable to see because unaccustomed to the dark, or having turned from darkness to the day is dazzled by excess of light. And he will count the one happy in his condition and state of being, and he will pity the other; or, if he have a mind to laugh at the soul which comes from below into the light, there will be more reason in this than in the laugh which greets him who returns from above out of the light into the den.

That, he said, is a very just distinction.

But then, if I am right, certain professors of education must be wrong when they say that they can put a knowledge into the soul which was not there before, like sight into blind eyes.

They undoubtedly say this, he replied.

Whereas, our argument shows that the power and capacity of learning exists in the soul already; and that just as the eye was unable to turn from darkness to light without the whole body, so too the instrument of knowledge can only by the movement of the whole soul be turned from the world of becoming into that of being, and learn by degrees to endure the sight of being, and of the brightest and best of being, or in other words, of the good.

Very true.

And must there not be some art which will effect conversion in the easiest and quickest manner; not implanting the faculty of sight, for that exists already, but has been turned in the wrong direction, and is looking away from the truth?

Yes, he said, such an art may be presumed.

And whereas the other so-called virtues of the soul seem to be akin to bodily qualities, for even when they are not originally innate they can be implanted later by habit and exercise, the virtue of wisdom more than anything else contains a divine element which always remains, and by this conversion is rendered useful and profitable; or, on the other hand, hurtful and useless. Did you never observe the narrow intelligence flashing from the keen eye of a clever rogue—how eager he is, how clearly his paltry soul sees the way to his end; he is the reverse of blind, but his keen eye-sight is forced into the service of evil, and he is mischievous in proportion to his cleverness?

Very true, he said.

But what if there had been a circumcision of such natures in the days of their youth; and they had been severed from those sensual pleasures, such as eating and drinking, which like leaden weights, were attached to them at their birth, and which drag them down and turn the vision of their souls upon the things that are below—if, I say, they had been released from these impediments and turned in the opposite direction, the very same faculty in them would have seen the truth as keenly as they see what their eyes are turned to now.

Very likely.

Yes, I said; and there is another thing which is likely, or rather a necessary inference from what has preceded, that neither the uneducated and uninformed of the truth, nor yet those who never make an end of their education, will be able ministers of State; not the former, because they have no single aim of duty which is the rule of all their actions, private as well as public; nor the latter, because they will not act at all except upon compulsion, fancying that they are already dwelling apart in the islands of the blest.

Very true, he replied.

Then, I said, the business of us who are the founders of the State will be to compel the best minds to attain that knowledge which we have already shown to be the greatest of all—they must continue to ascend until they arrive at the good; but when they have ascended and seen enough we must not allow them to do as they do now.

What do you mean?

I mean that they remain in the upper world: but this must not be allowed; they must be made to descend again among the prisoners in the den, and partake of their labors and honors, whether they are worth having or not.

But is not this unjust? he said; ought we to give them a worse life, when they might have a better?

You have again forgotten, my friend, I said, the intention of the legislator, who did not aim at making any one class in the State happy above the rest; the happiness was to be in the whole State, and he held the citizens together by persuasion and necessity, making them benefactors of the State, and therefore benefactors of one another; to this end he created them, not to please themselves, but to be his instruments in binding up the State.

True, he said, I had forgotten.

Observe, Glaucon, that there will be no injustice in compelling our philosophers to have a care and providence of others; we shall explain to them that in other States, men of their class are not obliged to share in the toils of politics: and this is reasonable, for they grow up at their own sweet will, and the government would rather not have them. Being self-taught, they can not be expected to show any gratitude for a culture which they have never received. But we have brought you into the world to be rulers of the hive, kings of yourselves and of the other citizens, and have educated you far better and more perfectly than they have been educated, and you are better able to share in the double duty. Wherefore each of you, when his turn comes, must go down to the general underground abode, and get the habit of seeing in the dark. When you have acquired the habit, you will see ten thousand times better than the inhabitants of the den, and you will know what the several images are, and what they represent, because you have seen the beautiful and just and good in their truth. And thus our State, which is also yours, will be a reality, and not a dream only, and will be administered in a spirit unlike that of other States, in which men fight with one another about shadows only and are distracted in the struggle for power, which in their eyes is a great good. Whereas the truth is that the State in which the rulers are most reluctant to govern is always the best and most quietly governed, and the State in which they are most eager, the worst.

Quite true, he replied.

And will our pupils, when they hear this, refuse to take their turn at the toils of State, when they are allowed to spend the greater part of their time with one another in the heavenly light?

Impossible, he answered; for they are just men, and the commands which we impose upon them are just; there can be no doubt that every one of them will take office as a stern necessity, and not after the fashion of our present rulers of State.

Yes, my friend, I said; and there lies the point. You must contrive for your future rulers another and a better life than that of a ruler, and then you may have a well-ordered State; for only in the State which offers this, will they rule who are truly rich, not in silver and gold, but in virtue and wisdom, which are the true blessings of life. Whereas if they go to the administration of public affairs, poor and hungering after their own private advantage, thinking that hence they are to snatch the chief good, order there can never be; for they will be fighting about office, and the civil and domestic broils which thus arise will be the ruin of the rulers themselves and of the whole State.

Most true, he replied. . . .

And so, Glaucon, I said, we have at last arrived at the hymn of dialectic. This is that strain which is of the intellect only, but which the faculty of sight will nevertheless be found to imitate; for sight, as you may remember, was imagined by us after a while to behold the real animals and stars, and last of all the sun himself. And so with dialectic; when a person starts on the discovery of the absolute by the light of reason only, and without any assistance of sense, and perseveres until by pure intelligence he arrives at the perception of the absolute good, he at last finds himself at the end of the intellectual world, as in the case of sight at the end of the visible.

Exactly, he said.

Then this is the progress which you call dialectic?

True.

But the release of the prisoners from chains, and their translation from the shadows to the images and to the light, and the ascent from the underground den to the sun, while in his presence they are vainly trying to look on animals and plants and the light of the sun, but are able to perceive even with their weak eyes the images[6] in the water [which are divine], and are the shadows of true existence (not shadows of images cast by a light of fire, which compared with the sun is only an image)— this power of elevating the highest principle in the soul to the contemplation of that which is best in existence, with which we may compare the raising of that faculty which is the very light of the body to the sight of that which is brightest in the material and visible world—this power is given, as I was saying, by all that study and pursuit of the arts which has been described.

I agree in what you are saying, he replied, which may be hard to believe, yet, from another point of view, is harder still to deny. This however is not a theme to be treated of in passing only, but will have to be discussed again and again. And so, whether our conclusion be true or false, let us assume all this, and proceed at once from the prelude or

6. Omitting εντανθα δε προζ φαντασματα. The word θεια is bracketed by Stallbaum.

preamble to the chief strain,[7] and describe that in like manner. Say, then, what is the nature and what are the divisions of dialectic, and what are the paths which lead thither; for these paths will also lead to our final rest.

Dear Glaucon, I said, you will not be able to follow me here, though I would do my best, and you should behold not an image only but the absolute truth, according to my notion. Whether what I told you would or would not have been a reality I can not venture to say; but you would have seen something like reality; of that I am confident.

Doubtless, he replied.

But I must also remind you, that the power of dialectic alone can reveal this, and only to one who is a disciple of the previous sciences.

Of that assertion you may be as confident as of the last.

And assuredly no one will argue that there is any other method of comprehending by any regular process all true existence or of ascertaining what each thing is in its own nature; for the arts in general are concerned with the desires or opinions of men, or are cultivated with a view to production and construction, or for the preservation of such productions and constructions; and as to the mathematical sciences which, as we were saying, have some apprehension of true being— geometry and the like—they only dream about being, but never can they behold the waking reality so long as they leave the hypotheses which they use unexamined, and are unable to give an account of them. For when a man knows not his own first principle, and when the conclusion and intermediate steps are also constructed out of he knows not what, how can he imagine that such a fabric of convention can ever become science?

Impossible, he said.

Then dialectic, and dialectic alone, goes directly to the first principle and is the only science which does away with hypotheses in order to make her ground secure; the eye of the soul, which is literally buried in an outlandish slough, is by her gentle aid lifted upwards; and she uses as handmaids and helpers in the work of conversion, the sciences which we have been discussing. Custom terms them sciences, but they ought to have some other name, implying greater clearness than opinion and less clearness than science: and this, in our previous sketch, was called understanding. But why should we dispute about names when we have realities of such importance to consider?

Why indeed, he said, when any name will do which expresses the thought of the mind with clearness?

At any rate, we are satisfied, as before, to have four divisions; two for intellect and two for opinion, and to call the first division science, the

---

7. A play upon the word νομος, which means both "law" and "strain."

second understanding, the third belief, and the fourth perception of shadows, opinion being concerned with becoming, and intellect with being; and so to make a proportion:

> *As being is to becoming, so is pure intellect to opinion.*
> *And as intellect is to opinion, so is science to belief,*
>   *and understanding to the perception of shadows.*

But let us defer the further correlation and subdivision of the subjects of opinion and of intellect, for it will be a long inquiry, many times longer than this has been.

As far as I understand, he said, I agree.

And do you also agree, I said, in describing the dialectician as one who attains a conception of the essence of each thing? And he who does not possess and is therefore unable to impart this conception, in whatever degree he fails, may in that degree also be said to fail in intelligence? Will you admit so much?

Yes, he said; how can I deny it?

And you would say the same of the conception of the good? Until the person is able to abstract and define rationally the idea of good, and unless he can run the gauntlet of all objections, and is ready to disprove them, not by appeals to opinion, but to absolute truth, never faltering at any step of the argument—unless he can do all this, you would say that he knows neither the idea of good nor any other good; he apprehends only a shadow, if anything at all, which is given by opinion and not by science;—dreaming and slumbering in this life, before he is well awake here, he arrives at the world below, and has his final quietus.

In all that I should most certainly agree with you.

And surely you would not have the children of your ideal State, whom you are nurturing and educating—if the ideal ever becomes a reality—you would not allow the future rulers to be like posts,[8] having no reason in them, and yet to be set in authority over the highest matters?

Certainly not.

Then you will make a law that they shall have such an education as will enable them to attain the greatest skill in asking and answering questions?

Yes, he said, you and I together will make it.

Dialectic, then, as you will agree, is the coping-stone of the sciences, and is set over them; no other science can be placed higher—the nature of knowledge can no further go?

---

8. γραμμαζ, literally "lines," probably the starting-point of a race-course.

I agree, he said.

But to whom we are to assign these studies, and in what way they are to be assigned, are questions which remain to be considered.

Yes, clearly.

You remember, I said, how the rulers were chosen before?

Certainly, he said.

The same natures must still be chosen, and the preference again given to the surest and the bravest, and, if possible, to the fairest; and, having noble and generous tempers, they should also have the natural gifts which will facilitate their education.

And what are these?

Such gifts as keenness and ready powers of acquisition; for the mind more often faints from the severity of study than from the severity of gymnastics: the toil is more entirely the mind's own, and is not shared with the body.

Very true, he replied.

Further, he of whom we are in search should have a good memory, and be an unwearied solid man who is a lover of labor in any line; or he will never to able to endure the great amount of bodily exercise and to go through all the intellectual discipline and study which we require of him.

Certainly, he said; he must have natural gifts.

The mistake at present is, that those who study philosophy have no vocation, and this, as I was before saying, is the reason why she has fallen into disrepute: her true sons should take her by the hand and not bastards.

What do you mean?

In the first place, her votary should not have a lame or halting industry—I mean, that he should not be half industrious and half idle: as, for example, when a man is a lover of gymnastic and hunting, and all other bodily exercises, but a hater rather than a lover of the labor of learning or listening or inquiring. Or the occupation to which he devotes himself may be of an opposite kind, and he may have the other sort of lameness.

Certainly, he said.

And as to truth, I said, is not a soul equally to be deemed halt and lame which hates voluntary falsehood and is extremely indignant at herself and others when they tell lies, but is patient of involuntary falsehood, and does not mind wallowing like a swinish beast in the mire of ignorance, and has no shame at being detected?

To be sure.

And, again, in respect of temperance, courage, magnificence, and every other virtue, should we not carefully distinguish between the true son and the bastard? for where there is no discernment of such qualities states and individuals unconsciously err; and the state makes a ruler, and the individual a friend, of one who, being defective in some part of virtue, is in a figure lame or a bastard.

That is very true, he said.

All these things, then, will have to be carefully considered by us; and if only those whom we introduce to this vast system of education and training are sound in body and mind, justice herself will have nothing to say against us, and we shall be the saviors of the constitution and of the State; but, if our pupils are men of another stamp, the reverse will happen, and we shall pour a still greater flood of ridicule on philosophy than she has to endure at present.

That would not be creditable.

Certainly not, I said; and yet perhaps, in thus turning jest into earnest I am equally ridiculous.

In what respect?

I had forgotten, I said, that we were not serious and spoke with too much excitement. For when I saw philosophy so undeservedly trampled under foot of men I could not help feeling a sort of indignation at the authors of her disgrace: and my anger made me too vehement.

Indeed! I was listening, and did not think so.

But I, who am the speaker, felt that I was. And now let me remind you that, although in our former selection we chose old men, we must not do so in this. Solon was under a delusion when he said that a man when he grows old may learn many things—for he can no more learn much than he can run much; youth is the time for any extraordinary toil.

Of course.

And, therefore, calculation and geometry and all the other elements of instruction, which are a preparation for dialectic, should be presented to the mind in childhood; not, however, under any notion of forcing our system of education.

Why not?

Because a freeman ought not to be a slave in the acquisition of knowledge of any kind. Bodily exercise, when compulsory, does no harm to the body; but knowledge which is acquired under compulsion obtains no hold on the mind.

Very true.

Then, my good friend, I said, do not use compulsion, but let early education be a sort of amusement; you will then be better able to find out the natural bent.

That is a very rational notion, he said.

Do you remember that the children, too, were to be taken to see the battle on horseback; and that if there were no danger they were to be brought close up and, like young hounds, have a taste of blood given them?

Yes, I remember.

The same practice may be followed, I said, in all these things—labors, lessons, dangers—and he who is most at home in all of them ought to be enrolled in a select number.

At what age?

At the age when the necessary gymnastics are over: the period whether of two or three years which passes in this sort of training is useless for any other purpose; for sleep and exercise are unpropitious to learning; and the trial of who is first in gymnastic exercises is one of the most important tests to which our youth are subjected.

Certainly, he replied.

After that time those who are selected from the class of twenty years old will be promoted to higher honor, and the sciences which they learned without any order in their early education will now be brought together, and they will be able to see the natural relationship of them to one another and to true being.

Yes, he said, that is the only kind of knowledge which takes lasting root.

Yes, I said; and the capacity for such knowledge is the great criterion of dialectical talent; the comprehensive mind is always the dialectical.

I agree with you, he said.

These, I said, are the points which you must consider; and those who have most of this comprehension, and who are most steadfast in their learning, and in their military and other appointed duties, when they have arrived at the age of thirty will have to be chosen by you out of the select class, and elevated to higher honor; and you will have to prove them by the help of dialectic, in order to learn which of them is able to give up the use of sight and the other senses, and in company with truth to attain absolute being: And here, my friend, great caution is required.

Why great caution?

Do you not remark, I said, how great is the evil which dialectic has introduced?

What evil? he said.

The students of the art are filled with lawlessness.

Quite true, he said.

Do you think that there is anything so very unnatural or inexcusable in their case? or will you make allowance for them?

In what way make allowance?

I want you, I said, by way of parallel, to imagine a supposititious son who is brought up in great wealth; he is one of a great and numerous family, and has many flatterers. When he grows up to manhood, he learns that his alleged are not his real parents; but who the real are he is unable to discover. Can you guess how he will be likely to behave towards his flatterers and his supposed parents, first of all during the period when he is ignorant of the false relation, and then again when he knows? Or shall I guess for you?

If you please.

Then I should say, that while he is ignorant of the truth he will be likely to honor his father and his mother and his supposed relations more than the flatterers; he will be less inclined to neglect them when in need, or to do or say anything against them; and he will be less willing to disobey them in any important matter.

He will.

But when he has made the discovery, I should imagine that he would diminish his honor and regard for them, and would become more devoted to the flatterers; their influence over him would greatly increase; he would now live after their ways, and openly associate with them, and, unless he were of an unusually good disposition, he would trouble himself no more about his supposed parents or other relations.

Well, all that is very probable. But how is the image applicable to the disciples of philosophy?

In this way: you know that there are certain principles about justice and honor, which were taught us in childhood, and under their parental authority we have been brought up, obeying and honoring them.

That is true.

There are also opposite maxims and habits of pleasure which flatter and attract the soul, but do not influence those of us who have any sense of right, and they continue to obey and honor the maxims of their fathers.

True.

Now, when a man is in this state, and the questioning spirit asks what is fair or honorable, and he answers as the legislator has taught him, and then arguments many and diverse refute his words, until he is driven into believing that nothing is honorable any more than dishonorable, or just and good any more than the reverse, and so of all the notions which he most valued, do you think that he will still honor and obey them as before?

Impossible.

And when he ceases to think them honorable and natural as heretofore, and he fails to discover the true, can he be expected to pursue any life other than that which flatters his desires?

He can not.

And from being a keeper of the law he is converted into a breaker of it?

Unquestionably.

Now all this is very natural in students of philosophy such as I have described, and also, as I was just now saying, most excusable.

Yes, he said; and, I may add, pitiable.

Therefore, that your feelings may not be moved to pity about our citizens who are now thirty years of age, every care must be taken in introducing them to dialectic.

Certainly.

There is a danger lest they should taste the dear delight too early; for youngsters, as you may have observed, when they first get the taste in their mouths, argue for amusement, and are always contradicting and refuting others in imitation of those who refute them; like puppy-dogs, they rejoice in pulling and tearing at all who come near them.

Yes, he said, there is nothing which they like better.

And when they have made many conquests and received defeats at the hands of many, they violently and speedily get into a way of not believing anything which they believed before, and hence, not only they, but philosophy and all that relates to it is apt to have a bad name with the rest of the world.

Too true, he said.

But when a man begins to get older, he will no longer be guilty of such insanity; he will imitate the dialectician who is seeking for truth, and not the eristic, who is contradicting for the sake of amusement; and the greater moderation of his character will increase instead of diminishing the honor of the pursuit.

Very true, he said.

And did we not make special provision for this, when we said that the disciples of philosophy were to be orderly and steadfast, not, as now, any chance aspirant or intruder?

Very true.

Suppose, I said, the study of philosophy to take the place of gymnastics and to be continued diligently and earnestly and exclusively for twice the number of years which were passed in bodily exercise—will that be enough?

Would you say six or four years? he asked.

Say five years, I replied; at the end of the time they must be sent down again into the den and compelled to hold any military or other office which young men are qualified to hold: in this way they will get their experience of life, and there will be an opportunity of trying whether, when they are drawn all manner of ways by temptation, they will stand firm or flinch.

And how long is this stage of their lives to last?

Fifteen years, I answered; and when they have reached fifty years of age, then let those who still survive and have distinguished themselves in every action of their lives and in every branch of knowledge come at last to their consummation: the time has now arrived at which they must raise the eye of the soul to the universal light which lightens all things, and behold the absolute good; for that is the pattern according to which they are to order the State and the lives of individuals, and the remainder of their own lives also; making philosophy their chief pursuit, but, when their turn comes, toiling also at politics and ruling for the public good, not as though they were performing some heroic action, but simply as a matter of duty; and when they have brought up in each generation others like themselves and left them in their place to be governors of the State, then they will depart to the Islands of the Blest and dwell there; and the city will give them public memorials and sacrifices and honor them, if the Pythian oracle consent, as demigods, but if not, as in any case blessed and divine.

You are a sculptor, Socrates, and have made statues of our governors faultless in beauty.

Yes, I said, Glaucon, and of our governesses too; for you must not suppose that what I have been saying applies to men only and not to women as far as their natures can go.

There you are right, he said, since we have made them to share in all things like the men.

Well, I said, and you would agree (would you not?) that what has been said about the State and the government is not a mere dream, and although difficult not impossible, but only possible in the way which has been supposed; that is to say, when the true philosopher kings are born in a State, one or more of them, despising the honors of this present world which they deem mean and worthless, esteeming above all things right and the honor that springs from right, and regarding justice as the greatest and most necessary of all things, whose ministers they are, and whose principles will be exalted by them when they set in order their own city?

How will they proceed?

They will begin by sending out into the country all the inhabitants of the city who are more than ten years old, and will take possession of their children, who will be unaffected by the habits of their parents; these they will train in their own habits and laws, I mean in the laws which we have given them: and in this way the State and constitution will gain most.

Yes, that will be the best way. And I think, Socrates, that you have very well described how, if ever, such a constitution might come into being.

Enough then of the perfect State, and of the man who bears its image—there is no difficulty in seeing how we shall describe him.

There is no difficulty, he replied; and I agree with you in thinking that nothing more need be said. . . .

Myths: Chaos, Daedalus and Icarus, the Golden Verses of the Pythagoreans.

Plato's divided line summarizes the possibilities of the individual soul and of the culture. For an individual, a culture, to be complete it must proceed to action and, therefore, training, by including *Chaos* as the foundation of the cosmos. Chaos is the region of origin of the gods, of the magician, of the hero and of those acts that create and renew the cosmos. If we cut off chaos from cosmos, our possibilities of renewal are diminished: we are left with the "shadow of knowledge," the world of cosmos, ghosts produced at our own expense. Identification of culture, or individuals, is acquired against others under the umbrella of one or another orthodoxy: this is the ground of separation, of ideology, of repression, inquisitions, imitation, the *simulacrum*, war, strife, discrimination. If, on the other hand, we accept chaos as the ground of the cosmos we need to include the gods, the hero, the magician and those acts they performed as the *models* of human acting. Needless to say, all the gods must be kept alive, particularly those of the middle ground, for if any one is missing then orthodoxy is around the corner and soon enough, deterioration, imitation, stagnation follow. But in order to keep this project of education alive we must include in education other acts beside those practiced within the region of the shadows of the cave. We need to recall the acts by which the sun is seen, even when it is night all around. We need to re-read the myths and Plato again to make them alive in the classroom. Let the students bring them to life the same way chaos brought cosmos to life, through the acts of self dismemberment, giving life with their own bodies to what is now dead.

Daedalus eventually tired of his life in Crete, and Minos would not let him go. He therefore contrived feathered wings, held together by wax, by means of which he and his son Icarus could escape. As they flew high above the sea, Icarus ignored his father's warning not to fly too close to the sun; the wax on his wings melted and he fell into the sea, which thereafter was called *Mare Icarium*. The story is told by Ovid (*Metamorphoses* 8. 200–230):

> When Daedalus the craftsman had finished [making the wings] he balanced his body between the twin wings and by moving them hung suspended in air. He also gave instructions to his son, saying: "Icarus, I advise you to take a middle course. If you fly too low, the sea will soak the wings; if you fly too high, the sun's heat will burn them. Fly between sea and sun! . . . Take the course along which I shall lead you."
>
> As he gave the instructions for flying, he fitted the novel wings to Icarus' shoulders. While he worked and gave his advice the old man's face was wet with tears, and his hands trembled with a father's anxiety. For the last time, he kissed his son and rose into the air upon his wings. He led

the way in flight and was anxious for his companion, like a bird that leads its young from the nest into the air. He encouraged Icarus to follow and showed him the skills that were to destroy him; he moved his wings and looked back at those of his son. Some fisherman with trembling rod, or shepherd leaning on his crook, or farmer resting on his plow saw them and was amazed, and believed that those who could travel through the air were gods. Now Juno's Samos was on the left (they had already passed Delos and Paros), and Lebinthos and Calymne, rich in honey, were on the right, when the body began to exult in his bold flight. He left his guide and, drawn by a desire to reach the heavens, took his course too high. The burning heat of the nearby sun softened the scented wax that fastened the wings. The wax melted; Icarus moved his arms, now uncovered, and without the wings to drive him on, vainly beat the air. Even as he called upon his father's name the sea received him and from him took its name.

Daedalus himself successfully reached Sicily.

GOLDEN VERSES OF THE PYTHAGOREANS

Preparation

> Offer to the immortal gods the sacred exercise;
> Center your faith: Bring to memory
> the illustrious heroes, demi-gods of the spirit.

CATHARSIS

> Become a good son, a just brother, a tender spouse, a good
> 　　father;
> Make friends only with the friend of virtue;
> Surrender to his soft advice; learn from his life,
> Do not reject him on the grounds of a slight insult;
> Bind yourself to him with the rigid law that binds
> Power to Necessity.
> For you may fight and conquer your foolish passions:
> Learn to conquer them;
> Be sober, active, chaste; avoid anger in any shape.
> Do not allow evil within you
> In public or in secret; and respect yourself above all.
> Do not speak nor act before you have had time to reflect.
> Be just. Remember that death is decreed
> By an invincible power; that easily acquired
> Riches and honors are as easy to lose.
> And all the evils that Destiny brings to you,

Judge them for what they are: endure them and try,
As much as you are able, to change their shape:
The gods have not freed the Sage from the most cruel ones.

Error, as much as Virtue, has its lovers:
The philosopher agrees or disagrees with prudence;
If Error wins, the philosopher leaves and waits.
Listen and write my words down in your heart;
Close your eye and ear to all prejudice;
Fear the example of others; think by yourself always:
Meditate, reflect, choose freely.
Let fools act aimlessly and with no cause.
In the present you should contemplate the future.

What you do not know do not pretend to know.
Instruct yourself: all comes with patience and time.
Watch over your health: with moderation feed
Nourishment to the body and peace to the soul.
Avoid receiving too much attention or too little;
For envy attaches itself equally to both extremes.
And the same happens with lust and avarice.
In all things choose a just and good mean.

PERFECTION

Your tired eyes should never be closed by sleep,
Ask yourself as a habit: What have I omitted, what have I done?
Abstain from doing evil; persevere in doing good.
Meditate on my councils; love them; follow them;
They will take you to the practice of divine virtue;
I swear it by what is written in our hearts:
The Divine Tetrad, universal and pure symbol,
Origin of Nature and model of the gods.
Let your soul, faithful to its virtue, and before anything else,
Invoke those gods with fervor, for your work begun
Only their help can bring it to an end.
Guided by the gods nothing will deceive you:
You shall sound the essence of diverse beings;
And you will know their origin and end.
If the heavens will it, you will know that Nature,
Alike in everything, is the same everywhere:
Enlightened by your own true rights
Your heart will no more feed on vain desires.
You will learn that the evils devouring men
Are the fruits of their choice; these unfortunates

Seek outside for the goodness they carry within.
Few know happiness: playthings of passions
They are tossed about by contrary waves,
They roll upon a shoreless sea, blindly,
Not able to fight or yield to the storm.
 God! You could save them by opening their eyes.
But no: it is the way of humans, within a divine race,
To discern Error and see the Truth.
Nature serves them. You who have reached its bottom,
Wise and happy man, rest on its shore.
But keep my laws, abstain from the things
Your soul fears, separate them well;
Let virtue be the habit of your body;
So that on rising over the Ether,
To the womb of the Immortals, you yourself become a god!
Trans. Antonio T. de Nicolas

Translator's Note: The verses above translated date back to the time of Pythagoras, though they are attributed to his disciple Lysis, who brought them to Greece. They summarize the life and doctrine of the Pythagoreans. By testimony given by Cicero, Horace, Seneca, and others, we know these verses were recited by every Pythagorean twice a day, in the morning on rising and at night before going to bed.

FOCUSING QUESTIONS

1. What is the difference between principles and origins?

2. How are principles achieved?

3. How are origins reached?

4. How are principles and origins related?

5. What is the relation between memory and imaging?

6. What is the relation between memory, will, imagining, and the body?

7. How are imaginings helpful in decision making?

8. Is education for contemplation or for decision making?

9. How did Plato in the *Republic* divide the acts of the mind following the divided line?

10. Who were the people in the cave facing the wall?

11. Who were the people behind the fire casting the shadows?

12. Where is the sun in the *Republic* when Plato talks about democracy?

13. Which are the technologies of the visible?

14. Which those of the intelligible?

15. Which part of the divided line is the visible and which the intelligible?

16. Why is Er so important to Plato?

17. What is recollection as used in the *Republic?*

18. Is there anyone outside of the cave?

19. Why does the prisoner who has left the cave return?

20. Why, according to Plato, is Homer a bad poet?

Summary
Philosophies of
Education

THEORY	CLAIM	KNOWLEDGE	VALUES	PHILOSOPHY
Realism	reality is objective made of matter and form; based on Natural Law.	sensation plus abstraction to the third degree	absolute. eternal natural law	Aquinas scholastics and "their" Aristotle
Idealism	reality is mental and unchanging	necessity of thought dialectically developed	Absolute Eternal	Berkeley Butler Froebel Hegel
	or material	scientific	Utopian	Marx
Pragmatism (experimental)	reality in constant change, built in interaction of individual with environment.	scientific method	relative	Dewey James Pierce
Existentialism	reality is subjective choice	knowledge is personal choice	values are freely chosen, but choice is inevitable	Sartre Marcel
Philosophical Analysis	reality verifiable through scientific method	knowing involves empirical verification or language analysis	values are emotions	Russell Moore

THEORY	CLAIM	KNOWLEDGE	VALUES	PHILOSOPHY
Paideia	exercise of all faculties builds soul-society.	only that which is imagined is real, music criteria built in as epistemology	eternal models. virtue may be taught as a habit of action; decisions are arrived at through the mediation of the original background.	Plato, Socrates; Legacy of oral cultures

Bibliography to the
First Five Chapters

Bloom, Allan. *The Closing of the American Mind*. New York: Simon and Schuster, 1987.

Barthel, Manfred. *The Jesuits: History and Legend of the Society of Jesus*. Translated by Mark Howson. New York: William Morrow and Co., 1984.

Bataillon, Marcel. *Erasmo y Espana*. Translated by Antonio Alatorre. Buenos Aires: Fondo de Cultura Economica Mexico, 1950.

de Nicolás, Antonio. *Avatára: The Humanization of Philosophy Through the Bhagavad Gítá*. Maine: Nicolas-Hays, 1976.

———. *Powers of Imagining:* Ignatius de Loyola. Albany, N.Y.: SUNY, 1986.

Durant, Will. *The Story of Civilization: The Reformation*, Vol. 6. New York: Simon and Schuster, 1957.

———. *The Story of Civilization: The Age of Reason Begins*. Contributor, Ariel Durant. New York: Simon and Schuster, 1961.

Koyre, Alexander. *Mystiques, Spirituels, et Alchemistes*. Paris, 1955.

Lincoln, Victoria. *Teresa: A Woman*. Albany, N.Y.: SUNY, 1984.

Manuel, Frank. *A Portrait of Newton*. Cambridge, Mass.: Harvard University Press, 1968.

Rattansi, P. M. "The Social Interpretation of Science in the Seventeenth Century." In *Science and Society,* Edited by P. Mathias. Cambridge, Mass.: Harvard University Press, 1972.

Toulouse, Teresa. *The Art of Prophesying: New England Sermons and the Shaping of Belief*. Athens, Ga.: University of Georgia Press, 1987.

Yates, Francis A. *Giordano Bruno and the Hermetic Tradition*. Chicago: University of Chicago Press, 1964.

———. *The Art of Memory*. London: Penguin, 1969.